The Encyclopedia of Exercise, Sport and Health

Peter Brukner, MBBS, FACSP, FACSM, FASMF, is currently Associate Professor in Sports Medicine at the Centre for Sports Medicine Research and Education at the University of Melbourne. Peter has been Clinic Director at the Olympic Park Sports Medicine Centre in Melbourne since 1987 and has served two terms as President of the Australian College of Sports Physicians. He is the co-author of *Clinical Sports Medicine* and is the Senior Associate Editor of the *Clinical Journal of Sport Medicine* and *The Physician and Sports Medicine*, as well as being a past editor of *Sport Health*. Peter was an Australian Team Physician at the Atlanta Olympic Games and Team Manager of the Australian athletics team at the Sydney Olympics.

Karim Khan, BMed Sci, MBBS, PhD, FACSP, is an Australian-trained sports physician and academic who has been at the University of British Columbia in Vancouver, Canada since 1997. He serves as a consultant physician at the Allan McGavin Sports Medicine Clinic and an Assistant Professor in Family Practice and Human Kinetics. Karim's care of sporting teams has included the Australian Women's Basketball team (the Opals) and the Australian Ballet. His research focuses on the role of exercise to promote bone health across the lifespan and on better understanding of painful tendons.

John Kron was born in Melbourne and graduated as a physiotherapist from Lincoln Institute of Health Sciences (now La Trobe University) in Melbourne in 1983. From 1984 until 1991 he lived in Israel, where he worked as a physiotherapist, first on a kibbutz and later in Jerusalem. After returning to Australia he began working as a freelance health writer and cartoonist. His articles on topics from exercise and sport through to children's and women's health have been published in a wide range of magazines and newspapers in Australia and overseas. From 1997 to 2000 he was the sports medicine writer for *Australian Doctor*.

The Encyclopedia of Exercise, Sport and Health

Dr Peter Brukner, Dr Karim Khan and John Kron

ALLEN&UNWIN

I 95/
29/
4-8-05

First published in 2004

Allen & Unwin
83 Alexander Street
Crows Nest NSW 2065
Australia
Phone: (61 2) 8425 0100
Fax: (61 2) 9906 2218
Email: info@allenandunwin.com
Web: www.allenandunwin.com

National Library of Australia
Cataloguing-in-Publication entry:

Brukner, Peter.
   The encyclopedia of exercise, sport and health.

   ISBN 1 74114 058 7.

   1. Sports - Encyclopedias. I. Khan, Karim. II. Kron, John.
   III. Title.

796.03

Set in 10/12 pt Electra by Bookhouse, Sydney
Printed by Ligare Pty Ltd, Sydney

10 9 8 7 6 5 4 3 2 1

Contents

Acknowledgements

Our gratitude goes to Debbie and Colin Golvan, who enabled an idea for a book to become a reality by finding it a home. Special thanks go to the publishing team, especially Annette Barlow, who saw the potential in this book and gave it a chance, and Colette Vella, who cared for and nurtured it through to publication with professionalism and patience.

Much of the information in this encyclopedia is based on Peter and Karim's bestselling textbook, *Clinical Sports Medicine*. Our thanks to all those contributors, proofreaders, models and others whose help in producing that book has also assisted us with this one.

Thanks also to Dr Michael Makdissi who painstakingly checked the initial manuscript for us, and to our colleagues at the Centre for Sports Medicine Research and Education at the University of Melbourne and the Department of Family Practice and School of Human Kinetics at the University of British Columbia who support our strange literary obsessions.

From Dr Peter Brukner:
I would again like to thank Diana, Julia, Charles, Joe and Bill for their tolerance and understanding of my literary obsessions. A special thanks to John Kron for providing the impetus for this book, and for his commitment and dedication to seeing the fulfilment of the project.

From John Kron:
To my colleagues, editors and fellow writers, who have given me the spark, ongoing encouragement and positive feedback to adopt and maintain a career as a writer. And my family and friends, who have continually provided me with joy and strength, especially my loving parents, Halina and David, and my wonderful and supportive partner, Sandy Saxon.

Introduction

The fitness boom was a phenomenon that emerged in the latter part of the 20th century, and it shows no sign of abating in the 21st. While competitive sport continues to be as popular as ever, more and more people have taken up exercise as recreation and as a means to improving their health. This exercise boom has not been restricted to any one group but is spread among men and women, old and young, competitive and non-competitive. It manifests itself in many ways, from the ultra-endurance iron man to the lunch-time jogger, from the competitive netballer to the family walking the dog, from the elite junior snowboarder to the child playing football in the park.

The benefits of exercise are now more readily understood and its positive effect on both physical and mental health appreciated by millions of participants throughout the world. Conditions such as coronary artery disease, cancer, gallstones, hypertension, obesity, osteoporosis, stroke, diabetes and depression have all been linked to inactivity. As a result there is enormous interest in training, fitness, nutrition, psychology and how to improve your health.

Unfortunately there is also a down side to exercise and that is the risk of injury associated with it. These injuries can be due to overuse, misuse or just plain bad luck. Those of us who love to exercise are desperate for knowledge on the prevention and management of injuries associated with exercise. A whole new medical specialty, sports medicine, has evolved over the last twenty years, and as a result we are far more knowledgeable about sporting injuries than we were in the days when all a doctor would recommend was that four-letter word, rest.

While there are many textbooks for the sports medicine and exercise health professional, there is a huge demand for information on these topics by the general public. It is to fill this need that we have written the *Encyclopedia of Exercise, Sport and Health*.

Sports physicians Peter Brukner and Karim Khan have combined with physiotherapist and health writer John Kron to provide an up-to-date, easy-to-read encyclopedia covering topics related to exercise, sport and health.

The A to Z format of the book enables you to go straight to your topic of interest by looking up a specific entry. We have tried to give you sufficient information in each of the entries, but have also extensively cross-referenced to avoid repetition —

cross-references appear in italics for easy reference. And we have tried to not be too technical or to mystify you with the use of medical or scientific jargon.

So if you have a pain in the knee and want information about the possible cause, go to knee pain. If you have already been diagnosed with an anterior cruciate ligament tear of knee osteoarthritis and want to know what that means, those entries are there for you. If you are overweight, look that up to see how to lose weight. If you want to improve your strength, read about it under strength training. If your child needs an ice pack following an injury, check the entry for ice. And if you can't find the entry you want, look in the index and it may be there under another name. With around 1500 entries and sub-entries you're sure to find an answer that you need.

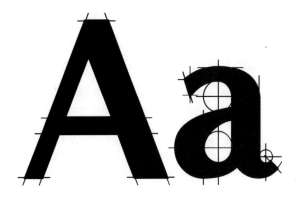

Abdominal injury

An acute injury caused by a sudden excessive force to the abdomen. It is most common in high-speed activities such as *motor sports* and *horse riding sports*.

The primary concern is damage to an organ, which can lead to severe blood loss. The most commonly injured organs include the *spleen, liver, kidney, bladder* and *urethra. Pelvis fracture* and acute injuries of the penis and *scrotum* in males may also occur.

Treatment

A suspected abdominal injury should be treated as a *medical emergency*, which includes ensuring that breathing and circulation are not compromised, followed by transport off the field of play to a hospital as quickly as possible.

Abdominal injury is suspected until proven otherwise by the following symptoms:

- Loss of consciousness, either soon after the injury, a few hours later or, in rare cases, days later
- Severe pain in the abdomen
- Hardness of the abdomen when pressed with the fingers.

Other symptoms specific for each organ include:

- Blood in the urine (kidney, bladder or urethra injury)
- Bruising over the middle or side of the back just below the ribs (kidney injury).

Abdominal toner

A rocker-shaped piece of fitness equipment designed to assist with sit-ups. Regular use can be an effective form of *strength training* for the lower abdominal muscles. However, it is no more effective than doing sit-ups without equipment. In addition, the claim that the abdominal toner can achieve *spot reduction* by decreasing fat from the abdomen does not have supporting research evidence.

Abduction

A movement of a joint in a direction pointing away from the midline of the body. For example, lifting your leg out to the side when standing up is called abduction of the hip joint. Abduction is also known as lateral flexion in some joints. It is the opposite of *adduction*.

ACE inhibitors

A drug used in the treatment of *hypertension* (high blood pressure). The full name is angiotensin converting enzyme inhibitor. It acts by reducing the amount of muscle contraction in blood vessels to minimise narrowing. It does not have a negative effect on people participating in exercise and sport.

Acetylcholine

An important neurotransmitter in exercise and sport that enables *neurons* (nerve cells) to trigger off *muscle contractions*.

Acetylcholine (ACh) is released from the end of a neuron in the *motor nervous system* after it receives an electric current. It crosses a tiny gap called a synapse and attaches to the cell wall of a nearby muscle fibre. This triggers a chain of events within the muscle fibre that leads to the muscle contraction.

Achilles paratenonitis

An injury that causes inflammation to the tendon sheath that covers and protects the Achilles tendon of the *calf* muscles. It is an overuse injury caused by a gradual accumulation of repeated excessive physical forces over a period of weeks, months or even years. It most commonly occurs in *running* sports, *jumping sports*, the *football* codes, *netball* and *basketball*.

Diagnosis and treatment
This *paratenonitis* injury causes pain felt above the site where the Achilles tendon attaches to the heel bone, tenderness when pressed firmly with the fingers, *swelling*, restricted *flexibility* and weakness of the calf muscle, and sometimes a 'creaking' noise, caused by the breaking of small adhesions (healing

scar tissue) which have developed between the *tendon sheath* and Achilles tendon.

Treatment includes *ice, non-steroidal anti-inflammatory drugs (NSAIDs), rest* from the aggravating activity, *massage, flexibility exercises* and *strengthening exercises*.

Achilles tendinitis

See *Tendinitis*.

Achilles tendinosis

An injury of the large tendon that connects the *calf* muscles to the heel bone (calcaneus). It is caused by a gradual accumulation of repeated excessive physical forces over a period of weeks, months or even years. It most commonly occurs in *running* sports, *jumping sports, football* codes such as *Australian Rules football, netball* and *basketball*.

Causes
The excessive forces may be associated with an abnormality of *running biomechanics*, especially *foot pronation*, sudden increases in training *overload* (usually intensity or volume), decreased recovery time between exercise sessions, poor selection of *running shoes*, poor running or training surfaces, reduced *flexibility* and *strength* of the calf muscles, and loss of ankle joint *range of movement*.

Initially the injury may cause inflammation of the tendon, called tendinitis. However, continued aggravation of the tendon rapidly leads to the development of *tendinosis*, a degenerative condition that breaks down the cells in the tendon and causes microscopic tears.

Diagnosis
The pain is felt within the tendon just above its attachment to the heel bone. It usually starts some time after activity is commenced or first thing the following morning. In the early stages the pain reduces during a warm-up or the aggravating activity, only to return after activity.

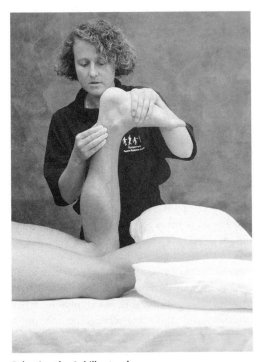

Palpating the Achilles tendon

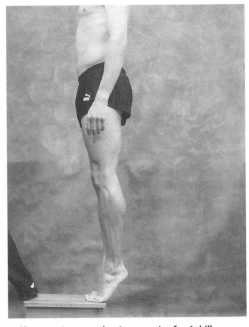

Calf eccentric strengthening exercise for Achilles tendinosis

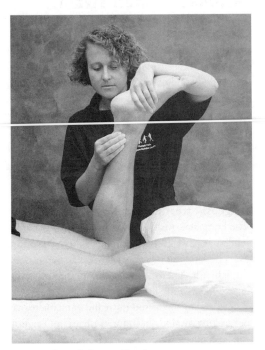

Massage for Achilles tendinosis

However, in the later stages the pain continues throughout activity. The tendon may be tender, or a hard focal point (called a nodule) may be felt when pressed firmly with the fingers.

Radiological investigations such as *diagnostic ultrasound* and *magnetic resonance imaging (MRI)* are used to help confirm the diagnosis.

Treatment and return to sport

The recommended treatments include *rest* from the aggravating activity, *ice*, *interferential therapy*, a heel raise (such as a wedge of rubber adhered to the inside sole of the shoe) and *massage*.

Correction of biomechanical abnormalities is essential for recovery and prevention of re-injury. Treatments may include *taping*, *motor re-education*, *flexibility exercises* and *strengthening exercises*, with emphasis on *eccentric* contractions. *Non-steroidal anti-inflammatory drugs (NSAIDs)* also may be recommended. *Corticosteroid* injection is generally not advised.

Return to sport takes at least 3 months if the injury is caught in the early stages and up to 6 months if it has been present for years. Light jogging can commence when the tendon is no longer tender when pressed firmly with the fingers. The intensity and volume (see *Overload*) can be increased as long as there is no increase in pain in response to the activity up until the next morning.

Surgery may be required if the above treatments fail to gain sufficient improvement after 6 months, which is more likely in males older than 40 and those with longstanding tendinosis. It involves removal of areas of degenerative tissue and repair of partial tears, followed by a *sport rehabilitation* program with an emphasis on eccentric strengthening. Return to sport can take up to 9 months after surgery.

Achilles tendon

The large tendon that connects the gastrocnemius and soleus muscles of the *calf* to the heel bone (calcaneus). (For injuries see *Calf and Achilles tendon pain and injuries*.)

Achilles tendon rupture

A complete tear of the large tendon that connects the *calf* muscles to the heel bone (calcaneus). It most commonly occurs in people in their thirties and forties playing sports such as *tennis* and *squash*. It is often described as feeling 'like a car crashed into the back of my leg'.

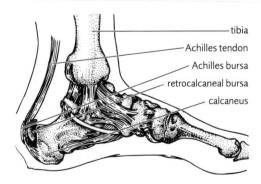

Anatomy of the Achilles tendon medial (inner side) view

Diagnosis, treatment and return to sport
The pain is felt immediately in the tendon, followed by a sudden loss of strength and inability to walk without an obvious limp, which is defined as a grade 3 *strain*. The injury may cause a loud snap when it occurs. Pressing the tendon with the fingers usually reveals a noticeable gap.

Surgery to reconnect the tendon is only recommended for elite or amateur athletes or people intending to remain as active as they were before the injury. Surgery is followed by *immobilisation* in a plaster cast for 4 to 9 weeks, then weight-bearing in a walking cast. Older aged people, or those who do not intend to be as active as they were before the injury, should only require immobilisation.

Treatment at the completion of the immobilisation involves intensive *sport rehabilitation*, including *mobilisation* for the ankle joint, and *flexibility exercises* and *strengthening exercises* to improve muscle *flexibility* and joint *range of movement*. Return to sport can take 6 to 8 months.

Achilles tendon strain (partial tear)

An injury of the large tendon that connects the *calf* muscles to the calcaneus (heel bone). It occurs due to a sudden and excessively forceful contraction of the muscles that the tendon cannot withstand, such as when lunging to play a *tennis* or *squash* stroke or jumping in sports such as *volleyball* and *basketball*.

It is associated with insufficient *warm-up*, reduced *flexibility*, excessive muscle fatigue and an abnormality affecting *running biomechanics*.

Diagnosis, treatment and return to sport
The immediate first sensation felt when the Achilles tendon is partially torn is pain in the back of the lower leg, and calf muscle weakness that makes walking difficult. There may also be an audible snap, crack or tear at the time of the injury.

Depending on the severity of the *strain*, there may be *swelling* around the injured site. The diagnosis can be confirmed with *diagnostic ultrasound* or *magnetic resonance imaging (MRI)*.

The recommended treatments begin with *rest* (possibly crutches to keep off the injured leg), *ice*, *compression* and *elevation*, followed by the same treatments as for *Achilles tendinosis*.

Acromioclavicular (AC) chronic joint pain

A shoulder injury that develops due to repeated minor *acromioclavicular (AC) joint sprains* or a single moderate to severe sprain (see *Shoulder joint*). Shoulder horizontal flexion movement (arm sweeping across the chest) is painful, and *shoulder impingement* is usually present.

Treatment includes *mobilisation, strengthening exercises* and, in some cases, *corticosteroid* injection. If the pain persists, surgery is recommended to remove the end of the clavicle (collarbone) that is closest to the shoulder joint.

Acromioclavicular (AC) joint sprain

An acute injury that tears the ligaments or joint capsule of the acromioclavicular (AC) joint at the top of the shoulder.

It is usually caused by a fall on to the point of the shoulder.

Diagnosis
The joint is located just above the *shoulder joint*, between the collarbone (clavicle) and shoulder tip (acromion). The structures that may be damaged by the *sprain* include the joint capsule, AC ligaments and coracoclavicular ligament (conoid and trapezoid ligaments).

Treatment and return to sport
Types I and II are treated with *conservative treatments* (non-surgical). In the past, most Type III sprains have been treated surgically, but conservative treatments have been found to be just as good. Surgery, which involves reattaching the ligaments, is now only recommended for Types IV, V and VI, and for Type III

Diagnostic classification system of acromioclavicular (AC) joint sprain

Type	Injury
I	Joint capsule damage that is especially painful with horizontal flexion movement (sweeping arm across the chest).
II	AC ligament complete tear with coracoclavicular ligament sprain.
III and V	Coracoclavicular ligament complete tear. Type V also involves significant associated muscle damage. X-rays can differentiate between them.
IV	Posterior (backwards) displacement of the clavicle.
VI	Inferior (downwards) displacement of the clavicle.

Note: Types IV, V and VI are less common than Types I, II and III.

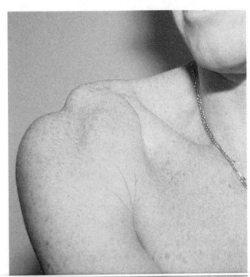

Step deformity, common in Types III and V acromioclavicular (AC) joint injury

cases that fail to respond adequately to conservative treatments.

Conservative treatments include *rest* and *ice* to reduce pain and inflammation, *immobilisation* of the arm in a sling for 2 to 3 days for mild Type I injuries or up to 6 weeks in severe Type II or Type III injuries, *mobilisation* of the AC joint and *isometric strengthening*.

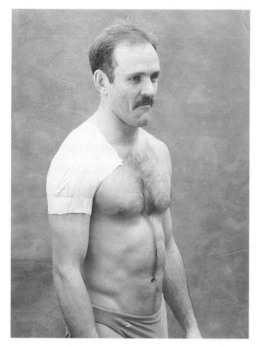

Protective taping for acromio-clavicular (AC) joint sprain

Return to sport is possible when there is no shoulder pain or tenderness and full *range of movement* has returned. Mild Type I and II injuries may take 7 to 10 days, and moderate cases 2 to 3 weeks. Up to 6 weeks may be required before playing *collision sports*. Severe injuries, particularly those requiring surgery, require up to 3 months. *Taping* can provide protection when returning to sport.

Active exercise

An activity that involves moving a part of the body without assistance from an outside force. For example, lifting the arm up in the air as high as possible above the head is an active exercise of the shoulder joint. A *passive exercise* is when the movement is performed with the assistance of an outside force.

Active exercises should be commenced as soon as possible within the limits of pain after an injury has occurred, subject to medical advice if the injury has been severe or involved surgery.

It is a form of *flexibility exercise*, which is used to restore *range of movement* and maintain normal function.

Active movement

A movement that is performed at a joint or muscle, without assistance from an outside force. For example, lifting the leg to the side is an active movement of the hip joint. A *passive movement* is when the movement is performed with the assistance of an outside force, such as a therapist lifting up the arm.

Diagnosis and treatment

Active movements are assessed in a *physical examination* to help provide a *diagnosis* for an injury. An observation is made as to whether the pain that is associated with the injury is reproduced or aggravated by a particular active movement. A measurement of the amount of movement, called *range of movement*, is also made for each available movement at the relevant joints.

Treatments that aim to improve the range of the active movement are called *active exercises*.

Acupuncture

A medical tradition dating back to the rule of the Shang Dynasty in China in 1558 BC that involves inserting needles of various lengths and diameters into designated points of the body. The word 'acupuncture' is derived from the Latin word 'acus' (needle) and means 'puncturing of bodily tissue for the relief of pain'. The practice is a branch of *Chinese medicine*.

Theory

In the early period of the development of acupuncture, treatises were written that were illustrated by anatomical drawings that related to these points along lines called meridians, or 'zing'. During the Sung Dynasty (AD 960–1279), Emperor Wei-yi ordered a bronze statue to be cast on which all acupuncture points were located.

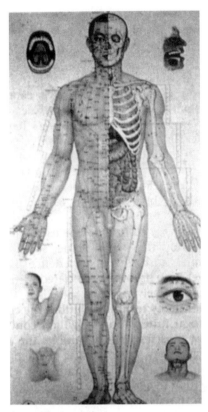

Acupuncture points

At approximately the same time, the relationship was established between the 12 meridians, or 'zing', and the body organs, which are divided into five 'zsang' (heart, liver, spleen, lungs and kidneys) and six 'fu' (stomach, gall bladder, large intestine, small intestine, bladder, and the function known as 'triple warmer'). To these 11 organs or functions, a twelfth meridian of the pericardium was added.

From a conventional medical perspective, the exact mechanism of action of acupuncture remains uncertain. Its effects may be explained by the gate control of pain in which stimulation of one part of the body may block pain from other parts of the body. The *autonomic nervous system* may also play an important role in mediating the acupuncture effect. In addition, acupuncture causes the body to release *endorphins* that may block signals in the pain pathways.

Current scientific evidence shows that it can be useful for reducing pain. In exercise and sport, it may be beneficial in the treatment of injuries such as an *ankle sprain, tennis elbow, low back pain (non-specific)* and *neck pain (non-specific)*.

Treatment

The needles are inserted to various depths, rotated, and either immediately withdrawn or left in place. The needles may also be stimulated electrically or by moxibustion (application of heat to acupuncture points by burning moxa, the dried leaves of Artemisia vulgaris). For example, needles may be placed at acupuncture points close to an ankle sprain. The aim of the treatment is to reduce pain and swelling and increase the rate of healing through increased microcirculation.

Using needles as a form of treatment without reference to acupuncture points or meridians is called *dry needling*.

Acute compartment pressure syndrome

An acute injury that causes excessive pressure on a group of muscles wrapped up in thick fascia, a layer of relatively inelastic, fibrous tissue.

It can occur due to a *fracture* (break) of a nearby bone or a blow leading to a *muscle contusion* (bruise) that leads to excessive pressure due to an accumulation of fluids in the fascia, which obstructs the flow of blood to the muscles and may lead to cell death if not treated in time.

The most common site is the anterior compartment of the *shin*, due to being struck by another player's foot or a piece of equipment such as a hockey stick. It may also occur in the forearm.

The symptoms include persistent pain (greater than one would expect given the nature of the injury), swelling, and pain when stretching the muscle. In severe cases, numbness and pins and needles may develop (on the top of the foot for a shin injury), along with muscle weakness. Emergency surgery is required to release the pressure, followed by a period of *sport rehabilitation*.

Acute injury

An injury that comes on suddenly due to a single incident with an obvious cause. The most common causes are a direct blow, such as being hit by equipment such as a bat or ball or colliding with another player, a twist or fall that causes a ligament sprain, or excessive exertion when performing an activity such as taking off for a sprint. In each case an energy exchange creates forces that are too great for the body part to withstand, leading to tissue damage.

Acute injuries can occur at one or more anatomical sites. For example, a twisted knee that causes a ligament tear often also damages the articular cartilage. An injury that develops over a period of time due to an accumulation of excessive forces is called an *overuse injury*.

Severe acute injuries may need to be treated as a *medical emergency* and require treatment in a hospital as soon as possible. If the injury is not a medical emergency, the first aid treatment varies according to the injury. For example, a dislocation usually requires reconnecting the bones in the joint, which is called relocation. A fracture may require a splint attached to it, preferably a medical piece of equipment or, if necessary, using sporting equipment such as a ski pole or paddle. Subsequent treatments for acute injuries depend on the nature, location and severity and usually include RICE (*rest, ice, compression and elevation*).

Addiction

See *Substance abuse*.

Adduction

A movement of a joint in a direction pointing towards the midline of the body. For example, from a starting position above the head, bringing both arms downwards past the ears to the side of the body is called adduction of the shoulder joint. Adduction is also known as medial flexion in some joints. It is the opposite of *abduction*.

Acute injuries according to type of body tissue

Body tissue	Acute injury
Bone	• *Fracture* • *Periosteal contusion*
Articular cartilage	• Osteochondral/chondral fractures (see *Articular cartilage acute injury*) • *Bone bruise*
Joint	• *Dislocation* • Subluxation
Ligament	• *Sprain/tear*
Muscle	• *Strain/tear* • *Muscle contusion* • *Muscle cramp* • *Acute compartment pressure syndrome*
Tendon	• *Strain* (complete rupture or partial tear)
Nerve	• Neuropraxia (see *Nerve injury*) • Axonotmesis • Neurotmesis
Skin	• Laceration and abrasion (see *Skin injury*) • Puncture wound
Bursa	• Acute haemorrhagic bursitis

Adductor muscle strain

An acute injury that causes a specific point of pain in the groin where the adductor muscle has been damaged, either right next to the pubic bone of the *pelvis* or a number of centimetres below it (see *Hip joint*).

Causes and diagnosis
The injury usually occurs during a sudden change of direction in running, which is common in sports such as *basketball, netball* and the *football* codes, leading to an immediate stabbing pain and inability to perform hip joint adduction (moving the thigh towards the other leg). It is more likely to occur in people with a biomechanical abnormality (e.g. *pelvis lateral tilt*).

The pain is reproduced when pressing firmly on or stretching the muscle and resisting hip joint adduction.

There are three degrees of muscle *strain*. Mild (grade 1) causes pain, but no loss of strength. Moderate (grade 2) causes reduced muscle strength and pain that limits movement. Severe (grade 3) causes significantly reduced strength, but may be less

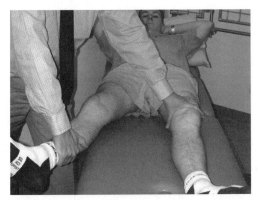

Resisting hip joint adduction for the diagnosis of adductor muscle strain

painful than a moderate strain. The diagnosis may be confirmed with *diagnostic ultrasound* or *magnetic resonance imaging (MRI)*.

Treatment and return to sport

The initial aim of treatment is to reduce bleeding and swelling with (RICE) *rest, ice, compression and elevation*. Gentle *flexibility exercises* and *strengthening exercises* should only be started 4 days after the injury to prevent the development of *adductor tendinosis*. Electrotherapy such as *laser therapy* may be helpful.

Return to running and performing sudden changes of direction should only be recommended once the adductor muscle has achieved a full *range of movement* and full *strength* compared to the uninjured muscle. For a mild strain this takes about 2 weeks, a moderate strain 4 weeks, and a severe strain 6 to 8 weeks.

Recurrent adductor muscle strain

It is not uncommon to suffer a recurrence of an adductor muscle strain, probably due to inadequate treatment, resuming sport too quickly, or if there is an abnormality of *running biomechanics*, particularly *pelvis lateral tilt*.

Adductor tendinosis

An injury of the adductor muscles that causes groin pain. The injury may develop as an *overuse injury*

due to a gradual accumulation of repeated excessive physical loads over a period of weeks or months, or following an *adductor muscle strain* that has been prematurely treated with *flexibility exercises*. It is most common in sports that involve running, twisting and kicking. Pain can also spread to the other groin or the pubic region if left untreated.

A physical examination usually finds tenderness over the adductor muscle tendons near the pubic bone of the *pelvis*. The groin pain is reproduced with *hip joint* abduction (moving the thigh away from the other leg) and resisted hip adduction.

The recommended treatment is the same as for *osteitis pubis*, except that improvement is usually achieved at a much faster rate. Return to sport may commence within 2 to 3 weeks for mild cases and up to 3 months for severe cases.

Adenosine diphosphate (ADP)

A compound produced by the body made up of the protein adenosine joined to a molecule of ribose and two phosphate groups. Adding a third phosphate group to this compound converts it into *adenosine triphosphate (ATP)*, the main source of energy for *muscle contractions*, which is constantly being done in muscles by metabolic processes such as *fat metabolism* and *carbohydrate oxidation*.

Adenosine triphosphate (ATP)

A compound produced by the body that is the main source of energy for *muscle contractions*. It is made up of the protein adenosine joined to a molecule of ribose and three phosphate groups.

Energy is released when the adenosine triphosphatase enzyme (ATPase) breaks the bond holding one of the phosphate groups. This energy is used to bind myosin and actin protein filaments in the sarcomere (see Muscle contraction) of muscle fibres, which in turn creates a muscle contraction. The leftover compound is called *adenosine diphosphate*

(ADP), which is recycled back into ATP by adding a phosphate group.

Adolescent

The period in life beginning with *puberty* and ending with the start of adulthood, when sexual and physical features fully mature. It is associated with psychological, emotional, social and economic aspects of growing up.

According to a strict definition, it ends when the diaphysis and *epiphysis* of the long bones such as the femur (thigh) have fused together and stopped growing, usually around 19 years in females and 22 years in males (see *Growth plate*).

The chronological age of adolescents is the most commonly used rule for deciding the level of participation in exercise and sport. However, it should be noted that each adolescent has his or her own rate of physical development, particularly around puberty.

For younger adolescents it can be useful to apply the Tanner system, a five-point rating based on secondary sex characteristics including pubic hair, breast and genital development for assessing age according to development. Other methods include the age of menarche (first *menstruation*) in girls and salivary testosterone level in boys. Slowly maturing children

can be assessed according to the average height and weight for their age.

Adolescents found to be developmentally advanced may be permitted to participate beyond the recommended age limits, although it is up to a school or club to decide if it is able to accommodate this exception. Many adolescent athletes participate as equals against adults in exercise and sport in their latter years.

During early adolescence, physical and emotional capabilities and responses to participation in exercise and sport change from those typical of childhood but remain unique and different to those of adults. As they mature through to late adolescence they become more like adults.

Physiology

The physiology of adolescence is a steady and gradual transition between childhood and adulthood. Rules adaptations and training alterations should be implemented for specific sports to better suit the physiological and psychological development of adolescents at different ages (see *Middle and long distance running for children and adolescents, Sprinting for children and adolescents, Throwing sports for children and adolescents, Jumping sports for children and adolescents, Swimming for children and adolescents* and *Strength training for children and adolescents*).

The bones of adolescents are more vulnerable to specific types of injuries usually not seen in adults, including *greenstick fracture, growth plate fracture, avulsion fracture, apophysitis* and *osteochondrosis*.

Males and females

At the start of puberty boys and girls possess more or less the same physical and physiological features. During puberty the main influence in boys is a massive increase in the sex hormone *testosterone*, which accelerates the growth of bone and muscle mass. In girls *oestrogen* is the most important sex hormone, which does not have as great an influence on muscle growth and, conversely, causes a relatively greater amount of fat to be deposited in the body, particularly around the hips and thighs. As a result the average adult male ends up taller, heavier and with a higher proportion of muscle mass compared to women.

A young adolescent participating in a walking event

Psychological and social development

Adolescence is a process of growing independence in terms of identity, beliefs and behaviour. This involves a change in relationships with parents—in particular, less financial and emotional reliance.

Areas of exploration and experience include sex, work, career, lifestyle choices such as smoking and drug-taking, and personal presentation, such as hairstyle and clothes. Role models can include adults at the local school and sport club or from the wider world, such as film and music stars, and, of course, leading sports people.

It is also a critical time for the development of self-esteem and self-confidence. Related to this are body image issues that may be accentuated by the rapid physical changes that occur. *Eating disorders* such as anorexia nervosa and bulimia are more likely when dieting and unrealistic body weight expectations are present.

The pressure to optimise performance or achieve a specific body shape for a particular sport can increase the risk of eating disorders. *Sports psychology for younger athletes* and *Sports nutrition for younger athletes* can play an important role in the above dynamics and situations.

Adrenaline

A chemical compound that is a *neurotransmitter* and *hormone*. *Sympathetic nervous system* neurons send instructions to the adrenal gland of the kidneys to produce and release adrenaline (also called epinephrine) into the bloodstream. As it flows around the body it affects many organs at the same time, including the heart, lungs, blood vessels and intestines.

This mass effect is called the 'fight or flight' response and occurs before and during exercise and sport and in reaction to feelings of fear. The sympathetic nervous system directly affects the same organs in the same way.

Adrenaline is also produced in synthetic form. It is used as a drug for emergency treatment for *anaphylaxis* and in special preparations together with *anaesthetics (local)*.

Aerobic capacity

See VO$_2$ *max*.

Aerobic fitness

The efficiency of muscles in the use of oxygen to break down foods such as carbohydrates and fats to release energy that is re-used to produce *adenosine triphosphate (ATP)*, the main source of energy for *muscle contractions*. Breaking down foods using oxygen is a form of *aerobic metabolism*.

The harder the muscles work, the more ATP is required. The greater the efficiency of oxygen usage, the easier it is to supply ATP. Aerobic fitness is also influenced by the combined effort of the lungs, heart and arteries to bring oxygen-carrying blood to the muscles.

People exhibit a wide range of levels of aerobic fitness. The activities that require a high level are those that involve being active for long periods of time, such as marathon runners. A person recovering from a heart attack usually has a low level of fitness. *Aerobic training* increases aerobic fitness.

Aerobic fitness can be measured in different ways. The more sophisticated methods use a treadmill or stationary bicycle to measure VO$_2$ *max*. Less exact, but simpler and more commonly used methods include *maximum heart rate estimation* and *perceived exertion*, such as the *Borg perceived exertion scale*.

Aerobic fitness is also called endurance fitness and cardiovascular fitness. It is the fitness most people are referring to when they say, 'I'm going to get fit.' However, it is just one of several types of *fitness*.

Aerobic metabolism

The chemical processes in the human body that use oxygen to help them proceed. The predominant system in exercise and sport is *carbohydrate oxidation*, which produces energy by using oxygen to break down the chemical bonds that hold together the single chain of carbon (C), oxygen (O) and hydrogen (H) atoms that make up carbohydrates.

Aerobic systems are significantly more productive and efficient over a long period of time than *anaerobic metabolism*, which does not use oxygen. However the latter is best for producing energy quickly, such as in a 100 m sprint. Other aerobic metabolic systems that are important in exercise and sport include *fat metabolism* and *protein oxidation*.

Aerobic training

Regular participation in activities that aim to increase *aerobic fitness*. It can prevent disease and illness, improve the health of a person who is already in poor health, and improve performance levels in people who participate in sport and exercise.

For example, a moderate gain in aerobic fitness achieves significant protection against *coronary heart disease*, *stroke*, *depression* and *diabetes*, and is an essential part of the treatment for people who have had a *heart attack*. A large gain in aerobic fitness can prepare a person to run a marathon.

Physiology

Training improves aerobic fitness by increasing the number of mitochondria in the muscles, the microscopic structures where oxygen is used in *aerobic metabolism* to produce *adenosine triphosphate* (ATP), the main source of energy for *muscle contractions*, which leads to an increased efficiency of oxygen usage in the muscles.

It also increases storage of muscle glucose, makes free fatty acids more available and increases the number of arteries in the muscles. In response to improved aerobic fitness, *heart rate* and *blood pressure* decrease and heart *stroke volume* rises. Aerobic training is also called cardiovascular training and endurance training.

Exercise and sport

Aerobic fitness increases in response to an *overload*, where activities are performed at a high enough volume and intensity to cause fatigue. Current aerobic fitness levels should be assessed beforehand to determine the required volume and intensity to achieve an overload.

The most accurate assessment of aerobic fitness is gained by measuring VO_2 *max* with specialised equipment. When equipment is unavailable or too costly, there are other acceptable methods including *maximum heart rate estimation* and *perceived exertion*, such as the *Borg perceived exertion scale* (see also *Breathing regulation*).

High increases in fitness require high-intensity training, such as fast jogging or swimming laps, for at least 20 minutes, three times a week. Moderate gains are sufficient when the goal is general health benefits, which can be achieved with brisk walking (see *Exercise for health*).

Aerobic *interval training* is a technique used by athletes training at the highest levels. It involves brief periods of increased intensity repeatedly performed throughout a training session, interspersed with less intensity or full *rest*. For example, performing a number of brief periods of fast swimming during a 4 km swim at a slow pace or including several brief uphill runs during a 10 km (6 mile) run on flat terrain.

Measures of the intensity of a physical activity are:
- Low intensity: equivalent to breathing exertion ranging from 'no effect on breathing' up to the point that 'shortness of breath is noticed' = 30–49 per cent of VO_2 *max* = 35–59 per cent of maximum heart rate estimation (220 – age) = 11 on the Borg perceived exertion scale.
- *Moderate intensity*: is equivalent to a range from 'shortness of breath is noticed' up to the point that 'whistling or normal continuous conversation is just possible' = 50–74 per cent of VO_2 max = 60–79 per cent of maximum heart rate estimation = 13 on the Borg perceived exertion scale.
- *High intensity*: equivalent to a range from the point that 'whistling or normal continuous conversation is just possible' up to the point that 'whistling or normal continuous conversation is impossible' = 75–84 per cent of VO_2 max = 80–89 per cent of maximum heart rate estimation = 15 on the Borg perceived exertion scale.

Rehabilitation

The best levels of aerobic fitness are often achieved by participating in the specific sport at competition level. However, maintaining aerobic fitness as much as possible is an essential component of the recovery process following an injury. Even though rest and treatment for an injury usually limit the ability to participate in activities, it should always be possible to select aerobic fitness exercises as part of a *sport rehabilitation* program.

For example, following a leg injury, activities such as cycling, swimming or water exercises can be performed instead of running. Once a full recovery and return to sport is achieved, it may be advantageous, particularly if it has been an overuse injury, to incorporate some of the alternative activities in the normal training program.

Activities

Aerobic training generally includes activities that use the large muscle groups for long duration—for example, walking briskly, *jogging*, running, *swimming*, *cycling*, *rowing*, *cross-country skiing* and *dancing*. Reduced-weight-bearing activities, such as rowing, swimming and *aqua running*, are preferable for people with lower limb *osteoarthritis* or as part of a sport rehabilitation program.

Aerobic training diet

The foods that are recommended for athletes participating in *aerobic training*. The most important goal is to ensure a sufficient carbohydrate supply to fill the glycogen storage sites in muscles and the liver.

Carbohydrates and fats

The ideal diet for most athletes is 60–70 per cent of the energy supply derived from *carbohydrates* and 25–30 per cent from *fats*. Inadequate carbohydrate supplies may eventually cause *carbohydrate depletion* over the long term and lead to excessive *tiredness*.

Endurance athletes performing more than 90 minutes of high-intensity activity (see *Aerobic training* and *Metabolic equivalent (MET)*) at training sessions need a daily carbohydrate intake of 8–10 g per kilogram (g/kg) (3.6–4.5 oz/lb) of body weight to fill up glycogen stores.

Protein

Repair of minor tissue damage that can be caused by aerobic training requires an adequate protein intake. In addition, protein makes a small contribution to energy supply.

The recommended protein intake is 1.2–1.6 g/kg (0.5–0.7 oz/lb) per day. The longer the duration of training, the greater the amount of protein required. A 60 kg (132 lb) long distance running athlete in heavy training would require 96 g (3.4 oz) of protein each day.

Aerobics

The term 'aerobics' was coined by US exercise physiologist Kenneth Cooper in the 1960s. By the 1970s it was a household word, due to its association with exercise to music. The large majority of participants are female.

Fitness, equipment and rules

Aerobics is performed to music according to a choreographed routine designed to elevate the heart rate, which is a form of *aerobic training*. Routines are categorised into different class types according to impact levels, including:

- High-impact: both feet simultaneously above the ground at some moments.
- Low-impact: at least one foot on the ground at all times.
- Step aerobics: stepping up and down a height-adjustable platform.
- Aquarobics: low-impact in a swimming pool.

The most appropriate footwear is the *cross training shoe*, and the best surface is wooden or carpeted floors, not concrete. Competition aerobics is similar to floor *gymnastics*.

Injuries

The most common injuries are *tibia stress fracture* (shin), *fibula stress fracture* (shin), *shin chronic compartment syndrome, patellofemoral joint syndrome* (knee), *Achilles tendinosis* (calf) and *low back pain (non-specific)*. Participants may face a risk of *eating disorders*.

Ageing

The changes that occur during adulthood with increasing age. These changes are influenced by a combination of one's inheritance or genetic programming, environment, and lifestyle (such as diet and exercise and sport).

The biological process that underlies ageing is still unclear. One prominent theory is that each time a cell replicates itself there is an increased chance for an error in DNA. Genes also influence vulnerability to illness and disease. There are, of course, individuals who have smoked and lived to 100 years. However, they are the exception to the rule that illness and disease can be prevented or delayed by avoiding unhealthy lifestyle habits.

Exercise and sport are permitted until any age as long as one is healthy enough and the level of participation is age appropriate (see *Older athlete*). A *medical clearance* is recommended for participants who have had a history of illness such as *coronary heart disease* or are planning to participate in exercise or sport that requires a greater effort than the equivalent of brisk walking. Participation in exercise and sport is often done under the auspices of *masters sports* organisations.

Aggression

A tendency to initiate attacks or offensive action with the intent to intimidate, harm or cause injury. It can be negative and inappropriate, such as punching an opposing player in a team sport. But it also can be positive and appropriate when it is within the rules of *collision sports* such as ice hockey and football.

The causes of inappropriate aggression are still not fully understood. There is little evidence that some people are born with an aggressive *personality* that is just waiting for a provocative situation to be expressed. It is generally agreed that aggression is a learnt behaviour that can be modified. It is more likely to occur when taking *anabolic steroids*, which is called 'roids rage'.

The most commonly used method of treating overly aggressive behaviour is anger management, where participants learn to identify the causes and their feelings that lead to acts of aggression and to counter them with alternative, non-violent feelings and behaviours.

Agility training

Regular participation in activities that aim to increase the ability to move quickly, lightly, nimbly and with good *balance* skills. The activities are usually sport-specific, such as performing cartwheels in gymnastics and running figures of eight for soccer, or injury-specific, such as *proprioception training* to improve balance skills after an ankle sprain. In addition, agility requires an appropriate level of *flexibility training*, *strength training* and *speed training*.

AIDS

See *HIV*.

Alcohol

A liquid made from the fermentation of *carbohydrates* that have been added to yeast. In social situations it is used to relax the nerves, reduce inhibitions and improve self-confidence. However, alcohol has a negative impact on participants in exercise and sport.

It acts as a depressant on the central nervous system, which dampens reaction times, balance and coordination. It increases urine production and, as a result, the risk of *heat illness*. Alcohol also increases the amount of *oedema* and *swelling* caused by an *acute injury* and should be avoided for up to 72 hours after the injury occurs. Even though alcohol has a high concentration of energy (1 g = 27 kJ/6½ Cal, compared to 1 g carbohydrates = 17 kJ/4 Cal), the energy cannot be used by the muscles or stored as *glycogen*. Lastly, there are long-term dangers associated with prolonged excessive use including liver and brain damage and vitamin and mineral deficiency.

The guidelines for the use of alcohol in exercise and sport are:

- Avoid binge drinking (see *Substance abuse*).
- Avoid drinking in the 24 hours prior to competition.
- Avoid drinking if injured.
- Be aware of the dehydrating effect of alcohol.
- When drinking, rehydrate beforehand with *water* or a *sports drink* and accompany alcohol with a nutritious meal.

Alcohol is not on the list of *drugs banned in sport* according to the International Olympic Committee (IOC). However, a sport organisation may request a breath test or blood alcohol test as a prevention measure against substance abuse.

Alexander technique

A method of increasing the efficiency of movements and improving postures such as sitting and standing to prevent and treat injuries, illness and disease.

It was developed by the Australian teacher, Frederick Matthias Alexander in the 1920s. It is currently taught in a wide range of fields, from drama schools for improving elocution through to physiotherapy for pain relief and posture improvement.

Altitude sickness

An illness that occurs when breathing in air at a significantly lower atmospheric pressure and oxygen content compared to sea level. The critical level begins from a height of 2400 m (8000 ft) above sea level. It is most commonly observed in mountain climbers and skiers (up to one in five people may experience it), especially those that do not allow themselves to acclimatise.

The best acclimatisation is to rest for a day or two at 2400 m (8000 ft) before ascending another 600–900 m (2000–3000 ft), or climbing no more than 300 m (1000 ft) a day from 3000 m (10 000 ft). Medical advice should be received before taking preventive medications such as dexamethasone.

Diagnosis and treatment

MILD (ACUTE)

Symptoms include headache, nausea, vomiting, shortness of breath and sleep disturbances (insomnia). They usually begin 6 to 96 hours after arriving at altitude. Treatment includes descending at least 600 m (2000 ft) and resting at that level for a day or two.

SEVERE

Severe altitude sickness is a life-threatening condition due to pulmonary oedema (water on the lungs) and, less commonly, cerebral oedema (water on the brain), which should be treated as a *medical emergency*, requiring treatment to ensure that breathing and circulation are not compromised.

Symptoms of pulmonary oedema include tiredness, severe shortness of breath, and coughing that brings up frothy, whitish sputum (phlegm). Treatment includes descending at least 600 m (2000 ft), receiving oxygen and *diuretics*, and is followed by a quick recovery.

Cerebral oedema causes severe headache, vomiting, poor coordination, confusion and hallucinations, seizures and loss of consciousness. Treatment is similar to pulmonary oedema; however, recovery may take days or weeks.

Altitude training

Training at heights of between 1500 and 3000 m (5000 and 10 000 ft) with the aim of gaining improvements in performance for an upcoming competition at sea level. The main benefits include stimulating *erythropoietin (EPO)*, which increases the numbers of red blood cells and improves haemoglobin levels. However, these benefits only last for a few days and need to be weighed against the disadvantages, including initial loss of fitness due to the need to train at a significantly reduced intensity during the first 2 weeks and the cost of moving the training to a new location.

Another reason for altitude training is to acclimatise to an upcoming competition located at a high altitude. Full acclimatisation requires 4 to 6 weeks' training, although significant adaptation can be achieved after 2 weeks. An alternative is to ensure that arrival at altitude and competition occurs within 24 hours, before the detrimental effects of altitude begin.

Alveolus

The tiny balloon-like space in the *lungs* filled with air that sits alongside a blood vessel, which allows the easy movement of oxygen and carbon dioxide gases between them. Groups of these spaces, called alveoli, are located in a cluster that looks like a bunch of grapes at the end of small tubes, called bronchioles (see *Respiratory system*). The movement of oxygen and carbon dioxide between the alveoli and blood is called *pulmonary diffusion*.

Amateur

See *Non-elite*.

Amenorrhea

Less than three menstrual periods in a year, or none in the last 6 months. The most common cause is *pregnancy*. Other causes include *eating disorders* such as anorexia, thyroid disease, *tumour* and *depression*. When it is associated with *disordered eating* and *osteoporosis*, the syndrome is called *female athlete triad*. A milder form of amenorrhea is oligomenorrhea, defined as infrequent menstrual periods, three to six in the past 12 months, and small amounts of blood loss.

Amenorrhea and oligomenorrhea are up to four times more likely to occur in women who regularly participate in excessive amounts of high-intensity exercise or sport. It is due to a combination of inadequate diet, low body fat, high levels of exercise and psychological stress, causing the hypothalamus of the brain to release less luteinising hormone (LH), which results in low levels of the hormones in *menstruation*, oestrogen and progesterone.

It is more frequent in *long distance running* and ballet *dancing* than in sports such as swimming and cycling.

Treatment

If the cause of amenorrhea and oligomenorrhea is excessive participation in exercise and sport, the recommended treatment is reducing the duration and intensity of training or increasing the percentage body fat through dietary changes. In rare cases it is recommended to increase oestrogen through the oral-contraceptive pill (see *Contraception*) or *hormone replacement therapy*. Women should not automatically assume that amenorrhea prevents pregnancy.

American football

In 1875, Harvard and Yale universities played the first inter-college game that was part soccer and part Rugby Union. Since then, American football has evolved to become a distinctive sport.

Rules and equipment

A game is played between two teams of 11 players on a rectangular field with goalposts at each end. Each team tries to score points by moving the ball over the opponent's goal line for a touchdown (by carrying or passing the ball to a teammate) or by kicking it between the goalposts (a field goal). A team must advance the ball 10 yards in four attempts, called downs. As the possession of the ball changes from side to side, defensive and offensive teams move on and off the field. Specialised equipment is worn, including *football boots*, protective padding, hard plastic shells and a *helmet*.

Fitness and injuries

Defensive players require more *strength training*, whereas offensive players need more *anaerobic training* for sprinting.

The most common injuries include *quadriceps contusion* (thigh), *hamstring strain* (thigh), *medial collateral ligament (MCL) sprain* (knee), *ankle sprain, clavicle fracture* (shoulder) *acromioclavicular (AC) joint sprain* (shoulder), *shoulder instability* (shoulder), *rotator cuff tendinosis* (shoulder), *Colles fracture* (wrist), *concussion, neck burner,* and *hand and finger pain and injuries.*

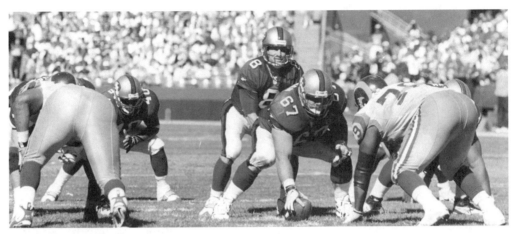

American football players

American football boots

See *Football boots*.

Amino acids

The basic building blocks of *proteins*. Each amino acid is made up of a nitrogen-based amino molecule and an acidic carboxyl molecule. There are 20 different types of amino acids in all the proteins in the human body. Of these 12 can be produced in the body and another eight have to be eaten in the diet, which are called essential amino acids. Only foods such as meat, eggs, poultry and dairy products contain all of the essential amino acids. Vegetables and grains have a limited number. Amino acids bonded together by peptide bonds make up a protein.

Supplementation

Amino acid supplementation provided as a powder, such as milk powder with additional vitamins or *colostrum* that is added to liquid, is often suggested for people participating in strength training such as lifting weights to help them achieve an adequate protein intake. However, a healthy diet of protein-rich foods should be sufficient (see *Strength training diet*). Supplementation of the amino acid glutamine may maintain the strength of the *immune system* in people participating in long distance sports such as

marathon running, which may help to prevent *over-training syndrome*. Valine, leucine and isoleucine, which are branched chain amino acids, are also suggested as a means to delay fatigue and aid recovery by promoting muscle growth.

Amphetamines

A stimulant drug that is used in the treatment of narcolepsy (excessive daytime sleepiness) and childhood syndromes such as attention deficit disorder (ADD). It was widely used several decades ago in sport to delay fatigue and increase alertness, until a number of deaths and dangerous side effects became a deterrent. It is a *drug banned in sport*.

The side effects include irritability, insomnia, restlessness, dizziness, tremor (trembling), confusion, paranoia, delirium, uncontrolled aggression, *hypertension* (high blood pressure), angina (chest pain), vomiting, abdominal pain and cerebral haemorrhage (see *Stroke*). Amphetamines are addictive, and withdrawal is associated with fatigue, lethargy and *depression*.

Amputation (traumatic)

Cutting off a part of the body, such as an arm, finger, nose or ear. The primary concern is blood loss, which can lead to loss of consciousness and, if severe, eventually death. The secondary concern is to save the amputated part so that it can be reattached with microsurgery.

The main aim of first aid treatment is to stop or minimise the loss of blood by applying pressure to the wound. This can be done by covering the stump with a sterile dressing that is held in place with a bandage, positioning the stump in a raised position, and transporting the injured person as quickly as possible to a hospital to perform microsurgery.

The amputated part should be wrapped in a moist sterile dressing, surrounded by aluminium foil and placed on ice. *Rehabilitation* treatments are required after successful reattachment.

If reattachment of a significant part of a limb is unsuccessful, rehabilitation may include learning to use a prosthesis and to participate in exercise and sport (see *Amputee athletes*).

Amputee athletes

People with at least one major joint in a limb missing, such as the elbow, wrist, knee or ankle, who participate in exercise and sport. In some sports they compete as *wheelchair athletes*.

Young people injured in a road or workplace accident make up the largest group of amputees and are the most likely to participate in sport and exercise. Another large group of amputees, older-aged people who have had *peripheral vascular disease* of the legs, are the least likely participants.

Exercise and sport

People with amputations participate in a wide range of sports, including track and field, swimming, shooting, cycling, table tennis and archery.

There are nine classes of disability determined by a combination of 'above- or below-knee amputations' and 'above- or below-elbow amputations'. The largest class is 'A4', comprising single below-knee amputees. The smallest class is 'A9', which includes athletes with up to three amputations. Class can restrict participation. For example, track and field athletes only include single and double below-elbow and single below-knee amputees, not double below-knee.

An A4 single below knee amputee athlete

The benefits of exercise and sport are the same as for the general population, including a reduced risk of being *overweight* and developing *coronary heart disease, diabetes* and *osteoporosis*.

Injuries

The most common problems are *blisters*, skin loss, *muscle contusion* (muscle bruise), local infection and pressure sores of the stump, most commonly in lower limb amputees participating in track and field and other running sports. These injuries are more likely in athletes with relatively shorter stumps—for example, a high above-knee amputation—which are more difficult to fit properly for a prosthesis.

Injuries also occur when repetitive forces cause the prosthesis to suddenly break during activity. This is more likely to occur to lower limb amputees during running. Muscle or bone injuries are possible at the time of failure if there is a heavy fall.

Treatment is generally the same as for the general population, including *rest* from *weight-bearing* and physical activity. For lower limb amputees, this means less time wearing the prosthesis and increased use of elbow crutches. Weight-bearing is only reintroduced for severe injuries after full healing has occurred. A gradual reintroduction is permitted during healing for mild injuries. *Ice* and *elevation* of the affected limb are recommended for bruising. *Antibiotics* also may be prescribed for local infections. There should be a greater emphasis on *cross training* to avoid loss of aerobic fitness—for example, swimming for track and field athletes.

Anabolic agents

A group of drugs that increase the size and bulk of muscles and reduce inflammation. There are two types of anabolic agents: *anabolic steroids* and *beta-2 agonists*. There is a total ban on the use of anabolic steroids. Beta-2 agonists are permitted for use in an inhaled form for the treatment of *asthma*.

Anabolic steroids

A group of drugs that have a similar effect to the male sex hormone *testosterone*. Doctors infrequently prescribe them to treat diseases such as breast cancer.

They are primarily used to increase muscle size and bulk by athletes in power sports such as *weight lifting*, *sprinting*, short distance *swimming*, *throwing sports* such as shot put, *bodybuilding* and *football* codes. There is also high usage among certain professions such as security services and the armed forces and in the general population to improve physical appearance. The World Anti-Doping Agency (WADA), International Olympic Committee (IOC) and other sporting organisations have banned the use of anabolic steroids (see *Drugs banned in sport*).

Many anabolic steroids are obtained through a flourishing black market that exists in some gymnasiums, health centres and clubs. Names of commonly used steroids include clostebol, fluoxymesterone, ethandienone, methenolone (Primobolan), nandrolone (Deca-Durabolin), 19-norandrostenediol, 19-norandrostenedione, oxandrolone, stano-

zolol, androstenediol, androstenedione, dihydrotestoserone and dehydroepiandrosterone (DHEA). The lack of regulatory control of these drugs means that the exact amount of steroids in each tablet is uncertain.

Steroids are usually taken in cycles that include heavy use alternating with drug-free periods that aim to reduce the side effects. The two cycle methods are: a 'pyramid' regimen, which commences with a low daily dose and gradually increases to a high dose, and a 'stacking' regimen, in which several different types of anabolic steroids, oral and injectable, are taken simultaneously.

Physiology

Anabolic steroids appear to increase muscle size and muscle strength, but only when performing intense *strength training* and eating an adequate *protein* intake. This occurs due to an anabolic stimulus, where the body uses the protein to build up the number and size of muscle fibres in response to the stimulus of lifting weights during strength training.

At the same time, steroids reduce the *inflammation* and the breakdown of proteins, called a catabolic effect, that occur during strength training. They allow quicker recovery between training sessions and an increased tolerance of training *overload*. Steroids also may increase aggressive behaviour, leading to greater participation in strength training.

Side effects

Most side effects are reversible when steroids are stopped. However, long-term use may cause permanent damage, even death.

The side effects for adults of both sexes include liver disorders, increased risk of tumours, reduced *high-density lipoproteins (HDL)* and increased *low-density lipoproteins (LDL)*, which is an increased risk for *coronary heart disease*, and *hypertension* (high blood pressure).

Other side effects include decreased effectiveness of the *immune system*, skin problems such as acne and rosacea (permanent redness of the cheeks and nose), increased body hair, irritability, mood swings, changes in libido and increased aggression, commonly known as 'roids rage', and, in severe cases, schizophrenia and psychosis.

Specific side effects for males are reduced testes size and sperm volume, and gynecomastia (development of breasts) because the steroids are converted into a form of *oestrogen*. Many steroids users counteract the latter by taking tamoxifen (Nolvadex).

In females the side effects include *menstruation* problems, deepening of the voice, baldness, hirsutism (increased facial and body hair), altered libido and enlargement of the clitoris. Steroids taken during pregnancy can cause foetal abnormalities or death.

Side effects for *adolescents* are acne, increased facial and body hair, premature closing of the growth plates in the *long bones*, penis enlargement, baldness, deepening of the voice and abnormal psychosocial maturation.

Anabolism

The chemical processes in the human body that use up energy to produce compounds or build up tissues. For example, adding a phosphate group to the adenosine diphosphate (ADP) creates adenosine triphosphate (ATP), the main source of energy for muscle contractions. Protein is used to build up the number and size of muscle fibres. It is the opposite of *catabolism*. The energy for anabolism mainly comes from breaking down foods such as *carbohydrates* and *fats*.

Anaemia

See *Iron deficiency*.

Anaerobic fitness

The efficiency of muscles to release energy by using chemical processes that do not use oxygen to produce adenosine triphosphate (ATP), the main source of energy for *muscle contractions*. These chemical processes are part of *anaerobic metabolism*.

This type of fitness is most important in activities that involve brief bursts of power, such as a 100 m sprint or *weight lifting*.

A direct method of measuring anaerobic fitness has yet to be found. The level of *lactate* in the blood is commonly regarded as the best of the indirect methods. The most effective method of increasing anaerobic fitness is through *interval training*.

Anaerobic metabolism

The chemical processes in the cells of the human body that do not need oxygen to proceed. The two most important anaerobic metabolic systems that produce adenosine triphosphate (ATP), the main source of energy for muscle contractions, are the *creatine phosphate system* and the *glycolytic system*.

The creatine phosphate system produces energy in muscles at the beginning of an activity. It does its best work for 6 to 30 seconds. By then the glycolytic system has kicked into action and takes over as the main supplier of energy.

Anaerobic threshold

See *Lactate threshold*.

Anaerobic training

Regular participation in activities that aim to increase *anaerobic fitness*. The most effective method is *interval training*. It involves performing brief periods of increased intensity of an activity followed by reduced intensity or *rest*, which is repeated throughout a training session.

For example, a 100 m sprinter may run 50 m at competition pace followed by a period of complete rest, repeated 20 times throughout a training session.

Athletes possessing a higher proportion of *fast-twitch (FT) muscle fibres* are considered to have an advantage in training to improve anaerobic fitness.

Improvements in anaerobic fitness are attributable to increased muscle strength, increased capacity in the muscles to delay *lactate fatigue* and increased *economy of effort*, the measure of the efficiency of energy-use during a specific activity. Taking *sodium bicarbonate* supplements to increase the concentration of bicarbonate in the blood also may reduce acidity, leading to a delay in lactate fatigue.

Anaesthesia

The absence of feeling or sensation. It can be due to an injury, such as *nerve root compression* caused by a prolapsed disc in the low back, which is also called *numbness*. It can also be intentionally induced for the whole body prior to surgery with general anaesthesia, for a large region with an epidural, or for a small region with *anaesthetics (local)* and *ice*.

Anaesthetics (local)

Drugs used to reduce or block out sensations. They are not banned in sport; however, the World Anti-Doping Agency (WADA) recommends specific restrictions. Only bupivacaine, lidocaine (lignocaine), mepivicaine and procaine are permitted in conjunction with vasoconstrictor drugs such as *adrenaline* in the area of injury or in joints and when medically justified, which should be notified to the relevant authorities in writing.

Analgesics

Medications that reduce *pain*. There are two types: *narcotics*, such as morphine and *codeine*; and non-narcotics, such as *aspirin* and *paracetamol*. These drugs may be swallowed as a pill, rubbed into the skin as a cream (see *Analgesics (topical)*) or given as an injection (see *Anaesthetics (local)*).

Paracetamol and codeine are the most commonly used analgesics by people participating in exercise and sport. They are usually recommended for a *headache* or an *acute injury* in the first 72 hours after

it has occurred. Subsequent use of analgesics for an injury depends on the amount and duration of pain. For example, pain reduction may make it easier to perform flexibility exercises.

The narcotics morphine and pethidine are *drugs banned in sport* by the World Anti-Doping Agency and International Olympic Committee (IOC).

Analgesics (topical)

A medication that is rubbed into the skin to reduce aches and pain. Some preparations—commonly known as sports rubs, heat rubs and liniments—are used to warm up the muscles and joints in preparation for exercise or sport.

Most topical analgesics contain a combination of substances such as menthol, methyl salicylate, camphor and eucalyptus oil. The two main effects are to widen the blood vessels and make the skin turn red, and to stimulate the pain and temperature-sensing nerve receptors. This stimulation can reduce pain through counter-irritation. Although the exact action of counter-irritation is still unknown, it is believed that it acts to distract one's perception of pain.

Topical analgesics should not be used for an *acute injury* of a structure just below the skin, such as a knee or finger injury, because it increases bleeding and the formation of oedema and *swelling* (see *RICE (rest, ice, compression and elevation)*). In some people they can also cause blistering or skin rashes.

Anaphylaxis

A life-threatening condition that causes symptoms including feelings of warmth, itching, skin redness, rashes and wheals (raised areas of skin), and swelling of organs such as the gastrointestinal system and upper airways, which can make speaking, swallowing and breathing difficult. It should be treated as a *medical emergency*, which requires mouth-to-mouth resuscitation, possibly cardiopulmonary resuscitation and an injection of a synthetic form of the neurotransmitter, *adrenaline*.

Exercise and sport

It is most likely to be triggered off by an allergy, often to a food such as eggs, nuts or seafood, or to a medication such as penicillin, which causes a sudden release of histamines. In rare cases, participation in a physical activity such as exercise or sport is the trigger.

Prevention measures are based on avoiding known allergic triggers. In exercise and sport, this may require reducing the intensity of *aerobic training* (also see *Metabolic equivalent (MET)*), avoiding exercise on warm and humid days, waiting 4 hours after a meal before exercising and taking *antihistamine* medication.

Making preparations for treating an attack, particularly an adrenaline injection, also may be recommended. At the first signs of an attack, such as itching, exercise should be stopped immediately.

Anatomical position

The position of the human body that is the starting point used for describing subsequent movements. In the anatomical position the human body is standing with the face forwards, arms by the side with palms facing forwards, legs together, feet flat on the ground and toes pointing forward.

Anatomy

The science that describes the structure of the human body in terms of its shape, size, composition and location of specific parts. It includes microscopic structures such as cells and tissues, and those that can be seen with the naked eye such as the organs and systems of the body. It is intimately related to physiology, which describes how the human body works and functions.

Angioedema

A non-itchy swelling in the deep skin most commonly found in the face and mouth, although it can occur in any part of the body. In most cases it is triggered off by an allergy; however, it can be due to participation in exercise. If the swelling is located in the throat, angioedema can be life-threatening (see *Anaphylaxis*). It can be prevented with *antihistamines*.

Angle and base of gait

The angle of gait is the angle between an imaginary straight line representing the direction of running and an imaginary line running parallel to the foot indicating the direction in which the toes are pointing. During walking, the foot tends to point at an angle of 10 degrees away from the direction of walking. As the speed of running increases, this angle gets smaller until in sprinting the toes are pointing in the same direction as the direction of running (an angle of 0 degrees).

Base of gait is the distance between the foot and an imaginary line down the middle of the body. During walking, the normal base is 2.5–3.0 cm (approx 1 in). As the speed of running increases, the base narrows. In sprinting it is zero.

Deviations from the above can reduce the efficiency of the gait technique (see *Economy of effort*), cause slower running times and be associated with problems such as increased risk of an *overuse injury* (see also *Biomechanical abnormality*).

Ankle

The joints, bones and muscles between the lower leg and foot. The bones are the lower shin bones (tibia and fibula) and the talus, a squat bone on top of the heel bone (calcaneus). There are three joints:
1) Ankle (talocrural) joint: between the lower end of the tibia and fibula, and the upper end of the talus. Movements: *plantar flexion* (foot downwards) and *dorsiflexion* (foot upwards).
2) Inferior tibiofibular joint: between the lower ends of the tibia and fibula. Movements: small rotation.
3) Subtalar joint: between the undersurface of the talus and the top of the heel bone (calcaneus).

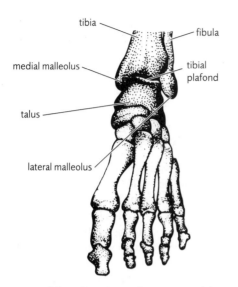

Bones of the ankle (talocrural) joint, viewed from above

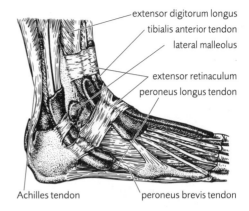

Tendons on the lateral (outer) side of the ankle

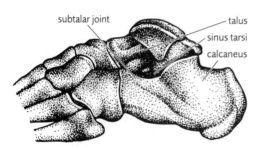

Bones of the subtalar joint of the ankle lateral (outer side) view

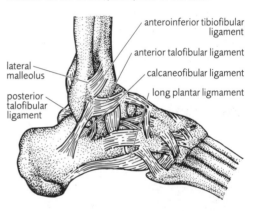

Lateral (outer side) ligaments of the ankle

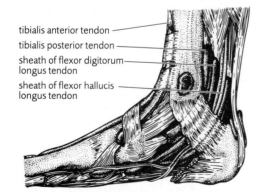

Tendons on the medial (inner) side of the ankle

Movements: *Supination*, part of inversion (turning sole of the foot towards midline), and *pronation*, part of eversion (turning sole to face outwards) (see *Foot and toes* and *Running biomechanics*). This joint permits the foot to adjust to uneven ground and remain flat on the ground when the leg is at an angle.

Ankle anterior impingement

Pain located at the front of the *ankle* joint due to the formation of bony spurs on the lower end of the large shin bone (tibia) and the top of the talus bone. The pain is produced during extreme dorsiflexion (foot upward movements) such as in kicking a football

Muscles involved in ankle movements

Movement	Primary movers	Secondary movers
Plantar flexion	• Gastrocnemius • Soleus (collectively called the *calf* muscles)	• Plantaris • Tibialis posterior • Flexor hallucis longus • Flexor digitorum longus
Dorsiflexion	• Tibialis anterior	• Extensor digitorum longus • Peroneus tertius • Extensor hallucis longus
Inversion	• Tibialis anterior • Tibialis posterior	
Eversion	• Peroneus longus • Peroneus brevis	

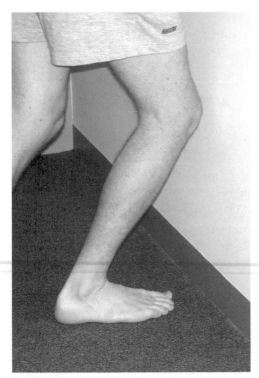

Reproduction of pain caused by ankle anterior impingement

and plie (lunge) movements in ballet dancing that press the spurs against nearby soft tissue such as the joint capsule. Spurs are more likely following an *ankle sprain* that does not heal fully.

The recommended treatment for mild cases is *rest* from aggravating activities, *mobilisation* of the ankle and foot joints, and *non-steroidal anti-inflammatory drugs (NSAIDs)*. If the pain persists, surgery may be required to remove the spurs.

Ankle equinus

A structural abnormality of the *ankle* joint that causes less than 10 degrees of dorsiflexion movement (lifting toes and foot upwards). It is a biomechanical abnormality of the foot that can lead to excessive *foot pronation*, which is associated with injuries including *metatarsal stress fracture*, *navicular stress fracture* and *Achilles tendinosis*.

Ankle equinus may be caused by an inherited bone defect or loss of flexibility of the gastrocnemius or soleus (calf) muscles. A bouncy running style is a sign of ankle equinus.

Ankle medial ligament sprain

A tear or excessive stretch of the medial (inner side) ligaments of the *ankle* joint due to a twist that turns the foot outwards in an excessive movement. It is a relatively uncommon ankle injury.

In some cases a medial ligament sprain occurs together with a *Pott's fracture*, *talar dome injury* or *ankle sprain*. The degrees of severity and treatment are the same as for ankle sprain; however, return to activity and sport takes nearly twice as long.

Ankle pain and injuries

Causes

Pain can be caused by an acute or overuse injury. An *acute injury* causes pain that begins suddenly due to a single incident, such as twisting the ankle.

An *overuse injury* causes pain that gets worse over a period of weeks or months due to an accumulation of excessive forces that cause microtrauma. In the early stages it causes only minor pain and stiffness. But later on, either gradually or following a sudden force, it becomes painful enough to seek medical care.

The joints, ligaments, bones, muscles and tendons of the *ankle* are the main sources of *pain*. In some cases the pain comes from another structure such as the low back, which is called *ankle referred pain*.

Causes of ankle pain and injuries

Common	Less common	Not to be missed
Acute injury		
• Ankle sprain (lateral ligament)	• Talar dome injury • Ankle medial ligament sprain • Pott's fracture • Fifth metatarsal base fracture	• Complex regional pain syndrome (CRPS)
Overuse injury		
Pain located on the medial (inner) side of the ankle		
• Tibialis posterior tendinosis • Flexor hallucis longus tendinosis	• Ankle referred pain • Talus stress fracture • Ankle posterior impingement	• Navicular stress fracture • Complex regional pain syndrome (CRPS)
Pain located on the lateral (outer) side of the ankle		
• Peroneal tendinosis • Sinus tarsi syndrome	• Ankle posterior impingement • Talus stress fracture • Ankle referred pain	• Fibula stress fracture • Complex regional pain syndrome (CRPS)
Pain located on the anterior (front) side of the ankle		
• Ankle anterior impingement • Tibialis anterior tendinosis		

Diagnosis

Making a diagnosis involves combining information gathered from the *history*, the *physical examination* and relevant tests.

For acute injuries it is important to recall the movement that caused the injury. For example, a twist that turns the ankle inwards causes an *ankle sprain*, whereas a twist that turns the ankle outwards causes an *ankle medial ligament sprain*. A twist when landing on the foot from a height may also cause a *talar dome injury*. If walking was not possible immediately after, due to severe pain, the injury is more likely to be a fracture, such as a *Pott's fracture* or *fifth metatarsal base fracture*.

For overuse injuries it is important to know the pain's location—medial (inner) side, lateral (outer) side or anterior (at the front)—and the activity that brings on the pain, such as running for *tibialis posterior tendinosis* and standing up on the toes in ballet dancing for *flexor hallucis longus tendinosis*. *Talus stress fracture* and *navicular stress fracture* bring on pain with running and possibly also when resting or at night.

Radiological investigations may be required, such as X-rays for a Pott's fracture and a *bone scan* or *magnetic resonance imaging (MRI)* for a talus stress fracture.

Ankle posterior impingement

Pain caused by the back of the heel bone (calcaneus) pressing against the rear portion of the large shin bone (tibia) when the foot is moved downwards (plantar flexion movement) into an extreme position (see *Ankle*). This movement commonly occurs in ballet *dancing* when standing up on the toes. In many cases the heel bone has an enlarged tubercle (bump) called an os trigonum, which occurs in 10 per cent of the population. The pain is also common in *gymnastics* and *football* codes.

The recommended treatment is *rest* from aggravating activities, *mobilisation* of the ankle and foot joints, *non-steroidal anti-inflammatory drugs (NSAIDs)* and correction of poor technique, such as forcing turnout of the foot in ballet dancers. If the pain persists, a *corticosteroid* injection may be recommended. If this fails, surgery may be required to remove an os trigonum.

Ankle referred pain

Pain in the ankle caused by a structure located a distance away, such as the low back joints. The diagnosis is based on excluding a local cause of pain, followed by positive signs that the cause is *referred pain*. For example, pain referred from the right side

QUICK REFERENCE GUIDE

Ankle

Acute injuries: Pain caused by a sudden force

Ankle sprain ....Did you twist your ankle by causing the foot to excessively turn inwards?

Ankle medial ligament sprain ......Did you twist your ankle by causing the foot to excessively turn outwards?

Talar dome injury.......................Did you twist your ankle when landing on the foot from a height?

Fifth metatarsal base fracture ....Did you twist your ankle by causing the foot to excessively turn, and now you feel pain on the outside border of the foot about half-way down?

Pott's fracture ....Did you twist your ankle by causing the foot to excessively turn inwards and then felt a sharp pain that immediately made walking difficult?

Overuse injuries: Pain that has gradually worsened over a period of weeks or months

Tibialis posterior tendinosis ....Do you have pain on the inside of your ankle associated with running activities?

Flexor hallucis longus tendinosis Do you have pain on the inside of your ankle associated with activities that involve standing up on the tips of your toes?

Peroneal tendinosis ....Do you have pain on the outside of your ankle during activities such as running on slopes?

Sinus tarsi syndrome ....Do you have pain on the outside of your ankle that is worse in the morning and can get better with exercise?

Talus stress fracture...................Do you have pain on the outside of your ankle that is felt even when at rest or at night?

Ankle posterior impingement......Do you have pain at the back of your ankle that is aggravated by kicking or going up on to your toes?

Tibialis anterior tendinosis ....Do you have pain at the front of your ankle?

Ankle anterior impingement ......Do you have pain at the front of your ankle associated with extreme movements of bending the foot upwards or kicking a football?

---

low back joints to the ankle is likely if *mobilisation* treatments reduce the pain.

Ankle sprain

A tear or stretch of the lateral (outer side) ligaments of the *ankle* joint due to a twist that turns the foot inwards in an excessive movement. This injury often occurs when suddenly changing directions during running, especially on uneven surfaces such as grass, or when landing on another competitor's foot from a jump. It is one of the most common injuries in *basketball, volleyball, netball* and most *football* codes.

Diagnosis

There are three degrees of severity of *sprain*: mild, moderate and severe. The amount of *swelling* and bruising is usually, but not always, an indication of severity. More important is the amount of disability, both immediately following the injury and later on. The sound of a 'snap' or 'crack' has no particular significance. Pain is mainly felt on the outer side of the ankle.

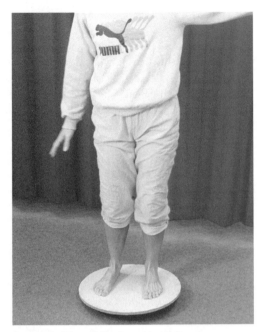

Proprioception training for ankle sprain

MILD (GRADE 1)

Most people are able to continue playing after the injury. Only a few ligament or joint capsule fibres are affected. The fibres are mostly stretched enough to cause pain, and minor swelling comes up after a few hours. A *physical examination* of the joint movements finds that stability is normal.

MODERATE (GRADE 2)

Usually unable to continue playing, but can walk with a limp. A large number of fibres are torn, which is also called a partial tear. It causes significant pain and swelling, perhaps bruising. The joint shows an abnormal amount of laxity and instability.

SEVERE (GRADE 3)

Usually unable to walk. The ligament or joint capsule is completely torn across the width. Also called a rupture. In many cases, less pain is experienced because the nerves are completely torn as well. Swelling and bruising can be severe. The joint shows an excessive amount of laxity and instability.

Treatment and return to sport

The treatment is the same regardless of the severity, except for the time required to return to sport. All sprains should be immediately treated with *rest* (crutches for moderate and severe sprains, although weight can be taken on the ankle after 24 hours and the crutches can be used less as long as walking causes no more than niggling pain), *ice, compression* and *elevation*.

Activities that increase swelling—such as hot showers, heat rubs, alcohol or excessive walking—should be avoided. Electrotherapy that decreases swelling, including *transcutaneous electrical nerve stimulation (TENS)*, *interferential therapy* and *magnetic field therapy, analgesics* for pain relief and, after 48 hours, gentle *massage* and *mobilisation* are recommended.

Flexibility exercises for all movements of the ankle, *strengthening exercises* for the muscles, and *proprioception training* using a wobble board for joint-sense awareness should start after 48 hours. Jogging can be started when walking is pain-free and proprioception is sufficient, as demonstrated by standing on the injured ankle on flat ground with the eyes shut for 30 seconds without overbalancing.

Return to sport is permitted when activities such as hopping and running figure eights can be performed without pain during or after activity (up until the morning after). The expected times are: mild—5 to 14 days; moderate—14 to 30 days; and severe—30 days to 6 months. Ankle protection should be worn, either *taping* or a *brace*, for 6 to 12 months after the injury.

Some cases of severe (grade 3) ankle sprain require *reconstructive surgery* of the lateral ligament, which involves taking a graft from a peroneal tendon or periosteum from the fibula, followed by the same treatments as above.

Persistent pain

Three to six weeks is a reasonable amount of time to assess whether the injured ankle is improving as expected. If pain, swelling and inability to walk or jog without pain persist, it may be caused by *complex regional pain syndrome* or an undiagnosed damaged structure that occurred at the time of the ankle sprain, such as a *talar dome injury, ankle posterior impingement, ankle anterior impingement, sinus tarsi syndrome* or a fracture such as a *fifth metatarsal base fracture*.

Ankylosing spondylitis

An inflammatory disease of the joints that causes loss of flexibility, morning stiffness and pain, often at night. It usually affects the *low back joints* and sacro-iliac joint (see *Pelvis*) and causes low back and buttock pain. In 30 per cent of cases the shoulder or hip joint is also painful. In severe cases permanent stiffness of the joints can eventually develop over a period of years, which is called ankylosis.

The condition most commonly affects men aged 18 to 40 years. The cause is unknown, though in 95 per cent of cases there is an increased amount of a marker in the blood called HLA B27.

The diagnosis of ankylosing spondylitis is based on the symptoms, *X-rays* and *magnetic resonance imaging (MRI)*. Treatments include *non-steroidal anti-inflammatory drugs (NSAIDs)*, *flexibility exercises*, *strengthening exercises*, *heat therapy (superficial)* and *hydrotherapy*.

Anorexia nervosa

See *Eating disorder*.

Anterior

The anatomical direction pointing towards the front of the body. It is used to describe the surface of any part of the body that faces the front and a body part located closer to the front of the body than another part. It is the opposite of *posterior*. Also called ventral, palmar (in the hand) and plantar (in the foot).

Anterior cruciate ligament (ACL) tear

An injury of one of the ligaments inside the *knee joint* caused by a sudden excessive force.

The injury usually occurs when pivoting or decelerating to change direction when running, causing the foot to be fixed to the ground, followed by an excessive *internal rotation* movement that overstretches the anterior cruciate ligament, which normally contributes to the stability of the knee joint by preventing this movement and anterior movement (forward slide). It can also be caused when another player falls across the front or back of the knee, or when landing awkwardly from a jump.

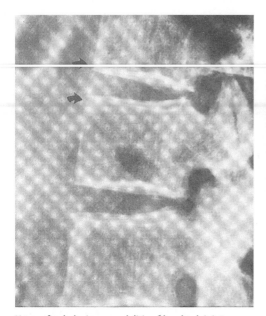

X-ray of ankylosing spondylitis of low back joints

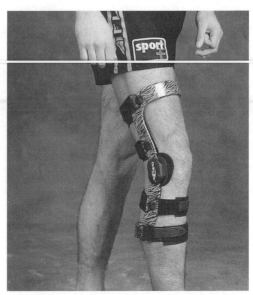

A limited motion brace for the knee after an anterior cruciate ligament tear

A strengthening exercise for the right leg quadriceps after an anterior cruciate ligament tear

It is most likely to occur in sports such as the *football* codes, *basketball, tennis, baseball* and *downhill skiing*. There may be a loud 'crack' or 'pop' at the time. In many cases, more than one knee joint structure is injured, such as a *meniscus tear* or *medial collateral ligament (MCL) sprain*.

Diagnosis

In contrast to other ligament *sprains*, an ACL injury is almost always a severe (grade 3) sprain, which is a complete tear or rupture across the width of the ligament. The diagnosis usually can be made based on the signs and symptoms, although in some cases it may need to be confirmed with *magnetic resonance imaging (MRI)* or *arthroscopy*.

A type of swelling called a *haemarthrosis* usually occurs within 2 hours due to bleeding into the joint. Intense pain within the first minutes settles down, but resumes over the next day or two before decreasing again. The knee often cannot be fully straightened (extended). *X-rays* are recommended to exclude bone fractures.

Treatment and return to sport

The recommended treatment during the first 48 to 72 hours is RICE (*rest, ice, compression and elevation*) and avoiding heat and alcohol consumption to minimise swelling, which can delay healing if it is excessive.

Afterwards, the two main types of treatment are surgery and conservative treatment (non-surgical). Balancing the pros and cons based on age, the demands of the sport, exercise goals, occupation, other injuries and personal factors can help make the decision on the treatment type. For example, a young person keen to keep skiing or playing *collision sports* such as the football codes requires a stable knee joint and should undergo surgery. However, surgery does require time off work and a commitment to a *sport rehabilitation* program for up to 1 year. Some people decide to change their sport and live comfortably without an intact ligament.

SURGERY

A graft (sliced section) is taken from another tendon, usually either the patella (kneecap) or hamstring tendon, and attached to the bones in place of the torn anterior cruciate ligament via an arthroscopy. The best time for surgery is when there is little or no swelling and full *range of movement* is available, often around 3 weeks after the injury occurred.

After surgery the knee joint is encouraged to start normal movement and regain strength as early as possible. Crutches are used for up to 2 weeks. A limited motion *brace* may be used for support. Other treatments include *strengthening exercises, flexibility exercises, massage*, electrotherapy such as *interferential therapy* and *ultrasound therapy*, and a *sport rehabilitation* program, which will vary according to the type of tendon graft.

Return to sport takes 9 to 12 months. In some elite sports people, it has been reduced down to 6 to 9 months. Complications can occur after surgery, such as the graft not fixing to the bone, joint stiffness and *patellofemoral joint syndrome*. New techniques are being developed to decrease the time required for recovery, including *gene therapy* and biosynthetic tissue treatments.

CONSERVATIVE TREATMENT

Beforehand, arthroscopy may be required to clean out the haemarthrosis and treat other damage that may be present, such as a meniscus tear. Afterwards, the conservative treatments are similar to the post-surgical treatments described above.

Anterior inferior iliac spine apophysitis

An injury of the *pelvis* bone in children and adolescents at the front of the lower abdomen, either on the left or right side, where the rectus femoris muscle tendon attaches.

It causes hip pain and is due to an accumulation of repeated, excessive physical loads on the bone and growing bone over a long period of time — weeks or months — such as doing an excessive amount of kicking.

Treatment for this *apophysitis* injury consists of *rest* from aggravating activities, *ice*, gentle *flexibility exercises* and *massage*.

Anterior inferior iliac spine avulsion fracture

An acute injury in children and adolescents that causes separation of the rectus femoris tendon and its attachment to a small piece of the *pelvis* bone. It is usually due to a sudden muscle contraction, such as kicking. The injury causes sudden pain in the hip region and loss of *range of movement* of the hip joint.

Treatment for this *avulsion fracture* injury is usually the same as for a severe muscle *strain*, including *rest* from aggravating activities such as kicking, *ice*, gentle *flexibility exercises* and *massage*. Surgery is recommended if the avulsed bone is greater than 3 cm (approx. 1 in) away from the rest of the pelvis.

Antibiotics

A group of drugs used to treat bacterial infections located in, for example, the gastrointestinal system or lungs. Antibiotics may be effective against specific bacteria or a wide range of infections. The four types of antibiotics include aminoglycosides, cephalosporins, penicillins and tetracyclines. Possible side effects include nausea, *diarrhoea*, skin rash, thrush (candidiasis) and an allergic reaction.

Antidepressants

Medications used primarily for the treatment of *depression*. They are also recommended in the treatment of chronic pain, *overtraining syndrome*, *chronic fatigue syndrome (CFS)*, *eating disorders* and *gambling addiction*.

There are four different sub-groups of antidepressant that have varying levels of effectiveness and side effects. For example, the brand name Prozac is a selective serotonin (5HT) uptake inhibitor that is often the first choice for mild to moderate depression, particularly when associated with generalised *anxiety* and sleep disturbances. It is considered moderately effective and has low levels of side effects such as drowsiness, sweatiness and reduced libido. If it fails, stronger drugs can be prescribed, such as tricyclic antidepressants; however, they also have stronger side effects.

Chronic pain

Antidepressant treatment for chronic pain should commence with a low bedtime dosage (for example, amitryptyline 10 mg) that can be increased slowly upward depending on the response. Side effects vary, but include excess daytime sedation, dry mouth, constipation, weight gain and, in older people, urinary retention. Antidepressants can be taken at the same time as other *analgesics* and *non-steroidal anti-inflammatory drugs (NSAIDs)*.

Antihistamines

A group of drugs used to counter the impact of histamines, a chemical produced in excessive amounts due to an allergic reaction such as *anaphylaxis* (allergic shock), *cholinergic urticaria* and *angioedema*.

Most current antihistamines do not cause side effects such as sleepiness and dizziness, which avoids the danger of accidents when driving or engaging in other activities requiring concentration. Antihistamines are sometimes used in medications for the *common cold* and *flu*.

Antihypertensives

A group of drugs prescribed in the treatment of *hypertension* (high blood pressure), which is associated with an increased risk of *heart attack* and *stroke*. They include *beta blockers*, *calcium channel blockers*, ACE *inhibitors* and *diuretics*.

Antioxidants

Chemical compounds that neutralise free radicals, which are molecules possessing unpaired electrons that are produced by oxidation reactions. Excessive amounts of free radicals are believed to contribute to molecular damage, leading to the development of disease and illness.

Free radicals keep cells and their chemical reactions humming along like an engine room furnace at a normal level of oxidation. However, when too many are produced, they are like an uncontained fire. For instance, excess free radicals may cause cancer by attacking a cell's genetic material. In *coronary heart disease*, free radicals can result in the formation of plaques that harden the arteries.

The main antioxidants are *vitamins* C and E; polyphenols, *flavonoids* and carotenoids such as beta-carotene and lycopene, which help make up the red, orange and yellow colouring in fruit and vegetables; lipoic acid; and N-acetyl-cysteine and selenium, both of which help to increase and maintain the activity of glutathione peroxidase, an enzyme involved in the repair of cells damaged by excessive physical activity.

Exercise and sport
Participation in exercise and sport can increase the body's natural level of antioxidants. In contrast, training at high *overload* levels, such as a significant increase in running distance or running speed, can decrease antioxidant levels.

Supplementation
Consuming antioxidant supplements may not have the desired effect of maintaining normal levels because the body's antioxidant system is highly complex, possessing many different components that work in interaction. As a result, even if a high dose of antioxidants bolsters one component, it may upset the balance of the whole antioxidant system and cause other components to become pro-oxidant—in other words, cause damage.

Maintaining a diet rich in all antioxidants, such as vitamins and minerals, is sufficient, rather than resorting to supplementation as a habit. The only need for supplementation is as a short-term measure, for a maximum of 2 weeks, during periods of training at high overload levels to help the body cope until its own internal system adjusts. Supplementation may also be recommended for people suffering a *vitamin and mineral deficiency*.

Anxiety

Unpleasant feelings of worry and nervousness about a current or future experience. In exercise and sport it can involve fear of injury, self-doubt about one's talents and skills, and concerns about the consequences of losing in a competition.

Some anxiety is usually necessary in exercise and sport. It can provide a healthy self-restriction from performing excessively dangerous activities and focus the mind on the requirements for success.

On the other hand, it can have a negative impact on performance by causing excessive *arousal* levels, leading to increased *muscle tone* and reduced concentration levels. Signs and symptoms that indicate a high level of anxiety are cold and clammy hands, needing to urinate frequently, talking down one's chances of success, excessive perspiration, butterflies in the stomach, nausea, vomiting, *headache*, dry mouth, sleep difficulties, heart *palpitations* and *shortness of breath*. It can also be a trigger for *asthma*.

Treatments that can help to reduce excessive feelings of anxiety are similar to those recommended for *stress* and *exercise for health*.

Aortic stenosis

A narrowed opening of the aortic valve, which is the structure that allows blood to flow into the aorta, the large artery that carries oxygenated blood from the left ventricle of the *heart* to the rest of the body. The narrowing makes the heart work harder to pump blood and can cause *syncope* (fainting), chest pain and *palpitations*. People with severe aortic stenosis should avoid high-intensity *aerobic training* because of the risk of having a *heart attack*. Mild cases can participate in all forms of exercise and sport.

Apophysis

A centre for bone growth in children and adolescents located at the site where a large strong muscle tendon attaches to the bone. Common sites include the attachment of the quadriceps (front thigh muscle) to the tibial tuberosity (just below the front of the knee joint) and the calf muscle to the calcaneus (heel bone).

The bone at these sites matures together with the *epiphysis*. An overuse injury at this site is called an *apophysitis* or *osteochondrosis*.

Apophysitis

An injury of the growing bone in children at a site where a large strong muscle attaches to the bone, called the *apophysis*. This *overuse injury* is an inflammation due to an accumulation of repeated, excessive forces on the growing bone over a period of weeks or months.

The main treatment is *rest* from the aggravating activity, which usually achieves significant improvement in a matter of weeks. Additional treatments include *ice*, correction of excessive repeated forces such as those caused by a *biomechanical abnormality*, followed by *massage, flexibility exercises, strengthening exercises* and *hydrotherapy*.

Most common apophysitis injuries

Injury	Site
Osgood-Schlatter disease	Tibial tubercle (below the knee)
Sinding-Larsen-Johansson disease	Inferior pole of patella (kneecap)
Sever's disease	Calcaneus (heel)
Ischial tuberosity apophysitis	Pelvis (buttock)

Appetite suppressants

A drug that reduces sensations of hunger and increases feelings of fullness in order to reduce the amount of food that is eaten and, as a result, achieve weight loss. Disadvantages include an overall reduction in nutrients such as *carbohydrates*, *vitamins* and *minerals* that are essential for maintaining energy levels. Side effects include a dry mouth, *anxiety*, insomnia, gastrointestinal disturbances, *headache*, drowsiness and nausea. It is a *drug banned in sport*, according to the World Anti-Doping Agency and International Olympic Committee (IOC).

Aqua running

An activity that involves running in the deep end of a pool using a floatation vest or belt to help keep the head above water. The impact of the feet striking the ground is eliminated because there is no contact with the bottom of the pool. It is performed during the recovery from a leg or foot injury in order to maintain aerobic fitness without aggravating the injury.

Aquarobics

See *Aerobics*.

Aromatherapy

A method of treatment that uses the healing powers of essential oils to enhance wellbeing and stimulate a healthy physical, mental and emotional state. Essential oils are pure extracts from aromatic plants. Aromatherapists select and blend essential oils for each individual's needs. The oils may be used on the skin as part of *massage* and through inhalation or water immersion.

Arousal

A state of excitement that leads to an action or response. Each person can have different amounts of arousal that have varying impacts on performance in exercise and sport.

The optimum arousal zone, described as feeling 'in the zone', is most likely to lead to the best performance. Under-arousal is associated with inappropriate recognition of and a poor response to activities in training or competition. Over-arousal also has a negative impact on performance by causing: excessive muscle tension; impairment of concentration, rhythm, coordination and timing; *anxiety*; and physical responses such as raised heart rate, breathing rate and sweating.

Artery

A strong, yet flexible tube, which carries *blood* from the heart to the cells of the body. The *heart* pumps blood from the left ventricle into the largest artery in the body, called the aorta. Branches coming out of the aorta are arteries with names based on their location in the body or their destination. Like a large tree trunk, each artery either divides into two or gives off branches that become smaller arteries called arterioles. The smallest type of blood vessel is called a capillary, where oxygen, carbon dioxide, nutrients and other substances are exchanged with the cells of the body.

Structure

Arteries are tough enough to withstand the pressure created by each *heartbeat* when blood is pumped through. At the same time they have the elasticity to recoil from the pressure and keep the flow of blood constant, rather than in stops and starts. Arterial disease reduces the artery's ability to withstand this pressure, decreasing the elasticity and causing blockages,

either partial or complete. If this occurs in the heart, it is called *coronary heart disease*.

Arthritis

The common name given to a group of joint diseases which affect up to one-third of people in countries such as the USA, UK and Australia. The largest group is *osteoarthritis*, which is due to excessive wear and tear in the joint. Other types include *rheumatoid arthritis, ankylosing spondylitis, gout, Reiter's syndrome* and *psoriatic arthritis*.

Arthroplasty

See *Joint replacement*.

Arthroscopy

A surgical procedure that involves inserting a fibre-optic telescope called an endoscope through a narrow opening into a joint. It has become increasingly used in surgical treatment and less so for diagnosis with improvements in radiological investigations such as magnetic resonance imaging (MRI).

Its great advantage over *open surgery*, which involves extensively cutting through the skin, is that recovery is much quicker. Depending on the type and severity of the injury, the time spent in hospital varies from just one day to a few days.

Arthroscopy is a well-established form of surgery for the knee, shoulder, elbow, ankle and, more recently, the hip and smaller joints, such as the wrist.

Method

A surgeon performs an arthroscopy. General anaesthesia is usually required, although occasionally spinal anaesthesia or a nerve block may be used. The *synovial joint* is filled with fluid to distend the joint capsule, irrigate the joint space and remove debris. A 3.2 mm/0.12 in fibre-optic telescope that has a small, fluid-submersible video camera to display the image on a television screen is usually used.

The optic fibre is inserted through a standard portal (narrow opening), while another portal is used to introduce an operating instrument, such as a miniature knife.

Use

An arthroscopy involves first assessing the damage done to specific structures in the joint, such as the *articular cartilage, synovium,* meniscus and cruciate ligaments of the *knee joint.*

The most common treatments include removal of a loose body within the joint due to *osteochondrosis* or bone fracture, particularly if it is causing *locking,* removal of a *meniscus tear* of the knee, and more complex reconstructive surgery such as repair of an *anterior cruciate ligament (ACL) tear.*

Arthroscopy has a low risk of infection. Occasionally, it can produce a persistent joint reaction manifesting as prolonged joint *swelling,* persistent pain and muscle *atrophy. Complex regional pain syndrome (CRPS)* also may occasionally develop. *Sport rehabilitation* and return to sport treatments are essential for a healthy recovery following surgery.

Articular cartilage

The layer of tissue covering the end of the bones that are connected together to form a *synovial joint.* It is exceptionally smooth and significantly reduces the friction between the two bones when they move over each other during joint movements. It is bathed in synovial fluid that acts as a lubricant.

Articular cartilage is also compressible, enabling shock absorption during weight-bearing activities, such as running and jumping. It is wear-resistant, too, and puts up with these forces for many years.

However, excessive wear and tear leads to a disease called *osteoarthritis.* Other joint diseases that target articular cartilage include *rheumatoid arthritis, ankylosing spondylitis, psoriatic arthritis, gout,* septic arthritis, inflammatory bowel disease arthritis and *Reiter's syndrome.*

It also can be damaged by a sudden excessive force, such as a knee sprain, that may be associated with a ligament injury such as *anterior cruciate liga-*

ment *(ACL) tear* or occurs alone, and does not heal well due to a poor blood supply (see *Articular cartilage acute injury*).

Anatomy

Healthy and young articular cartilage has a bright white, smooth and glistening appearance that can be 5–7 mm (0.2–0.25 in) thick in large joints such as the hip and knee. With age it thins down (to around 1–2 mm/0.04–0.08 in in small joints such as the fingers), becomes more brittle and has opaque yellow colour.

It is one of four different types of *cartilage* in the body. It is made up of cells called chondroblasts and chondrocytes embedded in a matrix of collagen fibres and gel-like ground substance and receives nutrition from the *synovium* of the *joint capsule,* synovial fluid and blood vessels of the underlying bone.

The deepest layer of articular cartilage contains a mix of articular cartilage and calcified cells that are typical of bone. The layer of bone that lies just below the articular cartilage is called *subchondral bone,* which is composed of deposits of calcium and phosphate embedded among bone cells, osteoblasts and osteocytes. These transitional layers from articular cartilage to subchondral bone are collectively called osteochondrum.

Articular cartilage acute injury

An *acute injury* to the layer of tissue covering the ends of the bones in a joint, due to a sudden, single external force. It causes pain, swelling and restricted movement of the affected joint and may increase the risk of developing osteoarthritis later in life.

Articular cartilage does not have pain nerve endings. Pain is caused due to exposure to mechanical forces on the *subchondral bone,* the layer immediately beneath. Injuries usually occur in combination with other joint injuries, including *dislocation,* subluxation, ligament *sprains* and tears, and meniscus damage.

Types

Injuries can be defined according to depth: (1) the outer surface of articular cartilage (2) the deepest

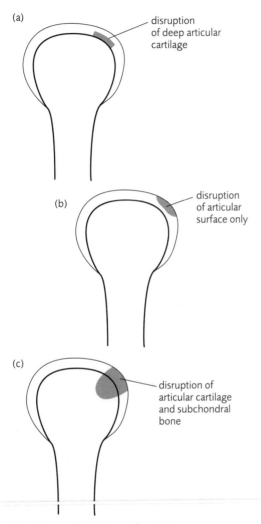

(a) disruption of deep articular cartilage

(b) disruption of articular surface only

(c) disruption of articular cartilage and subchondral bone

Three types of articular cartilage injury

layer of articular cartilage; and (3) subchondral bone, which is called a bone bruise.

Bone bruising usually occurs due to a sudden, forceful jarring movement of the joint. It should be suspected where other structures are found to be intact on clinical examination, the pain persists for longer than expected considering the low severity of the injury, and there is no swelling.

Location

The most common sites are the talar dome (the superior articular surface of the talus bone in the ankle), the femoral condyles of the knee joint, and the head of the humerus in the shoulder joint.

Diagnosis and treatment

It is difficult to diagnose this injury without an *arthroscopy, bone scan* or *magnetic resonance imaging (MRI)*. Initial X-ray examinations are often normal. Usually it is diagnosed after a simple joint sprain has not recovered within the expected time and continues to cause pain, swelling and restricted movement.

Conservative (non-surgical) treatment includes *immobilisation, rest, ice, flexibility exercises* and *strengthening exercises*. Arthroscopic treatment is more likely if there is a need to remove loose fragments of articular cartilage or smooth rough edges of cartilage. Return to sport is permitted after 2 to 3 months of *sport rehabilitation*.

Aspiration

A procedure that involves withdrawing fluid or tissue from the body. It is usually performed with a needle attached to a syringe. It may be done to obtain a *biopsy* (sample) that can be tested for disease. In joints and tendon sheaths it is used as a treatment to remove blood or *oedema* following an injury or the exacerbation of a disease such as *osteoarthritis* or a *wrist ganglion*.

Aspiration pneumonia is inflammation of the lungs caused by inhaling foreign material such as vomit, which can occur after *head injury*.

Aspirin

A medication that can reduce pain, fever and, inflammation and has anti-blood clotting effects. It belongs to a group of drugs called salicylates.

At low dosages, aspirin reduces pain and fever. At higher dosages it acts as an anti-inflammatory. However, it is not recommended for an *acute injury* because the anti-blood clotting effect may increase bleeding. *Non-steroidal anti-inflammatory drugs* (NSAIDs) are the preferred medication. Aspirin is also associated with an increased risk of side effects, including damage to the gastrointestinal system such as an *ulcer*.

Asthma

A disease of the *lungs* that causes temporary narrowing of the airways in response to one or more trigger factors. Narrowing of airways leads to symptoms including a wheeze when breathing, shortness of breath, a cough, chest tightness, palpitations, a fast pulse and feelings of anxiety. When symptoms appear it is called an asthma attack.

Potential triggers for an attack include well-known factors such as dust, fungal spores, pollens, animal fur, feathers, colds and flu, cold and dry air, cigarette smoke, exercise (see *Exercise-induced asthma*), side effects of drugs such as *beta blockers* and *aspirin*, *stress, anxiety* and, possibly, specific foods or food additives.

A trigger factor stimulates cells in the inner lining of the large airways to produce chemicals including histamine, leukotrienes and *prostaglandins* that cause inflammation (swelling) of the airways, which makes them narrower. This is accompanied by contraction of the smooth muscle in the airway walls (called bronchoconstriction) and, sometimes, increased mucous production. Some inflammation may remain after an attack has subsided, which makes the airways more sensitive to triggers later on.

Diagnosis

There are three degrees of severity for an asthma attack: mild, moderate and severe. The best measure of the severity is not the symptoms (although they are relevant), but *lung function tests*—especially FEV_1, the maximum amount of air that can be breathed out in one second. A *peak flow meter* can be used by the patient to give an approximate guide.

Mild = 10 to 25 per cent reduction in FEV_1; moderate = 25 to 50 per cent reduction in FEV_1; severe = > 50 per cent reduction in FEV_1. Severe attacks can cause blue colouring of the face and lips, difficulty speaking, no response to the usual medications, pale and clammy skin and, if not treated quickly, can lead to death.

Treatment

A severe attack can occur without warning. It is a *medical emergency* that requires immediate treatment to ensure that breathing and circulation are not compromised, followed by transport to a hospital, doctor, or other person trained in first aid as quickly as possible.

The main aim of asthma prevention is to avoid the trigger factors—for example, reducing the

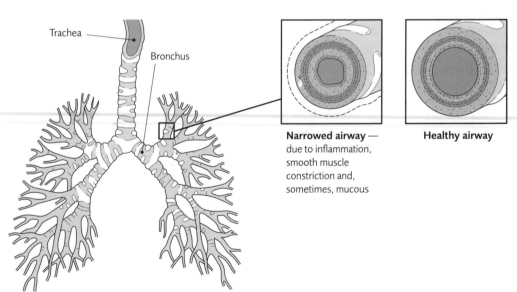

Trachea

Bronchus

Narrowed airway — due to inflammation, smooth muscle constriction and, sometimes, mucous

Healthy airway

Airway narrowing in asthma

amount of dust in the house, minimising the amount of inflammation in the airways with prevention medications such as *corticosteroids (inhaled)* and *sodium cromoglycate*, and having a plan for assessing the severity of an asthma attack and the appropriate response. *Bronchodilator* medications such as Ventolin should only be used for relief of mild to moderate symptoms. In moderate to severe attacks, corticosteroids (inhaled) should also be used.

Atherosclerosis

A disease of the arteries. The two most common types are *coronary heart disease* of the heart and *peripheral vascular disease* of the legs.

Athlete's foot

A skin infection between the toes due to the tinea fungus. The main symptoms are irritation and itching. The recommended treatment is an antifungal cream such as clotrimazole and, if the infection is moist, a drying powder applied two to three times per day for 2 to 4 weeks. Preventive measures include regular changes of socks, use of foot powders and regular cleaning of shower facilities.

Cathy Freeman, winner of the 2000 Olympics gold medal for the 400 m sprint

over 2 days, the winner being the person who accumulates the most points.

Athletics

A group of sports, including *jumping sports* (high jump, long jump and triple jump), *throwing sports* (shot put, javelin, hammer and discus), *pole vault*, *sprinting* (100 m, 200 m, and 400 m and 100 m, 4 × 100 m and 4 × 400 m relays, and 400 m hurdles), *middle distance running* (800 m, 1500 m, 5000 m and 10 000 m, cross-country running and 3000 m steeplechase), *long distance running* (marathon, half-marathon and fun runs) and race *walking*. Heptathlon (100 m hurdles, shot put, high jump, 200 m, long jump, javelin and 800 m), and decathlon (100 m, long jump, shot put, high jump, 400 m, 110 m hurdles, discus, pole vault, javelin and 1500 m) are held

Atrophy

A reduction in the size of a *tissue* or *organ* in the body. It is caused by injury, disease or lack of activity. In exercise and sport, it most commonly refers to *muscles*.

Muscle atrophy causes a loss of *strength* and *power* and may cause *instability* of a joint or region of the body, such as the low back or shoulder. The reduction in muscle size involves shrinkage of each individual muscle fibre and a decreased number of fibres in the muscle.

Significant atrophy is visible to the naked eye.

Diseases that cause atrophy include muscular dystrophy and multiple sclerosis, which damage nerves in the motor nervous system. It is also seen in *quadriplegia* and *paraplegia*. Atrophy is the opposite of *hypertrophy*.

Australian Rules football

The first recorded game, played in the winter of 1858 between two private schools in Melbourne, was a combination of Irish Gaelic football, Rugby Union and soccer, with around 40 players per side. The rules were first codified in 1866 and have been evolving ever since.

Rules
In the modern version there are 18 players on the field and four players on the bench. Play is started when the umpire bounces the oval ball and tall ruckmen jump to tap the ball. Subsequently the ball is moved around the field of play (a large, non-uniform sized oval) either by kicking or handpassing (no throwing is permitted). Running with the ball is permitted, with a bounce every 15 m. The aim is to kick the highest score: 6 points (= 1 goal) between the tall goalposts and 1 point (= 1 behind) between the shorter posts.

Australian Rules footballers

Fitness, skills and equipment
The fitness requirements include *aerobic training* for running, *anaerobic training* for sprinting, *strength training* and *skills training* for kicking, marking, jumping, handpassing, tackling and bumping. Required equipment includes *football boots* and *mouthguards*.

Injuries
The most common acute injuries include *hamstring strain* (thigh), *quadriceps strain* (thigh), *quadriceps contusion* (thigh), *back-related hamstring injury* (thigh), *medial collateral ligament (MCL) sprain* (knee), *anterior cruciate ligament (ACL) tear* (knee), *meniscus tear* (knee), *acromioclavicular joint sprain* (shoulder), *shoulder dislocation, concussion, rib fracture, nosebleed, navicular stress fracture* (foot), *Achilles tendinosis* (calf), *low back pain (non-specific)*, *osteitis pubis* (hip and groin) and *adductor tendinosis* (hip and groin).

Australian Rules football boots

See *Football boots*.

Autogenic training

A self-generated relaxation technique that is likened to self-hypnosis. It involves guiding oneself to a level of arousal between sleep and rest. The aim of this relaxation is described as switching on the 'life support systems', particularly the immune system, which controls the defence, recovery and recuperation after illness.

Autogenic training involves six graded steps of relaxation from the outer body through to the inner core that are learnt over a period of 4 to 8 weeks:
1) Deactivating the muscles of the face, arms and legs by feeling 'heaviness'.
2) Opening the circulation of the skin of the face, arms and legs by feeling a 'warm fuzziness'.
3) Slowing down the pulse rate by feeling that it has become 'calm and regular'.

4) Slowing down the breathing rate by feeling that it has become 'calm and regular'.
5) Placing the abdominal activities on hold by feeling 'warm throughout'.
6) Switching on the life support systems, associated with feeling a 'cooling' of the forehead.

Autonomic nervous system

The collection of *neurons* (nerve cells) that conduct the communications in the body that seemingly are not in our voluntary control. These communications occur to and from the internal organs, or viscera, such as the intestines, heart and lungs, and also the blood vessels throughout the body. The system has two divisions—the *sympathetic nervous system* and *parasympathetic nervous system*—which tend to work in opposition. For example, sympathetic nerves relax the bladder allowing it to fill up with urine. Parasympathetic nerves make the bladder muscles contract, forcing the urine out.

Avascular necrosis

An injury that means death of cells caused by a loss of blood supply. It can occur in conditions such as *osteochondrosis*, which is an overuse injury where excessive forces associated with an aggravating activity cause softening of a bone, or following an *acute injury*, such as a *scaphoid fracture* in the wrist or fracture of the neck of the femur (thigh bone) that contains the vessels that bring blood to the head of the femur in the *hip joint*.

Conservative treatment is usually recommended, including *flexibility exercises*, *strengthening exercises* and electrotherapy such as *ultrasound therapy*. If this fails, surgery may be required.

Avulsion fracture

A break in a bone where a large muscle, tendon or ligament is attached, which is most likely to occur in children and adolescents because of growth cartilage at the site of injury that constitutes the weakest link when subjected to strong external forces. The most common avulsion fractures are *anterior inferior iliac spine avulsion fracture* of the rectus femoris muscle attachment at the hip and *ischial tuberosity avulsion fracture* of the hamstring muscle attachment in the buttock.

Types, diagnosis and treatment

Diagnosis is made with a plain X-ray. Treatment of avulsion fractures of muscle tendons is similar to a grade 3 muscle *strain*, including reduction of pain and swelling, *flexibility exercises* and gradual introduction of *strengthening exercises*. Surgery is rarely necessary.

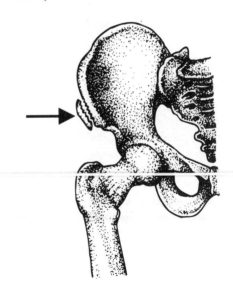

Avulsion fracture of the pelvis

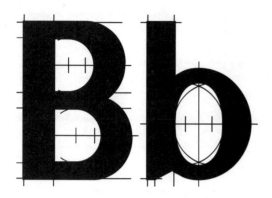

Back-related hamstring injury

A recurring hamstring (back of the thigh) pain referred from structures that are damaged in the low back and pelvis.

The most common causes include stiffness and loss of range of movement of the *low back joints*, *neural tension, lumbo-pelvic instability* and abnormalities of *running biomechanics* such as overstriding, which places excessive stretch on the hamstring muscle as it attempts to perform a contraction.

Treatment includes *mobilisations* for the low back joints and neural tension stretching (see *Low back pain (non-specific)*), *strengthening exercises, flexibility exercise* and *motor re-education*

Badminton

This sport took its modern name from Badminton House in Gloucestershire, England, the home of the Duke of Beaufort, where the sport was first played in 1873. It is a racquet sport where a shuttlecock is hit at speeds of up to 200 km/h (125 miles/h) over a raised

net on a court. A point is won when the server is the last one to successfully hit the shuttlecock over the net. The player who wins 15 points wins the game, and the first to win three games wins the match.

Injuries

The most common injuries include *rotator cuff tendinosis* (shoulder), *rotator cuff strain* (shoulder), *tennis elbow, thoracic pain (non-specific)* (middle back) and *patellofemoral joint syndrome* (knee).

Balance

The skill of maintaining the body in a fixed or moving position in relation to the ground or another object. For example, standing balance is the ability to keep upright without falling over. Cycling balance is the ability to keep upright on a bicycle. The skill involves complex coordination of the flow of information and instructions between the musculoskeletal system and the nervous system, particularly *sensory-motor integration*.

Information from the *sensory nervous system* is received in the brain about the position of the body and the environment. It comes from the eyes, the semicircular canals in the inner ears that act like spirit levels, and sensory receptors in the skin, muscles and joints. The brain processes and interprets this information according to cerebral instructions and then sends out instructions through the *motor nervous system* to the relevant muscles to relax or perform movements.

The key to balance during activities when the feet or hands are in contact with the ground is that the line of the *centre of gravity* is maintained within the *base of support*. For example, during walking when both feet are on the ground, the line falls between the two feet. During a step forward when one foot lifts off the ground and is in the swing phase moving towards heel strike, the base of support is under the opposite foot. Temporarily the line of the centre of gravity is shifted outside the base as it is transferred to the foot at heel strike before loss of balance can occur.

Hitter ready for the pitch in baseball

Basal metabolic rate (BMR)

See *Resting metabolic rate (RMR)*.

Base of support

The area within imaginary lines that connect between all the points of the body in contact with the ground. The area is usually square-like. For example, the base of support when standing up is within a line between the toes and a line between the heels, and includes the area in between and underneath the feet.

The base of support is important for *weight-bearing* activities such as standing, walking and running (see *Angle and base of gait*), and when maintaining *balance* in sports such as gymnastics.

Baseball

The British first brought the children's game called 'rounders' to North America in the 1600s, and this, in turn, developed into an adult game called Town

Ball in the 1830s. In 1845 a bank teller, Alexander Cartwright Jr, created a set of standard rules, leading to the first baseball league in the 1860s. Today, millions of people around the world play baseball.

Rules and equipment
Two teams of nine (if a designated hitter is used) or 10 players each take turns to bat and field. The hitter from the batting team stands at the 'home' base of a set of four bases arranged in a diamond. The pitcher from the fielding team throws the ball at the hitter with an overarm action. If a fielder catches the ball or the hitter misses three attempts to hit the ball (three strikes) or is tagged while not touching a base, the hitter is out.

Fitness, skills and injuries
The fitness requirements include *speed training* for sprinting and *strength training* (lifting weights). Eye–hand coordination is important for hitting, which can be improved with *skills training*.

The most common injuries include *rotator cuff tendinosis* (shoulder), *shoulder impingement*, *shoulder instability*, *glenoid labrum injury* (shoulder), *Little Leaguer's shoulder*, *elbow medial collateral ligament sprain*, *ulnar nerve compression* (elbow), *flexor tendinosis* (Golfer's elbow), *Little Leaguer's elbow*, *elbow apophysitis* and *Panner's disease* (elbow).

Basketball

Basketball was invented in the USA in 1891 by James Naismith, a physical education instructor at the YMCA Training School in Springfield, Massachusetts, who hung two peach baskets from the balcony of a gymnasium and threw a soccer ball into the baskets. (A ladder was used to get the ball out again). Today a braided cord net attached to a hoop is used.

Rules and skills
A formal game is played between two teams of five players on a small, wooden court. Players score points by throwing the ball into the hoop; two points from within the semi-circle and three points from outside. Free throws and foul shots are worth one point each. The winning team is the one that scores the most points.

The main skills include bouncing the ball with each step (called dribbling), accurately passing the ball and throwing into the basket, and jumping up to catch the ball (rebounding).

Fitness and injuries
The fitness requirements include *aerobic training* for long periods of running, *speed training* for sprinting, *strength training* for positioning against other players, and *skills training* for dribbling and throwing the ball into the basket. Properly designed *basketball shoes* are recommended.

The most common injuries are *ankle sprain*, *ankle medial ligament sprain*, *quadriceps strain* (thigh), *quadriceps contusion* (thigh), *patella dislocation* (knee), *anterior cruciate ligament (ACL) tear* (knee), *patellar tendinosis* (knee), shin periostitis, *PIP joint dislocation* (finger), *olecranon bursitis* (elbow), *low back pain (non-specific)* and *rotator cuff tendinosis* (shoulder).

Basketball shoes

Footwear that is designed for the physical demands of *basketball*, which involves frequent side-to-side movements and jumping. The upper section of the *shoe* should have a high-ankle cut for additional support, the midsole needs good shock absorption qualities similar to the *running shoe*, and the outsole requires an efficient tread for grip on the court surface. Many of the basketball shoes designed for teenage fashion wear possess excessively flexible midsoles and may increase the risk of injury.

Beach volleyball

See *Volleyball*.

Behaviour modification

Techniques that aim to change the way a person behaves when performing an activity or in a specific situation. Negative techniques include pointing out errors, and punishment for failure to make a change. Positive techniques involve increasing *motivation* and providing rewards. Psychologists tend to regard

Offensive play in basketball

positive techniques as being the most effective for achieving long-term changes. The *stages of change* theory has been used successfully to change health behaviours, such as giving up smoking or sticking with participation in exercise and sport.

Bends

See *Decompression sickness.*

Benign exertional headache

A *headache* that starts during a physical activity such as *weight lifting* or running, causing severe pain that lasts only seconds or minutes, followed by a dull pain that persists for a number of hours. Treatment can involve taking a preventive drug—for example, indomethacin—before the activity.

Bennett's fracture

See *Metacarpal fracture*

Beta blockers

A group of drugs commonly used in the treatment of *hypertension, cardiac arrhythmia, migraine, anxiety,* tremor and following a *heart attack.* They reduce blood pressure and heart rate by blocking receptors of *noradrenaline,* a neurotransmitter that increases the activity of the sympathetic nervous system, leading to changes such as making blood vessels narrower.

Athletes have been known to take them in sports such as shooting and archery that require reduced anxiety and tremor, and increased steadiness and eye–hand coordination. They are banned in these sports and in winter sports such as luge, bobsleigh and ski jumping.

Potential side effects include *asthma* symptoms, excessive *tiredness,* impotence, an increased risk of developing *peripheral vascular disease, depression,* nightmares, sexual dysfunction, and masking *hypo-*

glycaemia (low blood sugar levels) in people with diabetes.

Names of beta blockers include acebutolol, atenolol, metoprolol, oxyprenolol, sotalol, alprenolol, labetalol, nadolol and propranolol.

Beta endorphin

See *Endorphin.*

Beta-hydroxy methylbutyrate

An organic compound derived from the metabolism of the amino acid leucine. It acts to minimise the breakdown of *protein,* the main structural component of muscles, during high overload *strength training,* leading to an increase in muscle size and bulk. Beta-hydroxy methylbutyrate (popularly called HMB) is found in most foods but only in small amounts. As a result, taking supplements is required to gain the claimed benefits, as long as it is combined with strength training and eating an adequate protein intake. It appears to be safe, although the long-term effects are still not known.

Beta-2 agonists

Drugs used to reduce *asthma* symptoms. They are banned by the World Anti-Doping Agency and International Olympic Committee (IOC) when taken as a tablet or injected, because they act as a *stimulant* (delays fatigue and increases alertness) and increase muscle size and bulk, like *anabolic steroids.*

They are permitted in the inhaled form (see *Bronchodilators*) if a doctor writes a notification of asthma. Side effects can include nervousness, tremor (trembling), high *heart rate, palpitations,* headache, nausea, vomiting and sweating.

Banned beta-2 agonists taken as tablets or injected are bamuterol, clenbuterol, fenoterol, eformoterol (Oxis, Foradile), formoterol, reproterol, salbutamol (Ventolin), terbutaline (Bricanyl) and salmeterol

(Serevent). Only salbutamol, terbutaline and salmeterol are permitted by inhalation. A positive doping test for salbutamol is a urine concentration greater than 500 nanograms per millilitre (ng/mL).

Bicarbonate ions

Bicarbonate ions (HCO_3^+) are essential for absorbing excessive H^+ ions in the blood so as to maintain its acidity at a normal and tolerable range (pH 6.9 to 7.5) (see *Blood*). Maintaining an acid balance is important, because cells work most efficiently at an optimum level of acidity. Failure to achieve this level in the muscles can lead to *lactate fatigue* during an event. However, it may be prevented by taking *sodium bicarbonate* as part of a *pre-competition eating* program.

Biceps tendinitis

See *Tendinitis*.

Biceps tendinosis

An overuse injury of the long head of the biceps tendon that passes over the top of the *shoulder joint*. It is seen most commonly in people performing a large volume of *strength training*, such as bench presses. *Shoulder referred pain* and *rotator cuff tendinosis* are sometimes mistakenly diagnosed.

This *tendinosis* injury causes pain in the biceps tendon and loss of flexibility. Treatment includes *ice*, *flexibility exercises*, *mobilisation* and *massage*.

Biceps tendon (long head) rupture

An acute injury that completely tears the long head tendon of the biceps muscle at the front of the *shoulder joint*. It is most commonly seen in older-aged people. It occurs during a contraction of the biceps, causing a sharp pain in the front of the shoulder that quickly passes, followed by the biceps bunching up in the upper arm.

Surprisingly, it does not affect muscle strength for most people and does not require treatment, other than some *rest* and *ice*. The exception is in power sports such as *weight lifting* and *bodybuilding*, where surgery may be recommended.

Bicycle equipment

See *Cycling biomechanics*.

Biofeedback

A technique that aims to influence a body function that is not normally under conscious control or to increase conscious input. It is most commonly used in two applications: as a psychological technique, and for strengthening a specific muscle. It is achieved by attaching electrodes to the body to monitor the function and provide information about changes—for example, to pulse rate or muscle activity.

Psychological technique
When used as a psychological technique—for example, to reduce pulse rate—one pays attention to one's state of mind when the pulse rate decreases and uses this information to bring on a reduced pulse rate at a later time.

It is considered particularly useful for athletes who experience high levels of pre-competition *anxiety* and *stress*, and in sports where precision and accuracy are paramount, such as shooting and archery.

Relaxation techniques such as *progressive muscle relaxation* can be used at the same time to teach people how to achieve decreases in pulse rate. Other body functions that can be influenced include *blood pressure*, *muscle tone*, body temperature, sweating and *gastrointestinal system* activity.

Strengthening
The electrodes from a biofeedback machine are attached to the skin over the muscle that needs to be strengthened to measure the degree of muscle

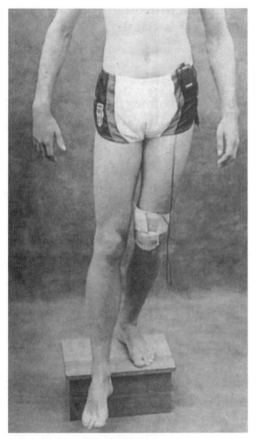

Biofeedback test of left leg quadriceps muscle

activity by recording action potentials from the contracting muscle fibres.

It may be recommended for strengthening the vastus medialis, one of the four parts that make up the quadriceps (front thigh muscle), that is weak and not contracting at the correct time, causing pain described as *patellofemoral joint syndrome*. Biofeedback aims to make sure the vastus medialis is being activated sufficiently and strengthened, rather than the other three parts.

Biomechanical abnormality

A deviation from the movement and posture that is normally observed during a specific activity. It is associated with an increased risk of developing an *overuse*

injury and reduced proficiency of performing the activity. For example, cocking the wrist too much during a tennis backhand stroke is an abnormal movement of the wrist that increases the risk of developing *tennis elbow*. It may also reduce the accuracy and power of the *tennis* stroke.

Injuries are made more likely because an abnormal movement can place joints and muscles under excessive forces. Sometimes the affected joint or muscle is located at a distance from the abnormality. For instance, the normal biomechanics of running includes movements and interactions between the joints and muscles of the foot, ankle, knee, hip, pelvis and lower back. An abnormal movement in the foot may be transferred up the leg to the low back joints and muscles, causing them to move in a manner that places them under increased stress.

Leg and foot injuries and the most common biomechanical abnormality causes

Injury	Common biomechanical abnormalities
Sesamoiditis (foot)	• Foot pronation • Abducted gait • Plantar flexed first ray
Plantar fasciitis (foot)	• Foot pronation/High arched foot • Abducted gait • Ankle equinus
Metatarsal stress fractures	• Foot pronation • Foot supination
Navicular stress fractures (foot)	• Foot pronation • Forefoot and rearfoot varus
Tibia stress fracture	• Foot pronation • Ankle equinus • Forefoot and rearfoot varus • Abducted gait
Fibula stress fractures (outer shin bone)	• Foot supination • Foot pronation • Forefoot and rearfoot varus
Patellofemoral joint syndrome (kneecap)	• Foot pronation • Pelvis anterior tilt • Forefoot, rearfoot and tibial varus • Abducted gait
Iliotibial band friction syndrome (outer side of knee/thigh)	• Forefoot, rearfoot and tibial varus • Pelvis lateral tilt
Hamstring strain (back of thigh)	• Pelvis anterior tilt

Types of abnormality

A biomechanical abnormality may be due to an anatomical (static) problem such as a short femur (thigh bone) that causes the leg to be shorter than the other, which is called a *leg length discrepancy*.

The other type of biomechanical abnormality is a functional (dynamic) problem. It may be due to an abnormality of a joint, ligament or muscle, such as a ligament sprain causing a joint *instability*, or too much strength in one group of muscles that leads to an imbalance of movement at a joint.

Another common cause of functional biomechanical abnormalities is poor technique in the performance of a particular activity. For example, poor throwing technique in a baseball pitcher may lead to the development of shoulder joint instability.

The following table is a list of technique-related causes of biomechanical abnormality and the associated injury according to different sports. More details can be found under *running biomechanics*, *walking biomechanics*, *throwing biomechanics*, *scapular biomechanics*, *tennis biomechanics*, *golf biomechanics*, *swimming biomechanics* and *cycling biomechanics*.

Diagnosis and treatment

Screening tests can be performed to detect abnormal biomechanics; however, most often they are found after an injury has occurred. A biomechanical exam-

Technique-related causes of injury according to sport

Sport	Technique	Injury
Tennis	• Excessive wrist action with backhand tennis stroke • Tennis service contact made too far back (i.e. ball toss not in front)	• Tennis elbow • Golfer's elbow
Swimming	• Insufficient body roll • Low elbow on recovery • Insufficient external rotation of the shoulder	• Rotator cuff tendinosis
Diving	• Shooting at the water too early (backward dives)	• Low back pain (non-specific)
Cycling	• Incorrect handlebar and saddle height • Toe in/out on cleats	• Thoracic joint pain (non-specific) • Patellofemoral joint syndrome
Weight lifting (Olympic)	• Bar position too far in front of body in clean phase/jerk phase	• Sacroiliac joint pain
Weight lifting (Power lifting)	• Toes pointing forward on squatting	• Patellofemoral joint syndrome
Javelin	• Poor hip drive	• Thoracic joint pain (non-specific)
Triple jump	• 'Blocking' on step phase	• Sacroiliac joint pain • Sinus tarsi syndrome
High jump	• Incorrect foot plant	• Patellar tendon strain • Sinus tarsi syndrome • Fibular stress fracture
Pole vault	• Too close on take-off • Late plant	• Low back pain (non-specific) • Talus stress fracture
Running	• Pelvis anterior tilt • Pelvis lateral tilt	• Hamstring tendinosis • Iliotibial band friction syndrome
Cricket bowling	• Mixed side-on/front-on action	• Pas interarticularis stress fracture
Baseball pitching	• Opening up too soon • Dropped elbow 'hanging'	• Shoulder joint instability • Medial collateral ligament sprains • Little Leaguer's elbow • Rotator cuff tendinosis
Gymnastics	• Excessive hyperextension on landing	• Pars interarticularis stress fracture
Rowing	• Change from bow side to stroke side	• Rib stress fracture
Ballet	• Sickling en pointe	• Second metatarsal stress fracture

ination should be a part of the *physical examination* for every *overuse injury*. It includes an assessment of *active movements*, *passive movements* and *flexibility*. A *video analysis* also is an effective technique. *Shoes*, equipment and sporting technique should be checked.

If a biomechanical abnormality is contributing to the injury, treatment to restore that body part back to normal is essential to improve the recovery process and reduce the risk of re-injury.

There are a number of treatments that may be used to restore normal biomechanics, including *flexibility exercises* for joints and muscles, *massage*, *mobilisation*, *strengthening exercises* for muscles, *motor re-education*, *taping*, appropriate shoe selection or modification, and *orthotics* such as a firm rubber wedge in the shoe for a leg length discrepancy.

Biomechanics

The study of the movements performed by the body as a whole and its individual parts during exercise and sport. Because the joints and muscles are interconnected, movements affecting one have an effect on the other.

Biomechanics is used to analyse common activities. For example, running biomechanics is an analysis of the movements and positions of the foot, ankle, knee, hip, pelvis and lower back, and how they affect each other. It is applicable to many sports.

Other common activities include *walking biomechanics*, *standing biomechanics* and *throwing biomechanics*. For example, throwing a ball in baseball, softball and cricket out-fielding is divided into four stages: preparation or wind up; cocking; acceleration; and deceleration or follow through. An analysis of a person's throwing biomechanics can have implications for both effectiveness (for instance, how far the ball is thrown), which is called *economy of effort*, and the chances of developing an injury, particularly an *overuse injury*.

Other analyses for specific sports include *swimming biomechanics*, *cycling biomechanics*, *tennis biomechanics* and *golf biomechanics*.

Efficient or correct biomechanics reduces the chances of developing an overuse injury. A *biomechanical abnormality* increases the chances of an injury. It may be detected before an injury occurs through a *screening* test or during the rehabilitation of an injury. *Video analysis* is a more sophisticated method of detecting abnormalities. The two types of abnormality are: anatomical, such as one leg being longer than the other and functional, which includes incorrect playing technique, such as cocking the wrist too much during a tennis backhand.

Biomechanist

A person working in the science of *biomechanics*. Many biomechanists are on the coaching staff for professional and elite sporting teams and individuals.

Biopsy

A sample of tissue or cells removed from the body and tested to help make a diagnosis of disease or illness, or in research. For example, a biopsy from a lump in the breast can be tested for cancer, or a biopsy of a muscle can help researchers improve understanding of the physiology of muscle fibres. The tissue and cells can be obtained through *aspiration* (needle and syringe), cutting open the skin, or *endoscopy*.

Black eye

A *bruise* to the area around the eye due to a direct blow. It is caused by damaged small blood vessels leaking blood into the skin around the eye, which is loose and transparent. *Ice* is the best immediate treatment to prevent the development of a black eye or reduce its severity.

Bladder

A hollow organ that collects and stores urine produced by the *kidneys* before allowing it to pass out of a long tube called the urethra (see *Urinary system* and *Reproductive system*). The outer wall of the bladder is made up of smooth muscle and the inner layer is called epithelium.

The bladder is shaped like an upside-down pyramid. It can expand and contain half a litre of urine in the average adult. The lower part, called the neck of the bladder, empties urine out into a long tube called the urethra. Normally the bladder neck is kept closed by a ring of muscle called a sphincter. Emptying the bladder involves relaxing the sphincter and a contracting of muscular walls. Involuntary leakage of urine from the bladder is called *incontinence*.

Injury

It is rare for the bladder to be injured in sport. It occurs due to a sudden blow or excessive force, for example, due to a high-speed collision in *motor sports* or a fall in *horse riding sports* (*Pelvis fracture* may also occur). Injury is suspected if there is pain just above the pubic bone above the genitals, blood in the urine (haematuria) or inability to urinate, and it should be treated as a *medical emergency* if there is loss of consciousness due to excessive blood loss. Minor injuries require rest and maintaining an adequate fluid intake. Major injuries require surgery.

Blisters

A small, round collection of body fluid just beneath the outer layer of the skin. It is the skin's response to excessive and repeated pressure and friction caused by shoes, clothing or equipment. For example, blisters on the feet are not uncommon when running in new shoes. Continued pressure and friction can lead to the area of the blister developing into thickened skin called a *callus*.

Prevention and treatment

Wearing-in new shoes, clothing or equipment can prevent blisters. Shoes should be first worn around the house. Petroleum jelly smeared over socks at sites of friction also helps to prevent blisters. An adhesive bandaid or skin-care pad should be applied at the first sign of a blister. Painful, fluid-filled blisters may be punctured, drained and treated with antiseptics to prevent infection.

Blood

A sticky fluid, which is pumped around the body transporting essential substances including oxygen, nutrients, minerals and wastes and hormones. It also plays a key role in temperature regulation, acid balance and removal of wastes from body tissues.

The average adult male has about 5–6 L (10–12 pt) of blood. Half the volume is a straw-coloured fluid called plasma, which is 90 per cent water and the rest is nutrients, minerals, wastes, *hormones* and other *proteins* such as antibodies which are important for fighting infections.

The other half is made up of blood cells, 99 per cent of which are *red blood cells* and the rest are *white blood cells* and platelets. Red blood cells are rich in *haemoglobin*, which attaches to oxygen. White blood cells play an essential role in fighting infection and also cause *inflammation*. *Platelets* are essential in blood clotting. The proportion of cells per unit of blood volume is called the *haematocrit*.

Exercise and sport

At rest the oxygen content of arterial blood is 20 mL per 100 mL of blood and for venous blood is 14 mL. During exercise and sport the oxygen content of venous blood drops to 2–4 mL.

The plasma volume can decrease by up to 20 per cent after prolonged periods of activity, primarily due to blood pressured through the capillaries into the space around the cells, as well as fluid loss through sweating, leading to an increased haematocrit, which is a benefit during activity.

Blood contributes to *temperature* regulation because working muscles give off heat, increasing the temperature of blood passing through, which carries off this heat to the skin and lungs.

At rest the blood is slightly alkaline with a pH of 7.4. The waste products of anaerobic metabolic processes in muscles—lactic acid, *lactate* and hydrogen ions (H^+)—increase the acidity.

Bicarbonate ions (HCO_3^+) and haemoglobin absorb the H^+ ions to maintain normal acidity (pH = 6.9–7.5). Bicarbonate ions form carbonic acid (H_2CO_3), which is converted in the lungs into water (H_2O) and carbon dioxide (CO_2). The body gets rid of the H^+ ions by breathing out CO_2. Excessive acidity can impede muscle contractions, called *lactate fatigue,* causing the lungs to increase the *breathing rate* and depth to clear out more CO_2 (see *Breathing regulation*).

Blood doping

A blood transfusion that is performed to increase the amount of *red blood cells* and related blood products in order to increase the oxygen-carrying capacity of the blood. It is a banned activity according to the International Olympic Committee (IOC) (see *Drugs banned in sport*).

The usual method of blood doping is to withdraw 2 units of an athlete's own blood 4 to 6 weeks prior to competition and transfuse it back again 1 to 2 days before the competition. Side effects include allergic reactions and the risk of bloodborne diseases such as *hepatitis* and *HIV* if someone else's blood is accidentally used. *Erythropoietin (EPO)* use has largely led to the abandonment of this activity.

Blood pressure

The pressure created by the blood as it flows through and presses against the walls of the blood vessels. It is like the pressure of water flowing from a tap, except that blood pressure increases and decreases in rapid cycles according to the *heartbeat.*

An increase in pressure is called the systolic pressure of the heartbeat and a decrease is called the diastolic pressure. The average healthy adult has a blood pressure of 120 mmHg (millimetres of mercury) systolic pressure and 80 mmHg diastolic pressure (120/80). Each beat of the *heart* pumps blood out of the left ventricle into the largest artery in the body, the aorta. It is so elastic that it recoils in response to the rush of blood from the ventricle and acts like a secondary pump, adding to the pressure of the flow into the large arteries that branch out further down.

Exercise, sport and health

The heart beats with greater strength during activity which temporarily increases the systolic pressure. If it is permanently above 140/90 it is a disease called *hypertension.* Abnormally low pressure, hypotension, occurs in response to *hypothermia* and during *pregnancy.* Blood pressure is usually measured using a sphygmomanometer, which is an inflatable cuff wrapped around the arm with a gauge for measuring the pressure.

Blood rule

See *Infectious disease prevention.*

Blood test

An analysis of the contents of blood to help confirm a diagnosis and monitor a disease. *Blood* contains many different substances and products—including blood cells, proteins, antibodies, hormones, minerals, foods, fluids, oxygen and carbon dioxide—that have a predicted normal range. A substance or product found to be outside the predicted normal level may indicate illness or disease. For example, high levels of glucose occur in people with *diabetes.*

There are three main types of blood test. Haematological tests assess the contents of the blood itself, such as levels of red and white blood cells. Microbiological tests look at the immune system and infective agents, such as bacteria and viruses. Biochemical tests measure contents, such as electrolytes, enzymes, *hormones* and gases.

Bludger

A person who doesn't put in the maximum effort or takes advantage of the privileges made available by the system. For example, giving up early when chasing after a faster opponent in a football game. This type of behaviour can be seen in individuals, but is more often noticeable in a group where *teamwork* is essential for success. It can be altered by a combination of counselling to find out the causes, and policing, such as appointing a staff member to keep an eye on a player's activities on the field.

Body composition

The relative proportions of the different types of tissue in a person's body. The body is made up of around 60 per cent water and the rest is divided between many types of tissue (including muscle, bones, fat stored in adipose tissue), and the organs (such as lungs, liver, intestines and the brain). In health, exercise and sport the main focus is on fat compared to other tissues, in particular muscle, which is called *relative body fat* and *fat-free mass*.

Excess body fat, particularly in the abdomen, increases the risk of *coronary heart disease, diabetes, stroke* and certain cancers. It is best measured by *waist–hip ratio* and *waist size*.

Exercise and sport

In exercise and sport the relative amount of fat and muscle in an athlete is a measure of fitness. Certain activities require small amounts of fat for optimum performance, such as *gymnastics, long distance running* and ballet *dancing*. Others require large amounts of muscle mass including *sprinting, throwing sports, weight lifting, bodybuilding* and the various *football* codes.

The commonly used *height–weight charts* and *Body-mass index (BMI)* are considered an unreliable guide of body composition because big isn't always fatter. For example, a person who is 190 cm (6 ft 3 in) and 100 kg (220 lb) may be bulked up with muscle, not overweight with fat.

The most practical method for assessing body composition in athletes is the *skin fold test*. Other methods include *densitometry, electrical impedance,* dual-energy X-ray absorptiometry (DXA) and *magnetic resonance imaging (MRI)*.

Bodybuilding

The first bodybuilding contest, held in London's Royal Albert Hall in 1901, was won by Germany's Eugene Sandow. The sport's later growth was largely due to Charles Atlas, world champion from the 1920s to 1960s. Arnold Schwarzenegger won the Mr Olympia title seven times (1970–75 and 1980).

Contests are judged according to muscle size, delineation between the muscles, evenness of proportion of the whole body, performing poses on request and individual poses performed to selected music. The most important fitness requirement is *strength training*.

Body-mass index (BMI)

A method of assessing if a person is *overweight* or underweight due to an *eating disorder*. It is calculated by dividing weight (kg) by height (metres)^2. For example, 85 kg divided by $(1.83 \text{ m})^2 = 25.3$. The alternative method is dividing weight (lb) by height (in)^2, multiplied by 703. For example, 187 lb divided by $(72)^2 \times 703 = 25.3$. The measurement is ranked according to the table below.

BMI	Ranking
under 20	Underweight
20–25	Healthy weight
25–29	Overweight
over 30	Obese

Body size

The height and weight of a person that may be more or less suitable for a specific sport. For instance, a 179 cm (5 ft 10 in) and 95 kg (210 lb) athlete is less likely to be suited to basketball than soccer, and a 193 cm (6 ft 4 in) and 100 kg (220 lb) athlete is more likely to be suited to Rugby League and American football than gymnastics.

Bone

A structure that forms the hard and rigid framework of the body, called the *skeleton*. Each bone has a distinctive shape and size. For example, the humerus is a long bone that connects the shoulder to the elbow. The carpal bones are small stone-like bones of the wrist that connect the forearm to the hand. Bone is composed of a tissue of the same name, and is regarded as a specialised type of *connective tissue*.

Anatomy

The hardness of bone tissue is due to the high concentration of deposits of phosphate and *calcium*. In fact most of the body's calcium is locked up in the bones.

Each bone is made up of layers. The surface is covered in a thin layer called *periosteum*. Beneath it is the compact bone that provides most of the rigidity. Further inside is the spongy or trabecular bone, which is similar to compact bone but more porous.

Last is the internal cavity called the medullary, which is filled with *bone marrow*. The appearance of each bone has distinctive *bone features*. In the arms and legs bones are divided into two groups according to size: *long bones* and *short bones*.

Physiology

Bone is an alive and regenerating tissue that changes throughout life. In the growing embryo it is in an immature state and predominantly made up of a tissue called hyaline cartilage. At the centre of each bone is a primary centre of *ossification* called the diaphysis, which first appears at around 7 to 8 weeks and is where hyaline cartilage cells (also called the protein matrix) are converted into cells called osteoblasts and osteoclasts.

Osteoblasts encourage deposits of calcium and phosphate to be laid onto the hyaline cartilage, whereas osteoclasts remove them. The balance of activity favours the osteoblasts throughout the

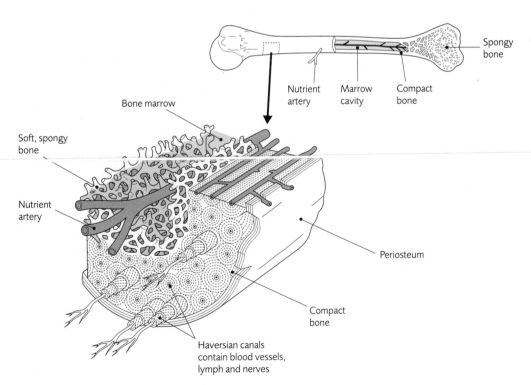

The structure of bone seen in a cross-section

growing life of bones due to the impact of hormones including *human growth hormone (HGH)*, *testosterone* and *oestrogen*. By birth most of the hyaline cartilage has completely ossified. The long bones also develop a secondary ossification centre called the *epiphysis*, which occupies the rounded ends of the bones.

Most of the growth in children and adolescents occurs at a plate of cartilage located between the diaphysis and epiphysis, called the epiphyseal plate or *growth plate*. As each layer of cartilage is converted into bone a new layer is produced, adding to the length of the bone until it reaches its characteristic adult dimensions. At this time the diaphysis and epiphysis fuse together and full bone maturation is completed. The exact age varies from bone to bone. The average female reaches maturation 2 to 3 years before the average male (see *Adolescent*).

At the start of adulthood the osteoclasts begin to slowly take over and cause a decline in calcium and phosphate deposits. If the process goes too far the bones can become excessively weak and thin, which is a disease called *osteoporosis*.

Bone bruise

An injury that causes an area of oedema (fluid) within the bone. It is usually due to a sudden, forceful, jarring movement, such as a fall onto the knee, that causes a bruise to the bone underlying the joint (see *Articular cartilage acute injury*). The bruise is not dissimilar to the injury caused by a direct blow in the shinbone.

Bone bruising most commonly occurs in the knee, ankle and shoulder. It should be suspected where other structures are found to be intact on clinical examination, if pain persists for longer than expected considering the low severity of the injury and if there is no swelling. It is best diagnosed with *magnetic resonance imaging (MRI)*.

Bone features

The common features that are used to describe the physical appearance of *bones*. They are given names

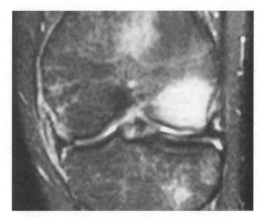

Magnetic resonance imaging (MRI) showing bone bruise in the outer side of the knee

in Latin or Greek to describe their shape and anatomical location. For example, the raised bone on the outside of the ankle is the lateral malleolus.

Bone graft

A surgical procedure that involves taking bone from one part of the body and placing it in another part that has been damaged by disease or injury. The bone graft usually dies off, but the protein component left behind forms a scaffold to allow new bone to grow in its place. The main reasons for a graft are to help two bones to reunite when they have failed to do so after a fracture, such as for a *scaphoid fracture*, or to fill a defect in a bone.

The most commonly used site for taking out the bone graft is the iliac crest of the *pelvis* (just above the hip). After the bone graft is inserted it is usually held down with metal wire, and that part of the body is placed in a plaster cast to prevent movement and allow the bone to grow.

Bone marrow

A soft and pulpy tissue found in the internal cavity of *bone*. It produces *red blood cells* and most of the *white blood cells* and *platelets* in the body. There are two types of marrow: red and yellow.

Description of bone features

Name	Description
Aperture	Large hole through a bone
Arch; pedicle; ramus	Rounded bar of bone
Articular surface	Area of bone that is in a joint
Attachment	Roughened area of bone where tendon attaches
Border	A long, thin raised area of bone
Canal	A long tunnel through a bone or bones placed in a row
Caput; head	Rounded end of a long bone
Cavity	Large articular surface
Condyle	Knuckle-shaped articular surface
Crest; line; lip; ridge	A long, thin raised area of bone
Epicondyle	A raised area of bone located next to a condyle
Facet	Small articular surface
Fovea	Small pit in a bone
Fissure	Cleft in a bone
Foramen	Hole through a bone
Fossa	Depression in a bone
Groove; sulcus	Long, canal-shaped depression in a bone
Lamina	Thin plate of bone
Malleolus	A raised area of bone
Neck	Junction between shaft and head of a long bone
Process	A general term for a bump or raised area of bone
Shaft	Tube of bone between two ends of a long bone
Spinous process	A pointed process
Trochanter; tuberosity; tubercle	A rounded bump of bone
Trochlea	Pulley-shaped articular surface

Red

At birth all the bones of the body contain red marrow. During childhood and adolescence the red marrow is gradually replaced by yellow marrow. By adulthood the only bones that still have red marrow are the spine, sternum (breastbone), ribs, clavicle (collarbone), scapula (shoulder blade), hip bone, skull and the upper ends of the humerus (upper arm) and femur (thigh).

Red marrow contains stem cells, the immature prototypes for all the blood cells and platelets. They are stimulated to form blood cells by a *hormone* called *erythropoietin (EPO)* produced by the kidney. The process of maturation is called erythropoiesis.

Yellow

Yellow marrow is made up of fat and connective tissue that can be converted into red marrow according to the body's needs.

Bone scan

A radiological investigation that is used to detect areas of increased blood flow and bone cell activity in bones. It is used in the diagnosis of *stress fracture*, *articular cartilage acute injury* of the subchondral bone and *scaphoid fracture* of the wrist.

It involves being injected with a radioactive substance that is carried by the blood to the bones. Images are produced in three phases or stages: the first are obtained immediately (the isotope angiogram), the second after 2 minutes (blood-pool phase) and the third after 2–4 hours (bone phase). This sequence of scans allows differentiation between soft tissue and bone injury. The full name for a bone scan is triphasic radio-isotopic bone scan scintigraphy.

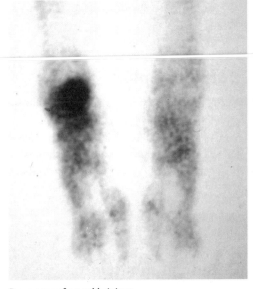

Bone scan of an ankle injury

Bone stress reaction

See *Stress fracture*.

Borg perceived exertion scale

A method of scoring the intensity of an activity based on subjective feelings of effort (see *Perceived exertion*). Sport science research has shown that it is accurate for assessing correct levels of *aerobic training* and correlates closely to more precise measures of intensity such as VO_2 *max*. It is based largely on the impact that exercise and sport have on *breathing regulation*, in particular breathing rate and depth.

6	No exertion at all
7	Extremely light
9	Very light
11	Light
13	Somewhat hard
15	Hard
17	Very hard
19	Extremely hard
20	Maximal exertion

The Borg scale also may be correlated with the three levels of intensity based on *metabolic equivalent (MET)*: low = up to 11; moderate = 13; high = 15 and above.

Born champion

A person who appears to possess the winning and successful qualities of a champion from a young age. While genes do give certain athletes the potential to be a champion, they are not the whole story. Environmental factors, particularly personal upbringing and training, also play a key role. Hard-working athletes can learn the mental and physical skills that are required to become a champion.

Botanical medicine

See *Herbal medicine*.

Bowed legs

See *Genu varum*.

Bowls

Lawn bowls originated in games played by Egyptian royalty 4000 years ago. The modern rules were developed in England in the 1700s. It is highly popular in Commonwealth countries such as Australia, which has nearly 300 000 participants, mostly male (61 per cent) and 77 per cent over 55 years old.

Rules and equipment

Players stand at one end of a grass area and roll large balls (called bowls) towards a white ball (the jack) at the other end. The game is played between two players (singles) or teams (pairs, triples or fours). Each side aims to roll more of their bowls nearer to the jack than the opposition.

Fitness, skills and injuries

Lawn bowls is low-intensity *aerobic training* suitable for people with conditions such as *osteoarthritis* or

Elite lawn bowls player, Adam Jeffrey

coronary heart disease. The main skill is eye–hand coordination.

The main health concern is aggravation of existing disease or illness such as *knee osteoarthritis, patellofemoral joint syndrome* (knee) and *low back pain (non-specific)*.

Boxer's fracture

See *Metacarpal fracture*.

Boxing

Boxing was a sport at the ancient Greek Olympics. The modern rules, including not hitting below the belt, were established in England in the 1700s. From the mid-1800s a system of rounds and the 10-second knockout were introduced.

Fitness and skills include *strength training, aerobic training, flexibility training* and *skills training*, particularly balance and spatial awareness. The most common injuries include *concussion*, eye and ear injuries (see *Face pain and injuries*), *metacarpal fracture, phalanx fracture, PIP joint dislocation* and *Boxer's fracture* (see *Hand and finger pain and injuries*).

Brace

A piece of equipment designed to protect and support muscles and joints. It may be specifically used to prevent injuries, protect an injury that is healing, reduce pain or retain heat.

Protection and support is achieved by increasing stability and providing joint and muscle position awareness (similar to *taping*, which involves the application of adhesive tape to the skin).

The advantages of a brace over taping include allowing athletes to put it on independently, whereas taping requires a *physiotherapist* or *sports trainer* to apply the adhesive tape. Even though the initial cost of a high quality, strong brace is much greater than using tape, it may prove to be cheaper over the long term and it is less likely to aggravate the skin.

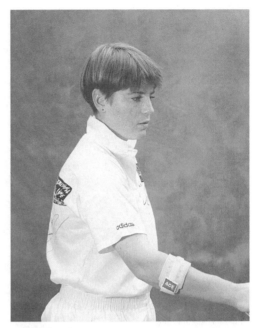

Tennis elbow brace

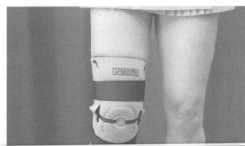

Hinged knee brace

However, there are disadvantages. A brace is more likely to slip off, it weighs more and there can be difficulties with pre-manufactured braces, such as

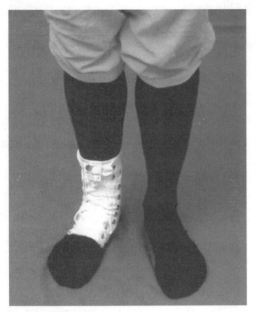

Lace-up ankle brace

finding the exact size and tailoring the stability to the needs of individual injuries. A brace can be custom-made by an orthotist, using thermoplastic material to create a splint, such as a hand and wrist splint for a *metacarpal fracture*.

A brace that is used for an injury protects a body part from excessive forces or blows, or prevents movement in a specific direction that would cause excessive stress on an injured structure while allowing other nearby non-injured structures to move. A brace that is worn to retain heat is called *thermal gear*.

Neck and shoulder
An elasticised brace pulls the shoulders back to help maintain an upright posture. It can prevent neck pain associated with *neck posture syndrome*.

Low back
An elasticised brace can be used to maintain the posture of lumbar lordosis (inward curve of the low back) to prevent *low back pain (non-specific)*.

Elbow
An elbow brace may be worn as part of the treatment for *tennis elbow*, in particular during return to sport.

Many people mistakenly assume it should be worn over the painful area itself, however the correct site is in the upper forearm, approximately 10 cm (4 in) below the elbow joint.

Wrist
A wrist guard should be made of a thermoplastic material that is flexible but provides a high degree of rigidity. It starts about 8 cm (3 in) above the wrist and maintains close contact with the upper palm and just below the proximal end of the thumb.

It is highly effective at reducing injuries including fractures of the wrist, such as *Colles fracture* and *scaphoid fracture* due to a fall on an outstretched hand in sports like snowboarding, skateboarding and rollerblading. In some cases it is used to allow a player to return back to sport earlier than normal.

Knee
A hinged knee brace prevents valgus (sideways) strain to protect a grade 3 (severe) *medial collateral ligament sprain*, while allowing the rest of the knee to move to prevent stiffness and maintain muscle strength. It is also called a limited motion brace.

Patellofemoral
A patellofemoral brace is worn by athletes who have had a *patella dislocation* and, in some cases, instead of taping for *patellofemoral joint syndrome*. These injuries are more likely in sports involving substantial running, jumping and twisting such as basketball, netball and gymnastics.

The brace is made of canvas or a flexible plastic material that fits around the knee and is centred on the patellofemoral joint at the front of the knee. It has a strap, positioned over the patella, which can be pulled and tightened to one side. This places pressure on the patella in a medial (sideways inwards) direction to counter the excessive lateral (sideways outwards) movement.

Ankle
Research shows conflicting results over whether an ankle brace protects an ankle from a first-time sprain in sports like basketball and netball. However there

is no doubt that a brace can help prevent re-injury after an *ankle sprain* has occurred.

Taping is preferred to wearing a brace because it can be tailored to a person's specific type of ankle sprain. However, a brace is better than nothing, and may be required if taping causes adverse skin reactions.

The lace-up or Velcro ankle brace made of canvas with plastic strips running the length of the brace on each side, beginning 10 cm (4 in) above the ankle and descending to encompass the heel, is better than pull-on elasticised braces.

Brain

The organ located inside the skull. It is the most important part of the *nervous system*, which controls much of the communications conducted in the body.

It is the starting point for any activity performed in exercise and sport. For example, swinging a golf club requires the brain to plan where to stand next to the ball, instructing the arms to strike it so that it lands near (or preferably in) the hole. The brain then receives information about how the ball was struck, such as visual information.

Structure and physiology

The average adult brain weighs about 1.4 kg (3 lb). It has the consistency of jelly. Even though it is mostly made up of nerve cells (see *Neuron*), it has no direct feelings itself. However, layers that cover the brain, called the meninges, do feel pain.

The three anatomical divisions are the forebrain, brainstem and cerebellum. The forebrain, also called the cerebrum, has a left and right hemisphere. It includes the primary motor cortex, where instructions to perform actions, such as swinging a golf club, take place (see *Motor nervous system*); the primary sensory cortex, where we feel sensations like pain, heat, touch, the weight of objects and more (see *Sensory nervous system*); and lobes for specific tasks, such as the occipital lobe for vision. Beneath the cerebrum are the corpus callosum, basal ganglia, pituitary gland, thalamus and hypothalamus.

Lower parts of the brain are not under conscious control. The brainstem contains, for example, the reticular formation, which has a role in *muscle tone*, *heart* and *lung* function. The cerebellum plays a crucial role in coordinating movements.

Bread

A food rich in *carbohydrates*. It comes in a wide variety of types in terms of nutritional content. Pita and Turkish bread are low in fat; focaccia is high in fat. Some types of white bread have a high amount of added sugar. Other products have added soya and linseed. Wholegrain and wholemeal breads are high in *fibre*, *vitamin* B and *iron*.

Until the 1990s people who were *overweight* were told to steer clear of bread. However, researchers found that many slices of bread need to be eaten before the body converts the carbohydrates into fat. The current advice is that eating bread itself is not fattening. The danger is the toppings used on bread, such as butter or margarine, that are high in *fat*.

Breasts

The breast is a sex organ that provides milk for infants after birth. It is also erotically stimulating, and a symbol of femininity and beauty. It is composed primarily of fatty tissue. Breast size and shape is largely determined by genetic predisposition but may be affected by general weight loss or weight gain. Breasts develop during *puberty*. Changes in size of up to 40 per cent can occur during the menstrual cycle (see *Menstruation*) and *pregnancy*. The *nipples* contain muscle fibres that respond to cold or rubbing stimulation.

Exercise and sport

The breasts may suffer an acute injury due to a sudden, direct blow from a ball, racquet or opponent during exercise and sport. Injuries usually cause bleeding and swelling. The recommended treatment is *ice*, *analgesics* and support. Occasionally a deep haematoma (see *Muscle contusion*) develops that requires *aspiration*.

Breath-hold diving

Diving under water by holding the breath as long as possible. It is performed for recreation and work, such as pearl diving. The maximum depth of diving is usually 20–30 m (60–95 ft). At this depth the water pressure has compressed the lungs down to its residual volume (the volume of air left in the lungs after fully breathing out). The usual depth is 5–6 m (16–20 ft). The maximum duration of a dive is usually determined by the amount of carbon dioxide in the blood, which forces an urge to breathe in.

Breathing

The act of moving air in and out of the *lungs*. Breathing in (inspiration) occurs due to the work of the breathing muscles, in particular the diaphragm and rib muscles, and the natural flow of air that occurs between the air outside and inside of the lungs due to pressure differences (see *Respiratory system*). Breathing out (expiration) involves the opposite actions.

Physiology

When the diaphragm and rib muscles contract they cause the wall of the chest to expand outwards. The lungs are attached to the chest wall, so they are stretched outwards too and this expansion increases the amount of space inside the lungs. According to the law of pressures, the same amount of air in an increasing space leads to an immediate decrease in air pressure.

Suddenly, with low air pressure inside the lungs, the outside air pressure, which hasn't changed and remains higher at 760 mmHg (millimetres of mercury), rushes in through the open mouth and/or nose.

The speed and amount of air that flows in depends on a number of factors, including the amount of expansion of the chest wall and the resultant decrease in air pressure. During rest the decrease may be as little as 5 mmHg. But during high-intensity activity, such as fast running (see *Aerobic training* and *Metabolic equivalent, MET*), it can be as much as 80 mmHg.

After contracting to create an inspiration, the breathing muscles relax and allow the chest wall to move inwards, which reduces the space inside the lungs, creating high air pressure. Naturally the air rushes out of the lungs to where the air pressure is low. During high-intensity activity the chest wall is moved inwards more quickly with the help of the intercostal, latissimus dorsi, quadratus lumborum and abdominal muscles.

Breathing control

A psychological technique used to take conscious control of *breathing* in order to make it smooth, deep and slower. It involves being focused on using the diaphragm, the main breathing muscle beneath the lungs (see *Respiratory system*). The diaphragm causes minimal lower chest and upper abdominal movement outwards, without hunching or raising the shoulders. Breathing out will cause it to move back in again.

Breathing control is an important part of *meditation*, *yoga* and many relaxation techniques that aim to reduce *anxiety* and *stress* levels, such as *centring*.

Breathing rate

The speed of breathing, as measured by the number of breaths per minute, is controlled by *breathing regulation* centres in the body. At rest the average adult breathes at 13 to 17 breaths per minute. During exercise and sport the rate can increase up to 60 breaths per minute in some athletes. A feeling of discomfort associated with increased breathing rate is called *shortness of breath*, which may be a symptom of an underlying disease such as a *heart disease* or *asthma*.

Breathing regulation

The combined effect of the different nerves in the body that control the breathing rate and breathing depth, thus determining the volume of air breathed in and out. Exercise and sport causes changes in the body, in particular an increased demand for oxygen to be supplied to the muscles and the need to remove carbon dioxide produced by the working muscles.

Physiology

Neurons (nerve cells) in the lower part of the brain called the respiratory centre send instructions through the phrenic nerve to the main breathing muscle, the diaphragm, to perform contractions. At rest the average adult has a *breathing rate* of 13 to 17 breaths per minute and breathing depth of 0.5–1.0 L (0.02–0.04 cubic ft) for each breath, which equals a breathing volume of 6.5–17 L (0.2–0.6 cubic ft) per minute.

Input from other nerve centres from around the body can change the instructions sent from the respiratory centre. There are *sensory nervous system* neurons located in the brain that detect changes in the level of carbon dioxide and acidity in the *blood* (as determined by the level of hydrogen, H⁺, ions). When carbon dioxide and acidity levels rise too high they instruct the respiratory centre to increase the rate and depth of breathing so as to blow off the excess carbon dioxide. Sensory neurons that also detect changes in oxygen levels of the blood are located in the aorta (largest artery in the body) and the common carotid artery in the neck. These have the same effect on breathing when oxygen levels drop too low.

Conscious control of breathing rate and depth can occur through meditation and other psychological methods. Unconscious input can occur through emotions such as *stress* and sexual excitement.

Exercise and sport

The increase in breathing rate and depth varies according to the intensity of the exercise and sport (see *Aerobic training* and *Metabolic equivalent, MET*). Low-intensity exercise only requires an increase in breathing depth. For example, when walking slowly, speaking is not affected by changes to breathing. At moderate-intensity, such as brisk walking, the breathing rate also begins to increase but not enough to disrupt speaking. However, at high-intensity, such as running, speaking is disrupted.

Exercise can cause a rapid and large increase in breathing volume. For example, from a total breathing volume of 6.5–17 L (0.2–0.6 cubic ft) per minute at rest, the increase can reach up to 100 L (3.5 cubic ft) per minute within 60 seconds of starting high-intensity exercise or sport. The response to excess carbon dioxide and acidity is an even more abrupt increase in breathing rate and depth in order to clear out carbon dioxide and hydrogen ions from the blood.

Breathing volume can increase to a range of 120–180 L (4.2–6.4 cubic ft) per minute during sustained high-intensity exercise, depending on the fitness level of the participant. At the end of high-intensity exercise, increased breathing rate and depth continues for a few minutes because it takes time for carbon dioxide and acidity levels in the blood to return to normal.

Increased *aerobic fitness* through *aerobic training* can increase the maximum breathing volume that can be achieved through increased breathing rates and depths. In highly trained athletes with large bodies, the breathing volume can reach up to 240 L (8.5 cubic ft) per minute. Increased fitness also lowers breathing rate at rest.

However, breathing regulation adapts well to the needs of the body during exercise and sport, even in unfit people. It is only elite endurance athletes, like marathon runners, that may experience limitations where oxygen consumption by the muscles is greater than the ability to absorb oxygen into the blood and causes oxygen levels to decrease and impact on performance.

The same limitations in performance can occur in people with lung disease, such as *asthma*, because narrowing of the lung airways decreases the amount of air breathed in. A *peak flow meter* can be used to assess breathing and lung volumes.

Bromelain

An enzyme derived from pineapple that breaks down *protein*, which may be recommended by natural health practitioners to treat *inflammation* and reduce *swelling* caused by injuries. It should not be taken together with conventional anti-inflammatory medications (see *Non-steroidal anti-inflammatory drugs (NSAIDs)* and *corticosteroids*).

Bronchodilators

Medications that aim to provide quick relief during an *asthma* attack and can also have a preventive effect. They work by relaxing the smooth muscles in the airways that cause bronchoconstriction and reduce the release of chemicals that cause airway inflammation.

However, excessive use of bronchodilators for prevention eventually leads to a reduction in its effectiveness. It is recommended to use other preventive medications, including *corticosteroids (inhaled)*, *sodium cromoglycate* and *nedocromil sodium*, and reserve the use of bronchodilators for when an attack occurs.

Short-acting bronchodilators, such as salbutamol and terbutaline, usually take effect within 5 minutes, reaching a peak within 15 minutes and lasting for 3 to 6 hours. Long-acting bronchodilators, including salmeterol, only start to take effect within 20 minutes, but last for at least 12 hours.

Bronchodilators belong to a group of medications called *beta-2 agonists*, which are regarded as *drugs banned in sport* by the International Olympic Committee (IOC) when taken as a tablet or injected.

Bruise

An area under the skin that has been discoloured by leakage from damaged blood vessels. It usually occurs due to a sudden direct blow to the skin or in association with another injury, such as an *ankle sprain*.

A bruise looks black or blue during the early stages and then gradually turns yellow as it heals. Anti-coagulant medication, which thins the blood to prevent disease such as *stroke*, increases the risk of receiving a bruise. A bruise to the eye region is called a *black eye*.

Ice is the best immediate treatment to prevent the development of a bruise or reduce its severity.

If a bruise does not clear within the expected time or appears suddenly for no reason, medical care should be sought in case there are problems with blood clotting.

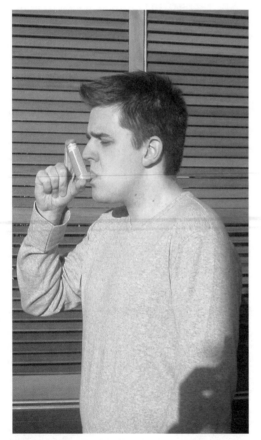

Salbutamol aerosol inhaler

Bulimia

See *Eating disorder*.

Bunion

See *Hallux valgus*.

Burnout

See *Overtraining syndrome*.

Bursa

A flattened sac filled with a lubricant called *synovial fluid* that protects a muscle tendon from excessive friction due to rubbing against a bone, ligament or another tendon. The inner lining of a bursa produces the synovial fluid and is similar to the synovium found in a joint capsule. Most bursae lie near joints in the shoulder, elbow, hip, knee and foot. Some are continuations of a joint cavity and share the same synovial fluid. Injuries of a bursa include *bursitis* and acute haemorrhagic bursitis.

Bursitis

An injury that causes inflammation of a *bursa*, a flattened sac filled with a lubricant called synovial fluid that protects a muscle tendon from excessive friction due to rubbing against a bone, ligament or another tendon. It is usually due to excessive and repeated forces associated with an aggravating activity experienced over a period of weeks or months.

The most common bursitis injuries include *olecranon bursitis* at the back of the elbow, *trochanteric bursitis* of the hip and Achilles bursitis of the retrocalcaneal bursa separating the *Achilles tendon* from the heel bone.

Diagnosis and treatment

Bursitis causes tenderness when pressed firmly with the fingers, and swelling and pain associated with specific movements. Treatments include *nonsteroidal anti-inflammatory drugs* (NSAIDs) and, if this is not successful, *aspiration* of the inflammatory fluid, sometimes accompanied by a *corticosteroid* injection. Occasionally surgery is required to remove the bursa.

Buttock

The large posterior region of the *pelvis* that connects the low back to the lower limbs. It contains a number of muscles, including the largest in the body, the gluteus maximus. These muscles help keep the pelvis

and lower trunk stable during activities (see *Lumbo-pelvic instability*). It also provides a passage for important nerves from the *low back joints* to the legs.

Buttock myofascial trigger point pain

Pain in the buttock that is produced by small tender areas located in tight bands of the gluteal muscles and the piriformis muscle (see *Piriformis impingement*). The pain also may spread into the back of the thigh. The tight bands are due to abnormal crosslinkages between muscle fibres that form in response to inflammation following an *acute injury* or due to a biomechanical abnormality such as *lumbo-pelvic instability* or *pelvis anterior tilt*. The tender areas cause pain due to hyperactive muscle fibres that are unable to stop muscle contractions.

The diagnosis is confirmed by pressing on the *myofascial trigger point* to reproduce the buttock pain. The most effective treatments include *dry needling* using acupuncture or conventional needles inserted into the trigger point, *ice*, stretching the muscle, *massage* and *corticosteroid* injection.

Buttock pain and injuries

Buttock pain is caused by overuse injuries, acute injuries and diseases. An *overuse injury* causes pain that gets worse over weeks or months due to an accumulation of excessive forces that cause microtrauma. In the early stages it causes only minor pain and stiffness. But later on, either gradually or following a sudden force, it becomes painful enough to seek medical care.

An *acute injury* causes pain that begins suddenly due to a single incident, such as a direct blow in a contact sport.

Causes

The *buttock* and associated structures are the main sources of *pain* in the region. However, it is not unusual for *referred pain* from another structure, which is called *buttock referred pain*.

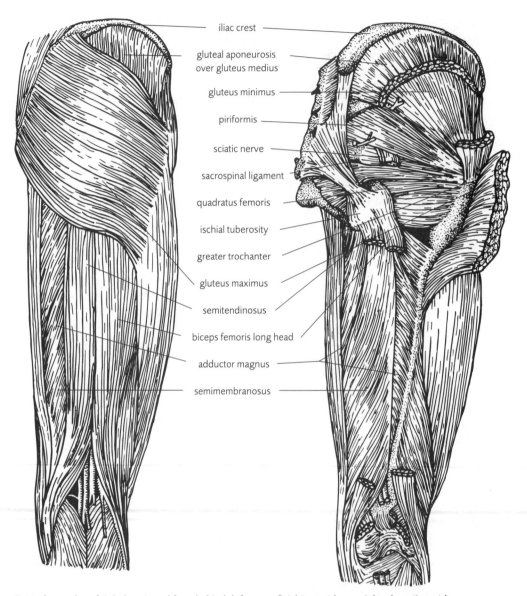

iliac crest

gluteal aponeurosis
over gluteus medius

gluteus minimus

piriformis

sciatic nerve

sacrospinal ligament

quadratus femoris

ischial tuberosity

greater trochanter

gluteus maximus

semitendinosus

biceps femoris long head

adductor magnus

semimembranosus

Buttock muscles of right leg viewed from behind: left, superficial (outer) layer; right, deep (inner) layer

Diagnosis

Making the diagnosis involves combining information gathered from the *history*, *physical examination*
and relevant tests.

A deep, aching, diffuse pain that is hard to pinpoint is an indication that the cause is *buttock referred
pain*. Pain located closer to the skin or easier to pinpoint is more likely to be a structure in the buttock.

For example, pain over the ischial tuberosity (protruding bone in the buttock) is usually a *hamstring
origin tendinitis* or *ischiogluteal bursitis*.

The time of day that pain is felt is also a good indication of the cause. Inflammatory arthritis such as
ankylosing spondylitis, *Reiter's syndrome* and *psoriatic arthritis* feel worse in the morning and improve
with light exercise. In some cases radiological investi-

Causes of buttock pain

Common	Less common	Not to be missed
• Buttock referred pain	• Piriformis impingement	• Tumour
• Hamstring origin tendinitis	• Ischial tuberosity apophysitis	• Ankylosing spondylitis
• Ischiogluteal bursitis	• Ischial tuberosity avulsion fracture	• Reiter's syndrome
• Buttock myofascial trigger point pain		• Psoriatic arthritis
		• Osteomyelitis
		• Pelvis fracture

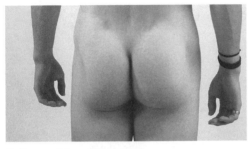

Surface anatomy of the buttock

gation can be useful, such as an X-ray for a *pelvis fracture* and *ischial tuberosity apophysitis* and tumours. Blood tests also may be used to confirm rheumatoid arthritis.

Buttock referred pain

Buttock pain caused by damaged structures in another location some distance away. The most common sources are myofascial trigger points in the low back or thoracic region, *neural tension* of the low back, the low back joints (see *Low back pain (non-specific)*) and the sacroiliac joint (see *Sacroiliac joint pain*). These structures may be the whole or partial cause.

Diagnosis and treatment

The diagnosis is based on excluding a local cause and looking for positive signs of *referred pain*. For example, pain referred from the right side low back joints to the right buttock is likely if a physical examination finds reduced range of movement of low back rotation (turning the trunk) and tender and stiff accessory (sliding) movements of the right side low back joints.

This diagnosis is tested with right side low back joints *mobilisation* treatments. If buttock pain is reduced, the diagnosis is correct. *Myofascial trigger points* are treated with *massage* and *dry needling*. *Neural tension* stretching may be required.

QUICK REFERENCE GUIDE

Buttock

Buttock referred pain	Is your pain centred around the low back, or in the junction between the spine and the pelvis, and spreading down into the buttock region?
Hamstring origin tendinitis	Is your pain centred around the bone that you sit on (called the ischial tuberosity)? Did the pain gradually get worse over a period of weeks or months?
Ischiogluteal bursitis	Is your pain centred around the bone that you sit on (ischial tuberosity)? Did the pain gradually get worse over a period of weeks or months?
Piriformis impingement	Is your pain centred in the middle of the buttock, aggravated by exercise and possibly associated with referral into the hamstring?
Ischial tuberosity avulsion fracture	Did an intense pain come on suddenly and is it associated with over stretching of the hamstring muscle?

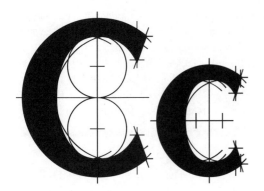

Caffeine

A stimulant drug that is found in coffee, tea, cola drinks, chocolates and medications for illnesses such as migraines. The amount of caffeine varies: 1 cup instant coffee (250 mL/8.5 fl oz) = 100 mg (3.5 oz); 1 cup strong tea (250 mL/8.5 fl oz) = 60 mg (2.1 oz); coca-cola (375 mL/12.7 fl oz) = 65 mg (2.3 oz); chocolate bar (family size) = 150 mg (5.25 oz); No-Doz tablet = 100 mg (3.5 oz).

The effects on the body, which are milder than other stimulants like *amphetamines*, include increased alertness, shortened reaction time, improved concentration and a diuretic effect (increased urination). Side effects include irritability, insomnia and increased *heart rate* and cholesterol levels.

Previously caffeine was a prohibited substance on the World Anti-Doping Agency (WADA) and International Committee (IOC) list, but it was removed on 1 January 2004.

Calcium

A mineral that gives *bones* their hardness and rigidity. It also has an essential role in nerves, blood clotting and *muscle contractions*.

The skeleton contains 98 per cent of the body's calcium. The amount of calcium in the average person is 1 kg (2.2 lb). Foods that are rich in calcium include milk, dairy products such as yoghurt and cheese, calcium-enriched soy drinks, bony fish such as sardines and salmon, tofu, tempeh, broccoli and dried beans (see *Minerals*).

The main risk of inadequate calcium in the body is the development of *osteoporosis*, which is a disease that results from thinning and weakening of the bones.

Calcium intake should be high during childhood and adolescence when the skeleton grows and becomes thick, in adults facing a high risk of calcium loss such as female athletes who have lost their menstrual periods (see *Amenorrhea*) and post-menopausal women.

Recommended daily intake for calcium

Age group (years)	Calcium (mg)
Children	
• 4–7	800
Boys	
• 8–11	800
• 12–15	1200
• 16–18	1000
Girls	
• 8–11	900
• 12–15	1000
• 16–18	800
Men	
• 19–64	800
• over 64	800
Women	
• 19–54	800
• over 54	1000
Pregnancy	1100
Breastfeeding	1200
Amenorrhaeic athletes	1200–1500

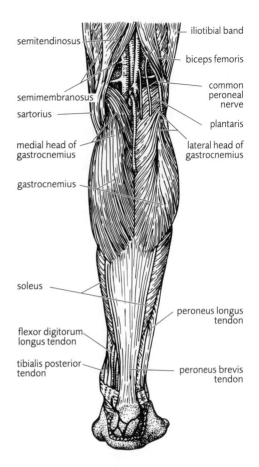

Calf muscles—superficial (outer) layer

Calcium channel blockers

A drug prescribed to treat conditions including *coronary heart disease*, particularly when associated with chest pain called angina, *hypertension* (high blood pressure) and *cardiac arrhythmias* (irregular heart beat).

They work by reducing the movement of calcium ions into muscles to prevent *muscle contractions* and slow the passage of nerve conduction through the heart to make the *heartbeat* more regular. Side effects include dizziness, *headaches* and face flushing. They may reduce *cardiac output* during exercise and sport, leading to reduced performance levels.

Calf

The back section of the lower leg between the knee and ankle. It contains the powerful gastrocnemius and soleus—the calf muscles. Both muscles join up at the *Achilles tendon*, attaching to the heel bone (calcaneus). They are surrounded by fibrous *fascia*, making up the superficial posterior compartment. The *shin* contains the other leg compartments.

Calf and Achilles tendon pain and injuries

Cause

Pain in the calf or Achilles tendon is caused by an acute or overuse injury or blood vessel disease. An *acute injury* causes pain that begins suddenly due to a single incident such as tearing a muscle.

An *overuse injury* causes pain that gets worse over a period of weeks or months due to an accumulation of excessive forces that cause microtrauma. In the early stages it causes only minor pain and stiffness. But later on, either gradually or following a sudden force, it becomes painful enough to seek medical care.

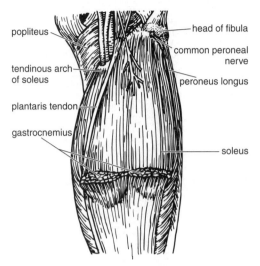

popliteus

head of fibula

common peroneal nerve

tendinous arch of soleus

peroneus longus

plantaris tendon

gastrocnemius

soleus

Calf muscles—deep (inner) layer, shown with gastrocnemius muscle removed

The gastrocnemius and soleus muscles, Achilles tendon and associated blood vessels are the main structures acting as sources of *pain*. In some cases the pain comes from another structure such as the low back (lumbar spine), which is called *calf and Achilles tendon referred pain*.

Diagnosis

A diagnosis involves combining information gathered from the *history, physical examination* and relevant tests.

For acute injuries, a sudden burst of acceleration, such as lunging to play a tennis stroke, followed by a sharp pain and an inability to run suggests a *gastrocnemius strain* or *soleus strain*. Achilles tendon pain, described as being 'hit by a car' or a loud snap, suggests *Achilles tendon rupture*. A blow to the calf can cause a *gastrocnemius contusion*.

Cramping episodes that come and go may be due to recurrent gastrocnemius or soleus strain, *calf and Achilles tendon referred pain* or a *deep vein thrombosis*, particularly if there has been a long car or airplane trip in the last 24 to 48 hours.

For overuse injuries, such as *Achilles tendinosis* and *retrocalcaneal bursitis*, the pain and stiffness is felt on rising in the morning, diminishes with walking, applying heat or during training, but comes back several hours afterwards.

Radiological investigations such as *diagnostic ultrasound* and *magnetic resonance imaging (MRI)* can provide supporting information. Doppler scan or venography may be required for confirming a deep venous thrombosis.

Calf and Achilles tendon referred pain

Pain felt in the calf or Achilles tendon caused by a damaged structure in a location some distance away. The most common are *posterior cruciate ligament (PCL) sprain* (knee), *neural tension* and *low back pain (non-specific)*.

Diagnosis and treatment

The diagnosis is based on excluding a local cause and looking for positive signs of *referred pain*. For

Causes of calf and Achilles tendon pain and injuries

Common	Less common	Not to be missed
• Gastrocnemius strain	• Sever's disease	• Deep vein thrombosis
• Soleus strain	• Achilles bursitis	• Achilles tendon rupture
• Muscle cramps	• Shin chronic compartment syndrome	• Peripheral vascular disease
• Calf and Achilles tendon referred pain	• Popliteal artery entrapment syndrome	
• Delayed-onset muscle soreness	• Fibula stress fracture	
• Gastrocnemius contusion	• Tibia stress fracture	
• Achilles tendon strain (partial tear)	• Varicose veins	
• Achilles tendinosis		
• Achilles paratenonitis		
• Retrocalcaneal bursitis		

Calf and Achilles tendon

Acute injury: Pain caused by a sudden force

Gastrocnemius strain, soleus strain ....Did you feel a strain, cramp or tear in your calf?

Achilles tendon strain (partial tear) ....Do you have pain in your Achilles that has come on gradually and is related to overuse (e.g. running)?

Achilles tendon rupture ....Did you feel a sudden snap or tear in the Achilles associated with weakness?

Overuse injury: Pain that has gradually got worse over a period of weeks or months

Achilles tendinosis,
Achilles paratenonitis,
rectocalcaneal bursitis ....Do you have pain in your Achilles that has come on gradually and is related to overuse (e.g. running)?

example, pain referred from left side low back joints to the left calf is likely if left side low back joint *mobilisation* treatments reduce the pain. The neural sheath is assessed with the slump *neural tension* test and treated with mobilisation and *flexibility exercises*.

Callus

A thickened layer of skin cells less elastic than normal skin that develop in response to repeated excessive pressure and friction, usually in the foot or hand. When the skin develops a layer of dead skin cells, it is called a corn. The pressure is usually due to a biomechanical abnormality, such as excessive *foot pronation* during running or poor fitting *shoes*.

Treatment involves seeing a podiatrist to remove the callus or corn with a scalpel and correcting the causes; for example, wearing the correct shoe size. Applying petroleum jelly over areas of skin subjected to excessive pressure, such as the top of the middle joint of the second and third toes and on the outside of the sock, can help prevent corns and calluses.

Calories

A measure of energy. One calorie equals the heat required to increase the temperature of 1 g of water by 1°C when the outside air is 14.5°C (58.1°F). The abbreviation is written as 'cal'.

The word 'Calorie' that is used more commonly actually is equal to 1000 calories. The abbreviation is written as 'Cal'. This is the amount of energy required to raise 1 kg of water by 1°C. Other measures of energy are *joules* and kilojoules (kJ). One calorie (cal) equals 4.2 joules. One Calorie (Cal) equals 4.2 kilojoules (kJ).

Cancer

A disease that causes unrestrained growth of cells that can eventually become life threatening. Cancers can be located in any organ or part of the body.

While the benefits of exercise for *coronary heart disease* and *diabetes* are already well known, there is a new and growing recognition that exercise and sport can be recommended for patients with cancer. One of the reasons for changing attitudes is the higher survival rate for many people after acute treatment for cancers such as breast cancer. Research has now found that exercise can help reduce symptoms associated with the cancer or treatment side effects, such as fatigue, poor sleep, weight gain, psychological stress and signs of *depression*. The main benefits of exercise include improvements in *aerobic fitness*, *flexibility* and *strength* and reductions in mood and sleep disturbances, weight loss, *swelling* and tiredness.

Treatment

Once medical treatment is determined, exercise selection should be made according to the preferences of the person with cancer wherever possible to help with motivation and regaining a sense of control in life.

The recommended intensity for improving aerobic fitness is moderate-intensity *aerobic training*, based on perception of effort or shortness of breath that still enables continuous conversation or whistling (see *Aerobic training* and *Metabolic equivalent (MET)*). This means no more than brisk walking for many people taking up exercise during acute treatment.

Participation in a group with similarly diagnosed patients, such as women with breast cancer, can be beneficial for peer support, though it should be kept in mind that some people prefer to exercise alone or in a mixed group.

A full medical check up conducted by a doctor is recommended to make sure that there are no additional problems preventing participation in exercise or sport. For example, a low haemoglobin count requires avoiding high-intensity activities, such as running, and bone pain means avoiding activities that increase the risk of fracture.

Cancer prevention

Regular participation in physical activity such as exercise and sport reduces the risk of breast, colon (large intestine) and bowel cancer, and possibly endometrial cancer and prostate cancer. A diet rich in *vitamins*, *minerals* and *fibre* and low in fat, particularly *saturated fats*, may also be protective.

Cannabinoids

A recreational drug derived from the marijuana plant that may act as a stimulant or depressant of the brain. It is usually smoked or eaten in leaf or leaf-derivative form, or as the resin that forms on the leaf, called hashish. The active ingredient is 11-nordelta-9-tetrahydrocannabinol-9-carboxylic acid (carboxy-THC).

The World Anti-Doping Agency does not regard it as a *drug banned in sport* outside of competition. However, because it is illegal in certain countries, it is banned during competition. A concentration in the urine of carboxy-THC over 15 nanograms per millilitre (ng/mL) is a positive test. Cannabinoids also have a negative effect on sport performance, including impairment of motor skills, perception of time and concentration.

Canoeing

The first sporting canoe club was established in England in 1866 by a lawyer named John MacGregor. Canoeing and kayaking (covered canoe) were included in the Olympics in 1936.

Olympic races have a simple code: K = kayak; C = Canadian canoe, followed by the number of paddlers: for example, C-1 means canoe singles. Contests are held over courses such as 1000 m flat-water or white-water slalom.

Fitness and injuries

The sport involves repetition of trunk and arm movements, which require *aerobic training* and *strength training*, as well as *flexibility training*.

The most common injuries include extensor tendinosis (*Tennis elbow*), flexor tendinosis (*Golfer's elbow*), de Quervain's tenosynovitis (wrist), *rotator cuff strain* (shoulder), *low back pain (non-specific)*, *lumbopelvic instability* (low back), *thoracic pain (non-specific)* (middle back) and *rib stress fracture*.

Capsaicin

An ointment that is used to reduce muscle aches and pains. It is made from the heat-causing ingredient in red peppers. Any benefits may be due to a painkiller effect. It also may cause an uncomfortable burning sensation.

Carbohydrate depletion

Excessively reduced carbohydrate supply in the body that can cause abnormal *tiredness* that leads to poor performance. Carbohydrates are stored in the muscles as *glycogen*, which is a long chain of bonded glucose molecules. *Carbohydrate oxidation* provides most of the energy for muscle contractions in high-intensity activities such as running, fast cycling and swimming laps.

Causes
If the *carbohydrate* supply is not fully replenished after a training session, a shortfall occurs. Over a period of weeks or months stores can become so low that not enough energy is supplied for the needs of training. People most at risk are those who don't eat breakfast, don't eat a snack made up of high-carbohydrate foods before and after exercise, or don't eat a full meal after exercise.

Treatment and prevention
Replenishment of the carbohydrate supply is achieved with a diet high in complex carbohydrates (see *Energy supply*). Snacking on carbohydrate-rich foods with a high *glycaemic index* (GI) such as bananas, low-fat muesli bars, confectionery (such as jelly beans) and sugary drinks before and after training is recommended.

The size of a snack eaten before an activity should be small enough not to cause indigestion problems during activity. It is important to note that the sooner carbohydrate is taken following a bout of exercise, the more effective the replenishment of stores. A snack should be eaten 15 to 20 minutes after activity has been completed.

Carbohydrate oxidation

The chemical processes that use oxygen to break down carbohydrates to produce adenosine triphosphate (ATP), the main source of energy for *muscle contractions*. They are a form of *aerobic metabolism*, which is the most productive and efficient system for supplying energy for activities lasting more than 1 minute.

For example, in a 100 m running sprint, *anaerobic metabolism* systems, such as the *glycolytic system* and *creatine phosphate system* which do not use oxygen, supply nearly 100 per cent of the energy. However in a 400 m sprint carbohydrate oxidation starts to kick in after 200 m and ends up supplying about 40 per cent of the energy. In a 1500 m race the body is overwhelmingly reliant on aerobic metabolism for energy. In ultra 'long' distance activities such as the Manhattan Island Marathon Swim (28.5 miles/45 km), *fat metabolism*, which is anaerobic and aerobic, is equally important as carbohydrate oxidation.

Physiology
Carbohydrate oxidation involves three processes: aerobic glycolysis, Krebs Cycle and electron transport chain.

Aerobic glycolysis breaks down pyruvic acid until it reaches an end product called acetyl coenzyme A (acetyl CoA). Pyruvic acid comes from the glycolytic system, which is an anaerobic metabolic system that begins the break down of *glucose* (also see *Carbohydrates*). Lactic acid and *lactate* are the end products. When oxygen is present lactic acid is converted into pyruvic acid.

In the **Krebs cycle**, Acetyl CoA is broken down in an 11-step process that produces 2 ATP. The end products are carbon dioxide (CO_2) and hydrogen atoms.

The **electron transport chain** process splits hydrogen atoms into electrons and hydrogen ions (H^+). The electrons are a form of energy that is used to produce another 34 ATP. The end products of all the processes are water (H_2O) and carbon dioxide (CO_2).

The aerobic system produces 36 ATPs compared to 3 ATPs for each molecule of glycogen (a long chain of bonded glucose molecules) produced by the anaerobic glycolytic system. In addition, the amount of oxygen required to produce ATP from the oxidation of carbohydrate is less when compared to fat metabolism.

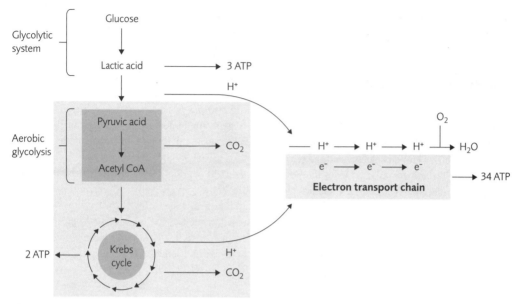

The stages of carbohydrate oxidation after glucose has been broken down into pyruvic acid

Carbohydrates

Chemical compounds composed of a combination of carbon (C), oxygen (O) and hydrogen (H) atoms, which are one of the main sources of energy during exercise and sport.

There are three types of carbohydrate compounds. Monosaccharides are made up of the simple sugars *glucose*, galactose and fructose. Disaccharides are composed of two simple sugars bonded together, such as maltose, lactose and sucrose (which is table sugar; a glucose bonded to a fructose). Monosaccharides and disaccharides are called simple carbohydrates.

Polysaccharides are more than two simple sugars bonded together. *Glycogen* is a long chain of glucose bonded together, which the body uses to store carbohydrates in the liver and muscles. Starch is an even longer chain of glucose that is also called a complex carbohydrate.

Disaccharides and polysaccharides have to be broken down into monosaccharides before they can be absorbed through the gut into the bloodstream and transported around the body.

Breakfast cereal is a rich source of carbohydrates

Carbohydrate content of foods

Food	Amount	Weight (g)	Weight (oz)	Energy (kJ)	Energy (Cal)	Carbohydrate (g)
Bread, wholemeal	1 slice	30	1	280	67	12
Bread roll, wholemeal	1/2 slice	30	1	300	72	13
Bread, pita	30 g	30	1	340	80	16
Muffin, English	half	40	1.3	330	80	15
Crumpet	1 average	50	1.7	390	93	20
Biscuit, plain, dry	20	20	0.7	270	65	13
Biscuit, plain, sweet	2 biscuits	17	0.6	320	76	12
Rice cakes	1 1/2 cakes	19	0.7	290	69	15
Oats, rolled, cooked	1/2 cup	195	6.9	410	99	17
Processed bran	1/2 cup	35	1.2	410	96	14
Weet-bix	1.5 biscuits	26	0.9	340	81	16
Vita brits	1.5 biscuits	26	0.9	340	81	16
Weeties	1/2 cup	25	0.9	350	84	17
Muesli, flakes	1/2 cup	22	0.75	350	84	15
Rice, brown, boiled	1/3 cup	60	2	370	88	19
Pasta, white, boiled	1/2 cup	75	2.6	370	89	18
Barley, pearl, boiled	1/2 cup	90	3	400	96	19
Potato, pale skin, baked	1 medium	100	3.2	310	73	15
Sweet potato, peeled, boiled	1/3 cup	71	2.5	220	52	12
Sweetcorn, frozen, on cob	1/3 cup	48	1.6	190	45	8
Pea, green, boiled	1 cup	165	5.8	340	80	11
Parsnip, peeled, boiled	1 cup	150	5.3	310	75	15
Beetroot, peeled, boiled	6 slices	180	6.3	310	74	15
Turnip, white, peeled, boiled	1 1/2 cup	360	12.7	320	77	14
Lentil, boiled	1/2 cup	105	3.7	310	74	10
Bean, kidney, fresh, boiled	1/2 cup	83	2.8	400	95	12
Bean, cannelloni, boiled	1/2 cup	86	2.9	220	80	11
Salad bean, commercial	1/3 cup	63	2.1	380	90	15
Soup, bean, lentil, homemade	150 g	150	5.3	530	126	15
Potato and leek soup	300 g	300	10.6	370	87	14
Soup, medium, canned, homemade	1 cup	264	8.9	420	100	17
Soup, light vegetable, canned	2 cups	528	17.9	520	125	18
Minestrone soup	300 g	300	10.6	280	67	13
Apple, golden delicious	1 average	123	4.3	220	53	13
Apricot, fresh, raw	3 medium	180	6.3	280	67	13
Banana, raw, peeled	1/2 average	50	1.75	200	48	12
Cherry, raw	25 medium	100	3.2	210	50	11
Custard apple, raw, peeled	1/4 medium	120	4	360	86	19
Fig, raw	4 pieces	160	5.6	270	64	13
Fig, dried	2 pieces	30	1	290	69	16
Grape, green sultana, raw	30 average	90	3	220	52	13
Kiwifruit, raw, peeled	2 medium	160	5.6	320	76	15
Melon, honeydew, raw	1 whole	240	8.5	320	76	16
Mango, raw, peeled	1 small	100	3.5	240	56	13
Mandarin, raw, peeled	3 whole	183	6.2	300	71	15
Nectarine, raw	3 medium	220	7.75	350	83	17
Orange, Valencia, raw	1 whole	160	5.6	240	58	12
Juice, orange, unsweetened	1 glass	204	6.9	290	69	16
Pear, Williams, raw, unpeeled	1 average	130	4.6	260	61	15
Peach, raw, unpeeled	2 medium	174	5.9	230	55	11
Peach, canned, in pear juice	2/3 cup	170	6	290	69	16
Tangerine, raw, peeled	2 large	200	7	200	48	10
Watermelon, raw, peeled	1 1/2 cup	293	10.3	280	67	15
Milk, skim	1 1/2 glass	300	10.6	430	102	15
Milk, whole	1 1/2 glass	300	10.6	520	195	14
Yoghurt, low fat, natural	1 tub	200	7	440	105	12
Ice cream, vanilla	1 1/2 scoops	67	2.4	570	136	14

Exercise and sport

An important feature of carbohydrates is how quickly they are broken down and absorbed into the blood, which is ranked according to the *glycaemic index (GI)*. Foods with a high GI quickly increase blood glucose levels. Low GI leads to a slow and gradual increase in blood glucose.

Chemical processes called the *glycolytic system* and *carbohydrate oxidation* break down glucose in a series of steps to produce adenosine triphosphate (ATP), the main source of energy for *muscle contractions*.

The energy content of carbohydrate is 1 g = 17 kJ (4 Cal). Alcohol is 1 g = 29 kJ (7 Cal).

Food

Carbohydrates are found in fruit, vegetables, legumes (such as beans and dried peas), breads, cereals, rice, pasta and other grains. Milk and other dairy products are also good sources of carbohydrates. All these foods contain other important nutrients such as vitamins, minerals and fibre. Sweets, honey, soft drinks, alcohol and table sugar are rich in carbohydrates but little else.

Carbohydrate content of drinks

Source	Amount	Carbohydrate (g)
Orange juice, 100% unsweetened	200 mL (6.75 fl oz)	15
Soft drink	200 mL (6.75 fl oz)	24
Low-fat milk	200 mL (6.75 fl oz)	11
Glucose powder	2 tsp	11
Polycose	1 tbsp	15
Ensure Plus	264 mL (9 fl oz)	47
Sustagen Sport	1 tbsp	13
Sustagen Gold	250 mL (8.5 fl oz)	35
Gatorade	200 mL (6.75 fl oz)	12

Cardiac arrhythmia

An irregularity or abnormality in the rhythm or rate of heart beats. A *heart beat* has a regular rhythm, which can be shown on an *electrocardiogram (ECG)* as a repeating series of spikes and dips. Irregularities include ventricular tachycardia and atrial fibrillation. Abnormal heart rate is called a tachycardia when it is greater than 100 beats per minute, bradycardia when less than 60 and atrial flutter for extremely high rates in the atrium only (200 to 400). Tachycardia can cause symptoms including *palpitations* in the chest.

The most common cause of cardiac arrhythmia is *coronary heart disease*. Rare heart problems include structural abnormalities such as congenital long QT syndrome, which is a cause of ventricular tachycardia. Drugs such as *caffeine* and certain *antidepressants* may also cause arrhythmias.

Diagnosis and treatment

The aim of making a diagnosis is to determine the specific cause of the arrhythmias. The physical examination includes heart testing, such as an *electrocardiogram (ECG)* and an *exercise stress test*, and assessing other causes such as a poorly functioning thyroid gland. A cardiologist should decide the most appropriate treatment, which may include medications and, in severe cases, a pacemaker.

Participation in exercise and sport is permitted in people with specific arrhythmias, but only following medical advice.

Cardiac output

The amount of blood pumped out of the left ventricle of the heart per minute. It is calculated by multiplying the *stroke volume* with the number of heartbeats per minute (see *Heart rate*). For example, the stroke volume in the average adult standing up and at rest is 70 mL (2.4 fl oz) and the average heart rate is 72 heart beats per minute. Therefore the cardiac output is 70 mL × 72 = 5040 mL = 5.04 L (10.6 pt) of blood per minute.

The average adult has about 5 L (10.5 pt) of blood in the body, which means at rest all of the body's blood is pumped through a cycle every minute. During exercise and sport the cardiac output can increase by 4 to 5 times (which equals 20–25 L/ 42–53 pt per minute) in order to keep up with the demand for oxygen and nutrients and clear the build up of waste products in the working muscles.

Cardiac rehabilitation

Activities that aim to restore the health of the heart. It involves participating in a formal program in a group, usually 2 to 3 times a week for 6 to 8 weeks. The program includes activities that improve *aerobic fitness* and *strength*, education about the *heart* and health, and learning to change unhealthy lifestyle behaviours such as smoking.

It is most commonly recommended after a *heart attack* or *heart surgery* including coronary bypass surgery, angioplasty, heart transplant and pacemaker implantation. Heart conditions that do not permit participation include severe *hypertension* (high blood pressure), severe *aortic stenosis*, uncontrolled *cardiac arrhythmias*, *myocarditis*, recent pulmonary embolism, recent *stroke* and fever.

Aerobic training

Low- to moderate-intensity *aerobic training* is recommended for most people. Intensity levels are based on perceived exertion of breathing. Measures of intensity of a physical activity are:

- Low-intensity is equivalent to breathing exertion ranging from 'no effect on breathing' up to the point that 'shortness of breath is noticed' = 30–49 per cent of VO_2 max = 35–59 per cent of *maximum heart rate estimation* (220 – age) = 11 on the *Borg perceived exertion scale*.
- Moderate-intensity is equivalent to a range from 'shortness of breath is noticed' up to 'the point that whistling or normal continuous conversation is just possible' = 50–74 per cent of VO_2 max = 60–79 per cent of maximum heart rate estimation = 13 on the Borg Perceived exertion scale.
- High-intensity is a range from the point that 'whistling or normal continuous conversation is just possible' up to the point that 'whistling or normal continuous conversation is impossible' = 75–84 per cent of VO_2 max = 80–89 per cent of maximum heart rate estimation = 15 on the Borg perceived exertion scale.

Strength training

People in cardiac rehabilitation may perform *strength training* at a reduced level and slower progression of the *overload* in terms of volume and intensity. The average person can start with lighter weights at 10 to 15 repetitions. People at low risk can perform heavy resistance for 12 to 15 repetitions until fatigue. High-risk people should keep their fatigue to a moderate level.

Other activities

Resumption of sex, housework and gardening should be guided by one's response to the aerobic training and strength training. If no unusual symptoms are present during the program, these activities are permitted.

Cardiac tamponade

Compression of the heart due to a build up of fluids, such as inflammation due to *myocarditis* or an acute injury to the chest that causes bruising of the heart muscle.

Treatment

This injury should be treated as a *medical emergency* including ensuring that breathing and circulation are not compromised and the injured person is transported as quickly as possible to a hospital.

It is suspected if the following symptoms are present:

- shortness of breath
- low blood pressure (hypotension)
- sudden loss of consciousness.

Cardiopulmonary resuscitation (CPR)

See *Medical emergency*.

Cardiovascular fitness

See *Aerobic fitness*.

Cardiovascular system

The tissues and organs responsible for the flow of blood to and from the cells of the body. *Blood* is a fluid that performs essential tasks in exercise and sport, including carrying oxygen, carbon dioxide, nutrients, wastes and hormones.

The central pumping station that produces most of the flow of blood in the cardiovascular system is the *heart*. It pumps oxygen-rich blood into large blood vessels (see *Artery*) that branch many times until they reduce down to blood vessels called capillaries, which are the width of a cell. The contents of blood move out of the capillaries into the fluid environment surrounding the cells where exchanges take place. For example, the oxygen in the blood is taken up by the cells for metabolism. Capillaries then join together to form larger vessels (see *Vein*)

that carry the oxygen-depleted blood back to the heart.

The cardiovascular system is divided into a number of smaller systems. The *peripheral vascular system* carries blood from the heart to all the cells of the body, except for the lungs, and back again. The *pulmonary vascular system* carries blood from the heart to the lungs and back again. The *lymphatic system* carries leftover fluid from around the cells that hasn't gone back into the veins back to the heart through lymph vessels.

Cardiovascular training

See *Aerobic training*.

Carpal joint dislocation

An acute injury that displaces one of the small joints that makes up the *wrist joint*. The displacement usually forces the lunate, one of the small bones located in the middle of the wrist, out of position.

The lunate may dislocate palm-side (anterior direction) as a result of falling onto the palm of the hand and forcing the wrist to bend backwards excessively. Alternatively, the force may push the rest of the carpal bones and hand excessively forwards and leave the lunate bone behind, causing a perilunar dislocation or, when associated with a *scaphoid fracture* it is called a trans-scaphoid perilunar dislocation.

Diagnosis, treatment and return to sport
The *dislocation* usually causes severe pain and obvious wrist deformity. Anterior lunate dislocation may compress the median nerve and cause pins and needles or numbness in the thumb, index and middle fingers and often half of the ring finger as well.

The diagnosis is confirmed with an X-ray. Treatment for both types of dislocation is surgery and ligament repair followed by 8 weeks *immobilisation* in a plaster cast. Median nerve compression may require surgery. Trans-scaphoid perilunar dislocation requires *open surgery* and *internal fixation* of the scaphoid fracture. It can take 3 to 6 months before a full return to sport is permitted.

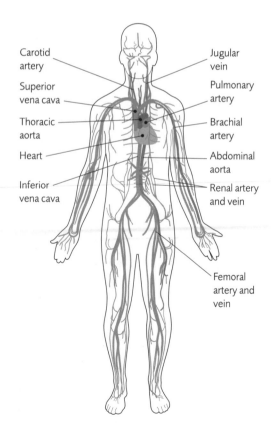

Carotid artery

Superior vena cava

Thoracic aorta

Heart

Inferior vena cava

Jugular vein

Pulmonary artery

Brachial artery

Abdominal aorta

Renal artery and vein

Femoral artery and vein

The cardiovascular system

Carpal tunnel syndrome

Pressure on the median nerve in the wrist that usually causes *numbness* or *pins and needles* in the thumb, index finger, middle finger and thumb-side of the ring finger and burning pain in the palm. These symptoms are often worse during the night. The pain also can spread into the forearm, elbow and shoulder.

The pressure in this *nerve entrapment* injury is usually due to swelling inside the carpal tunnel beneath the flexor retinaculum (fibrous band holding down the tendons) at the front of the *wrist joint*. The cause is often unknown, though it is more likely in people with *diabetes*.

Mild cases are treated with *non-steroidal anti-inflammatory drugs (NSAIDs)* and a splint, which is a form of *immobilisation*. Severe cases may require surgery to release the pressure on the nerve.

Cartilage

A specialised *connective tissue* that is rigid and strong, but also resilient and elastic. It can be thought of as the body's version of rubber. It is made up of a collection of cells called chondroblasts and chondrocytes embedded in a gel-like matrix substance and varying amounts of collagen and elastic fibres. The different types of cartilage are hyaline, *articular, fibrocartilage* and *elastic*.

It is also the word popularly used to refer to the meniscus in the *knee joint*. For example, a torn cartilage is a *meniscus tear*.

Cartilaginous joint

See *Fibrous and cartilaginous joints*.

CAT scan

See *CT scan*.

Catabolism

The chemical processes in the human body that release the energy contained in compounds by breaking them down into more basic components. For example, the *glycolytic system* and *carbohydrate oxidation* break down the chemical bonds that hold together the single chain of carbon (C), oxygen (O) and hydrogen (H) atoms that are contained in glucose. The end products are carbon dioxide (CO_2) and water (H_2O). It is the opposite of *anabolism*.

Caudal

See *Inferior*.

Cauliflower ear

An acute injury to the outer ear that mainly occurs in *Rugby Union, boxing* and *wrestling* due to a sudden forceful shearing blow that causes bleeding and *swelling* to be trapped between the skin and cartilage, leading to the cauliflower appearance. Treatment involves *aspiration* of the swelling with a needle followed by a *compression* dressing placed around the ear.

Cells

Microscopic structures that are the building blocks of the human body. Each cell has a unique shape, size and composition and performs a specific set of tasks. For example, a *red blood cell* carries oxygen and carbon dioxide around the body. It has a disc-like shape for maximising the absorption of these gases and contains iron, which holds onto them strongly.

There are billions of cells in the body including *neurons* (nerve cells), *bone* producing cells, *muscle fibres* and many more. They are organised in large collections called *tissues*.

All cells have common features including a tough protective outer layer called the membrane that actively selects the substances that move in and out.

Cells are mostly made up of fluid and contain even smaller structures within them called organelles, such as the nucleus that holds DNA and mitochondria for the production of adenosine triphosphate (ATP).

Central nervous system (CNS)

The *brain* and *spinal cord* are collectively known as the central nervous system (CNS). They are the central exchange for most of the communications conducted in the body. There is a two-way flow of sending instructions from the CNS and receiving back information. The CNS also communicates with itself. For example, the sensory section of the brain can feel your hand scratching your head. This information may be sent to the emotional section of the brain, which says to itself: 'That feels better.' There are over 100 billion *neurons* (nerve cells) in the CNS. *Hormones* and *neurotransmitters* also influence its activities.

Centre of gravity

The imaginary point that corresponds to the middle of the weight in an object in relation to the ground. It is usually just above the pelvis in the human body. Centre of gravity is important for *balance* in sports such as gymnastics and *weight-bearing* activities such as standing, walking and running. The higher the centre of gravity, the harder it is to keep the line of the centre of gravity within the *base of support* and maintain *balance*.

Centring

A psychological technique for relaxing muscles and reducing anxiety that involves taking in a long, deep breath and letting it out slowly. It can have a significant impact on decreasing levels of arousal in just a number of seconds, which makes it extremely useful during competition. It achieves this by focusing

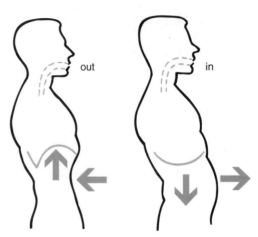

Taking a long deep breath using the diaphragm muscle

attention away from the source of *anxiety* to the centre of breathing.

Centring should be practised for 3 minutes each session for a total of 30 minutes a day. It is not uncommon at first for athletes to experience difficulty focusing on the breathing and achieving a positive level of attention. However, with practice, an athlete can learn to achieve significant relaxation with just a single breath.

Instructions
1) Sit in a comfortable chair.
2) To release muscular tension in the face, smile slightly so that the lips are apart.
3) Flick the arms and then roll the head slightly, attempting to consciously relax the arm and neck muscles.
4) Close the eyes and drop the chin towards the chest.
5 a) Take a long deep breath using the diaphragm, the main breathing muscle beneath the *lungs*. The diaphragm causes lower chest and upper abdomen movement without hunching or raising the shoulders. Breathe in through the nose and out the mouth.
  b) Thoughts should be solely focused on the movement of the lower chest and upper abdomen. Breathing in with the diaphragm will cause it to move gently outwards. Breathing out will cause it to move back in again.

c) As you breathe out, let yourself go and allow your muscles to relax. You will know that you have been successful if you feel a release of muscle tension and lowering of *muscle tone*.

6) Repeat the long, deep breath three times (if thoughts flash through your mind the breath should not be regarded as successful and must be repeated).

7) After completion of three breaths, immediately focus your attention on something in the environment; for example, a ball or target.

8) To finish, return to natural breathing and slowly open your eyes.

Cereals

A food yielded from a plant that produces an edible grain such as wheat, rye, oats, corn and rice. The same name is given to a food that is manufactured from these plants as a breakfast product.

Cereals are rich in *carbohydrates, proteins, fibre, vitamins* and *minerals* and are generally low in *fat*. The fat is usually either polyunsaturated or mono-unsaturated. Most of the food products made from cereals, such as pasta, rice and couscous, provide a nutritious addition to other foods such as meat, fish, vegetables and legumes.

Cerebral palsy

A disruption of the ability to move the body due to damage to the *brain* that causes a lack of muscle control. It usually occurs to the foetus during the later months of pregnancy as a result of poor supply of oxygen to the brain. Depending on the degree of cerebral palsy, it may not be recognised until well into the first year of life when an infant exhibits slower than normal development.

The different types of cerebral palsy include spastic paralysis (stiffness and excessive *muscle tone*), athetosis (involuntary writhing movements) and ataxia (impaired coordination and balance). There are great variations of severity and location within each of these types. For example, spasticity may affect any one or more of the limbs.

Cerebral palsy is often accompanied by other disabilities such as visual impairment, deafness and *intellectual disability*.

Exercise and sport

People with cerebral palsy participate in many forms of exercise and sport. There are eight classifications. CP1, CP2, CP3 and CP4 athletes use a wheelchair during competition (see *Wheelchair athletes*), while CP5, CP6, CP7 and CP8 don't use a wheelchair.

CP1
Unable to propel oneself in a wheelchair due to poor *range of movement* and *strength* and must use an electric wheelchair or other assistance for mobility.

CP2
Able to propel oneself in a wheelchair, but has range of movement and strength impairments.

CP3
A fair amount of trunk movement when pushing a wheelchair, but forward trunk movement is often limited during forceful pushing. Throwing is mostly from the arm.

CP4
Good functional strength with minimal limitations or control problems in the arms and trunk, but with poor overall *balance*.

CP5
Balance is normal when steady. However, during movement a slight shift of *centre of gravity* may lead to a loss of balance. Athletes may need an assistance device for walking, but not necessarily when standing or throwing. Running may be possible.

CP6
Incapable of remaining still. Athletes have involuntary cyclic movements and usually all four limbs are affected. Able to walk without any assistance. Usually have more control problems with the arms than the legs when compared to CP5, especially during running.

CP7
Uncontrollable muscular spasms in one half of the body. Athletes have good functional abilities in the *dominant side* of the body and walk without

assistance, but often with a limp due to uncontrollable muscular spasms in the leg. While running, the limp can almost totally disappear.

The dominant side has better development and good follow-through movement in walking and running. Arm and hand control is only affected in the non-dominant side, whereas good functional control is shown on the dominant side.

CP8

A minimum of uncontrollable spasms in one arm, one leg or one half of the body. Athletes need to have a diagnosis of cerebral palsy or other non-progressive brain damage to be eligible.

Injuries

The cerebral palsy athlete has the same injuries as the general population, though most likely at a higher rate due to the effect of spasticity on muscles, ligaments and joints. Spasticity can be treated with *flexibility exercises*. A *warm-up* routine is also an effective prevention measure.

Cerebrospinal fluid

The clear, water fluid that acts as a shock absorber for the *brain* against blows to the head. The fluid circulates within the cavities of the brain, called ventricles, and in the space between the two innermost layers protecting the brain and spinal cord, called the meninges. A lumbar puncture is a procedure used to take a sample of fluid to test for infections and to inject drugs such as anaesthetic during surgery, which is called spinal or epidural anaesthesia.

Cerebrovascular accident (CVA)

See *Stroke*.

Cervical joints

See *Neck joints*.

CFS

See Chronic fatigue syndrome.

Charley horse

See *Quadriceps contusion*.

Cheekbone fracture

A break to the cheekbone (zygomaticomaxillary complex) is usually caused by a direct forceful blow such as from a fist, hockey stick or baseball (see *Head*).

The fracture causes *swelling*, bruising such as a *black eye*, flatness of the cheek and jaw movement abnormalities. A severe fracture may also affect the orbital bone causing double vision, *numbness* of the affected cheek, restricted eyeball movement and asymmetry of the eyes. The recommended treatment is surgery to re-position the bone and, in severe cases, *internal fixation* with metal wires may be required.

Chest

The upper section of the trunk that connects to the arms and neck above and abdomen below. At the back it contains the 12 thoracic vertebrae that are connected together to form the *thoracic spine joints*. Each thoracic vertebra has a pair of ribs attached. Each rib is like half a circle beginning at the back and moving forward to the front to attach to the sternum (breastbone).

The 12 ribs form a bony cage for the contents of the chest, which include the *heart*, the largest blood vessels in the body (such as the aorta), *lungs*, *trachea* (windpipe), the main breathing muscle called the diaphragm and the digestive tube, called the oesophagus, that connects the throat to the stomach.

The chest is surrounded by muscles including the pectoralis major and pectoralis minor of the *shoulder joint* at the front, the intercostal muscles that are involved in *breathing* and at the back the muscles of

CHEST PAIN AND INJURIES

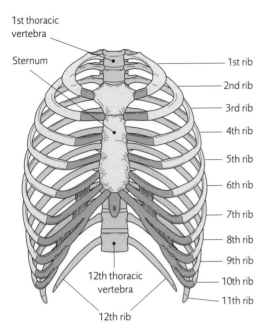

1st thoracic
vertebra

Sternum

1st rib
2nd rib
3rd rib
4th rib
5th rib
6th rib
7th rib
8th rib
9th rib
10th rib
11th rib

12th thoracic
vertebra

12th rib

Bones of the chest—anterior (front) view

the thoracic spine joints. Females also have *breasts* at the front. Both men and women have *nipples*.

Chest flail segment

An acute injury that causes fractures of two or more ribs in at least two places in each rib leaving that section of the chest excessively mobile. The injury is most commonly caused by a sudden forceful blow in high-speed activities such as *motor sports* and *horse riding sports*. It may be associated with a *pneumothorax* (punctured lung).

Treatment

A flail segment of the chest can compromise breathing. It should be treated as a *medical emergency* and the injured person transported as quickly as possible to a hospital. It is suspected if the following symptoms are present:
- shortness of breath
- the chest wall moves inwards instead of outwards when *breathing* in (inspiration).

Chest injury (severe)

An acute injury to the chest due to a sudden excessive forceful blow causing a concern that the heart and lungs have been damaged. The injury most commonly occurs in high-speed activities such as horse riding sports, *motor sports* like motorbike racing, and *downhill skiing*.

Treatment

A severe chest injury that is suspected of compromising breathing or the pumping of the heart should be treated as a *medical emergency*. The most common severe chest injuries include multiple rib fractures leading to *chest flail segment, pneumothorax, haemothorax* and *cardiac tamponade*. Any one of these should be suspected if the following symptoms are present:
- chest pain
- shortness of breath
- shifting of the windpipe (trachea) to one side
- coughing up blood
- open chest wound
- sucking noise from the chest wound.

Chest pain and injuries

Chest pain can be caused by an acute injury, overuse injury or underlying disease.

An *acute injury* causes pain that begins suddenly due to a single incident, such as a collision with another player causing a rib fracture or bruised rib.

An *overuse injury* causes pain that gets worse over a period of weeks or months due an accumulation of excessive forces that lead to microtrauma. Minor pain and stiffness can gradually become severe enough to seek medical care.

An underlying disease of one of the organs such as the *heart* or *lungs* may be exacerbated by participation in exercise or sport.

If either an acute injury due to a sudden excessive force (see *Chest injury (severe)*) or a life-threatening underlying disease or illness is suspected as the cause of the chest pain, it should be treated as a *medical emergency* unless proven otherwise, including checking that breathing and circulation are not compromised.

Cause

In the young, athletic population, chest pain is typically caused by an injury to a musculoskeletal structure such as a joint, muscle or bone. The most common injury is referred pain from the *thoracic spine joints*. But in some cases one of the organs of the chest may be the cause of pain, such as for a heart attack or angina pectoris. This is more common in older-aged or inactive people.

It is important to diagnose between *thoracic joint referred pain* and a *heart attack*. The differences are listed in the following table.

Pain accompanied by other symptoms such as *palpitations* is a warning sign of an exacerbated underlying heart problem. Other causes include *coronary heart disease, aortic stenosis, hypertrophic cardiomyopathy, myocarditis* and pulmonary embolism. A diagnosis is best confirmed by seeing a doctor as soon as possible.

Comparison of the clinical features and symptoms of chest pain referred from the thoracic spine joints and caused by a heart attack

Feature/symptom	Thoracic joint referred pain	Heart attack
Age	Any age, especially 20 to 40 years	Older, with an increased possibility with increasing age
History of injury	Sometimes	No
Location of pain	Back, arms, side and front of chest, abdomen	Behind the breast bone, jaw, neck, inner arms, upper abdomen
Type of pain	Dull, aching, occasionally sharp; the severity is related to activity, site and posture; suddenly starts and stops	Constricting, vice-like and may be burning; gradually starts and stops
Aggravating activities	Deep breathing in; certain activities like bending, walking upstairs, lifting; sitting for long periods; a slumped posture	Exercise, being active, heavy meals, cold weather, stress, emotion
Relieving activities	Maintaining an erect posture, lying down, firm pressure on the back (leaning against wall)	Rest; glyceryl trinitrate
Associated with	Chronic poor posture; employment requiring the same posture for long periods, such as keyboard operator	Cardiac risk factors such as heredity, obesity, smoking, shortness of breath, nausea, tiredness, sweating, vomiting

Causes of chest pain and injuries

Common	Less common	Not to be missed
• Rib fracture • Rib contusion • Thoracic spine joint referred pain • Sternoclavicular joint sprain	• Rib stress fracture • Breast injury	• Heart attack • Tumour • Gastrointestinal reflux • Lung infection • Pleurisy • Chest injury (severe) • Pneumothorax • Haemothorax • Chest flail segment • Cardiac tamponade • Pulmonary embolism • Aortic stenosis • Hypertrophic cardiomyopathy • Coronary heart disease • Myocarditis

Diagnosis

If pain begins due to a sudden, forceful, single incident such as a collision with another player and there are no symptoms of compromised breathing or circulation (see *Medical emergency* and *Chest injury (severe)*), the most likely cause is a *rib fracture, rib contusion* or *sternoclavicular joint sprain*.

For overuse injuries the most likely cause is *thoracic joint referred pain* and *rib stress fracture*, which is most common in sports such as *rowing* and *baseball* pitching.

Pain associated with coughing, especially when sputum is coughed up, suggests a *lung infection*. Indigestion (heartburn), which is relieved with antacid medication, can indicate that *gastrointestinal reflux* or *peptic ulcer* is the cause.

Radiological investigation with an *X-ray* may be required to confirm the diagnosis of a rib fracture. Heart tests such as *electrocardiogram (ECG)* and *exercise stress test* and gastroscopy for peptic ulcer may be needed.

Children

Childhood is the period in life from the age of 1 year until the beginning of *puberty*, which is usually around 10 years in girls and 12 years in boys. It is divided into an early stage corresponding to pre-school years and late childhood or primary school years.

The chronological age of a child is the most commonly used guideline for age-appropriate participation in exercise and sport. However, it should be

Children playing cricket

noted that each child develops and grows at a different rate, particularly in the years approaching puberty.

The Tanner system is a 5-point rating used for assessing growth and maturation, which is based on secondary sex characteristics including pubic hair, breast and genital development. Other methods include the age of menarche (first menstruation) in girls and salivary testosterone level in boys. Slowly maturing children can be assessed according to the average height and weight for their age.

Children found to be developmentally advanced may be permitted to participate beyond the recommended age limits. The final decision should be left to a school or club.

Exercise and sport

Children are not just mini-adults when it comes to participation in exercise and sport. They have unique physical and emotional capabilities and responses.

Their bones have features that make them relatively weaker and more vulnerable to injury compared to adults, including *greenstick fracture, growth plate fracture, avulsion fracture, apophysitis* and *osteochondrosis*.

Rules modifications and training alterations should be implemented for specific sports to better suit the physiological and psychological development of children at different ages (see *Middle and long distance running for children and adolescents, Sprinting for children and adolescents, Throwing sports for children and adolescents, Jumping sports for children and adolescents, Swimming for children and adolescents* and *Strength training for children and adolescents*).

Sports psychology for younger athletes can also be beneficial for children who are regularly participating in exercise and sport.

Fitness and training

In general children have the same potential for *aerobic fitness* as adults when size and weight differences are taken into account. However, the *anaerobic fitness* that can be achieved is poorer, probably due to a lower level of the enzyme phosphofructokinase in the *glycolytic system*.

Among children themselves, boys have a slightly greater aerobic capacity than girls, probably due to having more muscle mass and haemoglobin concentration. This difference increases in *adolescents*.

Children also exhibit varying aerobic fitness levels among themselves, though, unlike adults, this variation does not correlate with activity levels but is rather due to individual genetics and maturation, particularly *testosterone* production.

Training has much less of an effect on fitness levels of children compared to adults, perhaps as small as 25 per cent for the same effort. Children also have specific nutritional needs (see *Sports nutrition for younger athletes*).

In the *cardiovascular system* of children, the *cardiac output* is less than adults at any given oxygen uptake because the heart is proportionately smaller, which causes a relatively reduced *stroke volume*. The output is only slightly compensated by having a higher heart rate and an increased blood flow to exercising muscles.

The *respiratory system* of children when compared to adults has similar differences to those of the cardiovascular system. Children have a higher resting respiratory rate but breathe less deeply, therefore reducing the efficiency of blood oxygenation.

Children are able to recover quicker than adults after a bout of activity and are often willing to exert themselves again 30–45 minutes later, whereas adults may take many hours to recover.

The regulation of *temperature* in children is less efficient than in adults due to a greater surface area to body mass ratio, lower sweating rate (children have the same number of sweat glands but each produces less sweat), lower cardiac output (which causes less blood flow from internal organs the skin) and production of more metabolic heat per kilogram of body weight. These factors make children more susceptible to hyperthermia, such as *heat illness* (see also *Hydration for children*). In addition they face a greater risk of *hypothermia* (cold injury). They are most at risk to hyperthermia during endurance activities like long distance running. However, stop-start activities such as tennis, football and netball can also be dangerous.

The motor skills of children, such as coordination and sense of body position and movement, are less efficient than adults (see *Economy of effort*). For example, the running style of children often involves excessive and exaggerated movements of the arms, legs and pelvis. However, training can improve motor skills efficiency that, in turn, may be the main reason for the observed fitness improvements.

Strength training for children can lead to improvements, though, like women, it is not due to an increase in muscle mass and hypertrophy but rather improvements in the efficiency of nerves connecting to the muscles.

Chinese herbal medicine

A method of treating health problems based on releasing blockages of channels of energy in the body by using the healing powers of plants. It is a branch of *Chinese medicine*. Treatments are preparations using flowers, fruits, leaves, roots, bark or whole plants, in fresh, dried or powdered form, as infusions (hot water extractions) or tinctures (alcohol-based extractions).

Chinese medicine

A method of diagnosis and treatment of injuries, illness and disease that was founded thousands of years ago in China. It is based on the flow of energy called 'chi', which means the 'life-force', through channels in the body called meridians. Blockage of one or more meridians causes health problems, which are regarded as an imbalance between opposing forms of energy: the restraining yin and vigorous yang. Treatment aims to release blockages and restore the normal energy flow using techniques including *acupuncture*, acupressure and *Chinese herbal medicine*.

Chiropodist

See *Podiatrist*.

Chiropractor

A health practitioner who has completed training that is registered and recognised as being qualified to provide a diagnosis and treatment for injuries, illness and disease according to the chiropractic method.

Chiropractic began in the USA in 1895 when a teacher, Daniel David Palmer, restored the hearing of a man who had been deaf for 17 years by performing a spinal *manipulation*.

The central principle is the supremacy of the *nervous system*, which controls and coordinates the activities of all the other organs and structures. Ill health, including problems with the joints and muscles, may be due to an abnormally functioning nervous system.

The aim of an examination is to determine the diagnosis based on the presence and character of injuries (called subluxations), which may require X-rays. Treatments include adjustments or high velocity thrusts (usually called manipulations).

Chlorine

See *Minerals*.

Chocolate

A confectionery food made from cocoa, sugar and butter, which is high in *saturated fats* and *carbohydrates*. It is not harmful to have a small amount of chocolate in the diet. In fact recent research has shown that chocolate contains phenols that are *antioxidants*, which may be protective against *coronary heart disease*. In addition, the saturated fats in chocolate are less harmful when eaten in excess compared to those in red *meat*. Some people also claim it has aphrodisiac and libido-enhancing qualities.

Choking

A failure to perform to the best of one's ability when under pressure. It is attributed to internal thought processes that increase levels of *anxiety* and *stress* and lead to a sudden decline in skill levels and performance at an important time in a competition.

For example, at the start of the last round of the 1996 US Masters golf championship at Atlanta, Georgia, Greg Norman had a six stroke lead over his nearest rival. He shot a 78 to fall back into second place, five strokes behind the eventual winner, England's Nick Faldo. Norman and Faldo were coupled together for the final round. Faldo's score of 67 to win the championship was a stark contrast to Norman's collapse.

Cholesterol

A fat that has an essential role in the structure of the body, including the tough outer layer of cells and the production of bile salts, vitamin D and sex hormones. It is mostly produced in the *liver* and is one of a number of types of fat (also called lipid) that are transported around the body in the *blood* attached to proteins, called lipoproteins.

It was once thought that an excessive amount of cholesterol was bad for the health. However it is now realised that it is the specific types of lipoprotein that influence the risk of developing *coronary heart disease*. The two most important lipoproteins are *low-density lipoproteins (LDL)*, which are considered unhealthy in high amounts, and *high-density lipoproteins (HDL)*, regarded as healthy in high amounts.

Treatment

The best ways to control the level of cholesterol in the body are through exercise and sport, diet and, when necessary, cholesterol lowering drugs.

Regular participation in exercise and sport, especially *aerobic training*, is recommended because it significantly increases HDL, though it only achieves a small decrease of LDL. If coronary heart disease is also present, a combination of aerobic and strength training is recommended (see *Exercise for health*). A *medical clearance* is recommended before starting to participate in exercise and sport.

Foods from animals containing saturated fats, such as egg yolk, meat and poultry and whole-milk dairy products, contain high levels of cholesterol that raise the bad LDL and lower the good HDL. In contrast, foods like fruits, vegetables, grains, nuts and seeds are cholesterol-free.

Seafood (including fish) contains cholesterol too; however, it also has polyunsaturated fats such as omega 3 fatty acids that that decrease LDL and increase HDL levels. For good health it is recommended to limit the average daily cholesterol intake to less than 300 mg (see *Diet for good health*). People with coronary heart disease should have less than 200 mg.

Cholinergic urticaria

Raised skin bumps that occur in response to the body warming due to heat and humidity during exercise. Generally they appear first on the wrist or upper chest and spread to the limbs. Associated reactions, including fainting (see *Syncope*) and wheezing, are rare. The recommended treatment is *antihistamines*.

Chromium

A mineral that is essential in the breakdown of glucose. Only tiny amounts are needed in the body; 50–200 µg (micrograms) a day. Foods containing chromium include beans, legumes and poultry (see *Minerals*). Deficiency of chromium may reduce the impact of *insulin*, which is a hormone that stimulates cells throughout the body to absorb excess glucose.

Chromium picolinate has been promoted as a supplement for burning fat and increasing muscle size and strength, but studies have not shown any benefit. However some initial research has found it may increase carbohydrate transport into muscles, which could improve sprinting performance.

Chronic ankle sprain

See *Ankle sprain*.

Chronic compartment syndrome

An injury caused by excessive pressure exerted on a group of muscles. It is an overuse injury, where pain gradually builds up over a period of weeks or months due to an accumulation of excessive forces placed on the muscles.

It is most commonly found in the *shin* where muscles are grouped into compartments surrounded by fascia, a thick, slightly elastic and flexible layer of fibrous connective tissue. The excessive forces can include doing the activity too much, a *biomechanical abnormality*, poor technique and incorrect *shoe* and equipment selection. Some people are also simply born with an overly tight fascia.

Diagnosis
The main symptoms include pain, as well as a feeling of tightness and burning sensations. They usually begin during the aggravating activity and cease with rest in chronic compartment syndrome.

The diagnosis is made by differentiating chronic compartment syndrome from other causes of *overuse injury*.

In other overuse injuries, such as *tendinosis*, the pain is present at the start of the activity, then reduces further into the activity as the affected area warms up, only to return following cessation of activity.

Compartment pressures may be measured in the lower leg using a tube called a catheter. It is measured both at rest and during pain-provoking exercise.

Treatment
Rest from the aggravating activity, *massage* to increase the flexibility of the fascia and restore normal muscle function, and correction of a biomechanical abnormality may be helpful for mild cases. However, surgery is required if these treatments fail; either a fasciotomy (loosening of the fascia) or fasciectomy (removal of the fascia).

Chronic fatigue syndrome (CFS)

A disease that causes excessive tiredness that interferes with the ability to perform daily living and work activities, including exercise and sport. It does not have a specific cause like a virus. However, factors have been identified that increase the chances of developing the disease, including people with a history of *depression, anxiety* and previous viral infection.

It is also more common in females, high achievers, professionals, young adults and people who exercise and play sport at high *overload* levels, particularly those who combine a high level of commitment to their sport with full-time work, social and family commitments, and who continue to train and compete when suffering from a viral illness. There is an overlap in symptoms between *overtraining syndrome* and chronic fatigue syndrome (CFS), which suggests they both have similar causes.

Diagnosis

The diagnosis of CFS is based on confirmation that the sufferer is exhibiting a specific group of symptoms that have persisted or recurred during 6 consecutive months, and excluding other known causes of excessive tiredness.

The main symptom is excessive tiredness, especially after exercise, and four or more of the following symptoms: impairment in short-term memory or concentration, sore throat, tender neck or armpit lymph nodes, muscle pain, multi-joint pain without redness or swelling, chest and abdominal pains, headaches of a new pattern or severity and unrefreshing sleep.

Treatment

CFS usually improves over a period of months or years. The aim of treatment is to provide: psychological support; relief of symptoms with medications, including *analgesics* for pain relief; *antidepressants* for improved sleep quality; and a gradual return to activity, including an exercise program.

Exercise is usually commenced at low or moderate-intensity levels (see *Aerobic training* and *Metabolic equivalent (MET)*) for short durations, depending on the severity of the tiredness. The exercise should cause minimal or no aggravation of symptoms in the 24–48 hours post-exercise period. The increase in intensity and duration of the exercise should be very gradual. If adverse symptoms develop, a return to the previous level should be made, followed by an even slower subsequent build up.

Clavicle fracture

A break in the clavicle (collarbone) caused by an excessive, sudden force. This acute injury is one of the most common fractures in sport.

Causes and diagnosis

It is usually caused by a fall onto the point of the shoulder. For example, falling to the ground in horse riding or cycling, or forceful direct contact with opponents in sports such as *football*.

The *fracture* is extremely painful and also causes *swelling* and bony deformity. The diagnosis is confirmed with an X-ray. In most cases the break is located in the middle third (see *Shoulder joint*). Breaks in the distal third (closest to the shoulder joint) are the most complicated for treatment because many also damage the acromioclavicular and coracoclavicular ligaments and, as a result, are more likely not to heal properly (except in children).

Treatment and return to sport

For a middle third fracture *immobilisation* to allow the bone to heal involves 3 weeks in either a sling, figure-of-eight bandage or clavicle rings. During this time gentle *flexibility exercises* can be performed to a maximum of 90 degrees.

Distal third fractures that do not involve significant ligament damage are treated like a middle third fracture. *Open surgery* and *internal fixation* is often recommended for significant ligament damage.

Healing takes approximately 6 weeks in adults and 3 weeks in children. At this stage *strengthening exercises* can be recommended. Return to *collision sports* takes 2–6 months.

Clavicle osteoporosis

See *Osteolysis of the clavicle*.

Claw foot

See *Pes cavus*.

Cleats

Boots with spikes on the heels worn in *American football* when playing on grass fields. See *Football boots*.

Cloning

See *Therapeutic cloning*.

Closed chain exercise

Performing an arm or leg movement while maintaining the moving limb in constant contact with the ground. For example, squatting up and down while standing on one leg. It is the opposite of an 'open chain exercise' where the arm or leg is not fixed and allowed to move freely through space, such as lying on a bed and lifting the leg up. Closed chain exercise is considered to be a more advantageous form of *strengthening exercise*. It can also be performed for the upper limb, which is particularly useful during *shoulder rehabilitation*.

Cluster headache

A *headache* that causes an intense, disabling burning or 'boring' pain that may be associated with severe runny rose, nasal breathing obstruction, perspiration and watering eye. The attacks frequently begin in middle-aged people and may be triggered by *alcohol*. It is also called a histamine headache and Horton's headache.

Treatment with drugs depends on the age. Methysergide may be used in younger people, and either prednisolone or lithium or both in older people at the time and to prevent an attack. Inhalation of 100 per cent oxygen at 7 L per minute can help all ages at the time of an attack.

Closed chain knee extension (straightening) with foot immobile

Coach

A person who is appointed to lead, train and instruct a sports team or individual athlete.

The tasks of a coach include making decisions about tactics, strategies, team selection, team rules, disciplinary action, appointing team members to positions of responsibility (such as captain), choosing support staff, preventing injuries and supervising and implementing different types of training including *aerobic training*, *anaerobic training*, *strength training*, *speed training*, *agility training*, *flexibility training* and *skills training*.

Coaches take into account the needs, potential talents and *personality* of each player in their responsibility, including utilising techniques to foster *teamwork*, *gamesmanship*, *sportsmanship*, *situation awareness*, *goal setting* and clarifying one's *role*.

Players who have retired from active participation in a specific sport most commonly fill positions as coaches in that sport. The success or failure of a team or individual athlete is often considered the responsibility of the coach. Most coaches of teams or individual athletes that do not achieve stated goals in competition are forced to resign are sacked. Conversely, successful coaches are highly sought after.

Cobalt

See *Minerals*.

Cocaine

An illegal, highly addictive, stimulant drug that causes euphoria, a sense of wellbeing and a decrease in fatigue, while increasing awareness, activity, energy levels and talkativeness. It is mainly used as a recreational drug. 'Crack' is a purer form of cocaine.

The positive effects on athletic performance are minimal and tend to diminish with increased usage, along with increased detrimental effects such as impaired eye–hand coordination, distorted sense of time and inappropriate aggression. The side effects include *heart attack*, *stroke*, *seizures* and similar behavioural changes observed in *amphetamine* users.

Codeine

A medication that can reduce *pain*. It is more powerful than other *analgesics*, such as paracetamol and aspirin. It is a narcotic analgesic that was banned by the International Olympic Committee (IOC) until the mid-1990s.

Coenzyme Q10

A vitamin-like compound that assists with energy production in cells. It is suggested that coenzyme Q10 levels decrease in response to participation in high *overload* levels of *aerobic training*, such as

running longer distances or increasing the speed of running, and that supplementation is necessary to make up for the shortfall. Natural health practitioners may also recommend coenzyme Q10 in the treatment of *coronary heart disease*.

Cold

See *Common cold*.

Cold sores

See *Herpes simplex virus infection*.

Collagen

The most common fibre in structures such as *ligament*, *joint capsule*, *tendon*, *articular cartilage* and *fibrocartilage*. It provides strength and resilience at the same time as being flexible and pliant.

Each collagen fibre is shaped like a long rope made up of individual molecules of a *protein* called tropocollagen. Fibres are usually arranged in bundles. These bundles are arranged in distinctive patterns in each structure. For example, tendons have parallel bundles. Ligaments possess crisscross layers.

Collarbone

See 'clavicle' in *Shoulder joint*.

Colles fracture

A break of the lower end of the radius (outer forearm) and ulna (inner forearm) near the *wrist joint*. It usually occurs because of a fall onto an outstretched hand. It is quite common in older-aged people because of *osteoporosis* and in collision sports such as *football* codes, *downhill skiing*, *horse riding*, *trampolining*, *in-line skating*, *snowboarding* and *skateboarding*.

Diagnosis and treatment

The diagnosis of this *fracture* is usually easily made with an *X-ray*. In most cases the treatment is *immobilisation* for 6 weeks in a plaster cast that covers the lower half of the forearm, the wrist and the hand (leaving the knuckle (metacarpophalangeal) joints free to move), *flexibility exercises* and *strengthening exercises*.

Open surgery and *internal fixation* with a metal rod is only required for the most severe breaks. Return to *collision sports* usually takes 12 weeks after the injury occurs. A protective *brace* or wrist guards are often recommended to protect the bone after it has healed.

Collision sports

Sports in which physical contact between competing players is either legal and essential or a consequence of the game.

Sports where physical contact is legal include *soccer, American football, Australian Rules football, Rugby Union* and *Rugby League, martial arts, boxing, ice hockey, baseball,* and *basketball.*

Sports where physical contact is a consequence of participation include *gymnastics, motor sports, horse riding sports, downhill skiing* and *snowboarding.* Physical contact playing sport is also experienced by people with a disability, such as *wheelchair athletes.*

There is a high risk of an *acute injury* due to a sudden blow or force from an opposing player or piece of equipment that the body is unable to withstand without damage. *Protective equipment*, such as a helmet and mouthguard, is often worn in these sports. *Infectious disease prevention* rules, such as the blood rule, should be applied to collision sports. Participation in these sports during *pregnancy* may need to be reduced. Rules of the sport are modified for *children.*

Colostrum

Breast milk produced a few days before and after birth. The colostrum of cows is used in powder form as a food supplement because it is a rich source of proteins, such as casein and *whey protein, carbohydrates, fat,* minerals and vitamins. Research shows it can increase protein synthesis in muscle in people doing *strength training* leading to increase in muscle size and bulk, though the positive impact is likely to be reduced by poor absorption in the *gastrointestinal system.* The powder preparations also contain high levels of *insulin-like growth factor (IGF-1).*

Common cold

An infection in the *upper respiratory tract*, including the nose and throat. It is caused by the cold virus. The main symptoms are sneezing, mild fever, blocked or runny nose, sore throat, headache and coughing that can last for up to 2 weeks.

Exercise and sport

If there is no fever, participation in exercise and sport is permitted, but only at moderate levels, defined as 50 per cent of normal intensity. For example, an athlete who runs 5 km (3 miles) for training completes the same distance at half the usual pace. If fever, muscle aches, excessive fatigue and raised resting heart rate are present, complete rest from training is recommended to reduce the risk of developing *myocarditis* (heart inflammation).

The recommended treatment also includes drinking fluids, paracetamol (see *Analgesics*) and steam inhalation. Other medications include topical decongestants, such as phenylephrine or oxymetazoline for nasal decongestion, nasal anticholinergic spray for runny nose and dextromethorphan products for coughing.

Antibiotics do not help with treating a virus. Stronger medications, such as *ephedrine*, besides being a *drug banned in sport*, have side effects like tachycardia (raised heart rate), nervousness, dizziness, drowsiness and *hypertension* (high blood pressure).

Compartment syndrome

See *Chronic compartment syndrome* or *Acute compartment pressure syndrome.*

Complex regional pain syndrome (CRPS)

Excessive and prolonged swelling, pain and abnormal blood supply symptoms in response to an *acute injury*. It is usually located in the arm/hand and leg/foot. The blood supply problems may be indicated by either warmth and redness, or coolness (cyanosis (blue skin)) and mottling (splotches). It is also known as sympathetically mediated pain or reflex sympathetic dystrophy.

Prevention, diagnosis and treatment

It is less likely if the original injury experiences movement as early as possible after it has occurred. An injury should be assessed for CRPS if there is a delay beyond the expected recovery time and typical symptoms are present. The diagnosis is made based on the history and physical examination. A *bone scan* may be helpful.

Treatment includes an exercise program involving a gradual increase in activity, electrotherapy, such as *interferential therapy* and *magnetic field therapy*, and possibly paracetamol and central nervous system altering medications such as low dose tricyclic *antidepressants*. Recovery can take 6 months or longer.

Compression

A treatment for an *acute injury* that minimises bleeding and the formation of *oedema* and *swelling*. It should be done as soon as possible after an injury has occurred. Even firmly pressing one's hand over an injury when leaving the field can achieve substantial results. Compression should be applied for up to 72 hours. It should be done as part of the combination of treatments called *RICE (rest, ice, compression and elevation)*.

Method

Compression involves applying pressure to an injured area. An elasticised bandage is the best material, as crepe bandages tend to stretch and are ineffective after the first usage.

Bandaging should start just *distal* (away from the spine) to the site of bleeding with each layer of the bandage overlapping the underlying layer by one-half and eventually covering at least a hand's breadth *proximal* (closer to the spine) to the injury. The bandage should be applied firmly but not so tightly as to cut off circulation or cause pain. Blue colouring of the whole body part distal to the compression or loss of pulse is a sign of excessive tightness.

Concentration

The ability to focus one's thoughts or actions on a specific task. In exercise and sport it can include activities such as hitting a golf ball into the hole or following the coach's instructions in a football game. It involves blocking out negative thoughts, such as *anxiety*, and external distractions, such as the taunts of an opposition player and boos from the crowd. Players with good concentration usually possess *situation awareness*.

Concentric

A muscle contraction that causes a shortening in *muscle length*. An example of a concentric contraction of the quadriceps (front thigh muscle) is straightening the knee joint. Concentric is the opposite of *eccentric*. Both types of contraction have important roles in isotonic strengthening (see *Strengthening exercise*).

Conception

See *Reproductive system*.

Concussion

An acute injury of the *head* that causes a temporary loss of the normal function of the *brain*, including confusion, headache, dizziness, reduced concentration, nausea, blurred vision and impaired memory. Loss of consciousness (usually less than 5 minutes) may also occur.

A *head injury* is more likely to occur in collision sports, including the football codes such as *American football*, *Australian Rules football*, *Rugby League* and

Rugby Union, boxing, ice hockey, horse riding sports and the *martial arts*. The injury is usually either due to a direct blow to the head or a rapid and forceful rotation movement of the head.

Prevention

The chances of receiving a head injury can be reduced by changes to the rules in collision sports that minimise events where head injuries occur, such as penalising head-high tackles.

The use of helmets to prevent concussions in sports such as *Australian Rules Football* is still controversial as they have not been shown to reduce the number of concussions in players who wear them.

Diagnosis

It is important to recognise when a concussion has occurred so that the player can be treated appropriately. In some cases, particularly those that involve loss of consciousness, it is easy to tell that the player has had a significant head injury. However, in many cases it is difficult to tell that a player has been concussed. Often the player is keen to return to the game, so they don't admit to symptoms such as headache or blurred vision. One of the most useful practical ways to asses any player suspected of having a head injury is by a series of simple questions known as the Maddocks questions.

These include:
Which ground are we at?
Which team are we playing today?
Who is your opponent at the moment?
Which quarter is it?
How far into the quarter is it?
Which side scored the last goal?
Which team did we play last week?
Did we win last week?

Treatment and return to sport

Any player who has suffered a concussion must be assessed by a doctor prior to their returning to training or play. This should include a neuropsychological assessment such as the *digit symbol substitution test (DSST)*.

Rest from activity is required until all symptoms resolve. To put it another way, no player should be returned to play if they still have symptoms or they have not been cleared medically. Return to sport should be done initially at a reduced level and then slowly increased to full activity. If symptoms return, it indicates that the player has not yet fully recovered. In this case they should stop activity and be reassessed by their doctor.

Cases such as where a player has lost consciousness for more than 5 minutes should be treated as a *medical emergency*, and the player should be sent to hospital for observation and investigation.

Signs and symptoms that persist for a number of weeks are called *post-concussion syndrome*.

Conditioning

Regular participation in activities that aim to improve *fitness* levels. It is the first stage in *periodisation*, one of the four main principles of training. It is also a psychological technique, first identified by the Russian psychologist Pavlov, where an action or thought is produced as a learned response to a normally unrelated stimulus.

Confectionery

Foods that are often high in fat content, mainly *saturated fats*, such as *chocolate*, ice cream, biscuits and cake, or high in simple *carbohydrates*, such as sweets, lollies and soft drinks. In general, it is recommended to reduce the amount of confectionery in the diet and to choose products that are low in fat.

The exception may be sweets and lollies, which are a good supply of glucose with a high *glycaemic index (GI)* and which are quickly digested and absorbed, resulting in a rapid and high rise in blood glucose levels. They may be recommended after high-intensity activity such as a fast jog or football.

Connective tissue

A collection of *cells* imbedded in a matrix of fibres and ground substance that holds together and connects other types of tissue. For example, connective tissue holds together the bundles of individual nerve cells that together make up a whole nerve. A tendon is connective tissue that connects muscle to bone.

The cells in connective tissue can include any one or more of the following: fibroblasts, macrophages, mast cells, fat cells and lymphocytes. The most common fibres are *collagen* and elastin. The ground substance is like a gel.

There are different types of connective tissue. The mix and proportions of the above cells, fibres and ground substance determines the character and tasks performed by each type.

For example, a *ligament* is made up of parallel bundles of collagen fibres with fibroblasts imbedded among them. *Bones* and *cartilage* are considered to be specialised types of connective tissue. Bone includes cells called osteoblasts that lay down deposits of calcium and phosphate to create a hard and rigid supportive tissue. Cartilage is made up of cells called chondroblasts and chondrocytes that produce varying amounts of collagen and elastin fibres to create a tissue that is supportive, but more flexible than bone.

Conservative treatment

Treatments that do not involve surgery such as *massage, exercises, manipulation, mobilisation, electrotherapy, nutrition* and *psychology*. Conservative treatment is often considered the first choice for an injury because it is more effective, cheaper than surgery and avoids risks that can be associated with surgery including infection of wounds, *deep vein thrombosis*, pulmonary embolism and side effects of general anaesthesia.

Continuous training

Performing an activity for extended periods at less than competition intensity with the aim of improving fitness. The risk of injury is reduced with this type of training compared to *interval training*, which involves repeated bouts of high-intensity. However it can be dull and boring for some athletes and it does

not appear to be as effective as interval training at achieving fitness gains.

Contraception

Reducing the risk of fertilisation in order to prevent *pregnancy*. There are a number of methods including: abstinence from sexual intercourse on fertile days of the menstrual cycle based on the rhythm method, measuring body *temperature* and cervical mucous; withdrawal or coitus interruptus; barrier methods such as condoms and the diaphragm; intrauterine device (IUD); and medications like the oral-contraceptive pill.

Abstinence methods can be popular because they do not involve medications and are considered natural. However, they may be less effective with irregular menstrual cycles (see *Menstruation*), which is more common in women participating in high-intensity levels of exercise and sport.

Barrier methods have a number of advantages, though they are generally not as reliable as the pill or IUD, but are more reliable than the rhythm or withdrawal method. The diaphragm has virtually no side effects and when correctly fitted can be worn comfortably during exercise. The condom has had a resurgence in popularity due to the prevalence of AIDS and other sexually transmitted diseases. The effectiveness of the condom is increased if it is used in conjunction with a spermicidal cream or gel.

IUDs have the advantage of not having to be reapplied as with barrier methods. There is no hormonal interference, but side effects such as increased risk of *dysmenorrhea* (painful menstrual periods) and heavy bleeding may occur. Infections are a serious but uncommon side effect.

The oral-contraceptive pill can be safely recommended from the age of 16 years (or 3 years after the first menstrual period), either in the monophasic form as a constant daily dose or in the triphasic form with variable dosages throughout the cycle.

It is associated with a reduced risk of *dysmenorrhea, premenstrual tension* and *iron deficiency* due to excessive monthly blood loss. It may also be used to manipulate the menstrual cycle for exercise and sport events (see *Menstruation*). However in some women it is associated with weight gain, either due to fluid retention or appetite stimulation, and a possible increased risk of breast and cervical cancer.

Contusion

An injury to the tissue under the skin, such as muscle or bone, caused by a sudden and single blunt force, like an opposing player's knee striking the thigh (see *Muscle contusion* and *Periosteal contusion*).

Convulsions

See *Seizures*.

Cool-down

See *Warm-down*.

Copper

A mineral that is essential for the breakdown of glucose and production of haemoglobin. Only small amounts are needed in the body, 1.5 to 3 mg a day (see *Minerals*). It has been suggested that an imbalance between copper and *zinc* levels in the body may have a negative impact on performance.

Coracoid process stress fracture

An injury causing pain near the *shoulder joint* that is most commonly seen in the sport of trapshooting. The diagnosis and treatment is the same as for most other *stress fractures*.

Core stability

See *Lumbo-pelvic instability*.

Cork thigh

See *Quadriceps contusion*

Corneal abrasion

Damage to the cornea (white) of the *eye*, usually due to a scratch from a fingernail or sport equipment. It causes eye pain, a sensation that an object is present in the eye and blurred vision if the central cornea is damaged.

Treatment usually involves antibiotic eye drops and an eye pad. If the damage is a cut or chemical burn it should be treated as an emergency, requiring treatment at a hospital or from a doctor as quickly as possible.

Corns

See *Callus*.

Coronary heart disease

A disease that causes narrowing of the arteries that supply blood to the muscle fibres of the *heart*. The reduced flow of blood can cause problems such as angina pectoris (see *Chest pain and injuries*) and *heart attack*.

Causes

The coronary arteries become narrowed due to the development of atherosclerosis (the formation of fatty deposits in the walls of the artery called a plaque), that bulges inwards and makes them harder and less elastic. The arteries may become further narrowed or blocked by blood clotting around the bulge, called a thrombosis.

A number of factors are associated with an increased risk of developing coronary artery disease, including genetics, smoking cigarettes, *obesity*, lack of exercise, poor diet, *diabetes*, altered levels of blood contents (such as specific types of cholesterol) and *hypertension* (high blood pressure).

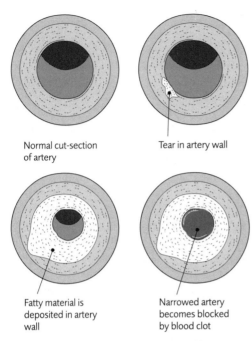

Normal cut-section
of artery

Tear in artery wall

Fatty material is
deposited in artery
wall

Narrowed artery
becomes blocked
by blood clot

**Narrowing of an artery in the heart caused by
atherosclerosis**

Coronary artery disease is the most common cause of exercise-related deaths in people aged over 35 years, and an infrequent cause of *sudden death* in athletes below that age.

Diagnosis

Coronary heart disease is often first noticed years after it has developed, when the arteries become so narrow that during exercise or a strenuous physical activity the muscle fibres do not receive enough blood, which leads to pain called angina pectoris that usually settles after resting for a minute or two.

Angina pectoris usually is a pressure-type pain in the chest or in the neck, jaw, shoulders, arms and back. It usually occurs at a predictable time during an activity, such as after 5 minutes of running or walking halfway up the hill to the bus stop. It should not be ignored and medical help should be sought as soon as possible (see *Chest pain and injuries*).

When blood clotting or spasm of the artery suddenly blocks off the blood supply, the heart muscle can be permanently damaged. This is what is commonly known as a *heart attack*.

Tests used to confirm a diagnosis of coronary artery disease include an *electrocardiogram (ECG)*, *exercise stress test*, *echocardiogram* and, in particular, a radiological investigation of the arteries called an angiogram.

Treatment

Angina pectoris is usually treated with drugs, such as *beta blockers* and *calcium channel blockers*, and lifestyle changes that include quitting smoking, a healthy diet (see *Diet for good health*) and exercise and sport (see *Exercise for health*). In severe cases, procedures such as angioplasty and coronary bypass surgery are recommended.

The positive impacts of exercise and sport include increased capacity for the heart to pump due to heart muscle hypertrophy (growth in muscle fibre size) and increased size of the diameter of the coronary arteries, enabling the muscle fibres to receive more blood. Being active also helps with negative factors, for example, reducing blood pressure, weight loss (see *Overweight* and *Fat-loss diet*) and improving blood cholesterol levels by reducing *low density lipoproteins (LDL)*, which are considered unhealthy in high amounts, and increasing *high density lipoproteins (HDL)*.

Participation in exercise and sport may also be associated with increased likelihood of quitting smoking and eating a healthy diet. A *medical clearance* is recommended before starting to participate in exercise and sport.

Corticosteroids

A medication that is a synthetic version of the natural human hormone corticosteroid, which has a strong anti-inflammatory effect. It may be recommended for some exercise and sports-related injuries including tendinosis, such as *tennis elbow* and *rotator cuff tendinosis, paratenonitis, ganglion, osteoarthritis, myofascial trigger point* pain and chronic *bursitis*.

Corticosteroids are also prescribed for *transplant recipients* and other conditions including eczema, intestinal disorders (such as colitis and Addison's disease) and as a preventive medication for asthma (see *Corticosteroids (inhaled)*.

Exercise and sport

Generally this medication should be restricted to injuries that have not responded to other forms of treatment. Corticosteroids are preferably given as an injection, rather than in pill form. A local injection of corticosteroid maximises its concentration at the site of the injury and minimises the risk of side effects. The oral form is also one of the *drugs banned in sport* by the World Anti-Doping Agency (see *Glucocorticosteroids*).

The number of injections to any one site should be restricted, and successive injections should not be performed within 3 to 4 weeks. It is important to rest the injury for a minimum of 2 to 3 days after the injection.

Corticosteroids (inhaled)

A medication that is a synthetic version of the natural human hormone corticosteroid, which has a strong anti-inflammatory effect on the tissues of the body.

When taken in inhaled form as an aerosol spray it reduces inflammation of the airways, which decreases symptoms in general and the airways' sensitivity to trigger factors that cause *asthma* attacks. The main side effects are candidiasis (fungal infection) of the mouth and speech disturbances, both of which can be reduced by rinsing the mouth following use of the medication.

Corticotrophin

A drug that stimulates the actions of hormones such as cortisol and aldosterone. It is rarely prescribed as an anti-inflammatory to treat *osteoarthritis* and hepatitis. Athletes use it like an *anabolic steroid*; however, research shows that it does not actually achieve the desired affects.

It is a *drug banned in sport* according to the World Anti-Doping Agency.

Cough

A sudden, forceful explosion of air breathed out of the *lungs*. It is a reflex action where the diaphragm, other breathing muscles and abdominal muscles contract to force air out. It occurs when sensory nerves in the lining of the airways are triggered off due to an irritant such as dust, smoke or excessive mucous, called sputum, produced by cells in the inner lining of the airways due to a *lung infection, common cold* or *asthma*. Other causes of a cough include *tumour, gastrointestinal reflux*, and certain drugs such as *ACE inhibitors*.

Associated symptoms, such as *fever, shortness of breath, chest pain* or *heartburn*, are important information for making a diagnosis. The treatment of a cough primarily involves treating the underlying cause. Medications, such as pholcodine, can be recommended just for the cough; however, most are *drugs banned in sport*.

Cranial

See *Superior*.

Creatine

An organic, ammonia compound that is found primarily in muscles in the body. It is an essential component of the *creatine phosphate system*, a metabolic system that produces adenosine triphosphate (ATP), the main source of energy for *muscle contractions*. The system produces energy for the muscles like using starter fuel for lighting a log fire.

The benefits of creatine are gained by loading up the creatine phosphate system, which aids recovery and delays tiredness when performing intermittent bursts of high-intensity exercise (6 to 30 second bouts) interspersed with short recovery intervals of 20 seconds to 5 minutes, like in *hockey (field)* and football codes such as *soccer, Australian Rules football, American football, Rugby Union* and *Rugby League*.

Creatine loading can be achieved by eating a low fat and high carbohydrate diet (see *Fat-loss diet*). It has been suggested that loading is improved by

Creatine supplements

taking creatine supplementation. Side effects of supplementation may include nausea, *gastrointestinal reflux* (heartburn), *headaches*, muscle cramping and possibly kidney failure.

Creatine phosphate depletion

Muscle fatigue due to a depleted *creatine phosphate system*. It is caused by excessive intensity at the beginning of an endurance event, such as running too fast at the start of a marathon, which severely reduces the system's available supply of energy. Lowering intensity at the start of an event can prevent it. *Creatine* supplementation may also be beneficial.

Creatine phosphate system

A metabolic system that produces *adenosine triphosphate (ATP)*, the main source of energy for *muscle contractions*. The system is like using starter fuel for lighting a log fire.

It immediately begins to produce ATP when muscles start contracting, but only has enough stores of ATP to work for 6 to 30 seconds. In contrast, the *glycolytic system* and *carbohydrate oxidation* can produce ATP for longer periods of time, but take more time to go into full production.

As a result, the creatine phosphate system is the most important producer of ATP during activities involving explosive strength such as 100 m *sprinting* or games where frequent and repeated short sprints are interspersed with short recovery intervals of 20 seconds to 5 minutes, like in *hockey (field)* and *football* codes. It is part of anaerobic metabolism because it does not need oxygen to proceed.

Physiology

The chemical process that drives the system includes an enzyme called creatine kinase (CK) that cuts off a phosphate group from the compound, phosphocreatine (PCr). This releases energy that is, together with the free phosphate group, immediately taken up by a nearby *adenosine diphosphate (ADP)* to create an ATP.

Cricket

Cricket originated from 13th century English bat-and-ball games using a tree stump. The earliest recorded game of 11 players a side was in 1697. In 1787 the Marylebone Cricket Club was established at Lord's. The first Ashes test between Australia and England was on 15 March 1877.

Wicket keeper and fielder watch an attacking batting stroke in a cricket match

Rules

Cricket is played between two sides of 11 players, including batsmen, bowlers and wicketkeeper. The pitch is 20.12 m (22 yards) long, with three sticks called stumps at each end. The bowler uses an overarm action (not throwing) to send a ball towards the batsman. The batsman tries to hit the ball and run to the other end. The team with the most number of runs wins the match.

Fitness and injuries

Cricket requires *aerobic training* and *skills training* for bowling, batting and fielding. The most common injuries are *pars interarticularis stress fracture* (back), *low back pain (non-specific)*, *rotator cuff tendinosis* (shoulder), *rotator cuff strain* (shoulder), *shoulder instability*, *hamstring strain* (thigh), *quadriceps contusion* (thigh) and *hand and finger pain and injuries*.

Cricket shoes

Footwear designed to cope with the physical demands of *cricket*. These demands vary according to the chosen position of each player. For example, bowlers require a *shoe* with a midsole with good shock absorption qualities similar to the *running shoe* because the front foot takes forces nine times the body weight when it pounds into the wicket on delivery. Their shoes also need an upper section with a high cut above the ankle and an outsole with spikes. Non-bowlers who are outfielders and can expect to run a lot also require good running shoes. Players who do a mixture of activities may be best to choose *cross-training shoes*.

Cross-country skiing

A snow sport that mainly requires *aerobic training* and *skills training* for the skiing technique. The most common injuries and illnesses are *rotator cuff tendinosis* (shoulder), *adductor tendinosis* (hip and groin), *patellar tendinosis* (knee), *ankle sprain*, *dehydration* and *hypothermia*. The sport is also called Nordic skiing.

Cross-country skiing machine

Fitness equipment designed for performing stationary cross-country skiing. Regular use can be an effective way to increase fitness through *aerobic training*. It doesn't achieve greater aerobic fitness than outdoors cross-country skiing, but it's clearly more convenient.

Cross training

Regular participation in different activities that aim to improve more than one type of fitness. For example, *strength*, *aerobic fitness* and *flexibility* are important components of training for basketball players. It is also used as a means of reinforcing fitness at the same time as reducing stress on a particular part of the body, such as a runner with a knee joint injury participating in swimming, which is an aerobic fitness activity.

One of the additional benefits of cross training is that the gains in the different types of fitness can overlap with each other. For instance, *strength training* may also be associated with a 50 per cent increase in *aerobic fitness*.

Cross-training shoes

Footwear designed for participation in different sports. It may also be suitable for *aerobics*. The physical features include reasonable shock absorption qualities and a semi-curved last (the shape of the shoe when viewed from below). It is preferable to select a *shoe* that is designed for a specific sport if you participate in that sport at least twice a week.

CT scan

A radiological investigation that produces images of muscle, tendon, ligaments and bone inside of the body, by combining *X-rays* and computer technology. CT means computed tomograph, which involves producing *X-ray* images that are slices of the body.

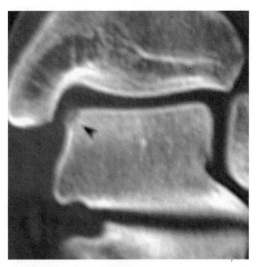

CT scan of a fracture in the ankle

In exercise and sport it is mainly used to assess the nature and severity of an injury after a diagnosis has already been made. It is particularly useful for injuries of the spine, *fractures* in small bones and fractures in anatomically complex regions such as the ankle, foot or pelvis. CT arthrography is performed after the injection of radio-opaque contrast medium into a joint cavity, most commonly the shoulder or ankle. CT scan is also used for other diseases and conditions, such as investigating the brain. It is also known as computed axial tomography (CAT) scan.

Curcumin

Yellow pigment that gives the herb turmeric its colour. It may be recommended by natural health practitioners to treat *inflammation* and reduce *swelling* caused by injuries. It should not be taken together with conventional anti-inflammatory medications (see *Non-steroidal anti-inflammatory drugs (NSAIDs)* and *corticosteroids*).

Cycling

Cycling is a recreational activity and sport. The different disciplines include: indoors track cycling (which was in the first modern Olympics in 1896), such as sprint, pursuit, time trial, points race and keirin (a motor-paced race); road cycling, such as point-to-point and circuit races, with single-day events of 240–280 km (148–174 miles) and racing on successive days such as in the Tour de France (first held in 1903); Cyclo-cross, cross-country cycling outdoors over rough terrain; mountain bike cycling, introduced into the 1996 Olympics; and BMX, which involves cycling over a circuit of rough terrain.

Long distance cycling mainly requires *aerobic training* and some *strength training*. Sprint cycling mainly requires *anaerobic training*.

Injuries are often related to *cycling biomechanics* abnormalities. The most common are *patellofemoral joint syndrome* (knee), *patellar tendinosis* (knee), *iliotibial band friction syndrome* (knee), *Achilles tendinosis* (calf), *low back pain* (non-specific), *neck pain* (non-specific), *ulnar nerve compression* (elbow), *de Quervain's tenosynovitis* (wrist) and *handlebar palsy* (wrist).

Cycling biomechanics

The movements and positions of the joints and muscles during cycling. The most important aspects of cycling biomechanics are the pedal cycle, set up and positioning on the bike and use of additional equipment. The aim of these is to enable the muscles to generate the greatest forces and power in the pedal cycle, maximise the aerodynamics and minimise the risk of injuries.

Pedal cycle

The down stroke is performed by the gluteals (*buttock* muscles) and quadriceps (front *thigh* muscles). The up stroke begins with the force of movement provided by the opposite leg that has just begun its down stroke, and may be assisted by muscles such as the hamstring (back *thigh* muscle).

Set up and positioning

The set up and positioning on the bike include the seat height, saddle fore/aft position and reach to the handlebars. The following are recommendations for

Optimal back position. In (a) the back is flat, which is less likely to cause injury

compared to a rounded back (b)

In (a) the right side is overstretching to reach the pedal

In (b) the level dots on the back show there is a correct reach

road cycling. Variations for different types of cycling are included later.

SEAT HEIGHT

Seat height is measured from a straight line taken from the bottom edge of a level placed on the saddle, down the seat tube to the crank axis plus the crank length.

Correct seat height in a cyclist who has good flexibility of the leg muscles (see *Range of movement*) is the same length as measured from the greater trochanter of the femur (the bony prominence of the thigh bone on the outside of the *hip joint*) to the sole of the foot with the ankle in the *neutral joint position*.

SADDLE FORE/AFT POSITION

The saddle fore/aft position should be set with the patellar tendon (located a few centimetres below the kneecap) directly above the axis of the pedal when they are both in the horizontal position.

REACH TO THE HANDLEBARS

The correct reach should be set with the rider's elbows slightly flexed (bent) when the hands are resting on the brake hoods. This involves raising or lowering the stem above the front wheel. As a result, the drop between the saddle and handlebars should be about 3–5 cm (1–2 in).

Other equipment

Cycling shoes need to be flexible yet give enough support to enable forces generated by the leg muscles to be transmitted through the pedals. Float pedals can minimise injuries without reducing the force generated. Cycling knicks (shorts) should be seamless and avoid chafing which can cause discomfort that interferes with the pedal cycle. *Helmets* should be firm-fitting and not fall over the eyes.

Variations

In mountain bike riding, the set up and positioning is less concerned with aerodynamics than control of the front wheel. For downhill mountain bike riding, the seat is positioned so as to lower the centre of gravity. *Triathlon* cycling is similar to road cycling except that the seat position is higher and more forward.

Aerodynamics

Wind resistance makes up 90 per cent of the retarding force in road cycling in windless conditions compared to 10 per cent from the ground (called rolling resistance). The single most important factor in wind resistance is the front surface area that the cyclist exposes to the wind.

Biomechanical abnormalities

A deviation from any of the above movements, poor technique or equipment selection is called a *biomechanical abnormality*. It is associated with an increased risk of developing an *overuse injury*. The two types are anatomical (structural) and functional (dynamic).

ANATOMICAL ABNORMALITIES

Foot pronation can lead to problems during the 'down-stroke' of pedal action by causing the foot to roll inwards, reducing its mechanical efficiency and possibly stressing the knee, hip or low back joints. This abnormality can be corrected with a cycling *orthotic* that fits in the shoe.

Excessive *genu varum* (bowed legs), *genu valgum* (knock knees), *tibial external tension* and *tibial internal torsion* are difficult to accommodate in the sport of cycling without the rider suffering some type of overuse injury.

FUNCTIONAL ABNORMALITIES

Lumbo-pelvic instability around the low back and pelvis due to poor abdominal muscle control may cause excessive rocking movement of the buttocks to one or both sides, which can increase the workload for the legs to achieve the same power output and, as a result, the risk of *low back pain (non-specific)* and *sacroiliac joint pain*. Pulling up too hard on the pedal cycle may cause an injury such as *hamstring origin tendinitis*.

Cyclist's nipples

See *Nipples*.

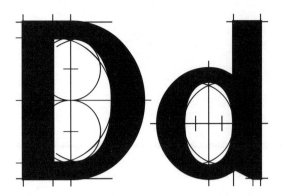

Dairy products

Foods such as milk, cheese, yoghurt and butter that are mostly produced from cows in Western countries. Similar products are made from goats, buffalo and other animals. They are rich in nutrients such as *protein*, *carbohydrates*, *vitamins* and *minerals*. They have varying amounts of *saturated fats*. It is recommended that babies and young children up to the age of five should be given full-fat products because they need the energy for growth. Older children should have reduced-fat products. Low-fat or no-fat products are recommended for adolescents and adults.

Dancing

Dancing is a creative activity and a form of exercise. Ballroom and line dancing are moderate-intensity, similar to brisk walking (see *Aerobic training* and *Metabolic equivalent (MET)*), and classical ballet, contemporary dance, many forms of folk dancing and tap dancing are high-intensity like running. Other

fitness requirements include *agility training* for balance, *flexibility training* and *strength training*.

Ballroom dancing—a moderate-intensity physical activity

Injuries

The most common injuries are *low back pain (non-specific), ankle anterior impingement, ankle posterior impingement, ankle sprain,* Achilles *tendinosis* (calf), *hallux valgus* (foot and toes), *hallux rigidus* (foot and toes), *metatarsal stress fracture* (foot and toes), *navicular stress fracture* (foot and toes), *Osgood-Schlatter disease* (knee) and *rotator cuff tendinosis* (shoulder). *Eating disorders* are also more common among dancers.

Darbepoetin

A drug that increases the amount of red blood cells and is used to treat people with anaemia. It is has a similar enhancing effect on performance in exercise and sport as *erythropoietin (EPO)*, except that it is considered to be ten times more powerful. It also is a *drug banned in sport*.

Dead arm syndrome

Sudden numbness and weakness of the arm lasting for a few minutes. Probably caused by traction or impingement on the nerves and blood vessels between the shoulder and *neck joints*. It is associated with *shoulder instability*.

Deaf athletes

People with a hearing impairment who participate in exercise and sport. It is the disability that has the least amount of impact on participation in exercise and sport, which enables these athletes to compete alongside able-bodied athletes. For instance, Dean Smith, a hearing impaired athlete, represented Australia in the decathlon at the 1990 Commonwealth Games.

The only adjustment required is to implement alternatives to audio cues. For example, instead of a starting gun in track and field events, tapping athletes on the shoulder.

Injuries and their treatment are the same as for the general population. Like *visually impaired*

athletes, they may face an increased risk of injuries associated with poor *proprioception*.

Decompression sickness

An illness caused by the development of bubbles in the body's tissues and blood due to ascending too quickly during *scuba diving*. The bubbles are made up of nitrogen gas, which is breathed in at a high pressure while under water and absorbed into the tissues.

When ascending slowly the gas leaches out into the blood gradually and is breathed out safely. However, a quick ascent allows the gas to form bubbles that cause symptoms including itchy skin and pain in the joints, most often the shoulders, elbows and knees. In severe cases air bubbles (air emboli) can block arteries in the heart, leading to a *heart attack*, or in the brain, causing a *stroke*.

The recommended treatment is to place the affected person inside a recompression chamber where the air is increased to simulate being under water and then gradually decreased. Prevention of decompression sickness is based on the depth and duration of a dive.

Deep

The anatomical direction pointing towards the inner core of the body or a body part located closer to the inner core. For example, the deep group of muscles in the front compartment of the forearm are located closest to the bones of the forearm. Also called internal for hollow structures such as blood vessels. It is the opposite of *superficial*.

Deep vein thrombosis (DVT)

A disease of the blood vessels that carry blood from the *calf* back up to the heart that causes the formation of blood clots. The risk is increased following long car trips or plane flights and after surgery.

The diagnosis should be suspected if there is constant calf pain, tenderness with firm pressure of the fingers, increased skin temperature and swelling. A clinical test is also used called Homan's sign, which involves passive *ankle* joint dorsiflexion movement (toes and foot moved upwards).

The diagnosis can be confirmed with a Doppler scan and venography. Treatment of a DVT includes anti-blood-clotting medications such as anticoagulants and *aspirin*.

In extreme cases a blood clot from a DVT can pass up to the heart and then into the lungs, which is called a pulmonary embolus. Symptoms include *shortness of breath*, dizziness and chest pain. If the pulmonary artery is completely blocked, it can cause sudden death.

Deep water running

See *Aqua running*.

Dehydration

Excessive water loss due to heavy sweating and inadequate fluid intake. It is believed to be associated with the symptoms caused by *heat illness*, including weakness, *muscle cramps*, headache, confusion and drowsiness, progressing to loss of consciousness.

Water levels in the body are determined by the balance between water loss and fluid intake. Water loss mainly occurs through sweating (see *Temperature*). A marathon runner can lose 6–10 per cent of body weight (4–8 L/8.5–17 pt in an 80 kg/176 lb runner) through sweating. Other mechanisms of water loss are humidified expired air, faeces and urine excretion.

Excessive water loss can be prevented by ensuring adequate fluid intake before, during and after exercise, called *hydration*. Additional measures are also required to prevent heat illness.

Thirst is an unreliable guide for deciding when to drink fluid. Exercise reduces the thirst sensation, and thirst may be quenched before the body is fully rehydrated. One method involves regular assessment of body weight. Each 0.5 kg (1 lb) lost should be replaced with about 500 mL (8 fl oz) of fluid. An alternative involves monitoring urine colour and volume. As water levels decrease the urine becomes more scant, concentrated and a dark yellow or orange, indicating the need for increased fluid intake. Clear urine excreted in copious amounts is an indication that water levels have returned to normal.

Chronic mild dehydration

Consistently low hydration levels (1–2 per cent less than normal) can cause abnormal *tiredness* and have a negative impact on performance levels. It should be suspected if only a small amount of yellow, highly concentrated urine is excreted every morning.

Delayed menarche

Starting menstruation at later than the average age, which is 12–13 years. Menarche usually occurs one to two years after the commencement of *puberty* in girls. If it has not occurred by age 16, a medical assessment is recommended. Delayed menarche is associated with delayed breast development, but not pubic hair growth.

Causes

The exact mechanisms that determine the timing of menarche are not known. Girls that participate in high levels of training before menarche such as ballet *dancing* and *gymnastics*, tend to have a later age of menarche than the general population. It may be that thinness, which may occur as a result of intense training, affects the hypothalamus of the brain and reduces the release of sex hormones.

However, girls genetically inclined to have a delayed menarche also may be more likely to participate in these sports in the first place because it is associated with a prolonged period of physical growth, which leads to longer legs, narrower hips, less weight per unit height and less relative body fat than the earlier maturing female.

Known causes of delayed menarche include *eating disorders* such as anorexia nervosa and, in rare cases, genetic abnormalities and ovarian failure.

Treatment

Assuming other causes are excluded, the recommended treatment includes a reduction in the level of exercise and dietary changes, in particular an increase in kilojoule intake and level of body *fat*. In rare cases, a form of oestrogen medication is recommended, such as *hormone replacement therapy* (HRT) or the oral-contraceptive pill (see *Contraception*).

Delayed-onset muscle soreness (DOMS)

Muscle aches and pain that develop up to 48 hours after an activity has been completed. It is due to an inflammatory response to microscopic *muscle fibre* damage, but it is not considered to be an injury.

In fact, a small degree of DOMS is normal in an athlete training to *overload*. However, excessive DOMS is caused by an intensity and volume of training that is too high or when too many *eccentric* muscle contractions are performed, such as squats to strengthen the quadriceps (front thigh muscle).

A *warm-down, post-activity massage, whirlpools and spas*, sleep and *rest, post-activity psychology* and *post-activity eating*, particularly consumption of *carbohydrates*, can reduce DOMS.

Densitometry

The science of measuring the density of a person's body, which is defined as mass/volume. It is used to make calculations of *body composition*, in particular the proportions of fat and muscle.

The mass is measured as the person's *weight* on standard scales. The volume can be measured by different methods. A common one is hydrostatic weighing, which involves weighing the person when totally immersed in water.

Depression

A group of symptoms including feelings of sadness, worthlessness and hopelessness, loss of interest in usual activities, sleep disturbances, tiredness, loss of appetite, weight loss, decreased sexual drive, difficulty concentrating and memory loss.

In most cases it is brought on by feelings of loss or difficulties coping with and adjusting to a new situation, such as a death or after the birth of a child (post-natal depression). Feeling down in these situations is normal; however, if the feelings and symptoms persist for at least 2 weeks and interfere with daily living, depression may have settled in.

There are specific types of depression including major depression, dysthymic and bipolar (manic depression, characterised by mood swings from mania to depression). Depression is also defined as mild, moderate or severe.

Exercise and sport

Regular participation in exercise and sport can reduce the risk of developing depression in the first place. If depression has been diagnosed (based on the symptoms and specific depression tests), it can help to reduce symptoms in mild to moderate cases in combination with other treatments such as psychotherapy and medications like *antidepressants* or the herb St John's Wort. Reduced use of alcohol and recreational drugs, regular sleep and supportive interpersonal relationships are also recommended. Moderate to severe cases usually require hospitalisation and/or medications as the main treatments.

Exercise and sport probably help with depression because it gives a sense of self-control over one's life, is a distraction from worries and fears and allows release from feelings of anger and frustration. Physical factors that may help include the release of *endorphins* and increased availability of *neurotransmitters* in the brain.

The only prerequisite for the choice of exercise or sport is that it be done regularly, in particular, at least five days a week, for at least 30 minutes on each of those days (see *Exercise for health*).

de Quervain's tenosynovitis

An overuse injury of the wrist that causes inflammation to the tendon sheath that covers and protects two thumb tendons, the abductor pollicis longus and extensor pollicis brevis. The symptoms can include pain and tenderness on the thumb-side of the wrist, swelling, reduced *range of movement* of the thumb and weakness.

This is a *paratenonitis* injury that most commonly occurs during sports such as *tennis, cycling, rowing, canoeing* and *golf*. For example, in golf the left thumb of a right-handed golfer is particularly at risk because of the hyperabduction movement required during a golf swing. The injury usually causes tenderness and swelling.

Treatment includes wearing a splint, which is a form of *immobilisation* called protected mobilisation, *non-steroidal anti-inflammatory drugs (NSAIDs)*, *mobilisation, flexibility exercises* and *strengthening exercises*. Writing with a pen with a diameter widened by rubber reduces pain. If the above treatments fail, a *corticosteroid* injection may prove helpful. In rare cases surgery is required.

Detraining

Taking a break from *training* between competitions or seasons. It is normal to experience a loss of *aerobic fitness* and *anaerobic fitness, flexibility* and possibly also skills that were gained during the previous training period. The losses may start to be noticeable after a few days. They can be prevented by continued participation in training at a lower intensity and volume.

Diabetes

A disease caused by reduced production of insulin by the pancreas, which leads to excessively high amounts of glucose (sugar) in the blood. *Insulin* is a *hormone* that is normally produced by the pancreas when blood glucose levels are high, which stimulates cells throughout the body to absorb glucose.

There are two types of diabetes: insulin dependent diabetes mellitus (IDDM), or type 1 diabetes; and the more common non-insulin dependent diabetes mellitus (NIDDM), or type 2 diabetes.

Type 1 diabetes is an inherited auto-immune disease, where antibodies are produced against the beta cells of the pancreas that produce insulin. It affects about 15 per cent of people with diabetes and usually starts during childhood and adolescence.

Type 2 diabetes is due to genetics and lifestyle, in particular poor diet and lack of physical activity. There is not only a reduced production of insulin, but muscles, fat tissue and the liver are also less sensitive to its effects. It is found in about 85 per cent of people with diabetes and usually begins in adulthood.

There are short- and long-term health problems associated with both types of diabetes. In the short term diabetes can cause excessive amounts of urine, thirst, hunger and fatigue. Hyperglycaemia (high blood sugar levels) can lead to dizziness, confusion and sweatiness, and in severe cases *ketoacidosis*, seizures, loss of consciousness and even death. Long term there is an increased risk of damage caused by hyperglycaemia, including *coronary heart disease, stroke, peripheral vascular disease*, kidney disease and eye disease such as *retinal detachment*.

Diagnosis and treatment

A simple urine test can confirm diabetes. Alternatively a blood test is required. The treatment of both types of diabetes aims to maintain blood glucose levels as close to normal as possible. For Type 1 this involves insulin injections, weight loss by eating a low-fat, low-simple-carbohydrate and high-complex-carbohydrate diet and regular participation in physical activity. Type 2 should not require any medication, just weight loss.

Exercise and sport

A full medical check up is required before starting a physical activity program to exclude heart, eye or foot problems.

People with diabetes also should have an identification card or bracelet identifying themselves as diabetic, keep an eye out for the early signs of *hypoglycaemia* for at least 6–12 hours after exercise, carry glucose tablets or an alternative source of glucose at all times and learn to check their own blood glucose levels before, after and sometimes during physical activity.

TYPE 1

Moderate-intensity activity (see *Aerobic training* and *Metabolic equivalent (MET)*) of less than 30 minutes rarely requires any insulin adjustment. The general rule for exercise greater than 30 minutes is the more intense and/or the longer the duration, the more reduction required. The only exception is in people with low insulin levels participating in high-intensity exercise. It is recommended that a doctor make the calculation for the insulin adjustment.

TYPE 2

Blood glucose levels can be maintained with diet alone in many people with Type 2 diabetes. Those who take oral hypoglycaemic drugs may need to halve their doses on days of prolonged exercise or withhold it altogether, depending on blood glucose levels.

Diet

Carbohydrate requirements for exercise vary considerably between individuals. Guidelines are useful, though only as a starting point. The key is checking blood glucose levels before, during and after exercise, learning the effects of different types of exercise under different environmental conditions on blood glucose levels, eating carbohydrate when exercise is completed, preventing dehydration by drinking adequate fluids before, during and after exercise and avoiding alcohol after exercise. The best time for training is 1 to 2 hours after a meal and eating extra carbohydrates during long duration exercise.

Kidney disease and eye disease

People with diabetes face an increased risk of eye disease and injuries. Jarring of the head during exercise in *collision sports* may cause *retinal detachment*. If eye disease is present, only low to moderate-intensity activities such as walking, swimming and stationary cycling are recommended to avoid excessively high blood pressure (*hypertension*). *Isometric strengthening*, such as *weight lifting*, also should be avoided. People diagnosed with kidney disease should avoid high-intensity activities and lifting heavy weights and wear well-cushioned *shoes*.

Adjustment of food intake during exercise for diabetes

Activity	Time	Blood glucose	Adjustment
Low-level	¹/₂ hr	under 5.5	10g (0.35 oz) carbohydrate (small serve fruit, bread, biscuit, yoghurt or milk)
		over 5.5	No extra food
Moderate-level	1 hour	under 5.5	20–30 g (0.7–1 oz) carbohydrate (1¹/₂–2 serves fruit, bread, biscuits, yoghurt and/or milk)
		5.5–10	10 g (0.35 oz) carbohydrate (small serve fruit, bread, biscuit, yoghurt or milk)
		10–16.5	No extra food (in most cases)
		over 16.5	No extra food. Preferably do not exercise, as blood glucose level may go up
Strenuous	1–2 hours	under 5.5	45–60 g (1.6–2.1 oz) carbohydrate (1 sandwich and fruit and/or milk or yoghurt)
		5.5–10	25–50g (0.9–1.8 oz) carbohydrate (¹/₂ sandwich and fruit and/or milk or yoghurt)
		10–16.5	15 g (0.5 oz) carbohydrate (1 serve fruit, bread biscuits, yoghurt or milk)
		over 16.5	Preferably do not exercise, as blood glucose level may go up
Varying intensity	Long duration		Insulin may be decreased (conservatively estimate the decrease in insulin peaking at time of activity by 10%; a 50% reduction is not common)
	¹/₂–1 day		Increase carbohydrate before, during and after activity
			10–50 g (0.35–1.8 oz) carbohydrate per hour, such as diluted fruit juice

Diagnosis

Identifying the location, severity and causes of an injury, disease or ill health.

The diagnostic process involves collecting information to answer the question 'What is the most likely diagnosis?' This includes answering questions, which is called obtaining the *history*, being subjected to a *physical examination* and appropriate tests and investigations.

A careful history taking, comprehensive physical examination and the judicious use of tests and investigations should make the diagnosis evident. It is also necessary to exclude diagnoses that may be life threatening or cause substantial damage, which are defined as 'not to be missed'.

Receiving a diagnosis should include an explanation of the location, severity and causes, followed by the proposed treatments. Do not be afraid to ask questions, especially if you do not understand something.

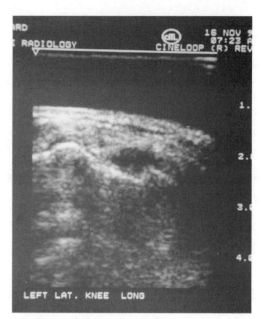

A diagnostic ultrasound scan of the patellar tendon of the knee

Diagnostic nerve block

A test used to check whether a zygapophysial joint in the spine is the cause of pain. It is used most often for *neck pain (non-specific)*, though sometimes also *low back pain (non-specific)*, when insufficient improvement has been achieved after 3 months of treatment.

The test begins with identifying the likely joints in the spine that are causing the pain (see *Neck joints*). For each joint, a needle is inserted into the neck (guided by a mobile X-ray machine) to the two small nerves that supply feelings of pain and an anaesthetic applied. If pain is reduced by the test, the joint is regarded as the problematic structure that requires treatment, usually *radiofrequency neurotomy*. The test takes up to 30 minutes.

Diagnostic ultrasound

A technique that uses invisible, high frequency sound waves to create an image of muscles, tendons and ligaments inside the body. It first became widely used as an investigative test in exercise and sports-related injuries in the 1990s. It is painless, and there is no radiation. In skilled hands it can provide a great deal of diagnostic information quickly and simply.

It is particularly helpful for confirming the diagnosis of tendon and muscle tears (see *Strain*), *tendinosis*, *muscle contusion* and calcification of a muscle (formation of bone-like material). The most commonly examined areas are large tendons (for example, the Achilles, patellar (kneecap), rotator cuff (shoulder)) and the muscles of the thigh. Real-time ultrasound examination during active movement can assist with the detection of an abnormality such as *shoulder impingement*.

Dialysis

A treatment that removes waste products from the blood and excess fluid from the body. It is performed when the *kidney* is not functioning properly due to disease. There are over 2000 people receiving dialysis treatment in Australia. Their ability to participate in exercise and sport is determined by the type of dialysis received and current health status.

Continuous ambulatory peritoneal dialysis (CAPD)

This treatment involves filling the abdominal cavity with 2 L (4.2 pt) of dialysate fluid through a catheter tube, allowing it to rest for a few hours while waste products empty out from the peritoneal membrane and then following this with drainage.

Exercise, such as walking, is highly recommended (see *Exercise for health*). Many people receiving CAPD have *diabetes*. Physical activity should be rigidly scheduled and structured around their diabetes treatment to fit in with eating and medication schedules. It should avoid high-intensity (see *Aerobic training* and *Metabolic equivalent (MET)*) because of susceptibility to blood sugar depletion. Aquatic, running and jumping activities are not permitted.

Haemodialysis

An artificial kidney machine is connected up to a vein in the leg via a plastic tube to receive blood that is filtered through membranes and then sent back into an artery. It is performed three times a week, either at a centre or home.

Most younger people requiring haemodialysis can participate in any exercise or sport without restrictions. They face an increased risk of developing anaemia (see *Iron deficiency*), particularly if they overdo their physical activity over the long term, and may need to take a medication called *erythropoietin* (EPO) to elevate red blood cell concentration.

Older aged people receiving haemodialysis are more likely to have *coronary heart disease*. A *medical clearance* and exercise prescription is necessary before commencing participation in exercise and sport.

Diaphysis

See *Bone*.

Diathermy

An electromagnetic wave treatment that heats up body tissues to increase blood flow in order to reduce chronic *swelling* and *oedema*. It is able to generate heat deep inside the body, such as at the hip joint, which is its advantage over other forms of heat delivery such as a hot water bottle (see *Heat therapy (superficial)*). Diathermy may be recommended for *hip osteoarthritis, low back pain (non-specific)* and *neck pain (non-specific)*. It should not be used for an *acute injury* during the first 72 hours after the injury has occurred. The wave frequencies include microwaves and short waves.

Diarrhoea

An increased amount, frequency or fluidity of faeces movement out of the bowels. The most common causes include food poisoning, gastrointestinal infection such as *traveller's diarrhoea*, and psychological factors such as *stress* and *anxiety*. It also is more likely to occur in people participating in sports involving high-intensity activities (see *Aerobic training* and *Metabolic equivalent (MET)*), particularly long distance running, and during competition rather than training.

The probable causes of exercise-related diarrhoea include a diversion of blood flow away from the *gastrointestinal system* to the exercising muscles, which is made worse with *dehydration*, and increased intestinal muscle actions.

Treatment

It is recommended to: 1) reduce dietary *fibre* 2 days prior to competition; 2) avoid solid foods 3 hours prior to event time, though fluids should still be taken during this time; 3) minimise *fat* and *protein* and eat a high proportion of *carbohydrates* in the meal prior to competition; 4) prevent dehydration by drinking 2 large cups (600 ml/20 oz) of fluid in the hour prior to competition and replacing fluids as much as possible during competition. For specific foods, see *Pre-event meal*.

Diet

A selection of specific foods and meals with the aim of achieving health, nutritional and weight goals. For example, a diet for a person with *diabetes* aims to maintain consistent levels of glucose in the blood.

A *strength training diet* aims to provide enough protein for muscle growth and carbohydrates for energy.

The word 'diet' has been replaced in many public health promotion campaigns by the term 'healthy eating' because diet is considered to have negative connotations following the production of hundreds of diets over the last few decades that lack scientific support and achieve poor results.

Part of the problem is that these diets are often too rigid and restrictive about the foods that are included and when they are eaten. A *diet for good health* is recommended as a more relaxed but still effective approach to food and meals.

Diet for good health

The foods recommended for achieving and maintaining good health. The diet aims to provide as many individual choices as possible within a set of general guidelines.

One problem with a diet that is too rigid is that it is less likely to be adhered to. Another concern is that it can miss out on nutritious foods that also provide vitamins, minerals and fibre. For example, an important general guideline is low-fat eating.

However, some people don't drink enough milk or eat cheese and other dairy products that are full of calcium, which is crucial for osteoporosis prevention. They don't realise low-fat dairy products have so little fat they could still gain the benefits of the calcium without eating too much fat. Besides, the body needs fat for the construction of body cells, particularly in nerves and the brain.

Another difficulty with having a rigid attitude to low-fat eating is deciding how much fat to eat. The specific public health target supported by health authorities is to have a daily fat intake of 30 per cent of total kilojoules eaten. However, not everyone is able to stay on top of all the mathematics and calculations.

For all the above reasons, the rules for healthy eating should not be overly structured when reducing fat at the same time as keeping nutrients, such as vitamins and minerals as well as fibre, in your diet. It involves eating from all the food groups, but some

Recommendations for a diet for good health

Eat small amounts	Oil, butter, margarine, alcohol, sugar, salt
Eat moderate amounts	
(2–3 servings)	Low-fat dairy products (milk, cheese, yoghurt), nuts, fish, eggs, lean meat, chicken without skin
Eat mostly	
(5–7 servings)	Fruit and vegetables
Eat mostly	
(6–11 servings)	Bread, cereals, rice, pasta, legumes and water

One serving of these foods is defined as:

Dairy products	275 mL (9.3 fl oz) milk/yoghurt, 40–50 g (1.4–1.8 oz) cheese
Meat, chicken or fish	50–75 g (1.8–2.6 oz)
Egg	One
Fruit	1 medium-sized apple, banana, orange, 75 g (2.6 oz) chopped, cooked or tinned, 200 mL (6.75 fl oz) fruit juice
Vegetables	100 g (3.5 oz) of raw leafy vegetables, 50 g of other vegetables (cooked or chopped raw), 200 mL (6.75 fl oz) vegetable juice
Bread, cereal, rice, pasta	1 slice of bread, 25 g (0.9 oz) of ready-to-eat cereal, 100 g (3.5 oz) of cooked rice, pasta or cereal

foods should be eaten more often than others. (See table 'Recommendations for a diet for good health'.) Starting and sticking with a good health diet may require planning such as using the *stages of change* model of behavioural change.

A healthy eating diet can also be helpful for people who are *overweight* or suffering from *obesity*, *coronary heart disease, stroke, varicose veins, diabetes, osteoarthritis, gout* and certain types of *cancer*.

Dietician

See *Nutritionist*.

Digestive system

See *Gastrointestinal system.*

Digit symbol substitution test (DSST)

A neuropsychological test used to assess the severity of *concussion* at the time that a head injury occurs and the progress of recovery afterwards to determine when return to sport is permitted. A full assessment of concussion also includes looking at signs and symptoms such as headache, dizziness and impaired memory.

The test measures the speed and efficiency of information processing. It is derived from the Wechsler adult intelligence scale. It involves substituting a symbol for a random succession of numbers. The injured athlete has 90 seconds to fill in as many symbols as possible and is given a score of correct answers. Athletes in sports with a high risk of concussion should be tested prior to the commencement of the season to provide a baseline score if concussion does occur.

Direct calorimetry

An accurate method of measuring the amount of energy a person uses up when performing an activity, such as running on a treadmill or riding on an exercise bike.

It measures the heat given off in a tightly enclosed chamber. The calculation is based on the fact that the processes of *metabolism* take out 40 per cent of the energy contained in foods like carbohydrates and fats to produce adenosine triphosphate (ATP), while the other 60 per cent gets burned as heat that is radiated out of the body. So, if two people run at the same speed and for the same time, the one that radiates more heat is using more energy to complete the same task.

Direct calorimetry is infrequently used because of the high cost of building a chamber that is large

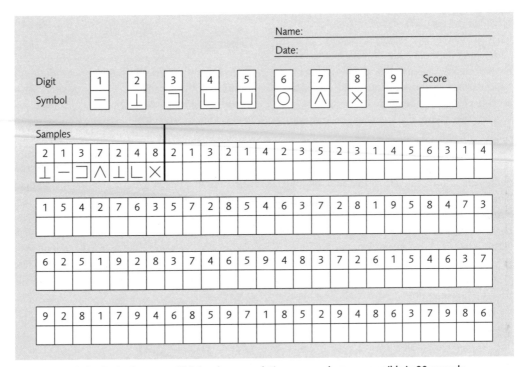

The Digit symbol substitution test, which involves completing as many boxes as possible in 90 seconds

enough for a person to be on a treadmill or bike. The more commonly used method is *indirect calorimetry*.

Disability

An ability that has been permanently or temporarily changed. There are many abilities that can be affected, including movement due to a loss of a limb, senses such as vision and hearing, and intellectual capacity. Aids or treatments are often provided to minimise the impact of a disability.

Exercise and sport

Just as in the general population, people with a disability exhibit a wide range of participation in exercise and sport from the sedentary through to the elite athlete.

There are 18 sports at the Paralympic Games. However, due to the physical demands of each sport, not all disability groupings can compete in each sport. For instance, only visually impaired athletes play judo and goalball, whereas swimming and athletics are open to all disability categories.

People with a disability who are regular participants in exercise and sport have unique health needs, but at the same time most of their needs are the same as athletes without a disability.

Over the last two decades each disability grouping has come to be represented by sporting organisations that aim to promote their members' interests, particularly giving them an opportunity to participate in physical activity that may not otherwise be available to them. This has usually meant participating with 'their own kind'. However, in recent years a trend has arisen to integrate people with disabilities into general community sporting organisations.

It should be noted that there are a number of people who prefer not to give a disability a negative value and simply see it as a different ability, in the same way as people have different coloured hair. Just as people without a disability vary in their level of skills and talents, the disabled athlete simply contributes to this variation.

Groupings

Athletes with a disability are placed in groupings according to the type and extent of disability to enable fair competition between similar performance capabilities.

The groupings are: *wheelchair athletes, amputee athletes, visually impaired athletes, intellectual disability, cerebral palsy, les autres, deaf athletes, transplant recipients* and people who receive *dialysis*.

Within groupings athletes may need to be divided according to different levels of impairment. For example, vision impaired athletes are categorised into three different classes: B1, totally blind; B2, athletes with minimum remaining light perception; and B3, athletes with some remaining light perception.

Classification systems differ from sport to sport, in accordance with the different skills required for performance. For example, a below-knee amputation means something different for a swimmer as compared to a volleyball player. Consequently, a below-knee amputee swimmer will be in a different class to a below-knee amputee volleyball athlete.

Disc

A *fibrous and cartilaginous joint* most commonly found in the spine between two vertebrae. It is shaped like a round plug containing a gel-like ball in the middle, called the nucleus pulposus, surrounded by a tough outer layering, called the anulus fibrosus.

The disc acts to provide stability between the two vertebrae at the same time as allowing a small amount of movement. It is also highly efficient as a shock absorber. However, excessive wear and tear can cause pain; for example, *low back pain (nonspecific)* and, in severe cases, *nerve root compression* due to a disc prolapse. Surgery to obliterate the disc in order to reduce severe low back pain is called a *spinal fusion*.

Disc prolapse

See *Nerve root compression*.

Dislocation

An injury that involves a severe disruption of the connection between the two bones that form a joint. It is most likely to occur in synovial joints that have the least stability, such as the shoulder joint and fingers. It is much less likely in a ball-and-socket joint, like the *hip joint* that is made up of a round ball at the end of the femur (thigh bone) that fits snugly in a deep cup in the pelvis. It is least likely to occur in *fibrous and cartilaginous joints*.

Diagnosis

Simply looking at the disrupted joint with the naked eye is usually enough to make the diagnosis. Signs and symptoms include deformity of the normal contours of the bones, soft tissue and skin; abnormal angulation of the limb; restricted movement; severe pain; swelling; and possibly bruising. A *subluxation* is a partial dislocation that produces less severe signs and symptoms. It is generally diagnosed and treated the same way; however, the recovery is quicker.

Checks should be made for any complications associated with the injury, including damage to nerves and blood vessels located next to the joint, such as the axillary nerve near the *shoulder joint* and brachial artery near the *elbow joint*, by checking for the nerve sensations and the *pulse* of the artery.

All dislocations should have an *X-ray* to check for associated bone fracture. *Articular cartilage acute*

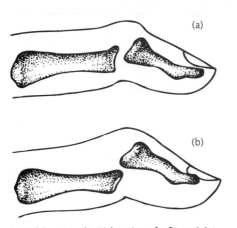

(a) Subluxation (b) Dislocation of a finger joint

injury is also not uncommon. Complications may need to be treated as a *medical emergency* and treatment received as soon as possible in a hospital.

Treatment

If there are no complications, such as nerve or blood vessel damage, the first aim of treatment is to reconnect the bones in the joint, which is called relocation. This may occur spontaneously, or can be performed by a medically trained person such as a doctor, physiotherapist or nurse. Occasionally drugs for muscle relaxation are required, such as valium. Much less frequently, general anaesthesia is required in a hospital.

After the relocation is complete, the aim of treatment is to prevent too much movement to promote healing of the joint capsule and ligaments (see *Immobilisation*), but at the same time allow gentle movement and *strengthening exercises* to provide joint stability, particularly *isometric strengthening*.

Once healing has been completed, ensuring full movement and maximum strength are the key to a full return to sport. A severe dislocation is more likely to be re-injured. Surgery may be required to prevent recurrent dislocations.

Disordered eating

A mild form of weight loss due to abnormal behaviour towards food and fluid intake. It is not as severe as *eating disorders*, such as anorexia nervosa and bulimia. Examples of disordered eating include an athlete limiting kilojoule intake and increasing the intensity of training in order to lose weight in the period leading up to a competitive event, and after the event allowing the weight to go up again. (A person with an eating disorder would maintain the same low weight after the event.)

Disordered eating is believed to increase the risk of developing *amenorrhea* (absence of menstrual periods), which leads to an increased risk of *osteoporosis*. A woman participating in excessive amounts of exercise and sport who suffers from disordered eating, amenorrhea and osteoporosis may be diagnosed with *female athlete triad*.

Distal

The anatomical direction pointing away from the trunk of the body. It is most often used in the arms and legs. For example, the elbow is distal to the shoulder and blood flowing from the knee to the ankle is moving in a distal direction. The opposite is called *proximal*.

Distal radioulnar joint instability

A displacement of the normal connection between the lower ends of the forearm bones (ulnar and radius) at the *wrist joint*. It is often due to a *triangular fibrocartilage complex sprain* that has not healed properly or has been re-injured, leaving the ligaments weakened, which allows the displacement to occur. It is also associated with repeated or forceful pronation movements (rotating the forearm inwards) performed during *tennis* and *gymnastics*. The recommended treatment is surgical repair.

Diuretics

A drug that increases urination to reduce the amount of fluid in the body. It is used to treat illnesses such as *hypertension* (high blood pressure) and excessive fluid in the body, as occurs in cardiac failure and pulmonary oedema (see *Altitude sickness*).

Side effects include *muscle cramps, dehydration* and electrolyte imbalance, especially in older aged athletes in hot weather and people who combine diuretics with other water-loss techniques such as using a sauna and restricting food and water. There is also a risk of increased blood sugar levels in people with *diabetes* and increased uric acid levels in those with *gout*. Hypotension (low blood pressure) is a risk for people also taking *antihypertensives* (for high blood pressure).

Diuretics are used in exercise and sport to rapidly lose weight prior to competition in sports with weight limits, such as *boxing, wrestling, weight lifting, martial arts*, lightweight *rowing* and horse racing. They are also used as a form of cheating to aid the excre-

tion or dilute the presence of *drugs banned in sport*, such as anabolic steroids, and are banned by the World Anti-Doping Agency (WADA).

Banned diuretics include acetazolamide (Diamox), bumetanide (Burinex), chlorthalidone, chlorothiazide (Chlotride), ethacrynic acid (Edecril), frusemide (Lasix, Urex), hydrochlorothiazide (Dyazide, Dichlotride, Moduretic), mannitol (only by injection), mersalyl, spironolactone (Aldactone, Spiractin) and triamterene (Dyazide).

Diving

A sport that involves explosive jumping followed by acrobatic manoeuvres in mid-air prior to entering the water. The physical requirements include *strength training, flexibility training* and *skills training*.

The most common injuries include *neck pain (non-specific), low back pain (non-specific), shoulder instability, shoulder dislocation, rotator cuff tendinosis* (shoulder), *triangular fibrocartilage complex sprain* (wrist), *shin chronic compartment syndrome*, shin periostitis, *gastrocnemius strain* (calf) and *soleus strain* (calf).

Dominant side

The tendency for a person to be more proficient with the right or left side. In exercise and sport about two-thirds of people are right-side dominant, about a quarter are left-side, and a small number use both sides equally well (called ambidextrous). It is believed to be an inherited physical characteristic. However, it is possible to increase proficiency of the non-dominant side, particularly in children up to the age of puberty when the brain is still growing.

Instructions for performing activities with the right hand come from the motor cortex of the left hemisphere, which also controls activities of the brain such as speech and writing. Creativity and visual/spatial referencing is centred in the right hemisphere. There is a theory that left-sided people have an advantage because their skills can better utilise the visual/spatial centre of the brain.

DOMS

See *Delayed-onset muscle soreness (DOMS)*.

Dorsiflexion

A movement of the *ankle* joint that involves moving the top of the foot in a direction that brings it closer to the front of the tibia (shin bone). It is also called *extension*.

Downhill skiing

A popular recreational activity and sport, including speed events, which are single runs featuring a small number of turns, and technical events such as the slalom and giant slalom, which are over courses through closely spaced gates.

Equipment, fitness and injuries

Correct *ski boots* prevent injuries, particularly bindings designed to release during a fall. Fitness requirements include *aerobic training* for long hours of skiing, *strength training* and *flexibility training* for the leg muscles.

Slalom downhill skiing

In the past 20 years, ankle and shin fractures have decreased due to improved binding designs. However, there has been a small increase in knee injuries, including *medial collateral ligament (MCL) sprain*, *anterior cruciate ligament (ACL) tear*, *tibial plateau fracture*, *meniscus tear* and *patellar dislocation*.

Other common injuries and illnesses include *shoulder dislocation*, *acromioclavicular (AC) joint sprain* (shoulder), *Colles fracture* (wrist), *skier's thumb* (wrist) (see *First MCP joint sprain*), *altitude sickness* and *hypothermia*.

Down's syndrome

An inherited abnormality of the chromosomes that causes intellectual disability and a distinct physical appearance. Instead of inheriting 46 chromosomes made up of 23 pairs, people with Down's syndrome receive an extra chromosome 21, making a total of 47. The most common cause is a faulty ovum, which is more likely in women aged 35 years and over.

Down's syndrome causes an *intellectual disability*, with the IQ varying from 30 to 80. People with an intellectual disability can participate in exercise and sport in the same manner as the general population. The typical personality of a person with Down's syndrome is friendly and cheerful.

Drugs and ergogenic aids

Substances that aim to gain an advantage over competitors. These substances can be divided into two groups: 1) *drugs banned in sport* such as anabolic steroids and erythropoietin; 2) *ergogenic aids* that are permitted, such as food supplements and alternative preparations including whey protein and creatine. Many medications are prescribed to heal injury, illness and disease (see *Drugs permitted in sport*).

Causes

A split second or fingertip can make the difference between winning and losing in sport. A determination to do anything possible to attain success, the public accolades and financial rewards that come with it and a belief that competitors are already taking drugs are often strong motivating forces.

In addition, there can be direct or indirect pressure from coaches, parents, peers and, in some countries, from governments or sport authorities. A lack of access to legal and natural methods to enhance performance, such as training methods, can also be a factor.

Drugs and ergogenic aids are also taken by people working in certain professions, such as security services, the military and entertainment industry, and also by the general public, usually to enhance physical appearance.

History

Drugs in sport are not a new phenomenon. Ancient Egyptian athletes favoured the rear hooves of an Abyssinian ass, ground up, boiled in oil and flavoured with rose petals and rosehip. The Norwegian warriors, the 'Berserkers', fortified themselves with psychoactive mushrooms that wildly affected their behaviour, leading to the word 'berserk' being introduced into our language.

In the modern era, the use of drugs in sport became widespread after World War II. *Anabolic steroids* were allegedly first used by Soviet Union athletes in the 1952 Olympics in Helsinki, and in western countries after the release of the steroid dianabol in 1958. *Amphetamines* were popular among cyclists, such as Danish cyclist Kurt Jensen who died from a heart related illness at the 1960 Rome Olympics. The first allegations regarding *blood doping* were made about Finnish distance runners in the 1970s.

More recently the use of the drug *erythropoietin* (EPO) has allegedly become widespread among endurance sports people, and may have contributed to the death of a number of European cyclists. In 1998 Chinese swimmers at the World Swimming Championships were caught trying to bring *human growth hormone (HGH)* into Australia.

Drugs banned in sport

Drugs used to enhance performance and gain an advantage over competitors. These drugs are banned because they are a form of cheating and may also have negative side effects on health.

The list of banned drugs produced by the World Anti-Doping Agency (WADA) is widely adopted around the world, though a number of sport organisations modify the list according to the requirements of their sport—and there are some that are less vigilant over detection and prevention of drug use.

There are also many drugs that are prescribed to heal injury, illness and disease and which are permitted for use in sport, especially if the need can be demonstrated (see *Drugs permitted in sport*).

Detection

Doping tests are crucial for effective policing of these drugs, and include: the establishment of agencies to perform testing such as the Australian Sports Drug Agency (ASDA); administrative measures, such as random testing and out-of-competition testing; the number of tests done each year; the type of samples taken such as urine and blood, and how they are taken.

For example, current testing procedures are structured in such a way that the risk of an athlete

---

Drugs banned by WADA (revised 1 Jan 2004)

1. Prohibited substances
   a) Stimulants: *amphetamines, ephedrine, cocaine*
   b) *Narcotics*: morphine, pethidine, heroin
   c) *Cannabinoids:* hashish, marijuana
   d) Anabolic agents: *anabolic steroids*, clenbuterol
   e) Peptide hormones: *erythropoietin (EPO), human growth hormone (HGH), insulin-like growth factor (IGF-1)*, chorionic gonadotrophins (HCG), gonadotrophins, insulin, corticotrophins
   f) *Beta-2 agonists*: salbutamol, terbutaline
   g) Agents with anti-oestrogenic activity: clomiphene, tamoxifen
   h) Masking agents: *diuretics*, epitestosterone, probeniciol
   i) Glucocorticosteroids: oral prednisolone, cortisone

2. Prohibited methods
   a) Enhancement of oxygen transfer: blood doping, modified haemoglobin products
   b) Pharmacological, chemical and physical manipulation
   c) Gene doping

3. Substances prohibited in particular sports
   a) *Alcohol*
   b) *Beta-blockers*
   c) *Diuretics*

---

substituting their urine with someone else's is minimal. Each athlete is accompanied by a chaperone (of the same gender) so that the urine sample is provided under direct supervision.

Techniques used in the laboratory are often playing a catch-up game with drug cheats. It was not until 1975 that mass spectrometry and radioimmuno assay techniques were developed for anabolic steroids. Eight athletes at the 1976 Montreal Olympic Games tested positive for anabolic steroid use for the first time; however, anabolic steroids had been used since the 1950s.

In 1990 erythropoietin (EPO) was added to the banned list. However, due to the technical difficulty of differentiating between the 'synthetic' form and the naturally produced hormone, effective testing was only developed in 2000.

Drugs permitted in sport

Despite the extensive list of *drugs banned in sport* by the International Olympic Organisation (IOC), athletes are permitted to use the majority of drugs that are prescribed for injury, illness and disease.

Most countries also now have a mechanism, either through a sport organisation or the IOC, where athletes can apply to use a banned drug for legitimate reasons. Generally the criteria necessary for granting a 'therapeutic use' include: 1) the athlete would experience significant impairment of health if the banned drug was withheld; 2) no enhancement of performance could result from the banned drug as medically prescribed; 3) the person would not be denied the drug if he/she was not a competing athlete; 4) no available permitted and practical alternative can be substituted.

Dry needling

A treatment that involves inserting needles into tender areas of muscles called *myofascial trigger points*. It has been found to be beneficial for chronic muscle problems such as *low back pain (non-specific)*, *neck pain (non-specific)* and *tennis elbow*.

Permitted drugs (with specific sports or drugs that are excluded)

Anti-inflammatory medications (*Non-steroidal anti-inflammatory drugs, NSAIDs*)
Aspirin, paracetamol, codeine (see *Narcotics*), dextropropoxyphene
Sleeping tablets (excluding modern pentathlon)
Antidepressants (excluding modern pentathlon)
Antihypertensives (excluding *beta-blockers*)
Antinauseants
Antidiarrhoeals
Bronchodilator inhalers (salbutamol and terbutaline, salmeterol only)
Antibiotics
Antihistamines
Eye medications
Skin creams and ointments
Oral-contraceptive pill (see *Contraception*)

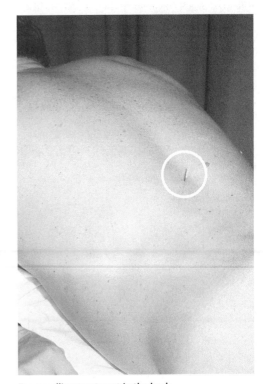

Dry needling treatment in the back

Either acupuncture or fine hypodermic needles may be used. They are inserted perpendicularly through the skin. When the needle makes contact with the trigger point an acute pain of varying intensity is felt at the site, in the area of pain referral or both. Up to three or four treatment sessions may be required to eliminate the trigger point pain. Following dry needling treatment there is usually some tenderness.

Dysmenorrhea

Painful cramps of the uterus during *menstruation*. Most women experience it at some time in their lives, most commonly in the teenage years and in the late 30s. It may be caused by excessive sensitivity to *prostaglandins*, a hormone-like chemical that causes swelling. There is an increased risk in women who use an IUD for contraception. Women who regularly participate in exercise and sport are less likely to experience dysmenorrhea. This may be due to increased levels of circulating *endorphins*.

Mild symptoms can be treated with simple *analgesics*, with little disruption in participation in exercise and sport. Moderate to severe cramping associated with heavy menstrual flow may adversely affect training or competition. Treatments include drugs such as mefenamic acid and *non-steroidal anti-inflammatory drugs (NSAIDs)*, which reduce the production of prostaglandins, or the oral-contraceptive pill (see *Contraception*).

Dyspnea

See *Shortness of breath*.

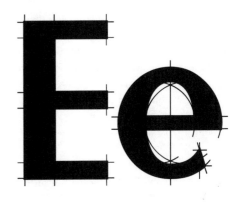

Ear infection

A common problem affecting swimmers due to excessive exposure to water and repeated rubbing and scratching of the external ear canal. It causes earache, itchiness, liquid discharge from the ear and impaired hearing.

Treatment includes cleaning, antibiotic cream and corticosteroid eardrops. Swimming should be stopped until the infection clears. Ear plugs achieve doubtful prevention benefits because they also damage the ear canal. Better prevention is achieved with alcohol ear drops (such as 5 per cent acetic acid in isopropyl alcohol) after each swimming session.

Ear injuries

See *Face pain and injuries*.

Eardrum rupture

Impaired hearing due to a damaged tympanic membrane caused by a sudden forceful blow across the side of the head in *collision sports*, such as boxing, and air pressure changes in the ear, most commonly seen in skydiving, paragliding and *scuba diving*.

It is due to dramatic changes to air pressure caused by an inability to equalise pressure between the ear and outside environment, normally performed by holding the nose and closing the mouth and blowing hard. In some cases there is also bleeding from the ear and pain. The rupture usually heals well by avoiding aggravating activities, though *antibiotics* are required to prevent infection.

Eating disorder

A severe form of weight loss due to abnormal behaviour towards food and fluid intake. The two most commonly diagnosed eating disorders are anorexia nervosa and bulimia. A milder form of abnormal eating is called *disordered eating*.

Eating disorders are estimated at 5–10 per cent among females and 1 per cent for males in the general population, though they may be higher because the condition is often denied. It can affect people from teenage years through to the 40s. The largest group is the post-puberty teenage years.

A number of sports are more likely to be associated with eating disorders, including aesthetic sports such as *gymnastics*, *diving*, figure *ice skating*, *aerobics* and *synchronised swimming*, where the athlete's physical appearance is taken into account when

117

awarding points during competition, with judges bringing their own preconceived notions of the ideal physical appearance (usually slim and trim).

Other at-risk sports are those where athletes are required to make a certain weight in order to participate in a competitive event, such as the *martial arts* (like judo and Tai Kwan Do) and *rowing*, and endurance athletes who discover they can run and swim faster and further if they have less weight to carry around, like *long distance running* and *triathlon*.

Causes

One theory about anorexia is that it is a true phobia about putting on weight. Others regard it as a symptom of an underlying mental health diagnosis such as *depression*, personality disorder, schizophrenia or as a disorder of the hypothalamus.

The most prominent psychological mechanisms that are observed include: excessive pressure to achieve through performance, not just in sport but other activities; anxiety to please important people, such as parents and the coach; and obsessional behaviour about habits as a way of exerting control over one's life.

Diagnosis

The diagnosis is made according to weight, with severe weight loss confirmed with the naked eye or less than 20 on the *body-mass index (BMI)* scale. Common symptoms include overactivity, obsessive exercising, tiredness and weakness, lanugo (baby-like hair on body), thinning hair on the head, extreme choosiness over food, binge eating, a distorted body image and intense fear of gaining weight. Bulimia is characterised by bouts of gross overeating usually followed by self-induced vomiting, and sometimes taking laxatives and *diuretics*. These activities are often kept secret. In severe cases there is an increased risk of suicide.

Severe weight loss associated with *amenorrhoea* (loss of menstruation) and *osteoporosis* is called the *female athlete triad*. Blood and urine tests and radiological investigations are used to monitor health: for example, bone density X-rays for *osteoporosis*.

Treatment

The recommended treatment approach is multidisciplinary, including counselling from a psychiatrist and/or psychologist, medications such as *antidepressants* and *sports nutrition* advice for athletes with a mild to moderate eating disorder. In severe cases hospitalisation is required to prevent permanent organ damage.

Eccentric

A muscle contraction that occurs at the same time as *muscle length* increases. For example, from a starting position of holding a heavy barbell up in the air with the arm straight above the head and, then moving the barbell slowly down to the level of your chest causes an eccentric contraction of your shoulder muscles, particularly the deltoids.

Eccentric *strengthening exercises* are an important part in the prevention of muscle or tendon *strain*

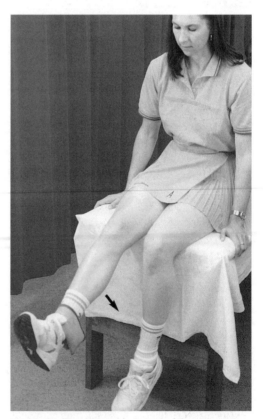

The black arrow shows the direction of an eccentric exercise of the quadriceps muscle

and the treatment of *tendinosis* injuries. For instance, for an *Achilles tendinosis* injury the aim is to eccentrically strengthen the calf muscles. An eccentric contraction involves standing on a step facing upwards, with the back half of the feet off the edge of the step, then allowing the heels to slowly descend.

This exercise can be made progressively harder by doing it on the injured leg only, then with a weight in the hands and lastly with a backpack filled with weights. However, an excessive amount of eccentric exercising can increase the risk of developing *delayed-onset muscle soreness (DOMS)*. Eccentric is the opposite of *concentric*.

Echinacea

A herbal preparation that may be recommended as a natural health medication to boost the immune system to prevent illness, such as the *common cold* and *flu*, or treat infections after they have started. It is

Echinacea medication

available in a number of forms, such as liquid, powder and tablets. For prevention and treatment it is recommended to take 150–300 mg of powder three times a day and 2–4 mL of fluid extract three times a day.

Echocardiogram

A technique that produces an image of the heart using *diagnostic ultrasound*, which is invisible high frequency sound waves. The technique involves sending ultrasound into the chest that is reflected from the different parts of the heart to provide a two-dimensional image.

Abnormalities such as an enlarged wall, defective heart valve or blocked blood vessels can be detected. It is used in the diagnosis of *hypertrophic cardiomyopathy*, *myocarditis* and *coronary heart disease*.

Economy of effort

A measure of the efficiency of energy-use during a specific activity. It involves assessing skill levels, maturity of coordination and *biomechanics*.

For example, swinging a golf club with poor skills takes more energy than good skills. Young children are not as efficient when running compared to adults because their coordination is less mature.

Women tend to have less economy of effort when running compared to men because of the biomechanics of the *pelvis* and hips which tend to be set widely apart. This anatomical feature, designed to facilitate childbirth, causes the thighs to be pointed in a medial (inwards) direction, which reduces the efficiency of forward propulsion of the legs.

Methods of improving economy of effort include *skills training*, treatments to correct biomechanics and coordination training.

EKG

See *Electrocardiogram (ECG)*.

Elastic cartilage

A rubbery and supportive tissue found in the larynx and epiglottis of the throat and outer ear. It is made up of cells, called chondroblasts and chondrocytes, embedded in a matrix of gel-like ground substance and predominantly elastic fibres.

Elbow and forearm pain and injuries

Cause

Elbow and forearm pain can be caused by overuse or acute injuries or diseases. An *overuse injury* causes pain that gets worse over a period of weeks or months due to an accumulation of excessive forces that cause microtrauma. In the early stages it causes only minor pain and stiffness. But later on, either gradually or following a sudden force, it becomes painful enough to seek medical care.

An *acute injury* causes pain that begins suddenly due to a single incident, such as falling onto the hand. Diseases that cause elbow pain include *osteoarthritis*, inflammatory arthritis such as *gout* and tumours.

The *elbow joint* and associated structures are the main cause of *pain* in the region. However, it is not unusual for another structure to be the cause, in particular the *neck joints*, called *elbow and forearm referred pain*.

Diagnosis

Making a diagnosis involves combining information gathered from the *history*, *physical examination* and relevant tests.

The pain's location is particularly important for an overuse injury. The three locations are lateral (outer side), medial (inner side) and posterior (back of the elbow).

Activities that bring on the pain also provide clues. For example, pain when gripping a racquet handle indicates *tennis elbow*. Throwing pain is associated with *elbow medial collateral ligament sprain* in adults and *Little Leaguer's elbow* in children. *Elbow and forearm referred pain* from the neck may be due to posture when working on a computer.

The diagnosis of acute injuries is more straightforward. For example, elbow pain after a fall onto the outstretched hand is most likely a *radius head fracture*. An X-ray can confirm a fracture. Other useful tests include *diagnostic ultrasound* for tennis elbow and blood tests for inflammatory arthritis.

Causes of elbow pain

Common	Less common	Not to be missed
Overuse injury		
Lateral (outer side) pain		
• Tennis elbow	• Posterior interosseus nerve entrapment	• Little Leaguer's elbow
• Referred elbow and forearm pain		• Panner's disease
		• Decompression sickness
Medial (inner side) pain		
• Golfer's elbow	• Elbow apophysitis	• Complex regional pain syndrome (CRPS)
• Elbow medial collateral ligament sprain	• Ulnar nerve compression	
• Elbow and forearm referred pain		
Posterior (back of the elbow) pain		
• Olecranon bursitis		• Gout
Acute injury		
• Radius head fracture		
• Supracondylar fracture		
• Olecranon fracture		
• Elbow posterior dislocation		

QUICK REFERENCE GUIDE

Elbow

Overuse injury: Pain that has gradually worsened over a period of weeks or months

Tennis elbow ....Do you have pain on the outside of your elbow, which is aggravated by activities that involve gripping (like tennis or golf)?

Elbow medial collateral ligament sprain ....Did you feel a pain on the inside of your elbow when performing an activity such as throwing a ball?

Posterior interosseus nerve entrapment ....Do you have pain on the outside of the forearm that is aggravated by turning your forearm to make the palm face upwards?

Golfer's elbow ....Do you have pain on the inside of your elbow, which is aggravated by activities that involve gripping (like tennis or golf)?

Ulnar nerve compression ....Did you receive a knock to the inside of your elbow and now you feel pins and needles, tingling or numbness on the inside of your forearm or hand?

Olecranon bursitis................................Do you have swelling and pain over the point of the elbow?

Acute Injury: Pain caused by a sudden force

Elbow posterior dislocation ....Did you fall on your elbow or receive a hard blow that caused the bones to 'pop out' of alignment?

Radius head fracture,
Supracondylar fracture and
Olecranon fracture ....Did you land on your outstretched hand and now feel a constant pain in the elbow?

Elbow and forearm referred pain

Pain felt in the elbow and forearm caused by a damaged structure in another location some distance away, usually the *neck joints, thoracic spine joints,* a muscle or *neural tension.* The *referred pain* may be wholly or partially the source of the pain. The diagnosis and treatment is the same as for *shoulder referred pain.*

Elbow apophysitis

An injury of growing bone at the site that the strong wrist flexor muscles attach near the inner side (medial epicondyle) of the *elbow joint.* It mostly occurs in children.

The *apophysitis* causes an inflammation of the bone due to an accumulation of repeated, excessive forces on the growing bone over a period of weeks or months (see *Osteochondrosis*). It is associated with excessive amounts of throwing and poor *throwing biomechanics.*

Elbow joint

A *synovial joint* linking the arm and forearm. It is made up of three smaller joints: two between the arm bone (humerus) and forearm bones (ulnar and radius), called the humero-ulnar joint and humero-radial joint, where bending (*flexion*) and straightening (*extension*) occur; the third joint connects between the ulnar and radius, called the superior (upper) radio-ulnar joint, where turning inwards (*pronation*) and outwards (*supination*) occurs.

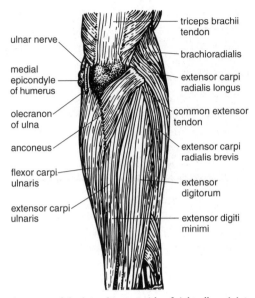

ulnar nerve

medial epicondyle of humerus

olecranon of ulna

anconeus

flexor carpi ulnaris

extensor carpi ulnaris

triceps brachii tendon

brachioradialis

extensor carpi radialis longus

common extensor tendon

extensor carpi radialis brevis

extensor digitorum

extensor digiti minimi

Anatomy of the lateral (outer) side of right elbow joint from behind

Muscles involved in elbow movements

Movement	Primary movers	Secondary movers
Flexion	• Brachialis • Biceps • Brachioradialis	• Pronator Teres
Extension	• Triceps • Anconeus	
Pronation	• Pronator quadratus	• Pronator teres
Supination	• Supinator	• Biceps

Elbow medial collateral ligament sprain

An injury of the ligament on the inner (medial) side of the *elbow joint*. It can occur due to an overuse injury or acute injury.

An overuse injury is caused by an excessive valgus stress on the elbow joint (excessive bending outwards movement) during throwing, particularly in *baseball* pitchers, javelin throwers and others involved in *throwing sports*, especially in those who 'open up too soon' (see *Throwing biomechanics*).

It initially causes inflammation, then scarring, calcification and occasionally ligament rupture.

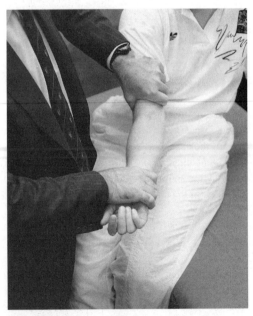

Testing for excessive valgus movement for elbow medial collateral ligament sprain

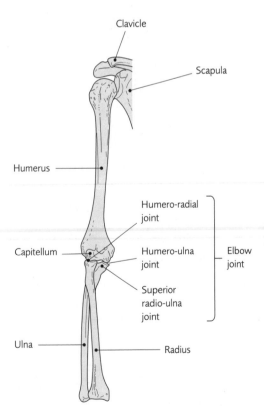

Clavicle

Scapula

Humerus

Humero-radial joint

Capitellum

Humero-ulna joint

Elbow joint

Superior radio-ulna joint

Ulna

Radius

Bones of the right elbow joint—anterior (front) view

An acute injury is due to a sudden force, such as a hard throw.

Diagnosis and treatment

There are three degrees of severity for a *sprain*. In most cases it is a mild sprain causing tenderness of the ligament, mild instability if excessive valgus movement is performed and loss of *flexibility* of the wrist flexor (bending forwards) muscles.

Treatment for the early stages of an overuse injury involves correction of faulty technique and any other *biomechanical abnormality*, electrotherapy such as *ultrasound therapy, massage, strengthening exercises* and medial side elbow *taping*. *Arthroscopy* may be required if the injury is severe. If an acute injury causes a grade 3 (severe) tear, surgical repair is usually required. Treatment for a grade 2 (moderate) tear includes *rest* and *ice*, protection in a *brace* and *strengthening exercises* for 3 to 6 weeks.

Elbow osteochondritis dissecans

See *Little Leaguer's elbow*.

Elbow posterior dislocation

An acute injury that displaces the joint between the bones of the *elbow joint*. The displacement forces the upper end of the radius and ulnar (forearm bones) in a backwards (posterior) direction. The *dislocation* usually occurs in either a contact sport or when falling from a height, such as during *pole vault*. In many cases there is also a *radius head fracture*.

Treatment and return to sport

Checks should be made that there are no complications, in particular making sure the blood supply to the forearm is intact by checking the radial *pulse* at the wrist. An absent pulse should be treated as a medical emergency requiring urgent hospital treatment. Reduction of the dislocation is performed as shown in the diagram. If a fracture is also present *immobilisation* in a sling is usually recommended for 2 to 3 weeks.

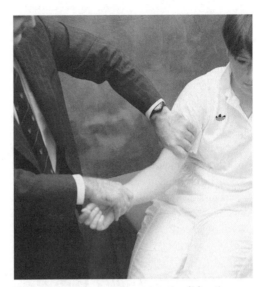

Technique used to put elbow posterior dislocation back into place

After the injury has been stabilised *flexibility exercises* are recommended as soon as possible to prevent loss of elbow movements, such as straightening (extension) and bending (flexion). *Non-steroidal anti-inflammatory drugs (NSAIDs)* should be taken for 3 months to prevent joint *ossification*, and *strengthening exercises* are also advisable. A full return to sport usually takes at least 12 weeks.

Electrical impedance

A reasonably accurate method of measuring *body composition*. It involves connecting four electrodes to an athlete's body, two at the wrist and two at the ankle. An electric current is passed through the body. Fat slows down the flow of electricity, whereas other tissues, such as muscle, increase the flow. The total amount of electric current flow is a measure of the *relative body fat*.

Electrocardiogram (ECG)

A diagnostic technique that measures the electrical activity and function of the *heart*. Each *heartbeat* produces a distinctive electrical pattern of peaks and dips, including the P wave, QRS complex and T wave. There are characteristic changes to the ECG pattern that may reflect an underlying problem with the heart, including *coronary heart disease, myocarditis* and *cardiac arrhythmia*.

An Ambulatory (Holter) ECG is a portable device for ECG monitoring during normal daily activity. It may be particularly useful in the diagnosis of arrhythmia or intermittent ischemia, the evaluation of drug therapy and in detecting a malfunction with a pacemaker. An ECG is an integral part of conducting an *exercise stress test*. ECG is called EKG in North America.

Electromyography (EMG)

A diagnostic test that checks how a muscle is working by measuring its electrical activity. It is used, for example, to confirm the diagnosis of a muscle disorder, such as muscular dystrophy or *nerve root compression* in the spine that has caused muscle weakness.

Electrodes are attached to the skin or inserted into the body via a needle that gives an electrical stimulus to *motor units*, which generate *muscle contractions*. These contractions are associated with a distinct pattern on a graph when muscles are working normally. Changes to this pattern indicate the presence of disease or injury.

Electrotherapy

A group of treatments provided by machines that are powered by electricity that generate different types of waves or energy, including ultrasound, low-voltage electrical stimulus or electromagnetic energy. They are often recommended for exercise, sports-related injuries and diseases such as osteoarthritis.

The machines, also called modalities, include *ultrasound therapy, transcutaneous electrical nerve stimulation (TENS), interferential therapy, high voltage galvanic stimulation, diathermy, magnetic field*

therapy, neuromuscular electrical stimulator (NMES) and *laser therapy*.

Elevation

A treatment for an *acute injury,* that aims to minimise the formation of oedema and *swelling*. It involves raising the injured part higher than or at the same level as the heart, such as lying on a couch and placing a sprained ankle on top of several pillows, or raising the injured part so that it is above the *proximal* part of a limb (the part that is closest to the spine), like placing an injured hand in a sling.

Elevation of the injured part reduces blood flow to the injured area and encourages the return of blood into the *veins* and lymph fluid into the *lymphatic system* to be carried back to the heart.

Elevation should be done as part of the combination of treatments called *RICE (rest, ice, compression and elevation)*.

Elite

Participation in a sport at a formal level where, in most cases, athletes can earn a partial or full income. Elite sports people have the opportunity to win prize money, sign a work contract and receive advertising sponsorship, payments for public appearances and government funds. They are also called sports professionals.

Endocrine system

Ductless glands that produce and release *hormones* into the blood. These hormones contain instructions to perform actions in specific tissues, such as *erythropoietin (EPO)* which is produced by cells in the kidneys that contain instructions for bone marrow cells to produce more red blood cells. EPO is released into the blood by the kidneys, but only communicates with bone marrow cells that have a special chemical site for receiving the hormone whereas other body cells do not.

Exercise and sport

The immediate role of the endocrine system and its hormones is in metabolism and hydration. For example, the pancreas releases the hormone glucagon during exercise that sends instructions to the liver to increase the supply of *glucose* into the blood that circulates to the muscles in the body.

Hormones are also involved in long-term changes in the body. For example, *human growth hormone (HGH)*, which is produced by the pituitary gland of the brain in response to exercise and training, sends instructions to the muscles of the body to grow larger.

Endorphin

A chemical substance naturally produced by the body that has a painkilling effect, similar to the drug morphine. The body produces more endorphins in people participating in endurance or long distance exercise or sports. A portable electrical device called a transcutaneous electrical nerve stimulation (TENS) may achieve endorphins release. They reduce *pain* by floating around the body in the blood and attaching to opiate receptors in the brain and spinal cord, the same ones that morphine acts on. They are also called beta-endorphins and may be regarded as a slow-acting *neurotransmitter*.

Endurance

Performing an activity continuously for a long time. It relies on the aerobic metabolic systems to supply energy to the muscles. For example, running a marathon (42.2 km/26.2 miles), swimming 1500 m, participating in a triathlon and going on a 3-day trek are endurance activities.

The ability to perform these activities is an indication of *aerobic fitness*, which can be improved by participating in *aerobic training*. Specific muscles also can increase their endurance strength (see *Endurance training for muscles*). Athletes born with a higher proportion of *slow-twitch (ST) muscle fibres* in their muscles are more likely to achieve higher levels of aerobic fitness and perform better in endurance activities.

Endurance training for muscles

Regular participation in activities that aim to increase a muscle's ability to sustain a contraction or perform repeated contractions. To gain muscle endurance it is necessary to improve aerobic fitness by increasing the oxidative enzyme capacity of the *slow-twitch (ST) muscle fibres* and increase the density of mitochondria in the muscle fibres.

This requires low load, high repetition exercise (see *Strength training*). The amount of resistance can be increased gradually. This will stimulate cellular adaptation and facilitate endurance strength gains.

Energy

The potential to perform an activity and the actual performance of an activity. In humans it can range from activities of the whole body, such as exercise and sport, down to microscopic activities, such as the biological and chemical processes that occur in individual cells.

The origin of energy in humans is the sun. Solar energy is converted into plant and animal growth. The gastrointestinal system breaks down these foods into a form that can be transported via the blood to the cells where chemical processes, which are part of *metabolism*, extract the energy for activities such as muscle contractions.

The energy that potentially can be yielded from food varies according to the type. For example, carbohydrate food contains 17 kJ (see *Kilojoules*) (4 Cal) of energy per gram compared to 37 kJ (9 Cal) per gram of fat. Energy is also measured in *kilocalories*.

Exercise and sport

The three main energy producing systems for *muscle contractions* in exercise and sport are: the *creatine phosphate system* and *glycolytic system*, both anaerobic systems that don't use oxygen; and the aerobic systems that do use oxygen, predominantly *carbohydrate oxidation*, which is assisted by *fat metabolism* and *protein oxidation*.

For example, in a 100 m sprint at the elite level the anaerobic systems, which can only work for a maximum of 20 seconds when performing at maximum speed, supply nearly 100 per cent of the energy. In a 400 m sprint, which is performed at less than maximum speed, the anaerobic system lasts slightly longer than 20 seconds and supplies about 60 per cent of the total energy needs of the muscles and then the aerobic carbohydrate oxidation system kicks in to supply the remaining 40 per cent to complete the race.

Of course, the total amount of energy required varies according to many factors, including the type of muscle fibres and fitness. For instance, 400 m sprinters need a high proportion of *fast-twitch (FT) muscle fibres* as well as good anaerobic fitness and aerobic fitness, defined as requiring a lower amount of energy to get the muscles to perform the same activity. A marathon runner needs *slow-twitch (ST) muscle fibres* as well as *aerobic fitness*.

Energy supply

The nutritional source of *energy* in the body. *Carbohydrate* and *fat* are the main sources during exercise and sport. *Protein* makes a relatively small contribution, except when there is an insufficient energy intake such as a depletion of carbohydrate stores. The primary need for energy during exercise and sport is to produce *adenosine triphosphate (ATP)*, which is used to produce *muscle contractions*.

Carbohydrate

Carbohydrates are categorised according to how quickly they are digested in the *gastrointestinal system*, absorbed through the gut and their subsequent affect on blood glucose levels, which is called the *glycaemic index (GI)*.

Foods with a high GI are quickly digested and absorbed, resulting in a rapid and high rise in blood glucose levels. This is particularly helpful for athletes who need an immediate external supply of carbohydrates during exercise.

Low GI foods are more slowly digested and result in a slower but continuous release of glucose into the blood. This can be beneficial for endurance athletes participating in activities lasting for an hour or

more when eaten in a *pre-event meal*. It also may help to replenish glucose stores after activity (see *Post-activity eating*).

Glucose is stored in the liver and muscles as *glycogen*, which is a long chain of glucose molecules bonded together. When energy is required, glycogen is broken down into glucose and released into the blood to be carried around the body.

Glycogen needs to be replenished everyday. The amount of stored glycogen varies according to the *aerobic fitness* levels. Unfit people eating a 50 per cent carbohydrate diet have muscle glycogen stores of 80–90 millimoles per kilogram (mmol/kg), whereas highly fit athletes have stores up to 135 mmol/kg. Eating a 60–70 per cent carbohydrate diet can increase these stores up to 200 mmol/kg.

Fat

Fat provides the body's largest store of potential energy. The average person has at least 294 000 kJ (70 000 Cal) of energy stored as fat in their body, which would be enough to let them run 1200 km (750 miles). In contrast, the average person's glycogen stores equals 8400 kJ (2000 Cal), which would provide energy for a 40 km (25 miles) run.

However, fat requires more oxygen to release its energy to produce adenosine triphosphate (ATP) (see *Fat metabolism*) compared to carbohydrates, which makes it less efficient, especially during high-intensity activities such as fast running.

Protein

The breakdown of protein contributes 5–10 per cent of total energy needs, which occurs through *protein oxidation*. The contribution of protein increases the longer the activity and as carbohydrate stores diminish. Protein is also used to repair damaged tissue, which often occurs during activities lasting more than an hour. As a result, the protein requirements are greater for an endurance athlete.

Short duration and high-intensity activity

In high-intensity activity (see *Aerobic training* and *Metabolic equivalent (MET)*) lasting 1 to 2 minutes, such as in an 800 m run, all of the energy is supplied from muscle stores of glycogen. Fat is too slow for supplying the energy required.

In addition, this type of activity relies on the anaerobic *glycolytic system* as well as aerobic carbohydrate oxidation to break down the glucose that comes from the glycogen. The former leads to a build up of lactic acid, which impedes the mobilisation of fat from adipose tissue where it is stored.

Moderate-intensity activity

The body prefers to use fat to supply its energy when doing moderate-intensity activities such as brisk walking. *Adrenaline* and *human growth hormone (HGH)* production is increased in people who regularly exercise at this intensity. These hormones promote the release of free fatty acids from fat stores in adipose tissue, which then undergoes *fat metabolism* to produce energy for muscle contractions. This level of intensity is recommended for weight loss (see *Fat-loss diet*).

Long duration

The longer the duration of an activity, the greater the supply of energy from fat. Fat may supply, for example, as much as 70 per cent of the energy needs of a moderate intensity activity lasting 4 to 6 hours.

Enkephalin

A chemical substance naturally produced by the body that is a painkiller like *endorphin*. It also can cause sedation (sleepiness) and is mood-altering.

Enlarged heart

See *Hypertrophic cardiomyopathy*.

Enzyme

A protein-based compound that triggers off or speeds up a chemical process. There are thousands of enzymes in the human body that play key roles in *metabolism*. Each one is designed for a specific chemical process. For example, when bread is eaten the enzymes in the digestive system break it down into its basic components, such as *carbohydrate* to glucose. The glucose is absorbed through the gut into the bloodstream and eventually transported to cells (as a long chain of bonded glucose called glycogen), where each glucose molecule is broken down by more enzymes into pyruvic acid in a 12-stage process called the *glycolytic system*.

Ephedrine

A stimulant drug that triggers the release of *noradrenaline*, a neurotransmitter involved in the 'fight or flight' response. It is used in many over-the-counter cold and flu and hay fever medications, such as Sudafed, Sinutab, Codral cold and flu, Demazin cold and flu, Benadryl and Dimetapp cough and flu tablets.

It is a *drug banned in sport* according to the World Anti-Doping Agency (WADA). Athletes use it for cheating to achieve similar effects as *amphetamines*. Side effects include *anxiety*, agitation, restlessness and *headaches*.

Epilepsy

A neurological disorder of the brain that causes a person to experience more than two *seizures*. In the large majority of cases the cause is unknown. The most common of the known causes are *head injury* and *stroke*. A seizure affecting most or all of the brain can cause daydreaming (petit mal) or a collapse into unconsciousness with jerky movements of the body (grand mal). A seizure affecting part of the brain can cause symptoms such as numbness, muscle twitching or psychological disturbances.

Diagnosis and treatment

The diagnosis involves combining information such as a description of a seizure by an observer, and results of an electroencephalogram (EEG) and *magnetic resonance imaging (MRI)*.

Treatments include anti-epileptic medications, exercise and sport (see *Exercise for health*) and avoiding aggravating factors such as sleep deprivation and drugs such as marijuana (see *Cannabinoids*).

Seizures finish spontaneously and are rarely life threatening. It is best to remain with the person, protect the arms and legs from injury and, immediately after the movements have finished, arrange medical care. Do not put an object in the person's mouth.

Exercise and sport

There is little or no increased risk of injury due to having epilepsy for most sports. The exception is that people with frequent seizures should avoid *scuba diving* and *horse riding sports*, and sports in which impairment in split-second timing is dangerous—for example, *downhill skiing*. *Swimming*, *cycling* and *cross-country skiing* should be done with a companion or under supervision.

Epinephrine

See *Adrenaline*.

Epiphysis

A secondary centre for *bone* growth in children and adolescents. It is located in the rounded ends of the *long bones* of the arms, hands, legs and feet.

Growth occurs through a process called *ossification* where hyaline cartilage is converted into hard and rigid bone tissue. The *diaphysis*, also called the primary ossification centre, first appears in the embryo at 7 to 8 weeks.

By the time of birth all long bones have also developed an epiphysis. In the arms and legs there is an epiphysis at each end of the bone. Only one epiphysis develops, usually at the distal end of the smaller long bones of the metacarpals, metatarsals and phalanges in the hands and feet.

Throughout childhood the epiphyses gradually ossify. An area in between the diaphysis and epiphysis, called the epiphyseal plate or *growth plate*, persists through into puberty and adolescence. It is a relatively clear area on an X-ray, which only shows ossified bone.

It is the site for continued bone growth until the diaphyses and epiphyses eventually join together and fuse, signalling full maturity of the skeleton (see *Adolescents*).

EPO

See *Erythropoietin* (EPO).

Equestrian

See *Horse riding sports*.

Ergogenic aids

Ingesting a nutrient, *vitamin* or *mineral* in addition to those eaten in foods with the aim of improving performance in exercise and sport.

The International Olympic Committee (IOC) and other organisations permit the use of ergogenic aids. However, many of them require more research to support the claimed benefits. For example, it is not enough for an ergogenic aid to have a plausible scientific explanation such as enhancing metabolism within a cell when it is questionable whether the substance even reaches the cell, due to not surviving the digestion process intact or having molecules that are too big to pass across the cell membrane. Greater care needs to be taken to ensure an ergogenic aid does what it claims to do and with a minimum of harmful side effects.

Commonly used ergogenic aids include *creatine, beta-hydroxy methylbutyrate (HMB), sodium bicarbonate, colostrum, fat-burning stacks, pyruvate, amino acids, antioxidants* and *vitamin and mineral supplementation*. Also called supplementation.

Ergolytic

A negative effect on performance in exercise and sport. It is opposite to the effect that *ergogenic aids* aim to achieve, which is to enhance performance.

Erythropoietin (EPO)

A synthetic form of the *hormone* that increases the amount of *red blood cells* and haemoglobin in the blood leading to increased oxygen-carrying capacity. It is used to treat people with anaemia due to kidney failure.

It is also a *drug banned in sport* according to the World Anti-Doping Agency (WADA). Athletes use it to improve endurance in sports, such as cycling and long distance running, because the extra oxygen leads to improved *carbohydrate oxidation* and *fat metabolism*.

The main dangers of EPO are blood clotting leading to *deep vein thrombosis* (DVT) and *stroke*, which have caused death in a number of endurance cyclists.

Eversion

A movement in the *ankle* joint and foot that means turning the sole of the foot so that it faces outwards, away from the midline (also see *Foot and toes*). For example, when both feet are next to each other with the ankle bones touching, it means turning the sole of the foot away from the other foot. Eversion is a combination of movements that occur at a number of joints, mainly the sub-talar and mid-tarsal joints, including pronation, abduction and dorsiflexion. It is the opposite of *inversion*.

Exercise

A physical activity that is performed in a structured and organised manner. Unlike sport, it does not involve participating in a competition or winning matches and is not governed by a set of rules and regulations.

Exercise is done for recreation and health, particularly the prevention and treatment of disease, illness and injury. For example, walking and slow jogging may be done as part of a *warm-up* before a run. An *exercise for health* program can reduce the risk of a wide range of conditions, including *coronary heart disease*, being *overweight*, *depression* and *stress*.

Treatment for a broken arm may include *flexibility exercises* to restore the normal movement of joints and muscles.

Exercise bike

Fitness equipment designed for stationary cycling. Regular use can be an effective form of *aerobic training*. An exercise bike also can be used to test *aerobic fitness*.

It was invented more than 150 years ago. Now there are hundreds of models on the market. Each bike provides resistance to pedalling. The various designs include: brake pad and strap-resistance that rely on friction; fan-wheel, which uses air-resistance; and magnets encased around the wheel that provide electro-magnetic-resistance. Some models include adjustable handles for simultaneous upper-body training.

Exercise bike

There are no indications that an exercise bike achieves greater aerobic fitness than outdoors cycling, though obviously it can be more convenient. A disadvantage is that some users may pedal at a fast speed, but not achieve an *overload* because the pedal resistance is too low. Poor body positioning may lead to a *biomechanical abnormality*, which can increase the risk of an *overuse injury*.

Exercise for health

Regular participation in activities that aim to prevent health problems and improve existing disease or illness. The main types of exercise that are good for health are *aerobic training* and *strength training*. In general it is recommended to combine the two types.

If the intention is to participate in high-intensity activities, such as jogging or squash, a *medical clearance* is recommended to check overall health and identify problems that may prevent or modify participation. This can be obtained from your doctor, *physiotherapist* or *fitness trainer* (also see

Cycling for pleasure is a moderate-intensity physical activity

Exercise prescription). Starting and sticking with regular physical activity may require planning such as using the *stages of change* model of behavioural change.

Aerobic training

This type of training improves aerobic fitness and can help prevent *coronary heart disease, stroke, diabetes, obesity*, being *overweight* and certain types of *cancer*. It is also beneficial for mental health problems, including *depression, anxiety* and *stress*.

The current public health recommendation for improving aerobic fitness is to do at least 30 minutes or more of moderate intensity *physical activity* on most if not all days of the week.

Moderate-intensity may be defined as any activity that expends energy that is the *metabolic equivalent* (3–6 METs or 4–7 kcal/min) of brisk walking, gentle swimming, gardening, ballroom dancing and doubles tennis.

For the average sedentary person this equals a brisk walk at a speed that quickens the breath but does not prevent a normal, flowing conversation. Physical activity does not have to be done in a single block of 30 minutes. It can be accumulated throughout the day, such as three times 10 minutes. High-intensity physical activity, such as jogging or swimming laps, can achieve a minor additional benefit over and above moderate intensity activity.

The main aim of losing weight is to reduce the amount of fat in the body. Carbohydrates are the main supply of energy in people participating in high-intensity exercise and sport. However, fat is the preferred energy supply in people participating in moderate-intensity activity such as brisk walking.

MEASURES OF INTENSITY OF A PHYSICAL ACTIVITY

Low-intensity is equivalent to breathing exertion ranging from 'no effect on breathing' up to the point that 'shortness of breath is noticed' = 30–49 per cent of $VO_2 max$ = 35–59 per cent of *maximum heart rate estimation* (220 – age) = 11 on the *Borg Perceived exertion scale*.

Moderate-intensity is equivalent to a range from 'shortness of breath is noticed' up to 'the point that whistling or normal continuous conversation is just possible' = 50–74 per cent of VO_2 max = 60–79 per cent of maximum heart rate estimation = 13 on the Borg Perceived exertion scale.

High-intensity is a range from the point that 'whistling or normal continuous conversation is just possible' up to the point that 'whistling or normal continuous conversation is impossible' = 75–84 per cent of VO$_2$ max = 80–89 per cent of maximum heart rate estimation = 15 on the Borg perceived exertion scale.

Strength training

The muscles that should be strengthened are the chest muscles, upper back muscles, shoulder muscles, buttocks, quadriceps and hamstring.

Strength increase is achieved when an *overload* is placed on a muscle, such as lifting a weight that is heavy enough to make it feel fatigued. It is recommended to train at 80 per cent of maximum strength, as measured by the maximum weight that can be moved in one full movement, which is called one *repetition maximum* (1-RM).

This weight should be lifted for a set of 10 repetitions repeated three times for a total of 30 repetitions in each session, three sessions per week. *Flexibility training* should be done at the same time to prevent reduced muscle flexibility.

Strength improvement can help treat *depression*, reduce the risk of *osteoporosis* and falling and also contribute to *coronary heart disease* and *stroke* prevention.

Exercise-induced asthma (EIA)

Asthma triggered off by participation in a physical activity such as exercise or sport. Physical activity is one of the most common triggers for *asthma*, which is defined as a disease of the lungs that causes temporary narrowing of the airways. It affects about 80 per cent of sufferers and is often the first form of asthma that leads to a diagnosis.

There are two theories about the process that causes the airways to release chemicals leading to airway narrowing including: 1) the airways become dehydrated; and 2) the airways are cooled during activity and then warm up again after cessation of activity, leading to a sudden increase in blood flow.

Despite the lack of certainty over the cause, it is known that breathing in dry air or cold air can trigger an attack. It is most commonly found in participants of *middle distance running, long distance running, downhill skiing, cross-country skiing, swimming, aerobics, cycling, dancing* and *basketball*.

Diagnosis

The severity of symptoms and attacks are the same as for other forms of asthma. Symptoms can begin from within a few minutes after commencement of exercise, up to 3 hours after cessation of exercise. A refractory response is another feature, where symptoms are less severe when renewing participation in exercise after an earlier attack.

The diagnosis is confirmed when preventive medication such as *sodium cromoglycate* or *nedocromil sodium* taken immediately before exercise prevents an attack.

More sophisticated tests exist, such as the exercise-challenge test, which involves measurements of breathing during high-intensity activity such as running on a treadmill, and bronchial provocation test, which involves breathing in saline in increasing dosages or voluntary hyperventilation of dry air to test if airway narrowing is triggered off.

Treatment

One general approach that is recommended is to take preventive medications such as sodium cromoglycate and nedocromil sodium, in combination with *corticosteroids (inhaled)* taken everyday to reduce inflammation, while keeping a *bronchodilator* in reserve for rescue medication if an attack occurs. Alternatively, it may be recommended to take short-acting bronchodilators 10 to 15 minutes prior to exercise or long-acting bronchodilators 15 to 30 minutes beforehand.

Other important measures include avoiding cold and dry air, performing an adequate *warm-up* and *warm-down*, and using equipment such as a *nasal dilator* and *nasal breathing* during activity to warm and humidify the air.

If an attack does occur the treatment should be the same as recommended for other forms of *asthma*. For example, if symptoms of an attack occur, participation in the activity should be stopped immediately.

If the attack is mild to moderate, take two puffs from a bronchodilator inhaler, waiting 4 minutes, followed by another two puffs and assess the response. If there is no improvement, or especially if symptoms worsen, medical care should be sought as soon as possible. If symptoms completely clear (this usually requires 15 to 60 minutes) participation in the exercise is permitted.

Exercise physiologist

A person working in the science of exercise physiology, which investigates and explains how the human body functions during exercise and sport. The work is usually performed for a professional team, sport institution or university. The practical aims of the work are to provide information and analysis to improve performance and prevent problems occurring during exercise and sport. Research is conducted in the laboratory and out in the field.

Exercise prescription

A detailed recommendation for exercise or sport given by a doctor or other health/fitness professional. It is beneficial for people with a specific health problem; for example, *coronary heart disease*, *osteoarthritis*, *asthma* and being *overweight*. It is also given to people starting out with a specific type of training, such as lifting weights for strength training.

A prescription includes choosing an exercise or sport that best suits your health goals. For example, a person who wants to lose weight may think that jogging is the best activity, and not realise that brisk walking is more effective for burning up fat.

A prescription involves deciding the intensity, duration and how often it should be done and how to prevent injuries. It should match one's skills and interests. It is also important to take into account that many people drop out of regular participation in exercise or sport within a year of starting. The *stages of change* model for health behaviour change provides a useful framework.

Exercise stress test

Exercise stress test is conducted to detect the presence of damage caused by heart disease. The measurements and assessment include an *electrocardiogram (ECG)*, *blood pressure*, *heart rate* and general symptoms.

It is the most commonly used test to diagnose *coronary artery disease* and provide a measure of the maximum permitted intensity levels for *aerobic training* in people who have a heart problem, such as after a *heart attack*.

It involves exercising on a treadmill or exercise bike and gradually progressing from low-intensity activity, such as slow walking, up to maximal-intensity activity, which varies according to fitness levels; for example, brisk walking in unfit people. The test is stopped if abnormalities occur, including significant chest pain, excessive fatigue, severe shortness of breath and abnormalities in the ECG such as *cardiac arrhythmias*.

Not all exercise stress tests are 100 per cent accurate at diagnosing coronary heart disease. For example, a test that finds the disease is present in a 55-year-old male with angina (chest pain) is associated with a 90 per cent probability of being correct. But in younger-aged people the result may be correct in only 10 per cent of cases.

As a result, doctors differ in their opinions as to the appropriate age that an exercise stress test should be recommended as part of a *medical clearance*.

Exocrine glands

Glands that produce substances that are released through a duct to a local area, such as the salivary glands in the mouth.

Expiration

Breathing air out of the lungs. It also refers to feelings of not being able to continue during an activity, usually due to overwhelming feelings of *tiredness* or fatigue.

Extensibility

The ability of a muscle to be stretched. See *Flexibility*.

Extension

A movement of a *synovial joint* that means straightening the elbow and knee and moving in a direction pointing towards the back of the body in other joints. For example, from a starting position by the side of your body, placing your hand into your back pocket produces extension of the shoulder joint. Extension is also known as dorsiflexion in the ankle joint (and sometimes in the wrist joint). It is the opposite of *flexion*.

Extensor tendinosis

The medical name for the injury popularly known as *tennis elbow*.

Extensor tendinosis (foot)

An overuse injury of the tendons that move the foot upwards, causes pain on the top of the middle of the foot. The *tendinosis* is caused by an accumulation of excessive physical forces on the tendon associated with running and wearing shoes with excessively tight laces.

Treatment includes *strengthening exercises*, particularly *eccentric* contractions and *mobilisations* of the first ray and midtarsal joints (see *Foot and toes*). Changing the lacing pattern on the shoes or placing adhesive foam to the underside of the tongue of the shoe also may be required.

External rotation

A turning movement of a *synovial joint* that produces a movement of a body part away from the midline of the body. For example, external rotation of the knee joint involves turning the front of the shin away from the other shin. It is similar to *supination*.

Extra corporeal shock wave therapy

A treatment that uses high frequency sound waves called ultrasound. Originally developed to treat kidney stones by breaking them down into fine powder, more recently it has been used to treat bone *fractures* that do not heal and unite properly, and injuries including *myositis ossificans*, *tennis elbow* and *plantar fasciitis*. However, its effectiveness is still under investigation.

Extreme sports

See *Snowboarding, Skateboarding, Cycling*.

Eye

The organ that enables vision. Each eye is made up of specialised structures. The outer, tough, transparent cornea and lens focus light that passes through the pupil to the back of the eyeball, called the retina, which contains millions of *neurons* that sense different types of light such as colour and shade. The neurons pass this information down the optic nerve to the occipital section of the *brain*, where it is understood as vision. The iris is the coloured part of the outer eye.

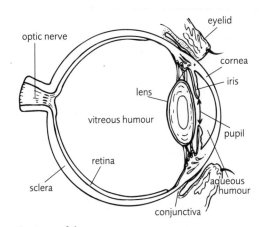

Anatomy of the eye

The two eyes work together to enhance the information they receive, such as determining the distance of an object's location.

Eye injuries

See *Face pain and injuries*.

Eyelid laceration

A cut to the eyelid due to a sudden forceful blow. A medical check-up is recommended to exclude damage to the *eye* itself and underlying bone. Treatment begins with *ice* and *compression* to reduce bleeding, followed by surgery to ensure each layer of the eyelid tissue is correctly repaired.

Face and scalp skin injury

Skin damage over the face and scalp is quite common in sports such as *Australian Rules football, Rugby League, Rugby Union, ice hockey, martial arts* and *squash*. The recommended first aid is to stop playing and place *ice* and *compression* on the wound to control bleeding. A physical examination by a doctor is also recommended to check for *concussion* or bone fracture. The treatment is the same as recommended for other *skin injury*. A bruise of the skin around the eye is called a *black eye*.

Face pain and injuries

Causes

In most cases pain is caused by an *acute injury* due to a sudden, single incident, such as a collision with an opponent damaging the teeth. Infrequently the cause is an *overuse injury*, where pain gets worse over

a period of weeks or months due to an accumulation of excessive forces.

In most cases the affected structures are easily identified based on the location of the pain. The diagnosis also requires defining the nature of the damage, such as a lens dislocation or haemorrhage of the retina.

Diagnosis

The diagnosis is made by combining information gathered about the *history*, *physical examination* and relevant investigations and tests.

An inability to bite down evenly suggests *maxilla fracture* or *jaw fracture*. Pain in one or both jaw joints may be due to a *temporomandibular joint sprain* or *temporomandibular joint pain*. Reduced sensation over the skin below the eye and the upper gum and lip, a protruding or sunken eye and double vision on upward gaze may be an *orbit blow-out fracture*.

Specific *eye* injuries include symptoms such as blurred vision (*corneal abrasion* or *lens dislocation*), sensitivity to light (*subconjunctival haemorrhage*),

Causes of face pain and injuries

Location	Common	Less common	Not to be missed
Face and scalp	• Face and scalp skin injury		
Nose	• Nasal bone fracture • Nosebleed		
Ear	• Cauliflower ear • Ear infection	• Eardrum rupture	
Eye	• Corneal abrasion • Black eye • Subconjunctival haemorrhage • Eyelid laceration	• Chemical burns • Hyphema	• Retinal detachment • Lens dislocation • Orbit blow-out fracture
Teeth	• Tooth fracture • Tooth avulsion		
Face bones	• Temporomandibular joint sprain • Temporomandibular joint pain	• Maxilla fracture • Jaw fracture • Cheekbone fracture	•

bleeding (*hyphema*) and flashes of light or the appearance of a 'curtain' spreading across the field of vision (*retinal detachment*).

Bleeding from the ear or impaired hearing suggests *eardrum rupture* of the eardrum. Earache, itchiness and impaired hearing are indications of an *ear infection*. An *X-ray* or other radiological investigation may be required to confirm a fracture.

Fainting

See *Loss of consciousness*.

Fair play

Participating in sport within the rules and spirit of the game. It follows the belief that each player should be enabled to perform at their best with the only hindrance coming from their skills, health and the vagaries of the environment, such as weather or variations in a playing field.

The rules of a game should be clearly understood by all participants. Players must allow a referee or umpire to decide whether a rule has been transgressed. However, players also have a responsibility to make the effort to play according to the rules. This may mean correcting an umpire's decision to one's own disadvantage, such as admitting that an opponent's tennis stroke bounced inside the court when it has been ruled out.

The spirit of the game refers to informal and unwritten rules, such as basic human decency, *sportsmanship* and not breaking the rules intentionally in the hope that you won't get caught. All sports pride themselves on some degree of fair play. It has been said that in recent decades acts of fair play have become less common.

Family physician

See *General practitioner*.

Fartlek

A type of *interval training* for long distance runners that aims to increase *anaerobic fitness* and *aerobic fitness*. Fartlek is the Swedish word for 'speed play'. It involves alternating between slow, moderate and fast running speeds during *long distance running*.

Fascia

A collection of *connective tissue* that surrounds an organ, connects together different body parts or forms a dividing layer between groups of muscles, such as in the *shin*.

Fast food

A meal that is provided quickly and conveniently by a restaurant or shop. Many contain high amounts of fat, particularly the unhealthy kind such as *saturated fats*, and low levels of healthy nutrients, such as *vitamins* and *minerals*.

There is nothing wrong with an occasional high-fat, fast food meal. However, when eaten too often it can increase the risk of becoming *overweight* or developing *obesity*, which is associated with an increased risk of *coronary heart disease* and certain types of *cancer*.

It is preferable to make fast food choices that have a lower fat content such as; two slices of vegetarian

Vegetarian pizza is a healthier fast food choice

or seafood pizza with a thin crust; vegetarian or seafood, tomato-based pasta; bread/pita with low-fat toppings such as tabouli; lightly fried vegetables, seafood or lean beef on steamed rice; chicken souvlaki; barbeque chicken with the skin removed; desserts such as fruit salad, sorbet, gelati and yoghurt-based ice cream.

It is recommended to avoid hamburgers with the lot, meat-lover's or salami pizzas, curries in coconut milk or ghee, fried rice or noodles, deep fried chips, chocolate, biscuits or cake, potato, corn chips and full-fat ice cream.

Fast-twitch (FT) muscle fibre

A *muscle fibre* that can contract quickly and is best suited for activities that require *power* and explosive strength like *sprinting*, *weight lifting* and swinging a golf club.

Physiology
FT muscle fibres switch on twice as fast as *slow-twitch (ST) muscle fibres*; 50 microseconds compared to 110 microseconds. This is due to fast ATPase, a fast-working enzyme for releasing the energy from *adenosine triphosphate (ATP)*, the main source of energy for muscle contractions.

FT fibres also absorb calcium ions at a faster rate which is important for muscle contraction. In addition the motor neurons (nerve cells) that bring signals from the brain to switch on muscle contraction are faster and reach more fibres than those supplying ST fibres.

Exercise and sport
The amount of power required for an activity determines the proportion of FT and ST fibres that are switched on. For instance, the faster you run the greater the number of FT fibres.

The proportions of FT and ST fibres that make up each muscle varies from person to person, with the average being 50 per cent each. A person born with a higher percentage of FT fibres is more likely to achieve high levels of fitness during *anaerobic training* and *strength training*.

Fasting

A method of achieving quick weight loss, often when *making weight* for a sport. While weight is certainly lost with this method, it is also accompanied by losses of *glycogen* stores, muscle mass and fluid, causing *dehydration*, tiredness and reduced ability to achieve optimal performance. If it is done repeatedly it can reduce the *resting metabolic rate (RMR)*, which makes it even harder to achieve weight loss.

Fat

A chemical compound made up of many carbon (C) and hydrogen (H) atoms and a few oxygen (O) atoms, which form basic units called fatty acids combined with glycerol molecules. It is also called a lipid.

The body uses fat for many essential functions: absorbing essentials *vitamins* from the gut into the blood including vitamins A, D, E and K; in the construction of myelin sheaths that surround many *neurons* (nerve cells) and the outer membrane of cells: and an insulating role to maintain body *temperature*.

It is also an important source of *energy* for sustaining human life and its activities. It contains the highest concentration of energy of any of the nutrients; 1 g = 37 kJ (8 Cal).

There are many forms of fat including: free fatty acids; *triglycerides*; and phospholipids, which have a role in transporting cholesterol around the body. Fat is mostly stored in the body in adipose tissue as triglyceride, which is made up of three fatty acids and one glycerol.

There are two types of fat: unsaturated and saturated. *Saturated fats* are found in foods such as red meat, dairy products and most confectionary. Unsaturated fats are divided between *monounsaturated fats* and *polyunsaturated fats*. Many foods tend to be dominant in one type. For example, olive oil and avocado mostly contain monounsaturated fats.

Diet

Fat is an essential part of our diet. But at the same time, a high-fat diet, particularly one containing an excessive proportion of saturated fats, is a cause of being *overweight* and *obesity*, which are associated with *hypertension* (high blood pressure), *coronary heart disease*, *diabetes*, gallstones and some types of *cancer*.

On the other hand, fats such as monosaturates and omega fatty acids have been found to have a protective effect against coronary heart disease, as long as they are eaten in moderate amounts.

Exercise and sport

Carbohydrates are the main supply of energy in people participating in high-intensity exercise and sport (see *Aerobic training* and *Metabolic equivalent (MET)*). However, fat is the preferred energy supply in people participating in moderate-intensity activity, such as exercise and sport that expends the equivalent amount of energy as brisk walking, which makes it the preferred exercise for weight loss (see *Overweight*).

In addition, the longer the duration of an activity the greater the usage of fat for energy. It is particularly important for *ultra long distance sports*.

A healthy diet for participation in exercise and sport, as well as disease prevention, includes a daily intake of 25–30 per cent of total energy needs derived from fat. For regular participation in moderate intensity activities this equals 70–80 g a day. For high-intensity activities it is 80–100 g a day.

Foods

Fat is found in a wide range of foods, including dairy products, soya products, red meat, chicken, fish, nuts, legumes and confectionary such as ice cream, cakes, biscuits and chocolate. Oils are liquid fats at room temperature. There is little to no fat in fruit and vegetables. Cereals and grains contain varying amounts.

Fat-burning stacks

A mixture of substances including herbs and drugs used to increase *fat metabolism* in order to increase weight loss. A non-herbal stack includes *caffeine*, *ephedrine* and *aspirin*. The herbal version contains guarana, ephedra and willowbark.

Fat content of foods

Food	Amount (Aust)	Amount (USA)	Energy (kJ)	Energy (Cal)
Milk, skim	1 cup/250 mL	8.5 oz	365	87
Milk, reduced fat	1 cup/250 mL	8.5 oz	505	120
Milk, whole	1 cup/250 mL	8.5 oz	675	160
Yoghurt, low fat, natural	1 tub/200 g	7 oz	500	120
Yoghurt, whole, natural	1 tub/200 g	7 oz	715	170
Yoghurt, flavoured/fruit	1 tub/200 g	7 oz	720	170
Cheese, cheddar processed	1 slice/30 g	1 oz	415	100
Cheese, ricotta	100 g	1.3 oz	615	145
Cheese, cottage, low fat	100 g	1.3 oz	610	145
Cheese, camembert	30 g	1 oz	390	93
Cheese, cream	30 g	1 oz	425	100
Ice cream, vanilla	100 mL/50 g	3.3 oz/1.75 oz	415	100
Beef, fillet steak, lean	85 g	3 oz	830	200
Chicken, breast, baked, no skin	90 g	3 oz	470	110
Pork, loin chop, baked, lean	70 g	2.3 oz	500	120
Ham, leg	50 g	1.7 oz	260	60
Lamb chops, lean	2 average pieces		470	110
Fish, steamed	150 g	5 oz	600	140
Oysters, raw	6 medium		180	40
Prawns, king, cooked	1		205	50
Egg, fried	1		410	100
Muesli flakes, 1 cup	40 g	1.3 oz	560	133
Weetbix, 2 biscuits	30 g	1	420	100
Cornflakes, 1 cup	30 g	1	475	110
Bread, wholemeal, 1 slice	30 g	1	280	66
Rice cakes	2		355	85
Crispbread, wholemeal, 4	25 g	0.9 oz	425	100
Biscuit, chocolate chip, 2	23 g	0.8 oz	450	110
Potato, cooked, 1 medium	150 g	5.3 oz	390	93
Rice, brown, boiled, 1 cup	160 g	5.6 oz	1000	240
Pasta, white, boiled, 1 cup	170 g	6 oz	845	200
Sweetcorn, frozen, on cob, 1 small	85 g	3 oz	470	110
Peas, green, boiled, 1/2 cup	80 g	2.8 oz	160	40
Broccoli, boiled	100 g	3.5 oz	100	25
Beans, green, boiled	100 g	3.5 oz	85	20
Apple, raw, unpeeled, cored, 1 small	100 g	3.5 oz	200	50
Pear, green, raw, unpeeled, 1 medium	160 g	5.6 oz	350	83
Orange, raw, peeled, 1 medium	180 g	6.3 oz	280	66
Banana, raw, peeled, 1 large	220 g	7.7 oz	585	140
Cantaloupe, raw, peeled, 1 cup, diced	150 g	5.3 oz	135	30
Grapes, green sultana	100 g	3.5 oz	255	60
Brazil nuts	50 g	1.8 oz	1410	335
Cashew nuts, raw	50 g	1.8 oz	1195	285
Almonds, unsalted	50 g	1.8 oz	1240	295
Peanuts	50 g	1.8 oz	1285	305
Baked beans, canned, in vegetarian sauce	250 g	8.8 oz	715	170
Lentils, boiled, red	190 g	6.7 oz	805	190
Beans, kidney, fresh, boiled	185 g	6.5 oz	890	210

Ephedrine and ephedra are not only *drugs banned in sport* according to the International Olympic Committee (IOC), they possess addictive qualities, and the amount of fat that is burned is minimal compared to conventional measures like a *fat-loss diet*.

Fat-free mass

The percentage of a person's total body weight that is composed of all tissues except for *fat*. It is an indication of the proportion of *muscle* in a person. The greater the fat-free mass, the higher the proportion of muscle. This is helpful for athletes participating in sports requiring strength, speed and power. It is also associated with a reduced risk of ill health and disease in the general population. The percentage of fat in a body is called *relative body fat*.

Fat-loss diet

The recommended foods for a person aiming to lose weight by reducing the amount of fat in the body. It involves eating a low-fat and high-carbohydrate diet. It can achieve weight loss at a rate of 0.5 to 1.0 kg (1–2 lb) per week when also combined with regular participation in exercise and sport (see *Overweight* and *Exercise for health*).

Method

The total energy intake must be appropriate for the person's height, weight, gender and level of activity. Regular participation in high-intensity activity (see *Aerobic training* and *Metabolic equivalent (MET)*), as performed by long distance running athletes, requires the highest intake. However, it should be 2000–4000 kJ (500–1000 Cal) less than the daily energy expenditure.

Of this total energy intake, 60 per cent should come from *carbohydrates*, 15 per cent *protein* and 25 per cent from *fat*. The type of carbohydrates should be complex, with a low to medium *glycaemic index* (GI). For high-intensity training, this is about 80–100 g of fat a day.

For people performing low- to moderate-intensity activity the recommendations for a weight loss diet for all adults is to eat 30–40 g of fat a day.

All foods should be nutritionally adequate and provide a complete range of essential *vitamins* and *minerals*. This includes a recommended *fibre* intake of 30–50 g a day and water intake of about 2–3 L a day. Alcohol intake should be kept to a minimum. Meals should be eaten three times a day and at regular intervals.

Fat metabolism

The chemical processes that break down *fats* to produce *adenosine triphosphate* (ATP), the main source

Fat-loss diet menu

Variety and taste are important factors influencing the ability of an athlete to adhere to a high-carbohydrate and low-fat diet. Some helpful suggestions include:

Breakfast
- Wholegrain cereal with low-fat milk and sliced fruit
- Wholemeal toast spread with fresh ricotta and fruit spread
- Toasted wholegrain muffin topped with baked beans
- Low-fat yoghurt and fresh fruit with a sprinkle of rice bran
- Pancakes topped with fromage frais and fresh strawberries

Lunch
- Wholemeal roll filled with chicken and salad
- Pita bread pocket, stuffed with tuna, tomato and spring onions
- Baked jacket potato topped with salmon and low-fat cheese
- Bowl of minestrone soup with fresh bread rolls
- Stir-fried rice with vegetables and a low-fat flavouring such as ginger

Dinner
- Lean grilled meat with jacket potatoes and steamed vegetables
- Taco shells filled with lean mince and red kidney beans served with brown rice and salad
- Vegetable lasagne made with low-fat cheese
- Stir-fried chicken with vegetables on brown rice
- Spinach fettuccine with lentil and vegetable sauce

Snacks
- Low-fat yoghurt and fruit
- Fresh, canned, stewed or dried fruit
- Raisin bread, crumpets or muffins topped with jam, honey or syrup
- Wholegrain breakfast cereal with low-fat milk
- Rice cakes topped with sliced banana and honey

of energy for *muscle contractions*. It involves four systems: lipolysis, beta oxidation, the Krebs Cycle and electron transport chain.

Physiology

Lipolysis is an anaerobic metabolic process (does not use oxygen) where an enzyme called lipase breaks down fat into glycerol and long chains of free fatty acids (FFA). *Adrenaline, noradrenaline,* cortisol and *human growth hormone (HGH)* are *hormones* involved in sending instructions to increase the activity of lipase in fat cells and the muscles that have stores of fat in them. At the start of an endurance activity the amount of cortisol produced is highest. But as the activity continues it drops off and adrenaline, noradrenaline and HGH take over.

The long chains of FFAs are transported into the mitochondria within cells by an amino acid called *L-carnitine*, where they are converted into acetyl coenzyme A (acetyl CoA) by beta oxidation, which is an aerobic metabolic process (uses oxygen). This compound then enters the Krebs Cycle and the electron transport chain (see *Carbohydrate oxidation*). FFAs and acetyl CoA are also involved in the production of ketone bodies.

Exercise and sport

The amount of oxygen required to produce ATP from the *aerobic metabolism* of fat is greater than carbohydrate oxidation, which means it is slower and less efficient. This makes carbohydrates the preferred fuel for activities such as long distance running, such as in a marathon.

However, fat is the fuel burned up towards the end of *ultra long distance sports*, such as open ocean swimming. It is also preferred during moderate-intensity activities, such as brisk walking (see *Aerobic training* and *Metabolic equivalent (MET)*), which are the recommended activities for *overweight* people who need to lose weight.

Fat pad

A tissue that fills up excess space in a *synovial joint* cavity, such as the *knee joint*. It is yellow, mainly made up of fat cells and grows as an extension of the synovium, the inner lining of the joint capsule. The main purpose of a fat pad is to even out the flow of synovial fluid, which is a lubricant that fills the joint cavity. A fat pad is also found in the deep skin tissue of the heel.

Fat pad contusion

Pain in the heel caused by landing on the heel from a height. In a few cases the pain may be an *overuse injury* due to excessive running on a hard surface and wearing *shoes* with poor heel cushioning. The recommended treatment is *rest* by avoiding the aggravating activities,

ice, wearing a heel cup (layer of cushion), *taping* and correct selection of *running shoes*.

Fat pad impingement

An overuse injury that causes pain in the front (anterior part) of the *knee joint* due to a pad of fat inside the knee joint getting caught between the kneecap (patella) and the underlying lower end of the bone. This catching occurs repeatedly over a period of weeks or months during activities that straighten out the joint such as kicking in swimming or standing for long periods of time, which causes pain to gradually get worse.

Treatment includes *taping* the patella so that it tilts forward and avoids catching the fat pad and *strengthening exercises*.

Fatigue

Feelings of tiredness. This can be a normal response to participation in training or a physical activity. However, when excessive, this can have a negative impact on a person's ability to perform an activity.

Fatigue that does not disappear after a three-day break from activity can have a number of causes, including serious disease and illness (see *Tiredness*).

Other causes are short term and often quickly reversible after an activity is completed, such as *creatine phosphate depletion, lactate fatigue,*

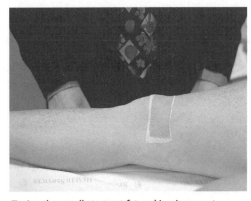

Taping the patella to treat fat pad impingement

neuromuscular fatigue, central nervous system fatigue and glycogen depletion (also called hitting the wall).

Feldenkrais

A method of increasing awareness and correcting poor methods of movement and posture that place excessive forces and stress on joints, muscles and bones. It was developed by Russian-born Israeli physicist, Moshe Feldenkrais (1904–1984). Treatment involves exercises that aim to reprogram the control of movement and improve posture, which can also benefit mental performance and achieve wellbeing and a more positive self-image.

Female athlete triad

A syndrome in women who have insufficient availability of energy during exercise and sport due to disordered eating that also leads to amenorrhea (absence of menstrual periods) and osteoporosis.

It is suggested that the disordered eating, which is a mild form of the eating disorders such as anorexia nervosa and bulimia, leads to the development of menstrual abnormalities over a period of months or years until amenorrhea is established. The possible causes of this development include reduced body fat or inadequate kilojoule/Calorie, protein or carbohydrate intake.

Amenorrhea is associated with loss of calcium in the bones, which increases the risk of developing osteoporosis (thinning and weakening of the bones), most likely due to reduced levels of oestrogen in the body. In the first 2 to 3 years following amenorrhea, the calcium loss is approximately 4 per cent per year. Loss of calcium and osteoporosis is associated with an increased risk of stress fractures.

Femoral head avascular necrosis

Degeneration and obliteration of the head of femur (thigh bone) in the hip joint due to loss of blood supply. The risk is increased following a neck of femur fracture, hip surgery and a corticosteroid injection into the joint.

It causes hip and groin pain, particularly during walking and running, and loss of flexibility and muscle weakness. The diagnosis is confirmed with X-rays or bone scans. The recommended treatments include flexibility exercises, strengthening exercises and avoiding activities that aggravate the pain. For the long term in many cases hip joint replacement surgery is required.

Femur fracture

An acute injury that causes a break in the long middle section of the thigh bone, usually due to a fall to the ground or contact with another player. It causes sudden and severe pain in the thigh and participation in the sport is immediately ceased.

The diagnosis of this fracture is made with an X-ray. Open surgery and internal fixation with metal rods are often required. A sport rehabilitation program is required to ensure a quick return to sport, which may take 3 months for non-collision sports and up to 6 months for collision sports such as football codes, ice hockey and basketball.

Femur neck stress fracture

A microfracture in the top end of the thigh bone that causes groin pain (see Hip joint). It develops gradually due to an accumulation of repeated, excessive physical loads associated with running over a period of weeks or months. The risk of this stress fracture is increased in female athletes with low oestrogen levels, such as women suffering from female athlete triad.

The pain is usually located in the groin, but is hard to pinpoint, and is made worse during a run. Bone scans and magnetic resonance imaging (MRI) are the most sensitive radiological investigations for confirming a diagnosis. The two types of fracture are 1) superior (upper) side and 2) inferior (lower) side.

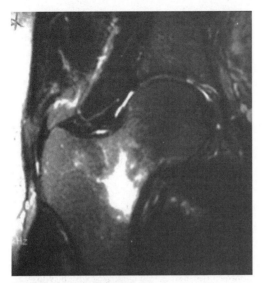

MRI of femur neck stress fracture

it doesn't affect menstrual cycles. However, a shorter luteal stage may precede menstrual abnormalities such as *amenorrhea* and *oligomenorrhea*.

Treatment

Ovulation and a normal menstrual cycle can be induced by decreasing the intensity and duration of exercise or by increasing the level of body fat. A good indication that ovulation has occurred in a particular cycle is the presence of either *premenstrual tension* or ovulation pain in the middle of the cycle. Ovulation may be confirmed by measuring the basal body temperature, which rises between 0.2–0.6°C (0.36 and 1.04°F) at the time of ovulation and remains elevated during the luteal phase.

Fever

A body temperature above the normal 37°C (98.6°F). It may cause symptoms including shivering, *headache*, sweating, flushed and hot skin and faster than normal breathing rate. Severe fever can also cause confusion or seizures.

Fever is usually due to proteins released by white blood cells of the *immune system* that are called up to defend the body against an infection of a virus or bacteria, which stimulate the body *temperature* centre in the brain. Medical care should be sought as soon as possible to make an exact diagnosis and receive treatment. Fever-reducing medications include *aspirin* and *paracetamol*.

Treatment and return to sport

Superior stress fracture requires immediate treatment, either *open surgery* and *internal fixation* or strict bed rest due to the risk of developing a complete fracture through the neck of the femur and *femoral head avascular necrosis*. Inferior stress fracture is treated with a period of *rest* for at least 6 weeks, at first using crutches and not bearing weight on the injured leg, followed by walking but not running. A gradual return to sport as part of a *sport rehabilitation* program is required, usually lasting 2 to 3 months.

Fertility problems

Women intensely participating in exercise and sport have greater difficulty becoming pregnant. It is often due to *menstruation* problems, though it may also occur with normal menstrual cycles due to luteal phase defects.

The luteal phase is normally associated with high levels of oestrogen and progesterone, lasting for 14 days after ovulation. A luteal phase of less than 10 days is common in women participating in high-intensity exercise, but is usually undetected because

Fibre

A substance that gives plants their rigidity. It is found in foods including fruit, vegetables, grains and cereals. The structure is made up of cellulose, lignin and pectin. It can't be digested in the human gastrointestinal system due to a lack of enzymes.

A diet high in fibre is associated with a reduced risk of intestinal illness and disease such as colon and bowel *cancer*. Fibre can absorb water, which adds bulk to the faeces and allows them to pass through the intestines more easily, which can help treat

Green peas are high in fibre

diarrhoea. The best way to increase fibre in the diet is by increasing the intake of fibre-rich foods (see p. 145).

Fibrocartilage

A *connective tissue* that is strong and highly elastic. It is mainly found in *joints*. For example, the *discs* of the spine are made of fibrocartilage. It is made up of cells called chondroblasts and chondrocytes, embedded in a matrix of gel-like ground substance, and a large amount of collagen fibres.

Fibrosis

Small areas of damaged muscle tissue that may be felt as firm, taut, thickened bands. It is an *overuse injury* caused by repeated excessive forces experienced by the muscle during an aggravating activity. The excessive forces cause microtrauma, including chronic *inflammation* with the development of adhesions between muscle fibres and the formation of cross-linkages in the fascia arranged in the direction of the stress or as large areas of increased *muscle tone*.

Fibrosis can cause pain in the muscle. In addition, it may compromise the ability of the muscle to contract and relax rapidly and, as a result, cause other structures, such as tendons, to become injured. It should be treated with soft tissue techniques, including *massage* and *flexibility exercises*.

Fibrous and cartilaginous joints

A joint that only allows a small amount of movement between the bones and provides a high degree of stability. For example, the pubic *symphysis* is the connection between the front ends of the pelvis bone situated near the genitals. A disc made of fibrocartilage that, acting like tough glue, connects the bones.

Fibrous and cartilaginous joints have *ligaments* to reinforce their stability. They may also exhibit some minor features that usually characterise *synovial joints*, such as hyaline cartilage on the articular surface and *synovial fluid*.

Other types of fibrous and cartilaginous joints include the sutures of the skull, syndesmosis, synchondrosis and gomphosis.

Fibula fracture

A break in the outer-side *shin* bone that is due to an excessive, sudden force, such as a direct blow in a contact sport. It usually causes pain in the outer-side of the shin and tenderness at the site of the fracture. Treatment usually only requires *rest* and *analgesics*.

Fibula stress fracture

A microfracture in the outer-side *shin* bone that causes pain that develops gradually due to an accumulation of repeated, excessive physical loads associated with running over a period of weeks or

Fibre content of foods

Food	Amount	Weight (g)	Weight (oz)	Fibre (g)
Bread, wholemeal	1 slice	30	1	2
Bread roll, wholemeal	1/2 slice	30	1	2
Bread, pita	30 g	30	1	1
Muffin, English	1 half	40	1.3	1
Crumpet	1 average	50	1.7	2
Biscuit, plain, dry	20	20	0.7	1
Biscuit, plain, sweet	2 biscuit	17	0.6	0
Rice cakes	1 1/2 cakes	19	0.7	1
Oats, rolled, cooked	1/2 cup	195	6.9	3
Processed bran	1/2 cup	35	1.2	14
Weet-Bix	1.5 biscuits	26	0.9	3
Vita Brits	1.5 biscuits	26	0.9	3
Weeties	1/2 cup	25	0.9	3
Muesli, flakes	1/2 cup	22	0.75	1
Rice, brown, boiled	1/3 cup	60	2	1
Pasta, white, boiled	1/2 cup	75	2.6	1
Barley, pearl, boiled	1/2 cup	90	3	3
Potato, pale skin, baked	1 medium	100	3.2	1
Sweet potato, peeled, boiled	1/3 cup	71	2.5	1
Sweetcorn, frozen, on cob	1/3 cup	48	1.6	2
Pea, green, boiled	1 cup	165	5.8	11
Parsnip, peeled, boiled	1 cup	150	5.3	4
Beetroot, peeled, boiled	6 slices	180	6.3	5
Turnip, white, peeled, boiled	1 1/2 cup	360	12.7	11
Lentil, boiled	1/2 cup	105	3.7	4
Bean, kidney, fresh, boiled	1/2 cup	83	2.8	9
Bean, haricot/cannellini, boiled	1/2 cup	86	2.9	8
Salad bean, commercial	1/3 cup	63	2.1	3
Soup, bean, lentil, homemade	150 g	150	5.3	3
Potato and leek soup	300 g	300	10.6	2
Soup, medium, canned, homemade	1 cup	264	8.9	1
Soup, light vegetable, canned	2 cup	528	17.9	3
Minestrone soup	300 g	300	10.6	4
Apple, golden delicious	1 average	123	4.3	2
Apricot, fresh, raw	3 medium	180	6.3	4
Banana, raw, peeled	1/2 average	50	1.75	1
Cherry, raw	25 medium	100	3.2	2
Custard apple, raw, peeled	1/4 medium	120	4	3
Fig, raw	4 pieces	160	5.6	4
Fig, dried	2 pieces	30	1	4
Grape, green sultana, raw	30 average	90	3	1
Kiwifruit, raw, peeled	2 medium	160	5.6	5
Melon, honeydew, raw	1 whole	240	8.5	2
Mango, raw, peeled	1 small	100	3.5	2
Mandarin, raw, peeled	3 whole	183	6.2	4
Nectarine, raw	3 medium	220	7.75	5
Orange, Valencia, raw	1 whole	160	5.6	3
Juice, orange, unsweetened	1 glass	204	6.9	1
Pear, Williams, raw, unpeeled	1 average	130	4.6	3
Peach, raw, unpeeled	2 medium	174	5.9	2
Peach, canned, in pear juice	2/3 cup	170	6	2
Tangerine, raw, peeled	2 large	200	7	4
Watermelon, raw, peeled	1 1/2 cups	293	10.3	2
Milk, skim	1 1/2 glasses	300	10.6	0
Milk, whole	1 1/2 glasses	300	10.6	0
Yoghurt, low fat, natural	1 tub	200	7	0
Ice cream, vanilla	1 1/2 scoops	570	2.4	0

months. It is less common than a *tibia stress fracture* of the shin.

Causes

The *stress fracture* is due to muscle traction and torsional forces on the bone associated with a biomechanical abnormality. People with excessive *foot pronation* have a tendency to develop outer-side (lateral) shin pain, especially when pronation occurs during toe-off. During this phase of *running biomechanics*, the peroneal muscles contract strongly in order to stabilise the foot for propulsion. It is the repetitive force of muscle contraction on the fibula that leads to stress fracture. In some cases it is associated with excessive *foot supination*.

Diagnosis, treatment and return to sport

The pain is located in the outer-side of the shin, is easy to pinpoint in the bone and gets worse with running or high-impact *aerobics*. The bone also feels tender when pressed firmly with the fingers. The diagnosis is confirmed with a *bone scan* or *magnetic resonance imaging (MRI)*.

The recommended treatment is *rest* from activity, especially running, until the bone tenderness clears. This usually takes 3 to 6 weeks. At this time slow jogging can be started again, with a gradual increase in activity as part of a sport rehabilitation program lasting for another 3 to 6 weeks. Any biomechanical abnormalities should be corrected.

Fifth metatarsal base fracture

A break of the base of the fifth metatarsal bone in the foot due to an excessive turning inwards movement of the foot, which may occur together with an ankle sprain.

It is an *avulsion fracture*, where the peroneus brevis tendon breaks off the bone (see *Foot and toes*). An X-ray can confirm the diagnosis. Treatment is usually *immobilisation* in a plaster cast for 1 to 2 weeks followed by the same treatments as provided for an *ankle sprain*. Occasionally surgery may be required.

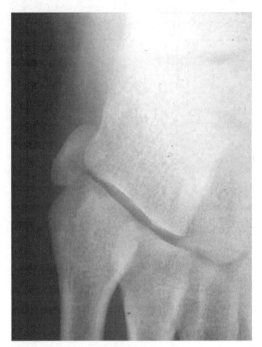

X-ray of fifth metatarsal base fracture

Fifth metatarsal shaft fracture

A break of the middle section of the long bone that connects to the little toe (see *Foot and toes*). It is most commonly seen in *dancing* when losing balance while on demi-pointe and rolling over the outer border of the foot.

The diagnosis of the *fracture* is confirmed with an *X-ray*. Treatment for a stable fracture is *rest* from aggravating activities. An unstable fracture requires *immobilisation* in a plaster cast for 4 to 6 weeks.

Fight-or-flight response

See *Adrenaline*.

Finger joints

See *Hand and finger joints*.

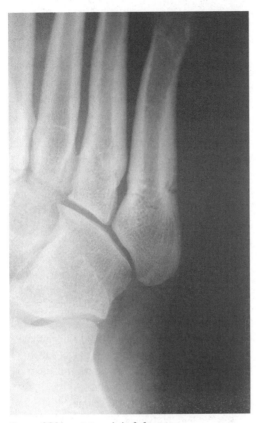

X-ray of fifth metatarsal shaft fracture

First MCP joint sprain

An acute injury that most commonly causes pain located in the palm at the base of the thumb, where the metacarpal-phalangeal (MCP) joint between the first metacarpal bone and proximal phalanx is located (see *Hand and finger joints*). Also popularly known as 'skier's thumb'.

It is one of the most common hand injuries in sport. It is usually caused when the thumb is forcefully moved backwards and outwards, damaging the ulnar collateral ligament of the first MCP joint. Less often, the movement is across the palm, damaging the radial collateral ligament.

Diagnosis, treatment and return to sport

In addition to pain, there is usually *swelling* and tenderness over the palm side of the first MCP joint and

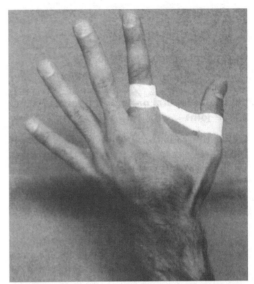

Taping the thumb to the index finger for first MCP joint sprain

possibly weakness of gripping strength between the thumb and index finger. The *sprain* of the ulnar collateral ligament may be a partial tear (grade 1 or 2) or complete tear (grade 3). Regardless of the severity, the initial treatment is *RICE (rest, ice, compression and elevation)*.

A partial tear is treated with *immobilisation* in a splint for 6 weeks. Further protective splinting with a *brace* is required during return to sport and for up to 12 months to prevent re-injury. *Taping* the thumb to the index finger also may be recommended.

A complete ligament tear requires surgical repair. If there is an associated fracture, *internal fixation* with a metal wire is necessary. After surgery the thumb is placed in a thumb spica plaster cast for 4 to 6 weeks, followed by protection in a *brace* during sporting activity for a further 3 months. Both partial and complete tears require hand and finger rehabilitation.

First metatarso-phalangeal (MTP) joint sprain

An acute injury of the joint in the ball of the foot due to a sudden and excessive amount of foot dorsiflexion (foot upwards movement) (see *Foot and toes*).

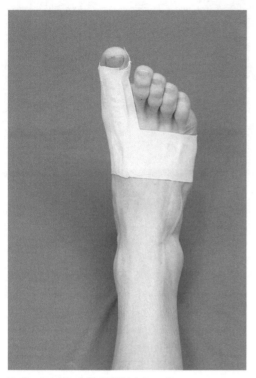

Taping to protect first MTP joint sprain

This *sprain* has become more likely on non-slip artificial playing surfaces and when wearing soft, flexible shoes. It is also called 'turf toe'.

Treatment includes *rest* from aggravating activities such as running, *ice* and *taping*. Wearing *running shoes* with a stiff sole is recommended. Return to sport is usually 3 to 4 weeks.

Fish

A food that contains essential nutrients including *protein*, *vitamins*, *minerals* and *polyunsaturated fats* called omega 3 fatty acids, which may have a protective effect against coronary heart disease. There is a low total amount of fat in white fish, such as bream, cod, flounder, John Dory, ling, perch, snapper, flake and whiting. Other seafood, such as prawns, shrimps, calamari and crab, have even less fat. A higher amount of fat is contained in fish such as gemfish, red fish, herring and salmon.

Fitness

The ability to do a physical activity. There are different types of fitness including *aerobic fitness* (also called cardiovascular and endurance fitness), *anaerobic fitness*, *strength*, *power*, speed, agility and *flexibility*. The aim of a *training* program is to increase fitness.

Fitness equipment

Equipment designed to make an activity more effective or easier to perform during training. For example, walking on a *treadmill* and cycling on an *exercise bike* for aerobic training and working out on a *weight station* for training to increase strength.

It should be noted that fitness equipment sometimes does not achieve greater training results than not using equipment. For instance, there is no further increase in aerobic fitness that can be achieved by using a treadmill compared to walking outdoors. In addition, there are pieces of equipment that make false claims and offer no benefit, such as the exercise belt and vacuum pants.

Other advantages of fitness equipment are convenience and comfort, such as a treadmill allowing walking without having to worry about the weather, and a short-term increase in motivation, particularly for people who enjoy exercising at home.

In addition to a treadmill and exercise bike, other commonly used equipment include the *abdominal toner*, *rowing machine*, *stepping (stair climbing) machine* and *cross-country skiing machine*. It may be worthwhile checking if you need to receive a *medical clearance* before using fitness equipment at home.

Fitness trainer

A person who has completed an education course and is recognised as being qualified to teach, supervise and provide advice about *training* programs and activities to improve *fitness*. A fitness trainer can work with one person at a time, called a *personal trainer*, or with groups of people, such as at a gymnasium, health centre, sport club and team. Fitness trainers working for elite and professional teams and individuals focus on the specific exercise and sport goals, such as a summer program to increase fitness prior to a football season.

Flat feet

A *biomechanical abnormality* in the structure of the foot that causes the medial (inner) arch to be lower (flattened), thus decreasing the height of the arch. It is due to excessive *foot pronation*.

Flavonoids

A group of pigments that give fruit and vegetables their red and yellow colouring, which may be recommended by natural health practitioners to treat *inflammation* and reduce *swelling* caused by injuries. It is also an *antioxidant* that may help prevent disease and illness and improve the repair of muscle fibres in people participating in exercise and sport. It should not be taken together with conventional anti-inflammatory medications (see *Non-steroidal anti-inflammatory drugs (NSAIDs)* and *corticosteroids*).

Flexibility

The stretchability of *muscles, joints, ligaments* and the neural sheath of *nerves*. It is assessed by the amount of movement that is achieved when stretching these structures. Another name for the flexibility of muscles is *muscle length*. The measurement of flexibility is called *range of movement*. It is performed in different ways according to the structure being measured.

Exercise and sport

Flexibility is important in exercise and sport for a number of reasons. It can be an essential part of a sport, such as *gymnastics*, which demands the performance of specific movements, such as bending backwards. It can also help prevent injuries by minimising the chances of the development of a *biomechanical abnormality* and making sure that a structure, such as a muscle, can withstand the forces that it is placed under. For example, the hamstring (back thigh muscle) can tear if it does not have sufficient flexibility when kicking a football.

Diagnosis and treatment

Flexibility is usually reduced following an *acute injury* due to a combination of a number of factors, including inactivity, *atrophy*, *spasm*, *inflammation*, *swelling* and *pain*. *Strength training* also can reduce flexibility. Occasionally an athlete may have too much flexibility, which is called hypermobility.

Reduced muscle flexibility may be associated with an *overuse injury*. Causes can include muscle *fibrosis* and *myofascial trigger points*. Some of the more common examples are included in the table, 'Muscles with reduced flexibility associated with injuries'.

Regaining full flexibility of muscles, joints, ligaments and the neural sheath is primarily achieved with *flexibility exercises*. Other recommended treatments include *massage, mobilisation, ice, heat therapy (superficial)* and *electrotherapy*. Additional treatments may be required for *myofascial trigger points*.

Flexibility exercises

An activity that aims to increase the stretchability and amount of movement performed at a joint, ligament,

Muscles with reduced flexibility associated with injuries

Muscles with reduced flexibility	Possible associated injury
Sternocleidomastoid	Neck pain (non-specific)
Psoas	Low back pain (non-specific)
Quadriceps	Patellar tendinosis (kneecap)
Vastus lateralis of the quadriceps, Iliotibial band and Tendon fascia lata	Patellofemoral joint syndrome (kneecap)
Soleus	Achilles tendinosis

Flexibility exercise for the hamstring muscle

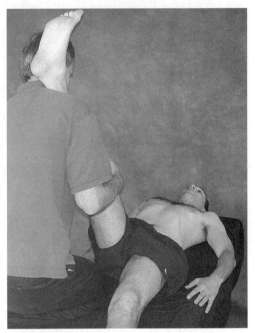

Using a proprioceptive neuromuscular facilitation (PNF) technique to improve hamstring muscle flexibility

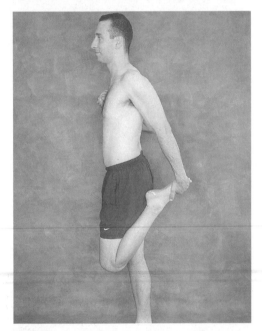

Flexibility exercise for the quadriceps muscle

muscle or the neural sheath. Other benefits include increased muscle relaxation, decreased muscle soreness, improved blood circulation, preventing excessive adhesions and promoting a flexible, strong scar. It may be recommended as treatment for an injury, in a *warm-up* and *warm-down* to prevent injury or with *strength training* to prevent loss of flexibility.

Method

An assessment of the amount of available flexibility, called the *range of movement*, should be made before performing flexibility exercises so that progress can be measured.

For joints and ligaments, flexibility exercises may be done as a *passive exercise*, with assistance from an outside force, or as an *active exercise*. *Neural tension* stretching is performed to increase flexibility of the neural sheath. For muscles, there are three types of stretching: 1) static; 2) ballistic; and 3) proprioceptive neuromuscular facilitation.

STATIC STRETCHING

The body part is moved slowly and gently until it can no longer be moved further without causing discomfort. It is held in this position for 5 to 60 seconds, depending on the amount of stretch required, followed by a further slight stretch. It is regarded as the safest flexibility exercise.

BALLISTIC STRETCHING

The body part is moved slowly and gently until it can no longer be moved further. A bouncing movement is performed to increase the stretch. The risk of injury makes this a less commonly selected flexibility exercise.

PROPRIOCEPTIVE NEUROMUSCULAR FACILITATION (PNF)

This technique involves performing alternating contractions and relaxations of a muscle. A disadvantage is that there is a tendency to overstretch the muscle.

General principles

- Gains in flexibility are based on the *overload* principle. Overload requires increases in intensity, duration, frequency and type of stretch over a period of time.
- Flexibility exercises should only cause a stretching feeling. Pain indicates that overstretching has occurred.
- They should be preceded by warm-up activities such as gentle jogging.
- *Heat therapy (superficial)* to increase tissue temperature can facilitate stretching.
- *Ice* may overcome pain and muscle *spasm* more effectively than heat in some people.
- Make sure the instructions for flexibility exercises are clearly understood, such as the correct starting position and movement to be performed.

Flexibility training

Regular participation in activities that aim to increase the stretchability of muscles, joints, ligaments and the neural sheath. The main activities are *flexibility exercises*. Flexibility training can be regarded as central to activities such as *yoga*. It is also called stretching.

Flexion

A movement of a joint, such as bending the elbow and knee. It also involves moving in a direction pointing towards the front of the body, like lifting the thigh up to take a step forward, which is called flexion of the hip joint. Flexion is also known as plantar flex-

ion in the ankle joint and palmar flexion in the wrist and hand. It is the opposite of *extension*.

Flexor hallucis longus tendinosis

An overuse injury causing pain on the inside of the *ankle* that gradually gets worse over a period of weeks or months due to repeated and excessive activity of the tendon. It is common in ballet *dancing* due to performing excessive amounts of toe-off or forefoot weight-bearing. There is an increased risk if excessive *foot pronation* or *ankle posterior impingement* is present.

The injury is initially a tendinitis that gradually leads to a *tendinosis*, which is a degeneration of the tendon. Treatment consists of *rest* from the aggravating activity, *analgesics* for pain relief, *ice*, *massage*, *strengthening exercises*, particularly producing *eccentric* muscle contractions, and *flexibility exercises*.

Flexor tendinosis

See *Golfer's elbow*.

Flotation tank

An enclosed bathtub half-filled with very salty water enabling a person lying inside to float comfortably without effort like a cork that is used as a form of relaxation.

Flotation tank

Research shows that it can decrease blood pressure and levels of cortisol, which is a hormone associated with *anxiety* and *stress*. Other relaxation methods include *centring* and *progressive muscle relaxation*. It also can be used with techniques that aim to improve performance in competition such as *visualisation*.

Flu

An infection of the *respiratory system* caused by the influenza virus. It spreads from virus-infected droplets floating in the air after sneezing and coughing. The people most vulnerable to the flu are older aged (greater than 65 years) and those with an illness that causes a depressed immune system, such as AIDS.

Flu vaccination may be recommended for sports people if there is a greater risk of exposure due to playing in a team. An infection may be carried through shared equipment such as water bottles, or via heavy respiration, coughing and spitting in sports where close physical contact occurs.

The recommended treatment is bed rest, drinking fluids, paracetamol for a high fever and headache (see *Analgesics*) and steam inhalation. *Antibiotics* do not help with treating a virus.

Exercise and sport

Complete rest from training is recommended if any of the following symptoms are present: *fever*, generally feeling ill, muscle aches, excessive fatigue and raised resting *heart rate*. The main concern is an increased risk of developing *myocarditis* (heart inflammation) and *dehydration*. There is also a detrimental impact on performance, including reduced muscle strength and endurance, and negative effects on the lungs, such as decreased *pulmonary diffusion*.

Training at 50 per cent of normal intensity can be commenced 7 days after complete resolution of signs and symptoms. For example, a 10 km (6 mile) swim at half the usual pace. If no problems arise following this training, intensity can be gradually increased until pre-illness intensity levels are regained after another 3 to 7 days. The build up is usually slower in athletes who have experienced severe prolonged fever.

Fluoride

See *Minerals*.

Foot and toes

The foot provides the link between the surfaces on which we stand, walk, run and jump and the *ankle* joint. It contains 26 bones and 30 joints that interact with each other, and many muscles providing complex movements.

REAR FOOT
Bones: calcaneus (heel bone), talus.
Most important joint: subtalar joint between the calcaneus and talus (also considered part of the ankle joint).

MID FOOT
Bones: navicular, cuboid, 3 cuneiforms (medial, intermediate and lateral).
Most important joint: midtarsal joint consists of two joints, the calcaneocuboid joint and the talonavicular joint.

FOREFOOT (INCLUDES THE TOES)
Bones: 5 metatarsals and 14 toe bones (2 phalanges for the first toe and 3 phalanges for each of the second, third, fourth and fifth toes).

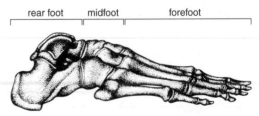

The regions of the foot—lateral (outer) side view

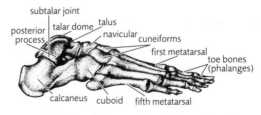

Bones of the foot and toes—lateral (outer) side view

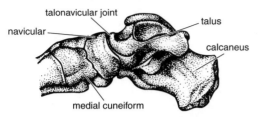

Bones of the foot and toes—medial (inner) side view

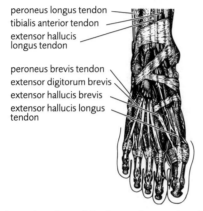

Muscles and tendons of the foot and toes—dorsal (top) view

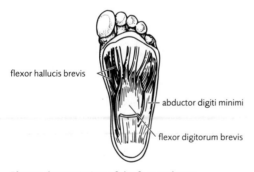

Plantar (bottom) view of the foot and toes

Most important joints: first ray (first metatarsal-medial cuneiform) joint; metatarso-phalangeal joints, particularly the first metatarso-phalangeal (MTP) joint.

Foot and toe movements

The foot moves as a single unit with specific contributions from the smaller joints within it. For example, *inversion* and *eversion* mainly occurs at the subtalar and midtarsal joints, with only a small contribution from the forefoot.

Muscles involved in ankle, foot and toe movements

Movement	Primary movers	Secondary movers
Ankle and foot		
Plantar flexion	• Gastrocnemius • Soleus (calf muscles)	• Plantaris • Tibialis posterior • Flexor hallucis longus • Flexor digitorum longus
Dorsiflexion	• Tibialis anterior • Peroneus tertius	• Extensor digitorum longus • Extensor hallucis longus
Inversion	• Tibialis anterior • Tibialis posterior	
Eversion	• Peroneus longus • Peroneus brevis	
Toes	**Primary and secondary movers**	
Flexion	• Flexor digitorum brevis and longus • Lumbricals • Interossei • Flexor hallucis longus • Flexor digiti minimi brevis	
Extension	• Extensor digitorum longus and brevis • Extensor hallucis longus	
Adduction	• Adductor hallucis • Interossei (plantar)	
Abduction	• Abductor hallucis • Interossei (dorsal) • Abductor digiti minimi	

At the same time, the foot can move together with the ankle. For example, *plantar flexion* (moving foot downwards) mainly occurs at the ankle joint with a smaller contribution from the foot. The toes are able to move on their own, but also often move together with the rest of the foot.

The complex interaction is called biomechanics and is usually described in detail for specific activities, such as *running biomechanics*.

Foot and toe pain and injuries

Causes

Pain in the foot is caused by an overuse or acute injury or disease. In an *overuse injury*, the pain gets

153

worse over a period of weeks or months due to an accumulation of excessive forces that cause micro-trauma. In the early stages it causes only minor pain and stiffness. But later on, either gradually or following a sudden force, it becomes painful enough to seek medical care.

An *acute injury* causes pain that begins suddenly due to a single incident, such as accidentally kicking a hard object. The most common diseases are inflammatory arthritis such as *gout* and *ankylosing spondylitis*.

The joints, ligaments, muscles and tendons of the *foot and toes* are the main sources of *pain*. In some cases the pain is referred from another structure, such as the low back, which is the same as *ankle referred pain*.

Diagnosis

The diagnosis involves combining information about the *history, physical examination* and relevant tests.

How the pain responds to exercise and changes through the day is important for overuse injuries. For example, rear foot pain is worse in the morning, improving with exercise and aggravated by standing suggests *plantar fasciitis*. Overuse injuries are also associated with a specific activity, such as running for *tibialis posterior tendinosis*.

Talus stress fracture, calcaneus *stress fracture*, *metatarsal stress fracture* and *navicular stress fracture* all cause pain located vaguely in the foot, rather than at a pinpoint, that gets worse with running and may cause pain at rest or at night. Pain between the third and fourth toe (or second and third) that gets worse

Causes of pain located in the rear foot (heel)

Common	Less common	Not to be missed
• Plantar fasciitis • Fat pad contusion	• Calcaneus stress fracture • Tarsal tunnel syndrome • Talus stress fracture • Retrocalcaneal bursitis	• Ankylosing spondylitis • Osteoid osteoma • Complex regional pain syndrome (CRPS)

Causes of pain located in the mid foot

Common	Less common	Not to be missed
• Navicular stress fracture • Plantar fasciitis • Midtarsal joint sprain • Extensor tendinosis (foot) • Tibialis posterior tendinosis	• Peroneal tendinosis • Tarsal coalition	• Lisfranc's fracture-dislocation • Osteoid osteoma • Complex regional pain syndrome (CRPS)

Causes of pain located in the forefoot and toes

Common	Less common	Not to be missed
• Callus (corns) • First metatarso-phalangeal (MTP) joint sprain • Subungual haematoma • Hallux valgus • Hallux rigidus • Morton's neuroma • Sesamoiditis • Metatarsal stress fracture • Fifth metatarsal shaft fracture • Ingrown toenail	• Freiberg's osteochondritis	• Complex regional pain syndrome (CRPS) • Gout

with tight shoes indicates *Morton's neuroma*. Pins and needles, or numbness, together with heel pain suggests tarsal tunnel syndrome. Base of the big toe joint pain that is felt at night and associated with morning stiffness, redness and *swelling* suggests *gout*.

For acute injuries, the movement that caused the injury is important. Rear foot pain due to jumping from a height onto the heel indicates a *fat pad contusion*.

Radiological investigations can confirm the diagnosis, such as an X-ray for a fracture, hallux rigidus or subungual exostosis, and a *bone scan* and *CT scan* or *magnetic resonance imaging (MRI)* for a stress fracture.

Foot pronation

A rotation movement of the foot that is essential for normal walking and running. It mainly occurs at the subtalar and midtarsal joints (see *Foot and toes*). It is the main component of foot *inversion*, which means turning the sole of the foot towards the mid-line. For example, when both feet are next to each other with the ankle bones touching, the sole of the foot is turned towards the sole of the other foot. It is the opposite of *foot supination*.

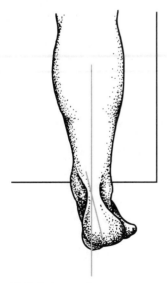

Right foot pronation

Running and walking

Running and walking movements involve a repeating cycle divided into two phases: stance and swing.

The stance phase is divided into three stages: contact, midstance and propulsive. In the swing phase, the foot is carried through the air towards the next heel strike. It is divided into three stages: follow through, forward swing and foot descent. The movements of the main sections in the foot, the subtalar joint, forefoot and first ray, are described in *running biomechanics*.

Biomechanical abnormality

If pronation occurs in an excessive amount or during a phase when supination is supposed to occur, it is regarded as a biomechanical abnormality that is associated with an increased risk of a number of overuse injuries. These include *sesamoiditis, callus* formation, *metatarsal stress fracture, navicular stress fracture* and *plantar fasciitis* of the foot, *flexor hallucis longus tendinosis* of the ankle, *Achilles tendinosis* in the calf, *peroneal tendinosis, shin chronic compartment syndrome, tibia stress fracture, fibula stress fracture* and *tibia periostitis* of the shin, *patellar tendinosis* and *patellofemoral joint syndrome* of the knee.

For example, excessive pronation causes increased ground-reaction forces on the medial (inner) aspect of the foot. This can lead to abnormal flattening of the medial longitudinal arch, placing an increased strain on the plantar fascia and resulting in the overuse injury, plantar fasciitis.

This abnormality also may occur due to an inherited (genetic) anatomical abnormality such as *forefoot varus*, poor *shoe* selection or following an injury that has healed incorrectly, such as muscle imbalance or loss of flexibility in a joint.

A physiotherapist, podiatrist or sports physician can identify excessive foot pronation, by checking the shoe and by other tests. Selecting the correct *running shoes* is important for prevention of injuries.

Foot supination

A rotation movement of the foot that is essential for normal walking and *running biomechanics*. It mainly

QUICK REFERENCE GUIDE

Foot

Overuse injury: Pain that has gradually worsened over a long period of weeks or months

Plantar fasciitis ....Is the pain located on the bottom (sole) of the foot and/or heel, that feels strongest during high-impact activities such as running and is worse in the morning, with the first steps very tender until the area warms up?

Calcaneus stress fracture ....Is your pain around the heel, making it difficult to walk, that tends to get worse with running and may cause pain when resting or at night?

Navicular stress fracture ....Is your pain over the top of your foot, perhaps extending down towards your toes, that tends to get worse with running and may cause pain when resting or at night?

Extensor tendinosis (foot) ....Is your pain over the top of your foot, perhaps extending down towards your toes, that feels worse when pointing the toes to the ground?

Metatarsal stress fracture..............Is your pain over the top of your foot, perhaps extending down towards your toes, that feels worse during exercise such as running and when pressing the bone firmly with the fingers?

Morton's neuroma.........................Do you have pain between the third or fourth toe (or second and third toe) that gets worse with tight shoes?

Sesamoiditis ....Do you have pain under your big toe that feels worse when putting weight through the ball of the foot and less painful when walking on the outside border of your foot?

Hallux rigidus ....Do you have pain at the base of the big toe and the joint is stiff?

Hallux valgus ....Do you have pain at the base of the big toe, which is in a position closer towards the second toe joint that creates a more prominent 'bump' on the inside of the foot?

Freiberg's osteochondritis ....Are you an adolescent (still growing) with pain over your toes, which is aggravated by standing on your toes?

Acute Injury: Pain caused by a sudden force

Fat pad contusion ....Do you have pain on the bottom (sole) of the foot and/or heel that suddenly began after landing on the heel on a hard surface from a height?

Midtarsal joint sprain....................Do you have pain around the middle of your foot that began after a sudden, twisting injury?

Fifth metatarsal base fracture ....Did you twist your ankle, excessively turning the foot inwards at the time, and now have pain on the outside border of the foot about half way down?

First metatarso-phalangeal ....Do you have pain at the base of the big toe after a sudden bending
(MTP) joint sprain   movement?

Subungual haematoma ....Do you have pain located in your toenail with obvious bleeding under the nail?

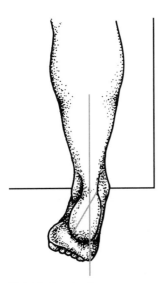

Right foot supination

occurs at the subtalar and midtarsal joints (see *Foot and toes*). It is the main component of the combination of movements that produce foot eversion, which means turning the sole of the foot so that it faces outwards, away from the midline. For example, when both feet are next to each other with the ankle bones touching, the sole of the foot is turned away from the other foot. It occurs in coordination with the opposite movement, *foot pronation*.

Biomechanical abnormality

If supination occurs in an excessive amount or during a phase when *pronation* is supposed to occur it is regarded as a biomechanical abnormality. It is associated with an increased risk of *sesamoiditis* and *fibula stress fracture* and *navicular stress fracture* because the supinated foot makes the foot excessively rigid resulting in poor shock absorption.

Excessive supination may occur to compensate for an anatomical abnormality of the foot, such as *forefoot valgus*. It may also occur due to: loss of *flexibility* in the subtalar joint; weakness of the peroneal muscles that perform pronation movement; or as a result of spasm or loss of flexibility in the supination

muscles, tibialis posterior and gastrocnemius and soleus (*calf*).

A physiotherapist, podiatrist or sports physician can identify excessive foot supination by checking the *shoe* and other tests. Selecting the correct *running shoes* is important for prevention of injuries.

Football

See *Australian Rules football, Rugby Union, Rugby League, American football* or *Soccer*.

Football boots

Footwear designed to cope with the physical demands of *soccer, Australian Rules football, American football, Rugby League* and *Rugby Union*. Each sport places similar physical demands on the feet. They need to be good *running shoes* with additional features that allow kicking and rapid changes in running direction, particularly on wet surfaces.

The *shoe* needs to have an upper section with adequate depth, a rigid heel counter, sufficient forefoot flexibility, a wide sole and a slightly curved last. Generally, the midsole should be completely flat; however, players with a history of *Achilles tendinosis* may need to wear boots with a midsole wedge that tilts the heel upwards.

Football boots

The outsole needs to have features that provide appropriate grip on different surfaces. The recommendations include: rubber outsoles (treads provide some grip but are only suitable for non-competitive play); moulded outsoles (low studs that are not replaceable and best suited for dry surfaces); and screw-ins (higher studs that are replaceable as they wear down and best suited for wet surfaces).

Over 15-year-olds in regular competition should own at least two pairs of boots: moulded outsoles and screw-ins. Under 15-year-olds should wear the boot that suits the playing conditions most commonly encountered on their homeground.

Specific recommendations for each sport include:
- Soccer: an upper with a low ankle cut.
- Rugby codes: an upper with a high ankle cut.
- Australian Rules football: an in-between cut.
- American football: spikes on the heels when playing on grass (called cleats), similar to the soccer boot.

Footballers' migraine

A migraine attack that causes severe head pain and neurological symptoms, particularly visual disturbances, associated with receiving a repeated number of blows to the head. It is common in *soccer* players, but also is seen in other *collision sports*. The recommended treatment is the same as for *migraine*.

Forefoot valgus

A defect in the structure of the foot that causes the front section of the foot and toes to point outwards, leading to excessive *foot supination* at the subtalar joint during walking and running.

Forefoot varus

A defect in the structure of the foot that causes the front section of the foot and toes to point inwards, leading to excessive *foot pronation* at the subtalar joint during walking and running.

Fracture

A break in a *bone* caused by a single event where the external forces are greater than the strength of the bone to withstand them. Healing of a fracture involves new bone tissue growing and reconnecting between the broken ends of the bone.

Types of fracture

Fractures are either non-displaced or displaced. Non-displaced fractures have the bone ends facing each other so that the alignment or position of the bone is the same as it was prior to the injury. In addition, the distance between the ends is sufficiently close to allow new bone tissue growth to rejoin them.

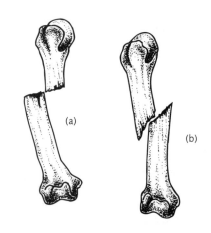

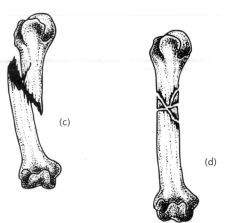

Types of fracture: (a) transverse; (b) oblique; (c) spiral; (d) comminuted

Displaced fractures are where the two bone ends are unaligned and/or have been forcibly separated by a significant distance.

Fractures may also be open or closed. Open (compound) fractures have one or more of the bone ends protruding through the skin. *Open fractures* should be treated as a medical emergency due to the risk of developing an infection. In closed (simple) fractures, the bone ends are contained under the skin.

Each fracture also has a distinctive shape and nature, which has a bearing on the treatment to realign the bone ends to maximise healing and the likely stability during the healing process. For example, an oblique fracture, where a lone bone is broken across the width, is more likely to slip apart during healing and may require surgery to insert metal pins to hold them together.

- Transverse fracture: This classical fracture is a break straight across the width of the bone.
- Oblique fracture: A break at an angle across the width.
- Spiral fracture: A break that twists across at an angle.
- Comminuted fracture: The bone shatters into more than two pieces.
- Compression fracture: The bone is crushed.
- *Avulsion fracture*: A piece of bone attached to a tendon or ligament is torn away.
- *Greenstick fracture*: Only occurs in children where the outer side of the bone breaks open.
- *Growth plate fracture*: Only occurs in children and adolescents.

Symptoms

A bone fracture usually causes *pain*, tenderness, localised bruising, *swelling* and, in some cases, deformity and restricted range of movement.

Associated injuries at the same time or later on as a consequence of the fracture include ligament, joint capsule, articular cartilage and muscle damage, nerve and blood vessel damage, *acute compartment pressure syndrome*, *deep vein thrombosis* (DVT) and abnormality in the growth of new bone tissue, which may lead to a delayed union, non-union or malunion between the broken bone ends.

Damage to soft tissues, nerves and blood vessels are due to the same external forces that cause the fracture. After the bone heals they may cause long-term problems, such as joint and muscle stiffness and loss of *range of movement*.

Swelling can develop into an acute compartment pressure syndrome in the limbs, particularly in the forearm and lower leg, where tight fascial sheaths completely enclose groups of muscles and entrap the fluids. The pain caused is much stronger than that of a normal fracture.

Deep vein thrombosis, the development of blood clots and blockages in the veins, can occur due to lack of activity of the muscles around the broken bone, which reduces the pumping of blood.

Delayed union, non-union and malunion tend to cause persistent pain and a reduced ability to move and perform activities of daily life.

First aid

Assuming the fracture is not a medical emergency due to an *open fracture*, nerve or blood vessel damage, the main aim of first aid is to prevent further injury. An injured limb should have a splint attached to it, preferably a medical piece of equipment or, if necessary, using a ski pole, oar, paddle, rolled up-blanket, pillows or adjacent limb.

It is also important to assess the *pulse*; for example, the radial and ulnar pulses in the wrist of the arm, and skin colour and temperature for a *supracondylar fracture* of the elbow.

Treatment

Treatment begins with realignment and re-apposition to ensure that the broken bone ends face each other so that new bone tissue growth rejoins them. This is followed by *immobilisation*, which means preventing too much movement between the bone ends so that the new bone tissue is not damaged and healing occurs.

For example, an unstable displaced fracture, like a spiral fracture, usually requires surgery to stabilise the bone ends with metal pins and plates, possibly followed by a plaster cast. Non-displaced or minimally displaced fractures usually need to be treated with a plaster cast or bracing.

Free radicals

See *Antioxidants*.

Freiberg's osteochondritis

A disease that softens the head of the second metatarsal bone that connects to the second toe, making it vulnerable to being deformed or separated from the main body of the bone (see *Foot and toes*). It is mostly found in adolescents aged 14 to 18. The diagnosis of this *osteochondrosis* injury is confirmed with an *X-ray*. Treatment involves taking excessive forces off the bone using padding and *orthotics*.

Frostbite

Damage to the skin and underlying tissues due to excessive and prolonged cold. The damage is caused by crystallisation of fluids. Low skin temperature and dehydration cause skin blood vessels to constrict and limit circulation. Water is drawn out of the cells and ice crystals cause mechanical destruction of the skin.

It most commonly occurs in the fingers and toes, tips of the nose and ears and the cheeks. *Cross-country skiing* races should be postponed if the temperature at the coldest point in the course is less than –20°C (–4°F) because of the severe *wind chill* generated during racing.

Diagnosis and treatment

Frostbite of the outer skin causes a burning pain with numbness, pale and grey skin and sometimes blisters. Direct body heat can treat superficial frostbite. Rubbing the part should be avoided because of a potential to cause skin damage.

Frostbite of the underneath layer of skin tissue is initially extremely painful and then becomes numb. The body part appears as a frozen block of hard, white tissue with areas of gangrene and, when severe, deep blisters.

The affected part should be rapidly re-warmed in a hot water bath of temperature 39–41°C (102–106°F). A whirlpool bath with added antiseptic is ideal. The re-warming process is often acutely painful and requires *analgesics*. Radiant heat from a fire or radiator (see *Heat therapy (superficial)*) should not be used because of the risk of skin burns. The tissue should continue to be warmed until it becomes soft and pliable and normal sensation returns. Intravenous infusion and *antibiotics* may be required.

Fruit and vegetables

Food produced by plants that is rich in *vitamins, minerals, antioxidants, fibre* and *carbohydrates* and usually low in *fat*. They are an essential part of a healthy diet, particularly for people participating in exercise and sport.

It is recommended to eat five to seven servings of fresh fruit and vegetables each day (see *Diet for good health*). A serving is, for example, 1 small tomato, 1 slice of melon, 1 half of a large orange. Produce should be as fresh as possible.

Functional exercises

The first activities introduced as part of the rehabilitation of an injury in preparation for a return to sport. The activities selected are the ones that form the basis of the sport. The most common functional exercises are walking and jogging.

They are usually begun in the intermediate stage of a *sport rehabilitation* program once a reasonable level of strength, power, endurance, flexibility and proprioception has been achieved. As recovery progresses, new functional exercises are introduced that are more demanding. Functional exercises are not a substitute for specific sport *skills training* in rehabilitation.

An example of progression of functional exercises for a severe leg injury is:
- walking
- jogging
  - jog 200 m (650 ft), walk 200 m (650 ft)
  - increase to jog 400 m (1300 ft), walk nil
  - increase jog to 1500 m (5000 ft)
  - increase jog to 3 km (2 miles)

- running
    - increase pace during 3 km run intermittently for 100 m at time (surge)
- sprint
    - accelerate for 20 m (65 ft), half pace for 40 m (130 ft), decelerate for 30 m (100 ft)
    - repeat up to 10 times
    - gradually increase pace to 60, 70, 80, 90 and 100 per cent

- figure of eight
    - run large (25 m/80 ft) figure-of-eight, 5 times
    - gradually increase speed
    - progress to smaller (15 m, 10 m, 5 m) (50 ft, 33 ft, 16 ft) figures
- agility drills
    - 45 degree zigzag slowly increasing speed
    - 90 degree cutting
    - run around square (forwards, sideways, backwards)
    - side to side (e.g. across tennis court)

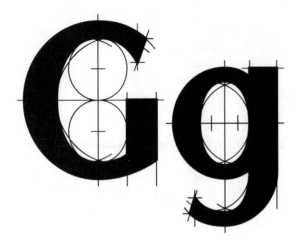

Gait cycle

See *Running biomechanics*.

Gambling addiction

Excessive spending on gambling activities leading to disruption of one's personal, social and working life. Even when large sums of money are lost, and family problems or criminal acts occur, the gambling addict is unable to resist the urge to gamble. The recommended treatment includes counselling and, if required, medications such as *antidepressants*.

Gamesmanship

Words or activities that aim to distract or worry opponents and diminish their performance level. The acceptability of gamesmanship is often in the eye of the beholder. An example more likely to be accepted is Australian cricketer Shane Warne's tactic of making a public announcement that he has developed a new secret ball. In some sports, physical intimidation is regarded as part of the game. In contrast, a tennis player disputing a close line call in order to delay the game and distract an opponent who is winning is usually considered unacceptable.

Ganglion

A word that has two different meanings:
1) A collection of *neurons* (nerve cells) that looks like a bean-sized ball and is part of the peripheral nervous system. They are located on the dorsal roots of each of the 31 pairs of *spinal nerves*, the sensory roots of several cranial nerves, including the facial nerve, and in a chain running up and down parallel to the spinal column as part of the *autonomic nervous system*.
2) An injury of a *tendon sheath* or weakness in a joint capsule that results in the formation of a cyst filled with synovial fluid. The size of a cyst varies from pea-size up to, less frequently, golf-ball-size. The most common location is a *wrist ganglion*. In most cases they do not cause pain. Those that are painful are treated with *aspiration* needle and possibly *corticosteroid* injection. If this fails surgery is recommended.

Gastrocnemius contusion

Damage to the calf muscle caused by a blunt sudden force, such as a direct blow from a part of the body of an opposing player or a piece of equipment. It is most common in collision sports, such as *soccer* and *basketball*, or ball sports like *hockey (field)*, *lacrosse* and *cricket* where the ball travels at high speed. The diagnosis, treatment and return to sport are similar to a *quadriceps contusion*.

Gastrocnemius strain

An acute injury of the large *calf* muscle caused by a sudden explosive force that either involves sprinting off from a stationary position with the ankle in dorsiflexion (bent upwards), lunging forward to play a tennis stroke or taking a running step onto a kerb and the ankle drops suddenly into dorsiflexion.

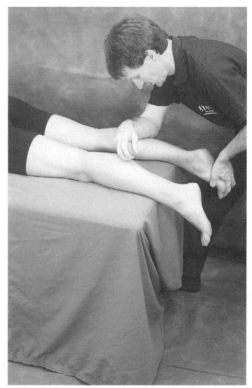

Massage treatment for gastrocnemius strain

Strengthening exercise for gastrocnemius strain

It mainly occurs in middle-aged participants in sports such as *basketball*, *volleyball*, *tennis* and *squash*. Insufficient *warm-up*, reduced *flexibility*, excessive muscle fatigue and muscle imbalance that creates an abnormality affecting *running biomechanics* are factors that increase the risk of this injury.

Diagnosis

The injury causes a stabbing pain or tearing sensation usually in either the inner (medial) side of the muscle belly or lower down just above the Achilles tendon. It also feels tender when pressed firmly with the fingers.

There are three degrees of muscle *strain*. Mild (grade 1) strain does not force a stop to participation in the activity but is usually noticed after cooling down or the following day. Moderate (grade 2) strain causes reduced muscle strength and pain that prevents continued participation as soon as the injury occurs. Severe (grade 3) strains immediately prevent continued participation, but may be less painful than moderate strains because pain-sensing nerves are ruptured too.

Treatment and return to sport

The recommended treatments for a mild and moderate strain include *rest* (moderate strains usually need to use crutches to reduce weight-bearing), *ice*, electrotherapy such as *transcutaneous electrical nerve stimulation (TENS)*, *magnetic field therapy*, *interferential therapy*, gentle *flexibility exercises* to the level of a feeling of tightness and *strengthening exercises* beginning 24 hours after the injury.

Massage should only be started when walking is pain-free. Return to sport for a mild strain is 10 to 12 days, moderate 16 to 21 days and severe strains 3 to 6 weeks. A heel raise should be worn during rehabilitation and on return to sport.

Recurrent gastrocnemius strain

Re-injury of a gastrocnemius strain may occur as an *overuse injury* or following inadequate sport rehabilitation of an acute injury. The recommended treatment is *massage*, *flexibility exercises* and *strengthening exercises*, particularly *concentric* and *eccentric* contractions.

Gastrointestinal bleeding

Bleeding in the *gastrointestinal system* that is observed either as red blood-stained or darkened faeces. There are many causes, including gastrointestinal *ulcers*, haemorrhoids, gastritis, cancer and ulcerative colitis. Gastrointestinal bleeding should be checked by a doctor as soon as possible.

There is also an increased risk of bleeding in endurance sports, particularly *long distance running*. The blood most often comes from the stomach or the large intestine, probably due to a diversion of blood flow away from the gastrointestinal system to the exercising muscles, which causes the inner lining tissues to break off, and the trauma of the diaphragm (main breathing muscle that is situated above the stomach) thumping down on the stomach (see *Lungs*).

Bleeding is also made worse by *dehydration* and certain medications, such as *aspirin* and *non-steroidal anti-inflammatory drugs (NSAIDs)*. It also may be a contributing cause of *iron deficiency*. Prevention is the same as recommended for *diarrhoea*, including diet and drinking fluids before competition.

Gastrointestinal reflux

A backflow of acidic contents from the stomach into the oesophagus that causes a burning pain in the chest (heartburn) due to relaxation of the gastro-oesophageal sphincter.

Reflux of the *gastrointestinal system* is not uncommon for people who exercise and play sport. It appears to be more likely during high-intensity *aerobic training*, which probably causes a delay in gastric emptying, especially when performed soon after a meal.

The types of food and drink in the stomach also affect emptying. For example, foods high in *carbohydrates* are more easily emptied from the stomach than high-*fat* and high-*protein* foods.

Alcohol, *caffeine* and peppermint also aggravate reflux because they relax the gastro-oesophageal sphincter.

Prevention of reflux involves reducing the contents of the stomach during exercise by eating at least 3 hours before participating in exercise or sport. Antacid medication, such as *sodium bicarbonate*, either in tablet or liquid form may be helpful. In severe cases stronger medications, including ranitidine and cimetidine, may be recommended.

Gastrointestinal system

The organs and tissues that bring the nutrients contained in food and fluids into the body to the cells. It can be regarded as a round tube that is 10 m (33 ft) long in the average adult, connected to a number of organs, such as the pancreas and gall bladder. It is also called the alimentary canal and digestive system.

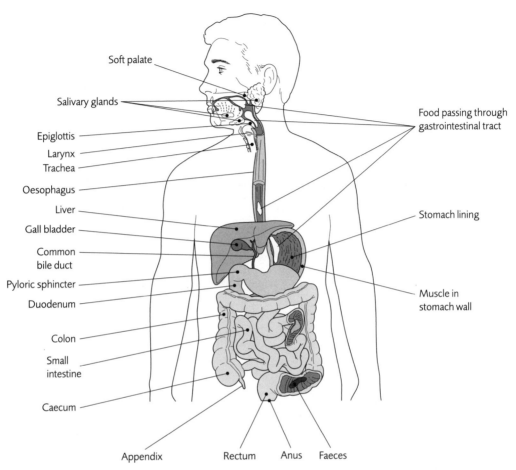

Soft palate

Salivary glands

Epiglottis

Larynx

Trachea

Oesophagus

Liver

Gall bladder

Common
bile duct

Pyloric sphincter

Duodenum

Colon

Small
intestine

Caecum

Appendix   Rectum   Anus   Faeces

Food passing through
gastrointestinal tract

Stomach lining

Muscle in
stomach wall

Gastrointestinal system

Physiology

The main task of the gastrointestinal system is to break down food into it's most basic components. For example, an orange is mostly made up of water, carbohydrates, fibre, vitamin C and other minerals. Carbohydrates are made up of three basic sugars: glucose, fructose and galactose.

The mouth chews and mashes up a piece of orange, which is swallowed down the throat into the oesophagus where it enters the stomach. The stomach is a muscle that churns the orange around. It also has cells that release acids and *enzymes*. After a few hours the orange moves into the small intestine, where bile and more enzymes are added from the liver, gallbladder, pancreas and cells lining the small intestine. By the end of the small intestine, made up of the duodenum, jejunum and ileum, the orange has been completely broken down and the carbohydrates absorbed through the intestinal wall and into the blood. It then enters the large intestine, made up of the caecum, colon and rectum, where the water and vitamin C are absorbed.

Fibre can't be broken down by the human body, but it serves an important role in adding bulk to the remaining undigested material, called faeces, allowing it to pass more smoothly through to the exit point, the anus.

The whole journey can take from 1 to 3 days. The movement of the food and fluids through the intestines occurs due to peristalsis, which are waves of contractions of the muscles in the intestinal wall, like a hand squeezing toothpaste out of a tube.

Illnesses and diseases

Exercise and sport may be associated with some illnesses and diseases of the gastrointestinal system, including *gastrointestinal reflux*, which is a backflow of acidic contents from the stomach into the oesophagus that causes a burning pain in the chest (heartburn), nausea, *vomiting* (often when activity is performed too soon after a meal), *stitch* (a sharp pain in the left or right upper abdomen underneath the ribs that is usually felt during high-intensity exercise) and *diarrhoea*.

Gastrointestinal bleeding may be observed either as red blood-stained or darkened faeces, and has a number of different causes that should be checked by a doctor. Another cause of gastrointestinal problems is *lactose intolerance*.

Gene therapy

A treatment that involves changing the activity of the genes in a cell in order to treat or prevent a disease or injury. Genes are the components that make up the nucleus of a cell, and act like a computer and manufacturing centre for proteins that are used to build structures or send messages. The genes are changed when a carrier, such as a harmless virus, contains new genes that are absorbed into the cells.

Gene therapy is a relatively new technology still under development. Research has been conducted for a number of exercise and sport injuries, including reconstructive surgery for *anterior cruciate ligament (ACL) tear* in the knee where the potential benefits include a quicker recovery. If it is successful, it is predicted that a full return to sport may be achieved after 6 weeks instead of 6 to 12 months.

General practitioner

A doctor who has received additional medical training to provide medical services including: being the first contact for people who need a diagnosis and treatment; deciding when to refer to another practitioner, such as a specialist; and providing ongoing treatment for a chronic illness or disease. These types of services are often called primary health care. A general practitioner (GP) is also called a family physician. Many GPs have a special interest in sports medicine.

Genitalia referred pain

Pain referred into the scrotum of males or labia of females. See *Sacroiliac joint pain*.

Genu valgum

A structural abnormality of the bones of the legs that causes excessive *foot pronation* and may be associated with an increased risk of injury.

Genu varum

A structural abnormality of the bones that causes bowed legs. It is associated with excessive *foot pronation* and an increased risk of injuries, including *patellofemoral joint syndrome*.

Ginseng

A herbal preparation that may be recommended by natural health practitioners to increase energy levels and produce a sense of wellbeing in people experiencing physical and psychological *stress* by stimulating the adrenal gland of the kidney. There are two types of ginseng: Siberian and Chinese.

Glandular fever

An infection of the white blood cells of the *immune system*, usually caused by the Epstein-Barr virus. It most commonly affects young people. Children with glandular fever only develop a flu-like illness. Adolescents and young adults have stronger symptoms, including severe *fever*, sore throat, general ill feeling, *headache*, swollen glands, spleen enlargement and sometimes muscles aches and pains, nausea and vomiting.

The virus is spread through close contact, especially saliva, such as kissing. It takes 30 to 50 days for symptoms to begin and lasts for 5 to 15 days. However, *tiredness* may be more prolonged and, in some cases, continues for a number of months.

Treatment includes medications to reduce fever, such as *paracetamol*, and rest to allow the immune system to destroy the virus. Return to exercise and sport should only commence after all symptoms have cleared. *Collision sports* should be avoided while the spleen is enlarged, due to the risk of rupture.

Glenoid labrum injury

An injury to the ring of fibrous tissue attached to the rim of the glenoid cavity, a shallow saucer-shaped bone, which expands its size and depth to increase the stability of the *shoulder joint*. The injury is a tear of the fibrous tissue.

Causes
An *acute injury* of the glenoid labrum can be caused by sudden trauma, such as a *shoulder dislocation*.

An *overuse injury* of the glenoid labrum is usually due to a gradual accumulation of forces over a long period of time, such as excessive amounts of throwing by *baseball* pitchers or serving by *tennis* players. There also may be an abnormality of the *throwing biomechanics* or *scapular biomechanics* leading to *shoulder instability*.

Diagnosis
There are two groups of injury: superior labrum anterior to posterior (SLAP) lesions; and non-SLAP lesions. Within each group the injury is either stable or unstable. An example of an unstable non-SLAP lesion is a Bankart lesion.

The main symptoms are a vaguely located pain in the shoulder, aggravated by arm overhead and behind-the-back movements. Popping or grinding sounds also may be present. A physical examination may find tenderness over the anterior (front) of the shoulder and pain during contraction of the biceps. *Magnetic resonance imaging (MRI)* may be ordered to confirm the diagnosis.

Treatment
Almost all glenoid labrum injuries should be treated initially with *rest* and *ice*, followed by *arthroscopy* to repair the tear. For example, an unstable SLAP lesion usually requires re-attaching the labrum to the glenoid cavity. A Bankart lesion should be treated with *internal fixation* (wire or screw). Stable SLAP lesions and non-SLAP lesions need debridement (scraping and cutting away) to eliminate mechanical irritation. An arthroscopy should be followed by *shoulder rehabilitation*.

Glucocorticosteroids

A group of *hormones* that are widely used as anti-inflammatory medications, such as *corticosteroid* injections for acute injuries and *corticosteroids (inhaled)* for *asthma*.

It is a *drug banned in sport* according to the International Olympic Committee (IOC) when taken in tablet form or injected to increase *cardiac output* of the heart, which can improve endurance in long distance activities.

Glucose

A chemical compound composed of carbon (C), oxygen (O) and hydrogen (H) atoms, which is the main source of energy sustaining human life and its activities. It provides much of the energy the body needs to keep all the basic body functions working, such as breathing, maintaining body temperature and heartbeat.

Glucose is primarily derived from foods containing *carbohydrates*. It belongs to a group of monosaccharides, or simple sugars, which also include galactose and fructose.

Carbohydrates are broken down by the *gastrointestinal system* into simple sugars, like glucose, absorbed through the gut into the bloodstream and transported around the body. Glucose is stored in the *liver* and muscles as *glycogen*, which is a long chain of bonded glucose.

When the bonds between the C, O and H atoms are broken down by the metabolic systems, such as the *glycolytic system* and *carbohydrate oxidation*, energy is released. In the muscles, this energy is used to produce a new compound, called adenosine triphosphate (ATP), which is then used to produce *muscle contractions*.

Of course, food is eaten at different times during the day. However, the levels of glucose in the blood are usually kept within narrow limits through the work of a number of *hormones*, except in people with uncontrolled *diabetes*.

The pancreas produces *insulin* when blood glucose levels are high, which stimulates cells throughout the body to absorb the excess. The glucose may be burned off to release cell energy, stored as glycogen in the muscles and liver, or converted into triglycerides.

Glucagon is another hormone produced by the pancreas that stimulates the break down of glycogen when blood glucose levels are low. *Adrenaline*, which has the same effect as glucagon, is produced in response to stress. *Human growth hormone (HGH)* also influences blood glucose levels by stimulating the breakdown of fats into glucose.

Gluteals

The muscles of the *buttock*, which include the gluteus maximus, gluteus medius and gluteus minimus.

Glycaemic index (GI)

A method of ranking the speed in which carbohydrate foods are broken down and absorbed from the gut into the bloodstream, and the resulting impact on blood glucose levels. It is commonly utilised by people with *diabetes* and athletes in training and competition (see *Energy supply*).

Foods with a high GI are quickly digested and absorbed, resulting in a rapid and high rise in blood glucose levels. Low GI foods are more slowly digested and result in a slower but continuous release of glucose into the blood.

It is also suggested that eating mostly low GI foods can help with weight loss—however, there is little research evidence to support this theory.

Glycogen

A long chain of bonded *glucose* molecules. Glucose is a *carbohydrate* that is the main source of energy for physiological processes that occur in the body, such as muscle contractions. It is stored in the body in the liver and muscles as glycogen. It provides an easily accessible supply of energy, particularly during exercise and sport.

When glucose levels in the blood are low, the pancreas produces a hormone called glucagon, which stimulates the breakdown of glycogen into glucose that passes into the blood to be carried around the body. High blood–glucose levels cause the pancreas to produce *insulin* to stimulate the conversion of glucose into glycogen.

Exercise and sport

Maintaining adequate glycogen stores through carbohydrate intake is an important part of the sports nutrition guidelines for people who are regularly participating in high intensity physical activities. Glycogen storage in the muscles and liver is limited and needs to be replenished after each session of activity.

Glycogen depletion during a competition event can severely reduce performance. Long-term excessively reduced supplies of glycogen that causes abnormal tiredness is called *carbohydrate depletion*.

Glycogen depletion

Muscle fatigue and tiredness that may be felt by athletes participating in endurance or long distance activities. For example, in marathon runners it usually occurs between 28 and 36 km (17–22 miles).

Glycaemic index (GI) of foods

Food group	Low GI (< 55)	Intermediate GI (55–70)	High GI (> 70)
Breakfast cereals	All Bran; muesli; oats; porridge; Special K; Guardian	Mini Wheats; Nutrigrain; Sustain; Vita Brits; Weet-Bix	Coco Pops; Corn Flakes; Puffed Wheat; Rice Bubbles; Sultana Bran
Breads	Fruit loaf; grainy breads; pumpernickel	Croissant; crumpet; pita bread; wholemeal	Bagel; rye; white
Crackers	Jatz	Ryvita; Sao	Kavli; puffed crispbread; water cracker
Grains	Buckwheat; bulgur	Taco shells	
Rice	Doongara	Basmati	Calrose; brown; long grain
Pasta	Instant noodles; egg; fettuccine; ravioli; spaghetti; vermicelli		
Sweet biscuits	Oatmeal	Arrowroot; shredded wheat; shortbread	Morning coffee
Cakes	Apple muffin; banana cake; sponge cake	Waffles	
Snack foods	Peanuts; potato crisps; chocolate	Popcorn; Mars Bar; muesli bar	Corn chips; jelly beans; Life Savers
Vegetables	Carrot; peas; sweet corn; sweet potato; yam	Beetroot; new potato; pontiac potato	Parsnip; baked potato; french fries; pumpkin; swede
Legumes	Baked beans; butter bean; chick peas; kidney beans; lentils; soya beans		Broad beans
Fruit	Apple; apricot (dried); cherries; grapefruit; grapes; kiwi fruit; orange; peach; pear; plum	Banana; mango; pawpaw; pineapple; raisins; rockmelon; sultanas	Watermelon
Dairy foods	Milk; flavoured milk; ice cream; yoghurt		
Drinks	Apple juice; orange juice	Cordial; soft drink	Lucozade

It is popularly called 'hitting the wall'. It may also be felt between competition events as a feeling of sluggishness, heavy legs, staleness and inability to maintain normal training intensity.

Physiology

It is due to a shutdown of the metabolic processes (the *glycolytic system* and *carbohydrate oxidation*) that produce adenosine triphosphate (ATP), the main source of energy for muscle contractions.It is caused by insufficient supply of *glycogen*, a long chain of glucose molecules that are stored in the muscles and liver.

Replenishing glycogen stores in the muscles and liver before an event (see *Pre-competition eating*) and maintaining a slower but steady pace during endurance activity can prevent glycogen depletion.

Glycolytic system

The chemical processes that do not need oxygen to break down glucose to produce *adenosine triphosphate (ATP)*, the main source of energy for *muscle contractions*. These processes are part of *anaerobic metabolism*.

The system is like kindling wood that gets a log fire burning stronger. When a muscle starts contracting, the *creatine phosphate system* immediately produces ATP, but fatigues after 6 to 30 seconds. By this time the glycolytic system has gone into full production to keep the supply of ATP going strong for a few minutes until carbohydrate oxidation finally kicks into action. The glycolytic system reaches it peak between 5 to 20 seconds and then starts decreasing.

Physiology

The glycolytic system uses *enzymes* in a 12-step process to break down glucose. It produces three ATPs for each molecule of glycogen (a long chain of bonded glucose molecules). At the end, glucose has been converted into lactic acid or *lactate*. If oxygen is present, the end product is pyruvic acid, which is broken down further through *carbohydrate oxidation*.

Exercise and sport

The glycolytic system is the main supply of energy for short bursts of activity, such as a sprint or lifting a weight. However, if it is used too quickly it can produce excessive amounts of lactate, called *lactate fatigue*. This limits the aerobic systems, such as carbohydrate oxidation, supply of energy for muscle contractions and as a result hinders the ability to continue performing an activity at the same intensity.

Goalball

See *Visually impaired athletes*.

Goal setting

Identifying a set of processes and results that are a product of participation in your chosen exercise or sport. Goals come in different forms, including subjective, objective, outcomes and task-oriented goals.

Subjective goals refer to personal feelings, such as 'I want to have fun'. Objective goals relate to performance, such as running times or swimming distance. Outcome-orientation is a focus on the results of a game, competition or tournament or being selected for a team. Task-orientation looks at the components of performance that leads to results, such as the proficiency of a tennis player's ground strokes.

Task orientation gives athletes goals that are immediate and in their direct control. It is a common belief that when an athlete achieves task-oriented goals, the outcomes will take care of themselves.

Golf

Golf originated in a game called 'paganica' played by Roman emperors hitting a feather-stuffed ball with a stick. The first modern golf club, the Company of Gentlemen Golfers, was established in Edinburgh in 1744. It has become one of the most popular sports in the world, with 23 million players in the USA and nearly 1 in 10 Australians playing golf every year.

Rules and equipment

A stick called a club is used to hit a small ball into a hole. A golf course generally has 18 holes. Play on each hole begins at the tee. The player with the fewest hits (strokes) to complete the course is the winner. The expected number of strokes is 'par'. For correct footwear, see *golf shoes*.

Fitness, skills and injuries

Players should have good eye-hand coordination and participate in *strength training*, *flexibility training* and *skills training*. Being *overweight* does not prevent playing good golf.

The most common injuries are *low back pain (non-specific)*, extensor tendinosis (*tennis elbow*), *Golfer's elbow* (flexor tendinosis), *de Quervain's tenosynovitis*

Champion golfer, Karrie Webb

(wrist), *rotator cuff tendinosis* (shoulder) and *rotator cuff strain* (shoulder) (see also *Golf biomechanics*).

Golf biomechanics

The movements and positions of the joints and muscles during the golf swing. The efficient golf swing is designed to strike the ball with the greatest impact and accuracy, with minimum strain to the muscles and joints.

Efficient biomechanics
The golf swing divides the body into three moving sections: the legs are the stable foundations; the trunk also provides stability and movement as it turns on it's axis like a rotating door; and the arms holding the club provide most of the power.

The golf swing is made up of four stages. Stage 1 is facing (addressing) the ball, standing with the trunk slightly bent forward. In stage 2, the right-handed golfer rotates the trunk to the right, maintains the bent forward position and lifts the arms holding the club behind and above the upper back on the right side. Stage 3 brings the arms back down to strike the ball with the club, rotating the trunk to the left. Stage 4 involves striking the ball and continuing the left rotation of the trunk as the arms swing up and above the upper back on the left side. At the same time the trunk straightens up from its bent forward posture.

Biomechanical abnormality
Any deviation from the above causes an inefficient golf swing and increases the risk of injury. For example, golfers who allow the trunk to bend or sway sideways during stages 2, 3 and 4 cause excessive stress on the lower back intervertebral disc and facet joints, increasing the risk of *low back pain (non-specific)*.

Golf shoes

The recommended footwear for *golf* is similar to the *running shoe* because of the large amount of walking in the sport, with spikes for the outsole to provide grip when hitting the ball.

Golfer's elbow

An overuse injury causing pain on the medial (inner) side of the *elbow joint* that gradually gets worse over a period of weeks or months, or suddenly starts after a single incident, like attempting a long tee off shot.

It is most common in golfers, but also can occur in *tennis* players who add extra top spin on their forehand shots. The injury primarily affects the pronator teres tendon, a muscle that starts at the medial epicondyle (inner side of the elbow) and passes into the forearm. The correct medical name is flexor *tendinosis*, which is a degenerative injury that may also have some inflammation.

The diagnosis and treatment is the same as for *tennis elbow*, except for the location. Particular attention should be paid to the golf swing technique, or tennis forehand shots to correct any *biomechanical abnormality* and prevent a re-injury.

Gonadotrophins

A synthetic form of the *hormones* that stimulates the ovaries and testes to produce oestrogen and testosterone. The two main types are human chorionic gonadotrophin (hCG) and pituitary gonadotrophins. They may be prescribed to stimulate ovulation in females and induce *puberty* in adolescent males who have delayed sexual development. Athletes use them for the same reasons as taking *anabolic steroids*, though they are considered less effective. They are *drugs banned in sport* according to the World Anti-Doping Agency (WADA).

Gout

A disease of a single joint that causes *inflammation, swelling,* loss of *flexibility,* pain and sometimes a mild *fever.* The pain usually begins as a severe attack lasting for 24 to 48 hours. The joint in the base of the big toe (first metatarsal-phalangeal (MTP) joint) and the elbow joint are the most commonly affected. It is caused by a disorder of the kidney that allows an excessive amount of uric acid in the blood (called hyper-uricaemia) to be deposited as crystals in the joint.

Diagnosis and treatment

The diagnosis is based on the symptoms, X-rays and tests of joint fluid taken by *aspiration* needle that check for uric acid crystals. Highly effective treatments include *non-steroidal anti-inflammatory drugs (NSAIDs)* and colchicine. Prevention of excessive uric acid in the blood is achieved by avoiding purine-rich foods, such as liver, drinking lots of fluids (see *Hydration*) and taking drugs that encourage uric acid excretion.

Gravity

One of the four forces of nature that gives humans and objects a *weight*. It creates an attraction in a direct line towards the centre of the earth and makes our bodies feel as if they are being pulled into the ground.

The effects of gravity are seen all the time in exercise and sport, though often we are not aware of them. A reminder is the high jump where athletes are attempting to overcome gravity. In everyday life the muscles of the body are continually working to keep the body upright as part of an activity, such as walking, or in exercise and sport, like hitting a golf ball.

Greenstick fracture

An incomplete break in a *bone* that looks like it has buckled on one side, which only occurs in children. Young bones are elastic compared to the hardness and rigidity of adult bone. The diagnosis is made with an X-ray. The treatment is usually a simple *immobilisation*, such as a plaster cast, which heals within 3 weeks.

Groin

The region of the body located between the lower abdomen and the inner, upper portion of the thigh adjacent to the genitalia (see *Hip joint*).

Growth plate

The section of growing cartilage between the diaphysis, the central shaft, and *epiphysis*, the rounded end of the *long bones* of the arms, hands, legs and feet. It is where much of the bone growth occurs that gives these bones their length and dimension.

Bone grows through a process called ossification, where soft cartilage is converted into hard and rigid bone tissue. This process begins in the embryo in the diaphysis, called the primary ossification centre. By birth most have been completely ossified. The epiphyses, called the secondary ossification centres, gradually ossify during childhood. The growth plate is a layer of cartilage that persists between the diaphysis and epiphysis.

As each layer of cartilage is ossified a new layer is put down, thus adding to the length of the bone. This process continues through puberty and adolescence. Full bone maturation occurs when the growth plate completely ossifies and the diaphysis and

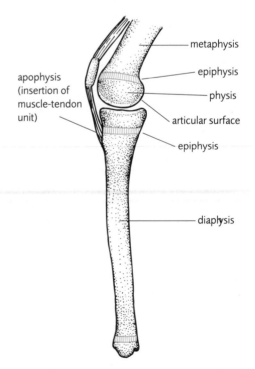

apophysis (insertion of muscle-tendon unit)

metaphysis

epiphysis

physis

articular surface

epiphysis

diaphysis

The growth plate is located between the diaphysis and epiphysis

epiphysis fuse together (see *Adolescents*). This occurs at varying ages according to each bone.

Growth plate fracture

A break in the section of bone in children and adolescents where much of the growth occurs that gives

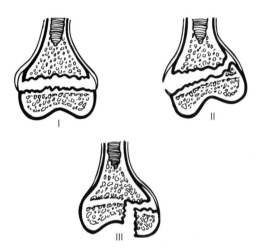

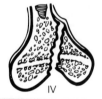

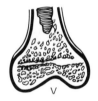

Salter and Harris classification of growth plate fractures

bones their length. The growth plate is located between the diaphysis, the central shaft and epiphysis, the rounded end of the long bones of the arms, hands, legs and feet. These *fractures* are of particular concern because of the dangers of interruption to the growth process.

Types, diagnosis and treatment

Growth plate fractures are classified according to the Salter and Harris method, which describes the location of the fracture. Salter-Harris Types I and II usually heal well with *immobilisation* because the fracture is only located within the growth plate. However, Types III and IV involve a fracture located in the *articular cartilage* surface as well as the growth plate, and have a high rate of complication, especially if they are not accurately realigned.

X-ray does not always detect a growth plate fracture. If a severe rotational or shear force caused the fracture, which was followed by swelling, bony tenderness and restricted movement and inability to do normal daily activities, a growth plate fracture should be suspected.

Gymnastics

The ancient Greeks and Romans invented gymnastics to prepare young men for war. During the 1800s the Germans and Swedish developed the modern rules. It was included in the first modern Olympics

Growth plate fractures, their treatments and potential complications

Site	Treatment	Potential complications
Wrist joint region • Radius (distal)	• Plaster cast for 3–4 weeks	• Not diagnosed early • Growth disturbance
Elbow joint region • Humerus (distal)	• Sling for 3 weeks	• Brachial artery damage • Median nerve damage • Malalignment
Shin region • Fibula (distal) • Tibia (distal)	• Plaster cast, non-weight-bearing for 4–6 weeks	• Growth disturbance • Premature fusion between diaphysis and epiphysis leading to angulation and leg shortness
Thigh region • Femur (distal)	• Realignment and re-apposition	• Growth disturbance

in 1896. The majority of participants are under 15 years old.

Fitness, skills and injuries

There are three disciplines: 1) Men's artistic gymnastics performed on the floor, pommel horse, vault, rings, parallel bars and horizontal bars; 2) women's artistic gymnastics on the floor, beam, asymmetrical bars and vault; and 3) rhythmic sportive gymnastics on the floor using hand apparatus including a ribbon, ball, rope, hoop or club. Gymnastics requires *flexibility training*, *aerobic training*, *agility training* and *skills training*.

The most common injuries include *triangular fibrocartilage complex sprain* (wrist), *distal radioulnar joint instability* (wrist), *Little Leaguer's elbow*, *low back pain (non-specific)*, *patellar tendinosis* (knee) and *Achilles tendinosis* (calf).

The most common *acute injury* is *ankle sprain*. There is also an increased risk of *eating disorders*.

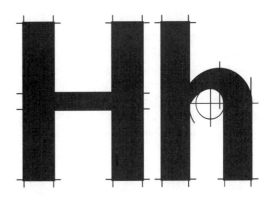

Haemarthrosis

Bleeding into a joint, which usually occurs due to an *acute injury* that is severe enough to rupture the blood vessels in a structure with access into the joint. For example, the anterior cruciate ligament, which passes through the inside of the *knee joint*. In most cases a haemarthrosis is an indication of the severity of an injury.

Diagnosis and treatment

A haemarthrosis causes sudden and severe *swelling* within 2 hours, which causes intense, sometimes throbbing, pain and the joint capsule can feel tight and tender. Walking is difficult or impossible, and active movements are restricted during the first 72 hours.

Immediate treatments, including *RICE* (*rest, ice, compression and elevation*), should be applied for up to 7 days. If pain is too severe, the blood can be withdrawn with a needle (*aspiration*). Subsequent treatment should be given for the injury (such as a torn ligament).

Haematocrit

The volume of blood cells, measured as a proportion of total blood volume. High haematocrit occurs as a natural response during exercise and sport when plasma volume decreases (up to 20 per cent after prolonged periods of activity), primarily due to increased blood pressure pushing it out of the *blood* through the capillaries and into the space around the cells. Fluid loss through sweating also contributes to decreased plasma volume.

A high haematocrit can be a benefit during activity because it increases the number of oxygen-carrying *red blood cells* per unit of blood, therefore increasing the availability of oxygen for working muscles. A low haematocrit can occur when the proportion of red blood cells decreases due to illness, such as *anaemia*.

Haematoma

See *Muscle contusion*.

Haematuria

Blood in the urine. The most common causes are *urinary tract infection*; trauma in *long distance running* from the repeated jarring that occurs with the impact of the foot striking the ground; and acute *abdominal injury* due to direct impact, including kidney, bladder or urethra injury. Jarring during running is reduced when wearing shock absorbent *running shoes* and running on good surfaces.

Haemoglobin

A protein-based, iron-containing molecule inside red blood cells which enables them to carry oxygen around the body. There are 250 million haemoglobin molecules in each red blood cell.

Physiology

The *iron* in haemoglobin has a strong chemical attraction for oxygen, which gives red blood cells their classic red colouring. Many factors influence the strength of the attraction for oxygen and, conversely, its tendency to release oxygen.

The amount of oxygen in red blood cells is called the oxygen saturation (in the average person the highest oxygen saturation is 98 per cent of all haemoglobin molecules). The lower the acidity and the more normal the temperature of the blood, the stronger the attraction, which is the usual condition in the blood vessels of the lungs.

However, in the muscles the acidity and temperature are higher, making it more likely for oxygen to be released. This tendency increases when the muscles are working hard due to metabolic processes and lactic acid and lactate production, which is an obvious benefit during exercise and sport.

A small part of carbon dioxide (CO_2) in the body, which is a waste product of working muscles, is attracted to the proteins in haemoglobin, giving *blood* carried in the veins and back to the lungs a blue colouring. However, most of the CO_2 is carried in the blood after it undergoes a chemical reaction with water (H_2O) in the plasma, changing it into *bicarbonate ions* (HCO_3^-) and hydrogen (H^+) ions.

Haemorrhage

Loss of blood from damaged blood vessels. It can be caused by an acute injury, such as a fall that twists the ankle and tears a ligament, or a sudden blow from a piece of equipment, such as a hockey stick causing a bruise. It may also be due to ongoing disease, like an aneurysm, in which an artery thins and weakens over a period of years until it bursts and *blood* escapes.

The body's response against bleeding is blood clotting, where *platelets* cause the blood to thicken and form a solid mass to block the opening in the blood vessel, and contractions of the muscles in the *artery* narrow it down and reduce blood flow.

Diagnosis and treatment

The signs and symptoms of a haemorrhage depend on the location. For example, bleeding into the cranial cavity can eventually lead to *loss of consciousness* and is life-threatening. So can internal bleeding into the abdomen where the blood volume and, as a result, the blood pressure drops too low. In exercise and sports-related injuries the usual sign is swelling. In a joint it is called a *haemarthrosis*, in a muscle it is a *muscle contusion* and in the skin it is a *bruise*.

Treatment depends on the location and the severity. Life-threatening haemorrhage is a *medical emergency*. Haemarthrosis, muscle contusion and bruising require *RICE* (*rest, ice, compression and elevation*).

Haemothorax

An acute injury that causes collapse of one of the *lungs* due to blood entering the pleural cavity, the space between the two layers of pleura that is normally only filled with a lubricant fluid. The causes and symptoms are similar to a *pneumothorax*. It should be treated as a *medical emergency*.

Hallux rigidus

An overuse injury that causes pain and stiffness in the first metatarso-phalangeal (MTP) joint located in the base of the big toe (see *Foot and toes*). It is due to an accumulation of excessive physical forces that build up gradually over a long period of time, often caused by a biomechanical abnormality called excessive *foot pronation*.

The pain is due to bony spurs that develop in the joint. Treatment involves *non-steroidal anti-inflammatory drugs (NSAIDs)* and *ice* to relieve the pain, and *orthotics* for correction of the biomechanical abnormality.

Hallux valgus

Pain at the base of the big toe, which has adopted a position closer towards the second toe joint, creating a more prominent bump (called a bunion) on the inside of the foot. It is an overuse injury due to an accumulation of physical forces over a period of weeks, months or years.

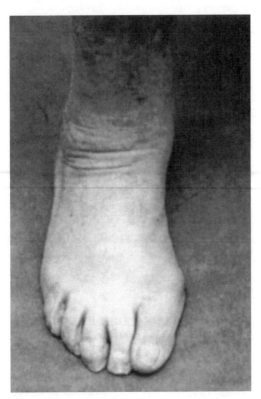

Hallux valgus of the big toe

It is often associated with excessive *foot pronation*, a biomechanical abnormality of walking or running, and wearing *shoes* that are too small. In cases of severe pain there are usually bony spurs in the first metatarso-phalangeal (MTP) joint (see *Foot and toes*).

Treatment includes padding to reduce the physical forces on the bunion, wearing the correct shoe size and correction of excessive foot pronation. *Open surgery* is occasionally required to remove bony spurs in the first MTP joint or, in severe cases, an *osteotomy*.

Hamstring contusion

Bruising of the hamstring (back *thigh* muscle) caused by a direct blow from a part of the body of an opposing player or a piece of equipment. It is most common in contact sports, such as the *football* codes and *basketball*, and ball sports such as *hockey (field)*, *lacrosse* and *cricket* where the ball travels at high speed. The diagnosis, treatment and return to sport are the same as for a *quadriceps contusion*.

Hamstring origin tendinitis

An injury that causes inflammation of the tendon of the hamstring (back of the *thigh* muscle) at its attachment in the buttock to a *pelvis* bone called the ischial tuberosity. It occurs frequently in sprinters.

This *tendinitis* injury is most commonly due to an overuse injury caused by an accumulation of excessive forces. In the early stages the inflammation causes only minor pain and stiffness, but with continued excessive forces it becomes severe enough to seek medical care. In a few cases it can be the result of an *acute injury* that is inadequately treated and does not heal properly.

Diagnosis, treatment and return to sport
The diagnosis is confirmed if pressing on the ischial tuberosity, stretching the hamstring and making the muscle work against resistance reproduces the buttock pain. There also may be reduced *flexibility* and weakness in the hamstring as well as their antagonists, the psoas major and rectus femoris muscles (see *Hip joint*).

177

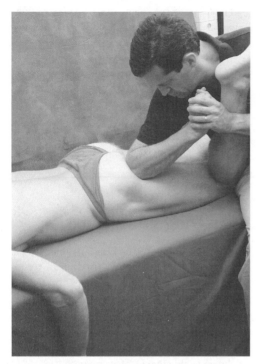

Massage treatment for hamstring origin tendinitis

The most effective treatment is *massage* of the tendon, using deep transverse frictions, and *ice* and *non-steroidal anti-inflammatory drugs (NSAIDs)* to reduce the inflammation, though there are doubts about the effectiveness of the latter.

Electrotherapy, such as *ultrasound therapy* and *high voltage galvanic stimulation*, may be helpful. *Flexibility exercises* for the hamstring, psoas major and rectus femoris muscles and *strengthening exercises* for the hamstring also may be required. If the above treatments are not successful, a *corticosteroid* injection may be recommended.

In general, mild cases take 1 to 2 weeks before making a return to sport. More severe cases may require up to several months, depending on the response to treatment.

Hamstring syndrome

In some cases, when tendinitis has been present for a long time, fibrous adhesions develop around the nearby sciatic nerve, a large nerve that begins at the low back and runs past the ischial tuberosity on its way down into the thigh. If the above treatments fail, surgery may be recommended to cut and loosen up the adhesions.

Hamstring strain

An acute injury of the back *thigh* muscle that causes sudden pain and a tearing sensation. It usually occurs during a running activity such as *sprinting*, hurdling, long jump (see *Jumping sports*), one of the *football* codes, *basketball* and *hockey (field)*. It is one of the most common injuries in sport. The older the athlete, the more likely it is to occur.

Causes

The injury usually occurs just before or after the leg strides forward and the foot hits the ground during running. In this position, the hamstring is stretched forward at the back of the hip and knee joints while it is working hard to slow down the leg.

The fact that the muscle spans those two joints is one reason it is particularly susceptible to injury. Other factors that may contribute to an increased risk include insufficient and inappropriate *warm-up*,

Flexibility exercise for hamstring strain

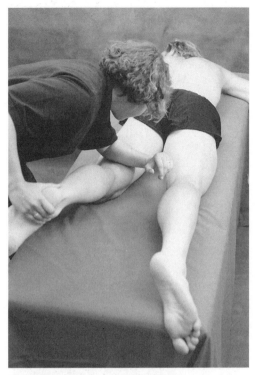

Massage treatment for hamstring strain

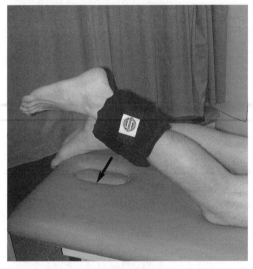

The black arrow shows the direction of an eccentric strengthening exercise for a hamstring strain

a rapid increase in the intensity of training (see *Overload*) combined with *lumbo-pelvic instability* or abnormalities of *running biomechanics* such as overstriding, which places excessive stretch on the muscle as it attempts to perform a contraction.

Diagnosis

There are three degrees of muscle *strain*. Mild (grade 1) strain does not force a stop to participation in the activity but is usually noticed after cooling down or the following day. Moderate (grade 2) strain causes reduced muscle strength and pain that prevents continued participation as soon as the injury occurs. Severe (grade 3) strains cause significantly reduced strength, a limp, muscle *spasm* and immediately prevents participation, though they may be less painful than moderate strains because pain-sensing nerves in the muscle have been completely torn. *Magnetic resonance imaging (MRI)* or *diagnostic ultrasound* may be helpful to determine the grade.

Treatment and return to sport

The initial treatment is *RICE (rest, ice, compression and elevation)* and *active exercises* for knee straightening (extension) in a sitting position following the ice treatment for 5 minutes to minimise loss of *flexibility* in the muscle.

The ice and exercises can be repeated as frequently as once an hour during the first 48 hours after injury. *Massage* should be only started 5 days after the injury to reduce the risk of developing *myositis ossificans*.

Other treatments include *mobilisation* for the low back joints if there is loss of range of movement, *neural tension* stretching and *flexibility exercises*, correction of any abnormalities associated with running biomechanics and *strengthening exercises*, which vary according to the sport; for example, *eccentric* contractions are important for sprinters.

Return to sport for a mild strain is usually 1 to 2 weeks; moderate 3 to 4 weeks; severe up to 10 weeks. In general it is essential not to do too much too early due to the high risk of re-injury. Running may be commenced in the first few days for mild strains, whereas a severe strain can require up to 3 weeks.

During a *sport rehabilitation* program it is recommended to focus on a type of running called 'run throughs', which involve acceleration over a fixed distance from a standing start, followed by constant speed over a fixed distance and then a final deceleration to a stop after a set distance. A 'run through' is made more demanding by decreasing the distance in the acceleration and deceleration phase.

Hamstring syndrome

See *Hamstring origin tendinitis.*

Hamstring tendinitis

An overuse injury that causes inflammation in the lower part of the back of the *thigh* muscle near the *knee joint.* It is often due to excessive training *overload* of knee flexion (bending) strength training and is most commonly seen in sprinters.

The recommended treatment for this *tendinitis* injury includes *non-steroidal anti-inflammatory drugs (NSAIDs), ice, massage,* electrotherapy such as *ultrasound therapy* and *high voltage galvanic stimulation, flexibility exercises* and *strengthening exercises.*

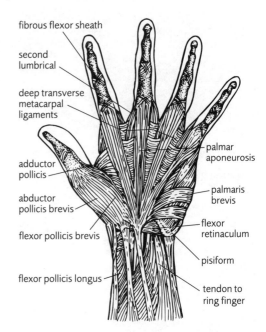

fibrous flexor sheath
second lumbrical
deep transverse metacarpal ligaments
adductor pollicis
abductor pollicis brevis
flexor pollicis brevis
flexor pollicis longus
palmar aponeurosis
palmaris brevis
flexor retinaculum
pisiform
tendon to ring finger

Anatomy of the hand and fingers—palmar (palm) view

Hand and finger joints

The hand is designed to sense and perform manipulation and prehensile activities. It is divided into four sections: the palm, back (dorsal), thumb-side (radial) and little-finger-side (ulnar). The fingers, or digits, are the thumb and the index, middle, ring and little fingers.

The hand contains five metacarpal bones connecting the *wrist joint* to the digit bones, called the phalanges (plural for phalanx). The thumb has two phalanges (proximal and distal) and the fingers have three phalanges (proximal, middle and distal). The joints between the metacarpals and phalanges are called metacarpal-phalangeal (MCP) joints.

The joint between the metacarpal of the thumb and first phalanx is the first metacarpal-phalangeal (MCP) joint. The remaining metacarpal-phalangeal (MCP) joints (knuckles) are numbered 2, 3, 4 and 5.

The joints between the phalanges are called interphalangeal (IP) joints. The one closest to the knuckle

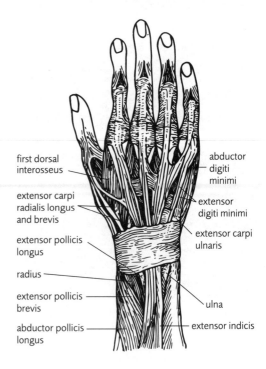

first dorsal interosseus
extensor carpi radialis longus and brevis
extensor pollicis longus
radius
extensor pollicis brevis
abductor pollicis longus
abductor digiti minimi
extensor digiti minimi
extensor carpi ulnaris
ulna
extensor indicis

Anatomy of the hand and fingers—dorsal (back) view

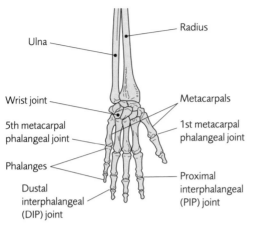

- Ulna
- Radius
- Wrist joint
- Metacarpals
- 5th metacarpal phalangeal joint
- 1st metacarpal phalangeal joint
- Phalanges
- Proximal interphalangeal (PIP) joint
- Dustal interphalangeal (DIP) joint

Bones of the hand and finger joints

Muscles involved in thumb movements

Movement	Primary movers	Secondary movers
Flexion	• Flexor pollicis brevis • Flexor pollicis longus • Opponens pollicis	
Extension	• Extensor pollicis brevis • Extensor pollicis longus	
Abduction	• Abductor pollicis brevis • Abductor pollicis longus	
Adduction	• Adductor pollicis longus	
Opposition	• Opponens pollicis • Flexor pollicis brevis	• Adductor pollicis • Flexor pollicis longus

is the proximal interphalangeal (PIP) joint, and the one closest to the finger tips is the distal interphalangeal (DIP) joint.

Many of the muscles in the forearm and elbow form tendons that pass through the wrist to move the hand and fingers. Also passing through the wrist are the major blood vessels and nerves, each called radial, median and ulnar respectively.

Hand and finger pain and injuries

Causes

Hand and finger pain is usually caused by an *acute injury* that begins suddenly due to a single incident, such as falling onto the hand.

The *hand and finger joints* and their associated structures are the main sources of *pain*. However, it is not unusual for referred pain to come from another structure, in particular the *neck joints*, which is called *hand and finger referred pain*.

Diagnosis

The diagnosis involves combining information gathered from the *history, physical examination* and relevant tests.

The activity and forces at the time of the injury are important clues. A direct, severe blow to the fingers may result in a *metacarpal fracture* or *phalanx fracture*. A blow to the point of the finger may produce a *MCP joint dislocation, PIP joint dislocation* or *first MCP joint sprain* (also called skier's thumb).

A punching injury also often results in a Bennett's fracture or boxer's fracture (see *Metacarpal fracture*). Grabbing an opponent's clothing while attempting a tackle in football suggests a *long flexor tendon avulsion*. An *X-ray* is recommended to detect fractures.

Muscles involved in finger (index, middle, ring and little) movements

Movement	Primary movers	Secondary movers
Flexion	• Flexor digitorum superficialis • Flexor digitorum profundus • Flexor digiti minimi	• Lumbricals • Interossei
Extension	• Extensor digitorum • Extensor Indicis • Extensor digiti minimi	
Abduction	• Interossei • Abductor digiti minimi	
Adduction	• Interossei (when fingers are straight) • Flexor digitorum superficialis • Flexor digitorum profundus (when fingers are bent)	

Causes of hand and finger pain and injuries

Most common	Less common	Not to be missed
• Metacarpal fracture	• MCP joint dislocation	• Long flexor tendon avulsion
• Phalanx fracture	• Boxer's fracture	
• PIP joint dislocation	• Mallet finger	
• First MCP joint sprain (skier's thumb)	• Hand and finger referred pain	
• PIP joint sprain		
• Subungual haematoma		
• Hand laceration and infection		

MCP = metacarpal-phalangeal, PIP = proximal interphalangeal, DIP = distal interphalangeal

QUICK REFERENCE GUIDE
Hand and fingers

Metacarpal fracture......................Do you have pain in the palm or back of the hand near the base of the fingers or knuckles that resulted from punching a hard object or falling onto your hand?

MCP joint dislocation....................Did a knuckle joint come out of place after receiving a sudden blow to the hand?

Phalanx fracture ....Did you receive a sudden blow to the lower part of the finger or thumb and now feel pain?

PIP joint dislocation......................Did a finger joint come out of place after receiving a sudden blow to the point of the finger?

First MCP joint sprain ....Do you feel pain located in the palm at the base of the thumb after the thumb was suddenly and forcefully moved backwards and outwards?

Hand and finger referred pain

Pain in the hands and fingers caused by a damaged structure in another location some distance away, such as the *neck joints*, *thoracic spine joints*, neural sheath of the *nerves* or *carpal tunnel syndrome* (wrist). The diagnosis and treatment is usually the same as for *shoulder referred pain*.

Hand laceration and infection

An open wound to the hand or fingers is a frequent occurrence in sport as a result of contact with equipment and opponents. All lacerations have the potential to become infected and should, therefore, be thoroughly cleaned with an antiseptic solution and observed closely for signs of infection (see *Skin injury*).

Of particular concern is a laceration of the hand (often over the knuckles) caused by the teeth, usually due to punching someone in the mouth. It should always be assumed that these injuries have been contaminated. They require immediate treatment in hospital for surgical debridement and *antibiotics*.

Handedness

See *Dominant side*.

Handlebar palsy

Pressure on the ulnar nerve in the wrist that causes pain and *numbness* or *pins and needles* in the little finger and inner side of the fourth finger. Muscle weakness may develop at a later stage. This *nerve entrapment* injury most commonly occurs due to *cycling* and *martial arts* such as karate. The compression is due to *swelling*, and is located between the pisiform and hamate bones (see *Wrist joint*).

Treatment for mild cases includes wearing a splint, a form of *immobilisation* called protected mobilisation, *non-steroidal anti-inflammatory drugs (NSAIDs)* and changing the grip on the bicycle handlebars. Surgery to drain the swelling may be required for severe cases.

Head

The head can be divided into two sections: 1) the skull and *brain* that sits inside and 2) the face, jaw, mouth and organs including the *eyes*, ears and nose.

The skull is made up of the occipital, parietal, frontal, sphenoid and temporal bones that form the rounded top section; and maxilla, zygomatic, nasal and vomer bones of the face, with the mandible (jaw bone) attached.

The bones are held together with a *fibrous and cartilaginous joint* called a suture, which permits little movement. The temporomandibular joint is a synovial joint that enables jaw and mouth movements.

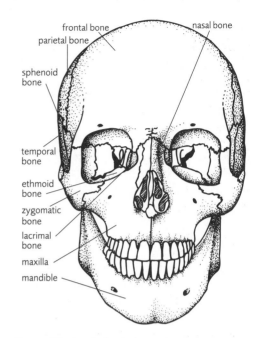

Bones of the head—front view

Pain and injuries to the skull and brain are in the *head injury* and *headache* sections. Pain and injuries for the rest of the head are in the *face pain and injuries* section.

Head injury

An acute injury to the head due to a sudden excessive force, such as a fall to the ground. The primary concern is brain damage.

Treatment

A suspected severe head injury, which also may be associated with a *spinal injury*, should be treated as a *medical emergency*. Recognising a severe head injury and transporting the injured person to a hospital as quickly as possible dramatically improves survival chances and reduces risk of long-term damage.

A severe head injury may be indicated by the following symptoms:

- Loss of consciousness for more than 5 minutes.
- Development of increasing headache, nausea and vomiting.

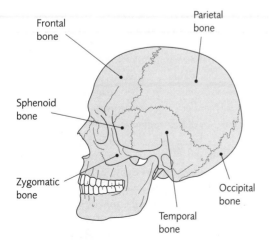

Bones of the head—side view

- Unequal size of the pupils of the eyes.
- Convulsions or seizures.
- Gradual increase in blood pressure or decrease in pulse rate.
- Deterioration of mental state such as becoming drowsy after being relatively alert or reduced concentration.

Mild and moderate, as well as severe head injuries, are described in more detail under *concussion*. A *skull fracture*, which also can occur due to a head injury, may require treatment.

Headache

Pain located in the head. In most cases, people who exercise and play sport have headaches as often as inactive people and for the same reasons.

However, there are causes more commonly experienced, such as *benign exertional headache*, where the headache comes on during exercise and stops with cessation, and *footballer's migraine*, due to repeated minor blows to the head.

Diagnosis

Many headaches do not require a medical assessment. However, if any of the following are present, it is recommended to see a doctor as soon as possible to exclude serious or potentially life-threatening causes:

- new or unaccustomed headache.
- stiff neck.
- *fever*, weight loss and malaise also present.
- neurological symptoms; for example, drowsiness, loss of *strength*, *numbness* or *pins and needles* in the limbs.
- headache increasing over a few days.
- sudden onset of severe headache.
- headaches that wake you up during the night or in the early morning.

The different types of headaches that are commonly experienced include:

1) Headache due to the *common cold* and *flu*.
2) Vascular headaches, including *migraine* and *cluster headache*, often associated with other symptoms, such as nausea and sensitivity to light, and cause more severe, throbbing pain relieved with sleep.
3) *Neck-related headache* is *referred pain* from the joints and muscles of the neck often associated with neck pain and stiffness and aggravating neck movements.
4) Tension headaches, or muscle contraction headaches, tend to cause minor pain daily.
5) Serious or life-threatening causes include *tumour*, intracranial haemorrhage, subdural haematoma and meningitis, which cause persistent and often severe pain, either suddenly or gradually.
6) Other causes can include *concussion* and side effects of drugs, such as *alcohol*, *analgesics*, antibiotics, *antihypertensives* for high blood pressure, *caffeine*, *corticosteroids*, cyclosporin, sedatives like nitrazepam, oral contraception and some *asthma* medications.

Healthy weight

A weight that achieves maximum prevention of ill health and disease. This weight can be calculated according to several methods including the *waist–hip ratio*, *waist size*, *height–weight chart* and *body-mass index (BMI)*.

Heart

The organ that is responsible for pumping blood around the body. It is a hollow, fist-sized muscle located in the *chest*. It is divided into a large left side and smaller right side. Each side is divided into an upper, small chamber called an atrium and a lower, larger chamber called a ventricle. The heart is the central part of the *cardiovascular system*.

Physiology

The flow of *blood* follows a cycle. It begins with red blood, rich in oxygen, flowing from the lungs into the left atrium, through the mitral (bicuspid) valve down into the left ventricle, which pumps it out through the aortic valve into the aorta and the arteries to the cells of the body.

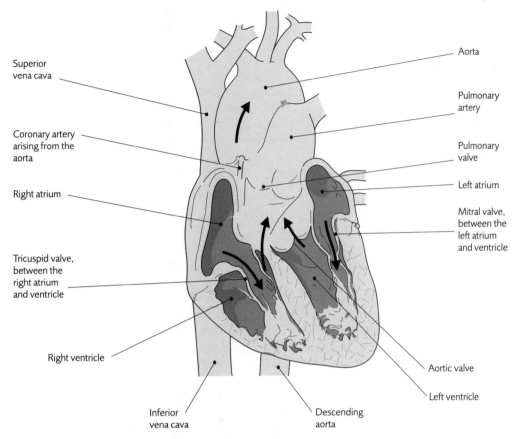

Superior
vena cava

Aorta

Pulmonary
artery

Coronary artery
arising from the
aorta

Pulmonary
valve

Left atrium

Right atrium

Mitral valve,
between the
left atrium
and ventricle

Tricuspid valve,
between the
right atrium
and ventricle

Right ventricle

Aortic valve

Left ventricle

Inferior
vena cava

Descending
aorta

The heart

From the cells, the blood depleted of oxygen flows back through veins (and with fluid in the lymph vessels) empties into the right atrium, which flows through the tricuspid valve into the right ventricle and then the pulmonary semilunar valve to the lungs where oxygen is absorbed into the blood—and once again the cycle begins.

The heart is made up of cardiac *muscle fibres*, which are designed to perform a *heartbeat* in a coordinated sequence. The frequency of heartbeats is called the *heart rate*. The amount of blood pumped out with each heartbeat is called *stroke volume*, which per minute is called *cardiac output*.

The coronary vascular system comprises the heart's own arteries for bringing blood from the left ventricle and veins for carrying away wastes. Reduced blood flowing through these arteries is called *coronary heart disease*. It is the main cause of a *heart attack*.

Heart attack

A sudden reduction in the flow of blood to the *heart* muscle. When the reduction is severe, or occurs for a long time, the heart muscle can be permanently damaged. If a large section of the heart muscle is damaged it causes sudden death. In very mild cases no symptoms are felt.

It is usually caused by narrowing of the arteries, called *coronary heart disease*. The narrowing is due to plaques that can trigger the formation of a blood clot, called a thrombosis, that completely blocks the artery. In other cases the muscles in the wall of artery temporarily go into spasm. It may also be caused by air emboli blocking arteries due to *decompression sickness*.

Diagnosis

The main symptom of a heart attack is chest pain, though not all causes of chest pain are due to a heart attack (see *Chest pain and injuries*). It may also cause pain in the jaw, neck, shoulder, inner arms and upper abdomen.

The type of pain is often described as vice-like and sometimes burning. It may be brought on by being active, such as participating in exercise or walking up stairs, or by heavy meals, cold weather, *stress* and emotion. Other common symptoms include *shortness of breath*, nausea, *tiredness*, loss of consciousness (*syncope*), sweating and *vomiting*.

Treatment

A heart attack is a *medical emergency* that may require immediate treatment to prevent sudden death and permanent damage to the heart muscle.

The recommended treatments afterwards depend on the severity of the attack. For example, in mild cases only drugs such as *beta blockers* may be recommended. In moderate to severe cases treatment in a coronary care unit of a hospital is required until the heart recovers, followed by *cardiac rehabilitation*. Long-term treatment may include coronary bypass surgery. In all cases lifestyle changes such as quitting smoking, *diet for good health* and *exercise for health* are recommended.

Heart disease

Heart disease is the most common cause of death. In Australia it claims a life every 18 minutes, in the USA every 34 seconds. It can occur in people of all ages, but is more likely with increasing age. It can also affect people who are active, including elite athletes, though inactive people face the greatest risk.

Performing a physical activity, such as exercise or playing sport, makes the *heart* work harder. As a result, people with heart disease can develop symptoms such as *palpitations, syncope, heart murmur* and chest pain (see *Chest pain and injuries*).

The most common types of heart disease that need special attention with regards to participation in exercise and sport include *hypertrophic cardiomyopathy, Marfan's syndrome, coronary heart disease, heart attack, aortic stenosis, mitral valve prolapse, mitral stenosis* and *myocarditis*.

Heart murmur

A sound heard with a stethoscope when blood is not flowing smoothly through the *heart*. It may be normal or a warning sign of an underlying problem, such as *aortic stenosis*. It may occur during different parts of the *heartbeat*, systolic (contraction) and diastolic (relaxation). All diastolic murmurs are abnormal. A normal murmur is usually a short systolic sound, unlike an aortic, which produces a harsh crescendo-decrescendo murmur radiating to the neck.

Heart rate

The frequency of *heartbeats*, usually stated as the number of heartbeats per minute. It can be measured in several ways. The easiest to feel is a *pulse*, usually the radial pulse in the wrist, and counting the number of beats in 20 seconds and multiplying by three. Doctors and other health professionals often use a stethoscope.

The most accurate method of measurement is a heart rate monitor, which is a device that detects the distinctive electrical pattern produced by each heartbeat. Monitors are often found in hospitals. Portable monitors can be strapped around the chest and used to measure heart rate during activities such as running.

The average heart rate for an adult at rest is 60 to 80 beats per minute. However, the range can vary enormously according to fitness. Unfit people can be as high as 100 per minute. Fit people can be as low as 28 per minute, mainly because they have a higher *stroke volume*, and their muscle fibres are efficient at absorbing and using oxygen from the blood and therefore they don't need as much blood pumped to them.

Exercise and sport

During exercise and sport the heart rate increases in direct proportion to the intensity of the activity until you reach a point of exhaustion (determined by your fitness levels) and then it levels off. A steady heart rate less than the maximum is an intensity of activity below the point of exhaustion, called sub-maximal exercise.

Heart surgery

An operation performed on the heart. Common operations for *coronary heart disease* include coronary bypass surgery, which involves using a piece of a healthy vein from the leg to divert blood around the narrowed section of diseased coronary artery, and angioplasty, where a balloon is placed inside a diseased artery to flatten the bulge causing the narrowing. Angioplasty is also used to open out narrowed valves, such as *aortic stenosis*.

Heart transplants are performed to replace hearts that are severely diseased, such as severe coronary heart disease and congenital diseases (see *Transplant recipients*).

Heartbeat

A contraction of the *heart* muscle which pumps blood from the right ventricle to the lungs and from the larger left ventricle into the arteries and to the cells in the rest of the body.

A heartbeat is felt in the chest where the left ventricle is closest to the surface. The *pulse* of an artery, such as the radial artery in the wrist, is produced by heartbeats.

Physiology

A heart muscle contraction occurs as part of a regular and coordinated sequence of instructions from the sinoatrial node, the heart control centre, and due to responses from the muscle fibres of the heart.

An *electrocardiogram* (ECG) shows the sequence as an electric wave.

It begins with the diastole, where the heart muscle is relaxed and blood flows into the atrium and ventricle of both the right and left sides. The end of the diastole begins when the sinoatrial node sends out an instruction to start a contraction.

This instruction begins at the right atrium and spreads quickly to the left atrium, causing the muscle fibres in their walls to perform a contraction, called the atrial systole, which pumps more blood into both ventricles to fill them up completely. Then the instruction spreads further down the heart to reach the atrioventricular node, which instructs the muscle fibres in the walls of both ventricles to perform a contraction, called the ventricular systole.

The frequency of heartbeats is called the *heart rate*. Heart beat irregularities are called *cardiac arrhythmias*.

Heartburn

A burning pain in the chest that is caused by *gastrointestinal reflux*. It is often associated with oesophageal muscular spasm that causes a pain in the upper abdomen that may be confused with the pain caused by a *heart attack* (see *Chest pain and injuries*).

Heat acclimatisation

Training in preparation for an upcoming competition in a different climate. For example, the body needs time to adjust to a hot and humid climate when coming from a winter location, in particular the ability to alter the sweating mechanism for maintaining core body *temperature*.

The best method is travelling to a location with a similar climate two weeks prior to the upcoming event. A heat chamber for 3 hours per day prior to departure is only partially effective and should be used as an adjunct rather than as a replacement for full acclimatisation. Wearing impermeable clothing while exercising may also make a small contribution to acclimatisation. The effectiveness of acclimatisation is reduced in athletes who are *tapering*.

Heat illness

An excessively high core body temperature, about 41°C (105.8°F) and above. It occurs when heat gain is greater than heat loss during participation in exercise and sport. At rest the normal temperature is around 37°C (98.6°F). During exercise and sport the muscles and metabolism produce heat. In response the body switches on sweating to provide heat loss through evaporation (see *Temperature*).

Causes and diagnosis

The outside environment is the main factor that reduces the ability to lose heat through sweating. In a dry environment sweat is evaporated efficiently. In a humid environment the high level of water vapour in the air limits evaporation. A combination of high temperature and high humidity makes sweating even less efficient. The level of *dehydration* is most likely another important factor.

Each person responds differently to increases in core body temperature. As the temperature approaches 41°C (105.8°F) and above, symptoms may appear, including dizziness, weakness, nausea, *headache*, confusion, disorientation, irrational behaviour including aggressiveness, brown-coloured urine and drowsiness deteriorating to loss of consciousness in severe cases.

Children, younger *adolescents, wheelchair athletes* who have a spinal cord injury and *transplant recipients* are the most vulnerable to heat illness.

Treatment

Severe heat illness (also called heat stroke) is a *medical emergency*, requiring immediate cooling and treatments to ensure breathing and circulation are not compromised.

The recommended methods of cooling include being placed in the shade and a bath of ice water (shivering indicates that core body temperature has decreased to 37°C (98.6°F) or below). In some cases, intravenous fluids for dehydration may be required.

Following correct treatment and a full recovery, walking may be permitted.

Prevention

1) Heat illness is less likely in people who achieve adequate *aerobic fitness* levels.
2) *Heat acclimatisation* is recommended when competing in unaccustomed heat or humidity.
3) Avoid training or competition during hot and humid weather. If this is unavoidable, schedule event for early in the morning, not between 11 am and 3 pm, the hottest part of the day.
4) Wear appropriate clothing. In hot conditions, wear a minimal amount of loose-fitting, light-coloured clothing. An open weave or mesh top is ideal.
5) Maintain adequate *hydration* before, during and after training or competition (also see *Hydration for children* and *older athletes*).
6) Have first aid support available for an emergency and a plan for taking someone with heat illness to the hospital.

Heat rub

See *Analgesics (topical)*.

Heat therapy (superficial)

A heat treatment that penetrates to the superficial layers of the body, including the skin, subcutaneous tissue and upper muscle layers and nearby joints and ligaments. The aim of the heat is to relieve chronic *swelling* and muscle *spasm*, reduce pain and promote healing. It should not be used to treat an *acute injury* for at least 72 hours after the injury has occurred.

Method

Increasing the temperature of body tissue widens the diameter of the blood vessels to increase circulation to help clear swelling, alters the conduction velocity of motor and sensory neurons (nerve fibres) to help reduce muscle *spasm* and *pain*, accelerates the *metabolism* of cells and increases the flexibility of the *collagen* in muscle, ligament and joint capsule.

Heat can be applied in different ways including a hot water bottle, warm shower or bath, warm whirlpools, heat packs and paraffin wax. Heat radiant lamps only penetrate a few millimetres.

At least three layers of towel should be used between the heat source and the skin to prevent excessive heating that can lead to a burn. Pain that is stronger than that caused by normal heating is a sign that the treatment is too hot. The recommended time for heating is 10 to 20 minutes. It should not be performed when the skin has reduced sensation, the area has poor circulation nor over open wounds.

Heel spurs

See *Plantar fasciitis.*

Height–weight chart

A method of assessing whether a person's weight is healthy. Though not as accurate as other methods, including *waist–hip ratio* for women and *waist size* for men, it is still useful for most men and women aged above 18 years (see *Overweight*).

Hellerwork

See *Rolfing.*

Helmet

A piece of equipment worn to protect the head and face from injuries, including fractures, concussion, lacerations and bruising (see *Face pain and injuries* and *Head injury*). It may also reduce the occurrence of *migraines*.

Helmets can reduce the likelihood of a skull fracture. Therefore they should be worn in sports where the head and face have a high risk of being struck, such as *motor sports, cycling, cricket, horse riding sports, ice hockey, American football* and snow sports

Height–weight chart

Height (no shoes)		Body weight (light clothing/no shoes)	
cm	ft/in	kg	lb
140	4'7"	39–49	86–108
142	4'8"	40–50	88–110
144	4'9"	41–52	90–114
146	4'9"	43–53	95–117
148	4'10"	44–55	97–121
150	4'11"	45–56	99–123
152	5'0"	46–58	101–128
154	5'1"	47–59	103–130
156	5'1"	49–61	108–134
158	5'2"	50–62	110–136
160	5'3"	51–64	112–141
162	5'4"	52–66	114–145
164	5'5"	54–67	119–147
166	5'5"	55–69	121–152
168	5'6"	56–71	123–156
170	5'7"	58–72	128–158
172	5'8"	59–74	130–163
174	5'9"	61–76	134–167
176	5'9"	62–77	136–169
178	5'10"	63–79	139–174
180	5'11"	65–81	143–178
182	6'0"	66–83	145–183
184	6'0"	68–85	150–187
186	6'1"	69–86	152–189
188	6'2"	71–88	156–194
190	6'3"	72–90	158–198
192	6'4"	74–92	163–202
194	6'4"	75–94	165–207
196	6'5"	77–96	169–211
198	6'6"	78–98	172–216
200	6'7"	80–100	172–220

such as *downhill skiing*. However, there is no clear evidence that wearing a helmet reduces the chances of concussion.

Types of helmets
The two types of helmets are hard and soft shell. Hard shell is generally considered more effective at preventing head and face injury than soft shell. However, soft shell helmets can be worn to reduce the impact of blows to the head that trigger migraine.

Wearing any type of helmet is not necessarily better than not wearing protective headgear. A helmet is only worth wearing if it is the correct design for the sport and made according to an approved national standard.

Helmets

For example, an American football helmet consists of a hard plastic shell, foam pads that cushion the head and a strap that runs underneath the chin to keep the helmet in place during activity. The helmet also has holes near each ear to allow the player to hear and a facemask. Structural features that can reduce protectiveness include interference with the athlete's visual field, which may raise the risk of collisions, and reduced heat exchange through the head can increase the risk of *heat illness* and dehydration.

Hepatitis

An inflammation of the *liver* that can cause symptoms including nausea, *vomiting*, loss of appetite, pain in the abdomen, jaundice, which is a yellowing of the skin and whites of the eyes, *fever* and muscle aches.

In chronic cases cells of the liver are damaged, which leads to fatigue and a general feeling of illness. In many cases the cause of inflammation is one of the number of different viruses (A, B, C, D or E).

Other causes include medications such as paracetamol (see *Analgesics*), and *alcohol* abuse.

Hepatitis A, which is the most common cause of hepatitis in young people, is transmitted by faeces. It causes fever, nausea and vomiting, abdominal pain and loss of appetite, followed by jaundice 3 to 7 days later. Treatment involves rest until the symptoms subside, and then a gradual resumption of activity as tolerated leading to a full recovery. Hepatitis A vaccination is available.

Hepatitis B is transmitted sexually or by direct contact with contaminated needles, infected blood and body fluids in sexual contact. It causes similar symptoms to hepatitis A; however, exercise should be avoided until symptoms have completely disappeared and the results of liver function tests return to normal. Prevention of hepatitis B in *collision sports* is achieved by removing players with open, bleeding wounds (see *Infectious disease prevention*). A hepatitis B vaccine is available, which is 90 per cent effective after a course of three injections.

Hepatitis C is the most common hepatitis virus. It is probably transmitted through sex or infected blood, but is less contagious than hepatitis B.

Treatment for hepatitis C is with the antiviral drug, interferon. Exercise guidelines for those infected are similar to those for hepatitis B. There is no vaccine available for hepatitis C.

Herbal medicine

A method of diagnosis and treatment of health problems based on the healing powers of plants. Treatments are preparations of flowers, fruits, leaves, roots, bark or whole plants in fresh, dried or powdered form, as infusions (hot water extractions) or tinctures (alcohol based extractions).

Herpes simplex virus infection

An infection of the skin caused by the herpes simplex virus that causes small, fluid-filled blisters that are irritating in mild cases, and painful and cause fever when severe. The virus is transmitted through skin-to-skin contact. It is most commonly seen in *wrestling* (herpes gladiatorum) and *Rugby Union* forwards (scrum pox). In *collision sports* it is usually found on the head, eyes and lips (cold sores).

The recommended treatment is medication, called acyclovir, to reduce the irritation and pain, and rest from exercise, especially *collision sports*, until the blisters have healed, which can take 10 to 21 days. Symptoms can recur because the virus can't be completely eliminated. They usually occur at times of *stress*.

High-density lipoprotein (HDL)

A type of *cholesterol* that is associated with a decreased risk of *coronary heart disease* and *stroke* when found in high amounts in the blood.

Coronary heart disease is a narrowing of arteries in the heart due a disease called atherosclerosis, which is a build up of thick, hard deposits called plaques—made up of fat, cholesterol, calcium and

other substances from the blood—in the artery walls. The benefit of HDL is that it carries cholesterol away from the arteries and back to the liver, where it is broken down, or it may also take cholesterol out of the artery walls.

The recommended level of HDL for men is at least 35 per decilitre (mg/dL) (0.9 mmol/L) and for women at least 45 mg/dL (1.2 mmol/L). The best advice for keeping up HDL is to eat a *diet for good health*, including avoiding *saturated fats*, quit smoking cigarettes and regular participation in exercise and sport (see *Exercise for health*).

High protein/low carbohydrate diet

A type of *diet* that is often the underlying basis of many of the weight-loss diets that falsely claim to be highly effective. While it is true that they can achieve remarkably quick weight loss in the short term, in most cases it is not sustainable.

The problem is that eating low carbohydrates forces the body to use up its *glycogen* stores in the muscles and liver. Each glycogen molecule is attached to water molecules. Using up the glycogen releases the water, which is excreted out of the body as urine. Each litre of water equals one kilogram (2.2 lb) of weight.

In addition, without sufficient carbohydrates the body turns to protein for its energy supply, but often the protein in these diets is not enough, so muscle is used up instead. Finally, the diets are so restrictive in the types of food that can be eaten and the time of eating that most people find they can't stick to it.

High voltage galvanic stimulation

An electrical stimulation treatment that is recommended for *pain* relief and reduction of *swelling*, oedema and muscle *spasm*. High voltage galvanic stimulation transmits more than 100 volts via electrodes or pads held to the skin at the location of the pain or muscles that require stimulating.

Hip and groin pain and injuries

Causes

Hip and groin pain can be caused by an acute or overuse injury or disease. An *acute injury* causes pain that begins due to a single incident, such as a blow from an opponent or piece of equipment.

An *overuse injury* causes pain that gets worse over a period of weeks or months due to an accumulation of excessive forces that cause microtrauma. In the early stages it causes only minor pain and stiffness. But later on, either gradually or following a sudden force, it becomes painful enough to seek medical care.

Diseases that cause hip and groin pain include *osteoarthritis* and *ankylosing spondylitis*.

The *hip joint* and *pelvis* and associated structures are the main sources of *pain* in the hip and groin. However, it is not unusual for the source to come from another structure, in particular the low back joints, which is called *hip and groin referred pain*.

Diagnosis

Making the diagnosis involves combining information gathered from the *history*, *physical examination* and relevant tests.

An acute injury with easy to pinpoint groin pain is most likely an *adductor muscle strain*. A vaguely defined pain felt in different areas simultaneously, is more likely an *inguinal hernia, hip osteoarthritis* or *iliopsoas muscle tightness*.

For overuse injuries, such as *adductor tendinosis* and hip osteoarthritis, the pain is usually worse after exercise, especially the following morning, but gradually reduces during exercise. Progressively worse pain during exercise suggests a pubic ramus *stress fracture*. Pinpoint outer-side hip pain may indicate *trochanteric bursitis*.

Specific activities provide good clues. For example, groin pain associated with kicking movements suggests *adductor muscle strain*. Pain felt during sit-ups indicates rectus abdominis *tendinitis* or *inguinal hernia*.

The hip joint also can cause front of the knee pain, usually a dull ache. A clicking or catching sensation in the hip joint in children aged between 5 and 12 indicates *Perthes' disease*.

A radiological investigation, such as *X-rays*, may reveal characteristic changes of *osteitis pubis*. *Magnetic resonance imaging (MRI)* is used to detect *hip joint labral tear*.

Hip and groin referred pain

Pain in the hip or groin caused by a damaged structure in another location some distance away. Usually it is due to the sacroiliac joint, *low back joints*, lower part of the *thoracic spine joints*, a muscle or neural sheath (see *Neutral tension*).

Diagnosis and treatment

The diagnosis is made by excluding a local cause of pain and finding positive signs of *referred pain*. For example, pain referred from the right side low back

---

Causes of hip and groin pain

Common	Less common	Not to be missed
• Adductor muscle strain	• Iliopsoas muscle tightness	• Urinary tract infections
• Adductor tendinosis	• 'Snapping hip'	• Appendicitis
• Trochanteric bursitis	• Femur neck stress fracture	• Femoral head avascular necrosis
• Osteitis pubis	• Hip and groin referred pain	• Hip osteoarthritis
• Hip joint labral tear	• Hip pointer	• Urinary tract infection
	• Obturator nerve entrapment	• Perthes' disease
	• Inguinal hernia	• Ankylosing spondylitis
	• Anterior superior iliac spine apophysitis	• Tumour (testicle)
	• Anterior superior iliac spine avulsion fracture	• Osteomyelitis

QUICK REFERENCE GUIDE

Hip and groin

Adductor muscle strain ....Do you have pain that is easy to pinpoint in the groin and started suddenly?

Adductor tendinosis ....Did your pain start gradually over a period of weeks or months during participation in sports that involve running, twisting and kicking?

Osteitis pubis ....Do you have pain that started gradually over a period of weeks or months that is centred at the middle of the pelvis and aggravated by running, kicking or twisting?

Hip joint labral tear ....Do you have groin pain, possibly accompanied by low back pain, caused by a twisting injury or during running or due to a fall or motor car accident?

Trochanteric bursitis ....Do you have pain on the outside of your hip that eases off with exercise but gets worse after you cool down?

Femur neck stress fracture ....Is your groin pain a deep ache that started after performing excessive amounts of running over a period of weeks or months?

Snapping hip ....Do you hear a snapping noise in the hip region during activities such as ballet dancing, gymnastics or hurdling that is not associated with painful and clears with rest?

Iliopsoas muscle tightness ....Is your pain a deep ache in one side of the groin that is associated with repeated and excessive amounts of kicking a ball?

Inguinal hernia ....Do you have groin pain and a dragging sensation to one side of the lower abdomen that is aggravated by coughing or flatulence?

---

joints is considered likely if *mobilisation* treatments reduce the pain.

If the cause is *myofascial trigger points*, the recommended treatment is *massage* and *dry needling*. The neural sheath is treated with the slump and prone knee bend *neural tension* tests and stretching.

Hip irritability

See *Irritable hip*.

Hip joint

A ball-and-socket joint made up of the round head of the femur (thigh bone), which sits in the acetabulum, a cup-like cavity in the lower, outer side of the pelvis, located deep beneath muscle and other soft tissues.

The shapes of the two bones fit extremely well and provide the joint with a large amount of stability, which is necessary for the significant forces experienced during activities such as running and jumping. Several strong ligaments reinforce the stability of the joint.

Hip joint labral tear

An acute injury of the acetabular labrum, a ring of fibrous tissue attached to the rim of the acetabulum, the cup-like cavity of the *hip joint*. It is usually caused by a twisting injury, but also may occur during running or due to a fall or motor car accident.

The injury causes groin pain and, in many cases, also low back pain. *Magnetic resonance imaging (MRI)* can confirm the diagnosis. The recommended treatment is an *arthroscopy* to repair the tear.

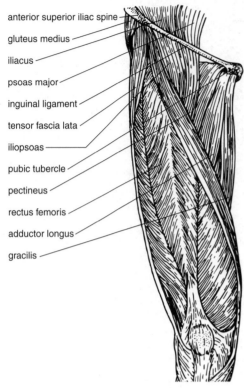

anterior superior iliac spine

gluteus medius

iliacus

psoas major

inguinal ligament

tensor fascia lata

iliopsoas

pubic tubercle

pectineus

rectus femoris

adductor longus

gracilis

Muscles in the hip joint and groin region

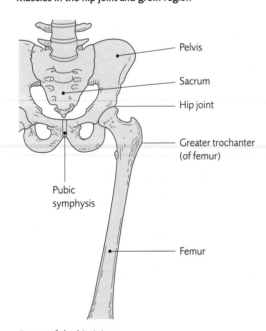

Pelvis

Sacrum

Hip joint

Greater trochanter (of femur)

Pubic symphysis

Femur

Bones of the hip joint

Muscles involved in hip movements

Movement	Prime movers	Secondary movers
Flexion	• Iliopsoas	• Rectus femoris • Sartorius • Adductor longus • Pectineus
Extension	• Gluteus maximus • Hamstring	
Abduction	• Gluteus medius • Gluteus minimus	• Tensor fascia latae • Sartorius
Adduction	• Adductor longus • Adductor brevis • Adductor magnus	• Gracilis • Pectineus
External rotation	• Obturator muscles • Quadratus femoris • Gemelli	• Piriformis • Gluteus maximus • Sartorius
Internal rotation	• Tensor fascia latae • Gluteus medius • Gluteus minimus	

If left untreated the injury may increase the risk of developing *hip osteoarthritis*.

Hip joint replacement

A surgical procedure that involves inserting an artificial joint in place of a diseased or injured *hip joint*.

A total hip replacement involves replacing the joint articular surfaces, which includes the round femur head (thigh bone) and cup-shaped acetabulum of the pelvis. It is usually done for a diseased joint such as *osteoarthritis, rheumatoid arthritis* and *avascular necrosis*. A half-joint replacement involves replacing the femur head only, most often for a fractured neck of femur.

Hip joint replacement was one of the first *joint replacement* surgery procedures. Developed by British orthopaedic surgeon Sir John Charnley in the 1960s, with some small variations, it continues to be followed and has remained highly successful.

The prosthesis (artificial joint) is a metal stem and ball, and shell made of either metal, polyethylene plastic or ceramic.

The prosthesis parts are either glued to the bone with cement or, more commonly these days, the stem and back of the shell are designed with pores so that the new bone is attracted to grow into the surface and hold them in place. Because the latter method requires a longer healing time and a prolonged period of avoiding activity compared to a cemented prosthesis, it is most often recommended for people under 50 years of age who are more likely to achieve good bone growth and recover fitness and strength.

Method

Joint replacement surgery is performed under general anaesthesia and involves major trauma to the hip, including cutting through the skin and moving aside muscles. It also involves dislocating the diseased hip from its socket and cutting and chipping bone with an electric saw and chisel. Once all the parts are in place the new artificial joint is moved about to test that it is secure.

Recovery

The hospital stay for a hip replacement is usually 1 to 2 weeks. Care must be taken not to dislocate the new joint by avoiding movements such as crossing the legs or sitting too low. Instructions from a physiotherapist can help, especially with practical activities such as walking using crutches or a walking frame, which can be performed after 1 to 2 days, and exercises for the hip and whole leg.

Following discharge from hospital a prolonged period of *rehabilitation* lasting for 3 to 6 months is required. Treatments include *flexibility exercises* to increase range of movement, *strengthening exercises* for the muscles and instructions regarding daily activities, such as getting into a bath, and leisure activities like walking and playing sport.

It is generally recommended to be as active as possible after joint replacement of the hip or knee, but avoid high-impact activities such as competitive tennis, skiing and jumping activities. Low-impact activities, such as swimming, walking and cycling, are associated with a longer lasting prosthesis.

Hip osteoarthritis

A disease of the *hip joint* due to wear and tear over a number of decades that leads to degenerative changes of the articular cartilage, joint capsule and ligaments. The signs and symptoms include joint *inflammation*, pain in the thigh, hip and groin region, loss of flexibility and *range of movement*, and decreased *strength* of the hip joint muscles.

The hip is one of the joints most commonly affected by *osteoarthritis* in the general population. The risk of developing the disease increases with age. Other risk factors include being *overweight* and inadequately treated injuries in the past, combined with participating in sports.

Treatment

Regular exercise is essential to reduce pain and muscle weakness and increase joint flexibility and aerobic fitness. The key is doing it at a level that does not aggravate the disease (see *Osteoarthritis*).

Other treatments include *non-steroidal anti-inflammatory drugs* (NSAIDs), *corticosteroid* injection and *hyaluronic acid therapy*, which is a lubricating substance injected into the joint. If the disease degenerates and causes pain that is persistently severe, *hip joint replacement* surgery should be considered.

Hip pointer

An acute injury that causes damage to the periosteum of the iliac crest of the *pelvis* due to a sudden, blunt force. It is most likely to occur in collision sports, such as the *football* codes, *hockey (field)* and *basketball*.

This *periosteal contusion* injury can be extremely painful and cause momentary paralysis of muscles in the region. Treatment includes *rest*, *ice* and *non-steroidal anti-inflammatory drugs* (NSAIDs). The time required before return to sport ranges from 1 week for mild cases up to 3 weeks when severe. Protective equipment, such as a hip guard, should be worn afterwards.

History

A series of questions asked by a health practitioner in order to gather all the relevant information about a person's presenting health problem in order to make a diagnosis of an injury, illness or disease.

The diagnostic process also includes conducting a *physical examination* and, where required, tests and investigations. However, in many cases, a diagnosis is already reasonably clear after the history has been completed.

The history should include the exact circumstances of the injury. For example, a twisted ankle caused by a turning inwards movement strongly suggests a lateral ligament injury.

The specific details of the *pain* should include:
1) Location.
2) The speed in which the pain appears for an *overuse injury*, and for an *acute injury*, if there was a snap or other sensation.
3) Severity of the pain, which can be felt as mild, moderate and severe, or using a pain scale of 1 to 10.
4) The level of activity required to provoke the pain, and how long it takes to settle down.
5) The quality of the pain, such as 'knifelike' when a slipped disc presses against a nerve root in the back.
6) Constant or intermittent (comes and goes) and how it varies during a 24-hour day.
7) An activity or posture that aggravates the pain.
8) An activity or posture that reduces the pain.
9) Abnormal sensations, such as pins and needles, tingling or numbness.

Immediate *swelling* following an injury may indicate a severe injury, such as a major ligament tear accompanied by bleeding into a joint. Instability is indicated when a part of the body gives way during an activity. Details should be given about treatment already received, such as *ice* or a firm *compression*, and what effect it had on the pain.

Information about a previous similar injury, general health (such as weight loss) and general malaise is important.

Training history and use of equipment, such as a tennis racquet, are essential for overuse injuries associated with *overload* or a *biomechanical abnormality*. Symptoms such as excessive fatigue and recurrent illness may point to *overtraining syndrome*. Injury also can be caused or aggravated by *anxiety* and *stress*. Inadequate *nutrition* may play a role in the devel-

opment of sports-related illness, such as excessive *tiredness*.

Lastly, the level of commitment to exercise or sport has a bearing on the decisions that are made about treatment and how to manage the return to activity during *rehabilitation*.

Hitting the wall

See *Glycogen depletion*.

HIV

Human immunodeficiency virus (HIV) is transmitted sexually, or by contact with blood or blood products.

Infection with HIV initially causes a flu-like illness. This is followed by a symptom-free period, where the HIV virus replicates and antibodies form. The length of this period is variable but may last for months or years.

If acquired immunodeficiency syndrome (AIDS) develops, it may present as a variety of diseases associated with the suppression of the *immune system* including lung infection, such as Pneumocystis carinii pneumonia, and tumours, such as Kaposi's sarcoma.

Prevention
The presence of HIV antibodies can be detected a short time (usually within three months) after the initial infection. Practising safe sex and avoiding direct contact with blood or blood products can reduce the risk of infection.

The risk of catching HIV from a contact on the sporting field with an HIV carrier bleeding from an open wound or from bloodstained clothing is extremely low, estimated to be between one in a million and one in 85 million game contacts. This risk is reduced when following the *infectious disease prevention* guidelines.

Exercise and sport participation
A healthy, symptom-free HIV-infected person should be able to participate in exercise and sport without restriction, but should avoid overtraining. People with

AIDS may remain physically active and continue training on a symptom-related basis, but should avoid high-intensity activities (see *Aerobic training* and *Metabolic equivalent (MET)*) and endurance exercise. Activity also should be reduced during acute illness.

HMB

See *Beta-hydroxy methylbutyrate*.

Hockey

See *Hockey (field)* or *Ice hockey*.

Hockey (field)

The origins date back to Egyptian tomb drawings in 2050 BC depicting a 'stick and ball' game. The word 'hockey' was first used in the 1600s, probably deriving from the French 'hoquet', meaning shepherd's crook. The modern game was developed in England during the 1700s. Hockey first appeared at the modern Olympics in 1908. It is the second most popular team sport in the world after soccer.

Hockey is an outdoor game played on a large rectangular field between two opposing teams of 11 players. The aim is to strike the ball with a stick with a curved end into the opposing team's goal.

Fitness, skills and injuries

The fitness demands include *aerobic training* for endurance, *strength training* for positioning and *speed training* for sprinting.

The most common injuries in hockey are *low back pain (non-specific)*, *hamstring strain* (thigh), *back-related hamstring injury* (thigh), *medial collateral ligament (MCL) sprain* (knee), *anterior cruciate ligament (ACL) tear* (knee), *meniscus tear* (knee), *tibia stress fracture* (shin), *gastrocnemius strain* (calf), *soleus strain* (calf), *ankle sprain*, *Sever's disease* (ankle), *metacarpal fracture* and *phalanx fracture* of the hand and fingers.

Elite hockey players

Home-field advantage

An improved chance of success due to playing on familiar territory in front of a supporting crowd or audience. It applies to both team sports such as football, baseball and cricket, and individual sports, such as Olympic athletes from the host-nation.

It is based on possessing better knowledge of the physical characteristics of the home field and the encouragement and positive feedback from fans for achievements made during the competition, which increases the motivation to perform well.

Home-field advantage is not a guarantee of success. Teams and athletes that travel frequently become aware of different playing conditions. Home players also have reported that there are times where they can feel too much pressure to succeed that leads to excessive *arousal*. In addition, there are some opponents who say they feel extra motivation to prove themselves in front of non-supportive crowds.

Homeopath

A health practitioner who has completed training and is recognised as being qualified to provide a diagnosis and treatment for injuries, illness and disease according to the method of homeopathy, which is based on the principle of using small amounts of a substance to produce the same or similar signs and symptoms of an illness or disease. For example, for *diarrhoea* a person would be given a laxative substance. These substances are usually derived from plants, chemicals or minerals.

Hormone

A chemical substance that is released by an endocrine gland into the blood that contains instructions for specific tissues located in another part of the body to perform actions. Hormones are also taken by some athletes to try to improve performance in exercise and sport, which is potentially unhealthy and is considered a form of cheating (see *Drugs banned in sport*).

Physiology

Hormones only communicate with target cells. This occurs because each hormone is like a key and a target cell is like a lock. Only a specific key can open the lock. The locks are found either inside the cell or on the cell membrane. Hence, there are two types of hormones, steroid and non-steroid.

Steroid hormones can easily enter cells, whereas non-steroid hormones find it much harder. Each target cell can have from 2 to 10 000 locks. The number of locks changes all the time. Usually they increase when less hormones are circulating around in the blood, and decrease when there are more hormones.

Endocrine glands get switched on and off to produce hormones, like a thermostat for a heater. For example, *erythropoietin (EPO)* is a hormone produced by cells in the kidneys that contains instructions for bone marrow cells to produce more red blood cells. When the number of red blood cells falls too low, the kidneys get switched on to produce EPO. When enough red blood cells are circulating around the body the kidneys are switched off from producing EPO.

Exercise and sport

The natural activity of hormones during exercise and sport is to make sure that enough *glucose* is supplied to the muscles so the metabolic systems can produce

adenosine triphosphate (ATP), the main source of chemical energy in *muscle contractions*.

Glucose is stored in the liver and muscles as a long chain of bonded glucose molecules called glycogen. *Glycogen* can be broken down into glucose that then enters the blood and circulates around the body, where muscles scoop it up and use it in metabolism.

Hormones instruct the liver to perform this breakdown and make sure that enough glycogen is broken down to keep the amount of glucose in the blood at sufficient levels for the metabolic needs of the muscles. These hormones include glucagon, produced by the pancreas, and *adrenaline, noradrenaline* and cortisol, a corticosteroid produced by the adrenal glands of the kidneys.

The amount of glucose released by the liver into the blood is associated with the intensity and duration of the activity. Short bursts of high-intensity activity, such as a running sprint, use the glycogen stored in the muscles immediately. Glucose in the blood is used more for endurance activities and for replenishing the muscles after activity has been completed.

Insulin, another hormone produced by the pancreas, is essential for making sure that the muscles do take up the glucose passing by in the blood. Exercise appears to increase the sensitivity of muscles to the effects of insulin, which means only low levels of insulin are needed during exercise (see *Diabetes*). This is important because insulin has the opposite effect to glucagon, which sends instructions not to break down glycogen.

Hormones also make sure *fat* can be used as an energy source during endurance activities, including ultra long distance events such as open ocean swimming.

For fat to be used as an energy source it has to break down into free fatty acids. The enzyme lipase is the key to this metabolic process. The hormones adrenaline, noradrenaline cortisol, and *human growth hormone (HGH)* send instructions to fat cells and muscles that have stores of fat in them to regulate fat breakdown. During endurance activities, the production of cortisol drops off and adrenaline, noradrenaline and HGH increase to take over fat break down.

Hormone replacement therapy (HRT)

Medications that aim to increase the amount of hormones in the body that have been reduced due to disease, illness or a stage in life. It is often prescribed for severe symptoms of *menopause*, the cessation of menstrual periods that is associated with reduced oestrogen, and *osteoporosis*, which is a weakening of the bones caused by excessive loss of bone minerals.

It also may be recommended for female teenagers experiencing *delayed menarche* (excessively late first menstrual period). The medication is made up of a synthetic form of *oestrogen* and some progesterone. Possible side effects include light menstrual period, *breast* discomfort, mood changes and a potential increased risk of breast and cervical cancers.

Horse riding sports

Horse riding sports include horse racing, trotting, show jumping, dressage, cross country, hunting, polo, rodeo and the Sunday afternoon leisurely ride. The physical requirements include *aerobic training*, particularly for cross country, *strength training* and *skills training*, especially for jumps.

A *helmet* made according to correct standards, sturdy, long riding boots and stirrups 2–3 cm (1 in) wider than the boot are recommended.

The most common injuries include *head injury*, *abdominal injury*, *Colles fracture* (wrist) and *clavicle fracture* (collarbone), *adductor tendinosis* (hip and groin), *quadriceps strain* (thigh) and *low back pain (non-specific)*.

Human growth hormone (HGH)

A hormone that increases the production of protein in muscles and the metabolism of fats (see *Hormone*). It is rarely used to treat teenagers with retarded physical growth and chronic kidney disease.

It is a *drug banned in sport* according to the World Anti-Doping Agency (WADA). Athletes use it to increase muscle size and bulk and to reduce fat content in the body, similar to *anabolic steroids*. Side effects include excessive growth leading to gigantism in adolescents, hypothyroidism, *coronary heart disease*, *diabetes*, impotence, *osteoporosis*, *menstruation* problems and Creutzfeldt-Jakob disease.

Currently researchers are developing a doping test that can detect the difference between natural HGH produced in the body and the form taken as a drug.

Humerus neck fracture

A break in the humerus (arm bone) just below the *shoulder joint* due to a fall on the outstretched hand or a direct blow. It occurs most commonly in older aged people. *Immobilisation* involves either a broad arm sling for minimal *fracture* displacement, collar and cuff for 6 weeks for significant displacement and surgery if *shoulder dislocation* also occurs.

Hyaluronic acid therapy

A treatment for *osteoarthritis* using a polysaccharide carbohydrate substance naturally found in many body tissues, including *synovial fluid*, the aqueous humour of the eye, skin and cartilage. Hyaluronic acid is produced in healthy joints, but it breaks down in people with osteoarthritis, which increases the susceptibility of the articular cartilage to wear and tear.

Hyaluronic acid is prepared as a medication by obtaining it from humans or genetic engineering. The treatment is given as an injection into the joint. Significant improvements may be achieved with three to five injections given once a week. Side effects are uncommon, but may include gastrointestinal discomfort and joint *swelling*.

Hydration

The amount of water contained in the body. In general it is around 60 per cent of body weight. About two thirds of the water in the body is locked up inside the cells. This watery environment is ideal for all the

Drinking to replace water loss

chemical activities and metabolism that takes place. Outside of the cells water provides the medium via which compounds and substances can be brought to the cells and away from them, such as the watery component of blood called plasma.

Insufficient water in the body is life threatening. Maintaining adequate levels is essential for optimal performance in exercise and sport. One of the specific roles of water is the regulation of body *temperature*. Another role for water is to maintain the volume of *blood*. Reduced blood volume has an impact on *cardiac output*, which is the amount of blood pumped by the heart with each heartbeat.

Maintaining hydration

Water levels in the body are a balance between fluid intake and water loss, which is due to a combination of sweating, humidified expired air, faeces and urine excretion. A decrease in water levels is called dehydration, or *heat illness*, which can be prevented by ensuring adequate fluid intake.

Thirst is an unreliable guide for deciding when to drink fluid. Exercise reduces the thirst sensation and thirst may be quenched before the body is fully rehydrated. The most accurate method of ensuring adequate fluid intake during exercise and sport is by assessing body weight, replacing each 0.5 kg (1 lb) reduction with 0.5 L (1 pt) of fluid.

An easier method is monitoring urine colour and volume. As water levels decrease the urine becomes more scant, more concentrated and a darker yellow or orange, indicating the need for increased fluid intake. When the urine has become clear again and is excreted in copious amounts, water levels have returned to normal.

Fluids

The recommended fluids for people participating in exercise and sport are plain *water* and *sports drinks* containing carbohydrates and electrolytes or salts. Drinks containing *caffeine*, such as tea, coffee, energy drinks and certain soft drinks, are not advisable. *Alcohol* also should be avoided.

Before exercise

Drinking fluids prior to exercise or sport, whether it is during training or competition, can minimise the impact of losses during exercise. During the 24 hours prior to competition, drink enough to ensure that urine output is clear and of good volume. It is recommended to drink 500 mL (17 fl oz) of cold water 1 to 2 hours before training or competition, followed by up to 600 mL (20 fl oz) of cold water or a carbohydrate-electrolyte sports drink 10 to 15 minutes before the activity.

During exercise

Fluid during exercise or sport can ensure performance levels are not affected detrimentally, particularly in activities lasting for an hour or more. It is recommended to drink 120 to 150 mL (4 to 5 fl oz) every 10 to 15 minutes. A cooled drink is more palatable and helps to lower body temperature. During short events water is sufficient. A sports drink is especially useful for athletes participating in day-long, multiple events where carbohydrate replenishment is required but eating solid foods is too difficult.

After exercise

Fluid replacement after exercise rehydrates the body and should be continued until the urine is clear and excreted in copious amounts. For athletes participating in moderate-intensity activity in moderate temperature, cool water is recommended.

Athletes training regularly at high-intensity or in high temperatures may suffer from a prolonged state of dehydration. A fluid containing small amounts of mineral salts, such as sports drinks, may help with rehydration by increasing thirst and reducing urine excretion. A sports drink or soft drink can help with carbohydrate replenishment.

Hydration for children

Children face a greater risk of developing *heat illness* compared to adults. They have a larger body surface-area-to-weight ratio, which makes heat loss through radiation, convection and sweating less effective. They also have a lower capacity to sweat (see *Temperature*) and reduced *cardiac output*, which decreases the transfer of heat away from muscles to be lost through evaporation. Children also produce more heat during activity due to a reduced *economy of effort*.

Maintaining hydration

Children should drink 300–400 mL (10–13 fl oz) of fluid 1 to 2 hours before activity and 10 to 15 minutes beforehand. During activity it is recommended to drink 100 mL (3.5 fl oz) every 20 minutes.

Hydrotherapy

A treatment that involves doing exercises and performing movement in a heated pool. The benefits include the buoyancy of the water, which enables weak muscles to perform movements easier than on dry land, and the warmth of the water has therapeutic effects, including relaxation, relief of *pain* and reduced muscle *spasm*.

It is recommended for both *overuse injuries* and *acute injuries* after the inflammatory response has finished (usually 3 to 7 days) and as part of a *sport rehabilitation* program.

Hyperbaric oxygen

A treatment that involves breathing in 100 per cent oxygen and being subjected to pressure greater than the normal atmospheric pressure at sea level in a special chamber.

It is used to treat injuries including *acute compartment pressure syndrome*, bruises, *tendinitis*, *paratenonitis*, bone *fracture*, post-surgical *oedema*, joint *swelling* and ligament *sprains*.

Method

The treatment was first developed for *decompression sickness* associated with scuba diving, air embolism and carbon monoxide poisoning. It has since been applied to people suffering from severe burns and crush injuries.

It works by reducing excessive interstitial fluids (clear fluid from the blood that immerses the cells of the body) that have accumulated due to the formation of oedema and swelling in response to *inflammation*. It is also believed that it can inhibit the release of oxygen free radicals and enhance collagen deposition as part of the healing process.

Sports medicine research is still being conducted to confirm the effectiveness of hyperbaric oxygen. So far there is only good evidence for the treatment of acute compartment pressure syndrome. It is unlikely to help injuries that cause bleeding because once blood has entered the tissues it can't be reabsorbed back into the circulation like oedema and swelling.

Hyperglycaemia

Excessively high levels of glucose in the blood (see *Diabetes*).

Hypertension

Excessively high blood pressure when at rest and inactive. It is associated with an increased risk of disease such as *coronary heart disease*, which can lead to a *heart attack*, and *stroke*. Hypertension also can lead to end-stage renal disease, bleeding in the eye and *retinal detachment*, which can cause visual impairment.

Causes

A healthy *artery* is flexible and elastic. With each heartbeat it normally expands with the extra flow of blood, which is measured in the average person as 120 mmHg (millimetres of mercury) systolic pressure, and as the heart prepares for the next beat the pressure decreases to 80 mmHg diastolic pressure = 120/80 (see *Blood pressure*).

Atherosclerosis is a disease that causes hardening of the arteries. As a result, with each heartbeat the arteries resist the flow of blood, which causes increased pressure. Genetics and an unhealthy lifestyle, including smoking, poor diet (high-fat, high-salt and excessive alcohol), lack of physical activity and possibly stress, are the main risks for hypertension. It may also be a symptom of hyper-reflexia, which is a physiological reaction to a full bladder, full bowel or gluteal abscess in *wheelchair athletes*.

Diagnosis

Hypertension usually doesn't cause symptoms for many years. It is often found when seeing a doctor for another problem. Adults who have not been to the doctor for 5 years should make arrangements to get blood pressure checked using a device called a sphygmomanometer.

Level	Blood pressure reading
Normal	less than 140/90
Borderline	between 140/90 and 160/95
High	equal to or more than 160/95
Very high	equal to or more than 200/120

If a check finds normal levels (120/80), a follow up check is required in 5 years. If the result is 135/85, the next check should be in a year or two. Above 140/90 requires closer attention and possibly treatment.

Treatment

The aim is to reduce blood pressure to 140–160/90 or below. Very high blood pressure requires immediate drug treatment with *antihypertensives*, including *diuretics, beta blockers, ACE inhibitors* and *calcium channel blockers*. High blood pressure (between 160/95 and 200/120) is treated with a change in lifestyle factors, such as healthy eating (see *Diet for good health*), exercise and sport and quitting smoking.

A *medical clearance* is recommended before starting exercise or sport, which may include an *exercise stress test*.

The main focus of activity is on aerobic training (see *Exercise for health*). The training intensity should be maintained within 65–70 per cent of maximum pulse rate as measured by an exercise stress test or from the calculated formula called *maximum heart rate estimation* (220 – age) or 13 on the *Borg perceived exertion scale*.

The initial conditioning period should last for 12 to 16 weeks and then, if blood pressure is adequately reduced, antihypertensives may be cut back under the supervision of a doctor.

Hypertrophic cardiomyopathy

An inherited disease that causes an abnormally large left ventricle of the *heart*. It occurs in up to 2 per 1000 births. The most common symptoms are excessive *shortness of breath* with activity, chest pain, *palpitations* and *syncope* (fainting). An *echocardiogram* usually finds an exceptionally thickened heart muscle wall.

Even though some athletes with hypertrophic cardiomyopathy can compete at very high levels, there is no way of identifying those at risk of sudden death due to a *heart attack*. As a result, once a diagnosis is made only very low-intensity *aerobic training* is permitted.

Hypertrophy

An increase in the size of a muscle. It occurs in response to *strength training*, and is associated with gains in muscle strength. It is caused by an increase in the size of individual *muscle fibres* in each muscle. It also may be due to an increase in the number of muscle fibres. A temporary increase in the size of muscles immediately after a training session that lasts for a few hours is called *transient hypertrophy*.

Hyperventilation

Breathing at a rapid rate and depth that excessively reduces carbon dioxide and acidity levels in the *blood*. Symptoms are felt quickly due to the body's great sensitivity to low acidity levels, including feeling light headed, fainting (see *Syncope*), *numbness* in the hands or feet and not being able to take a full breath.

It may occur due to *anxiety* prior to exercise or sport, in response to pain during childbirth or due to illnesses such as *diabetes*. Some sprint swimmers believe that hyperventilating on purpose can improve performance by reducing the breathing rate during an event. However, it also may prevent the adequate supply of oxygen and have a negative impact on performance.

Hyphema

Bleeding into the anterior chamber of the *eye* due to ruptured blood vessels in the iris (coloured part of the eyeball). It may be only visible after the blood settles in the lower part of the eye, like fluid in a bowl. It causes loss of sharpness of vision. Treatment involves rest in bed for 3 to 5 days until the blood clears.

Hypoglycaemia

Excessively low levels of glucose in the blood. It most commonly occurs in people with *diabetes* in response to treatments that reduce glucose levels, including physical activity, low carbohydrate intake and *insulin* injections. People with diabetes who participate in physical activities should know the warning signs of hypoglycaemia and have an action plan for immediate treatment.

Diagnosis

The initial symptoms include sweating, *headache*, nervousness, trembling and hunger. Unfortunately some of these symptoms are a normal response to high-intensity activity (see *Aerobic training* and *Metabolic equivalent* (MET)).

Hypoglycaemia also may occur at night during sleep following late-afternoon or evening exercise. Symptoms include night sweats, unpleasant dreams and early morning headaches. The symptoms of severe hypoglycaemia include confusion, abnormal behaviour, *loss of consciousness* and seizures.

Treatment

At the first indication of hypoglycaemia, oral *carbohydrates* in solid or liquid form (such as glucose tablets, barley sugar or *sports drinks*) should be taken immediately. Severe hypoglycaemia is a *medical emergency* that requires immediate treatment to ensure that breathing and circulation are not compromised.

Hyponatremia

An illness caused by low sodium levels in the blood due to drinking excessive amounts of plain water. It is more likely to occur in people at the end of *ultra long distance sport* events, such as running more than a marathon, which is 42.1 km (26.2 miles).

It can cause symptoms including diluted urine and a bloated or 'swollen' feeling. In severe cases it causes *loss of consciousness*, which is a *medical emergency* requiring immediate hospital care, where attention needs to be paid not to misdiagnose the symptoms as *heat illness* or dehydration, because giving intravenous fluids can lead to death.

Hypothermia

Excessively low core body *temperature* (below 35°C/95°F) due to heat loss greater than heat gain. When the body is immersed in water heat loss is 23 times greater than in air. Wet clothing has a similar effect. The *wind chill* is another important factor.

Sports with a particularly high risk of hypothermia include *long distance running, cross-country skiing, downhill skiing, cycling*, hiking, caving, *windsurfing, canoeing* and *scuba diving*. The risk is increased by lack of preparation, pushing oneself to exhaustion, ignoring early warning signs and inadequate protection from the weather.

Diagnosis

Ideally a rectal thermometer should be used to check the temperature. Skin temperatures can drop to as low as 21–23°C (70–73°F) before any decrease in core body temperature is detected. Symptoms can also provide a guide to the temperature and severity.

Mild hypothermia (33–35°C or 91–95°F) causes cold extremities, shivering, extremely high *heart rate* and *breathing rate,* urge to urinate and slight incoordination.

Moderate hypothermia (31–32°C or 88–90°F) causes increased incoordination and clumsiness, fatigue, reduced shivering, slurred speech and amnesia, weakness and drowsiness, apathy, poor judgment and *dehydration.*

Severe hypothermia (under 31°C or 88°F) causes total loss of shivering, inappropriate behaviour (like removing clothes), reduced level or loss of consciousness, muscle rigidity, hypotension (low *blood pressure*), bradycardia (slow heart rate), pulmonary oedema (water on the lungs) and *cardiac arrhythmias*. The *heartbeat* can be so slow (down to 6 beats per minute) that a person may appear to be dead.

Treatment

MILD HYPOTHERMIA

Move out of the cold, insulate appropriately with a blanket or clothes and give a warm, sweet drink.

Alcohol should be avoided. Re-warming should occur safely.

MODERATE HYPOTHERMIA

Move out of the cold and insulate appropriately. Immediate emergency medical help is required because, even though moderate hypothermia is not usually life-threatening, there is a high risk of worsening to severe hypothermia.

SEVERE HYPOTHERMIA

Severe hypothermia is a *medical emergency*. The hypothermic person should be handled as little and as gently as possible because of the risk of ventricular fibrillation (rapid, uncoordinated heart beat) that can cause a *heart attack*. The best treatment is quick transport with minimal handling to a hospital equipped with an intensive care unit.

Prevention

It is advisable to wear a number of layers of clothing rather than one thick layer. If clothing becomes wet, it should be changed as quickly as possible. Clothing should be made of a good insulating material, such as wool, wool blends or polypropylene. Cotton should be avoided.

In rain or snow, adequate waterproof outer clothing should be worn. The outer jacket should also offer adequate protection against wind. Recommended materials include nylon and Goretex. In cold conditions, extremities such as the head, face and hands should be covered.

When running in cold conditions, two pairs of socks should be worn, the inner pair made of polypropylene and the outer pair of wool. Drink lots of fluids to prevent dehydration. In water sports, wetsuits with coverings for extremities are highly recommended because of excessive heat loss in water.

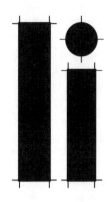

Ice

A treatment for an injury, that minimises bleeding and the formation of oedema and swelling and reduces pain and muscle spasm.

A frozen gel pack for ice treatment

It is most effective when applied within 24 hours after the injury has occurred and should be continued up to 72 hours. It is often done as part of the combination of treatments called *RICE (rest, ice, compression and elevation)*. It also can be beneficial after 72 hours, particularly if an injury has been aggravated. Children can receive the same ice treatments as adults, though they may require assistance to become accustomed to them the first time.

Method

An acute injury, such as a twisted ankle or direct blow to a muscle, can cause damage to blood vessels and *inflammation*, which widens the diameter of blood vessels that leads to *oedema* formation and swelling. Cooling below 37°C (99°F) narrows the blood vessels, decreases the *metabolism* rate, increases *blood* viscosity and slows down pain-sensing *neurons* (nerve fibres).

Treatment

Crushed ice formed into an icepack is the easiest and cheapest method. An icepack is prepared by wrapping crushed ice in a towel dripping wet with cold water. Three layers of towel between the ice and skin prevents cold injury.

Reusable frozen gel packs are relatively inexpensive. Care should be taken not to use these packs straight out of the deep freeze, which can cause a cold injury. Instant ice packs, which rely on a chemical reaction to provide instant cold, are convenient but can only be used once.

Cold sprays provide rapid skin cooling, though they are used mainly as temporary pain relief rather than reduction of swelling. Spraying more than 6 seconds at a time can cause a cold injury.

The following recommendations apply to crushed ice, reusable frozen gel packs and instant ice packs. The treatment should be applied for 15 minutes, longer for deeper tissues; for example, 20 minutes for a *quadriceps contusion* (cork thigh), and less for superficial injuries, for instance, 10 minutes for the fingers.

For an *acute injury*, it should be done every 1 to 2 hours during the first 24 hours after the injury has occurred or, at a minimum, at least three times. Then the frequency can be gradually reduced during the next 48 hours. After 72 hours it should be applied according to need.

Dangers

Ice should not be used where the underlying circulation is poor, such as *peripheral vascular disease*, or if there is hypersensitivity to cold.

Signs of excessive cold include pain, the icepack sticking to the skin and excessive redness or a feeling of burning. Damage caused by excessive cold includes nerve damage and blisters or in extreme cases, skin necrosis (death).

Ice hockey player on the attack

requirements include *aerobic training* and *strength training*.

The most common injuries are *quadriceps contusion* (thigh), *acromioclavicular (AC) joint sprain* (shoulder), *face pain and injuries, concussion, medical collateral ligament (MCL) sprain* (knee), *anterior cruciate ligament (ACL) tear* (knee), *ankle sprain* and *low back pain (non-specific)*.

Ice hockey

Ice hockey originated from both a Canadian Indian and Irish game using a 'hurley' stick and wooden block. The first recorded indoor ice hockey game was in Montreal between McGill University students in 1875.

Rules, equipment and fitness

A game is played between two teams of six players. Each player wears a *helmet* and padding, and uses a long stick with a horizontal end to hit a rubber puck into a net. It is the fastest team sport in the world, with players reaching 50 km/h (30 miles/h) making frequent physical contact. The main physical

Ice skating

Organised ice skating sports include speed skating, figure skating and ice dancing. International competitions were first held in the 1800s and it was included in the first Winter Olympics in 1924. Ice dancing was first included in 1976.

Fitness and injuries

Sprint speed ice skaters require *strength training* and *speed training*. Longer distances require *aerobic training*. Figure skating and dance skating are similar to *gymnastics* and *dancing*.

The most common injuries are *patellofemoral joint syndrome* (knee), *patellar tendinosis* (knee), *ankle sprain, low back pain (non-specific), neck pain (non-specific)* and *concussion*.

Iliac artery endofibrosis

Narrowing of a blood vessel in the pelvis that causes pain in the thigh, usually the front and outer side, though sometimes the back. It is most commonly seen in *cycling* and *triathlon*. The pain may arise after 15 to 20 minutes of exercise but usually ceases immediately with the end of exercise.

A physical examination with a stethoscope finds a bruit (the sound made by turbulent blood flow due to *artery* narrowing) during the exercise. Diagnosis may be confirmed with echography or arteriography. If the condition is affecting performance the recommended treatment is either surgery or balloon dilation of the narrowed artery.

Iliopsoas muscle tightness

An overuse injury of the iliopsoas muscle that causes a deep ache in one side of the groin that is associated with repeated and excessive amounts of *hip joint* flexion (moving the thigh upwards), such as kicking a ball.

A physical examination usually finds loss of *flexibility* of the iliopsoas muscle, low back joints and femoral nerve *neural tension* test. Treatment includes *rest* from the aggravating activity, *flexibility exercises* for the iliopsoas muscle and femoral nerve neural tension stretching and low back joint *mobilisation*.

Iliotibial band friction syndrome

An overuse injury that causes pain on the outer (lateral) side of the knee that is associated with excessive amounts of running downhill or walking downstairs. It is also commonly seen in association with ballet *dancing* and *cycling*.

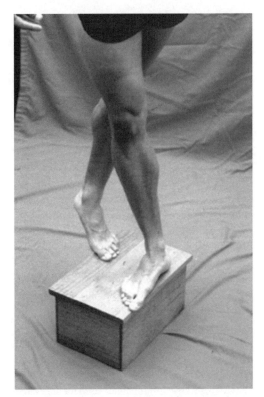

Flexibility exercise for iliotibial band friction syndrome

The iliotibial band begins in the upper thigh near the outer side of the pelvis and runs down the side of the thigh to attach to the upper end of the large, front shin bone (tibia) near the *knee joint*. The injury is due to a gradual accumulation of excessive friction where the band passes over the outer (lateral) side of the lower end of the thigh bone (femur) that causes inflammation.

The recommended treatments include *ice, nonsteroidal anti-inflammatory drugs (NSAIDs)*, electrotherapy such as *interferential therapy* and *ultrasound therapy, massage, flexibility exercises, mobilisations* and *strengthening exercises* for the gluteus medius muscle to correct *pelvis lateral tilt* abnormality, which is a common contributing factor.

In some cases a *corticosteroid* injection may be required, or surgery to loosen the iliotibial band to reduce friction. Return to sport for mild cases requires up to 2 weeks, moderate cases 2 to 4 weeks and severe cases up to 3 months.

Imagery

See *Visualisation*.

Immobilisation

A treatment that prevents movement of a body part to allow an acute injury to heal. It is mostly used for broken bones (*fractures*), severe joint and ligament *sprains*, severe muscle and tendon *strains* or tears, severe *articular cartilage acute injury*, severe *nerve injury*, some *stress fractures* and *dislocations*.

Though immobilisation is essential for healing, it is also associated with a number of detrimental effects on tissues when applied for lengthy periods including *swelling*, reduced joint and muscle *flexibility*, degenerative changes in articular cartilage and muscle *atrophy* and loss of *strength*.

Immobilisation for a bone fracture can be achieved with *surgery* or conservative (non-surgical) treatment. Surgery involves *internal fixation* and external fixation, and is only performed for bone fractures. Conservative treatments are used for bones and all other damaged tissues, such as joints, ligaments, muscles and tendons, and include a rigid *brace*, air splint, *taping*, thermoplastic material, fibreglass cast and, most commonly, a plaster cast.

Internal fixation
Surgery is performed to insert pieces of metal to hold the broken bone pieces together. It has advantages over conservative immobilisation, such as a plaster cast, by allowing joints and muscles to commence movement at an earlier stage and reducing the risk of non-union. There are different types of metal

Immobilisation in plaster cast

pieces that can be inserted, including a plate, wire, rod or long nail and screws.

External fixation
The surgical insertion of a piece of metal into the bone that extrudes through the muscles and skin. Pieces include pins, screws and rods. There is a slightly increased risk of infection with external fixation. The metal is removed after the bone has healed.

Plaster cast
Even though plaster has the disadvantage of being relatively heavy, prone to damage and not water-resistant, it is cheap, easy to make and can be easily moulded to the body part. However, fibreglass casts are preferred for undisplaced fractures and immobilisation of soft tissue injuries because they are light, strong and waterproof.

Protected mobilisation
A rigid brace, air splint and taping can be used to provide protected mobilisation, which prevents movement in a specific direction that would cause excessive stress on an injured structure at the same time as allowing non-injured structures to move.

Immune system

The organs and tissues that defend the body in the fight against infections caused by viruses, bacteria and fungi, the development of cancer and in response to physical injury.

Physiology
The system works in different ways depending on what it is fighting against. For example, fighting infection first involves recognising whether a cell or organism that has invaded the body is a friend or foe which is determined by the structure of the outside wall. If it is a foe, it acts to neutralise or destroy it.

A part of the knowledge of the immune system is inherited at birth, but mostly it is learnt as we go through life. An example is measles, an illness caused by a virus. After recovering from measles infection the body remembers the virus and recognises any future exposures so as to muster up a quick and strong protective response. Vaccinations work the same way. By injecting a tiny amount of, for example, a flu virus, the body remembers to protect against a future exposure.

Once the immune system decides that a foreign body is a foe it starts a general all-out attack mounted by antibodies, which signals to *white blood cells* called phagocytes to gobble up the foe.

The phagocytes then release fragments of the foe out into the blood, called antigens, which stimulate an adaptive immune response. This involves anti-bodies that recognise the foe and signal a gathering of other white blood cells called lymphocytes. These cells are capable of multiplying millions of times over, and spread throughout the body to attack viruses everywhere.

Inflammation is a part of the immune system. It can appear due to an infection, such as a *common cold* that causes a runny nose (called rhinitis or nose inflammation), an allergy, diseases including *asthma* and also in response to damage to cells and tissue fol-lowing a physical injury such as an *ankle sprain*.

Exercise and sport

It is commonly stated that there is a strong relation-ship between exercise and vulnerability to infection. Moderate-intensity *aerobic training* is supposed to reduce vulnerability, while high-intensity increases it. The standard explanation is that high-intensity exercise suppresses the immune system.

However, there is a lack of evidence supporting the latter view. Blood tests of elite athletes that suffer symptoms such as swollen glands, headaches and feeling feverish often do not show any infection.

An alternative suggestion is that they may be pre-senting with infection-like symptoms, due to increased levels of circulating cytokines (immune cells secreted by macrophages), which can be defined more accurately as an over-reactive immune system.

Another theory is that immune cells are at normal levels; however, they are not being moved efficiently around the body. This type of malfunction is called a 'trafficking problem'. Lastly, there is the theory that symptoms are glandular fever-like due to reactiva-tion of a latent Epstein-Barr virus.

In the zone

A state of mind characterised by being in the opti-mum level of *arousal* for achieving the best perfor-mance possible during competition or training. It involves not feeling too anxious, but feeling enough stress to respond appropriately.

Athletes can learn to be 'in the zone' by becom-ing more aware of their arousal levels, identifying the correct level that achieves the best performance, recognising situations that disturb their arousal level during performance, and utilising psychological techniques that can control these levels before, during and after competition, including developing a *routine, visualisation, biofeedback, progressive muscle relaxation, centring* and positive self-talk. It is also called 'feeling in sync' and 'in the flow'.

Incontinence

Involuntary loss of urine that has become a social or hygienic problem. It most commonly affects women. There are three main types of incontinence: stress, urge and overflow.

Stress incontinence usually occurs during a particular activity, such as a golf swing, coughing, laughing, sneezing or a change of body position, like getting up from bed in the morning. Leakages tend to be small volumes. They are due to weakness of the pelvic floor muscles, which normally act to squeeze and close the urethra, the tube that carries urine out of the bladder (see *Urinary system*). It is more likely in women who have had a vaginal deliv-ery during labour.

The risk of having stress incontinence is also increased by activities involving repeated and exces-sive pressure on the pelvic floor such as jumping, running, *gymnastics, basketball, trampolining, martial arts, horse riding sports, bodybuilding, weight lifting* and *strength training* with heavy weights. Low-risk activities include *swimming, cycling*, walking, *rowing* and gentle forms of *yoga* and *Tai Chi*.

Urge incontinence is due to an inability to stop the bladder muscle contracting to release urine (called detrusor instability), which may be triggered by the sight of a bathroom, cold weather or the sound of running water. Leakages tend to be large volumes and may occur during the night.

Constant leakages not associated with an activity or specific stimulus are likely to be overflow incontinence.

Treatment

The recommended treatments for stress incontinence include pelvic floor exercises to increase the *strength* of the muscles. It involves learning to contract the correct part of the pelvic floor that feels as if it is stopping urine flow or the passage of a stool by firmly tensing around the vagina and anus and inwardly lifting and squeezing.

A *strengthening exercise* program involves doing six to eight sets of exercises per day. Each set equals a 4-second pelvic floor contraction repeated five times, with a 5-second relaxation between each contraction. Ensuring an adequate fluid intake is also important (see *Hydration*).

Other treatments that may be recommended until pelvic floor strength has increased sufficiently include placing a moistened tampon sideways inside the vagina, vaginal pessaries, such as incontinence rings and contraceptive diaphragms, and taking medications such as *hormone replacement therapy (HRT)* and anticholinergics if urge incontinence is also present. If the above treatments fail, surgery may be recommended.

Incorrect biomechanics

See *Biomechanical abnormality*.

Indirect calorimetry

A method of calculating the amount of *energy* a person uses during an activity by measuring the amount of oxygen breathed in and carbon dioxide breathed out. It involves, for example, running on a treadmill with a mask over the mouth and nose that has long tubes connected to a computer for measuring gases. It can be done in a laboratory or out in the field.

The measurement is performed in a series of steps. A computer usually calculates the respiratory exchange ratio, which is the amount of carbon dioxide breathed out divided by the amount of oxygen breathed in. A table of standard values gives a measure of the energy released per litre of oxygen.

Individuality

Selecting activities for a *training* program that best suit the participant's ability to increase fitness and improve performance according to their genetic makeup, previous training history, age and current state of fitness.

Factors that should be taken into account include tolerance to training *overload*, speed of recovery, psychological makeup, nutritional intake and lifestyle habits. A *personal trainer* provides this service for an individual. A *fitness trainer* does this for people at gymnasiums and health centres and elite, professional and non-elite sportspeople.

Infection

An invasion of an organ or tissues by viruses, bacteria or fungi. The invaders multiply and directly cause damage to the organ or tissues and other organs and tissues by releasing toxins into the bloodstream. Infections usually provoke a defensive response from the body's *immune system*, in particular a *fever*. The treatment for bacterial infection is *antibiotics*.

Infectious disease prevention

Sports medicine authorities in many countries have produced guidelines for the prevention of infectious diseases with particular reference to *HIV* and hepatitis B (see *Hepatitis*), particularly for body contact and *collision sports*.

Infectious diseases such as HIV and hepatitis may be spread by contact with infected blood, saliva (not for HIV), perspiration (not for HIV) and semen and vaginal fluids. The following recommendations will reduce the risk of disease transmission.

Players

1) It is the players' responsibility to maintain strict personal hygiene, which is the best method of controlling the spread of disease.
2) It is strongly recommended that all participants involved in contact sport be vaccinated with hepatitis B vaccine.
3) Players with prior evidence of these diseases must obtain advice and clearance from a doctor prior to participation.

Team areas

1) It is the clubs' responsibility to ensure that the dressing rooms be clean and tidy. Particular attention should be paid to hand basins, toilets and showers.
2) Communal bathing areas (e.g. spas) should be strongly discouraged.
3) Spitting or urinating in team areas must not be permitted.
4) All clothing, equipment and surfaces contaminated by blood must be treated as potentially infectious. Clothing soiled with blood and other body fluids should be washed in hot, soapy water.
5) Sharing of towels, face washers and drink containers should be avoided.
6) All personnel working in team areas should be vaccinated against hepatitis B.
7) Open cuts and abrasions must be reported and treated immediately.

Referees and game officials

1) Open cuts and abrasions must be reported at the first available opportunity. This includes removing players from the field of play.
2) Those who officiate in body contact and collision sports should be vaccinated against hepatitis B.
3) All contaminated clothing and equipment must be replaced prior to the player being allowed to resume play.
4) If bleeding should recur, the above procedure must be repeated.
5) If bleeding cannot be controlled and the wound securely covered, the player must not continue in the game.

Infectious mononucleosis

See *Glandular fever*.

Inferior

The anatomical direction pointing downwards in the body towards the feet. It is used to describe the surface of any part of the body that faces downwards, or a body part located below another part. It is the opposite of *superior*. Also called caudal.

Inflammation

The initial response of the body when cells and tissues are damaged. It occurs regardless of the cause, whether the damage is due to, for example, a bacterial infection or a twisted ankle.

It is essential for the healing and recovery processes. However, it is better designed to respond to infection, where the inflammation only continues as long as the infective agent is present.

In exercise or sports-related injuries the initial cause of the injury is quickly gone (e.g. twisting the ankle), but the inflammation continues for days afterwards, causing too much inflammation, which can delay recovery and lead to poor long term outcomes.

Pathophysiology

Inflammation due to an injury begins when damaged cell membranes rupture and release arachidonic acid that is converted by a number of enzymes, in particular cyclo-oxygenase (COX), into *prostaglandins*, thromboxane and prostacyclins, which act as mediators of the inflammatory response.

This involves widening the local blood vessels (see *Artery*) leading to leakage of watery fluid into the area that has been injured, called *oedema*. Death of the damaged cells occurs quickly, which releases lysin that stimulates further oedema formation which can spread into nearby uninjured areas, sometimes within minutes, leading to increased intercellular pressure and possibly additional damage to the cells and tissues. When oedema is visible it is called *swelling*.

Among the helpful cells that are attracted into the injured area are *white blood cells* that destroy invading micro-organisms and are later involved in the healing process, including the recruitment and proliferation of mesenchymal stem cells that later differentiate into new cells that make up ligaments, muscles and bone.

The length of the inflammatory period depends on the severity of the injury. Severity is often determined by the mechanism of the injury, in particular the speed and force of impact.

Mild injuries can last from 5 minutes up to 24 hours. Moderate injuries up to 48 hours. Most severe injuries last up to 72 hours, though some can continue for 7 days.

Diagnosis and treatment

The main symptom of inflammation for an acute injury is *pain*. It is caused by chemical stimulation of pain-sensing nerve endings, called nociceptors, due to the release of prostaglandins into the injured area by the damaged cells and mechanical stimulation caused by increased intercellular pressure.

The extent of swelling should be assessed using methods such as a tape measure to measure the circumference or other dimensions of the swollen part. Other signs can include heat and redness.

The main aim of treatment is to reduce the amount of inflammation. Treatments include *RICE* (*rest, ice, compression and elevation*), *active movement* exercises, *electrotherapy, massage, non-steroidal anti-inflammatory drugs* (NSAIDs), *corticosteroids, acupuncture*, and natural health supplements including *bromelain, curcumin* and *flavonoids*.

Influenza

See *Flu*.

Ingrown toenail

Pain caused by the edges of the toenail, usually of the big toe, growing abnormally into the surrounding skin. In some cases the nail becomes infected. It is often associated with wearing an incorrect *shoe* size and poor nail cutting. This injury is also called onychocryptosis.

Treatment involves removing the ingrowth and repairing the nail and, if required, taking antibiotics for the infection. Prevention measures include wearing the correct shoe size, cutting toenails once a week and not leaving sharp edges pointing down towards the skin.

Inguinal hernia

Protrusion of part of the intestine into the inguinal canal, a passage that normally only contains the vas deferens, a tube that carries the sperm from the testes to the penis (see *Reproductive system*). The injury is much less common than was previously believed for people who play sport. As a result, terms like footballer's hernia have gone out of fashion. Other injuries, such as *osteitis pubis*, are more likely to be the source of groin pain (see *Hip and groin pain and injuries*).

A hernia causes groin pain and a dragging sensation to one side of the lower abdomen that is aggravated by coughing or flatulence. A physical examination occasionally finds obvious swelling. The recommended treatment is surgery.

In-line skating

In-line skating is a hybrid of *roller skating* and *ice skating*. Invented by Minneapolis ice hockey player, Scott Olson, in 1979, his company was bought in the early 1980s and eventually became Rollerblade Inc., hence the popular name 'rollerblading'.

Equipment

In-line skaters move at speeds of up to 50 km/h (30 miles/h) using a similar technique to ice skating. Quad hockey and in-line hockey and Street and Vert (performing tricks) are in-line skating sports. Wrist guards and *helmets* are important protective gear.

Fitness and injuries

In-line skating involves agility, *aerobic training* and *skills training* for correct use. The most common

In-line skating (rollerblading)

injuries are *Colles fracture* (wrist), *scaphoid fracture* (wrist), *quadriceps contusion* (thigh), patella fracture (knee), *patellofemoral joint syndrome* (knee), *tibia stress fracture* (shin), *shin chronic compartment syndrome* and *tibia periostitis* (shin).

Inspiration

Breathing air into the lungs. It is also an emotion associated with increased motivation to achieve in exercise and sport.

Instability

Reduced stability of a joint or region that can cause pain or an injury. It is most commonly found in the shoulder and low back/pelvis.

For instance, the stability of the *shoulder joint* is provided by, in small part, ligaments, joint capsule and a fibrocartilage structure called the glenoid labrum and, mostly, from the rotator cuff muscles that surround the joint and work to hold it together. Injury to the ligaments or weakness of the muscles reduces stability at this joint.

Abnormal timing of the two trunk muscles, the transversus abdominus and multifidus that minimise movement of the pelvis and low back to keep it as a stable base while the legs are moving during running and jumping, can cause *lumbo-pelvic instability*.

Muscles that provide stability are called stabilisers. Treatments for an injury that is due to instability include muscle *motor re-education, flexibility exercises, strengthening exercises, taping* and *biofeedback*.

Insulin

A *hormone* produced by the pancreas when blood glucose levels are high, which stimulates cells throughout the body to absorb the excess. It plays an essential role in the metabolism of carbohydrates in exercise and sport. Reduced level of insulin production causes a disease called *diabetes*.

It is also a *drug banned in sport* according to the World Anti-Doping Agency (WADA). Athletes use it for an anabolic effect, which includes increased protein synthesis leading to increased muscle size and bulk, similar to *anabolic steroids*. It is mainly used in power sports, such as *weight lifting* and *bodybuilding*. It is less popular among sprinters because it also increases the storage of fat in the body. One of the dangerous side effects is *hypoglycaemia*.

Insulin-like growth factor (IGF-1)

A drug used to treat some types of growth problems in *children, diabetes, osteoporosis, coronary heart disease* and *osteoarthritis*.

It is a chemical that achieves similar effects as *human growth hormone (HGH)* and also is a *drug banned in sport*. *Colostrum* powder, which is used as a food supplement, contains high levels of IGF-1. However, it is questionable whether IGF-1 can be absorbed through the gastrointestinal system.

Intellectual disability

An IQ less than 70, and a history of developmental delay in childhood that causes limitations in two or more of the following areas: communication, self-care, home living, social skills, community use, self-direction, health and safety, functional academics, leisure and work.

Intellectual disability is the largest single group of disabilities. The majority are mild and have unknown causes.

The severe disabilities usually have a physical cause. About 25 per cent are due to *Down's syndrome*, another 25 per cent due to inherited or congenital conditions such as phenylketonuria and 35 per cent are due to trauma or infection at birth or during early childhood. The remaining 15 per cent have unknown causes.

Exercise and sport
Exercise and sport can be greatly beneficial for people with an intellectual disability, particularly those living in homes, sheltered workshops or community centres, because they are more prone to being *overweight* and face a higher risk of *coronary heart disease* and *diabetes*.

Additional benefits include reduced rates of *depression*, and improved self-esteem and social skills due to being part of a group and participating according to team sport rules.

People with an intellectual disability can participate in exercise and sport in the same manner as the general population.

Injuries
The injuries also are the same as those seen in the general population. The only exceptions may be a need for increased supervision and more time spent on instructions regarding treatment, delayed timing of a return to sport and measures to prevent re-injury.

Intensity of training

See *Overload*.

Interferential therapy

An electrical stimulation treatment that is recommended for *pain* relief, reduction of *swelling*, oedema and muscle *spasm* and producing *muscle contractions*.

Method
Four electrodes that produce two alternating medium-frequency electric currents (one current for each pair of electrodes) are simultaneously applied to the skin. The currents become superimposed on each other at their intersection, causing wave interference that results in a modulated frequency equal to the difference in frequency of the two original waves, called the beat frequency.

All beat frequencies achieve pain relief in the same manner as *transcutaneous electrical nerve stimulation (TENS)*. Different beat frequencies have varying effects on circulation.

At 90–100 Hz (hertz), vasodilatation (blood vessel widening) occurs, while at 0–10 Hz, muscle stimulation occurs to assist removal of fluid into the veins and lymph vessels, which reduces swelling and oedema. The electric currents are felt as comfortable pins and needles on the skin.

Internal fixation

A surgical treatment that involves inserting pieces of metal to hold together the broken bones in a fracture.

It has advantages over conservative (non-surgical) methods of immobilisation, such as a plaster cast, because it allows joints and muscles to commence movement at an earlier stage and reduces the risk of non-union of a *fracture*.

However, the decision to choose surgery must be weighed up against other negative factors, including the risk of infection, complications of anaesthesia, the cost and long-term plans for participation in exercise or sport.

Method

The metal is inserted by cutting open the body (see *Open surgery*). It has to be strong enough to withstand the forces of daily living and sport, and minimise the chances of corrosion and an allergic reaction.

There are different types and shapes of metal that can be inserted. Screws are the most commonly used piece, either with other pieces such as holding a plate securely into the bone or alone for a small piece of bone that has broken away, like an avulsion fracture.

A plate is like an internal splint. A wire is used together with larger pieces of metal, like a plate, or alone in small bones, such as in the hand or foot. A rod or long nail are recommended for long bones, such as the femur (thigh bone), and placed through the hollow centre that contains the marrow.

Internal rotation

A turning movement of a *synovial joint* that produces a movement of a body part towards the midline of the body. For example, internal rotation of the *hip joint* involves turning the front of the thigh towards the inner side of the opposite thigh. It is similar to *pronation*.

Interval training

Performing an activity in repeating cycles, beginning with increased intensity followed by reduced intensity during a training session. It is used to improve anaerobic fitness and aerobic fitness, in particular for endurance activities such as running a marathon.

For example, interval training for a 400 m running sprinter may require repeated, short, intense bouts of running at just under competition pace followed by complete rest for one minute.

For a 5000 m runner it may involve a smaller increase in intensity compared to a 400 m sprinter, but for longer distances, such as 500 m, and shorter rest periods in between of up to 15 seconds. Interval training has a higher risk of injury and *overtraining*

syndrome compared to *continuous training*. *Fartlek* is a form of interval training.

Inversion

A movement used in the *ankle* joint and foot that means turning the sole of the foot so that it faces towards the midline. For example, when both feet are next to each other, the sole of the foot is turned towards the other foot (see *Foot and toes*). Inversion is a combination of movements that occur at a number of joints, mainly the subtalar and midtarsal joints, including supination, adduction and plantar flexion. It is the opposite of *eversion*.

Iodine

See *Minerals*.

Iron

A mineral that has an essential role in the transportation and storage of oxygen in the body. It is found in *red blood cells*, in a protein called haemoglobin that transports oxygen around the body, and in myoglobin, a protein that briefly stores oxygen in muscles once it arrives prior to being used in metabolic processes that produce muscle contractions.

Foods rich in iron include liver, meat, cereals, fish, green leafy vegetables, nuts and beans (see *Minerals* for an extensive list). There are two forms of iron in foods; haeme iron is in all meat, poultry, fish and dairy products and is easily absorbed; non-haeme iron is in nuts, legumes, cereals, leafy green vegetables and dried fruit and is less well absorbed. A lack of iron in the body can cause *iron deficiency* and anaemia.

Iron deficiency

A lack of iron in the body, which may have a negative impact on the transportation and storage of oxygen in the body. Not eating enough iron in the

Baked beans are a good source of iron

Recommended daily intakes (RDI) of iron

Age group (years)	Iron (mg)
Children	
• 4–11	6–8
Adolescents	
• 12–18	10–13
Men	
• 19–64	7
• over 64	7
Women	
• 19–menopause	12–16
Post menopause	5–7
Pregnancy	an extra 10–20
Breastfeeding	no extra

diet, loss of *blood* or decreased iron absorption are the main causes. As a result, new *red blood cells* produced in the bone marrow have a reduced amount of iron in them.

It is a common problem in the general population, with estimates of up to one in five people affected at one time in their lives. In particular, women need extra iron during *pregnancy* to ensure healthy development of the foetus, as do people on severe weight-loss or low-energy diets.

It is also found at high rates in people participating in exercise and sport, particularly female endurance athletes, such as those performing *long distance running*, who eat little or no red meat. Without enough iron to enable the body to meet its oxygen needs, it is not surprising that one of the prob-

lems caused by a deficiency is poor performance levels.

Causes

Blood loss can be menstrual, gastrointestinal, urinal or muscular. Heavy periods, called menorrhagia, can take a toll on iron stores in women who may find it hard to sufficiently build them up.

Gastrointestinal bleeding is common in athletes, though usually it is present in small amounts and is not noticeable in the faeces. It is caused by jarring of the large intestine associated with running, or damage resulting from the diversion of blood flow away from the gut to exercising muscles.

Medications including *non-steroidal anti-inflammatory drugs (NSAIDs)* and *aspirin* increase the risk of bleeding. Occasionally there may be a problem unrelated to exercise and sport, such as a bleeding gastric *ulcer* and inflammatory bowel disease. *Haematuria* is also caused by jarring during running that damages the walls of the bladder. Trauma to muscles is associated with destruction of red blood cells with subsequent iron loss.

Decreased iron absorption is more likely to be a problem in vegetarians. There are two forms of iron in food: haeme iron is in animal products and is easily absorbed; whereas non-haeme iron in nuts, legumes, cereals, leafy green vegetables and dried fruit is less well absorbed. In addition, other substances in the diet severely reduce iron absorption, such as phytic acid in cereal fibre and tannin in tea.

Some research also shows that regular participation in high-intensity exercise (see *Aerobic training* and *Metabolic equivalent (MET)*) and sport may have a negative impact on absorption.

Symptoms and diagnosis

The symptoms depend on the severity. The most severe form is anaemia, which is rarely seen in people who participate in exercise and sport. It can cause abnormal *tiredness*, headache, pale skin and reduced levels of performance in exercise and sport. It is diagnosed with a blood test of haemoglobin: less than 11 per decilitre (g/dL) (6.8 mmol/L) in females and < 13 g/dL (8mmol/L) in males.

Iron depletion is a milder form, which can cause tiredness and poor performance. It is diagnosed with low serum ferritin levels (less than 30 mg/mL in females and less than 50 mg/mL in males), a protein that stores iron and is used to transport it in the blood.

Blood tests should be done regularly for elite athletes and those who are at risk, such as vegetarians and female endurance athletes.

Treatment

Treatment is directed at the causes. For example, blood loss due to diversion of blood flow from the gastrointestinal system to the exercising muscles, can be reduced by measures such as ensuring adequate *hydration*.

Iron intake and absorption can be improved by the following measures:

- Eat at least small amounts of red lean meat three to four times a week.
- Eat liver and kidney occasionally.
- Eat skinless poultry and fish regularly.
- Include food and drinks rich in vitamin C with each meal to increase the absorption of non-haeme iron.
- Increase consumption of wholegrain breads and iron-enriched breakfast cereals.
- Vegetarians need to eat foods rich in iron and vitamin C at every meal.
- Avoid drinking tea with meals.

Iron supplementation may be necessary if the above measures do not raise serum ferritin and/or haemoglobin levels. The supplement contains ferrous sulphate, ferrous gluconate or ferrous fumarate.

Irritable hip

An injury in children that causes a limp, hip and groin pain that is hard to pinpoint, and loss of flexibility of the *hip joint* movements. It does not have a known diagnosis. Radiological investigations such as *X-rays* are normal. It usually settles down with a period of bed *rest*.

Ischial tuberosity apophysitis

An overuse injury of the ischial tuberosity bone of the *pelvis* at the attachment of the hamstring tendon (see also *Buttock*).

It is due to an accumulation of repeated, excessive physical forces on the growing bone during running activities performed over a period of weeks or months that leads to buttock pain. *Apophysitis* mainly affects adolescents. Treatment consists of *rest* from running activities, *ice*, gentle *flexibility exercises* and *massage*.

Ischial tuberosity avulsion fracture

An acute injury that causes the hamstring tendon and a small piece of the ischial tuberosity bone in the *buttock* to become detached from the rest of the *pelvis*.

An *avulsion fracture* usually occurs in adolescents due to the relative weakness of the bone compared to adults who are more likely to tear the tendon.

An *X-ray* is required to confirm the diagnosis. The treatment is usually the same as for a severe (grade 3) tear of the hamstring muscle (see *Hamstring strain*). Surgery is recommended if the avulsed bone is greater than 2 cm (1 in) away from the pelvis.

Ischiogluteal bursitis

An injury that causes inflammation of the *bursa* that protects the hamstring muscle tendon from excessive friction due to rubbing against a ischial tuberosity bone in the *pelvis*. It is an overuse injury that is usually due to excessive and repeated physical loads on the bursa over a period of weeks or months. It may occur together with *hamstring origin tendinitis*.

Diagnosis and treatment

It is difficult to differentiate between ischiogluteal bursitis and hamstring origin tendinitis because both usually cause pain that is aggravated by *sprinting*, hamstring stretching and resisted muscle contraction.

One indication that the injury may be a *bursitis* is that *massage*, the main treatment for hamstring origin tendinitis, fails to relieve the pain. A quicker method is *diagnostic ultrasound*, which may find a fluid-filled bursa.

The recommended treatment for ischiogluteal bursitis is a *corticosteroid* injection into the bursa and *strengthening exercises* for the hamstring muscle.

Isokinetic strengthening

Activities that aim to improve a muscle's ability to move a weight or load at a constant speed. It is achieved using specialised equipment, including the Ariel, Biodex, Cybex, Kincom, Lido and Merac machines. It is most commonly performed to test whether an injured muscle has recovered sufficiently to permit return to sport.

The ability of a muscle to generate force to move the same weight varies during a movement, which is mainly determined by the *muscle length*. In midrange the muscles can generate maximum force. As a result, when lifting a weight the speed tends to be quickest during mid range and is slowest at the start and end of range.

The main disadvantages of isokinetic machines is the high cost, and that exercises are less functional than isotonic *strengthening exercises* or *strength training* with free weights or using the body such as when doing a squat.

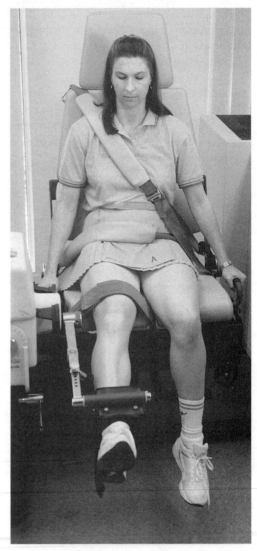

Isokinetic strengthening of the right quadriceps muscle

Isometric

A muscle contraction that does not produce any movement at a joint. For example, an isometric contraction of the abdominal muscles involves tensing them up (as if in preparation to withstand a punch in the stomach) without moving the trunk or spine. The contraction does cause shortening of the *muscle*

Features of Isokinetic strengthening machines

Machine	Type of system	Operational modes	Maximum speed	Accessories	Relative disadvantages	Special features
Ariel	Passive	Isometric Isokinetic Concentric	1000°/sec	Back/trunk accessories are available	Service availability limited. Not accessories for all joint movements	Not used clinically. Also manufacture multijoint isokinetic computerised exercise equipment (e.g. leg press)
Biodex	Active	Passive motion Isometric Isotonic Isokinetic (eccentric and concentric)	450°/sec (concentric) 120°/sec (eccentric)	Accessory chair for specific patterns. Back/trunk accessories for flexion/extension		Front panel control offers flexible rehabilitation protocols
Cybex	Passive/ active	Passive motion Isometric Isokinetic (concentric and eccentric)	500°/sec (concentric) 120°/sec (eccentric)	Upper body exercise table and accessory cart. Back attachment for existing system or separate back system		
KinCom	Active	Passive motion Isometric Isotonic Isokinetic (concentric and eccentric	210°/sec	Accessory chair for specific joint stabilisation. Back/trunk for flexion/extension	Insufficient numerical data	
Lido	Active and passive available	Passive motion Isometric Isotonic Isokinetic (concentric and eccentric	400°/sec (concentric) 250°/sec (eccentric) 120°/sec (passive)	Back attachment for existing system or separate back system		Sliding cuff on lever arm to minimise minor joint axis malalignment
Merac	Passive	Isometric Isotonic Isokinetic (concentric only). Dynamic variable resistance	500°/sec (isokinetic)	Accessories for specific joint patterns. Back/trunk flexion/ extension table available	Lacks eccentric mode	Uses little floor space

fibres, which is exhibited as an increase in tension, for instance, when showing-off the size of your biceps muscle.

Isometric strengthening

Activities that aim to improve a muscle's strength to perform a contraction that does not cause joint move-ment. It can prevent atrophy (shrinkage) of a muscle and reduce swelling through a pumping action to remove accumulated fluid.

Isometric strengthening is often recommended after surgery, during *immobilisation* of an injury in a plaster cast and the rehabilitation of a severe injury such as a joint *dislocation*.

The exercises are commenced as soon as pain permits. They may also be done at a later stage of

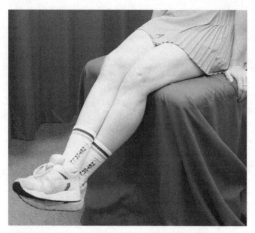

Isometric strengthening of the left quadriceps muscle—the right leg holds the left leg so that it doesn't move

a *sport rehabilitation* program as part of *motor re-education* to treat instability at a joint.

Strengthening involves performing a contraction for 5 seconds followed by a rest for 10 seconds, repeated ten times in each set. This set should be done repeatedly throughout a day for up to 200 repetitions. Progress of strengthening is made from sub-maximal to maximal contractions within the limitations of pain (see *Overload*). After isometric strength has improved, isotonic *strengthening exercises* may begin.

Isotonic strengthening

See *Strengthening exercise*.

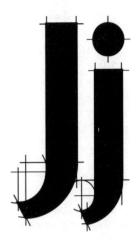

Jaw fracture

A break in the jaw bone (mandible), usually caused by a direct, forceful blow by equipment, such as a bat, stick, ski, or from collisions with opponents or the ground.

The jaw tends to break in more than one place, often on opposite sides (see *Head*). The *fracture* may be undisplaced or displaced.

Undisplaced jaw fractures are painful, tender and swollen, and need to be treated with *analgesics*, *rest* and only soft food can be eaten for up to 4 weeks (advice from a nutritionist is recommended). Displaced jaw fracture is a more severe injury that requires first aid to make sure the breathing passages remain unobstructed.

Most require external fixation (see *Immobilisation*) to hold the bones together for 4 to 6 weeks. If this fails, *open surgery* and *internal fixation* with a metal wire is recommended. In all cases *flexibility exercises* for opening and closing the mouth should be commenced as soon as pain permits. Return to sport takes 1 to 2 months after external fixation is removed or earlier for internal fixation.

Jet lag

A lack of adjustment to a time-zone shift when travelling overseas that may cause fatigue, loss of concentration and memory, a strong desire to sleep in the middle of the day and wakefulness during the middle of the night.

It is associated with brain hormone melatonin levels being out of sync with the day–night cycle, called the circadian rhythm. It is worse when travelling eastwards.

Prevention and treatment

Prevention measures prior to departure include making an adjustment to regular eating, sleeping and training times towards those of the destination. Once the trip begins, set your watch to the time at the destination, and eat, sleep and try to remain active according to this time.

During the trip, avoid dehydration by drinking adequate fluids (see *Hydration*), don't drink alcohol and *caffeine*-containing fluids, don't have an excessive food intake, avoid sleep deprivation (ear plugs and eyeshades can be helpful) and stretch and walk around the plane and break up the flight with a stopover. Melatonin medication has varying effects on each individual and is not recommended.

Upon arrival at the destination it is recommended to adopt the local time and eating habits, make every effort to stay awake during the day even if feeling very tired, exercise to prevent dozing off, avoid sleeping tablets at night (because they delay return to normal circadian rhythm) and try to spend some time in natural sunlight.

Jock itch

A skin infection of the groin area caused by the tinea fungus. The main symptoms are irritation and itching. It is more likely to occur due to excess sweating and insufficient ventilation.

The recommended treatment is an antifungal cream applied two to three times per day for 2 to 4 weeks. Preventive measures include regular changes of shorts and underwear, and regular cleaning of shower facilities.

Jogging

Running at a speed slower than sprinting. It is a recreational fitness activity that first became popular during the 1970s.

For mild to unfit people, it is regarded as a moderate to high-intensity activity (see *Aerobic training* and *Metabolic equivalent (MET)*). The recommended time for a jog is up to each individual jogger. For weight loss or general health, a common range is from 30 up to 60 minutes. The most common injuries are similar to *long distance running*. Correct *running shoes* are recommended.

Joint

A junction where two or more *bones* are connected together. The main types are synovial joints, and fibrous and cartilaginous joints. Most joints in the body, such as the knee, elbow and shoulder, are synovial.

A *synovial joint* is a flexible connection that allows smooth and easy movement. At the same time it provides a significant degree of shock absorption, and is stable and tough to withstand forces that attempt to separate it.

The amount of stability varies according to the type of synovial joint. For example, the knee joint permits a large amount of bending and straightening. It also ensures that the thigh connects firmly with the lower leg and is able to absorb the forces of running and jumping. *Instability* is an injury, for example, that commonly affects the shoulder joint and the low back and pelvis regions (see *Lumbopelvic instability*).

The main features of a synovial joint include the *joint capsule*, synovium, *synovial fluid*, *articular cartilage* and *ligaments*.

A *fibrous and cartilaginous joint* is inflexible and only allows a small amount or no movement. Its main role is to be solid and provide stability. For example, the pubis symphysis connects the front ends of the *pelvis* near the genitals. Little movement occurs at this joint, so that the whole pelvis can provide a solid base for the large movements performed by the legs.

Joint capsule

A tissue that securely connects bones together in a synovial joint. It is tough and unyielding, at the same time as being flexible and pliant to allow smooth and easy movement.

Anatomy
Joint capsule is shaped like a tube. Each end of the tube fits over and is attached firmly around the circumference of one of the two bones (see *Synovial joint*).

This creates an enclosed *joint cavity* that is filled with a lubricant called *synovial fluid*, produced by the inner lining of cells of the joint capsule, called the synovium. Joint capsule is made up of *connective tissue* containing mostly fibroblast cells that produce collagen fibres.

A capsule may possess one or more *ligaments*, a thickened part that provides additional support and keeps the connection secure. Accessory ligaments are rope-like ligaments that are not part of a capsule.

Joint cavity

The enclosed space within a synovial joint. The borders of this space are the ends of the bones that are connected together, ligaments and the tube-shaped joint capsule that fits over them.

In *synovial joints* the cavity is mostly filled with a lubricant called *synovial fluid*. Some joints have one or more *tendons* or *ligaments* pass through the cavity, such as the anterior cruciate ligament of the knee joint. The knee also contains a *fat pad*, which is an extension of the inner lining of the joint capsule called the synovium. *Fibrous and cartilaginous joints* tend to be mostly or completely filled with fibrocartilage or ligament.

Joint replacement

A surgical procedure that involves inserting an artificial joint, called a prosthesis, in place of a diseased or injured joint. Joints that are most commonly replaced are the hip and knee. The shoulder, elbow and finger are less common.

Causes

Joint replacement is recommended when pain and stiffness is so severe and disabling that it interferes with activities of daily living or if there is a deformity that needs to be corrected, most commonly due to *osteoarthritis* and *rheumatoid arthritis*.

Joint replacement has a high rate of success. It is performed mostly for people aged 60 years or older, though it is not uncommon for younger people. A prosthesis has a lifespan, assuming there are no complications such as infection, that may be regarded as being like a car engine. It is associated with the amount and type of weight-bearing activity that wears down the prosthesis, rather than a function of time. It may range from 10 years in a highly active person, up to 25 years for someone less active.

Types

Total joint replacement involves the removal of all the articular surfaces and insertion of two new joint components. This is usually done for conditions such as osteoarthritis and rheumatoid arthritis.

Half joint replacement involves removing just one half of the articular surfaces and leaving the other half in place. A common example is following a fracture to the neck of femur, requiring the round head and neck of the femur to be replaced with a metal prosthesis.

Method

Surgery can take from 1 to 3 hours, depending on the joint. It requires anaesthesia, usually a general anaesthetic or an epidural. The joint is opened up and the diseased portions of the joint are removed to make way for the new joint.

A prosthesis can be made of plastic, ceramic or metal. A cementless prosthesis, where bone actively grows around the prosthesis to provide a firmer hold, is more commonly performed now than using cement.

The stay in hospital may be 1 to 2 weeks, followed by 3 to 6 months of *rehabilitation*, including exercises, until a full recovery is made. Certain movements must be avoided at all costs, such as bending the hip upwards too far by sitting in a seat that is too low, which may cause *dislocation*.

Other complications associated with open surgery include nerve damage, excessive *oedema* and *swelling*, infection and blood clotting such as *deep vein thrombosis (DVT)*. Loosening or breakage of the prosthesis causes pain and requires additional surgery to fix it more securely or replace it.

Joules

A measure of *energy*. One joule equals the heat required to increase the temperature of 1 gram of water by 1°C (when the outside air is 14.5°C/58.1°F) divided by 4.2. One *calorie* equals 4.2 joules. A joule is a bit less than a quarter of a calorie (0.24). There are 1000 joules in *a kilojoule*. The abbreviation for a joule is written as 'j'.

Jumper's knee

See *Patellar tendinosis*.

Jumping sports

A group of sports that includes high jump, long jump and triple jump. High jump involves jumping over a cross bar and landing on a padded mattress. In 1968 it was revolutionised by the 'Fosbury flop' developed by US athlete Dick Fosbury, which enabled jumps higher than 2 m (6 ft 9 in). Long jump was in the ancient Greek Olympics. The current world record is nearly 9 m (29.5 ft) for males.

Triple jump may have its origins in ancient games of hopscotch. It involves a hop, step and then a jump.

Fitness, skills and injuries

The requirements for the sport include *skills training* to develop a good technique, *anaerobic training* and *strength training*.

The most common injuries are *hamstring strain* (thigh), *quadriceps strain* (thigh), *patellar tendinosis* (knee), *patellofemoral joint syndrome* (knee), *tibia stress fracture* (shin), *ankle sprain*, *Achilles tendinosis* (calf), *navicular stress fracture* (foot and toes), *metatarsal stress fracture* (foot and toes), *sinus tarsi syndrome* (foot and toes) and *low back pain (non-specific)*.

Jumping sports for children and adolescents

There are recommended training guidelines for children and adolescents participating in *jumping sports*, such as long jump, triple jump, high jump and pole vault, which are a precautionary measure to minimise the risk of injuries.

The number of training sessions per week for children and adolescents up to the age of 14 should not exceed three, with a maximum of 10 jumps per session. From the age of 15 to 18, the maximum number of training sessions per week is five, with a maximum of 20 jumps per session. The amount of time per training session should not exceed 1½ hours including a warm-up.

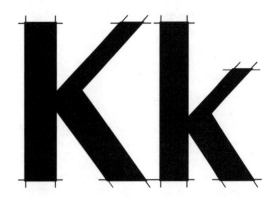

Kayaking

See *Canoeing*.

Ketoacidosis

An excessive amount of ketones in the body, most commonly seen in people with *diabetes* and during *fasting* and crash diets. It occurs when glucose is unavailable, or can't be utilised in the body, and fat is used instead for energy needs. *Fat metabolism* is a process that breaks down free fatty acids (FFAs) that eventually are converted into ketones, a chemical similar to acetone, the smell associated with bubble gum.

In diabetes, for example, it occurs when there are excessively high blood glucose levels, insufficient insulin to use it and participation in high-intensity activities. Symptoms include sweet-smelling breath, nausea, vomiting and gastrointestinal pain. Diagnosis is confirmed with a urine test. Participation in exercise should not be permitted if ketones are present in the urine.

Ketosis

See *Ketoacidosis*.

Kidney

The organ responsible for filtering the blood to take out waste products of cells and excess water, salts and acids. There are two kidneys, each one resting on either side of the spine just above waist level (see *Urinary system*). They are about 10–12 cm (4–5 in) in length. A kidney that is not functioning properly may require *dialysis*.

Physiology

About 1500 L (400 gallons) of blood a day, at a rate of 1 L (2 pt) every minute, flows through the kidneys. Filtering the *blood* takes place in the nephron. There are 2 million nephrons in the kidneys.

The content of urine varies. For example, when the body is dehydrated due to exercise, the antidiuretic hormone (ADH or vasopressin) makes the concentration of urea higher, giving urine a strong yellow colour.

Urine is passed into the collecting region of the kidney, the medulla, and then down a long tube, called the ureter, into the *bladder*, then is excreted through the *urethra*. The kidneys also contain the adrenal glands that produce hormones, including *erythropoietin (EPO)*, adrenaline, noradrenaline and corticosteroids.

Injury

The kidney can be injured due to a sudden blow or excessive force such as a high-speed collision in motor sports or *collision sports* such as the football codes. It should be suspected if there is pain or bruising in the middle or side of the back just below the ribs or if there is blood in the urine (haematuria).

It should be treated as a *medical emergency* if there is loss of consciousness due to excessive blood loss. Minor injuries require rest and maintaining an adequate fluid intake.

Kienbock's disease

A disease that causes softening of the centre of the lunate, a small bone in the *wrist joint*, which makes it vulnerable to being deformed. It is an overuse injury that belongs to a group of injuries called *osteochondrosis*, and is associated with repeated excessive forces on the wrist.

It causes pain, either on the palm-side or back of the wrist, and loss of strength. It is most commonly seen in people aged in the 20- to 30-year-old age group. The best radiological investigation is a *bone scan* or *magnetic resonance imaging (MRI)*. In the early stages *immobilisation* and *flexibility exercises* are recommended. If the pain persists, surgery may be required to relieve the pressure on the bone.

Kilocalorie

See *Calories*.

Kilojoules

A measure of *energy*. One kilojoule (2.2 lb) equals the heat required to increase the temperature of 1 kg of water by 1°C (when the outside air is 14.5°C/58°F), divided by 4.2. One *Calorie* equals 4.2 kilojoules. A kilojoule is a bit less than a quarter of a *Calorie* (0.24) and equals 1000 joules. The abbreviation for kilojoule is 'kJ'.

Kinesiology

Originally the science of human movement studied in medical and physical education academic institutions. It is also now practiced separately as a natural health therapy.

Science of human movement

An analysis of the movements of the *elbow joint* identifies three muscles that are involved in supination, which is an outward rotation of the forearm so that the palm of the hand moves from facing downwards to facing upwards.

The supinator is the prime mover muscle and the biceps muscle is the assistant. However, when the biceps muscle contracts it also produces flexion movement, bending at the elbow. As a result the triceps muscle has to contract at the same time, but only strong enough to oppose the flexion produced by the biceps and keep the elbow steady.

The kinesiological roles of these muscles are: the supinator is the agonist, biceps is the *synergist*; and the triceps is the antagonist. In addition, the supinator produces *concentric* contractions and triceps produces *isometric* contractions.

In kinesiology emphasis is also placed on the type and shape of a joint, including features like the mechanical axis. For example, at the elbow joint four movements occur: supination and its opposite, pronation (inwards rotation); flexion (bending) and its opposite, extension (straightening).

Kinesiology is mostly studied in academic circles. It is also practised as a form of alternative therapy. *Biomechanics* is the preferred term for the science of human movement in conventional sports health professions.

Natural health therapy

The therapy believes that the body has innate healing energy, but sometimes it needs to be helped into a better position to achieve this care. It also recognises flows of energy within the body, similar to *acupuncture*, that relate not only to the muscles but also every tissue and organ.

These energy flows are evaluated by testing the muscles for imbalances, which in turn reflect the body's overall state of structural, chemical or emotional balance. The aim is to restore the balance between muscles with treatments such as *massage* and exercises. Kinesiology is also called muscle balancing or energy balancing.

Knee articular cartilage acute injury

An acute injury of the layer of tissue that covers the ends of the two bones and the kneecap within the *knee joint*. It is usually due to a sudden excessive force such as falling onto the knees.

It is more common than previously realised since the widespread use of *arthroscopy* and *magnetic resonance imaging (MRI)* in the 1980s and 1990s. It is associated with an increased risk of developing *osteoarthritis*.

Diagnosis, treatment and return to sport

Knee *articular cartilage acute injury* causes *pain*, *swelling*, reduced *range of movement* and difficulty walking.

The diagnosis can be confirmed with MRI, which may be ordered if the above signs and symptoms persist for more than 4 days and there are no other obvious causes that are diagnosed. It also may occur together with another injury, such as *anterior cruciate ligament (ACL) tear*, *meniscus tear* or *bone bruise*.

Treatment during the first 48 to 72 hours is *RICE* (*rest, ice, compression and elevation*) and avoidance of heat and alcohol consumption to minimise

swelling, followed by *flexibility exercises* and *strengthening exercises*. Return to sport can take up to 6 weeks, depending on the severity of the injury.

Arthroscopy may be recommended if there are loose fragments of articular cartilage aggravating the joint or to perform a chondroplasty, followed by a *sport rehabilitation* program. Return to sport is permitted 2 to 3 months after surgery.

Knee joint

The joint that links between the thigh and lower leg and foot. It is the largest *synovial joint* in the body. It is made up of the connection between the round end of the thigh bone (femur) and the slightly concave upper end of the front shin bone (tibia).

The movements are bending (*flexion*) and straightening (*extension*), and small amounts of rotation and side-to-side.

The patellofemoral joint is created by the round kneecap bone (patella) in front of the lower end of the femur, embedded within the quadriceps (front

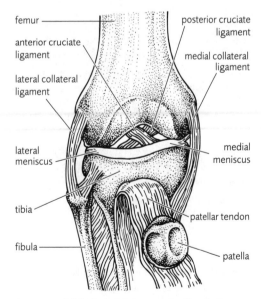

Anatomy of right knee joint—anterior (front) view (patella pulled downwards to reveal inside of knee joint)

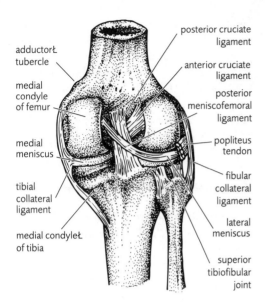

Anatomy of right knee joint—posterior (back) view

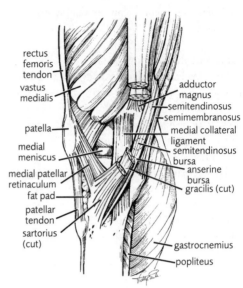

Muscles, tendons and other structures of the right knee joint—medial (inner) side view

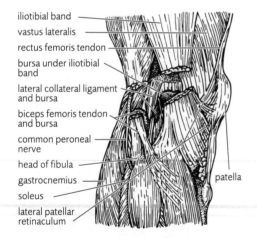

Muscles, tendons and other structures of the right knee joint—lateral (outer) side view

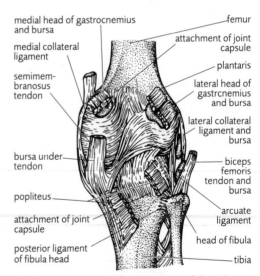

Muscles, tendons and other structures of the right knee joint—posterior (back) view

thigh muscle) tendon. The patella protects the femur and improves the efficiency of the quadriceps during knee straightening.

The large *range of movement* at the knee joint requires strong ligaments to maintain stability, including the anterior cruciate ligament (ACL), posterior cruciate ligament (PCL), medial collateral ligament (MCL), lateral collateral ligament (LCL) and iliotibial band.

Muscles involved in knee movements

Movement	Primary movers	Secondary movers
Extension	• Quadriceps	
Flexion	• Hamstring	• Gastrocnemius • Popliteus • Sartorius • Gracilis
Internal rotation	• Popliteus • Hamstring (semimembranosus and semitendinosus)	• Sartorius • Gracilis
External rotation	• Hamstring (biceps femoris) • Popliteus	

Additional stability is provided by two C-shaped fibrous cartilages, horizontally positioned in the joint, the medial and lateral meniscus, which are also shock absorbers for the articular cartilage.

Knee joint replacement

A surgical procedure that involves inserting an artificial joint in place of a diseased *knee joint*. The surgery removes the diseased articular surfaces of the joint: the upper part are the two rounded ends of the femur (thigh bone); and the lower part are the two shallow cup-shaped ends of the tibia (leg bone). They are replaced with metal and plastic parts that aim to be strong enough to bear the mechanical forces of walking and allow some movement.

Most knee joint replacement is performed for joints affected by *osteoarthritis* or *rheumatoid arthritis* that are causing excessive pain and stiffness that interferes with the ability to do normal daily activities, such as walking.

The first knee joint replacement was performed in 1968. In the early years the procedure was less successful than *hip joint replacement* because of difficulties finding materials that could withstand the mechanical forces experienced in the knee and designing a prosthesis that provided enough stability. However, new materials and designs have been developed and high success rates are now being achieved.

After surgery

A stay in hospital of 3 to 7 days is required after surgery, followed by 3 to 6 months of *rehabilitation*, including *flexibility exercises* to increase range of movement, *strengthening exercises* of the muscles and instructions regarding leisure activities such as walking and playing sport. Potential problems include loosening, breakage and dislocation of the prosthesis, lengthening or shortening of the leg, nerve damage, infection and blood clotting leading to *deep vein thrombosis*.

It is generally recommended to be as active as possible after joint replacement of the hip or knee, but to avoid high-impact activities such as competitive tennis, skiing and jumping activities. Low-impact activities, such as swimming, walking and cycling, are associated with a longer lasting prosthesis.

Knee osteoarthritis

A disease of the articular cartilage of the *knee joint* due to a gradual accumulation of excessive physical loads over a period of years that eventually cause pain, usually either on the outer (lateral) side or medial (inner) side of the knee.

The pain is particularly associated with weight-bearing activities, such as running and walking. It also may be aggravated by low-intensity sports such as lawn *bowls* where many bowlers stand with their knees slightly bent prior to delivery, followed by (for right handers) stepping forward with the left leg and transferring 95 per cent of body weight over the left knee as the bowl is delivered. Morning stiffness that is relieved within half an hour of walking is a common symptom. In severe cases pain is felt at night that may disturb sleep.

Diagnosis of *osteoarthritis* is confirmed with an *X-ray*. The recommended treatment includes *analgesics, non-steroidal anti-inflammatory drugs (NSAIDs)*, reducing the amount of weight-bearing activities; for example, replacing walking and running with swimming, *flexibility exercises* and *strengthening exercises*. In severe cases *knee joint replacement* surgery is required.

Knee osteochondritis dissecans

An injury in children that causes softening of a bone in the *knee joint* that makes it vulnerable to being deformed or separated from the main body of the bone, which is called a loose body. This *osteochondrosis* injury mostly occurs in teenagers and adolescents.

A diagnosis is confirmed with an X-ray or *magnetic resonance imaging (MRI)*. The recommended treatment is usually reduced amounts of activity for 3 to 6 months. In severe cases surgery is required to reconnect a loose body, followed by *rest* from activity for 6 weeks, *flexibility exercises* and *strengthening exercises*, with a full return to sport taking 8 to 12 weeks.

Knee pain and injuries

Causes

Knee pain can be caused by an acute or overuse injury or diseases. An *acute injury* causes pain that begins suddenly due to a single incident, such as a twisting fall.

An *overuse injury* causes pain that gets worse over a period of weeks or months due to an accumulation of excessive forces that cause microtrauma. In the early stages it causes only minor pain and stiffness. But later on, either gradually or following a sudden force, it becomes painful enough to seek medical care.

The *knee joint* and associated structures are the main sources of *pain*. However, it is not unusual for pain to come from another structure, in particular the low back joints, which is called *knee referred pain*.

Diagnosis

Making the diagnosis involves combining information gathered from the *history, physical examination* and relevant tests.

For acute injuries, an important clue is pain location. For example, inner (medial) side pain may suggest a *medial collateral ligament (MCL) sprain*.

The number of hours after the injury for *swelling* to become obvious is also important. Less than 2 hours usually means bleeding, called a *haemarthrosis*, which may indicate an *anterior cruciate ligament (ACL) tear* or *patella dislocation*. Six to 24 hours suggests a *meniscus tear*. No swelling indicates a medial collateral ligament (MCL) sprain.

How the injury occurred is important. A blow to the front of the knee that causes excessive knee straightening (hyperextension) may cause a *posterior cruciate ligament (PCL) sprain*. A fall onto the knees compressing the kneecap (patella) against the underlying bone suggests *knee articular cartilage acute injury*. The knee twisting with the foot stuck to the ground indicates a *meniscus tear*. Compression from landing on both feet, such as in skiing and wave-jumping, can cause *tibial plateau fracture*.

For overuse injuries, the pain location is important: inner side (medial), outer side (lateral), back (posterior) or front (anterior). For example, medial side pain is most likely to be caused by *patellofemoral joint syndrome*.

Overuse injuries are also associated with a specific activity. For instance, pain just below the kneecap is most likely to be due to *patellar tendinosis* if it is associated with *basketball, volleyball* and *jumping sports* such as high jump, whereas in swimmers it is more likely to be *fat pad impingement*.

Lateral pain with excessive downhill running is associated with *iliotibial band friction syndrome*. Posterior pain while doing sprinting or kicking activities suggests *hamstring tendinitis*. Clicking and pain on the medial or lateral side associated with twisting activities such as getting out of the car may be due to *meniscus degeneration*. A feeling that the kneecap is moving sideways (laterally) suggests *patellofemoral joint instability*.

Radiological investigations may be required, such as *magnetic resonance imaging (MRI)* for ligament

Causes of knee pain and injuries

Common	Less common	Not to be missed
Acute injury		
• Meniscus tear	• Patella dislocation	• Tibial plateau fracture
• Medial collateral ligament (MCL) sprain	• Lateral collateral ligament (LCL) sprain	• Decompression sickness
• Anterior cruciate ligament (ACL) tear	• Fat pad impingement	
	• Patella fracture	
• Posterior cruciate ligament (PCL) sprain		
• Knee articular cartilage acute injury		
Overuse injury		
Pain located in the front (anterior) of the knee		
• Patellofemoral joint syndrome	• Osgood-Schlatter's disease	• Knee referred pain
• Patellar tendinosis		• Tumour
• Fat pad impingement		• Slipped capital femoral epiphysis
• Patellofemoral joint instability		• Perthes' disease
		• Knee osteochondritis dissecans
Pain located on the outer (lateral) side of the knee		
• Iliotibial band friction syndrome		• Slipped capital femoral epiphysis
		• Perthes' disease
Pain located on the inner (medial) side of the knee		
• Patellofemoral joint syndrome	• Knee joint synovial plica	• Tumour
• Meniscus degeneration	• Pes anserinus tendinitis	• Slipped capital femoral epiphysis
	• Knee osteoarthritis	• Perthes' disease
Pain located in the back (posterior) of the knee		
• Knee referred pain		• Deep vein thrombosis
• Hamstring tendinitis		• Peripheral vascular disease

injuries and *knee articular cartilage acute injury*, diagnostic *ultrasound* for tendon injuries, and *X-rays* for tibial plateau fracture, *patella fracture* and *knee osteoarthritis*.

Knee referred pain

Pain may be felt in the knee that is caused by a damaged structure some distance away, usually in the low back, sacroiliac joint or hip joint. *Referred pain* on the inner (medial) side of the knee is more likely to come from the *hip joint*, such as *hip osteoarthritis*. Pain in the back (posterior), front (anterior) and outer (lateral) side of the knee is more likely to be associated with *low back pain (non-specific)* or *sacroiliac joint pain*.

The diagnosis first requires excluding a local cause of pain. Second, an assessment is made for positive signs that the cause is referred pain. For example, a diagnosis of pain referred from the right side joints of the low back to the back of the knee is considered likely if *mobilisation*, a treatment involving a practitioner pushing the joints with the hands, reduces the pain.

If a muscle is referring pain, such as *myofascial trigger points*, the recommended treatment is *massage* and *dry needling*. The neural sheath is assessed with the straight leg raise *neural tension* test and treated with *flexibility exercises*.

Knock knees

See *Genu valgum*.

QUICK REFERENCE GUIDE

Knee

Acute injury: Pain caused by a sudden force

Anterior cruciate ligament (ACL) tear ......Did you land on your feet from a jump or pivot or decelerate suddenly while running, which caused immediate pain and obvious swelling within 2 hours?

Posterior cruciate ligament (PCL) sprain....Did you receive a blow to the front of the knee causing the joint to hyperextend (over-straighten)?

Meniscus tear ....Did you twist the knee with the foot stuck to the ground, which caused pain and obvious swelling 6 to 24 hours later?

Medial collateral ligament (MCL) sprain ....Did you have a player fall across the outer side of your knee or bend it in an inwards direction during a slow twisting fall when skiing, which caused pain on the inner side of the knee but no obvious swelling?

Lateral collateral ligament (LCL) sprain ....Did you have a player fall across the inner side of your knee when your foot was fixed to the ground, which caused pain on the outer side of the knee?

Knee articular cartilage acute injury ....Did you a fall onto your knees and compress the kneecap against the underlying bone?

Tibial plateau fracture ....Did you land on both feet, such as in skiing and wave-jumping, and compress the knee joint bones against each other?

Patella dislocation ....Did your kneecap suddenly pop out of place, which caused pain and obvious swelling within 2 hours?

Overuse injury: Pain that has gradually worsened over a period of weeks or months

Patellofemoral joint syndrome ......Do you feel pain in the front or inner side of the knee that comes on after running, walking, walking up stairs or sitting down for an extended period of time such as at the movies or during a long car ride?

Patellar tendinosis.........................Do you feel pain located in the front of the knee just below the kneecap that is aggravated by playing basketball, volleyball or training for jumping sports like high, long or triple jump?

Fat pad impingement....................Do you have pain in the front of your knee just below the kneecap associated with activities that straighten out the joint, such as kicking during swimming or standing for long periods of time?

Iliotibial band friction syndrome ....Do you have pain on the outside of the knee that is associated with excessive amounts of downhill running?

Hamstring tendinitis ....Do you have pain in the back of your knee associated with sprinting or kicking activities?

Meniscus degeneration ....Do you have a clicking noise and pain (on either the inner or outer side) brought on with certain twisting activities such as rolling in bed or getting out of the car?

Patellofemoral joint instability ......Do you have a feeling that the kneecap is excessively moving sideways?

Lacrosse

Lacrosse originated from the North American Indian game called 'baggataway'. Players used a long stick with a small cross at the end to hold a net for catching a ball, which reminded French immigrants of a bishop's crozier ('la crosse'). It is played between two teams of 10, with the winner scoring the most goals within a set time, usually four 15 minute quarters.

Lactate

A molecule produced when lactic acid dissolves in liquid and loses a hydrogen ion (H⁺). Lactic acid is the end product of the *glycolytic system*, which produces adenosine triphosphate (ATP), the main source of energy for *muscle contractions*. It is used interchangeably with lactate.

An accumulation of lactate and H⁺ ions is a normal response to activity. After cessation of activity they are gradually cleared out of the muscles by the blood, which can take up to a few hours to complete. This process can be made quicker by performing a *warm-down*, such as doing the same activity at 50 per cent intensity, which maintains a steady flow of blood.

Lactate and H⁺ ion levels in muscle and blood can become excessive if a person performs an activity at an intensity that is too high for their aerobic fitness levels. This causes an acidic environment, particularly inside the muscles. It involves crossing the *lactate threshold*, and when it occurs during training or a competition activity it is called *lactate fatigue*

Lactate fatigue

Feelings of tiredness and inability to continue performing an activity at the same level of intensity and control due to a build up of excessive amounts of *lactate* in the muscles and blood. It can occur at any time during participation in exercise and sport. For example, in the middle of a marathon or towards the end of a 100 m swimming sprint.

Physiology

Lactate is produced by the *glycolytic system*, which is an anaerobic metabolic system that produces energy for muscles by breaking down glucose without using oxygen. In a 100 m swimming race this system provides the main supply of energy for the muscles in the first 50 m, then the aerobic systems (that use oxygen) also begin to supply energy.

However, if a swimmer goes too fast at the start, it can make the glycolytic system produce excessive amounts of lactate. This is associated with high levels of hydrogen ions (H^+), leading to increased acidity in the *blood* and muscles, which hinders the work of the aerobic systems. All of a sudden the swimmer is overwhelmed by a loss of energy due to lactate fatigue, which is also called 'a bear jumped on my back' or 'feeling awash in a sea of lactic acid'.

Lactate fatigue can be avoided by timing the speed of activity in order to use up energy gradually, as well as methods of anaerobic training such as *anaerobic training, interval training* and *aerobic training*. *Lactate threshold* is a method of measuring aerobic fitness during aerobic training.

Lactate threshold

A method used to measure *aerobic fitness*, particularly for endurance sports such as *long distance running*. The specific measurement is the point where the level of *lactate* and hydrogen (H^+) ions in the muscles and blood suddenly increase above the normal range.

This sudden increase is usually due to an inability to cope with an increase in the volume or intensity of an activity, such as the distance that needs to be run in a marathon or an increase in speed during a marathon.

Crossing the lactate threshold is a signal for an impending onset of *lactate fatigue*, including feelings of tiredness that have a negative impact on ability to continue performing at the same intensity.

Testing

The most accurate method of testing lactate threshold is to take a blood sample to measure levels of lactate. In adults lactate threshold is 4 millimoles per litre (mmol/L) (36 mg/dL) and in children, 2.5 mmol/L (23 mg/dL).

The test involves an athlete, for example, performing a series of runs at gradually increasing speeds. At the end of each run a blood sample is taken. The speed at which the athlete has a blood lactate level of 4 mmol/L (36 mg/dL) or above is the athlete's level of aerobic fitness. *Aerobic training* to increase fitness should enable the athlete to achieve a faster running speed at a subsequent test.

An indirect method of assessing lactate threshold is noticing when breathing rate and depth suddenly increases during an activity. It occurs because of the body's need to get rid of excess carbon dioxide from the blood, which is associated with high levels of H^+ ions.

Lactate threshold can also be expressed as a percentage of VO_2 *max*, another measure of aerobic fitness, defined as the highest amount of oxygen that can be consumed by a person during an activity. Unfit people have a lactate threshold of 50–60 per cent VO_2 max. Fit athletes have a threshold of 70–85 per cent VO_2 max.

Lactic acid

The end product of the break down of glucose in the *glycolytic system*. It is used interchangeably with *lactate*.

Lactose intolerance

An inability to digest the milk-sugar lactose due to a lack of the enzyme lactase. It can cause stomach cramps, flatulence and diarrhoea. The recommended treatment is to avoid all normal dairy products, eat only lactose-reduced products, and take alternative sources of *calcium* and *protein* to ensure an adequate dietary intake.

Laser therapy

A treatment for injuries using highly concentrated beams of pure light or amplified luminous energy. They are called cold lasers because there is no

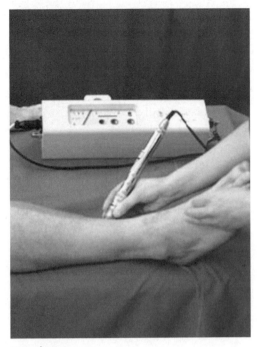

Laser therapy

measurable heat. The helium neon laser has a penetration of up to 8 mm (0.3 in). The gallium arsenide laser, with a longer wavelength, has a penetration depth up to 20 mm (0.75 in).

Tissue healing is best stimulated by low doses, while higher doses should be used for the relief of *pain*, muscle *spasm* and *oedema*.

Due to the small width of the laser beam and relatively superficial penetration, it is recommended for small tendon *strains*, *sprains* of ligaments and joints near the skin such as fingers and *myofascial trigger point* pain.

Lateral

The anatomical direction pointing outwards from the midline towards the side of the body. It is used to describe the surface of any part of the body that faces away from the midline, or a body part located further from the midline than another part. For example, the lateral surface of the thigh is the outside of the thigh. Lateral is the opposite of *medial*.

It is also called radial in the forearm and fibular in the lower leg.

Lateral collateral ligament (LCL) sprain

An uncommon acute injury of the ligament on the outer side of the *knee joint* due to a sudden excessive force that causes it to be overstretched. It occurs when the knee is bent outwards at the same time as the foot is fixed on the ground, such as a player falling across the inside of the knee.

The recommended treatments during the first 48 to 72 hours include *RICE* (*rest, ice, compression and elevation*) and avoiding heat and alcohol consumption to minimise swelling. Surgery is required if the severity of the injury is a grade 3 *sprain*. For grade 1 (mild) and grade 2 (moderate) sprains, treatments include *strengthening exercises*, *flexibility exercises*, *massage* and a *sport rehabilitation* program.

Lateral epicondylitis

See *Tennis elbow*.

Lateral flexion

See *Abduction*.

Lateral rotation

See *External rotation*.

L-carnitine

An *amino acid* that plays a central role in *fat metabolism* by transporting long chains of free fatty acids (FFAs), the basic building blocks of fat, through the membranes of mitochondria in cells where they are broken down to release energy for activities such as muscle contractions.

More than half of the body's daily requirements for L-carnitine is normally supplied by the diet from meat, poultry, fish and some dairy products, and the rest are produced within the body by converting other amino acids.

The aim of L-carnitine supplementation is to improve long distance, endurance and aerobic fitness, and help with weight loss by reducing fat content in the body. It is commonly suggested for sports such as *wrestling, rowing, gymnastics* and *bodybuilding*. However, research does not show any benefit during *aerobic training* at a high *overload*. The most effective method of losing fat is a *fat-loss diet* for a person already performing sport and exercise.

Leadership

The behaviour of an individual in a team who shows the way forward to achieving the team's goals. Leaders include people such as the *coach*, captain, head of a team section, team manager and gym directors. Leadership involves providing guidance, direction and opinions, taking the initiative, helping to bring the best out of all the individuals in the team, and plays an important role in *teamwork*.

Leaders vary according to their *personality* type. A quiet person of few words may be just as effective as an extroverted and talkative person. However, there are common features of successful leadership, including giving feedback, having good relationships with members of the team, and knowing when and how to influence decisions and team behaviour and performance.

Leg length discrepancy

A *biomechanical abnormality* that makes one leg shorter than the other. It can be caused by an anatomical abnormality of a bone or a functional problem, such as excessive *pelvis lateral tilt*.

It should be suspected if any of the following are noticed: head tilt and shoulder drop, often towards the longer leg; asymmetry of arm swinging motion during walking or running; increased speed of arm swing during walking or running; the position of the *pelvis* being higher on the side of the longer leg; longer leg being swung outwards in a circle (circumduction) when moved forward during walking or running; and pain or injury on the side of the shorter leg. In severe cases a surgical procedure called *osteotomy* may be required.

Legumes

A pod or seed vessel of plants. Common legumes include beans, lentils and peas. They are rich in *protein, carbohydrates, fibre, vitamins* and *minerals*, are low in *fat* and are often used in salads and soups and prepared as spreads, such as hummus, though the latter usually has added oil. They are also called pulses.

Lens dislocation

A sudden forceful blow to the *eye* can cause the outer lens to come away. Partial dislocation causes few symptoms; however, complete lens dislocation results in blurred vision. Surgery is often required.

Les autres

The French word for 'the others' is a term used to describe athletes with a disability caused by a wide range of conditions which result in impairment of walking and running that doesn't fit into the traditional classification systems of the established *disability* groups. An example is dwarfism.

Life expectancy

The age that a person born today can expect to live to. It is calculated as an average of the total population of people who have died. Life expectancy was around 50 years in 1900, and has increased to around 80 years today and continues to improve.

Women tend to live longer than men, mainly due to less frequent participation in risk-taking activities that lead to accidental deaths in young adults, a tendency for more men to smoke cigarettes compared to women and because *oestrogen* naturally protects women against *coronary heart disease*.

The older a person is today, the greater the life expectancy. For example, the average healthy 70 year old can expect to live to around 85 years. The few people who live beyond 100 years probably have a genetic advantage for living a long life.

Ligament

A rope or strap-shaped bundle of *connective tissue* that supports a structure or organ. It is made up of parallel bundles of collagen fibres embedded with fibroblast cells that make it tough and unyielding, yet flexible and pliant.

In a *synovial joint*, a ligament provides additional support to the *joint capsule* that connects together the two bones that form the joint. Most joint ligaments are a thickening of the joint capsule in the form of a distinctive bundle. Less commonly a joint may have an accessory ligament that is separate to the capsule, such as the anterior cruciate ligament of the knee joint.

Ligaments are also found in *fibrous and cartilaginous joints*, where they act like superglue to hold the bones together and only allow a small amount or no movement.

Examples of ligaments that support organs include the abdominal cavity ligaments of the *bladder* and uterus, and pectoral ligaments that help maintain the shape of the *breasts*.

Ligament sprain

See *Sprain*.

Liniment

See *Analgesics (topical)*.

Lisfranc's fracture dislocation

Displacement of the joints between the cuneiforms and cuboid bones and their corresponding metatarsals and, in some cases, a broken bone. The injury can result in damage to the dorsalis pedis artery if it is unstable (see *Foot and toes*).

The *dislocation* and *fracture* cause pain in the middle of the foot, difficulty walking and generalised *swelling*. If it is severe the blood flow to the toes can be compromised. A diagnosis is often confirmed with *CT scan*. Treatment involves *immobilisation* in a plaster cast for 6 weeks. Severely unstable injuries require *open surgery* and *internal fixation*.

Lithotripsy

See *Extra corporeal shock wave therapy*.

Little Leaguer's elbow

An injury caused by softening of a section of bone and articular cartilage in the *elbow joint*, leading to their separation from the rest of the bone. The section of bone most commonly affected is the capitellum, which is the outer side of the lower end of the humerus (arm bone). Separation can lead to small pieces of bone floating in the joint called loose bodies.

It is most commonly seen in children and teenage athletes in *throwing sports*, particularly *baseball* pitchers, and in *gymnastics*.

The injury is an *osteochondrosis*, also known as osteochondritis dissecans. It is believed to be due to a problem with the blood supply that is brought on by an accumulation of repeated, excessive physical loads on the bone over a long period of time, weeks or months. For example, in baseball pitchers it is due to repeated throwing and the forces caused by an abnormality of *throwing biomechanics*. Restrictions should be placed on the amount of throwing done by children and adolescents (see *Throwing sports for children and adolescents*).

Diagnosis, treatment and return to sport

Pain is usually felt in the outer side of the elbow. Other signs include reduced *flexibility* and bony thickening of the elbow joint. Diagnosis is confirmed with an X-*ray*.

The recommended treatment for mild cases (indicated by a slightly reduced *range of movement* of elbow joint straightening movement) is a splint, which is a form of *immobilisation* called protected mobilisation, for 6 weeks and *flexibility exercises*, followed by a return to sport after 9 weeks.

Surgery may be required for severe cases to reattach the section of bone with *internal fixation* and remove any loose bodies. Return to sport may require up to 6 months of *sport rehabilitation*.

Little Leaguer's shoulder

An overuse injury due to a separation between the mature and growing bone (epiphysis) in the rounded head of the humerus (arm bone) in the *shoulder joint*. It is caused by an accumulation of repeated excessive physical loads over a period of weeks or months during *throwing sports* such as *baseball* and javelin. It usually affects teenagers aged between 12 and 15.

The diagnosis of this injury to the *epiphysis* is confirmed with a *bone scan*. Treatment for mild cases involves *rest*, usually for at least 6 weeks, by reducing the amount of throwing (such as changing from pitching to being on first base), *ice* and *flexibility exercises*. Severe cases require *immobilisation* in a plaster cast until the pain is gone.

Liver

A large organ in the upper right and central side of the abdomen (see *Gastrointestinal system*). The upper portion of the liver is protected by the lower ribs. The liver is responsible for producing and regulating many of the chemicals, *hormones* and compounds in the *blood* such as *cholesterol*. For example, it produces protein-based compounds for the blood, such as the globin part of *haemoglobin*, stores *glucose*

as glycogen molecules that are released into the bloodstream to circulate around the body to supply energy to the muscles, and clears the blood of excessive chemicals such as alcohol.

Disease and illness of the liver include *hepatitis* (viral infection), many causes of cirrhosis (chronic damage), including excessive use of alcohol and medications like *non-steroidal anti-inflammatory drugs (NSAIDs)*, and liver cancer.

Injury

The liver can be injured due to a sudden blow or excessive force during *collision sports* such as *motor sports*. It is suspected if there is upper right side abdominal pain, lower right side *rib fracture* and loss of consciousness. It should be treated as a *medical emergency*.

Load

The amount of work that needs to be produced by a person or a specific muscle in order to perform an activity. Examples of activities are lifting a 5 kg (11 lb) weight, a push up, doing a vertical jump and running 200 m (660 ft). If the load is high enough to lead to fatigue it is called *overload*.

Locking

Joint movement that is blocked by a damaged structure inside the joint. An example is when a torn piece of *knee joint* meniscus gets trapped between the bones inside the joint as it is being bent or straightened out and the movement is brought to a complete and sudden halt. It also may be due to a loose body of bone floating inside the joint caused by *osteoarthritis*, *osteochondrosis* or a *fracture* affecting a joint.

Locking is associated with pain. Most of the time the piece can be freed with subsequent attempts to move the joint. However, an *arthroscopy* may be required to remove a loose body to prevent further locking.

Long bones

The *bones* of the arms, legs, hands and feet with elongated shafts with expanded ends that form *joints*. They have a thick layer of compact bone to bear the brunt of the mechanical forces and stresses of movement.

Long distance running

Long distance running was in the ancient Greek Olympics. Today, the events include the 10 000 m, marathon (42.195 km/26.16 miles, the distance from Windsor Castle to London's White City stadium) and half-marathon (20.097 km/13.08 miles). Fun runs vary, such as Sydney's City to Surf (14 km/8.7 miles). Cross-country running is an 8–12 km (5–7.5 miles) run outdoors.

Fun runs are great for all age groups

Fitness, equipment and injuries

The fitness requirements are *aerobic training*, *interval training* and *flexibility training*. Injuries are associated with abnormalities of *running biomechanics*. Wearing correct footwear is recommended (see *Running shoes*).

The most common injuries and illnesses are *tibia stress fracture* (shin), *fibula stress fracture* (shin), *shin chronic compartment syndrome*, *patellofemoral joint syndrome* (knee), *iliotibial band friction syndrome* (knee), *Achilles tendinosis* (calf), *plantar fasciitis* (foot and toes), *navicular stress fracture* (foot and toes), *heat illness*, *gastrointestinal reflux* and *gastrointestinal bleeding*.

Long flexor tendon avulsion

An injury that causes an inability to bend the end of the finger at the distal interphalangeal (DIP) joint. It is due to the tendon of the flexor digitorum profundus muscle snapping when grabbing an opponent's clothing, which forces the end of the finger to suddenly straighten out. The ring (fourth finger) is most commonly affected (see *Hand and finger joints*).

The snapped tendon takes off a small piece of the bone of the distal phalanx, which is called an *avulsion fracture*. An X-ray is used to confirm the diagnosis. The recommended treatment is surgery to reconnect the tendon, which must take place within 10 days of the injury.

Loss of consciousness

A loss of being awake and awareness of oneself and surroundings. It can occur during exercise and sport due to trauma or an underlying disease or illness. Other symptoms that are sometimes associated with loss of consciousness include *vomiting*, nausea, paleness, ashen-grey colour of the face and the body bathed in cold perspiration (see *Syncope*).

Each cause of loss of consciousness should be treated as a *medical emergency*.

Low back joints

The spine that connects the *thoracic spine joints* to the sacrum of the *pelvis*. It is made up of five bones in a column, collectively called the lumbar vertebrae and numbered from top to bottom, L1 to L5.

Each vertebra has three joints with the vertebra below: the central and forward-located (anterior) joint is the lumbar *disc* and two backward-located (posterior) *synovial joints*, one on each side, the zygapophysial joints (Z-joints). The lumbar spinal column curves inwards in the middle, called a lordosis.

Lumbar joint muscles also are essential for keeping the pelvis stable during movements of the legs (see *Lumbo-pelvic instability*).

The spine protects the *spinal cord*. At each lumbar vertebra level there are two large branches, the ventral and dorsal nerve roots. They form a larger *spinal nerve*, which exits the spinal canal through the intervertebral foramen. Each spinal nerve is named according to the vertebra level; for example, L5 spinal nerve.

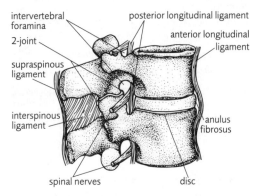

intervertebral foramina
2-joint
supraspinous ligament
interspinous ligament
spinal nerves
posterior longitudinal ligament
anterior longitudinal ligament
anulus fibrosus
disc

Anatomy of low back joints—lateral (outer) side view

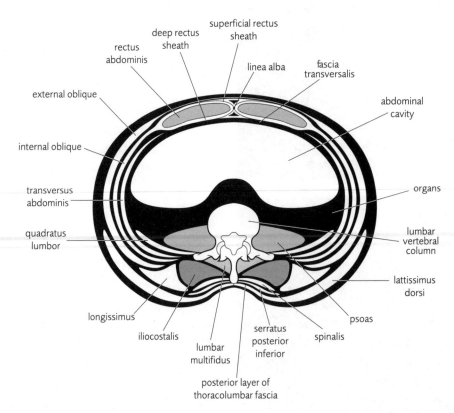

rectus abdominis
deep rectus sheath
superficial rectus sheath
linea alba
fascia transversalis
external oblique
abdominal cavity
internal oblique
transversus abdominis
organs
quadratus lumbor
lumbar vertebral column
longissimus
lattissimus dorsi
iliocostalis
psoas
lumbar multifidus
serratus posterior inferior
spinalis
posterior layer of thoracolumbar fascia

Anatomy of low back joints and muscles of the abdomen—cross-section showing a superior (from above) view

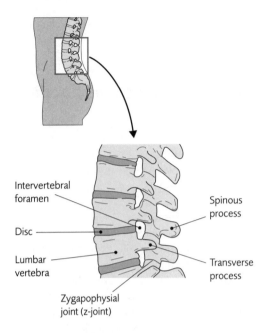

Intervertebral foramen

Spinous process

Disc

Lumbar vertebra

Transverse process

Zygapophysial joint (z-joint)

Bones of the low back joints

Low back muscle contusion

Bruised low back muscles caused by a blunt sudden force, such as a direct blow from a part of the body of an opposing player or a piece of equipment. It is most common in *collision sports* such as the *football codes, basketball, ice hockey* and *lacrosse*.

Diagnosis, treatment and return to sport

The *muscle contusion* causes a specific area of tenderness, *swelling*, discoloration due to bleeding, and pain that is aggravated by bending backwards. In severe cases the *pain* may interfere with sleep.

The most important period in the treatment is in the first 24 to 48 hours following the injury when *rest*, *ice* and *compression* and avoiding heat and drinking alcohol are essential to minimise the bleeding. Afterwards, *passive exercises* and later *flexibility exercises* to prevent loss of range of movement of the muscle is recommended. *Massage* should not be started in the first 48 hours, and then only gently.

The timing of return to sport is mainly guided by pain and response of the muscle to treatment. General guidelines based on the severity are: mild contusion, 3 days to 2 weeks; moderate, 2 to 4 weeks; severe, 4 to 6 weeks. Prevention of another contusion can be achieved by wearing low back padding.

Low back pain and injuries

Causes

Low back pain can be caused by an overuse or acute injury, or disease. In most cases it is an *overuse injury*, where the pain gets worse over a period of weeks or months due to an accumulation of excessive forces that cause microtrauma. In the early stages it causes

Low back joint range of movement and muscles

Movement	Range of movement	Muscles producing movement
Flexion (bending forwards in the middle)	75 to 90°	• Rectus abdominus
Lateral flexion (bringing trunk sideways to the left and right)	25°	• Iliocostalis lumborum • Longissimus lumborum • Transversus abdominus
Extension (bending backwards)	20°	• Multifidus • Spinalis lumborum • Iliocostalis lumborum • Longissimus lumborum
Rotation (turning trunk to the left and right)	90°	• Rotatores lumborum • Semispinalis lumborum • Obliquus abdominus • Multifidus

only minor pain and stiffness. But gradually it becomes severe enough to seek medical care. Often a single incident such as lifting a heavy weight makes the overuse injury worse.

An *acute injury* causes pain that begins suddenly due to a single incident such as a blow with a piece of equipment. Diseases that cause low back pain include tumours and *osteoporosis*.

The *low back joints* and associated structures are the main sources of *pain*. However, there is little consistency to the type and location of the pain produced by each structure (see *Pain*). Only about 10 per cent have an exact diagnosis. The rate has improved with new techniques, *diagnostic nerve blocks* and provocation discography, but currently they are only recommended if pain has not improved after 3 months.

Diagnosis

The 90 per cent of people with low back pain that can't be easily given an exact diagnosis are described as having *low back pain (non-specific)*. Fortunately the success rate of treatment is very high.

Of the causes of low back pain that have an exact diagnosis, an overuse injury aggravated by bending backwards movement and repetitive actions, such as fast bowling in cricket or *throwing sports*, may indicate a *pars interarticularis stress fracture*. Sacrum pain (at the top of the buttocks) aggravated when walking up stairs or rolling over in bed suggests *sacroiliac joint pain*.

Pain that has appeared after receiving a sudden, forceful blow to the low back indicates a *low back muscle contusion*. Knife-like pain in the low back and/or leg, possibly with pins and needles or numbness, suggests *nerve root compression* due to a slipped or prolapsed disc.

Radiological investigations such as X-rays, CT scan and *magnetic resonance imaging (MRI)* are rarely required because the results usually can't iden-tify the painful structure. The exceptions include diseases such as *tumours* and *osteoporosis*.

Low back pain (non-specific)

Pain located in the low back that does not have an exact diagnosis. Fortunately in more than 90 per cent of cases it is unnecessary to identify the structure causing the pain because treatments can achieve improvement anyway.

Diagnosis and treatment

The pain may be located in the lower back, either centrally, on one side or both sides. It may also be *referred pain* to the buttocks, thigh or lower leg below the knee. Movements may be extremely difficult to perform due to aggravation of the pain. It may be associated with poor posture, most commonly a reduced lumbar lordosis (inward curve of the low back).

If the pain is severe the initial treatment involves *ice, analgesics, non-steroidal anti-inflammatory drugs (NSAIDs)* and adopting a position of greatest comfort in bed and avoiding aggravating activities for up to 48 hours, though brief amounts of walking, such as to the toilet, should be performed even if they aggravate the pain. After 48 hours, or when the pain settles down, more walking and light activities around the house are recommended, as long as they only slightly aggravate the pain.

Subsequent treatments are based on detection of abnormalities of muscles, joints and the neural sheath (see *Low back joints*) using the techniques detailed below.

One abnormality is treated at a time. The effect of the treatment is assessed by comparing the amount of pain and movement before treatment and afterwards. If the technique is not effective, a different technique should be attempted.

Causes of low back pain

Common	Less common	Not to be missed
• Low back pain (non-specific)	• Nerve root compression	• Osteosarcoma
• Sacroiliac joint pain	• Spondylolisthesis	• Osteoid osteoma
• Pars interarticularis stress fracture	• Low back muscle contusion	• Osteoporosis

QUICK REFERENCE GUIDE

Low back

Nerve root compression.................Do you have pain that is knife-like, located in the low back and/or leg in a well-defined area and possibly also pins and needles or numbness?

Pars interarticularis stress fracture Do you have back pain aggravated by bending backwards movements and associated with repetitive movements such as fast bowling, throwing or gymnastics?

Sacroiliac joint pain ....Do you have pain over the sacrum (the top of the buttocks) that is aggravated when walking up stairs or rolling over in bed?

Low back muscle contusion ....Do you have low back pain after receiving a sudden forceful blow in the low back?

Low back pain (non-specific) ....Do you have pain in the low back and/or buttock, hip or leg that doesn't have an exact diagnosis?

Extension (back bending) exercises to reduce pain and improve flexibility for low back pain (non-specific)

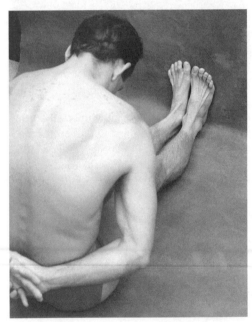

Flexibility exercise to improve slump neural tension for low back pain (non-specific)

Poor posture can be treated with *taping, motor re-education* and a lumbar foam roll to support the lordosis. In severe cases of low back pain a surgical procedure called a *spinal fusion* may be required.

Muscles

Abnormalities that are often found include *myofascial trigger points* in the paraspinal muscles,

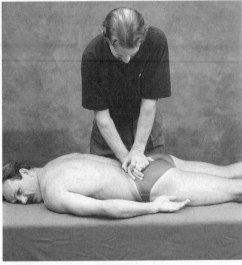

Mobilisation treatment for low back pain (non-specific)

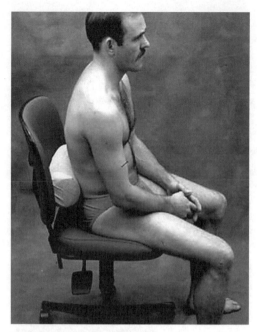

Lumbar support using a foam roll

quadratus lumborum and gluteal muscles, general areas of *fascia* thickening, and loss of *flexibility* and weakness associated with *lumbo-pelvic instability*. The recommended treatments include *massage* and *dry needling* for myofascial trigger points, *flexibility exercises* and *strengthening exercises*.

Joints

The most common abnormalities are pain and loss of *range of movement* in one or more of the joints. Treatments include *mobilisation*, *manipulation* and *traction*.

Neural sheath

The neural sheath (the outer layer covering the *nerves*) most commonly causes pain when stretched, or there is a loss of range of movement. The recommended treatments include *mobilisation* of the straight leg raise and slump *neural tension* test and *flexibility exercises*.

Posture

Taping, posture training through *motor re-education* and lumbar support using a foam roll aims to

increase stability, prevent aggravating movements and provide joint and muscle position awareness to help maintain a lumbar lordosis. It is most often used during the early stage of low back pain.

Low density lipoprotein (LDL)

A type of cholesterol that is associated with an increased risk of *coronary heart disease* and *stroke* when found in high amounts in the blood. For example, coronary heart disease is a narrowing of arteries in the heart due to a disease called atherosclerosis, which is a build up of thick, hard deposits called plaques— made up of fat, cholesterol, calcium and other substances from the blood—in the artery walls.

High levels of LDL lead to more *cholesterol* to be deposited in the *artery* walls, where it can accumulate and harden.

The recommended level of LDL cholesterol is less than 130 per decilitre (mg/dL) (3.38 mmol/L). Avoiding foods containing *saturated fats* can help keep down LDL levels (see *Diet for good health*).

Lumbar joints

See *Low back joints*.

Lumbar roll

A foam roll or rolled-up towel that is used to help maintain the normal posture of the low back, an inward curve called the lumbar lordosis, in the treatment of *low back pain (non-specific)*.

Lumbo-pelvic instability

Abnormal timing of the trunk muscle contractions that increase the risk of developing low back pain. The trunk muscles work to keep the pelvis and low back joints relatively stable during activities such as running so that all the movement occurs in the legs, in the same way as the body of a moving car is a stable platform for the rolling wheels.

The trunk muscles are the transversus abdominus, one of the deep abdominal muscles and multifidus, a large muscle located in the back (see *Low back joints*). In normal timing they are activated as soon as a person starts running. In abnormal timing the pelvis and low back joints become unstable, which causes excessive forces, which can be felt in the low back. It can also increase the risk of recurring hamstring strain, called *back-related hamstring injury*.

Treatment involves *motor re-education* to retrain the muscles to start contracting at the start of running and *strengthening exercises*. This takes place in three stages, with the central focus on performing a contraction of the transversus abdominus called 'abdominal wall drawing in' and an isometric contraction of multifidus at the same time.

The first stage begins with learning to do these contractions in the kneeling on all fours position, and progresses to the sitting and standing positions. In the second and third stages the contractions are performed while doing light activities such as driving a car or sitting at a desk, progressing to walking and finally the specific activities of each sport such as running, jumping and throwing a basketball or running and playing groundstrokes in tennis.

Lung function tests

A number of tests used to assess the nature and quality of breathing. For example, a *peak flow meter* is used to assess *asthma* or the severity of an asthma attack by measuring the maximum rate at which air can be breathed out of the lungs. Another test involves using a spirometer, which is a piece of equipment that measures volume of air breathed out in 1 second, called the FEV_1 and the total volume of air breathed out, called the forced vital capacity (FVC).

In lung disease, such as asthma, emphysema and chronic bronchitis, the FEV_1/FVC ratio is reduced due to the slowness of breathing out caused by airways narrowing.

Lung infection

An invasion of the *lungs* by viruses, bacteria or fungi. For example, bronchitis is an infection of the bronchi, the large airways. Pneumonia is an infection of the microscopic *alveolus*, where exchange of gases between the air and blood take place. A common viral infection is the *flu*. Streptococcus pneumoniae is a bacterial pneumonia. Fungal infections, such as candidiasis, are relatively uncommon.

A lung infection can cause any one or more of the following symptoms including *cough, fever,* sputum production and chest pain. In some cases the infection can spread to the pleura, causing *pleurisy*, which may cause pain in the *shoulder joint*.

Lungs

A respiratory organ located in the *chest*, made up of round tubes that are responsible for bringing oxygen into the body from the outside air and removing carbon dioxide out of the body.

Structure
The tubes can be thought of as a large, leafy tree that is upside down (see *Respiratory system*). The trunk of the tree is a hollow tube called the upper respiratory tract, including the mouth, nose, and throat. The throat divides into two, one tube continuing down to the stomach, the other tube called the *trachea* (windpipe) connecting with the lungs. The trachea divides into two tubes, the left and right bronchus, each connecting with the two lungs, left and right.

In each lung the bronchus repeatedly divides into smaller branches called bronchioles. The inner lining of both bronchi contains cells that produce mucous and cells that have cilia (tiny hair-like structures) that can capture unwanted particles like dust and carry them back up to the throat.

The smallest branches end up at a tiny air-filled space called an *alveolus* (which functions like a leaf). Microscopic-thin membranes separate this air space from tiny blood vessels called capillaries, where oxygen passes in and carbon dioxide passes out of the blood flowing past (see *Heart* and *Blood*).

Breathing in and out occurs due to the activity of the diaphragm muscle and rib muscles.

Both lungs are enclosed in a thin membrane called the *pleura* and sit freely inside the chest, unattached to the ribs. Nerves instruct muscles in the tubes of the lungs to make their diameter narrower or wider, and also the muscles that control breathing.

Lymphatic system

The vessels that collect fluid called lymph and carry it back to the heart. Lymph is produced when *blood* flows out of capillaries and bathes the cells. Most flows back into the capillaries for the return journey to the heart (see *Vein*). The rest flows back to heart via the lymphatic system. The largest lymph vessels empty into the subclavian veins under the clavicles (collarbones). The flow of lymph is kept one-way due to valves and muscle contractions.

Lymph vessels occasionally have areas called lymph nodes (glands) that contain a high number of *white blood cells* called lymphocytes, which are essential in the *immune system*'s fight against bacteria and viruses, and are most numerous in the groin, neck and armpits.

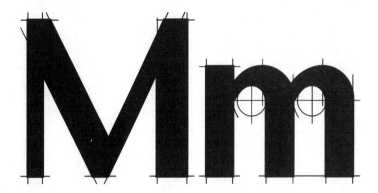

Magnesium

A *mineral* that is essential for the formation of the bones and teeth. It may also have a role in the break down of glucose and producing muscle contractions. It is mostly found in the bones and teeth. The average person has 35 g in the body.

During prolonged exercise magnesium levels in the blood may decrease, possibly lost through sweating. The recommended daily intake is 270 mg in women and 340 mg in men. There is no evidence that magnesium supplementation achieves any improvement in performance in exercise and sport. A diet rich in magnesium should be sufficient.

Magnetic field therapy

An electromagnetic treatment that is recommended for the reduction of *swelling* and *oedema* in injuries. An alternating current running through a coil applicator generates a magnetic field inside the coil. Most units use low frequencies (20 Hz) with variable intensity and duration. It is also called pulsed magnetic field therapy. Although little research has been performed on magnetic field therapy, the primary effect may be on the surface of the cell membrane.

Magnetic resonance imaging (MRI)

A diagnostic technique that uses a magnetic field to create images by detecting hydrogen atoms in water (H_2O). Tissues that contain a high content of water show up on these images differently to those with a low content. These images are of a high quality and can be cross-sections or three-dimensional.

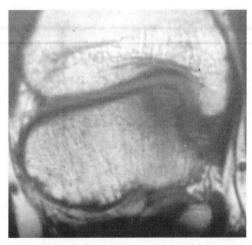

Magnetic resonance imaging (MRI) of a fracture of the talar dome in the ankle

MRI is particularly useful for detecting spinal disc injuries such as *nerve root compression*, bone marrow cancer, *articular cartilage acute injury* and *bone bruising*. It is a relatively new form of investigation. Practitioners are still developing its suitability in the diagnosis of injuries. One main disadvantage is the cost. An advantage is that a magnetic field is not a form of radiation as are *X-rays*.

Making weight

Losing weight to fit within a specific weight category in sports such as *boxing*, horse racing, *martial arts*, *weight lifting* and *rowing*.

The most commonly used methods are *fasting* and reducing water levels in the body through reduced fluid intake, saunas, *diuretics* and sweat suits. These measures can present considerable risks to health and performance, including muscle strength loss, defective kidney function, *heat illness* and, in extreme cases, poor mental skills and loss of consciousness. Long-term weight reduction through a *fat-loss diet* is a more effective and safer method.

Mallet finger

An acute injury that causes an inability to straighten the end of the finger, which is called a flexion deformity. It is usually due to a direct blow to the fingertip forcing the finger to suddenly bend forwards, which snaps off the extensor tendon that normally straightens the end of the finger (see *Hand and finger joints*).

The blow is usually caused by a ball and is most frequently seen in *baseball* catchers and fielders, *American football* receivers and *basketball* players. The snapped tendon takes off a small piece of the bone of the distal phalanx, which is called an *avulsion fracture*.

An *X-ray* is usually required to confirm the diagnosis. If the injury involves the joint or occurs in a growing child or teenager, the recommended treatment is *open surgery* and *internal fixation*. If the fracture is stable the recommended treatment is *immobilisation* in a splint for 8 weeks, followed by

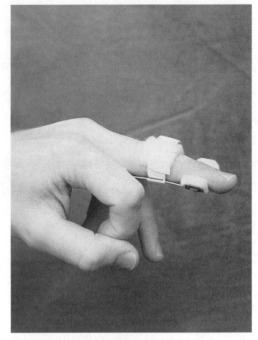

A splint for mallet finger injury

rehabilitation and wearing a splint during sport and at night for 6 to 8 weeks. If the fracture does not heal properly a chronic flexion deformity can develop.

Manganese

See *Minerals*.

Manipulation

A treatment that involves a practitioner using the hands to move a joint in a sudden forceful thrust. It is usually done for a pain-free but stiff joint, with the aim of improving the range of movement and flexibility, or for a painful joint that is locked and unable to move.

The manipulation occurs without assistance from the patient. It is done so quickly that a patient is unable to prevent it from happening and is often accompanied by a 'pop' or 'click' sound. It is usually performed on joints in the spine, though it can be done for the upper and lower limbs.

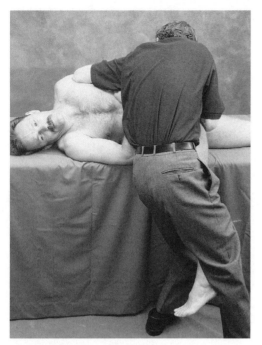

A manipulation treatment for the low back using rotation (turning) movement

The technique can be very effective and achieve dramatic and quick improvements. It is, however, also associated with considerable risks if performed inappropriately or with faulty skills. Only fully qualified practitioners who have had formal training in manipulation, including *chiropractors*, *physiotherapists* and some doctors, should be allowed to perform a manipulation.

It should not be performed on a joint that may be affected by cancer, infection such as *osteomyelitis*, spinal cord or cauda equina compression, vertebral artery insufficiency of the neck, *rheumatoid arthritis* of the atlanto-occipital and C1 joints of the neck, *spondylolisthesis* of the spine, *children* whose bones have not yet fully matured, during the last trimester of *pregnancy* and after a recent *whiplash* injury.

Manual therapy

A group of treatments that are produced by the hands of a medical or health practitioner, including manipulative therapy, which is made up of *mobilisation* and *manipulation* techniques, *traction*, *massage*, *muscle energy techniques* and *neural tension* stretching.

Marfan's syndrome

An inherited disease that causes abnormalities of connective tissue in many organs around the body, in particular, an increased risk of a burst aorta, the large artery that carries oxygenated blood from the left ventricle of the *heart* to the rest of the body, which can cause sudden death.

Skeletal features of Marfan's syndrome include high arched palate (upper roof of the mouth), long tubular bones, wide-arm span and hyper-flexible joints. The latter features are more likely to be found in *basketball* and *volleyball* players. The athlete with an abnormal aorta due to Marfan's syndrome should avoid high-intensity *aerobic training*.

Marijuana

See *Cannabinoids*.

Martial arts

The martial arts were first developed and established in India, China, Korea, Okinawa, Japan, Indonesia and the Philippines. They later became popular in the West, including Australia, UK and USA.

There are hundreds of different systems of fighting techniques throughout the world today, divided into two categories: percussive and non-percussive. In percussive martial arts, participants strike blows with the hands and feet. Non-percussive involves throwing, locking and neutralising the opponent. Competition events are between two contestants. Coloured belts designate skill levels. The main martial arts are:
- Judo: Translated as gentle (ju) way (do), a non-percussive sport developed in Japan in 1882.
- Karate: Translated as empty (kara) hand (te), a percussive sport involving striking blows to vital anatomical points of the opponent.

• Tae kwon do: Translated as foot (tae) fist (kwon) way (do), a Korean form of karate developed in 1955.

Injuries

The most common injuries are *quadriceps contusion* (thigh), *medial collateral ligament (MCL) sprain* (knee), *acute compartment pressure syndrome* (shin), *tibia fracture* (shin), *shin chronic compartment syndrome*, shin periostitis, *metatarsal fracture* (foot and toes), *rotator cuff tendinosis* (shoulder) and *metacarpal fracture* (hand and fingers).

Massage

A treatment that involves applying direct physical contact with the hands on the skin, muscles, tendons, ligaments and fascia. It is used to reduce *pain*, *swelling*, *spasm*, promote healing of injured tissue and increase the *flexibility* of these tissues.

For example, injured muscle fibres are often replaced with connective tissue called scar tissue, which is less flexible and more likely to cause pain when stretched compared to healthy muscle fibres. Massage can loosen up the scar tissue, making it more flexible and less painful, and at the same time can stimulate the growth of new muscle fibres in its place.

Massage is also used as a psychological technique to provide feedback about muscle tension and to achieve deep relaxation, particularly when used together with *progressive muscle relaxation*.

Massage methods include Rolfing, shiatsu, Hellerwork and Swedish. In many cases the recommended choice of method is largely a matter of personal preference.

Method

Each massage practitioner should first assess the patient and determine the aims of the massage. The techniques that are frequently selected for sports injuries can be defined according to the Granter-King scale of depth of treatment based on pain levels and resistance (the amount of give in the tissues being massaged).

Prior to the massage the muscles should be as relaxed as possible by using *heat therapy (superficial)*,

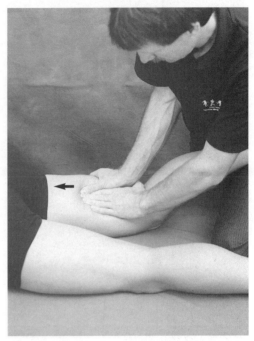

Massage treatment for the hamstring. The black arrow shows direction of movement for the longitudinal technique

Grading system for depth of massage (the Granter-King scale)

Grade	Effect on massage therapy
Patient's pain response	
I	No pain perceived
II	Commencement of pain
III	Moderate level of pain
IV	Severe level of pain (seldom used)
Resistance to palpation (pressing down with the fingers/hands)	
A	No sense of tissue resistance
B	Onset of tissue resistance
C	Moderate tissue resistance

such as a heat pack, and placing the muscle in a shortened position.

A lubricant is often applied to the skin to aid both comfort and the practitioner's ability to feel abnormalities in the tissue. Suitable lubricants are deodorised vegetable oils, such as safflower, soy and almond oils. Inexpensive, highly refined, clear mineral oils are also a suitable medium. Massage should be avoided in the 72 hours immediately after an *acute injury* has occurred due to the risk of developing *myositis ossificans*.

Massage should start with gentle broad contact stroking at a grade IA depth to minimise the consolidation of oedema and swelling, which may result in a reduction of pain-producing chemicals.

Increasing the strength of treatment is done gradually up to IB, and then IIB about one week after the injury. More than one week after the injury the massage can be given at IIC and then IIIC. Specific massage techniques are used to treat *myofascial trigger point* pain.

Massage therapist

A health practitioner who has completed training and is registered and recognised as being qualified to provide *massage* treatments.

Masseur

See *Massage therapist*.

Masters sports

Exercise and sport organised for the skills and abilities of *older athletes*. The starting age for participation is usually around 40 years, though many organisations allow younger participants.

Participants compete with each other according to age groups so that performances are more evenly matched. For example, the US Masters Swimming organisation has competitions according to five-year increments up to 95 and over age bracket. Events include 100, 200, 800 and 1500 m freestyle, backstroke, breaststroke, butterfly and individual medley. National championship and international championships are conducted periodically by Masters swim organisations in countries throughout the world. Masters Games are held every four years, similar to the Olympic Games.

A *medical clearance* is recommended for participants who have had a history of illness, such as *coronary heart disease*, or are planning to participate in exercise or sport that requires a greater effort than the equivalent of brisk walking. In some sports *rules modifications*, such as enforced breaks and reduced playing time, are considered appropriate to reduce the risk of injury or illness.

Maxilla fracture

A break to the bone in the middle of the face, which is usually due to a direct crushing blow from equipment such as a baseball or collision with another player (see *Head*).

This *fracture* causes the face to appear longer than usual, an inability to close the mouth normally and restricted nasal breathing. It should be treated as soon as possible in a hospital to make sure that breathing does not become fully obstructed. The recommended treatment is *open surgery* and *internal fixation* with metal wires, screws or a plate.

Maximal oxygen uptake

See VO_2 *max*.

Maximum heart rate estimation

A method used to make recommendations for *aerobic training* to increase aerobic fitness that is used to measure the intensity of a physical activity.

It involves calculating the theoretical maximum heart rate by subtracting your age from 220. For example, for a 30-year-old it is $220 - 30 = 190$ beats per minute. The following are commonly used levels of intensity for aerobic training:

- Low-intensity is equivalent to breathing exertion ranging from 'no effect on breathing' up to the point that 'shortness of breath is noticed' = 35–59 per cent of maximum heart rate estimation (220 – age).
- Moderate-intensity is equivalent to a range from 'shortness of breath is noticed' up to 'the point

that whistling or normal continuous conversation is just possible' = 60–79 per cent of maximum heart rate estimation.

- High-intensity is a range from the point that 'whistling or normal continuous conversation is just possible' up to the point that 'whistling or normal continuous conversation is impossible' = 80–89 per cent of maximum heart rate estimation.

Other measures of intensity for aerobic training include VO₂ *max* and *Borg perceived exertion scale*.

McConnell technique

A diagnostic and treatment technique that was invented and first described by Australian physiotherapist Jenny McConnell in 1986. (See *Patellofemoral joint syndrome*.)

MCP joint dislocation

An acute injury that displaces a joint between the metacarpal bone of the hand and the proximal phalanx of the finger. It usually occurs in the thumb or index finger (see *Hand and finger joints*).

The injury is usually caused by a blow to the thumb or finger that pushes the metacarpal bone towards the back of the hand. It should be suspected if the injured thumb or finger appears hyperextended (excessively bent backwards) and bent across the finger next to it.

The recommended treatment for the *dislocation* is surgery, possibly including *internal fixation* with a metal wire if a fracture into the joint has also occurred, followed by *immobilisation* in a splint for 5 to 6 weeks and *rehabilitation* treatments.

Meat

A food that contains essential nutrients, including *protein*, *vitamins* and *minerals*, particularly *iron*. In general it is recommended to eat lean meat that has had the fat trimmed off and only has a minor level of marbling. The fat in red meat is *saturated*

fat which, when eaten in excess over a lifetime, is associated with an increased risk of being *overweight* and developing coronary heart disease and certain types of cancer.

Medial

The anatomical direction pointing inwards from the side of the body towards the midline of the body. It is used to describe the surface of any part of the body that faces towards the midline or a body part located closer to the midline than another part. For example, the medial surface of the thigh is the inner thigh. Medial is the opposite of *lateral*. Also called ulnar in the forearm and tibial in the lower leg.

Medial collateral ligament (MCL) sprain

An acute injury of the ligament on the inner side of the *knee joint* due to a sudden excessive force that causes it to be overstretched. It occurs when the knee is bent inwards (valgus stress) and the foot is fixed on the ground, such as a player falling across the outside of the knee or a twisting fall during skiing when the ski boot binding does not release. There may be a loud 'crack' or 'pop' as it occurs.

Diagnosis, treatment and return to sport

There are three degrees of severity for a medial collateral ligament (MCL) *sprain*. Grade 1 causes tenderness on the inner side of the joint, but no laxity when bent inwards. Grade 2 causes pain and some laxity. Grade 3 is a complete tear or rupture of the ligament that makes it 'wobbly' and unstable.

All grades of sprain should be treated during the first 48 to 72 hours with *RICE* (*rest, ice, compression and elevation*) and avoiding heat and alcohol consumption to minimise *swelling*. Treatments are similar for all grades, except the time required for healing. Surgery is not required. Grade 1 requires 3 to 6 weeks for a return to sport, and Grades 2 and 3 require 8 to 12 weeks. Grade 2 and 3 sprains are usually kept in a hinged *brace* for 4 to 6 weeks.

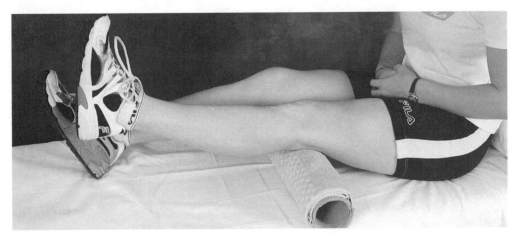

Strengthening exercise for the left quadriceps muscle for medial collateral ligament sprain

The recommended treatments include *strengthening exercises, flexibility exercises, balance* exercises, *massage,* electrotherapy such as *interferential therapy* and *ultrasound therapy,* and a *sport rehabilitation* program. A brace or *taping* may be recommended after return to sport.

Medial flexion

See *Adduction.*

Medial rotation

See *Internal rotation.*

Medial tibial stress syndrome

See *Tibia periostitis.*

Medical clearance

A doctor's examination that gives the 'all clear' to start participating in exercise or sport. The main aim is to prevent life-threatening events, such as a heart attack, as well as muscle, joint and bone injuries. In addi-

tion it may be important to receive advice about exercise and sport, called an *exercise prescription.*

Requirements

Not everyone needs to have a medical clearance. It depends on the type of activity you intend to participate in and your current health and age. For example, walking briskly for 30 minutes each day does not require a medical clearance if you are healthy, regardless of age.

However, a high intensity activity (see *Aerobic training* and *Metabolic equivalent (MET)*) such as running does require a medical clearance for men aged 35 years and over and women aged 40 years and over. Anyone who has been diagnosed with *coronary heart disease* also should get a medical clearance before starting exercise or sport.

Method

The examination includes assessing the *cardiovascular system, nervous system, musculoskeletal system* and *respiratory system.* An *exercise stress test* is not recommended as part of a medical clearance, except in some people who have recently had a heart problem.

Medical emergency

An injury or illness that requires immediate treatment to prevent permanent damage or death.

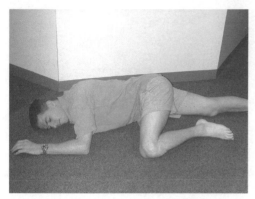

Lying in a sideways position to check the airways of an injured person

Emergencies in exercise and sport are usually caused by: trauma to a previously well person such as a severe head injury or spinal injury; aggravation of a previously recognised medical problem, such as coronary heart disease, asthma or diabetes; or aggravation of a previously undiagnosed medical problem.

Method

The first step is to assess whether the person is conscious or unconscious. If the person is lying face down, he or she needs to be brought to the face-up or facing sideways position by rolling the body.

Consciousness is checked by asking simple questions, such as 'What is your name?' or 'Can you open your eyes?'

If conscious, make the person comfortable but avoid bending or turning the neck if there has been an injury to the head or spine. Stop any bleeding by covering the wound with a sterile dressing held in place with a bandage. Immediately transport the person to a hospital or a doctor.

If unconscious, follow instructions according to ABC = Airways, Breathing and Circulation.

Airways

Make sure the person is lying sideways to clear the airways. Partial airway obstruction is characterised by noisy breathing. Clear the mouth of all blood clots, secretions, vomit, teeth or other debris. Do not tilt the head backwards if there has been an injury of the head or spine.

Breathing

Check for *breathing* by looking for the rise and fall of the lower chest and upper abdomen. Listen and feel for air from the nose and mouth.

If there is no breathing, perform mouth-to-mouth resuscitation.

Circulation

The *pulse* is checked by feeling for the carotid artery in the side of the neck next to the Adam's apple. If there is no pulse, start cardiopulmonary resuscitation (CPR) (see Table, Mouth-to-mouth resuscitation, below).

Causes of medical emergency

Trauma	Disease or illness
• Head injury	• Heart attack
• Spinal injury	• Stroke
• Throat injury	• Heat illness (hyperthermia)
• Chest injury (severe)	• Hypothermia (cold)
Chest flail segment	• Hypoglycaemia (low blood sugars)
Haemothorax	• Hyponatremia (low blood sodium)
Pneumothorax	• Asthma attack
Cardiac tamponade	• Pneumothorax (spontaneous)
• Abdominal injury	• Anaphylaxis (allergic or exercise
Liver	related)
Spleen	• Syncope (fainting)
Kidney	
Bladder	
Urethra	
Scrotum	
Pelvis	
• Amputation (traumatic)	

Mouth-to-mouth resuscitation

An emergency treatment for a person who has suddenly collapsed and stopped breathing:

1) Place the person on their back.
2) Tilt the head back gently, holding the jaw and top of the head. The person's mouth should be partially open.
3) Take a deep breath and place your mouth over the person's mouth, with your cheek against the nostrils, and blow in firmly.
4) Perform five breaths in 10 seconds, removing your mouth to allow air to escape between each breath.
5) Check the person for a pulse at the carotid artery in the side of the neck next to the Adam's apple.
   If there is no pulse: Start cardiopulmonary resuscitation (CPR) (see below).
   If there is a pulse: Check breathing again.
   If there is no breathing: Continue mouth-to-mouth resuscitation, performing one breath every 4 seconds.
6) After 1 minute, check the pulse and breathing again and continue to do so every 2 minutes until medical help arrives.

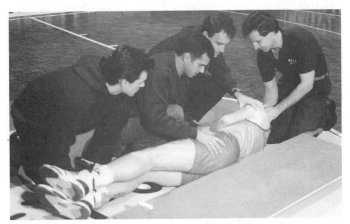

Removing an unconscious person from the court in three stages: a)

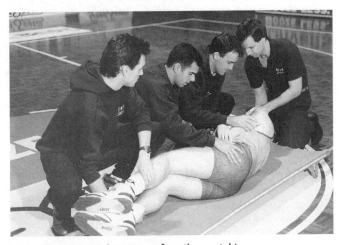

Removing an unconscious person from the court: b)

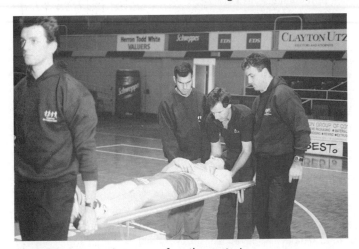

Removing an unconscious person from the court: c)

Cardiopulmonary resuscitation (CPR)

An emergency treatment for a person who has suddenly collapsed and stopped breathing and the heart has stopped beating. It involves combining mouth-to-mouth resuscitation with external cardiac compression (ECC). It can be done by two people at a ratio of 5 cardiac compressions per breath. If alone, perform 15 compressions every second breath.

External cardiac compression (ECC)

1) Kneel next to the person's chest.
2) Locate the middle part of the breastbone by pressing your fingers firmly into the chest.
3) Place the heel of your hand closest to the person's head firmly on the breastbone. Then place your other hand on top, interlocking the fingers.
4) Keep your arms straight above the breastbone.
5) Press down 4–5 cm in one firm, quick movement and then release allowing the chest to come back up.
6) The compressions should be done rapidly one after the other. For example, 15 compressions should be done in 10 to 12 seconds followed by the two breaths in 3 to 5 seconds.
7) After 1 minute check the pulse and breathing again and continue to do so every 2 minutes until medical help arrives.
8) After breathing and pulse has re-started closely observe the person until medical help arrives.

How to prepare for a medical emergency

• Preparing for a medical emergency involves having the appropriate equipment, people and training.

• At a minimum there should be a first aid kit, (including bandages, slings, rubber gloves and more), stretcher, crutches and possibly specialised equipment that requires proper training such as a defibrillator for a *heart attack*, spinal board and cervical (neck) collar for moving a person after a *spinal injury* and *head injury*.

• Some sports require specific equipment, such as a screwdriver for American football to help release helmets if facemasks are being worn. In hot weather, ice and cool water or a sports drink should be available for *heat illness*.

• One person who has at least completed a first aid training certificate should be present at each training or sport event. This may be a coach, parent or even a competitor. For the removal of a severely injured player from the field of play, four or five persons are required.

• If cardiopulmonary resuscitation (CPR) is required, it is advantageous to have two people trained in CPR performing the procedure. If a doctor is not designated to be present, an emergency plan to move a person as quickly as possible to the nearest hospital should be prepared beforehand.

Meditation

Focusing the mind on a single sound or image with the aim of reaching a specific psychological and physical state of being. For example, repeating a word or phrase in the mind to block out other thoughts may lead to an altered state of consciousness associated with feeling relaxed.

Meditation has been practised by religions such as Buddhism for centuries. It became popular in Western countries in the 1960s through the teachings of Maharishi Mahesh Yogi, an Indian monk who developed a form of meditation, called Transcendental Meditation, that could be easily practised as a lifestyle or recreational activity.

The research and writings of Dr Herbert Benson from the Harvard Medical School in the 1970s first consolidated the scientific evidence that meditation may also have physiological benefits in the prevention and treatment of illness and disease. Called the 'relaxation response', meditation was found to induce changes that were the opposite of the 'fight-or-flight response' (see *Adrenaline*), including a slowing down of the *heart rate*, respiration and brain waves, reduction in *muscle tone* and *stress*-related hormones.

It is recommended to meditate for 20 minutes, twice a day, everyday, for general health benefits. In exercise and sport it can be part of a pre-competition *routine* as a relaxation technique to prevent over *anxiety* and stress.

Meniscus degeneration

An overuse injury of the one of the two C-shaped fibrous cartilages in the *knee joint*. It is caused by a gradual accumulation of repeated excessive physical loads over a period of years.

It most cases the outer (lateral) side meniscus is injured, causing pain on that side of the knee that is brought on by sudden twisting activities such as getting out of the car or rolling in bed. Clicking and joint *locking* are also common.

The recommended treatments include *ice, rest* from running activities, *flexibility exercises* and *strengthening exercises*. If this fails, *arthroscopy* to remove the meniscus may be required.

Meniscus tear

An acute injury of one of the fibrous C-shaped cartilages that separate the two bones of the *knee joint*. These structures act as shock absorbers within the knee to cushion and protect the *articular cartilage*. The inner side meniscus, called the medial meniscus, is injured more often than the outer side meniscus, the lateral meniscus. The injury is usually a tear across or along the length of the meniscus.

The most common cause of a meniscus tear is a twist of the knee when the foot is anchored to the ground in competition sports such as *football* codes and *basketball*. It may also occur due to minimal trauma in older aged athletes with *meniscus degeneration*.

Diagnosis
A small tear may not cause obvious signs and symptoms. However, more severe tears, such as a 'bucket-handle tear', cause pain, often *swelling* after 6 to 24 hours, a limp, weakness, a sensation of the knee 'giving way', clicking noises and an inability to fully straighten (extend) the knee, called *locking*. *Magnetic resonance imaging (MRI)* or *arthroscopy* may be recommended to confirm an unclear diagnosis.

Treatment and return to sport
The recommended treatment for mild to moderate injuries during the first 48 to 72 hours is RICE (*rest, ice, compression and elevation*). The meniscus is unable to heal by itself because it has a poor blood supply. An arthroscopy is recommended to remove the torn portion, and the rough edges are smoothed to maintain what is left of the meniscus as much as possible for its shock absorption features, which reduce the risk of developing *knee osteoarthritis*.

Recovery normally takes 6 weeks. *Strengthening exercises* and *flexibility exercises* as part of a *sport rehabilitation* program are recommended.

Menopause

The end of *menstruation* in women. It usually occurs between the age of 45 and 55 years. The ovaries of the *reproductive system* stop producing and releasing eggs and there is an associated reduction in the female sex hormone, *oestrogen*.

In the short term this can cause symptoms including hot flushes, night sweats, vaginal dryness, mood changes, loss of memory and concentration and reduced interest in sex. In the long term it is associated with an increased risk of developing *incontinence, coronary heart disease, stroke* and *osteoporosis*. This risk can be reduced by regularly participating in exercise and sport (see *Exercise for health*). Medication treatment includes *hormone replacement therapy (HRT)*.

Menstruation

The periodic loss of blood and tissue from the lining of the uterus that occurs in women. A normal menstrual cycle varies between 23 to 35 days. The average is 28 days. Menstruation is regulated by the hypothalamus in the brain, which produces gonadotrophin-releasing hormone (GnRH) to stimulate the pituitary hormones.

The first half of the cycle (follicular phase) is characterised by an increase in follicle-stimulating hormone (FSH), which results in *oestrogen* production by the ovaries. These hormones stimulate the formation of the primary follicle and growth of the lining of the uterus. The follicular phase ends with rupture of the follicle and release of the ovum (see *Reproductive system*) approximately 14 days before the next menstrual bleed begins.

The second half begins with the luteal phase. It also lasts around 14 days and is marked by a surge in luteinising hormone (LH) triggered by rising levels of oestrogen. A resulting increase in progesterone stimulates maturation of the follicle and ovulation. If fertilisation of the ovum by male sperm does not occur, luteal function declines and brings on a rapid decrease in oestrogen and progesterone, leading to menstruation.

Menstruation ceases in women when the ovaries release their last ovum, usually between the age of 45 and 55, which is called the *menopause*.

Exercise and sport

There is no scientific evidence that performance levels are affected, positively or negatively, at any particular stage of the menstrual cycle. In fact world best performances have been recorded at all stages of the menstrual cycle, including the premenstrual and menstrual phases.

However, for the women who feel they are affected by a stage of the menstrual cycle, a low-dose oral contraceptive (see *Contraception*) to avoid that stage coinciding with a major event may be beneficial. This manipulation should not be used on a regular basis.

The pill can be ceased 10 days prior to an event, which will usually induce a withdrawal bleed. A new packet of the pill can either be resumed at the end of menstruation or following the completion of the event. If this method is used, suppression of ovulation may fail and additional methods of contraception such as condoms, must be used until 2 weeks after recommencing the pill.

A second way involves omitting the 7-day tablet-free interval (or sugar pills) and continuing to take the pill throughout the event to prevent menstruation occurring prior to or during the event. This method is simpler to use with monophasic pills than with triphasic pills.

For women who do not wish to use the oral-contraceptive pill, a menstrual bleed can be induced 10 days prior to the event with administration of a progesterone derivative for 10 days duration, finishing the course 10 days prior to the event.

Menstrual problems

Abnormalities of menstruation include *dysmenorrhea* (painful menstruation), *premenstrual tension (PMT)*,

delayed menarche (late age of starting menstruation in teenage girls), *amenorrhea* (absence of menstruation) and oligomenorrhea (infrequent menstruations or small amount of blood loss).

Metabolic equivalent (MET)

A measure of the intensity of an activity based on the predicted amount of energy expended by an average person in the general population. Energy is measured according to the oxygen consumed: the greater the amount of oxygen that is required, the higher the intensity of the activity performed. Metabolic equivalent can be used to provide guidelines for participation in *aerobic training* to increase fitness.

The baseline level is the *resting metabolic rate* (RMR) which in the average person = 3.5 mL oxygen per kilogram of body weight per minute (3.5 mL/kg/min) = 1.0 metabolic equivalent (MET).

Walking up stairs is an everyday activity with a high-intensity metabolic equivalent

METs for everyday physical activities, exercise and sport

Low (under 3.0 METs or 4 CAL/min)

- Walking slowly (strolling) (1.5–3 km/h or 1–2 miles/h)
- Cycling stationary (under 50 Watts)
- Swimming or treading water slowly
- Conditioning exercise, light stretching
- Golf using power cart
- Bowling
- Fishing (sitting)
- Home care; carpet sweeping
- Mowing lawn riding on mower
- Home repair (carpentry)

Moderate (3–6 METs or 4–7 Cal/min)

- Walking briskly (4–6 km/h or 2.5 miles/h)
- Walk/jog combination (jogging less than 10 minutes)
- Cycling for pleasure or transportation (under 16 km/h or 10 miles/h)
- Swimming leisurely, not lapping
- Conditioning exercises, general callisthenics
- Dancing, ballroom
- Tennis (doubles), table tennis
- Tai Chi
- Aerobics (low impact)
- Golf pulling own cart or carrying clubs
- Volleyball
- Basketball, shooting baskets
- Water activities, surfing, windsurfing
- Canoeing leisurely
- Home care, general cleaning
- Mowing lawn with power mower
- Home repair, painting

High (over 6.0 METs or over 7 Cal/min)

- Walking briskly uphill or carrying a load
- Jogging or running
- Cycling, fast or racing (over 16 km/h or 10 miles/h)
- Swimming, lapping, breaststroke, butterfly, crawl
- Conditioning exercise, stair ergometer
- Dancing, ballet, modern, aerobic, twist
- Tennis, singles
- Aerobics, high impact
- Volleyball, beach
- Basketball, competition
- Water activities, scuba diving
- Canoeing over 6 km/h (4 miles/h)
- Home care, moving furniture
- Mowing lawn by hand

METs for everyday physical activities, exercise and sport are divided into three levels of intensity. Other measurements of intensity of activity include VO_2 max and *Borg perceived exertion scale*.

Metabolism

The chemical processes in the cells of the human body that are involved in the production and breakdown of compounds.

Many different chemical processes are in action at the same time throughout the body. They can be thought of as a sprawling and criss-crossing network of railway lines and stations. The passengers on this network are foods such as *carbohydrates*, *fats* and *proteins*. Each train trip is like a chemical process. The train drivers that decide on the speed of the chemical process are the *enzymes* and the chemical contents of the internal and external environment of the cells. The foods can get on and off at many different points where railways lines interconnect.

Metabolism is made up of two parts; anabolism uses up energy to produce compounds: catabolism produces energy by breaking down compounds into more basic components. *Aerobic metabolism* uses oxygen for its chemical processes. *Anaerobic metabolism* does not use oxygen.

Metacarpal fracture

A break in the one of the five long bones that runs between the wrist and the thumb and fingers (See *Hand and finger joints*).

First metacarpal (Bennett's fracture)

The *fracture* is usually located in the base of the bone, just above the wrist joint. This injury commonly occurs as a result of a punch connecting with a hard object, such as an opponent's head or a fall on the thumb.

An *X-ray* is required to confirm the diagnosis. If the fracture in the bone does not involve the first carpometacarpal (CMC) joint, the recommended treatment is *immobilisation* in a short arm spica plaster cast.

If the fracture is located in the joint, which is called a Bennett's fracture, the recommended treatment is *open surgery* and *internal fixation* with a wire, followed by *immobilisation* in a plaster cast for 4 to 6 weeks. If an early return to sport is required, a protective *brace* should be worn.

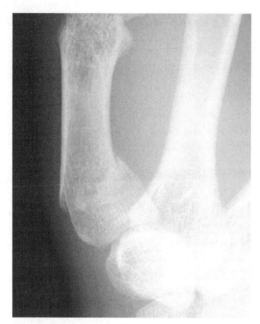

X-ray of a fracture at the base of the first metacarpal bone (Bennett's fracture)

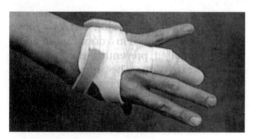

A protective brace for a Bennett's fracture

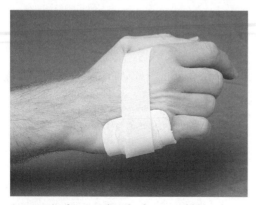

A protective brace (splint) for fracture of fifth metacarpal

Second to fifth metacarpals

A break of the fourth or fifth metacarpal (boxer's fracture) are the most common, usually as the result of a punch. An X-ray is required to confirm the diagnosis.

The treatment of a fracture that does not involve a joint is immobilisation in either a splint or plaster cast for 2 to 3 weeks. Sport can be resumed immediately with a protective brace. Open surgery for internal fixation with a metal pin may required if the fracture is located in a joint, followed by *rehabilitation* treatments.

Metatarsal stress fracture

A microfracture of one of the long bones that connects to the toes that develops gradually due to an accumulation of repeated, excessive physical loads over a period of weeks or months, often due to running and ballet *dancing*.

The second metatarsal is the most commonly injured. The pain is felt in the forefoot. A physical examination usually finds tenderness when pressed firmly with the fingers (see *Foot and toes*).

A diagnosis of this *stress fracture* is confirmed with *bone scan* or *magnetic resonance imaging (MRI)*.

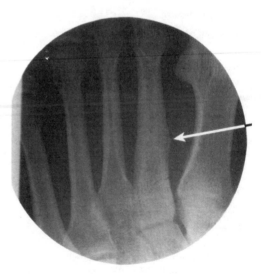

X-ray of a stress fracture of the second metatarsal bone

Treatment involves *rest* by avoiding the aggravating activity for 4 to 8 weeks, followed by a gradual return to sport as part of a *sport rehabilitation* program.

Middle and long distance running for children and adolescents

The recommended maximum running event distances and training guidelines for children and adolescents participating in *middle distance running* and *long distance running*, which are a precautionary measure to minimise the risk of injuries.

Running events

Age	Distance
Under 9	3 km (2 miles)
9–11	5 km (3 miles)
12–14	10 km (6 miles)
15–16	21.2 km (13 miles) (half marathon)
17	30 km (19 miles)
18	42.2 (26.2 miles) (marathon)

Training

The weekly training distance should not be more than twice the recommended running distance for a competition race, for example, 6 km (4 miles) per week for under 9 year olds. Races of up to 10 km (6 miles) can be held at a maximum of once a week. Races over 10 km (6 miles) require longer recovery periods.

The number of training sessions per week should not exceed three up to the age of 14 years. Training can be held up to five times per week from the age of 15 years. The general recommendations for *running shoes* also apply for children and adolescents. Hard surfaces, such as bitumen and concrete, should be avoided and grass and dirt used as much as possible.

Middle distance running

Running sports including 800 m, 1500 m and 5000 m and 3000 m steeplechase and cross-country running (outdoor distances of 4 km/2.5 miles).

Running 800 m involves running fast, but at less than 100 per cent of maximum speed. At the start the muscles rely on *anaerobic fitness*, then before 400 m *aerobic fitness* kicks in for the remaining distance. For 1500 m most of the run is aerobic; however, the anaerobic system is required for sprints such as towards the finishing line. The fitness requirements include *aerobic training* based on *periodisation, interval training* and *fartlek*. Injuries experienced by middle distance runners are similar to those seen in *long distance running*.

Midtarsal joint sprain

A tear or excessive stretch of the joints in the middle of the foot (see *Foot and toes*). It is seen most often in *gymnastics, jumping sports* and *football* codes.

Treatment for this *sprain* involves RICE (*rest, ice, compression and elevation*), *analgesics* for pain relief and, after 48 hours, *flexibility exercises, strengthening exercises* and *proprioception training* to improve joint-position awareness.

Migraine

A headache that is usually associated with nausea, vomiting, diarrhoea and weight gain. In the classic migraine attack, painless sensory neurological symptoms, such as visual disturbances, sensitivity to light, pins and needles and dizziness (vertigo), precede the headache.

The pain is sharp, intense and often throbbing, commonly located in the temple or forehead on both sides. If the *headache* is intense, it may spread to the back of the head. Nausea, vomiting and dizziness are common during or after the attack. After the headache, frequent urination, diarrhoea, euphoria or a surge of energy are common. Most people can identify a trigger that brings on the headache such as exercise, sex, *menstruation, stress*, lack of sleep, foods like *chocolate* or nuts, and *alcohol* and drugs, especially red wine.

Treatment

Most people choose to lie quietly in a dark room or sleep during a migraine attack. A high dose of *aspirin*

(1200 mg) may also bring relief. Migraine sufferers with a known trigger may find that taking aspirin beforehand can prevent attacks. A herbal treatment that may be helpful is 'feverfew'.

Minerals

A group of inorganic substances that is essential for health. The amount required is called the recommended dietary intake (RDI), which varies according to age, gender, state of health and levels of participation in physical activity. There are minerals that need to be taken in greater amounts of at least 100 mg a day, whereas others are required in trace elements.

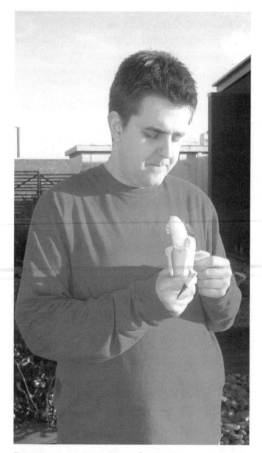

Bananas are a great source of potassium

The minerals that are most important in exercise and sport are *iron, calcium, magnesium, zinc, selenium, copper* and *chromium*.

Mitral stenosis

A narrowing of the mitral valve, which controls the flow of oxygenated blood between the left atrium and left ventricle of the *heart*. It forces the left ventricle to work harder to pump blood. The impact on the heart is similar to that of *mitral valve prolapse*.

Mitral valve prolapse

A defect in the mitral valve, which controls the flow of oxygenated blood between the left atrium and left ventricle of the *heart*.

It occurs in 5 per cent of the population. Most are able to exercise and play sports without restriction. However, a small number face the risk of *heart attack* during exercise and sport, especially those who have had someone in the family die from a heart attack and have symptoms including dizziness, *syncope, palpitations* and *shortness of breath*.

Mobilisation

A treatment provided by a practitioner using the hands to move a joint in order to reduce pain and improve flexibility. It is a passive movement technique in which the practitioner moves the joint without assistance from the patient, such as moving the arm up above the head.

The Maitland method of mobilisation is the most widely used in the world. It involves moving a joint with a rhythmic and oscillatory (back and forth) manner. Grades I and II are used primarily to reduce *pain*. Relief may be achieved through changes to the transmission of signals from pain-sensing nerve receptors and, in the spine, reduced pressure in the discs and improvements in the circulation. In pain-free joints that have reduced *flexibility* and *range of movement*, grades III and IV are used. Improvements are achieved by stretching of the connective tissue within

Minerals: Food sources, functions and possible importance in exercise and sport

Mineral	Some food sources	Some major functions	Possible importance
Macronutrients			
Calcium	Milk, cheese, yoghurt, green leafy vegetables, canned fish, sesame seeds	• Bone structure • Blood clotting • Transmission of nerve impulses • Muscle contraction	• Muscle contraction • Glycogen breakdown
Chlorine	Common table salt	• Maintenance of electrolyte and fluid balance	
Magnesium	Most foods, especially whole grain products, green leafy vegetables, fruits and other vegetables	• Involved in regulation of protein synthesis, muscle contraction and body temperature regulation • Essential cofactor in most energy production pathways	• Muscle contraction • Glucose metabolism
Phosphorus	Milk, poultry fish and meat	• Formation of bones and teeth (with calcium) • Essential to normal functioning of B group vitamins • Important role in the final delivery of energy to all cells, including muscle, in the form of ATP	• Formation of the ATP creatine phosphokinase • Release of oxygen from red blood cells
Potassium	Abundant in most foods, especially meat, fish, poultry, cereals, oranges, bananas, fresh vegetables and milk	• Muscle function • Nerve transmission • Carbohydrate and protein metabolism • Maintenance of body fluids and acid-base balance of blood	• Nerve transmission • Muscle contraction • Glycogen storage
Sodium	Table salt, soy sauce, seafoods, dairy products, yeast spread	• Important co-role with potassium to carry out functions mentioned above	• Nerve impulse transmission • Water balance
Micronutrients			
Chromium	Traces in meat and vegetables	• Functions with insulin to help control glucose metabolism	• Glucose metabolism
Cobalt	Meat, liver, milk, green leafy vegetables	• Component of B_{12} • May help prevent anaemia and nervous system disorders	
Copper	Meat, vegetables, fish, oysters, drinking water from copper pipes	• Component of many enzymes • Role in haemoglobin formation	• Oxygen transportation and utilisation • Linked with iron
Fluoride	Water supplies, tea and some small fish	• Prevention of tooth decay • Possible role in prevention of osteoporosis	
Iodine	Iodised salt, seafood	• Component of thyroid hormones that regulate metabolic rate	
Iron	Liver, heart, lean red meat, dried apricots, kidney beans and green leafy vegetables	• Formation of compounds essential to the transport and utilisation of oxygen	• Oxygen transport by red blood cells • Muscle metabolism
Manganese	Whole grain cereals, green leafy vegetables, wheat germ, nuts, bananas	• Involvement in bone structure and nervous system activity • Co-factor in carbohydrate metabolism	• Energy metabolism
Molybdenum	Liver, legumes, whole grains	• Component of certain enzymes	
Selenium	Mainly high protein foods, wholegrain products	• Component of antioxidant enzyme helping to protect cells from oxidation by free radicals of oxygen	
Zinc	Meat, eggs, liver, oysters, wholegrain products, legumes	• Component of many enzymes • Aids in wound healing • Co-factor in protein and carbohydrate metabolism	• Energy production in muscle cells
Cadmium, nickel, silicone, tin, vanadium	In most animal and plant foods	• Uncertain	• Uncertain

Iron, magnesium and zinc content of common foods

Food	Amount	Magnesium (mg)	Iron (mg)	Zinc (mg)
Beef, fillet steak, grilled, lean	100 g	22	4.1	4.5
Lamb, chump chop, grilled, lean	100 g	29	3.5	4.8
Chicken, beast, baked, lean	100 g	23	0.9	1.7
Pork, boneless, cooked, lean	100 g	22	1.4	3.1
Veal, boneless, cooked, lean	100 g	23	2.1	3.8
Beef, liver, simmered	100 g	24	6.5	5.3
Pate, liver	30 g	5	2.8	1.1
Fish, steamed	100 g	31	0.4	0.7
Oyster, raw	1 dozen	30	2.3	38.7
Scallop, raw	6 average	17	0.6	2.1
Crab, boiled	100 g	27	1.0	9.1
Sardine, canned in oil, drained	6 whole	54	2.4	1.6
Tuna, canned in brine, drained	100 g	27	1.3	1.2
Salmon, canned in brine	100 g	25	1.7	2.1
Egg, whole, hard-boiled	1 medium	5	0.9	0.4
Broccoli, boiled	1 cup	32	1.5	1.0
Zucchini, green skin, boiled	1 cup	22	0.9	0.5
Spinach, English, boiled	1 cup	94	4.4	0.9
Silverbeet, boiled	1 cup	28	2.5	0.6
Pea, green, boiled	1 cup	35	1.8	1.3
Bean, green, boiled	1 cup	24	1.5	1.1
Lettuce, common, raw	2 leaves	8	0.6	0.2
Muesli flakes	1 cup	33	6.9	0.5
Allbran	1 cup	184	5.6	3.5
Weeties	1 cup	110	3.2	1.2
Bread, wholemeal	1 slice	18	0.7	0.4
Crispbread, rye	2 biscuits	13	0.5	0.3
Rice cakes	1 serve	44	0.4	0.8
Baked beans, canned in sauce	1 cup	68	4.4	1.4
Lentils, boiled	1 cup	53	4.2	1.9
Cashew nuts, roasted	30 g	75	1.4	0.6
Peanuts, raw	30 g	48	0.7	0.9
Sesame seeds	15 g	51	0.8	0.8
Rice, brown, boiled	1 cup	88	0.9	1.6
Pasta, wholemeal, boiled	200 g	78	3.6	1.2

the joint capsule and ligaments and reduction in muscle *spasm*.

Molybdenum

See *Minerals*.

Monounsaturated fats

A type of *fat* that is found in foods made from plants such as olive oil, canola oil, certain types of margarine and avocado. When eaten in excessive amounts it is associated with being *overweight* and *obesity*.

At the same time, it is not as harmful to health as saturated fats. It may even be protective against coronary heart disease by decreasing bad cholesterol, called *low density lipoprotein (LDL)*, and increasing the levels of good cholesterol, *high density lipoprotein (HDL)*.

A healthy diet should include no more than 30 per cent of total energy needs from fat that is evenly divided between the three types: *saturated fats*, *polyunsaturated fats* and monounsaturated.

Morton's neuroma

Pain between the third and fourth toes, occasionally between the second and third toes, and in some cases

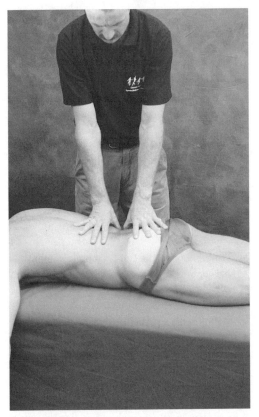

A mobilisation treatment for a low back joint

Grades of mobilisation

Grade	Degree of mobilisation
I	Small amplitude movement performed at the beginning of range
II	Large amplitude movement performed within the free range but not moving into any resistance or stiffness
III	Large amplitude movement performed up to the limit of range
IV	Small amplitude movement performed at the limit of range

also numbness caused by pressure on a nerve. It is due to an accumulation of physical forces over a period of weeks or months that causes *swelling*, placing pressure on the nerve. These forces are associated with a biomechanical abnormality of walking and running called excessive *foot pronation*, and also wearing *shoes* that are too small.

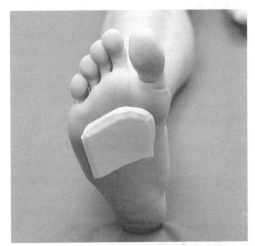

Padding worn to reduce the pressure for Morton's neuroma injury

Treatment includes *ice*, padding inside the shoe to reduce the pressure and correction of foot pronation. If this fails, a *corticosteroid* injection or surgery to remove the nerve is recommended.

Motivation

Psychological factors that have a strong influence on making a person act and behave in a particular way. They can determine whether a person seeks to achieve a specific outcome and the amount of effort put in to achieving it.

Each person has their own unique set of factors for being involved in exercise and sport. For example, a previously inactive person may start jogging in order to lose weight and reduce *stress*. An elite athlete may perform an excellent pre-season training to resurrect her career after the coach has talked about trading her to another team.

Motivation is often described in terms of extrinsic (external) and intrinsic (internal) rewards. Extrinsic rewards include prize money, trophies, medals and any form of recognition from others. Intrinsic rewards can be described as a love for a particular exercise or sport, and personal feelings such as contentment, satisfaction, fun and excitement that are directly generated by successfully performing the skills involved.

Both types of motivation are important, though intrinsic rewards are believed to be the most potent. *Psychologists* aim to identify these rewards and motives and build on them.

Motor nervous system

The neurons (nerve cells) that send out instructions from the brain and spinal cord to the rest of the body to perform actions such as walking, running, jumping, kicking a ball and drinking water. The cell body of a motor nervous system *neuron* can trigger off an electric current that is passed along its nerve fibre (also called an axon).

The collection of motor neuron cell bodies in the *brain* is called the motor cortex. A bundle of motor neuron nerve fibres that pass through the brain and down into the spinal cord is called a motor nerve tract or pathway. Sections of motor nerve fibres branch off from the tract to form part of a *spinal nerve*. The end of a motor nerve fibre is called the motor endplate. If it ends up in a muscle it forms part of a *motor unit*. This system is also called the efferent nervous system.

Motor program

A *motor skill*, such as a tennis serve or riding a bicycle, that has been learnt previously and stored in the brain and can be accessed after a prolonged break, even decades later. For example, when the motor skill is learnt for the first time it may be performed with a degree of difficulty that only reduces with practice until, for many people, it can be done almost unconsciously. Storage of the motor program is most likely in the sensory and motor cortex of the cerebrum of the *brain*.

Motor re-education

Activities that improve the strength of muscles and the timing of their contractions in order to increase the stability of a joint or region. For example, if the transversus abdominus (deep abdominal muscle) does not contract when a person starts running, the *pelvis* and *low back joints* become unstable causing excessive stress, which can lead to pain (see *Instability*).

Method

Motor re-education involves learning to execute the required contraction in an easy position and, later on, during the activity. For the transversus abdominus muscle, exercises may be commenced lying on the back. As timing and strength improve, progress can be made to doing the exercise kneeling, then standing and, eventually, during running (see *Functional exercises*).

Other techniques used to improve motor re-education include:
- *Visualisation* of the correct muscle action.
- *Taping* the skin can assist by increasing postural awareness.
- *Flexibility exercises* to treat a lack of flexibility that prevents a particular movement.
- *Strengthening exercises* to treat a weak muscle.

Motor skill

A movement or activity such as swinging the arm to perform a tennis stroke, and forcefully moving the leg forward to kick a ball. Motor skills are divided between fine skills, that involve movements of the hand and fingers, and gross skills, involving the whole arm, leg or trunk. It requires *sensory-motor integration* between the nervous system and muscles to work effectively.

Motor sports

There are three types of motor sports: cars, bikes and karts. Protective designs and safety equipment worn by drivers reduce the risk of injuries. The most common injuries are *head injury, skin injury, chest injury (severe), abdominal injury, neck pain (non-specific)* due to the weight of the helmet and high G-forces when going around corners, *low back pain (non-specific)* from prolonged sitting, and *heat illness* due to wearing fire-protection suits.

Motor unit

A single motor *neuron* (nerve cell) and the *muscle fibres* that are switched on by it to produce a *muscle contraction*. Motor units vary in the number and type of muscle fibres that get switched on. For example, a motor unit of slow-twitch muscle fibres usually includes from 10 to 180 fibres. In the calf muscle up to 2000 fast-twitch muscle fibres are switched on by each motor nerve, which is one of the reasons that it is the most powerful muscle in the body.

It takes more than one signal from a motor neuron (see *Motor nervous system*) to switch on a muscle contraction. The number of signals that are required is like a heater thermostat that gets switched on according to a temperature setting. This is called an 'all-or-none' response, where the motor unit is either 'on' or 'off'.

Motor units are gradually switched on when doing a specific action so that the correct strength is produced for the action. Only a few are required for picking up a delicate object, but many more when hitting a ball with a tennis racquet.

Mountain sickness

See *Altitude sickness*.

Mouth-to-mouth resuscitation

See *Medical emergency*.

Mouthguard

A piece of equipment worn inside the mouth to prevent injuries to the teeth, cheeks and lips (see *Face pain and injuries*). It can also decrease the risk of a *jaw fracture* by dispersing the force from a blow to the jawbone.

It is compulsory for sports such as *Rugby League, Rugby Union, Australian Rules football, American football, boxing* and *hockey (field)*. It is also recommended for sports that may be regarded as involving

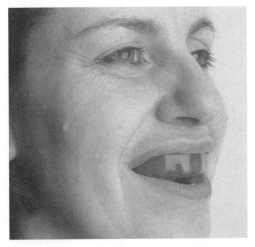

Mouthguard

less physical contact but still have a risk of being hit in the mouth or jaw, such as *basketball, cricket, squash* and highboard *diving*.

Protecting the teeth is particularly important because they have a lower potential for returning to their previous healthy state compared to other body parts.

The recommended standard for a mouthguard is custom-fitted by a dentist and made from laminated plastic. It is the most expensive, but provides an accurate fit that is made more protective with additional layers of plastic onto the areas most needed, the chewing surfaces of the teeth.

The cheapest but less protective type is the do-it-yourself mouthguard. It is less able to absorb forces due to an inaccurate fit, and requires athletes to clench the teeth to hold it in, which interferes with breathing, and is more likely to dislodge and block the airway.

A middle-priced mouthguard is called the vacuum-form, which can be made by some dentists. They fit better than the do-it-yourself types, but the method of forming the plastic is thinnest at the chewing surface where most protection is required.

Muscle

The tissue that is responsible for creating movement in the human body. It is made up of specialised cells that have the ability to contract. For example, the biceps muscle is attached at one end to a bone in the forearm and at the other end to bones in the shoulder. A *muscle contraction* pulls on the forearm bone and makes it move up, creating a bending movement of the elbow.

There are three types of muscles in the body: skeletal, cardiac and smooth. Skeletal muscle creates the movements required in exercise and sport, such as running, swinging a racquet and throwing a ball. Cardiac muscle creates the pumping action of the heart that sends blood flowing around the body. Smooth muscle is found in organs, such as the walls of the *gastrointestinal system* and blood vessels such as an *artery*. It creates movements such as peristalsis, the movement of food through the intestines, and tightens or widens the diameter of an artery.

Muscle also has the ability to relax and be made longer or be stretched. For example, the biceps muscle is made longer when straightening the elbow. In a blood vessel relaxation of the smooth muscle allows a widening of the diameter to let more blood flow through. In addition, muscle can produce a contraction at the same time as being stretched, which is an *eccentric* contraction.

The cells in muscles are called *muscle fibres*. They contain a smaller structure called the sarcomere that is the basic unit responsible for producing *muscle contractions*. Muscles also contain neurons from the *motor nervous system* and *sensory nervous system*, blood vessels and connective tissue, which holds muscle fibres together in bundles.

Muscle cell

See *Muscle fibre*.

Muscle compartment

A group of *muscles* wrapped up in thick *fascia*, a layer of relatively inelastic, fibrous connective tissue. Muscle compartments are located in the forearm and lower leg (see *Shin*).

Muscle conditioning

Regular participation in activities to improve the fitness of muscles. There are four types of muscle conditioning: *strength training*; training to increase power, including *plyometrics* and *Olympic-type weight lifting*; *endurance training for muscles*; and *motor re-education*.

Muscle contraction

The generation of force in a muscle that creates movement in the human body. It is produced in the basic unit of the muscle called the sarcomere. Muscle is made up of cells called *muscle fibres* that contain bundles of long, tube-like myofibrils filled with sarcomeres. The number of sarcomeres in each muscle varies. The largest muscles, like the gluteus maximus, contain more than 1 billion.

Physiology

Each sarcomere has two filaments or rods, one made up of the *protein* myosin and the other, actin. Myosin is thick and folded to form a globular head at one end like a hook. Actin has one end attached to a fixed point in the sarcomere, the Z-disk, and the other end floats freely near the myosin hook.

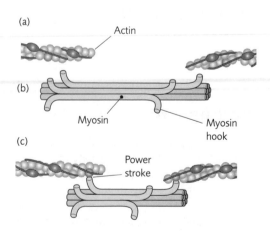

The filaments in the sarcomere, the basic unit of the muscle, producing a muscle contraction. (a) Actin rod; (b) Binding to myosin hook; (c) Sliding over it in a power stroke

A signal received from a neuron in the *motor nervous system* triggers a chain of events. The neuron releases a *neurotransmitter*, acetylcholine (ACh), that causes the release of calcium ions stored inside the muscle fibres, which makes the myosin hook bind with the actin rod.

This binding occurs in a way that tilts the myosin hook, called a power stroke, and slides the actin over the myosin filament, like fingers interlocking. This action drags the Z-disks closer to each other. Because this is occurring at thousands of Z-disks throughout the muscle fibre, the overall effect is a shortening.

Energy is needed to bind the myosin hook and actin rod. It is supplied by the compound, *adenosine triphosphate (ATP)*. When the adenosine triphosphatase enzyme (ATPase) cuts off one of the phosphate groups from ATP it causes a release of energy that is used to make the binding and power stroke.

A muscle contraction ends when calcium is taken back into storage in the muscle fibre, which weakens the attraction between the myosin hook and actin until the binding is released and the actin slides back to its original position.

The different types of muscle contractions are *concentric*, *eccentric* and *isometric*.

Muscle contusion

An injury to muscle caused by a sudden and single blunt force, like an opposing player's knee striking the thigh. It is most common in *collision sports* such as *football* codes, *ice hockey*, *martial arts*, snow sports such as *downhill skiing* and *basketball*. The most common sites include the quadriceps (also called a cork thigh or charley horse), hamstring and calf muscles. The force causes primary damage to muscle fibres, connective tissue and blood vessels.

Diagnosis and treatment

The main symptoms are pain, stiffness, restricted movement, bruising in the area of the blow and, occasionally, further down in the limb, blood trickling down due to gravity.

MILD (GRADE 1)

Tenderness at the site of the blow and *flexibility* (stretching) of the muscle is reduced by 5–20 per cent when compared to the uninjured side. In many cases the incident is not remembered and activity is continued afterwards.

Treatment aims to minimise the bleeding and swelling with *RICE* (*rest, ice, compression and elevation*). Heat, provided by a hot bath or hot packs, alcohol and vigorous *massage* should be avoided because they make the bleeding worse.

MODERATE (GRADE 2)

Some pain on resisted contraction and a 20–50 per cent restriction of stretching. Moderate cases can usually walk, though with a limp.

The recommended first aid is the same as for a mild injury. After 2 to 3 days the recommended treatment includes encouraging resorption of the blood clot with electrotherapy, such as *interferential therapy* and *ultrasound therapy*, *flexibility exercises* and *strengthening exercises. Sport rehabilitation* for return to sport usually takes 1 to 2 weeks.

SEVERE (GRADE 3)

Severe pain is felt with resisted contraction and there is a 50 per cent restriction of stretching range. First aid and treatments are the same as for grade 2; however, with greater care to ensure full healing and rehabilitation. Return to sport requires 3 to 4 weeks.

One of the complications of a muscle contusion is *myositis ossificans*, where the healing tissue absorbs calcium deposits that can be detected on an *X-ray* about 10 to 14 days after the injury. It should be suspected when a contusion does not heal within the expected time.

Muscle cramps

Sudden, involuntary muscle contractions that cause pain and restricted movement, and which have a negative impact on ability to perform activities. The most common site is the calf; however, it can occur in any muscle in the body.

The causes are still not fully understood. Current theories suggest it is associated with loss of fluid and loss of salts, such as sodium and potassium, due to dehydration, carbohydrate depletion, reduced *flexibility* of a muscle and disturbances of the motor nerves that control muscle contractions.

There are no proven strategies for prevention. The recommendations that have the best supporting evidence include maintaining good flexibility, correct muscle balance and posture, fitness, avoiding drugs that provoke cramps such as *diuretics*, keeping up adequate carbohydrate stores by eating a high carbohydrate meal 2 to 3 hours before exercise, and ensuring a healthy fluid and salt intake before and during activity (see *Hydration*).

Other strategies such as *plyometrics*, muscle *strengthening exercises*, particularly *eccentric* contractions, and treating *myofascial trigger points*, still require further research.

The immediate aim of treatment for muscle cramps is to stop the muscle contractions, which can be achieved by stretching the muscle (see *Flexibility exercises*).

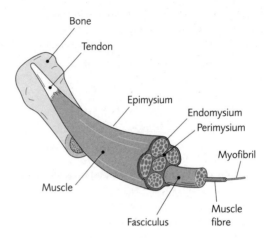

Skeletal muscle fibre structure

Muscle energy technique

A treatment that aims to correct asymmetrical movement and posture between the two sides of the body. It is part of osteopathy (see *osteopath*) and based on the assumption that if the body's posture is not symmetrical it faces an increased risk of injury and pain.

Asymmetry may develop as a result of an injury. For example, a moderate strain of the left-side hamstring (back thigh muscle) can cause a change in the posture of the pelvis on the left side, making it asymmetrical with the posture on the right side. After the hamstring muscle has healed the asymmetry may remain and cause continuing pain and an increased risk of re-injury.

The technique is used most commonly for pain in the legs, pelvis, low back, neck and shoulder.

Muscle fibres

Specialised cells that are the building blocks of a *muscle*. The main feature of a muscle fibre is the ability to produce contractions that create move-

ment. There are three types of fibre: skeletal, cardiac and smooth. While all muscle fibres are long and tube-like, each type produces movement differently.

Skeletal muscle fibre

The longest fibre type. It reaches a maximum length of 15 cm (6 in). Fibres line up end on end in muscles so that a contraction produces movement in a single direction. Each fibre contains from 200 to 2000 myofibrils that contain the basic contractile unit, the sarcomere (see *Muscle contractions*). A single skeletal muscle fibre, for example, may contain up to 500 000 sarcomeres. In the calf muscle, which has 1 million muscle fibres, there are 500 million sarcomeres.

Skeletal muscle fibres are switched on to produce a contraction by neurons from the *motor nervous system* in a structure called the *motor unit*. Neurons from the *sensory nervous system* in the muscle sense the strength of the contraction and send signals to the brain to decide whether it needs to be altered.

Fibres are held together in bundles and surrounded in a sheath of *connective tissue* called the endomysium and perimysium. Skeletal fibres come in two types: *slow-twitch (ST) muscle fibres* that are best suited for long distance events, and *fast-twitch (FT) muscle fibres* for short distances.

Cardiac muscle fibre

Only found in the *heart*. It is shorter than skeletal muscle fibres, and contains branches that interlink with each other. This makes it easier to perform the coordinated and regularly timed contractions called *heartbeats*. The heart has a nerve centre called the sinoatrial node, which sends out a signal to the fibres to start a contraction. The shape and size of cardiac muscle fibres increase the speed of the signal as it spreads from fibre to fibre. Heartbeats are also triggered by *hormones*.

Smooth muscle fibres

Not as efficient or coordinated as skeletal and cardiac fibres. They are short, like cardiac fibres, but taper at the ends and are loosely woven together so a signal to start a contraction spreads from fibre to fibre at a relatively slower speed. Contractions also can be triggered by hormones and may occur spontaneously.

Skeletal and cardiac muscle fibres are called striated muscle because stripes running across them are visible under a microscope. Smooth muscle fibre is non-striated.

Muscle fibrosis

See *Fibrosis*.

Muscle inhibition

Loss of the ability of a muscle to perform a contraction due to pain caused by an injury or *swelling* in a nearby joint. The loss is a reflex reaction triggered by *neurons* (nerve cells) in the joint that sense the increased pressure created by the swelling and send signals via the spinal cord to inhibit the muscles that normally move the joint.

Muscle length

The distance of a *muscle* from end to end. It varies according to the *flexibility* of a muscle. Muscle length is usually described as an angle that is measured in degrees using the position of a joint or other anatomical parts as a starting-off point. It is also called *range of movement*.

Muscle-length relationship

The length of a muscle influences how much strength can be generated by a muscle contraction. Muscles are weaker at the start and end of the range of movement. For example, sitting down with your feet flat on the floor and straightening the knee involves the quadriceps muscle (front thigh) performing a range of movement of 90 degrees.

The quadriceps is weakest at the start (90 degrees bent) and at the end (0 degrees bent or fully straightened) and strongest in the mid-range between 30 and 60 degrees. Muscle-length relationship is a factor that needs to be taken into account during *isokinetic strengthening*.

Muscle soreness

Muscle aches and pain that develop after an activity has been completed that has not been caused by an injury. Immediately after an activity the soreness is due to the accumulation of swelling and waste products of metabolism, often associated with *transient hypertrophy*, and usually passes within a few hours.

A *warm-down* can speed up the recovery by helping to maintain a steady flow of blood to clear the waste products. *Post-activity massage, whirlpools and spas*, sleep and *rest, post-activity psychology* and *post-activity eating* may also be helpful. Muscle aches and pains that develop within 48 hours of the completion of an activity are called *delayed-onset muscle soreness (DOMS)*.

Muscle strain

See *Strain*.

Muscle tension

An excessive level of background muscle contraction when the body is at rest. It is associated with *anxiety*, *stress* and difficulty achieving a state of relaxation. Background muscle contraction, which is called *muscle tone*, is important for keeping the muscles in a state of readiness for quick action.

However, when the level is set too high it can be associated with injuries such as *neck-related headaches* and *low back pain (non-specific)*. It can also interfere with performance during competition by making movements less coordinated or less able to maintain precision and accuracy.

Muscle tone

The background level of contraction in the muscles. The lowest background level of *muscle contraction* occurs during sleep or unconsciousness. The next level is a state of relaxation that can be achieved through various techniques, such as *meditation, yoga, autogenic training* and *progressive muscle relaxation*.

The next highest level is a state of rest where there is enough tone to maintain basic activities, such as stopping your body from falling out of a chair, and enable the muscles to quickly spring into action as required, as when walking or jumping. The higher levels are associated with being active, such as playing sport, and performing mental tasks requiring great alertness and concentration, such as air traffic control. It is also associated with *anxiety* and *stress*.

There are also diseases that damage the brain and spinal cord that can cause the nerves to create excess tone, called hypertonia, which is seen in spastic cerebral palsy and *stroke*. Too little tone is called hypotonia, which is found in *paraplegia, quadriplegia* and muscular dystrophy.

Musculoskeletal system

The *skeletal muscles, bones, joints* and their associated *nerves* and blood vessels that combine to produce movement of the body as a whole and its specific parts.

The system creates all the actions and activities collectively known as exercise and sport, as well as the structures most likely to get injured during exercise and sport. It also interacts extensively with the *cardiovascular system, nervous system* and *gastrointestinal system*.

Music

A psychological technique that can help an athlete prepare for a competition by inducing specific mood states. For many athletes it is a fixed part of their pre-competition *routine*. The best music is the one that achieves an optimum state of *arousal*. When used regularly it can help to reduce *stress*. It is recommended to have several different types of music to choose from.

Myocardial infarction

See *Heart attack*.

Myocarditis

Inflammation of the *heart* muscle. In many cases it does not cause symptoms. However, in some people there may be chest pain, *tiredness, shortness of breath,*

Australian medley swimmer Matt Dunn listening to music before a competition event

palpitations, cardiac arrhythmias, and an increased risk of a *heart attack* during participation in exercise and sport.

People who have the flu, in particular symptoms such as fever and muscle aches, and participate in high-intensity *aerobic training*, such as running or jogging, face a higher risk of developing myocarditis. The diagnosis is made with a blood test, *electrocardiogram (ECG)* and *echocardiogram*. Competitive sport is not permitted for 6 months following myocarditis.

Myofascial trigger points

Small tender areas located in tight bands of *muscles* that produce pain. The tightness is due to abnormal cross-linkages between muscle fibres that form in response to inflammation following an injury.

The trigger points cause pain in a predictable pattern when pressed firmly with the fingers. For example, trigger points in the back muscles can refer pain down into the buttocks and upper thigh.

The exact mechanisms that lead to pain are not fully understood. One theory is that hyperactive muscle fibres in the trigger point that are unable to stop *muscle contractions* are responsible. The hyperactivity is due to an excessive build up of calcium ions, which keeps the myosin and actin filaments bonded together and prevents relaxation of the muscle fibres. This theory is supported by *electromyograph (EMG)* evaluation showing unique, prolonged and rapid activity of muscles with active trigger points.

Diagnosis and treatment
The key to diagnosis is pressing on a trigger point to reproduce the pain that a person is complaining about (see *Physical examination*). If it is reproduced then the conclusion is that the trigger point is contributing to or solely causing the pain.

The aim of treatment is to reduce the sensitivity of the trigger point. Suggested methods include *ice*, stretching the muscle, electrotherapy such as *laser therapy* and *ultrasound therapy*, *massage*, injections of local anaesthetic or *corticosteroid* and *dry needling*, which uses acupuncture or conventional needles.

Myositis ossificans

A bruise to the quadriceps (front *thigh* muscle) or, less commonly, hamstring (back *thigh* muscle) that does not heal correctly and develops bone-like calcium deposits. It can be detected with an *X-ray* after 3 weeks. After 6 or 7 weeks the bone growth ceases and a lump in the muscle can often be felt. The body then slowly resorbs the bone though a small amount of bone may remain.

The causes are unknown, though the more severe bruises (*muscle contusions*) are more likely to develop *myositis ossificans*. Inappropriate treatment such as heat or massage within the first 48 hours after a contusion, or massage that is too aggressive, may increase the risk.

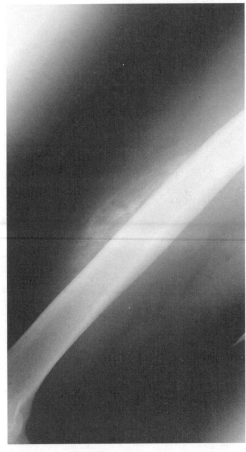

X-ray of myositis ossificans

Diagnosis and treatment

Myositis ossificans should be suspected if the pain gets worse with activity, starts to be felt during the night and if the *flexibility* of the muscle begins deteriorating.

Little can be done to speed up the bone resorption process. The only recommended treatment is gentle, painless *flexibility exercises. Corticosteroid* injection is absolutely forbidden, and surgery is not recommended. *Extra corporeal shock wave therapy,* which uses high frequency sound waves called ultrasound to break down the calcium, is a new treatment that may have some success.

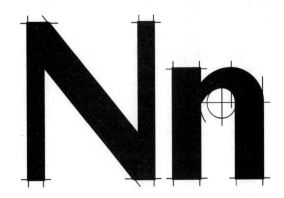

Narcotics

A group of drugs derived from the opium poppy, including codeine, morphine, pethidine and heroin. They are commonly used to treat moderate to severe pain, but are highly addictive. Recreational use of these drugs is illegal. Pain relief also can be achieved with non-narcotic *analgesics*.

Narcotic *drugs banned in sport* according to the International Olympic Committee (IOC) include buprenorphine (Temgesic), heroin, morphine, pethidine, dextromoramide, methadone and pentazocine. They are banned because they enable athletes to reduce pain and continue playing sport despite injuries or illness.

Permitted narcotics include codeine, dextromethorphan, dextropropoxyphene, dihydrocodeine, diphenoxylate, ethylmorphine, pholcodine, propoxyphene and tramadol.

Side effects of narcotics include mood disturbances, drowsiness, mental clouding, constipation, nausea, vomiting and, in high doses, respiratory depression, hypotension (low *blood pressure*) and significant withdrawal effects

Nasal bone fracture

A break of the nasal bones behind the nose due to a sudden forceful blow to the front of the face causing pain, nosebleed and swelling (see *Head*). Deformity and excessive mobility of the nose is an indication of a displaced *fracture*.

The treatment begins with controlling the *nosebleed*, followed by diagnosis of the type of fracture. Undisplaced fractures do not require treatment. Displaced nasal fractures require surgery to put the bones back in their correct position if the deformity is a cosmetic concern or causing obstruction of the nasal passages. However, it is preferable to delay this treatment for 7 days to reduce the risk of damaging a nearby artery. Some people choose to wait until a more convenient time, such as at the end of a season or upon retirement.

Nasal breathing

A technique used to prevent *exercise-induced asthma (EIA)* attacks by making breathing easier.

It involves a conscious effort to breathe in only through the nose.

Air breathed in through the nose achieves a higher degree of warming and humidification than *breathing* in through the mouth, which is less harsh on the airways of the lungs. In addition, the turbulent passage of air through the nose catches a greater amount of dust and other particles compared to the mouth.

Asthma attacks are less likely in people who increase the amount of nasal breathing during exercise. However, during high-intensity activity, such as running, the demand for air forces breathing to also occur through the mouth.

Nasal dilator

A piece of equipment worn on the nose to reduce the risk of an attack of *exercise-induced asthma (EIA)*. It may also improve the performance of athletes regardless of whether they have asthma or not.

It is a thin plastic strip with an adhesive on one side that is placed on the nose at the start of the cartilage, just below the junction with the nasal bones. It is cheap, easy to use and can be worn by athletes participating in any sport, including water sports.

The nasal dilator widens the diameter of the nasal passages, which can lead to a substantial increase in airflow that makes breathing through the nose easier. Nasal breathing humidifies the inspired air to a greater degree than mouth breathing. This makes episodes of exercise-induced asthma (EIA), which can be triggered by breathing dry air, much less likely.

Increasing the ease of nasal breathing may also help athletes who don't have exercise-induced asthma. Research has found that an increase in blood flow to the leg muscles in running sports is achieved when overall breathing, including nasal breathing, is made easier.

Natural health supplements

Supplements recommended by natural health practitioners, such as herbalists and naturopaths, to help achieve maximum performance and minimise the strain and stresses of exercise and sport.

This may include taking supplements for prevention including *vitamin and mineral supplementation* such as vitamin B complex, which is lost more rapidly during exercise, *calcium* and *magnesium* for women for bone strength and muscle and nerve function, and *iron* for athletes at risk of iron-deficiency which affects blood oxygenation.

Recovery from injuries may be assisted with *antioxidants*, including vitamins A, C and E, beta-carotene and selenium, *amino acid* supplementation for increasing muscle strength and bulk, and enzymes, such as *coenzyme Q10*, and *ginseng* for increasing energy and endurance.

Naturopath

A health practitioner who has completed training and is recognised as being qualified to provide a diagnosis and treatment for injuries, illness and disease according to the method of naturopathy, which regards the body, mind and spirit as possessing an inherent capacity to generate self-healing in appropriate conditions. The role of the naturopath is to facilitate this process using a range of diagnostic techniques such as iridology and treatments including *herbal medicine*, diet and *nutrition* and *massage* therapy such as *Rolfing*.

Nausea

An unpleasant sensation of feeling the urge to vomit. The causes are usually the same as *vomiting*.

Navicular stress fracture

A microfracture in the small bone on the inner arch of the foot that develops gradually due to an accumulation of repeated, excessive physical loads over a period of weeks or months. It is associated with *athletics*, including hurdling and sprinting, and sports that involve running and jumping, including football codes such as *soccer* and *Australian Rules football*.

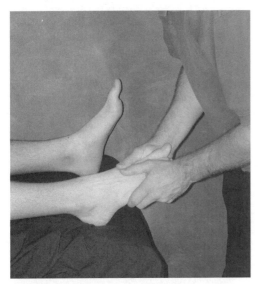

Looking for tenderness caused by navicular stress fracture called the 'N spot'

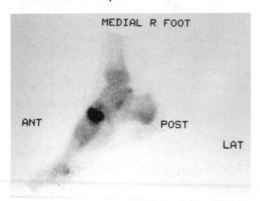

MEDIAL R FOOT

ANT

POST

LAT

Bone scan of navicular stress fracture

It is more likely in people with biomechanical abnormalities, particularly excessive *foot pronation* and loss of *range of movement* of ankle joint dorsiflexion (moving foot upwards).

Diagnosis, treatment and return to sport

The pain comes on during the aggravating activity, and is usually vaguely located over the top of the foot (see *Foot and toes*). However, unlike most *stress fractures*, the pain settles quickly with rest. A physical examination finds tenderness when the bone is pressed firmly with the fingers, called the 'N spot'.

The diagnosis is confirmed with a *bone scan* or *magnetic resonance imaging (MRI)*. Treatment involves not taking weight on the foot during *immobilisation* in a plaster cast for a minimum of 6 weeks. In most cases by this time the 'N spot' is no longer tender. However, if it is, another 2 weeks immobilisation is required.

A *sport rehabilitation* program should follow, including correction of any biomechanical abnormality, *mobilisation* of ankle and foot joints, *massage*, *flexibility exercises* and *strengthening exercises*. Return to full training and sport should take at least 6 weeks (12 weeks from the start of immobilisation).

Neck burner

A sudden stretch of the nerves of the *neck joints* and *shoulder joint* (brachial plexus) causing a burning pain, pins and needles, numbness and weakness located in the neck and, in some cases, also spreading down the arm into the hand.

The injury is due to a sudden downward displacement of the shoulder at the same time as bending the neck sideways towards the opposite side. It is seen most often in *American football*. It is also called a 'stinger'.

No treatment is required. Mild cases clear up on their own after a few minutes, and in severe cases after a few days.

Neck joints

The upper spine that connects the head to the middle back and shoulder region. It is made up of seven bones in a column, which are collectively called the cervical vertebrae and numbered from top to bottom: C1 to C7.

Each vertebra, beginning with C2, has three joints with the vertebra below: the central and forward-located (anterior) joint is the *disc*; and two backward-located (posterior) *synovial joints*, one on each side, the zygapophysial joints (Z-joints). The cervical column curves inwards in the middle, which is a lordosis.

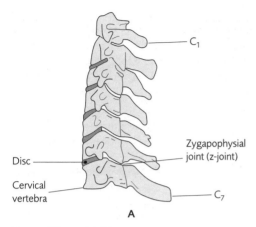

Bones of the neck joints

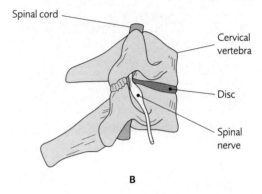

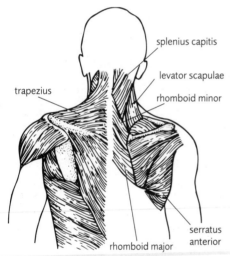

Anatomy of the neck—posterior (behind) view (trapezius removed on right side to show scapular muscles)

The neck joints allow six types movements, as shown in the table, 'Neck joint range of movement and muscles'.

Muscles also keep the neck steady and stable during movements of the arms and hands, in co-ordination with the shoulder region.

The spine protects the *spinal cord*, and at each cervical vertebra level two large branches come off,

the ventral and dorsal nerve roots. Within the spinal canal they form a larger *spinal nerve*, which exits through a hole called the intervertebral foramen. Each spinal nerve is named according to the vertebra level it exits from the spinal canal; for example, C7 spinal nerve.

The neck region also contains vital arteries and veins that run between the heart and head and brain, as well as nerves such as the vagus nerve.

Neck pain and injuries

Causes

Neck pain can be caused by overuse or acute injury, or disease. In most cases it is an *overuse injury*, where the pain gets worse over a period of weeks or months due to an accumulation of excessive forces that cause microtrauma. In the early stages it causes only minor pain and stiffness. But later on it becomes severe enough to seek medical care, either gradually or due to a sudden event that aggravates it.

An *acute injury* causes pain that begins suddenly due to a single incident, such as whiplash following a car accident. A severe acute injury of the neck, usually associated with a severe *head injury* and *spinal injury*, should be treated as a *medical emergency*. Diseases that cause neck pain include osteoarthritis and *tumours*.

Neck joint range of movement and muscles

Movement	Range of movement	Muscles producing movement
Flexion (bringing chin to the chest)	45 degrees	• Longus colli • Longus capitis • Sternocleidomastoid muscles
Lateral flexion (bending head sideways to the left and right)	45 degrees	• Scalenus anterior and medius • Sternocleidomastoid • Splenius cervicis and capitis
Extension (lifting head backwards)	60 degrees	• Longissimus capitis • Semispinalis capitis and cervicis • Splenius cervicis and capitis • Rectus capitis posterior major and minor • Trapezius
Rotation (turning head to the left and right)	80 degrees	• Sternocleidomastoid • Scalenus anterior • Obliquus capitis inferior • Semispinalis capitis

The *neck joints* and the associated ligaments, muscles and neural sheaths are the main sources of pain. However, there is little consistency to the type and location of neck *pain*. An accurate technique called *diagnostic nerve blocks* is currently only used for people with pain that has not improved after 3 months. Fortunately over 90 per cent of people with neck pain get better without an exact diagnosis.

Diagnosis

In the majority of neck pain cases the structure causing the pain can't be identified, which is described as *neck pain (non-specific)*.

Exact diagnoses include: *wry neck*, sharp neck pain and difficulty moving the head after a sudden, quick movement or sleeping; *whiplash*, after a car accident or collision with an opponent; *neck posture syndrome*, excessive spine lordosis; and *neck burner*, also called a stinger, which causes neck and arm burning pain, numbness, pins and needles and weakness, usually less than 5 minutes.

Neck *osteoarthritis* is more likely in older-aged people, causing pain felt worse in the morning, but improving with movement during the day. The neck joints also can cause *neck-related headache*.

Radiological investigations, such as *X-rays, CT scan* and *magnetic resonance imaging (MRI)* are rarely required because the results can't confirm if a specific structure is causing the pain.

Neck pain (non-specific)

Pain in the neck that does not have an exact diagnosis. Fortunately in more than 90 per cent of cases treatment can achieve improvement anyway. If pain has not improved after 3 months, further investigation may be recommended.

Non-specific neck pain requires careful assessment and detection of abnormalities of muscles, joints and the neural sheath, which are treated using techniques detailed below.

One abnormality is treated at a time. Comparing the amount of pain and movement before and after the treatment provides an assessment of the its effectiveness. If the treatment is not effective, a different technique should be attempted.

Muscles

Abnormalities of muscles that may be found include *myofascial trigger points* in the suboccipital, sternomastoid, scalenes, trapezius and levator scapulae muscles, general areas of *fascia* thickening, loss of *flexibility* of the trapezius and levator scapulae and

QUICK REFERENCE GUIDE

Neck

Overuse injury: Pain that has gradually worsened over a period of weeks or months

Neck pain (non-specific) ....Do you have pain in the neck, shoulder, arm or hand that doesn't have an exact diagnosis?

Neck posture syndrome ....Do you have neck pain that is made worse by staying in the same position for long periods of time?

Acute Injury: Pain caused by a sudden force

Wry neck ....Do you have sharp neck pain and difficulty moving the head after a sudden, quick movement or after waking up?

Whiplash ....Do you have neck pain after a car accident or collision with an opponent or equipment?

Neck burner ....Do you have a burning pain in the neck and arm, numbness, pins and needles and weakness that last for a short time (usually less than 5 minutes)?

weakness of the rhomboids (see *Neck joints*). The recommended treatments include *massage* and *dry needling* for myofascial trigger points, *flexibility exercises* and *strengthening exercises*.

In many people neck pain is also associated with *stress* that can lead to excessive muscle tone. It may be reduced with techniques such as *yoga* and *meditation*.

Joints

The most common abnormalities are pain and loss of *range of movement* in one or more of the joints. The recommended treatments include *mobilisation*, *manipulation* and *traction*.

Neural sheath

The neural sheath (the outer layer covering the *nerves*) most commonly causes pain when stretched or there is a loss of range of movement. The recommended treatments include mobilisation of the upper limb *neural tension* test and flexibility exercises.

Neck posture syndrome

Posture of the neck that is abnormally curved inwards (kyphosis) causing the chin to protrude forwards,

leading to a burning or aching pain across the shoulders and neck, or pain in the upper *neck joints* near the back of the head.

The pain is made worse by staying in the same position for hours. *Neck-related headache* is also common. It is more likely to occur in sports where a constant posture is required, such as in *cycling* and for *baseball* catchers, and in jobs such as visual display unit operators, painters and production-line workers.

Treatment follows the same approach to *neck pain (non-specific)*. In addition, postural retraining is essential by using *motor re-education* and *taping*.

Neck-related headache

Pain felt in the head that is caused by a distant damaged structure, usually the neck joints, ligaments or muscles.

The headache occurs because pain-sensing nerve receptors in the neck send their signals to the brain via nerves in the spinal cord that also connect with other pain-sensing receptors in the head. As a result, instead of receiving a signal from the neck, the brain ends up perceiving that the pain is coming from the head (see *Referred pain*).

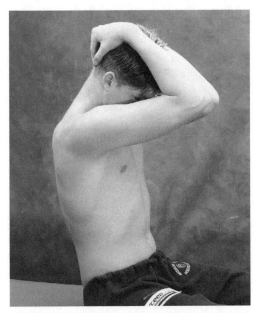

Flexibility exercises of the upper cervical extensor muscles for neck-related headache

The pain is usually described as a pulling or gripping feeling, or a tight band around the head. It is felt continuously, often on one side but sometimes both sides, usually in the back of the head, though also in the forehead, upper sides and behind the eyes. It is more likely in people who have had a *whiplash* injury.

Diagnosis and treatment

The diagnosis starts with excluding a local cause of *headache*, followed by identifying positive signs that the pain is being referred from a distant structure.

For example, a physical examination of a person with headache on the right side of the head may find reduced range of movement of neck lateral flexion (sideways bending) and tender and stiff accessory movements of the right side *neck joints*. This diagnosis can be tested with right side neck joint *mobilisation*, a treatment involving a therapist pushing the joints with the hands. If the headache is reduced, the diagnosis is considered to be correct.

Treatments include mobilisation, *non-steroidal anti-inflammatory drugs* (NSAIDs), analgesics, *flexibility exercises* and *motor re-education* to correct posture.

Muscles in the neck, shoulder, upper thoracic spine and scapular regions may also refer pain into the head, particularly *myofascial trigger points* in the suboccipital, upper trapezius, splenius capitis and cervicis and sternomastoid muscles, which can be treated with *massage* and *dry needling*. *Neural tension* stretching (upper limb tension test) is also recommended if the neural sheath is involved.

Nedocromil sodium

A medication that prevents an *asthma* attack by reducing the release of chemicals that cause narrowing of airways. However, it does not reduce symptoms once an attack has occurred. The usual dose is 4 mg, which lasts for up to 4 hours. Although it has minimal side effects, some people complain about an unpleasant taste.

Nerve

A tissue made up of thousands of nerve fibres. Each nerve fibre, also called an axon, is a long thin single branch that comes out of a *neuron* (nerve cell). It has the ability to conduct an electric current, which is used to produce most of the communications between the brain and the body.

Structure

Each nerve is made up of bundles of nerve fibres. These bundles and the nerve itself are wrapped in connective tissue, called the neural sheath, which has a blood and nerve supply including pain-sensing nerve fibres. Reduced neural sheath flexibility is called *neural tension*.

Physiology

Twelve pairs of cranial nerves originate from the *brain*, and 31 pairs of spinal nerves from the *spinal cord*. The cranial and spinal nerves are the largest in the body. They give off branches, which form nerves that usually end up in the same part of the body such as the vagus nerve, which goes to the heart. All the above nerves make up the *peripheral nervous system*.

Each nerve conducts a two-way flow of communications that are passed along by nerve fibres that come from different systems, including the *motor nervous system, sensory nervous system, somatic nervous system* and *autonomic nervous system*. For example, a nerve can simultaneously send information telling a muscle to contract, an artery to increase blood flow, and report to the brain about skin sensations.

Nerve conduction test

A test to check if a nerve's ability to conduct has been diminished. This may be required if it has suffered degeneration, due to swelling or scarring caused by a *nerve entrapment*, or following an acute *nerve injury*.

It involves placing electrodes on the skin near the nerve and the muscles that it connects to and sending bursts of electricity to stimulate the nerve to activate the *motor units* in muscles. The more electricity required, the greater the degree of degeneration.

Nerve entrapment

An overuse injury of a *nerve* that causes pins and needles, numbness and muscle weakness. It is due to compression of the nerve caused by swelling or scarring in the surrounding muscle and soft tissues or anatomical abnormalities.

Diagnosis of nerve entrapment may require performing a *nerve conduction test* to check the impact on the nerve's function. The recommended treatment for a nerve entrapment is usually surgical decompression.

A chronic mild irritation of a nerve may result in damage called *neural tension*. An acute injury of a spinal nerve root, usually in the low back, is called *nerve root compression*.

Nerve injury

An acute injury of a nerve caused by a direct blow or an overuse injury due to an accumulation of forces over a long period of time.

An acute injury can lead to three types of damage, which can be assessed with a *nerve conduction test*:
- Neuropraxia: The nerve temporarily loses function, in mild cases causing numbness or pins and needles for a few days, or when severe, also causes loss of muscle strength, and may last up to 6 weeks.
- Axonotmesis: Damage leads to degeneration of the nerve, requiring slow nerve re-growth to recover and possibly surgery.
- Neurotmesis: The nerve is cut and re-growth is slow, possibly requiring surgery.

An overuse injury can cause pain associated with *neural tension* and *nerve entrapment*.

Nerve root compression

Excessive pressure on a nerve root caused by prolapse of a spinal disc. In most cases the injury occurs in a *low back joint*.

The prolapse involves the gel-like nucleus of the disc extruding through a break in the tough outer covering, called the anulus fibrosus. The gel either escapes or causes the anulus fibrosus to bulge outwards, reducing the narrow space in the spinal canal where the nerve root is located (see *Spinal nerves*).

Diagnosis
The disc prolapse can occur following a relatively simple movement, such as bending forward or twisting the spine, as well as through more complex and forceful movement of the spine.

In most cases it is usually easily identified by the particular type of pain it causes and its location. In some cases a diagnostic technique called *selective nerve root block* (SNRB) is recommended. Radiological investigation such as an X-ray usually isn't necessary.

The pain usually begins suddenly and is located in the low back and leg. It is often described as knife-like, sharp, shooting and accompanied by pins and needles, numbness or weakness in the legs. It may be associated with an inability to stand up straight, and made worse by sitting, bending, lifting, coughing or sneezing.

Treatment and return to sport

In a few cases the compression on the nerve root requires immediate treatment in a hospital if it causes numbness felt in the saddle (genital and anal region) and if there is difficulty with urination.

Bed rest and lying in the most comfortable position is recommended. In some cases the compression eases off after a few days and treatments such as *mobilisations*, *traction* and *active exercises* can be commenced.

In other cases *periradicular injection* is recommended. Recovery usually takes from 3 weeks in mild cases and up to 4 months in severe cases. If weakness, numbness and pins and needles get worse, then the best treatment is surgery such as *spinal fusion*, laminectomy or percutaneous discectomy using needle aspiration, all of which require 6 to 8 weeks for return to being active and up to 3 or 4 months for return to contact sports.

Nervous system

Tissues and organs that provide communications throughout the body. The two main types are motor and sensory. In the *motor nervous system* the brain sends out instructions to perform an action. In the *sensory nervous system* the brain receives back information about the action and also the outside world.

For example, at the moment brain *neurons* (nerve cells) are sending instructions to the hand muscles telling them to hold this book in front of your eyes. At the same time eye neurons are detecting areas of colour, light and shade on the page, which your brain interprets as words.

The central nervous system (CNS) includes two organs, the *brain* and *spinal cord*. The *peripheral nervous system* includes all the neurons that go to the rest of the body. The somatic nervous system refers to communications that are in our conscious voluntary control.

The autonomic nervous system conducts communications that are relatively less conscious, which control organs such as intestines, heart and lungs. Its two divisions are the *sympathetic nervous system* and *parasympathetic nervous system*, which oppose each other.

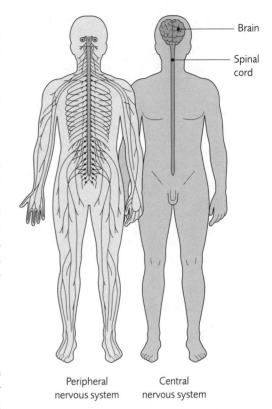

Peripheral nervous system   Central nervous system

Nervous system

Neurons communicate like the electric circuits in a machine. Each neuron has a single long branch, called a nerve fibre, that is like an electric wire. Thousands of nerve fibres in a bundle is called a *nerve*. A network of criss-crossing nerves is called a *plexus*. Nerves that connect with the cell bodies of other neurons form a *ganglion*. Other communications in the body are conducted by the endocrine system, which produces *hormones*. Though slower than the nervous system, the effects are generally longer lasting.

Netball

A game played between two teams of seven players. The ball is passed from player to player. Running with the ball is not permitted. A goal is scored when the ball is thrown into the ring. Netball is the most popular team sport in countries such as Australia.

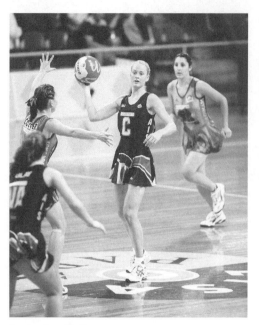

Passing in netball

Neural tension slump test

Fitness and injuries

The main fitness requirements include *aerobic train-ing*, *strength training* and *anaerobic training*. The most common injuries are *ankle sprain, anterior cruciate ligament (ACL) tear* (knee), *medial collateral ligament (MCL) sprain* (knee), *patellar tendinosis* (knee), *shin periostitis, gastrocnemius strain* (calf), *soleus strain* (calf) and *hand and finger pain and injuries*.

Netball shoes

The best footwear choice for netball is similar to a *basketball shoe*, particularly an upper section of the *shoe* with a high ankle cut or, at a minimum, a rigid heel counter.

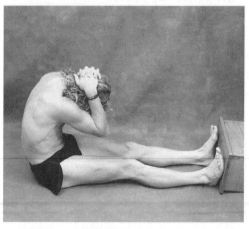

Flexibility exercise for the slump test

Neural tension

Abnormal mechanics of a *nerve* leading to increased tension that can result in pain. It is similar to a joint or muscle that has become stiff or tight and the flex-ibility has been reduced.

The source of the pain is pain-sensing nerve receptors in the neural sheath, the connective tissue component of neurons.

The assessment of nerve mechanics and neural tension is an important component of a *physical examination* for injuries and pain. Factors that can cause a loss of flexibility include scar tissue, tight sur-rounding muscles and adhesions within nerves. *Ankle sprain, hamstring strain* and *tennis elbow*, for example, have been shown to be associated with abnormal nerve mechanics.

Diagnosis

A test of neural tension involves performing movements of the body that stretch specific nerves. An abnormality is present (called a positive result) if the test reproduces the symptoms, which should lead to further physical examination to determine whether it is the sole cause or associated with another injury. The main neural tension tests are: straight leg raise, slump test, prone knee bend and upper limb tension test.

Treatment

The aim of treatment is to increase the flexibility of a nerve in order to make the mechanics normal. *Flexibility exercises* can be performed that are the same as the neural tension tests. Particular care must be taken in painful injuries that are easily provoked. Stretches should always begin gently and gradually increase under close supervision of an experienced practitioner, such as a physiotherapist. Additional treatments can be beneficial, such as *mobilisations* for spinal joints; for example, for *neck pain (non-specific)*.

Neuromuscular electrical stimulator (NMES)

An electrical stimulation treatment that produces muscle contractions to maintain strength, minimise

atrophy during the healing process and re-educate poorly controlled muscles. It is produced in a similar way to *transcutaneous electrical nerve stimulator (TENS)*.

Neuromuscular fatigue

Feelings of tiredness caused by a temporary reduction in the activity of the *motor units* in muscles. It is an uncommon problem, and is more likely to occur during endurance activities such as *long distance running*. It may be due to a slower than usual release of the *neurotransmitter* acetylcholine by neurons from the motor nervous system, or muscle fibres may develop a decreased sensitivity to acetylcholine during *muscle contractions*.

Neuron

The cell that is the basic building block of the *nervous system*, which is responsible for much of the internal communications in the body. Also called a nerve cell, it has the ability to create and conduct an electric current.

Structure

Each neuron is made up of two parts: the cell body, and the branches that stretch out from the cell body. The classical neuron has many short spiky

Neural tension tests

Neural tension test	Nerves stretched by test	Pain and injuries that can be associated with tension in the neural sheath
Straight leg raise	Lumbar nerve roots Lumbar-sacral plexus Sciatic nerve	Leg pain Low back pain Headache
Slump test	Lumbar nerve roots Lumbar-sacral plexus Thoracic nerve roots	Thoracic pain Back of knee pain Hamstring (back thigh muscle) pain
Prone knee bend	Femoral nerve Third lumbar nerve root (L3)	Quadriceps (front thigh muscle) pain
Upper limb tension test	Cervical nerve roots Brachial plexus Thoracic pain Headache	Tennis elbow Neck pain

branches, called dendrites, located on one side of the cell body. A dendrite receives an electric current from other neurons and passes it on to the cell body.

Coming out of the other side of the cell body is a long single branch called a nerve fibre or axon. The longest branch in the body runs from the brain down to the end of the big toe. Nerve cell bodies are only found in the *brain*, *spinal cord* and *ganglions*. Nerve fibres go to all parts of the body. A bundle of thousands of nerve fibres is a *nerve*. The end of a nerve fibre is the axon terminal.

Physiology

An inactive neuron has an electric charge of –70 microvolts (mV). It is created by a sodium-potassium pump in the membrane (wall), which pumps a high concentration of potassium ions (K+) into the cell, while the outside of the cell has a high concentration of sodium ions (Na+).

A stimulated neuron causes the sodium-potassium pump to let in a rush of Na+ ions and push the electric charge above +30 mV, triggering an electric current that is sent down the nerve fibre (axon). In nerve fibres wrapped in highly conductive myelin sheath, the electric current can travel at speeds of up to 100 m (330 ft) a second, taking 0.02 seconds from the brain to the foot. Nerve fibres without myelin are up to 50 times slower.

A *neurotransmitter* is released when an electric current reaches the axon terminal, which moves across a gap called a synapse and attaches to the wall of another neuron or a nearby cell such as a muscle fibre to cause a *muscle contraction*.

Neuropraxia

See *Nerve injury*.

Neurotransmitter

A chemical substance that enables a *neuron* (nerve cell) to communicate with another cell at the end of its nerve fibre, such as another neuron, a muscle fibre or gland cell.

The gap between the end of a nerve fibre and another cell is called a synapse. When an electric current reaches the end of a nerve fibre (also called an axon terminal), the release of a neurotransmitter is triggered off, which moves across the synapse and attaches to the wall of the other cell. If the cell across the synapse is a muscle fibre, the effect of the neurotransmitter is to trigger off a muscle contraction.

More than 50 neurotransmitters are at work in the body. They can be divided into two groups: fast-acting and slow-acting. Fast-acting neurotransmitters that are most important in sport and exercise are *adrenaline*, *noradrenaline* and *acetylcholine*. Slow-acting neurotransmitters include *endorphin* and enkephalin.

Neutral joint position

The position of a joint that is the starting point for describing subsequent movements. For example, the neutral position of the *shoulder joint* is when the arm is resting by the side of the body. It is understood as having 0 degrees of movement. Flexion movement of the shoulder joint involves lifting the arm forwards and upwards away from the neutral position. When the arm is raised fully so that the hand is above the head the shoulder joint it is described as being in a position of 180 degrees flexion.

Each *joint* in the body has a neutral position. The *anatomical position* is a starting point that is used for the whole body or regions of the body.

Nipples

A small protrusion of skin in the front of the chest. In women they are specifically located at the front end of the *breast*. The colour is usually darker than the surrounding skin. In women nipples are usually larger and contain an opening through which milk can pass during breastfeeding. They contain muscle fibres that respond to cold or rubbing stimulation to make them stand erect.

Exercise and sport

The nipples can become irritated and abraded by excessive rubbing against clothing during long distance activities, often called runner's nipples and cyclist's nipples. This injury is more common in males than females because they are less aware of the sensitivity of the tissue.

It is more likely to occur in cold weather, especially due to *wind chill* in cyclists, which causes the nipple to be more prominent and harder. It may be prevented by placing petroleum jelly or tape over the nipples, wearing a seamless bra and wind-breaking clothes over the chest.

Nitrogen narcosis

An illness that causes symptoms similar to alcohol intoxication due to nitrogen breathed in during *scuba diving* acting like an anaesthetic gas. It is most likely to occur during deep dives more than 30 m (100 ft). At this depth it is recommended to use compressed air mixed with helium rather than nitrogen.

Non-elite

Participation in a sport at a formal level where competition may involve winning prize money; however, participants do not expect to earn a living income. Amateurs are included at this level.

Non-steroidal anti-inflammatory drugs (NSAIDs)

Medications that are used to reduce inflammation. They are widely recommended in the treatment of exercise and sports-related injuries, *headache*, menstrual pain and arthritic conditions including *osteoarthritis, rheumatoid arthritis* and *gout*.

Inflammation begins when damaged cell walls release arachidonic acid, which is converted by a number of enzymes, in particular cyclo-oxygenase (COX), into prostaglandins, thromboxane and prostacyclins that act as mediators of the inflammatory response. NSAIDs interfere with the conversion of arachidonic acid to prostaglandin by inhibiting the action of cyclo-oxygenase.

Suitability

NSAIDs have been found to be extraordinarily helpful for arthritic conditions. However, despite the widespread use of NSAIDs by people who participate in exercise and sport, there are no convincing scientific research data proving their effectiveness in the treatment of *acute injury* or *overuse injury*. As a result, NSAIDs for injuries remains a topic for debate among sports medicine professionals.

Selection

Research has failed to show that one NSAID is consistently more effective than any other. At the same time, individuals can find that one NSAID is more effective for them, so a selection may require a 'hit-or-miss' approach.

Generally the choice is based on the dosage schedule and limiting the potential for side effects. Recently a new group of NSAIDs have become available, the Coxibs (COX-2 inhibitors), that appear to be associated with reduced risk of side effects.

Side effects

In general, NSAIDs are regarded as safe drugs with minimal serious side effects in the short term; however, long-term side effects are of concern, particularly *gastrointestinal bleeding*, *ulcers* and kidney disease.

The problem lies with cyclo-oxygenase (COX), which exists in two forms. Kidney and gastrointestinal cells produce COX-1, whereas COX-2 is expressed in response to an inflammatory stimulus. Most NSAIDs can't differentiate between them, and inhibit COX-1 as well as COX-2, thereby increasing the risk of the gastrointestinal and kidney side effects.

Medications called Coxibs have been developed to only inhibit COX-2 and hence reduce inflammation without inhibiting COX-1. The newest NSAIDs and enteric-coated forms of aspirin also have a considerably lower incidence of gastrointestinal

Commonly used non-steroidal anti-inflammatory drugs (NSAIDs) and Coxibs (COX-2 inhibitors)

Drug	Trade names	Usual dose (mg)	Daily doses (tablets)
Non-steroidal anti-inflammatory drugs (NSAIDs)			
Aspirin	Ecotrin, SRA, ASA	650	3–4
Diclofenac	Voltaren	25–50	2–3
Ibuprofen	Brufen, Motrin, Advil	400	3–4
	Nurofen	200	4–6
Indomethacin	Indocid, Indocin	25–50	3
Naproxen	Naprosyn, Anaprox	250–500	2
Piroxicam	Feldene	10–20	1–2
Coxibs (COX-2 inhibitors)			
Celecoxib	Celebrex	200–400	2
Rofecoxib	Vioxx	12.5–50	2

symptoms compared to aspirin, though there is individual variation in response to each drug.

In general, the risk of these side effects can be lowered by taking the minimum effective dose, taking the drug with or immediately after food or milk, or using antacids. Alcohol, cigarettes and coffee may aggravate side effects. Certain NSAIDs are available in suppository form and ointment preparations (see *Non-steroidal anti-inflammatory drugs (NSAIDs) topical*).

Other less common side effects include asthma, allergic rhinitis, rashes, tinnitus, deafness, headache and confusion. NSAIDs can also have dangerous interactions with other drugs, including *antihypertensives* and *diuretics*.

Non-steroidal anti-inflammatory drugs (NSAIDs) topical

Medications that are rubbed into the skin to reduce inflammation. They are recommended for injuries located close to the skin surface, such as *tennis elbow* and *ankle sprain*.

They are associated with reduced side effects, though not completely eliminated, compared to most *non-steroidal anti-inflammatory drugs (NSAIDs)* in pill form that are taken by mouth. They are not effec-

tive for treating large anatomical areas or deep injuries, such as a swollen knee joint and low back pain.

Commonly used medications include benzydamine (brand name, Difflam), adrenocortical extract (Movelat), indomethacin (Indo-spray, Elmetacin) and diclofenac gel (Voltaren). Application usually involves massaging the medication into the skin 2 to 3 times a day. Local skin reactions, such as irritation, erythema, pruritis, rashes, contact dermatitis and photosensitivity, may occur, though they are rare.

Noradrenaline

A chemical compound that acts as a *neurotransmitter* and *hormone* and affects specific cells throughout the body.

As a neurotransmitter it is used by the neurons of *sympathetic nervous system* to pass on communications that increase activity of organs in the body, such as instructions from the brain to make the heart beat faster. The sympathetic nervous system sends instructions to the adrenal gland in the kidneys to release noradrenaline as a hormone into the bloodstream, which increases blood pressure by narrowing the diameter of blood vessels, which is part of the 'fight or flight' response and also associated with the release of *adrenaline*. Noradrenaline is also called norepinephrine.

Nordic skiing

See *Cross-country skiing*.

Norepinephrine

See *Noradrenaline*.

Nose injuiries

See *Face pain and injuries*.

Nosebleed

Bleeding from the nose due to a sudden forceful blow that damages the rich supply of blood vessels in the nasal septum. Severe nosebleed may be a sign of septal haematoma, which causes a red, cherry-like swelling inside the nose and requires a different treatment including antibiotics.

Treatment begins with *ice* and *compression*, by applying firm pressure with the fingers on the lower nose for up to 20 minutes while sitting upright. If bleeding continues seek medical help. Nosebleed is also called epistaxis.

Numbness

The absence of feeling or sensation, caused by disruption or damage to a sensory nerve.

Disruption can occur, for example, after falling asleep on an outstretched arm, which places pressure on nerves passing through the upper arm. It is temporary and soon recovers, usually within minutes, once the pressure is released.

Damage can occur in a number of ways. A direct blow causes a *nerve injury*, which is also associated with pain and pins and needles. Numbness can last from a few hours for mild damage, and up to 6 or more weeks when damage is severe.

A *stroke* causes numbness due to permanent damage to nerves in the brain. Damage to the spinal cord due to a *spinal injury* is similar.

Nutrition

The scientific study of the amount and type of food and fluid requirements, which varies according to factors such as age, gender, state of health and physical activity levels.

Foods are made up of essential nutrients including *fats*, *carbohydrates*, *proteins*, *vitamins*, *minerals*, *fibre* and water (see *Hydration*). *Sports nutrition* is a specialised field that deals with the nutritional needs of people participating in exercise and sport.

Nutritionist

A health practitioner who has completed training that is registered and recognised as being qualified to provide diagnosis and treatment for illnesses and diseases that affect a person's *nutrition*, in particular, food and fluid intake. A nutritionist may have a specialisation in sport and exercise, called *sports nutrition*.

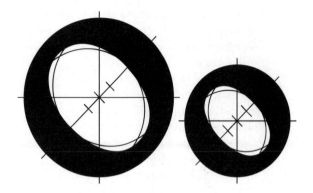

Obesity

A body weight that is excessively greater than normal for the average person of the same height and frame. Obesity occurs when the energy intake is greater than the amount of energy burned by participating in physical activity and also tends to run in families. It is defined as a *body-mass index (BMI)* greater than 30.

It is associated with an increased risk of *coronary heart disease, stroke, varicose veins, diabetes, osteoarthritis, gout* and certain types of *cancer*. The recommended treatments are the same as for people who are *overweight*, which include improvements in diet and the amount of physical activity. In severe cases medications and surgery may be recommended.

Obesity in children

A body weight that is excessive for the average child of that age, height and body shape. The main causes are a combination of genetic inheritance and a lack of participation in physical activity. It is becoming a greater problem in modern and industrialised nations.

The required treatment involves increasing the amount of physical activity, following similar recommendations for all people who are *overweight*. This is best achieved if the family participates in activities together.

The main features of a physical activity program include choosing enjoyable activities that are moderate-intensity (see *Aerobic training* and *Metabolic equivalent (MET)*), performed for up to 1 hour per day (activities can be done in 10 to 15 minute blocks). The general limitations on *children* participating in exercise and sport should also be taken into account.

Caution also should be taken in hot weather because obese children tolerate heat poorly and adapt slowly to changes of temperature, making them more vulnerable to *heat illness*. Adequate *hydration for children* during exercise in the heat is also required.

Obturator nerve entrapment

A nerve in the *groin* region compressed by swelling or scarring in the surrounding adductor muscles. In the early stages of the injury the pain is usually located in the upper groin. Later on it can spread down to the inside of the thigh. People often complain of weakness during running.

The recommended method for making a diagnosis of this *nerve entrapment* injury is to exercise to the level that reproduces the pain and conducting a physical examination afterwards to find weakness of the adductor muscles and numbness over the lower inside thigh. The diagnosis can be confirmed with a *nerve conduction test*.

The recommended treatment is surgery to release the muscle and free up the obturator nerve, followed by a gradual return to sport over 4 to 6 weeks. Treatments such as *massage* and *flexibility exercises* are generally unsuccessful.

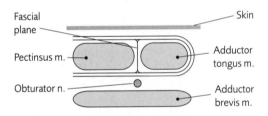

Obturator nerve entrapment caused by the nerve being compressed between adductor muscles

Oedema

An excessive accumulation of fluid in body tissue that indicates an injury or disease is present. For example, a twisted ankle causes oedema around the damaged ligament and surrounding tissue. Visible oedema is called *swelling*.

It occurs because an injury damages cells that release chemicals, which trigger off *inflammation*, a process that brings in other chemicals that encourage the nearby capillaries to widen and let in more fluids.

Oestrogen

A female sex hormone. It is essential for sexual and physical development during *puberty* and adolescence and for the normal functioning of the reproduction system and *menstruation*.

Oestrogen is mainly produced in the ovaries, and during *pregnancy* also by the placenta. Synthetic versions of oestrogen are used in *hormone replacement therapy* (HRT) and in the oral-contraceptive pill (see *Contraception*).

Oestrogen has specific effects on the body. It reduces the risk of *coronary heart disease* and *stroke* by decreasing total cholesterol and low-density lipoproteins (LDL) and increasing high-density lipoproteins (HDL), and protects against *osteoporosis* by increasing mineral uptake in bones.

It also increases the deposits of fat in the breasts, buttocks and thighs and increases the storage of carbohydrates as *glycogen* in muscles and liver, which is beneficial for *ultra long distance sports*.

Older athlete

An older aged person participating in exercise and sport. Older athletes can participate in almost all the same sports and according to the same rules as younger athletes. Increasing numbers of older aged people are doing so.

A *medical clearance* is recommended for older aged people who have had a history of illness, such as *coronary heart disease*, or who are planning to start participating in exercise or sport that requires a greater effort than the equivalent of brisk walking.

Physiology

While many fit and trained older athletes can perform as well as younger competitors, the average older athlete exhibits a slow deterioration in physical abilities and performance levels, usually beginning between 30 and 40 years. For example, world record times for the 100 m sprint according to age decline by 1 second every decade (though the fastest 50-year-old still beats most 30-year-olds).

Older-aged athletes waiting for the start of a running event

The deterioration observed in people who are inactive is even larger due to disuse. Notably, an unfit older person who starts training can achieve the same amount of improvement and at the same rate as a younger person.

Muscles

Muscle *strength* and size decrease from the age of 30. The rate of decrease is faster after the age of 60, and even faster when unfit and untrained. The average 30-year-old doing strength training is about 30 per cent stronger than the average strength-trained 80-year-old.

Reduced muscle size is predominantly due to possessing fewer *muscle fibres* rather than a decrease in the size of each fibre caused by decreased protein synthesis. It particularly affects the proportion of *fast-twitch (FT) muscle fibres*, which are responsible for sudden bursts of muscle activity, such as swinging a golf club.

In addition, the proportion of body fat increases as people get older. Combined with less muscle strength, this can make it harder for an older participant in exercise and sport to perform physical activities and daily activities. For example, the average 30 year old standing up from a chair only needs to use 50–60 per cent of the strength of the quadriceps (front thigh muscle). The strength required by the average 90-year-old is 95 per cent. An illness or injury could cause a 90-year-old an additional loss of strength and make it impossible to rise up from a chair.

The response to *strength training* is the same in older and younger people. Strength gains are achieved in the same amount and at the same rate, albeit from a lower level for the average older person.

Bone

Bone mass and bone density decreases slowly from a peak reached between 20 and 30 years. The rate of decrease is influenced by the amount of activity performed and hormone levels. The spine is particularly affected around menopause in women. Men are also affected, though at two-thirds the rate of women. Too little activity is associated with an increased risk of *osteoporosis*.

Aerobic fitness

The decline in aerobic fitness begins from around the age of 20. It is due to changes in the heart, blood vessels and lungs. The maximum *heart rate* that can be achieved declines by 1 beat per year. *Stroke volume* declines with age. The combined effect is that the average older athlete has 20 per cent less maximum *cardiac output* compared to the younger adults. Respiratory capacity declines due to reduced resting volume of the lungs and decreased lung compliance and joint mobility.

Aerobic training produces similar gains in the older and younger athlete. The improvements in the older athlete are due to increased efficiency of the aerobic metabolism in the muscles, such as *carbohydrate oxidation*.

Nerves

The speed of nerve conduction slowly decreases with age making older athletes slower in their responses to physical activities, such as preventing a fall when losing balance.

Temperature regulation

The older athlete faces a greater risk of developing *heat illness* due to a reduced sweating capacity and tendency to respond less to thirst and subsequently drink less. It is recommended to drink 500–600 mL (17–20 fl oz) of fluid one to two hours before activity and 10 to 15 minutes beforehand and during activity, 120–150 mL (4–5 fl oz) every 20 minutes.

Olecranon bursitis

Inflammation of the olecranon bursa, a flattened sac filled with synovial fluid beneath the skin surface at the back of the elbow.

The *bursitis* is most commonly seen in *basketball* players who frequently fall on the elbow after 'taking a charge', and people who rest the elbow on a desk for long periods, known as 'student's elbow'. Treatment includes *non-steroidal anti-inflammatories (NSAIDs)*, *rest* and firm *compression*. If these fail, *aspiration* and *corticosteroid* injection are recommended.

Olecranon fracture

A break of the point of the elbow at the upper end of the ulnar (inner forearm bone). It is usually due to a fall onto an outstretched hand or a direct blow to the elbow.

If the *fracture* is not displaced and stable, the recommended treatment is a splint (a form of *immobilisation* called protected mobilisation) for 3 to 6 weeks. More often it is displaced and unstable, which requires *open surgery* and *internal fixation* with metal wires. Return to sport can occur after 6 to 8 weeks.

Oligomenorrhea

See *Amenorrhea*.

Olympic-type weight lifting

A type of *strength training* that aims to increase muscle power in order to improve performance in a wide range of other sports such as football and golf.

Olympic-type weight-lifting includes the power clean, snatch, and clean and jerk. It uses a greater number of muscles than simple lifting of weights such as a bench press. However, the risk of injury is

higher and participants must be taught the correct technique. A weight belt can be worn to prevent *low back pain and injuries*.

Omega fatty acids (3 and 6)

See *Polyunsaturated fats*.

Onychocryptosis

See *Ingrown toenail*.

Open chain exercise

See *Closed chain exercise*.

Open fracture

An acute injury that causes a piece of broken bone to stick out through the skin. The recommended treatment for this *fracture* is to clean and cover the exposed bone and open wound using sterile dressings soaked in saline or antiseptic solution. The protruding bone should not be pushed back into the wound. However, a splint should be applied to the injured limb, followed by transport to a hospital as quickly as possible.

Open surgery

A surgical procedure that involves cutting open the skin to get inside the body. General anaesthesia is usually required, followed by an extended period of recovery of weeks or months. Examples include *joint replacement* surgery for severe hip osteoarthritis, inserting metal to hold together a bone fracture, called *internal fixation*, and coronary bypass surgery of the heart.

It has become less common as methods of endoscopy, which involve inserting a fibre-optic telescope into the body such as *arthroscopy*, have been

293

more widely developed and applied over the last few decades.

The disadvantage of open surgery is an increased risk of complications such as infection, and recovery is slower than arthroscopy. *Sport rehabilitation* and return to sport treatments are essential for a healthy recovery following open surgery.

Opposition

An active movement of the thumb that mainly involves rotation to touch the tip of any one of the fingers. It allows the hand to grip large objects such as a racquet or bat handle, down to small objects such as picking up a needle (see *Hand and finger joints*). Anthropologists suggest that opposable thumbs made a significant contribution to the evolution of human beings, in particular, technological advancements over other animals.

Optimal weight

A weight that enables athletes to perform at their best. This weight varies according to the sport played and, where relevant, the position in that sport. The best weight is one based on *relative body fat*, which is the proportion of fat in the athlete's body.

It can be measured using a *skin fold test*. Women tend to have a higher measure than men. For example, for tennis the optimal weight for men is 6–14 per cent relative body fat and for women it is 10–20 per cent.

Oral-contraceptive pill

See *Contraception*.

Orbit blow-out fracture

A break in the bone behind the eyeball due to a sudden forceful blow such as that produced by a fist, cricket ball, baseball or squash ball (see Head).

It can cause a protruding or sunken eye, double vision on upward gaze and numbness of the cheek. The diagnosis of this *fracture* is confirmed with an *X-ray* and *CT scan*. The recommended treatment is to immediately take antibiotics, followed by *immobilisation* or surgery in some cases.

Organs

A large collection of different types of *cells* and *tissues* that form a distinct structure performing a specific set of functions. For example, the *heart* is made up of muscle, blood vessels, connective tissue and nerves. Its main function is pumping blood around the body.

Orthopaedic surgeon

A doctor who has received an additional medical degree that is recognised as a specialisation to perform surgery and other treatments for injuries and disease affecting the bones, joints, tendons and muscles of the body. Many orthopaedic surgeons provide services primarily for people participating in exercise and sport, and specialise in one area of the body, such as knee surgery.

Orthotic

A solid object used to correct an abnormality in the structure of the body or the manner in which movement is performed. For example, an orthotic can be used to correct a *leg length discrepancy* for a leg that is shorter than the other leg, or be placed inside a shoe to reduce excessive *foot pronation* (inward rotation) movement.

An orthotic is most commonly produced by an orthotist as well as *podiatrists*, *physiotherapists* and occupational therapists. They are usually used together with other treatments to correct a biomechanical abnormality.

Types of orthotics

NON-CASTED

A non-casted orthotic is made of rubber, cork or plasterzote. It is usually used to treat a *biomechanical abnormality* in the foot. For example, a wedge of rubber can be adhered to the inside sole of the shoe.

The disadvantage of this type is a relatively reduced rate of correcting an abnormality and poor durability. On the other hand, they are extremely easy to produce and cheap, which makes them useful for giving an indication of whether or not a more effective and durable, rigid or semi-rigid casted orthotic may be helpful.

Casted

This type of orthotic is made of a polyethylene or polypropylene plastic material that is constructed from a plaster cast of the patient's foot or body part in a *neutral joint position*. The labour and material is relatively more costly; however, it is more effective and longer lasting.

Orthotist

A health practitioner who has been trained to produce *orthotics* (also see *Podiatrist*).

Osgood-Schlatter disease

An overuse injury in children and adolescents (10- to 15-year-olds) at the site where the large patellar tendon attaches to a bony protrusion at the upper end of the large, front shin bone (tibia), called the tibial tuberosity below the knee joint (see *Shin*).

The injury is an inflammation of the growing bone, called an *apophysitis*, which is due to an accumulation of repeated, excessive physical loads over a period of weeks or months that leads to pain located just below the kneecap.

It is a self-limiting condition that settles spontaneously after several months. Participation in sport should be guided by the amount of pain caused by activity. The main treatment is *ice* and *rest* from the aggravating activity if the injury is moderate or severe,

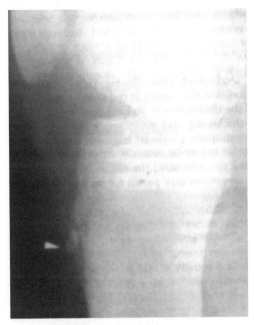

X-ray of Osgood-Schlatter's disease

which usually achieves significant improvement in 1 to 3 weeks. Additional treatments include *massage, flexibility, strengthening exercises* and *hydrotherapy*.

Ossification

The physiological process that results in *bone* growth. It involves converting soft hyaline cartilage cells into cells called osteoblasts that encourage the deposit of calcium and phosphate deposits, which produce hard and rigid bone.

Ossification begins in the embryo at the age of 7 or 8 weeks where each bone in the immature hyaline cartilage skeleton forms a primary centre called a diaphysis. By birth at least one secondary centre of ossification, called the *epiphysis*, also develops in each of the long bones.

During the growing years of infancy, childhood, puberty and adolescence bone tissue gradually replaces the hyaline cartilage and the bones increase in size. In the long bones the diaphysis and epiphysis eventually grow and spread out to fuse together, which signifies the end bone growth in *adolescents*.

A bone that has suffered a *fracture* is repaired through ossification.

Osteitis pubis

An inflammation of the pubic bone and pubic symphysis that causes pain in the groin. It is an *overuse injury* that causes pain that gradually builds up over a period of weeks or months. This injury used to be called pubic symphysitis.

Causes and diagnosis
The exact causes are still not fully understood. It may be that not treating other injuries such as *adductor tendinosis* and *obturator nerve entrapment* eventually causes them to develop into osteitis pubis.

The injury is associated with repeated excessive force on the pubic symphysis at the front of the *pelvis*, caused by repeated participation in activities that involve, for example, twisting and turning while running and kicking.

Pain is usually felt in both groins, though it can be centred in the lower abdomen or inguinal regions. A physical examination usually finds that the pain can be reproduced with tests such as passive movement of hip joint abduction (moving the thigh away

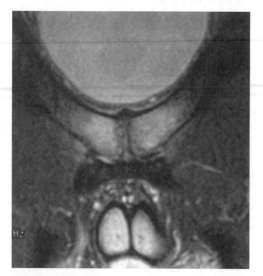

MRI of osteitis pubis

from the other leg), resisted adductor muscle contraction and adductor muscle squeeze test.

The radiological investigation most likely to detect osteitis pubis is *magnetic resonance imaging (MRI)*. A *CT scan* is also recommended for chronic osteitis pubis.

Treatment and return to sport
The recommended treatments begin with relative rest, which is reduced activity, not complete *rest*. The level of reduction depends on the severity of the pain. For example, if the adductor squeeze test is painless prior to and after exercise, then the activity level is correct and can be gradually increased using this test as a guide.

Massage of the adductor muscles, *mobilisation* of the low back joints and *neural tension* stretching are also recommended. *Non-steroidal anti-inflammatory drugs (NSAIDs)* may provide some pain relief. Recent experience shows that *lumbo-pelvic instability* treatments can have a dramatic, positive effect.

A full return to sport can be made after 4 to 6 months following the above treatments. Surgery is usually not recommended, except for some chronic cases.

Osteoarthritis

A disease of a *synovial joint* caused by wear and tear over a number of years, usually decades. It leads to degenerative changes of the articular cartilage, joint capsule and ligaments.

The symptoms include inflammation, swelling, pain, morning stiffness, creaking sensations, loss of flexibility and range of movement, and muscle weakness. The disease is most likely to cause *hip osteoarthritis* and *knee osteoarthritis*, as well as osteoarthritis of the neck joints and low back joints.

Causes
The risk increases with age, though it is not confined to older people and can be experienced by the younger aged (less than 45 years old). Other factors that increase the risk include *obesity*, being *overweight* and injuries to joints, especially when the rehabilitation has been inadequate, or there has been

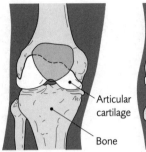 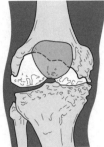

Healthy synovial joint

Degenerative changes of articular cartilage, with associated bone spurs

Osteoarthritis

damage to the shock absorbing components of a joint, such as the articular cartilage, sub-chondral bone and meniscus.

However, as long as there has been no injury, participating in high-impact and high-loading sports over a long period of time, such as in long distance running, does not increase the risk.

Diagnosis

The diagnosis is mainly based on the *history*, including the activities that cause the pain and *physical examination*, particularly joint movements. An *X-ray* can be misleading. Many people have joint degenerative changes but never experience symptoms.

Treatment

Regular participation in physical activities, such as exercise and sport, is essential to reduce pain and muscle weakness and increase joint *flexibility* and aerobic fitness. The key is being active at a level that does not aggravate the disease.

This requires checking the joint to determine whether it is in an acute, sub-acute or post-acute phase. If the disease degenerates and causes pain that is persistently severe surgery should be considered, such as *hip joint replacement* and *knee joint replacement*.

ACUTE PHASE

There is joint *inflammation* causing constant pain, difficulty performing movement and activities, and possibly *swelling*, redness and heat.

The recommended treatments include *non-steroidal anti-inflammatory drugs (NSAIDs)*, *corticosteroid* injection, *passive exercises* and gentle *mobilisations* by a physiotherapist.

SUB-ACUTE PHASE

There are the first signs of decreasing inflammation and intermittent periods of being pain-free. *Active exercises*, such as one set of five to seven repetitions daily, gradually increasing to several sets of 10 repetitions, and gentle *flexibility exercises* also can be introduced.

POST-ACUTE PHASE

The inflammation has mostly cleared; however, reduced range of movement and weakness may remain. Strengthening should begin with *isometric strengthening* exercises, which are muscle contractions without moving the joint, performed for 3 to 6 seconds with a 20-second rest period, three times a day. As the muscle gets stronger the contraction time should be gradually increased to 30 seconds.

Strengthening exercises with isotonic contractions, which are muscle contractions that result in joint movement, should begin next, with low *overload* and through a small range of movement.

Hydrotherapy and stationary cycling with low pedal resistance are frequently recommended forms of gentle isotonic exercise. Strengthening can later progress to activities such as *swimming*, *walking* and *Tai Chi*. A reasonable starting dosage for walking is 10 to 15 minutes on every second day.

MAINTENANCE

Hyaluronic acid, a lubricating substance that is injected into the joint, may achieve significant improvement and reduce the chances of subsequent inflammation.

For physical activity, a reasonable long-term goal is moderate-intensity activity such as brisk walking (see *Aerobic training* and *Metabolic equivalent (MET)*) for 30 minutes a day on most, preferably all, days of the week.

Unfit people may require up to 12 months to reach their best level of physical activity, while the more fit may only require 3 to 4 months. In general, participation in exercise or sport is usually less likely to cause aggravation in the morning hours when the joint is less sensitive.

Other forms of exercise and sports that can be safely recommended include *golf*, recreational *swimming*, stationary and recreational bicycling, *bowls* and aquarobics (see *Aerobics*).

Osteochondrosis

A softening of bone that makes it vulnerable to being deformed or separated from the main body of the bone. It mostly occurs in children and adolescents, though it can be found in people in their twenties and thirties. The exact cause of this overuse injury is often unknown, though it is believed to be due to a problem with the blood supply associated with excessive forces experienced during an aggravating activity.

Osteochondrosis is usually located in the *epiphysis* (the growing bone at the end of a long bone), or within a short bone such as a vertebra of the spine. A similar injury that affects growing bone that has a large strong tendon attached is called an *apophysitis*.

Osteochondrum

See *Articular cartilage*.

Osteoid osteoma

A benign cancer of a bone that is usually non-fatal and causes exercise-related bone pain and tenderness.

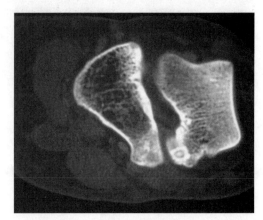

X-ray of osteoid osteoma of talus (ankle bone)

It is not infrequently misdiagnosed as a stress fracture, because the results of the radiological investigation of a *bone scan* are similar. This tumour usually causes pain during the night, which can be relieved with *aspirin*. Surgery is the preferred treatment.

Osteolysis of the clavicle

Weakening and loss of density of the collarbone at the end that is closest to the *shoulder joint*. It is most commonly found in people who do *strength training*, particularly large numbers of bench presses or push-ups.

It causes a dull ache in the acromioclavicular (AC) joint that tends to be worse at the beginning of exercise. The loss of density is a type of *osteoporosis* and is seen clearly on an X-ray. *Rest* from the aggra-

List of types of osteochondrosis

Type	Condition	Site
Joint	• Perthes' disease	• Femoral head (hip joint)
	• Kienbock's disease	• Lunate (wrist)
	• Kohler's disease	• Navicular (foot)
	• Freiberg's disease	• Second metatarsal (foot)
	• Osteochondritis dissecans	• Medial femoral condyle (knee)
		• Talar dome (ankle)
	• Little Leaguer's elbow	• Humerus capitellum (elbow)
Other	• Scheuermann's disease	• Thoracic spine (middle back)
	• Blount's disease	• Tibia (shin bone)

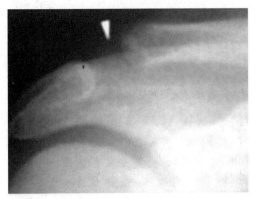

X-ray of osteolysis of the outer end of the clavicle (collarbone)

vating activities usually clears the pain. If it fails surgery may be required to remove the thinned bone, which achieves good results. This injury is also called clavicle osteolysis.

Osteomyelitis

A bacterial infection of a bone, usually by staphylococcus aureus. It is more common in children than adults. Symptoms include *fever*, severe bone pain and tenderness when pressed firmly with the fingers and *swelling*. Treatment begins with *antibiotics* and, if this fails, surgery to remove the infection and clean the bone.

Osteopath

A health practitioner who has completed training and is recognised as being qualified to provide a diagnosis and treatment for injuries, illness and disease according to the osteopathic method.

Dr Andrew Taylor Still founded osteopathy in 1892 in Missouri, USA, after concluding that the conventional medicine of his day was inadequate. Osteopathy is based on a number of principles, in particular that mechanical dysfunctions of the body can disturb fluid flow, especially in the veins and lymphatic system, leading to problems in the joints, muscles and bones.

Specific osteopathic treatment techniques that are commonly used include *manipulation, massage, muscle energy techniques* and craniospinal fluid therapy. Osteopaths in the USA can prescribe medications.

Osteoporosis

Weakening of the bones caused by excessive loss of bone mineral. It is due to the osteoclasts, cells that remove calcium from *bone*, winning out over the osteoblasts, the cells that encourage new bone formation.

Calcium loss begins at the start of adulthood and then accelerates in later years in women during *menopause* when levels of oestrogen (a hormone that maintains bone mass) drop dramatically. Men are less commonly affected, because the hormone testosterone usually drops gradually with age. It is also

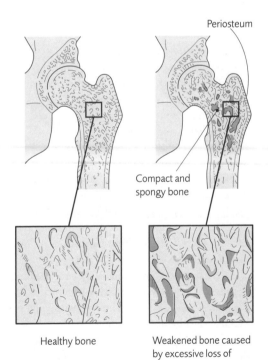

Periosteum

Compact and spongy bone

Healthy bone

Weakened bone caused by excessive loss of bone mineral

Osteoporosis

more common in smokers, *wheelchair athletes* and people with emphysema and chronic bronchitis.

When osteoporosis is associated with *disordered eating* that also leads to *amenorrhea* (absence of menstrual periods), it is a syndrome called *female athlete triad*.

Diagnosis

Osteoporosis may not cause symptoms for years. Pain can be the first symptom, often located in the low back. In other cases a normally non-traumatic fall may cause a fracture in the weakened bone, such as a *Colles fracture* (wrist) or a fracture of the femur (thigh bone) near the hip joint. The diagnosis is based on the symptoms and radiological investigations including *X-rays* and dual energy X-ray absorptiometry (DXA scan), which is the most accurate measurement of bone mineral density.

Treatment

The lost calcium can't be replaced; however, the rate of loss can be slowed down. Treatments include regular participation in exercise and sport, *hormone replacement therapy (HRT)* for post-menopausal women to increase the amount of oestrogen (which has potential side effects, including a small increase in breast cancer risk), a diet rich in *calcium* including dairy products, citrus fruits and green leafy vegetables, and in some cases, calcium supplements.

Exercise and sport

Physical activity for osteoporosis should include a combination of *aerobic training* and *strength training* for both the arms and the legs. Aerobic training involves activities such as walking, cycling, swimming, aquarobics and *aerobics*, where the aim is to do at least moderate-intensity activities for 30 minutes on most days of the week.

Strength training involves activities such as lifting weights, sit ups, push ups or even just practising standing from a seated position. The *overload* should be kept light; for example, performing sets of 8 to 16 repetitions with a weight no more than 80 per cent of the maximum weight that can be moved in one full movement, called a one *repetition maximum (RM)*, and not working to excessive fatigue with each set.

Osteosarcoma

A malignant cancer of the bone, which is usually located in the end of one of the *long bones*. It is more commonly found in the legs, such as in the femur (thigh bone) that causes pain in the front of the *thigh*. It is more common in children and adolescents than adults.

The cancer may be diagnosed with an X-ray, which reveals a moth-eaten appearance. It can send metastases (cancer cells) to other parts of the body, such as the breast, lung and prostate, and often becomes progressively worse leading to death.

Osteotomy

A surgical procedure that involves cutting out a piece of bone to change its length or restore a joint to its correct position. For example, a deformity called *hallux valgus* where the first toe, instead of pointing straight forward, is bent in a fixed position that presses up against the second toe. A wedge of bone is cut out to enable the bone to be straightened.

Osteotomy may be done when pain is severe or disabling, or when a deformity causes associated problems such as *leg length discrepancy* due to a shortened femur (thigh bone) that places excessive stress on the low back. The bone needs to heal after surgery, much like a bone fracture. Full recovery can take months or even a year.

Outcome and process

The outcome is the end result of a competitive activity, such as kicking a goal from a penalty in soccer or scoring a three-pointer in basketball. While the outcome can make all the difference between a win and loss, it is not the be all and end all of competition. The process that leads to the outcome is just as, if not more, important. It is said that if you take care of the process, then the outcome will take care of itself.

For example, a soccer penalty can be kicked perfectly each time, but come up with two different results. That is because the result, a goal or not a goal, is also dependent on other factors. In this case, the ability and luck of the goalkeeper, who may pull off a miraculous save and prevent a goal. Players should know that if they have kicked the ball perfectly then they have done the best they can do.

Overconfidence

An excessive expectation of success that is beyond one's level of competence to perform. In exercise and sport it can lead to a lack of preparation for an upcoming competition or game, such as failing to improve physical skills or fitness, or underestimating the strengths of the opposition. It is usually based on real past experiences, such as when the top-placed team plays the bottom-placed team.

Overload

A level and amount of training that results in an improvement in fitness, strength or skills. For example, the weight of a dumbbell must be sufficiently heavy and lifted the correct number of times to increase muscle strength. In particular, it has to be enough to cause fatigue.

Volume of training
Defined as the amount of time spent doing a specific activity during a training session. For example, it can be measured in minutes such as a 30-minute brisk walk or lifting a dumbbell for three sets of 10 repetitions = 30 repetitions. Increasing the volume would involve walking 40 minutes or lifting a dumbbell for three sets of 12 repetitions = 36 repetitions.

Intensity of training
Defined as the effort to perform a specific aspect of an activity. For instance, the speed of running can determine intensity. Running fast is more intense than slow running. Running uphill is more intense than running along the flat ground. Increasing the weight of a dumbbell from 5 kg to 8 kg (or 10 to 15 lb) is an increase in intensity.

The intensity of an activity varies from person to person according to fitness. For example, someone who is unfit will find that running fast is a high intensity activity whereas a fit person will find that it is low to moderate intensity.

The measures of intensity of a physical activity for *aerobic training* are:

- Low-intensity is equivalent to breathing exertion ranging from 'no effect on breathing' up to the point that 'shortness of breath is noticed' = 30–49 per cent of VO_2 max = 35–59 per cent of *maximum heart rate estimation* $(220 - age)$ = 11 on the *Borg perceived exertion scale*.
- Moderate-intensity is equivalent to a range from 'shortness of breath is noticed' up to 'the point that whistling or normal continuous conversation is just possible' = 50–74 per cent of VO_2 max = 60–79 per cent of maximum heart rate estimation = 13 on the Borg perceived exertion scale.
- High-intensity is a range from the point that 'whistling or normal continuous conversation is just possible' up to the point that 'whistling or normal continuous conversation is impossible' = 75-84 per cent of VO_2 max = 80–89 per cent of maximum heart rate estimation = 15 on the Borg perceived exertion scale.

Progressive overload involves gradually increasing a load during a training program as improvements are achieved. This is done to ensure that the training is consistently performed at the correct overload.

Generally it is recommended that increases in volume precede increases in intensity. It also should be noted that increasing the load too much and too quickly raises the risk of suffering an injury or other health problems, such as *overtraining syndrome*.

Overreaching

Temporary symptoms including *tiredness*, fatigue, decreased performance, feelings of depression and altered moods, which is resolved with three days of rest and long, undisturbed sleeps. It is regarded as a milder form of *overtraining syndrome*.

Overtraining syndrome

An illness of the nervous system and endocrine (hormone) system due to excessive training and insufficient recovery time. The main symptoms are persistent or abnormal tiredness and poor performance, which is not relieved with three days of rest.

It is most likely to occur in elite sportspeople involved in high-intensity training (see *Overload*); amateur and recreational athletes in sports such as *triathlon*, where extensive training is required in running, swimming and cycling; and people who train without a coach or training group and do not set appropriate training programs. The illness gradually accumulates over a period of weeks or months. It may be preceded by a milder form called *overreaching*.

Diagnosis

There is no test for overtraining syndrome. The diagnosis is based on the symptoms and excluding other known causes of persistent tiredness (see *Tiredness*).

Persistent tiredness and poor performance may be accompanied by one or more of the following: muscle soreness, psychological signs such as appetite loss, sleep disturbance, irritability, *depression*, feelings of increased *stress*, increased risk of overuse injuries, and frequent *common cold*, *flu* and upper respiratory tract infections.

A physical examination and tests may also find loss of body mass, cardiovascular changes such as increased early morning *heart rate* or resting *blood pressure*, and hormonal changes.

Treatment

The primary focus of treatment is to restore the balance between activity and recovery. This involves training at lower levels of intensity (see *Aerobic training*), training for less time at each session and having proper breaks in between sessions.

The return to normal training levels is based on improvement of symptoms and may take weeks or months. Progress can be measured using a training diary that records feelings of stress, fatigue, muscle soreness, quality of sleep and irritability. Medications, such as *antidepressants*, and psychological counselling may be recommended. Maintaining a healthy nutritional intake and adequate *hydration* is also essential.

Prevention

Periodisation, which involves dividing a program into three stages with the aim of building up to peak levels of fitness and performance, is the best method of achieving the correct balance between training and recovery. Training with a coach or training group can provide this type of appropriate training program. Another key factor of prevention is recognising early symptoms such as overreaching.

Overuse injury

An injury that develops gradually due to an accumulation of excessive forces that cause microtrauma. In the early stages the microtrauma only causes minor pain and stiffness and does not prevent activity. But later on, either gradually or following a sudden excessive force, it can become painful enough to seek medical care.

Diagnosis

Making a diagnosis requires taking a comprehensive *history* of when the pain started, the nature and site of the pain, training, technique and biomechanics, followed by a thorough *physical examination* and relevant tests and investigations.

Overuse injuries of bones and the periosteum include *stress fracture, osteitis pubis, periostitis, apophysitis, osteochondrosis* and *avascular necrosis*.

Chronic compartment syndrome, fibrosis, tendinosis, tendinitis and *paratenonitis* are overuse injuries of muscles and tendons.

Other overuse injuries include *bursitis*, skin *blisters, nerve entrapment* and *complex regional pain syndrome (CRPS)*. In most cases a *sprain* is an acute injury, except for injuries such as an *elbow medial collateral ligament sprain*, which can be both.

The common signs and symptoms are: pain associated with an aggravating activity, though it may not appear until the next morning in some cases; tenderness when pressure is applied to the correct location of the injury; swelling and warmth over the area in some cases; a crackling sound during movement may be associated with a tendon overuse injury; and pins and needles and numbness with a nerve overuse injury.

It is essential for the treatment and future prevention to identify the causes of the overuse injury during the diagnosis. Causes may be grouped into: extrinsic factors, such as the amount and type of training, running surface, shoes, equipment and environmental conditions; and intrinsic factors associated with a *biomechanical abnormality* such as malalignment, leg length discrepancy, muscle imbalance, muscle weakness and lack of flexibility.

Treatment

Treatments include relative *rest*, which means only doing activities that don't aggravate the injury, *ice*, various electrotherapy treatments such as *interferential therapy* and *ultrasound therapy*, soft tissue techniques such as *massage*, and medications such as *non-steroidal anti-inflammatory drugs (NSAIDs)*.

Treatments for the causes can include correction of a biomechanical abnormality, improving playing technique, *motor re-education* for a muscle imbalance, selection of correct *shoes* and running *surface*, planning a training program with the appropriate *overload* in terms of volume and intensity, *flexibility exercises* for tight structures, *strengthening exercises* for weakness, *orthotics* for leg length discrepancy and more.

Overweight

A body weight that is greater than normal for the average person of the same height and frame. The main health concerns of being overweight are an increased risk of developing *coronary heart disease*, *stroke*, *diabetes*, *osteoarthritis* and certain types of *cancer*.

Definition

There are a number of definitions of being overweight. The standard measure is the *height–weight chart*. This method is still useful for most men and women aged above 18 years, but is not as accurate as body-mass index (BMI), waist-hip ratio and waist size.

Factors associated with overuse injuries

Extrinsic factors	Intrinsic factors
Training errors	**Malignment**
• Excessive volume	• Pes planus
• Excessive intensity	• Pes cavus
• Rapid increase	• Rearfoot varus
• Sudden change in type	• Tibia vara
• Excessive fatigue	• Genu valgum
• Inadequate recovery	• Genu varum
• Faulty technique	• Patella alta
	• Femoral neck anteversion
Surfaces	
• Hard	
• Soft	
• Cambered	
Shoes	
• Inappropriate	
• Worn out	
Equipment	**Leg length discrepancy**
• Inappropriate	
Muscle imbalance	
Environmental conditions	**Muscle weakness**
• Hot	
• Cold	
• Humid	
Psychological factors	**Lack of flexibility**
	• Generalised muscle tightness
	• Focal areas of muscle thickening
	• Restricted joint range of motion
Sex, size, body composition	**Other**
	• Genetic factors
	• Hormonal factors
	• Metabolic conditions

Body-mass index (BMI) takes into account the proportion of the body weight that is made up of body fat, which is considered a risk for coronary heart disease and stroke.

Waist size and *waist–hip ratio* are methods that include body fat, but also where it is located in the body. The benefits of this measure include taking into account that people doing strength training have much less fat and more muscle on their body. In addition, body fat distributed around the abdomen is considered high risk for coronary heart disease and stroke, whereas fat around the hips is not. Abdominal fat is absorbed into the walls of the heart's arteries, which form 'plaques' and cause narrowing or a blockage that reduce the flow of blood to the heart. As a result, an apple-shaped body, indicating a big gut, is less healthy than a pear-shaped body.

Weight loss

The recommended ways to lose weight involve regular participation in physical activity and eating a healthy diet.

PHYSICAL ACTIVITY

The main aim of participating in physical activity is to reduce the amount of fat in the body. *Carbohydrates* are the main supply of energy in people participating in high-intensity exercise and sport.

However, *fat* is the preferred energy supply for people participating in moderate-intensity activity such as brisk walking. Therefore the recommendation for weight loss is to participate in moderate-intensity activities (see *Exercise for health*).

Measures of intensity of a physical activity are:

- Low-intensity is equivalent to breathing exertion ranging from 'no effect on breathing' up to the point that 'shortness of breath is noticed' = 30–49 per cent of VO_2 max = 35–59 per cent of *maximum heart rate estimation* $(220 - age) = 11$ on the *Borg perceived exertion scale*.
- Moderate-intensity is equivalent to a range from 'shortness of breath is noticed' up to 'the point that whistling or normal continuous conversation is just possible' = 50–74 per cent of VO_2 max = 60–79 per cent of maximum heart rate estimation = 13 on the Borg perceived exertion scale.
- High-intensity is a range from the point that 'whistling or normal continuous conversation is just possible' up to the point that 'whistling or normal continuous conversation is impossible' = 75–84 per cent of VO_2 max = 80–89 per cent of maximum heart rate estimation = 15 on the Borg perceived exertion scale.

DIET

The recommendations for a weight loss diet are for all adults to eat 30–40 g of *fat* a day, which should be about 25 per cent of total energy intake. Combined with regular participation in physical activity, weight loss should be about 0.5–1.0 kg (1–2 lb) a week, which equals 13–26 kg (28.5–57 lb) in 6 months. See also *Diet for good health* and *Fat-loss diet*.

Oxidative capacity

The maximal capacity of a muscle to use oxygen during the *aerobic metabolism* of carbohydrates and fats. It is determined by a number of factors, including the proportion of *slow-twitch (ST) muscle fibres* and, of course, the supply of oxygen. The latter depends on the amount of oxygen carried by the blood to the muscles and the local conditions that influence the tendency of the haemoglobin in the blood to release the oxygen.

Oxidative system

The metabolic systems that use oxygen to produce adenosine triphosphate (ATP), the main source of energy for muscle contractions. The systems include *carbohydrate oxidation, fat metabolism* and *protein oxidation*. In general they are more efficient at producing ATP compared to anaerobic metabolism, which does not use oxygen. Carbohydrate oxidation is the most efficient of them all.

Oxygen

An atmospheric gas that is essential for life. In humans it is breathed in through the nose and mouth, down into the lungs, where it is absorbed into the blood and attaches to red blood cells that carry it around the body to the cells. In the cells it is used in the *aerobic metabolism* of foods, mainly carbohydrates and fats, to release the energy contained in them. Oxygen does not have a colour or smell. It makes up 21 per cent of the earth's atmosphere.

Oxygen poisoning

An illness caused by excessively high levels of oxygen in the blood. It may occur when breathing in compressed air during *scuba diving*. Symptoms include visual disturbances, shortness of breath and *seizures*.

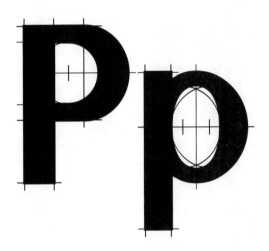

Pain

An unpleasant sensation or feeling that is usually a sign that a tissue or organ in the body has been damaged. It is mostly caused when the *neuron* (nerve cell) endings that sense pain are stimulated and send signals to the brain.

Pain nerve-cell endings, called nociceptors, are found throughout the body, including bone, joint capsule, ligaments, muscle, tendon, fascia, bursa, neural sheath and skin. Articular cartilage and the brain don't have nociceptors. Many of the other organs are poorly supplied.

Different nociceptors perceive specific types of pain, including pressure, stretching, cutting, prickling, heat and cold. An injury causes inflammation, including the release of chemicals called *prostaglandins* that stimulate nociceptors.

Pain location

An inconvenient aspect of pain is that just because you are feeling it at one location in the body it doesn't mean the anatomical structures at that location are causing all, or even any, of that pain.

This can make it difficult at times to arrive at an accurate *diagnosis*. General rules that govern the location of pain and the structure causing it are:

1) The closer the structures are located to the skin, the more likely they are to cause pain in the same area. For example, the *knee joint* structures are more likely to cause local knee pain. In contrast the *hip joint*, which is buried beneath layers of skin and muscle, has a greater chance of referring pain away from the joint, such as into the front of the thigh or knee.

2) The closer the structures are located to the spine, the more likely they are to cause pain to be felt at a distance, called *referred pain*, such as referred pain in the leg coming from the low back.

The lack of accuracy occurs because pain is a feeling that is perceived in the brain, which has a reasonably accurate map of the skin but not of the location of joints, ligaments, muscles and tendons.

Another problem is that nociceptors can send signals to the brain via nerves that connect with other nociceptors. For example, a low back ligament nociceptor sending a signal to a nerve that connects to a leg nociceptor. Instead of receiving a signal from the low back, the brain perceives that the signal has come from the leg.

Diagnosis and treatment

The relative contribution of each pain-causing structure usually can be accurately determined based on the *history, physical examination*, tests and investigations.

If not, the method used is to treat the most likely structures and then assess the effect on the perceived pain. For example, if the physical examination has found reduced flexibility of the low back joints on the right side in a person with buttock pain, treatment to increase the flexibility of these joints is provided. Despite sounding like a hit and miss approach, it is often highly effective. For drug treatments see *Anaesthetics (local), Analgesics* and *Non-steroidal anti-inflammatory drugs (NSAIDS)*.

Painful arc

See *Shoulder impingement*.

Palmar flexion

See *Flexion*.

Palpitations

A feeling in the *chest* that is also described as 'pounding', 'fluttering', 'flopping' and 'skipping' during participation in exercise or sport. In most cases it is a normal response. However, infrequently it is a warning sign of a health problem that requires seeing a doctor as soon as possible.

Palpitations may be a sign of tachycardia (extremely high heart rate), which is a *cardiac arrhythmia* (abnormal or irregular heart beat) usually caused by *coronary heart disease*. Other causes of abnormal palpitations include thyrotoxicosis (thyroid gland problem), hypoglycaemia (low blood sugars) in people with *diabetes, stress, anxiety,* adrenaline-producing *tumour, fever* and drugs including tobacco, *caffeine* products, *alcohol, ephedrine* and thyroid medication.

Panner's disease

An injury caused by softening of the capitellum, the rounded lower end of the humerus (arm bone) on the outer side of the *elbow joint*.

The injury belongs to a sub-group of *osteochondrosis* that usually affects under 11-year-olds. It is an overuse injury, due to repeated excessive forces on the elbow, in particular excessive throwing and abnormal *throwing biomechanics*.

Pain on the outside of the elbow is the main symptom. The recommended treatment is *rest* and *immobilisation*. If this fails surgery may be required.

Paracetamol

A medication that can reduce pain and *fever*. It may be prescribed for a *headache* or an acute injury; however, it does not have an anti-inflammatory effect such as *non-steroidal anti-inflammatory drugs (NSAIDs)*.

Paralympics

A gathering of athletes with a wide range of disabilities every four years to compete in different sports. The word is a shortening of 'parallel with' the Olympics.

The disability groupings that usually participate are *wheelchair athletes, amputee athletes, visually-impaired athletes*, athletes with an *intellectual disability, cerebral palsy* and *les autres* (others).

Paraplegia

Partial or complete loss of the ability to move the legs and lower part of the trunk and feel sensations, often accompanied by bladder control impairment.

It is due to damage to the *spinal cord*. The impact on muscles is hypotonia (see *Muscle tone*) and *atrophy*. The most common cause is a road accident. Twice as many males are affected. The largest age group is 19- to 35-year-olds. Moving around can be achieved by using a wheelchair. Participants in exercise and sport are called *wheelchair athletes*.

Parasthaesia

See *Pins and needles*.

Parasympathetic nervous system

A collection of *neurons* (nerve cells) that conduct communications with specific organs in the body, such as the heart and lungs. The communications involve sending instructions to reduce their level of activity when the body is resting from exercise and sport. For example, they make the *heartbeat* slower, decrease the amount of blood pumped by the heart and narrow the diameter of the lungs' airways after they have been widened during exercise.

It makes up one half of the autonomic nervous system. The other half is the *sympathetic nervous system*, which works in opposition; for example, by making the heartbeat faster. The sympathetic system dominates during exercise and sport, and also tends to have a mass response affecting organs at once, which is called the 'flight or fight' response. In contrast, the parasympathetic system affects organs selectively.

Paratendinitis

See *Paratenonitis*.

Paratenonitis

A group of injuries that cause inflammation to the *tendon sheath* that covers and protects a tendon. The symptoms can include pain, tenderness, swelling, restricted movement and weakness. It is usually due to excessive forces associated with an aggravating activity.

The specific injuries include paratendinitis, tenosynovitis (when the tendon sheath is a single layer of tissue covering the tendon) such as *de Quer-*

vain's tenosynovitis at the wrist, and tenovaginitis (double-layered tendon sheath).

It is more likely to occur in tendons that rub over a bony prominence, which directly irritates the tendon sheath. It is also seen in association with partial tears of a tendon and *tendinosis*. The recommended treatments are the same as for a *tendinitis*.

Pars interarticularis stress fracture

A microfracture in the rear part of one or more of the spinal bones (vertebrae), most commonly in the low back.

It causes pain that develops gradually due to an accumulation of repeated, excessive physical forces associated with activities that require excessive arching or rotation of the lower back, such as *gymnastics*, fast bowling in *cricket*, *tennis*, *rowing*, *dancing*,

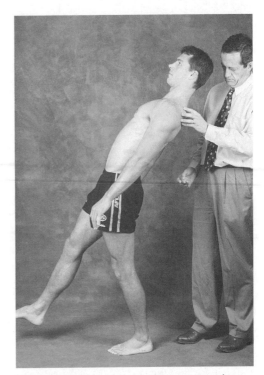

A single-legged hyperextension movement used to confirm diagnosis of pars interartciularis stress fracture

weight lifting, pole vault, and any throwing sports such as baseball pitching, javelin, discus and hammer throw.

Diagnosis, treatment and return to sport

The pain is easy to pinpoint in one of the bones in the low back, usually on one side of the spine, though sometimes both sides, and occasionally spreading into the buttocks (see Low back joints).

It is made worse during aggravating activities such as single-legged hyperextension and sports such as those listed above. In a few cases it does not cause pain, and is discovered coincidentally following an X-ray of the lower back for another problem. The diagnosis is confirmed with an X-ray, a SPECT bone scan or magnetic resonance imaging (MRI).

The recommended treatment is rest from aggravating activities, flexibility exercises for hamstring and gluteal muscles, and strengthening exercises of the abdominal and back extension muscles as soon as pain eases off.

When the aggravating activities no longer cause pain, they can be resumed and made gradually more difficult over a period of 4 to 6 weeks. Any biomechanical abnormality should be corrected, such as changing fast bowling technique from the mixed front-on and side-on technique to either a purely front-on or side-on technique as part of a lumbar rehabilitation program. Moderate to severe cases can take 3 to 9 months for a full return to sport.

Passive exercise

An activity that involves moving a part of the body with assistance from an outside force. This assistance may be provided by the hands of a person; for example, a physiotherapist, a piece of equipment like a pulley or the athlete's other limb, such as sitting down and resting the left foot on top of the right foot which is then lifted up. An active exercise is when the movement is performed without assistance.

Passive exercises should be commenced as soon as possible within the limits of pain after an injury has occurred, subject to medical advice if the injury has been severe or involved surgery. It is a form of

flexibility exercise, which is used to restore range of movement and maintain normal function.

Passive movement

Movement that is performed for a joint, ligament, muscle or the neural sheath with the assistance of an outside force. This assistance may be provided by another person; for example, a physiotherapist, a piece of equipment, or by oneself, such as lifting one foot with the other foot.

Passive movements are assessed in a physical examination to help provide a diagnosis for an injury. A number of observations are made including whether the pain that is associated with the injury is reproduced or aggravated by the passive movement. A measurement is also made of the amount of movement, called range of movement.

Passive exercises are performed as a treatment to improve the range of movement of structures including joint, ligament, muscle and neural sheath. The measurement from the physical examination is used to assess the progress achieved during rehabilitation.

Patella dislocation

An acute injury that displaces the normal position of the kneecap (patella) in the knee joint. The patella is an oval-shaped bone that sits within the patellar tendon, which connects the quadriceps (front thigh muscle) to the top end of the large, front shin bone (tibia).

In most cases the dislocation forces the patella towards the outer side of the knee. It is usually due to a sudden blow to the knee that makes it pop out of place, which causes pain and obvious swelling within 2 hours. In some cases, usually female teenagers, it is due to a naturally lax joint capsule.

Diagnosis

If the kneecap displacement wasn't observed, this injury appears similar to an anterior cruciate ligament (ACL) tear. The diagnosis is confirmed with the apprehension test, which involves performing quadriceps contractions that makes the patella feel as if it is about to pop out again.

Treatment and return to sport

The patella usually returns to its original position spontaneously, soon after the initial dislocation. The recommended treatments during the first 48 to 72 hours include *RICE* (*rest, ice, compression and elevation*) and avoiding heat and alcohol consumption to minimise swelling, which can delay healing if excessive.

It should be followed by *strengthening exercises* for the inner, lower part (medialis obliquus) of the quadriceps, *mobilisations* of the lateral (outer side) knee joint capsule and wearing a *brace* to protect and support the joint. Occasionally an *arthroscopy* is required.

Patellar tendinitis

See *Tendinitis*.

Patellar tendinosis

An overuse injury of the patellar tendon in the front of the *knee joint*. It is caused by a gradual accumulation of repeated excessive physical loads over a period of weeks or months in sports involving jumping, hopping and bounding activities such as *basketball*, *volleyball*, *jumping sports* such as high jump, long jump and triple jump and *weight lifting*.

Initially the injury causes inflammation of the tendon called *tendinitis*. However, continued aggravation of the tendon rapidly leads to the development of *tendinosis*, a degenerative condition that breaks down the cells in the tendon.

Diagnosis, treatment and return to sport

The pain is located in the front (anterior) of the knee. A mild injury causes pain that is felt some time after an aggravating activity has been completed or first thing the following morning, and it is reduced by a warm-up. A moderate injury causes pain that comes on during an aggravating activity and continues through the activity. A severe injury causes pain that

An eccentric strengthening exercise of the quadriceps muscle for patellar tendinosis

is felt all the time, even at rest. The diagnosis may be confirmed with *diagnostic ultrasound* or *magnetic resonance imaging* (MRI).

The recommended treatment includes *ice*, electrotherapy such as *ultrasound therapy* and *interferential therapy*, *flexibility exercises*, *massage* of the tendon and *strengthening exercises* with emphasis on *eccentric* contractions. Continued participation in the aggravating activity is permitted at a reduced intensity for a mild injury.

Moderate to severe injuries require a complete *rest* from jumping for 2 to 4 weeks. A full return to sport is a gradual process that can take from several weeks up to 6 months in the worst case. In chronic cases *thermal gear* such as a brace may be beneficial. If the above treatments fail a *corticosteroid* injection may be prescribed. If all this is not successful surgery may be required.

Patellofemoral joint instability

Reduced ability to maintain the normal connection between the patella and lower end of the thigh bone (femur) in the *knee joint*. It may be due to repeated *patella dislocation* or subluxation that damages the joint capsule, or a severe form of *patellofemoral joint syndrome*. Treatment is the same as for patellofemoral joint syndrome. Is this fails, surgery is required.

Patellofemoral joint syndrome

An overuse injury that causes pain in the front (anterior) and inner (medial) side of the knee. The pain usually starts gradually over a period of weeks or months during squatting, walking, walking up stairs or running activities and gradually gets worse during the activity.

Causes

During bending and straightening of the *knee joint* the kneecap (patella) normally moves up and down

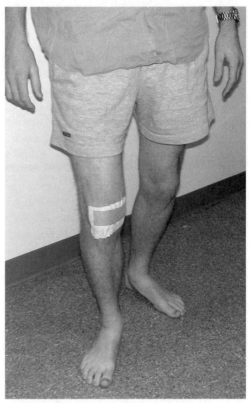

Strengthening exercise for vastus medialis muscle for patellofemoral joint syndrome

smoothly in a groove or rounded gutter in the underlying bone of the lower end of the femur (thigh bone).

In patellofemoral joint syndrome the patella veers excessively to the outer side of the groove, usually due to poor coordination of the vastus medialis muscle, one of the four parts that make up the quadriceps (front *thigh* muscle). The repeated veering excessively stretches the joint capsule, leading to pain.

The main causes of this poor coordination include a previous knee injury, a congenital *biomechanical abnormality*, knock-knees, teenage growth spurts and excessive tightness of the lateral (outer side) structures such as the iliotibial band.

Diagnosis

The diagnosis is confirmed if the McConnell technique reduces the pain during an aggravating activity, such as squatting or jogging on the spot.

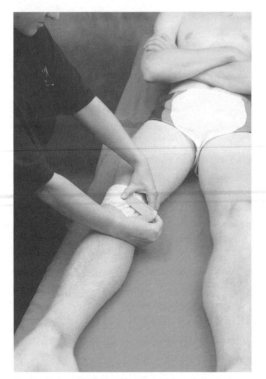

Taping for patellofemoral joint syndrome

The McConnell technique involves a practitioner pushing the patella towards the inner (medial) side with the hands and placing a long piece of tape across the patella starting from the lateral (outer) side of the knee so that the tension of the tape maintains the patella in a more medial position.

Treatment and return to sport

The aim of treatment is to relieve pain in the short term with the McConnell technique, and improve vastus medialis coordination and strength in the long term, mainly with *motor re-education* and *strengthening exercises* utilising *biofeedback. Massage* or *mobilisation* of tight structures such as the iliotibial band may be required.

Return to sport is often immediately permitted because the McConnell technique is highly effective. In severe cases 1 to 2 weeks rest is required. *Taping* is usually continued for up to 6 weeks (when severe, 3 months may be required). In some cases a patellofemoral *brace* may be recommended.

Pathology

The science of the causes and effects of injury, illness and disease. A *diagnosis* gives a specific name to the pathology. It is described in terms of the physical and psychological presentation of a person as a whole, including the signs and symptoms, and of the affected parts including the cells, tissues, organs and systems.

For example, the cause of the common cold is a cold virus infection of the nose and throat. The infection causes an inflammation that leads to symptoms including sniffing, sneezing, a runny nose, sore throat, headaches, tiredness and irritability.

Pathophysiology

The science of the physiological processes that lead to injury, illness and disease. A *diagnosis* gives a specific name to the pathophysiology. It is explained in terms of the physical and chemical activities that take place in the cells, tissues, organs and systems of the body, and how they relate to the signs and symptoms.

Peak flow meter

A hand-held device that measures the maximum speed that air can be breathed out of the lungs. It is used to measure the severity of an *asthma* attack during the recovery from an attack, such as the response of the airways to medication, and as a method of self-monitoring the condition of the airways.

Making a measurement with a peak flow meter involves taking a deep breath in and then breathing out into the device's mouthpiece with the maximum effort possible.

Peak performance

Timing one's training so that fitness and skill levels are at their best for a specific competition. A single competition event, such as a triathlon, may involve a period of rest beforehand, called *tapering*, to ensure peak performance on the day.

If competition is spread out over a season the aim is to maintain high performance levels and then rise to peak levels for the finals. Peak performance is an important goal of *periodisation*, one of the four main principles of training.

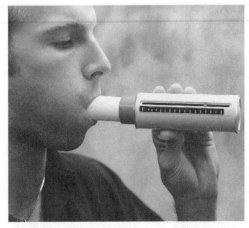

Peak flow meter used to measure airway narrowing

Pelvic floor

See *Incontinence*.

Pelvis

A large ring-shaped bone that connects the low back and lower abdomen to the hips, thighs and groin.

The pelvis is made up of three parts: a left and right pelvic girdle, and the sacrum bone. Each pelvic girdle is made up of three smaller bones (ilium, ischium and pubis) that are fused together through *ossification* during childhood and adolescence.

Each pelvic girdle is connected together at the front by a strong fibrous and cartilaginous joint called the pubic *symphysis*. The sacrum lies at the back of the pelvis and is connected to each pelvic girdle by a synovial joint called the sacroiliac *joint*. The upper section of the sacrum connects to the lowest *low back joint*. Each side of the pelvis also contains a cup that forms one half of the *hip joint*.

The pelvis performs two main roles. It protects important organs within the ring of bone, such as the large intestine, rectum, bladder, and female sex organs including the uterus and vagina. Second, it acts as a stable base for movements of the legs and, to a lesser extent, of the low back. The muscles that produce these movements are located in the lower abdomen, low back, buttock, hip, groin and thigh.

Pelvis anterior tilt

A forward rotation movement of the pelvis bone that is essential for normal biomechanics of walking and running.

Movements of the *pelvis* occur in relation to the low back and hips through a combination of movements at the sacroiliac joints and *hip joints*. In the anterior tilt, the pelvis can be thought of as a vertical flat square board with the genitals at the front and buttocks at the back. The forward rotation turns the front of the board to face downwards.

When the heel strikes the ground at the start of the stance phase of walking or *running biomechanics* the pelvis is in the *neutral joint position*. From contact through to propulsive stages of the stance phase there is an anterior tilt movement.

Biomechanical abnormality

An excessive amount of anterior tilt is a biomechanical abnormality that is associated with injuries. It can be due to weakness of the abdominal, gluteus medius and minimus, hamstring and external hip rotator muscles, which normally provide stability of the pelvis, and loss of *flexibility* of the hip flexor muscles. It may be associated with *low back pain (non-specific)*, *sacroiliac joint pain* and *patellofemoral joint syndrome*.

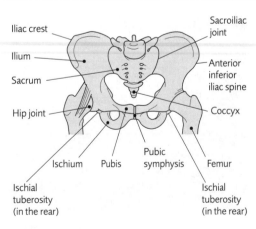

Bones of the male pelvis

Iliac crest
Ilium
Sacrum
Hip joint
Ischium
Pubis
Pubic symphysis
Femur
Ischial tuberosity (in the rear)
Ischial tuberosity (in the rear)
Sacroiliac joint
Anterior inferior iliac spine
Coccyx

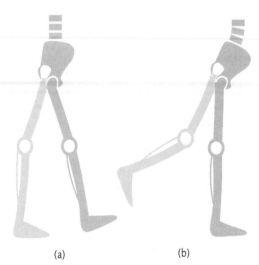

(a) (b)

Pelvis anterior tilt during walking

Treatment

Flexibility exercises and *massage* are performed to reduce the tightness of the hip flexor muscles. *Motor re-education* and *strengthening exercises* are recommended for the abdominal, gluteus medius and minimus, hamstring and external hip rotator muscles.

Pelvis fracture

An acute injury of the *pelvis* is most commonly due to a sudden excessive force, such as a collision in high-speed car racing, that causes a fracture. Most *fractures* are treated with 3 weeks rest in bed and *analgesics* as required. Severe injuries are associated with *abdominal injury* to the bladder, urethra or rectum, which require immediate transportation to a hospital (see *Medical emergency*).

Pelvis lateral tilt

A sideways rotation movement of the pelvis bone that is essential for normal walking and running biomechanics. The movement occurs in relation to the lower back and hips. It involves one side (or buttock) being raised upwards while the other side is lowered downwards. The *pelvis*, which is ring-shaped, can be thought of as being like a wheel; turning the wheel causes one side to rise and the other side to fall.

When the heel strikes the ground at the start of the stance phase of walking and running the pelvis is in the *neutral joint position*. In the midstance stage there is an upward lateral tilt that is a result of a downward lateral tilt of the pelvis on the other side, which occurs because the leg is going through the swing phase.

Instability due to poor control of the hip abductor and adductor muscles causes excessive lateral tilt, which is a biomechanical abnormality that may lead to overuse injuries such as *adductor muscle strain*, *trochanteric bursitis* and *iliotibial band friction syndrome*. The recommended treatments include *motor re-education* and *strengthening exercises*.

Pelvis posterior tilt

A backward rotation movement of the *pelvis*. It occurs in relation to the lower back and hips. In this movement the pelvis can be thought of as a vertical, flat square board, with the genitals at the front and buttocks at the back. The backward rotation turns the front of the board to face upwards. It causes the lower back to flatten out and decrease its arch.

Pelvis transverse rotation

A movement of the *pelvis* that can be thought of as being like a merry-go-round in relation to the lower back and hips. The forward rotation of one side (or buttock) of the pelvis occurs at the same time as the other side rotates backwards.

Perceived exertion

Subjective feelings of effort when participating in a physical activity. It is used as an approximate measure of the intensity of the activity during participation in *aerobic training*.

These feelings differ in people performing the same activity according to their aerobic fitness levels. For example, jogging is perceived as very hard for someone who is unfit, whereas it is less difficult for a fit person.

A formal method of measuring perceived exertion is the *Borg perceived exertion scale*. The simplest and most commonly used method is based on quickness of breath during participation in the physical activity (see *Breathing regulation*):

- Low-intensity is equivalent to breathing exertion ranging from 'no effect on breathing' up to the point that 'shortness of breath is noticed' = 30–49 per cent of VO_2 *max* = 35–59 per cent of *maximum heart rate estimation* (220 – age).
- Moderate-intensity is equivalent to a range from 'shortness of breath is noticed' up to 'the point that whistling or normal continuous conversation is just possible' = 50–74 per cent of VO_2 max = 60–79 per cent of maximum heart rate estimation.

- High-intensity is a range from the point that 'whistling or normal continuous conversation is just possible' up to the point that 'whistling or normal continuous conversation is impossible' = 75–84 per cent of VO_2 max = 80–89 per cent of maximum heart rate estimation.

Periodisation

Dividing a *training* program into three stages with the aim of building up to peak levels of fitness and performance. The stages are called conditioning, followed by pre-competition and competition. It reduces the risk of injuries and illness, such as *overtraining syndrome*.

Conditioning stage

In this stage the emphasis is on *aerobic training*, *anaerobic training*, *strength training*, *skills training* and psychological and teamwork sessions. Participants often feel fatigued because they are training to *overload* and, if asked to compete, would perform poorly.

The *overload* of volume and intensity of training should be reduced at regular intervals in order to decrease the risk or injury. Participants should be given at least one day off a week, called an 'easy day', and an 'easy week' every three or four weeks.

Precompetition stage

The focus is on technique and skills improvement while maintaining fitness levels. It may also involve *tapering* if the athlete is due to participate in a competition event such as swimming heats and finals. *Pre-competition eating* is also important.

Competition stage

The aim is to reach *peak performance* in this stage. In sports where the competition season lasts for a large part of the year, such as football and basketball, the conditioning extends and overlaps into the competition phase. However, the aim is still to peak at the most important time of year, in the finals or championship. Most of the training involves maintaining fitness and skills, and concentrating on

psychological factors, strategies and tactics. *Pre-event meal* recommendations also should be followed,

Adequate recovery time (4–6 weeks) before recommencing the next conditioning stage is necessary to ensure complete recovery from the physical and mental stress of the training program. This period may be associated with *detraining* effects.

Periosteal contusion

An acute injury caused by a sudden, blunt force to the *periosteum*, the external thin outer layer of bone. It is most likely to occur in contact sports, such as *hockey (field)*, *basketball*, and *football* codes, such as *soccer*.

It can be extremely painful and cause momentary paralysis of nearby muscles. Examples include a *hip pointer*, to the iliac crest of the pelvis, and *tibia periosteal contusion* in the front of the shin.

The time required before return to sport ranges from 1 week (mild) up to 3 weeks for severe contusions. Protective equipment, such as a hip guard or *shin guard*, should be worn to prevent or reduce the severity of an injury or re-injury.

Periosteum

A thin membrane that covers the entire surface of *bones*, except where they form joints. It is made up of *connective tissue* and bone-producing cells, called osteoblasts, and is rich in nerves and blood vessels. Damage to the periosteum is the main source of pain when a bone is broken. The blood vessels in the periosteum also supply nutrients to the underlying compact bone.

Muscle tendons, ligaments and joint capsules that attach to bones blend together with the periosteum. The structure that connects a *tendon* and periosteum is called the tenoperiosteum.

Periostitis

An inflammation of the *periosteum* of a bone that gradually builds up over a period of weeks or months, due to repeated excessive traction forces exerted by muscles experienced during a particular activity such as running. The excessive forces are often associated with a *biomechanical abnormality* and muscle *fibrosis*.

The most common site for this overuse injury is the tibia (shin bone), which is called *tibia periostitis* and is popularly known as shin splints.

A diagnosis may be confirmed with a *bone scan*. Tenderness along the bone when pressed firmly with the fingers corresponds with the area of increased uptake found on the bone scan. The area of increased uptake on a bone scan is larger than that found in a bone *stress fracture*.

The treatment includes reducing excessive forces by correcting the biomechanical abnormality and *massage* to treat the muscle fibrosis. This injury is also called tenoperiostitis.

Peripheral nervous system

All the nerves located outside the *central nervous system*, which is made up of the brain and spinal cord. The peripheral nervous system is mostly made up of the 12 pairs of cranial nerves that originate from the brain, and 31 pairs of *spinal nerves* that originate from the spinal cord. Most of these branches continue onwards to their target destinations, such as muscles, joints and more, though a few get sidetracked into a *ganglion*.

Peripheral neuropathy

A disease, inflammation or damage of the nerves located in the *peripheral nervous system* in the arms, legs or trunk. Symptoms include weakness if motor nerves are involved, and numbness, pins and needles and pain if sensory nerves are damaged.

The most common cause of peripheral neuropathy is *diabetes*, which leads to loss of sensation. It usually begins in the ends of the arms and/or legs and moves towards the shoulders and/or hips, often described as a 'glove and stocking' distribution. Pain is also common. Lack of sensation can lead to the development of skin *ulcers*.

Regular close inspection of the feet by a podiatrist and wearing the correct *shoes* is important. Exercise that may cause trauma to the feet, such as *jogging* or high-impact *aerobics*, should be avoided in preference for swimming, cycling and arm exercises. Feet and toes should be kept dry and clean, and socks should be kept dry.

Peripheral vascular disease

Disease that damages blood vessels that carry blood between the cells of the body and the heart, except for the lungs. The most common conditions are atherosclerosis of the leg arteries, *varicose veins* and *deep vein thrombosis (DVT)*.

The risks of developing peripheral vascular disease are increased by genetics, smoking cigarettes, *obesity*, lack of exercise, poor diet, *diabetes* and *hypertension* (high blood pressure).

Atherosclerosis
Atherosclerosis is a disease that causes narrowing of an *artery* due to fatty deposits forming in the walls, called plaque, that bulge inwards and also make them harder and less elastic. It most commonly affects the calf or thigh in middle-aged inactive people, though some *older athletes* may be affected.

The first symptoms are usually aching and tiredness during leg activities, such as running or walking. As it gets more severe, cramp-like (claudicant) pain develops that is relieved with rest.

The diagnosis is confirmed with a doppler ultrasound and angiogram. Bypass surgery is the most commonly used surgical treatment. In severe cases amputation is required (see *Amputee athletes*).

Peripheral vascular system

The arteries and veins carrying blood to and from all the cells of the body, except the lungs. Blood with a high content of oxygen, which has a bright red colour, is pumped by the left ventricle of the *heart* into the arteries which branch and divide and get smaller until they reach the cells where the contents, also including nutrients and other substances, are absorbed into the cells.

Wastes from the cells are collected into the blood, which flows mostly back into the smallest veins, called venules, that join up with each other to form larger vessels, called *veins*, which take the blood, now with a low oxygen content, back to the right atrium and ventricle ready to be pumped into the *pulmonary vascular system*. Left-over fluid, called lymph, that does not enter the veins is returned to the heart via the *lymphatic system*.

Periradicular injection

A treatment used to reduce pain caused by *nerve root compression*. The technique is the same as a *selective nerve root block (SNRB)* injection, except that *corticosteroids* are used instead of anaesthetic.

Peroneal tendinosis

An overuse injury causing pain on the outside of the ankle that gradually gets worse over a period of weeks or months due to repeated and excessive activity of the tendons. It is common in activities involving *ankle* eversion (turning outwards movement), such as running on slopes, *basketball* and *volleyball*, and if excessive *foot pronation* is present.

Treatments for this *tendinosis* include *rest* from the aggravating activity, *ice* and, if required, *analgesics* for pain relief. *Mobilisation* of the ankle joint, *strengthening exercises*, particularly *eccentric* muscle contractions, *massage* and *flexibility exercises* are also recommended.

Personal trainer

A *fitness trainer* who provides services for just one person at a time. It can be the most effective method of achieving one of the main principles of training, called *individuality*, where activities are selected that best suit that person's ability to increase fitness and

improve performance, and provides psychological benefits such as helping to maintain motivation.

Personality

The sum of the personal characteristics of an individual. It is made up of distinguishing features, called traits, and typical behaviours influenced by past experiences that are brought out in common situations. Personality is considered to be a product of one's hereditary and environmental factors.

There are a number of models that categorise common personality types. For example: Type A personality is hyperactive, easily aroused and competitive; and Type B is more laid back, relaxed and less competitive. However, these models have a limited ability to make accurate predictions about people's behaviour, including their performance in exercise and sport.

It is possible to be more accurate when referring to mental skills that produce specific behaviours. For instance, an athlete who copes well with adversity, is free of excessive *anxiety* and concentrates on sport-specific goals is more likely to be successful.

Perthes' disease

A disease that causes softening of the head of the femur (thigh bone) in the *hip joint* that makes it vulnerable to being deformed or separated from the rest of the femur.

The injury is an *osteochondrosis* that is believed to be due to a loss of blood supply to the bone, though the causes are still not fully understood. It may be associated with delayed bone maturity. It most commonly affects children aged 4 to 10 years.

Diagnosis, treatment and return to sport

The injury is usually first noticed when it starts causing a limp and minor ache in the thigh, groin or referred pain in the knee. A physical examination usually finds loss of *flexibility* of the hip joint. An X-ray may show increased density and flattening of the *epiphysis*.

The recommended treatment is *rest* from aggravating activities and *flexibility exercises*. The

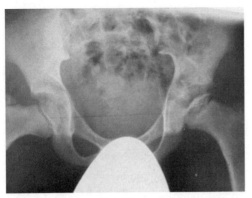

X-ray of Perthes' disease

condition usually resolves with time, and return to sport is possible when there is no pain and the X-ray shows some improvement. The main long-term concern is early onset of *hip osteoarthritis* due to irregularity of the joint surface.

Pes anserinus tendinosis

An overuse injury of the tendons of the inner thigh muscles and inner part of the hamstring at their attachment to the large shin bone (tibia) near the *knee joint*. It is most commonly associated with an accumulation of excessive physical loads over a long period, usually weeks or months, during *swimming*, particularly breast-stroking, *cycling* and *running*.

The injury causes pain located on the inner (medial) side of the knee. Treatment includes *ice*, electrotherapy such as *ultrasound therapy* and *interferential therapy*, *flexibility exercises* and *massage* of the tendon.

Pes cavus

A defect in the structure of the foot that causes the medial (inner) arch to be excessively raised, increasing the height of the arch and positioning the forefoot lower than the rear foot (see *Foot and toes*).

It may be caused by an abnormality of the position of the calcaneus (heel bone) or excessive *foot supination* due to, for example, reduced *flexibility* of

the Achilles tendon or *tibial external torsion*. It is also called 'claw foot'.

Phalanx fracture

A break in one of the bones of the thumb and fingers. There are three phalanges in each finger and two in the thumb (see *Hand and finger joints*). In most cases these fractures require an X-ray to confirm the location of the fracture, and *rehabilitation* treatments after the fracture has been stabilised.

Proximal phalanx
The *fracture* is located in the phalanx located closest to the knuckles. The recommended treatment is *immobilisation* with a splint. Weekly X-rays are required to ensure the fracture is healing correctly. The splint is removed after 3 to 4 weeks, and buddy taping continued for another 2 weeks for full healing.

Middle phalanx
The fracture is located in the middle of the finger. It can be treated with *immobilisation* in a splint for 3 weeks. However, if the bones are unstable or the fracture involves a joint then *open surgery* and *internal fixation* with a metal wire is recommended.

Distal phalanx
The fracture is located in the end of either the thumb or finger. It is usually due to a crushing injury, such as the fingers being jammed between a fast moving ball and a stick in *hockey (field)* or *lacrosse*.

In many cases the pain is mainly caused by a *subungual hematoma* (bleeding under the nail), which may require surgery to remove the nail if the bleeding is extensive. The recommended treatment is *immobilisation* in a splint and *compression* dressing. Most fractures heal in 4 to 6 weeks.

Phenylpropanolamine

A stimulant drug that is a common ingredient in diet pills or appetite suppressants, and is banned by the

World Anti-Doping Agency (WADA). Side effects can include *hypertension* (high blood pressure).

Phosphocreatine (PCr) system

See *Creatine phosphate system*.

Phosphorus

See *Minerals*.

Physical activity

All forms of being active including *exercise, sport* and the activities that are part of day-to-day life, such as washing the car by hand and walking up stairs.

Regular participation in any type of physical activity is a form of *aerobic training* that can improve fitness, which is associated with a reduced risk of disease and illness such as heart attack, stroke and diabetes. The recommendation to increase physical activity on a regular basis is called *exercise for health*.

Physical examination

Gathering all relevant information about a person's presenting health problem by checking the body and conducting physical tests in order to make a *diagnosis* of an injury, illness or disease.

Together with the *history*, it is usually able to provide a clear idea of the likely diagnosis. Appropriate additional tests and investigations can be ordered afterwards to further confirm it. An accurate and complete physical examination should include the following general principles and examination routines.

General principles
- Aggravating activities or movements may be required to reproduce the pain.
- Where relevant, the non-injured side is examined.
- Assess local tissues around the injury.

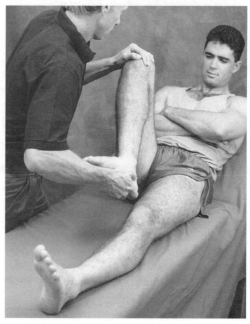

A test for the stability of the knee joint during a physical examination

- Look for other possible causes, such as *referred pain* or pain associated with a *biomechanical abnormality*.

Physical examination routine
- Inspection: The injured area is closely inspected for any evidence of deformity, asymmetry, bruising, *swelling*, skin changes and muscle *atrophy* (wasting).
- Range of movement: This involves measuring the amount of movement of the joints, ligaments, muscles and the neural sheath, including *active movements*, *passive movements* and *neural tension* tests.
- Palpation: Using the fingers or hands to feel and press the relevant body parts, both injured and uninjured, to determine the exact location of the tender structure that is the source of the pain.
- Ligament testing: Moving a joint to place stress on a particular ligament to examine it for range of movement, laxity and pain.
- Muscle *strength* testing: Methods include manual muscle testing, functional testing such

as jumping; and isokinetic strength testing using a machine such as the KinCom (see *Isokinetic strengthening*).

- Biomechanical examination: Assessing for abnormalities of the biomechanics, the movements and positions of the body and its parts. *Video analysis* may be helpful.
- Technique and equipment: Assessing the manner in which activities and skills are performed and the equipment used such as shoes, racquet and bicycle.

Physiology

The science of how the human body works and functions. It includes the physical and chemical activities that take place in the cells, tissues, organs and systems, and how they interact with each other.

Different types of physiology describe specific functions. For example, exercise physiology is the science of how the body works during exercise and sport, and cardiac physiology is the science of how the heart works.

Physiology is intimately related to *anatomy*, which describes the structure of the human body in terms of shape, size, composition and location. *Pathology* is the science of the causes and effects of injury, illness and disease. *Pathophysiology* is the science of the processes underlying pathology.

Physiotherapist

A health practitioner who has completed training and is registered and recognised as being qualified to provide diagnosis, treatment and rehabilitation for a wide range of injuries, illness and disease that primarily affect the bones, joints, muscles and nerves of the body.

Treatments include *electrotherapy*, manual therapy such as *mobilisation* and *manipulation*, *traction*, *massage*, *muscle energy techniques* and *neural tension* stretching. Many physiotherapists have an area of specialisation, such as *sports medicine, cardiac rehabilitation, incontinence, stroke* rehabilitation and occupational health.

Pilates

A method of training emphasising the importance of muscle control that was developed by Joseph Pilates (1880–1967). Ballet dancers and performers at his New York clinic, which was established in 1923, adapted his philosophy and techniques.

Pilates is based on eight principles: relaxation, concentration, alignment, breathing, centring, co-ordination, flowing movements and stamina.

Initially the exercise programmes for dancers were extremely complex and performed on special machines. But in recent years the principles have been adapted to simplify and break down the exercise programmes into stages. Doing the exercises on mats on the floor are now considered to have equal effect.

Pilates is regarded as achieving similar benefits to *motor re-education*, which is used to treat *instability* of joints and body regions such as the low back and pelvis (see *lumbo-pelvic instability*).

Pins and needles

An abnormal prickling sensation of the skin that is caused by an injury or disease. It occurs because the information carried by neurons in the *sensory nervous system* is altered due to a disruption or damage. For example, sitting with the leg bent underneath the buttock for a prolonged time can cause pins and needles that are relieved by straightening the leg. A direct blow to a nerve can cause damage, which is called a *neuropraxia* (see *Nerve injury*).

PIP joint dislocation

An injury that displaces a joint between the proximal phalanx and middle phalanx in one of the fingers, which is called the proximal interphalangeal (PIP) joint (see *Hand and finger joints*).

Most commonly it is due to a sudden blow that pushes backwards one of the bones, often when playing a ball sport. In some cases the injured person repositions the bone while still on the playing field.

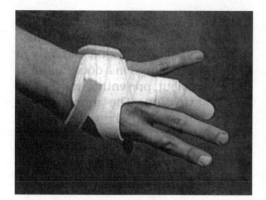

A splint for a PIP joint dislocation

Treatment for this *dislocation* is *immobilisation* in a splint for several days, then buddy *taping* to an adjacent finger to allow motion and an elastic pressure bandage to reduce *swelling*, followed by *rehabilitation* treatments.

If there is an associated fracture *open surgery* and *internal fixation* with a metal wire is recommended. If an open wound is also present, immediate treatment in hospital is required to prevent infection.

PIP joint sprain

An injury of the collateral ligaments of a joint between the proximal and middle phalanx of the one of the fingers (see *Hand and finger joints*). The most common cause is a sudden sideways force.

The *sprain* may result in a partial tear (grade 1 or 2) that causes pain but leaves the joint stable, or a complete tear (grade 3) that causes marked instability when bending the joint sideways. A partial tear is treated with buddy *taping*. Complete tears should ideally be treated with surgery, although in most cases *immobilisation* with a splint provides an adequate result. Both partial and complete tears require *rehabilitation*.

Piriformis impingement

An injury that causes buttock pain that may spread into the back of the thigh and calf due to pressure

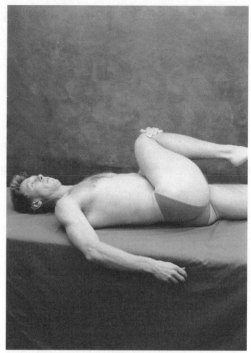

A flexibility exercise for piriformis impingement

on the sciatic nerve as it passes through the piriformis, a muscle located between the front surface (anterior) of the sacrum bone and the upper end of the femur (thigh bone) near the *hip joint*.

The recommended treatment is *flexibility exercises* and *massage* for the piriformis. Surgery may be required if this treatment fails.

Pitcher's elbow

See *Golfer's elbow*.

Plantar fascia sprain

A tear or excessive stretch of the thick band of fibrous connective tissue that runs from the bottom of the heel bone (calcaneus) forwards through the sole of the foot to the base of the toes (see *Foot and toes*).

The *sprain* causes pain in the middle of the foot. Treatment includes *rest, ice, massage, flexibility exer-*

cises and *taping*. Return to sport is usually permitted after 2 to 3 weeks.

Plantar fasciitis

An overuse injury that causes pain located on the sole of the foot or heel. The pain usually feels strongest during activities such as running and dancing, and is worse in the morning but improves after warming up.

Causes
The pain usually builds up gradually over a period of weeks or months due to an accumulation of excessive forces on the plantar fascia, a thick band of fibrous connective tissue that runs from the bottom of the heel bone (calcaneus) forwards through the sole of the foot to the base of the toes (see *Foot and toes*).

The plantar fascia plays an important role in stabilising the arch of the foot, particularly when the forefoot and toes push off during the propulsive stage of *running biomechanics*.

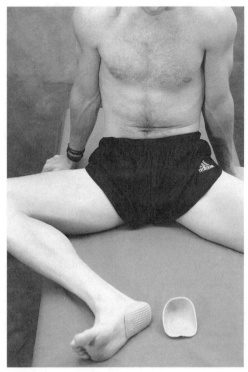

An orthotic heel cup for plantar fasciitis

Excessive forces are often associated with a biomechanical abnormality such as excessive *foot pronation*, for example, caused by loss of *flexibility* of the calf muscles or poor selection of *running shoes*.

Diagnosis, treatment and return to sport
It is not uncommon for an *X-ray* to show a calcaneal bony spur. However, many people have spurs but never experience pain. As a result, the previously popular diagnosis 'heel spurs' is now considered inaccurate.

The source of the pain is *inflammation* of the fascia where it attaches to the bone. The diagnosis may be confirmed with *diagnostic ultrasound*.

The recommended treatment aims to reduce the inflammation with *non-steroidal anti-inflammatory drugs (NSAIDs)*, *ice*, *rest* that avoids the aggravating activity and *taping* or an orthotic to correct excessive foot pronation. *Flexibility exercises*, *massage* and a night splint are also helpful. *Extra corporeal shock wave therapy* (high frequency sound waves) may have some success.

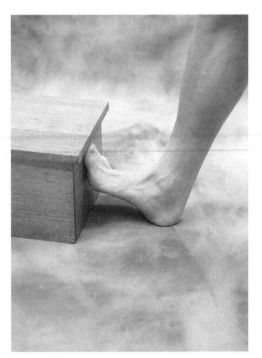

Flexibility exercise for plantar fasciitis

Return to sport such as running usually requires at least 6 weeks, with severe cases taking up to 1 year. A *corticosteroid* injection may be required if the above treatments are not successful. If this fails surgery to lengthen the fascia may be recommended.

Plantar flexion

A movement of the *ankle* that involves moving the sole of the foot in a direction away from the front of the tibia (shin bone). It is also called *flexion*.

Plantarflexed first ray

A defect in the structure of the foot that causes the first (big) toe and metatarsal bone to excessively bend downwards in relation to the other toes and metatarsals, leading to excessive *foot supination* during walking and running.

Platelets

The smallest cells in blood that are essential for *blood* clotting (called coagulation), which occurs when these cells aggregate together to form a sticky clump. Platelets are also called thrombocytes.

Pleura

A thin membrane that is wrapped around both *lungs* that lubricates and enables smooth movement within the chest during *breathing*. The membrane is made up of two layers, with a lubricant fluid contained in the cavity in between that maintains an even, negative pressure to help the lungs remain inflated. A punctured pleural cavity is a *pneumothorax*.

Pleurisy

An inflammation of the *pleura*, the membranes that form a lining of the lungs. It is usually caused by a *lung infection*, such as pneumonia or a viral infection of the pleura. Pleurisy causes sharp chest pain that is made worse when breathing in. Pain may also be felt in the shoulder on the same side. Treatment is recommended for the underlying cause, and *analgesics* can be prescribed for the pain itself.

Plexus

A network of criss-crossing and interwoven nerves derived from *spinal nerves*, which branch off from the spinal cord. The advantage of having a plexus is that paralysis is less likely if one nerve gets damaged.

The largest plexuses are near the spinal cord, including the cervical plexus, brachial plexus, lumbar plexus, sacral plexus, and plexuses of the *sympathetic nervous system* and *parasympathetic nervous system* such as the cardiac plexus of the heart. Small plexuses are found in the arms and legs.

A plexus of blood vessels is also called an anastomosis.

Plyometrics

Training that involves sudden and explosive activities that aim to achieve an increase in muscle *power*. The most common activities are hopping, jumping and bounding.

For example, the lateral bound involves a starting position of standing next to a wooden block in a semi-squat position with the back straight, head up and arms at the side. The sudden and explosive movement is a rapid thrust of the arms forwards and upwards, and jumping up and sideways over a wooden block. Immediately after landing on the ground, the starting position is adopted again and the lateral bound repeated back in the opposite direction. As little time as possible is spent in contact with the ground.

The physiological mechanism underlying this training is to maximise the impact of eccentric and concentric muscle contractions (see *Strengthening exercises*). Muscles fatigue quickly during plyometrics, and sessions should only be performed once or

Plyometrics lateral jump over a wooden block

twice a week to permit sufficient recovery time and to minimise the risk of injury.

Pneumonia

See *Lung infection*.

Pneumothorax

An acute injury that causes a collapse of one of the *lungs* due to air entering the pleural cavity, the space between the two layers of pleura that is normally filled with a lubricant fluid.

It may occur spontaneously due to an underlying disease, such as *asthma*. Not exhaling to allow compressed air in the alveoli to escape from the lungs during ascent in *scuba diving* is another cause.

In *collision sports* it is usually due to sudden trauma, and may be associated with other injuries including multiple fractured ribs leading to a *chest flail segment* and heart muscle bruising, which may result in a *cardiac tamponade*.

A pneumothorax should be suspected if a person has an obvious chest wound or shortness of breath and shifting of the windpipe (trachea) to one side.

Treatment

The injury should be treated as a *medical emergency*, ensuring that the breathing and circulation of the injured person is not compromised. Once breathing and circulation are in order, clothing should be removed and if there is an open wound the hand can be placed over it to stop air entering into the pleural cavity.

Afterwards the wound can be covered with a sterile dressing or any available object, such as a credit card, that can be held down with tape to make it airtight on three sides, except for one side that allows air under pressure to escape. Hospital treatment includes removing the air, closing the pleura and reinflating the lung.

Podiatrist

A health practitioner who has completed training that is registered and recognised as being qualified to provide diagnosis, treatment and rehabilitation for injuries, illness and disease that affect the feet.

Treatments include *orthotics* for foot pain, advice on selecting the correct *shoes* for exercise and sport, and the application of specialised dressings and local anaesthetics. In North America podiatrists are licensed to perform specific foot surgery procedures.

Pole vault

Pole vaulting originated in ancient times when Greeks and Cretans used wooden poles for recreational jumping. In the modern era, fibreglass poles are used. Physical requirements include *skills training*, *anaerobic training* and *strength training* for the arms and upper body.

The most common injuries are *hamstring strain* (thigh), *tibia stress fracture* (shin), *fibula stress fracture* (shin), *shin chronic compartment syndrome*, *ankle sprain, talus stress fracture* (foot and toes), *sinus tarsi syndrome* (foot and toes), *pars interarticularis stress fracture* (low back), *rotator cuff tendinosis* (shoulder), *shoulder instability, head injury, elbow posterior dislocation* and *wrist joint sprain*.

Polyunsaturated fats

A type of *fat* found in large amounts in foods from plants and fish. There are two types of polyunsaturates: omega 6 fatty acids from plants like sunflower, corn and soybean; and omega 3 fatty acids, mainly in fish.

In a *diet for good health* it is important to keep an equal balance between omega 3 and omega 6, because eating too much of one reduces the impact of the other. Polyunsaturated fats should be eaten in equal amounts as *saturated fats* and *monounsaturated fats*.

Popliteal artery entrapment syndrome

Excessive pressure on the popliteal artery as it passes near the *knee joint* into the calf region, usually as it goes through the upper portion of the gastrocnemius muscle. The pressure restricts the flow of blood to the calf muscles. The lack of blood during exercise, such as walking or running, causes calf pain, and in some cases, shin pain.

Diagnosis and treatment

It is sometimes mistakenly diagnosed as the superficial posterior type of *shin chronic compartment syndrome*. However, the pain from a compartment syndrome is often more severe on the second day when exercise is attempted on consecutive days, whereas popliteal artery entrapment syndrome pain is unaffected by exercise on the previous day.

A stethoscope can sometimes identify a popliteal artery bruit (sound of turbulent blood flow). The diagnosis is confirmed with an angiography (radiological investigation of the artery). Treatment involves surgery to free up the popliteal artery from the structures restricting the blood flow.

Post-activity eating

The foods that are recommended after training and competition in order to maximise recovery.

The main concern is to prevent *glycogen depletion*. A high carbohydrate diet may restore normal glycogen levels within 24 to 48 hours. Resynthesis of glycogen is fastest during the first 15 minutes after activity and remains high for 2 hours. Up to 3 g of carbohydrates per kilogram of body weight may be required.

Simple and complex *carbohydrates* restore glycogen levels equally as effectively in the 24 hour post-event period. Complex carbohydrates, such as cereals and fruits rather than confectionery, are more effective over the next 24 hours.

A simple carbohydrate sports drink and confectionery such as lollies or sweets are recommended immediately after activity as a practical method of combining glycogen restoration with the *warm-down* activities. This should be followed by a meal rich in complex carbohydrates about 2 hours later.

Post-activity massage

A treatment that involves applying direct physical contact, usually with the hands, on the body, especially the skin, muscles and tendons. It is done to prevent *muscle soreness* and *delayed-onset muscle stiffness* (DOMS) after high-intensity training and competition.

The aim of the treatment is to increase blood flow to the muscles and loosen up formations of scar tissue. The *massage* techniques that are recommended are the same as those used in the treatment of injuries.

Post-activity psychology

Treatments that reduce high *arousal* levels and excessive fatigue after high-intensity training and competition. Commonly used techniques include *floatation tanks, music* and *visualisation*.

The fatigue may be due to overactivity of the *sympathetic nervous system*, which responds to exercise and sport with a fight-or-flight response caused by a release of *adrenaline* that increases the heart rate and cardiac output, widens the airways, and reduces glycogen stores in the liver and muscles.

Post-concussion syndrome

Signs and symptoms of *concussion* that persist for more than 2 weeks, including headache, dizziness, poor memory, slow decision-making, reduced concentration, irritability and tiredness.

Investigations of the brain such as *CT scan*, *magnetic resonance imaging (MRI)* and *digit symbol substitution test (DSST)* are recommended to exclude an underlying abnormality. If these are normal the recommended treatment is rest until all signs and symptoms have cleared for at least 1 week.

Posterior

The anatomical direction pointing towards the back of the body. It is used to describe the surface of any part of the body that faces the back, and a body part that is located closer to the back of the body than another part. For example, the buttock is commonly called 'the posterior'. It is the opposite of *anterior*. Also called dorsal, or the dorsum, in the hand and foot.

Posterior cruciate ligament (PCL) sprain

An acute injury of the ligament inside the *knee joint* that normally contributes to the stability of the joint by preventing backward sliding (posterior) movement. The injury is caused when a sudden excessive force causes overstretching, usually a sudden blow received to the front of the knee or upper shin.

Diagnosis, treatment and return to sport
This *sprain* causes pain and reduced range of movement. Usually, there is minimal swelling of the knee joint.

Treatment during the first 48 to 72 hours is *RICE* (*rest, ice, compression and elevation*) and avoidance of heat and alcohol consumption to minimise

A strengthening exercise of the right quadriceps muscles for posterior cruciate ligament sprain

swelling, followed by *strengthening exercises, flexibility exercises, balance* exercises, *massage*, electrotherapy such as *interferential therapy* and *ultrasound therapy*, and a *sport rehabilitation* program that emphasises strengthening of the quadriceps muscle. A brace or *taping* may be recommended after return to sport.

Return to sport is 2 to 4 weeks for mild injuries, 4 to 6 weeks for moderate injuries and 6 to 8 weeks for severe injuries. In a few cases surgery is performed if other structures in the knee joint have been damaged such as a *meniscus tear*.

Posterior interosseus nerve entrapment

A nerve compressed by swelling or scarring in surrounding muscle and fibrous tissue just below the *elbow joint*. It causes pain in the outer side of the elbow and forearm. Often there is also numbness on the outer side of the elbow and in the hand. A *nerve conduction test* may be performed to confirm the diagnosis.

Treatment of this *nerve entrapment* injury consists of *massage* to the muscle at the site of entrapment and, if required, *neural tension* stretching. If this fails, decompression surgery may be recommended, which has a high success rate.

Post-natal exercise

Participation in exercise and sport after a normal vaginal delivery of a baby can begin with gentle exercises, such as walking or stretching, the day after and be gradually increased according to comfort.

Care should be taken in the first 6 weeks after delivery because the changes in the body caused by *pregnancy* may take some time to return to normal. Avoidance of excessive stretching or lifting is advisable in this period. Pelvic floor exercises to prevent or treat *incontinence* are also recommended.

After a Caesarean section, strenuous activity should be avoided for 6 weeks, and heavy weight training for 12 weeks. *Strengthening exercises* under the supervision of a physiotherapist or fitness trainer is recommended for the abdominal muscles. Breastfeeding women need to pay special attention to adequate fluid and caloric intake. A good supportive *sports bra* is also important for exercise during this period.

Potassium

See *Minerals*.

Pott's fracture

A break in both or one of the lateral or medial malleolus bones of the *ankle*. It is usually due to a twist that turns the foot excessively inwards in a similar way to a twisted ankle, often causing a sharp pain that immediately makes walking difficult.

An *X-ray* may be required to confirm the diagnosis of this *fracture*. Treatment is usually either *immobilisation* in a plaster cast for up to 6 weeks if the fracture is stable, or *open surgery* and *internal fix-*

ation. Both should be followed by the same treatments as recommended for an *ankle sprain*.

Poultry

A food that contains essential nutrients, including protein, vitamins and minerals. It should be eaten without the skin, which reduces the *saturated fat* content. Turkey has less fat compared to chicken and duck.

Power

The maximum amount of *strength* that can be produced by a muscle or group of muscles during a fixed amount of time. For example, the time it takes for the quadriceps (front thigh muscle) to straighten the knee lifting a maximum weight eight times in a row. A quick time is an indication of greater power.

Power is more important in sports where the ability to produce strength quickly enables an athlete to win a competition, such as a 100 m sprint. It is also a contributing factor in ball sports such as baseball, cricket and golf.

Plyometrics and *Olympic-type weight lifting* are training programs that aim to increase power.

An athlete born with a higher proportion of *fast-twitch (FT) muscle fibres* is more likely to achieve high levels of *anaerobic fitness* and perform well in power activities.

Pre-competition eating

The foods that are recommended during the week before a competition event in order to maximise performance levels and reduce the risk of problems of the *gastrointestinal system* during competition. Specific recommendations for the day of competition are called the *pre-event meal*.

Carbohydrate loading and reduced overload
Sports that require high levels of aerobic fitness, such as long distance running lasting for an hour or more,

or sports that involve intermittent activity, such as football, basketball, baseball and squash, require adequate glycogen stores to prevent early fatigue called *glycogen depletion*.

A combination of moderate-intensity *aerobic training* and dietary manipulation through carbohydrate loading can increase glycogen stores by up to 100 per cent and make the muscles more likely to utilise *fat metabolism* to supply energy, which preserves glycogen stores for longer.

Carbohydrate loading involves reducing the *overload* of training 1 week prior to the event (see *Tapering*), but maintaining moderate to high carbohydrate levels in the diet (about 60 per cent of energy intake). Three to 4 days before the event the overload should be reduced further, and the carbohydrate intake increased to 70–80 per cent.

Athletes participating in events lasting up to an hour do not require carbohydrate loading because they are highly unlikely to deplete glycogen stores. However, stores should be maintained by slightly reducing the overload of training while maintaining normal carbohydrate intake.

Carbohydrate loading should be avoided by athletes participating in power sports such as the 100 m sprint because when glycogen is stored in the body it is attached to water molecules, which can add up to 1.5 kg (3.3 lb) in weight and have a detrimental effect on performance.

Bicarbonate loading

This technique involves consuming 200–300 mg of *sodium bicarbonate* (baking soda) per kilogram (90–180 mg per lb) of body weight. It may be useful for athletes performing high-intensity anaerobic activities, such as an 800 m run or a 200 m swimming race, which produce lactic acid that, when levels are too high, causes excessive acidity leading to *lactate fatigue*.

Bicarbonate maintains normal levels of acidity in the blood and muscles because bicarbonate ions (HCO_3^+) soak up the hydrogen ions (H^+) that are a by-product of lactic acid.

Potential side effects include nausea, *vomiting*, flatulence, *diarrhoea* and muscle cramps. It should not be attempted for the first time in an important competition. It should be tested in training beforehand.

Pre-event meal

The foods that are recommended on the same day as a competition event in order to maximise performance levels and reduce the risk of problems of the *gastrointestinal system* during competition.

Constituents

In general the food should be high *carbohydrate* and low *fat*. High carbohydrate provides enough energy to prevent feelings of hunger. A total energy intake of 2000–4000 kJ (500–1000 Calories) is recommended. Fat should be avoided because it is slower to digest and causes feelings of heaviness.

The meal also should contain a low to moderate amount of *fibre*. Even though fibre is generally good for an athlete's diet, it increases faecal bulk, which stimulates the urge to move the bowels and may cause excessive gas production and discomfort.

Specific suggestions include:
- Breakfast cereals and low-fat milk
- Fruits and fruit juices
- Bread, toast, crumpets, muffins and pancakes
- Suitable toppings such as banana or honey
- Potatoes, rice, pasta, noodles.

Athletes who find it hard to eat solid food, usually due to nerves, may prefer liquid meal preparations.

Mealtime

It is recommended to eat the meal 2 to 3 hours before the event. This allows time for the contents to empty out of the stomach and avoid the discomfort caused by competing when feeling full.

It also reduces bloodflow to the gastrointestinal system and leaves more blood available for the muscles, and helps to ensure that *insulin*, which stimulates cells throughout the body to absorb excess glucose from the blood, is maintained at a normal level for competition.

Athletes competing several times a day, such as with track and field heats and finals, also need to eat solid food to replenish glycogen stores and combat feelings of hunger in between events.

If there is insufficient time then a liquid meal preparation may be a good alternative solution. This also helps to maintain normal *hydration* levels. Sports drinks, fruit juices and cordial are recommended.

Pregnancy

The fertilisation of a female egg by a male sperm, followed by growth of the embryo and foetus and concluding with the birth of a baby. After fertilisation the embryo sits within the placenta that is attached to the wall of the uterus. After the eighth week of pregnancy the embryo has grown and developed into a foetus, with some of the basic features recognisable in a baby.

This growth and development continues until around the fortieth week of pregnancy when the birth of the baby occurs. Pregnancy is divided into three stages: first trimester (0 to 12 weeks); second trimester (13 to 28 weeks); and third trimester (29 to 40 weeks).

Exercise and sport

The advantages of participating in exercise and sport during pregnancy include less weight gain and increased fitness, which may enable better coping with labour and reduced risk of developing illnesses such as *diabetes*. *Post-natal exercise* after childbirth is also recommended.

At the same time, it has been suggested that there may be risks such as injury to the foetus from a direct blow, hyperthermia, which is a rise in core body *temperature* of the mother above 39°C (102°F) that may lead to malformations in the foetus, and lastly, an association with low birth weight of the baby. However, the question of risks is still an area under research, with conflicting opinions from medical experts (see below; Specific recommendations).

Pregnant women themselves may face a higher risk of injuries, especially *low back pain (non-specific)*, probably due to postural changes and the hormone relaxin, which loosens the body's ligaments in preparation for labour. Another potential problem is hypotension (low *blood pressure*) when exercising on the back. *Strengthening exercises* for the abdominal muscles are recommended for all pregnant women because as the foetus grows the muscles become stretched and weaker.

General recommendations

Pregnant women with illnesses such as *coronary heart disease* and *hypertension* (high blood pressure) should not participate in exercise and sport. *Iron-deficiency* anaemia and *diabetes* may not exclude being active; however, they do require a medical assessment.

If there are no health problems, participation in low and moderate-intensity activities (see *Aerobic training* and *Metabolic equivalent (MET)*) such as brisk walking and gentle swimming, are permitted throughout pregnancy. For women who weren't active before pregnancy, activities should be no more than low-intensity. Discomfort may force a reduction in intensity in pregnant women regardless of fitness levels from around the end of second trimester.

All pregnant women participating in exercise and sport should note the following:
1) Avoid exercising when lying on the back.
2) Avoid hyperthermia (see *Heat illness*), especially during the first trimester, by:
   - participating, if possible, in only moderate-intensity activities.
   - not training or competing during the hottest time of day (usually 11am to 4pm).
   - ensuring proper fluid intake (see *Hydration*)
   - wearing light-coloured, open weave clothing made of natural fibres such as cotton.
   - in team sports, allowing regular interchange for cooling off.
3) Perform a good *warm-up* and *warm-down*.
4) Avoid excessive stretching during *flexibility exercises*.
5) Wear a firm supportive *sports bra*.
6) Perform pelvic floor exercises to prevent *incontinence*.
7) Cease activity immediately if any abnormal symptoms develop, such as pain, uterine contractions, vaginal bleeding or leakage of amniotic fluid, dizziness, faintness, shortness of breath, heart *palpitations*, excessively high *heart beat*, nausea, vomiting, pins and needles, numbness or visual disturbances.

Specific recommendations

Recent research has shed new light on the issue of making exercise and sport-specific recommendations. Certain recommendations (listed below) are considered by some medical experts to be excessively restrictive, though there are others that insist they should still be applied.

The research has found, for example, that despite the concerns about a direct blow to the foetus, a check of hospitals and medical journals shows that there are no reported cases of such an injury to a foetus from a mother playing sport. That doesn't mean that there has never been an injury to a pregnant woman in a contact sport resulting in harm to the foetus. But the lack of any reports appears to make the likelihood of such an incident low.

As a result, while it is important to discuss one's situation with a doctor beforehand, the research suggests that there is no evidence for a blanket ban on all pregnant women playing, for example, netball in the third trimester. However, because of the conflicting opinions, it may be recommended to adhere to all of the following exercise and sport-specific recommendations:

- Not permitted during pregnancy: *scuba diving* deeper than 10 m (33 ft), *horse riding sports*, water skiing, *downhill skiing, gymnastics, Valsalva manoeuvre* and sky diving.
- Only permitted during first trimester: *soccer*, touch football, *hockey (field), martial arts, softball, volleyball, basketball* and *lacrosse*.
- Only permitted during first and second trimesters: *netball, baseball, cycling, trampolining*, racquet sports such as *tennis*, indoor *cricket*.
- Permitted throughout pregnancy: walking, stationary cycling, *swimming* and low-impact *aerobics* (see *Exercise for health*).

Premenstrual tension (PMT)

Emotional and physical symptoms occurring in the week or two leading up to *menstruation*. Symptoms may include *anxiety, depression*, mood swings, *headaches*, fluid retention, breast soreness and breast enlargement. These symptoms disappear after menstruation starts. Regular participation in exercise and sport may reduce the severity of symptoms.

Treatments for athletes affected by fluid retention include *diuretics*, though they are *drugs banned in sport* according to the International Olympic Committee (IOC), avoiding *dehydration* by reducing *caffeine* and salt intake during the 2 weeks leading up to menstruation and taking primrose oil supplements.

Pre-syncope

See *Syncope*.

Prevention

Activities that aim to reduce the occurrence of injury, illness or disease. For example, drinking enough fluids before and during running a marathon can prevent *dehydration*. Taking antihypertensive medication reduces high blood pressure and the chances of a *heart attack*.

The most important prevention measures in exercise and sport include correction of a *biomechanical abnormality*, performing a *warm-up* and *warm-down, flexibility exercises, taping*, wearing a *brace*, using the correct *protective equipment* and exercise and sport-specific equipment such as tennis racquets, wearing the correct *shoes*, training on suitable *surfaces* and implementing appropriate *training, sports psychology* and *sports nutrition* techniques and advice.

Pritikin diet

A food program that aims to prevent ill health and disease and achieve wellbeing and weight loss. It is high in *carbohydrates* and *fibre* and very low in fat (less than 10 per cent of the total energy intake).

Specific foods that are not permitted include coffee, tea, alcohol, butter, margarine, oils, eggs and most dairy products. Salt and sugar intakes are kept to a minimum. In general the nutritional guidelines are acceptable, except there is a risk of inadequate intakes of iron, zinc and calcium.

Progressive muscle relaxation

A psychological technique that can reduce the level of tension in the muscles. It involves placing the body in a relaxed posture, such as lying down, and then progressively contracting and relaxing specific muscles one by one. It is recommended for people who are feeling excessive *stress*.

It teaches awareness of the difference between tense and relaxed muscles, and improves one's ability to concentrate on a specific part of the body.

Muscle tension is also called *muscle tone*, which means the background level of muscle contractions. Muscles have the lowest level of contractions during sleep. When at rest, the muscles are contracting slightly in preparation for activities that might be performed such as walking or running. The level of background contraction is raised in people who experience excessive stress and *anxiety* and high levels of *arousal*.

Method

Progressive muscle relaxation involves following a series of steps. Many people find it helpful to use a recorded tape of instructions as reminders for each step.

1) In a quiet room with dim lights and minimal intrusions from the outside world, place the body in a relaxed posture.
2) You can begin with any part of the body and the muscles that control it. For example, clench your right hand and make a fist, holding it as tight as possible for 1-2-3-4-5 seconds. Notice how much tension is created in the muscles of the hand. Then allow it to unfold and relax. Notice the difference between the tension created by making a fist and the relaxed state.
3) After 10 seconds of focusing on this relaxed state, repeat the same action with your left hand.
4) Repeat the same action progressively, moving up different sections of the right arm to the shoulder.
5) Repeat the same for the left hand and arm, then both hands and arms together, followed by the neck.
6) The same progression occurs from the feet to the hips and pelvis, then the muscles of the back, abdomen, chest and finally the face, mouth, jaws and forehead. In each case the key is to increase awareness of the reduction in muscle tension that occurs when allowing them to relax.

Progressive muscle relaxation was first developed by US psychologist Edmund Jacobson in the 1930s and has been incorporated into or adapted to many relaxation techniques. Other methods of relaxing muscles include *autogenic training, meditation, visualisation, stress inoculation, biofeedback, centring, flotation tank, music* and *massage*.

Progressive overload

See *Overload*.

Pronation

A movement of a *synovial joint* that means rotation in a direction pointing towards the midline of the body. For example, turning the hands so that the palms face downwards involves pronation of the elbow joint.

The mechanical axis of the rotation is usually through the centre of the bone that is moving, similar to a pen that is being rotated between your thumb and fingers. It is most commonly used to describe movement in the *elbow joint, ankle* and foot (see *Foot and toe joints*).

Pronation is also known as internal rotation at the *shoulder joint* and *hip joint*. It is the opposite of *supination*.

Proprioception

An unconscious sensory perception of joint position and movement that is particularly important for maintaining balance and coordination, and performing an activity with precision and skill.

It is produced by combining information gathered by different types of nerve receptors in the *sensory nervous system*, such as mechanoreceptors in ligaments and muscle spindles and golgi tendon organs in muscles.

This information is sent to nerves in the *central nervous system*, including the spinal cord and cerebellum of the brain, that send signals back with instructions telling the muscles about which movements and postures they should produce.

Proprioception training should begin as early as possible following an injury of a ligament, such as an *ankle sprain*.

Proprioception training

Regular participation in activities to improve the unconscious sensory perception of joint position and movement that is important for maintaining balance and coordination.

Nerve receptors can be damaged by an injury, which may lead to impaired balance and decreased coordination, diminished joint position sense, a tendency for the joints to give way and altered reflexes when performing specific or general movements. It is most commonly observed in the legs, particularly after an *ankle sprain*.

Method

Proprioception exercises should begin as early as possible in a *sport rehabilitation* program. The most

Proprioception training on a ski stimulator

simple lower limb proprioception exercise is to stand on one leg. Standing on the toes only, closing the eyes, using a moving surface such as ski simulators (Fitters) or a rocker or balance board, increases the difficulty.

After these tasks are mastered more complex tasks such as hopping and walking on soft, uneven or sloped surfaces may be introduced. In the later stages *agility training* and *skills training* encourage further improvement.

Proprioception exercises are also important in the rehabilitation of arm and hand injuries. Initially, exercises are performed with a light-weight in the available pain-free range. Exercises may progress to weight-bearing exercises in different positions; for example, push-ups either seated, kneeling, lying face down or standing against a wall.

Prostaglandins

A chemical substance produced by most cells in the body in response to an injury or specific hormones. Prostaglandins are similar to *hormones*, except that

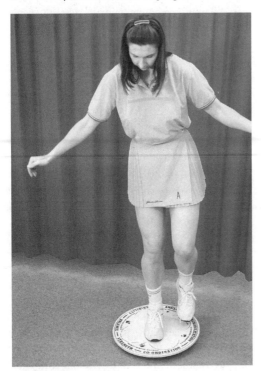

Proprioception training on a rocker board

Ankle proprioception training

Partial weight-bearing

- Walking with support (crutches) ensuring correct heel movement
- Seated with feet on rocker board, forward/backwards rocking for 2 minutes pain-free, first with both legs, then with one leg

Full weight-bearing

- Multiaxial rocker (both legs)
  - 2–3 minutes each way circling
  - Attempt to balance for 15 seconds, rest 10 seconds
  - Progressively increase complexity: arms out in front of body; arms crossed; eyes closed; knee bends; other leg swinging; bounce/catch ball
- Balance on minitrampoline
  - Same progression as above
  - Hop and land
  - Hop and land with one-quarter turn and return
  - Progress to half turn, three-quarter turn and full turn
  - Rhythmical hopping, alternatively placing toe forwards and sideways
  - Rhythmical hopping across a line, forward/backwards, sideways
- Jumping
  - Various patterns
- Hopping without rebounder
  - Alternatively two hops on one leg, two hops on other leg
- Skipping
  - On spot, both legs, forwards/backwards/sideways
  - Single leg, two hops on one leg, two hops on other leg
- Advanced tasks
  - Walk/run across a steep hill each way
  - Run sideways up and down hill, each way
  - Walk along balance beam, then bounce and throw ball while walking
  - Sideways step-ups, gradually increasing height of step
- Running drills
  - Straight
  - Backwards
  - Sideways
  - Circle (5 m/16 ft diameter)
  - Cutting 90 degrees
  - Zigzag through cones set at 45 degrees

they usually act on the local area rather than entering the blood to travel around the body.

There are many types of prostaglandins with different effects. For example, following an injury they cause blood vessels to widen their diameter and increase their permeability, which leads to *inflammation* and swelling. They may cause problems such as painful menstruation, called *dysmenorrhea*. In an *asthma* attack they cause inflammation of the airways of the lungs.

Protective equipment

Equipment designed to shield various parts of the body against injury from direct blows without interfering with the sporting activity. It can also be used for protection of an injury that is still healing or is at risk of re-injury.

The most commonly used and important pieces of equipment include *helmet, mouthguard*, forearm guard, *thigh padding*, shoulder pads, chest pad and *shin guard*.

Protein

A compound that is made up of a very long chain of amino acids held together by peptide bonds. Each protein is made up of hundreds or thousands of amino acids. There are 20 different types of *amino acid*, which is a nitrogen-based amino molecule attached to an acidic carboxyl molecule.

There are two types of proteins, fibrous and globular. Fibrous proteins are found in *muscles, tendons* and *connective tissue* such as *ligaments*, hair and skin. Globular proteins are found in *enzymes*, which are involved in metabolic processes such as the breakdown of glucose to release energy, and *hormones*, which promote physiological processes such as puberty.

Diet

Foods that are rich in protein include red meat, eggs, poultry, dairy products, vegetables, nuts and grains. The *gastrointestinal system* breaks down protein into amino acids that are absorbed through the gut into the blood to be transported to cells and used to build more proteins.

Exercise and sport

Protein is important in exercise and sport for the repair of damaged tissue and building new tissue, such as muscle in people who are lifting weights. It also makes a small contribution to the *energy supply* (usually 5–10 per cent).

The recommended daily protein intake for endurance athletes such as those participating in

Protein content of foods

Food	Amount	Weight (g)	Weight (oz)	Energy (kJ)	Energy (Cal)	Protein (g)
Milk, skim	1 cup	259	9.1	380	90	9
Milk, reduced fat	1 cup	260	9.1	540	129	10
Milk, whole	1 cup	258	9.1	700	167	9
Yoghurt, low-fat, natural	1 tub	200	7	450	108	12
Yoghurt, low-fat, flavoured	1 tub	200	7	630	151	10
Yoghurt, flavoured/fruit	1 tub	200	7	810	193	10
Cheese, cheddar	1 slice	20	0.7	340	81	5
Cheese, ricotta	20 g	20	0.7	120	29	2
Cheese, cottage, low-fat	20 g	20	0.7	75	18	4
Cheese, camembert	20 g	20	0.7	260	62	4
Cheese, cream	1 tbsp	20	0.7	280	67	2
Ice cream, vanilla	60 g	60	2.1	480	114	3
Beef, fillet steak, lean	120 g	120	4.2	990	235	36
Chicken, boneless, baked, lean	120 g	120	4.2	940	224	34
Turkey, breast, baked, lean	120 g	120	4.2	780	186	35
Pork, boneless, cooked, lean	120 g	120	4.2	850	204	37
Ham, non-canned, lean and fat	1 slice	25	0.9	150	36	4
Lamb, boneless, cooked, lean	120 g	120	4.2	940	225	37
Fish, steamed	150 g	150	5.3	780	187	36
Oysters, raw	1 dozen	60	2.1	180	44	7
Prawns, king, cooked	100 g	100	3.5	440	104	24
Egg, whole, hard boiled	1 medium	47	1.7	300	71	6
Muesli flakes	1 cup	43	1.5	690	164	4
Weet-Bix	2 biscuits	30	1	400	95	3
Corn Flakes	1 cup	30	1	470	113	2
Bread, wholemeal	1 slice	30	1	280	67	3
Rice cakes	1 serve	13	0.5	190	46	1
Crispbread, rye	1 biscuit	8	0.3	100	24	1
Biscuit, plain, dry	10 g	10	0.4	140	33	1
Potato, baked flesh	1 medium	100	3.5	310	73	3
Rice, brown, boiled	½ cup	90	3.2	570	135	3
Pasta, white, boiled	½ cup	75	2.6	370	89	3
Sweetcorn, frozen, on cob	½ cup	72	2.8	270	68	3
Pea, green boiled	½ cup	83	2.9	170	40	4
Broccoli, boiled	1 cup	152	5.4	150	37	7
Bean, green boiled	1 cup	140	4.9	100	23	2
Apple, raw, unpeeled	1 medium	120	4.2	250	59	0
Pear, yellow green, raw, unpeeled	1 medium	150	5.3	320	76	0
Orange, raw, peeled	1 medium	120	4.2	190	45	1
Banana, raw, peeled	1 average	140	4.9	420	100	2
Cantaloupe, raw, peeled	0.5 whole	120	4.2	110	26	1
Grape, green sultana	30 average	90	3.2	230	55	1
Brazil nut	20 g	20	0.7	560	133	3
Cashew nut	20 g	20	0.7	480	115	3
Almonds, unsalted	20 g	20	0.7	470	112	3
Peanuts, roasted, salted	20 g	20	0.7	520	124	5
Baked beans, canned in sauce	1 cup	272	9.6	775	185	13
Lentils, boiled	1 cup	211	7.4	620	148	14
Beans, kidney, fresh, boiled	200 g	200	7	960	229	26

long distance running, is 1.2–1.6 grams per kilogram (g/kg) (0.5–0.7 g per pound (g/lb)) of body weight, which is considerably higher than the 0.75 g/kg (0.3 g/lb) of body weight that is recommended for less active people.

The exact amounts required can be found according

to the guidelines of the *strength training diet* and *aerobic training diet*. The energy content from protein metabolism is 1 g = 16 kJ (4 Cal).

Some groups of athletes may be at risk of inadequate protein intake, which is called *protein depletion*, including children and adolescents, lactating and pregnant women and vegetarians.

Protein depletion

Excessively reduced protein supply in the body that can cause abnormal *tiredness* leading to poor performance.

Protein only provides 5–10 per cent of energy needs during exercise and sport through conversion of amino acids to glucose in a metabolic process called *protein oxidation*. However, the longer the duration of an activity, the more the carbohydrate supply diminishes and the contribution of protein increases.

Protein is also used to repair damaged tissue, which occurs during endurance activities lasting more than an hour. As a result, the protein requirements are greatest for endurance athletes (see *Energy supply*).

Protein oxidation

The chemical processes that break down proteins to produce adenosine triphosphate (ATP), the main source of energy for *muscle contractions*. Protein normally supplies only a small part of the total energy needs of muscles compared to carbohydrates and fats in a healthy person.

Physiology

A number of processes are involved in the oxidation of protein. Each one converts *amino acids* (the basic components of protein) into different types of *carbohydrates*. For example, amino acids are converted into glucose through gluconeogenesis. Other processes convert amino acids into acetyl coenzyme A (acetyl CoA), which is broken down by the *carbohydrate oxidation* metabolic system.

Proximal

The anatomical direction pointing towards the trunk of the body. Most often used in the arms and legs. For example, the elbow is proximal to the hand and blood flowing from the knee to the hip is moving in a proximal direction. The opposite is called *distal*.

Pseudoephedrine

A decongestant drug that has a similar effect to *ephedrine*. Previously it was a banned drug, but now it is permitted, though it is being monitored for misuse by the World Anti-Doping Agency (WADA).

Psoriasis

See *Psoriatic arthritis*.

Psoriatic arthritis

An inflammatory disease of the joints that causes loss of flexibility, morning stiffness, pain and fever, in association with psoriasis, a skin disease that causes thickened patches of red and inflamed skin. The cause of psoriasis is unknown.

The skin symptoms are due to cell growth that is 10 times faster than normal. The arthritis usually affects more than one joint, in particular the low back joints and sacroiliac joints, which causes low back and buttock pain.

There is no curative treatment for psoriasis. Treatments for the arthritis include *non-steroidal anti-inflammatory drugs* (NSAIDs), *flexibility exercises* and *strengthening exercises*.

Psychologist

A health practitioner who has completed training and is registered and recognised as being qualified to provide diagnosis and treatment for the internal workings of the mind, including emotions, thoughts, memory, intelligence, learning and motivation, and manifestations of the mind such as behaviour and physical health.

A number of psychologists have a specialisation in sport and exercise, called *sports psychology*.

Psychology

The science of the internal workings of the mind, including emotions, thoughts, memory, intelligence, learning and motivation, and their impact on behaviour and physical health.

Sports psychology is a specialised field that deals with people participating in exercise and sport.

Psychology of rehabilitation

The relationship between the workings of the mind and return to sport after an injury. Responses to injury that can have a negative impact on recovery include excessive focus on pain and fears of re-injury.

A psychological response experienced by some athletes with a severe injury that forces them out of full training and competition for months or a year, includes loss of lifestyle and personal goals that may lead to an excessive grief response.

Grief response

There are five stages in a healthy grief response:
1) Denial: 'I'm not that badly injured'
2) Anger: 'Why me?'
3) Bargaining: 'If you can get me through the game I'll give it a rest after that'
4) Depression: 'It'll never get right'
5) Acceptance.

However, some people can get stuck at one of the stages. For example, unrealistic bargaining with a doctor, such as demanding a medication to fix the injury as a trade off for the recommended *sport rehabilitation* program. Signs of poor coping include non-compliance to the program, consistent denial of the extent of injury and signs of *depression*.

Treatment

High self-esteem can assist with dealing with grief and achieve a more successful recovery from injury. Good psychological skills also help with coping with external sources of pressure, such as not worrying too much about missing important events, being permanently replaced in the team and financial loss.

Self-esteem can be learnt through counselling, which may raise psychological issues in a non-confrontational and empathetic manner. For example, acknowledging the loss and the need to accept the situation.

Techniques such as *visualisation* (using the imagination to picture the injury healing) and *progressive muscle relaxation* can also help. In addition, it may be useful to plan a structure to the day and fill the week with new activities.

Goal-setting is crucial to allow a step-wise approach and ensure concentration on short-term treatment goals rather than becoming anxious about the long-term outcome.

Puberty

The period of life where sexual maturation is achieved. It begins with physical changes such as budding breasts or pubic hair in girls, usually around the age of 10, and growth in the size of the scrotum and penis or pubic hair in boys, around the age of 12.

For most girls it ends around 13 or 14, when a regular menstrual cycle and the ability to get pregnant become present. For most boys it is around 14 or 15, when sperm production and the ability to cause pregnancy are present.

Puberty occurs due to the influence of the sex hormones, produced by the pituitary gland and ovaries in girls and testes in boys. The main sex hormone for boys is *testosterone* and for females, *oestrogen*. Though the sexual maturation process follows the same order in girls and boys, it can progress at different rates in each.

The changes in girls include the growth of breasts, pubic hair, *menstruation*, widening of hips and enlargement of the uterus. The first period is more likely to occur later in girls who are elite athletes such as gymnasts and ballet dancers, called delayed menarche. It is unclear whether this is because of the training or that the later the first period, the more likely an athlete will continue training and reach the elite level.

In boys the changes include sperm production, enlargement of sexual organs, pubic hair, widening of the shoulders and voice deepening.

Exercise and sport

Physical changes important to exercise and sport include growth in height and body weight, and a maturation of bones, muscles, nerves and other organs and the way they function in exercise and sport.

The physical maturation continues after puberty finishes until adulthood is reached, around 19 years in women and 22 in men. Puberty is the first part of being an *adolescent*, which also includes psychological, emotional, social and economic aspects of growing up.

Pubic symphysitis

See *Osteitis pubis*.

Pulmonary diffusion

The movement of oxygen and carbon dioxide between the tiny air-filled space in the lungs, called the *alveolus*, and a nearby capillary that contains flowing blood. The movement involves oxygen (O_2) taken out of the air and into the blood and carbon dioxide (CO_2) moving in the opposite direction, from the blood and into the air.

Physiology

The outside air is breathed in through the mouth and/or nose into the *lungs* and down the bronchioles until it reaches the alveoli. It is a mixture of different gases including oxygen (20.93 per cent), nitrogen (79.04 per cent) and carbon dioxide (0.03 per cent).

Each gas exerts a partial air pressure that is equal to its proportion of the total outside air pressure that is, at sea level, 760 mmHg (millimetres of mercury). This means the outside air has a partial pressure of oxygen (pO_2) of 20.93 per cent $\times$ 760 mmHg = 159 mmHg.

The alveolus contains its own mixture of gases, most notably, pO_2 = 100 mmHg, much less than the outside air. The air in the alveoli is separated from the blood flowing by in the blood vessel by an extremely thin membrane, a mere 0.5 to 4 micrometres (2/100 000 to 1.6/10 000 in) thick.

The blood, which has come from the cells of the body that have used up much of the oxygen in it, has a relatively low pO_2 = 40 mmHg. The movement of oxygen from the alveolus into the blood occurs due to the natural laws of pressure (it flows from high to low pressure).

Similarly, the blood contains a partial pressure of carbon dioxide (p CO_2) = 46 mmHg, whereas the alveolus has a pCO_2 = 40 mm Hg. CO_2, a waste product produced by the cells, moves out of the blood into the alveolus and is then breathed out of the lungs.

Exercise and sport

During exercise and sport a greater amount of oxygen and carbon dioxide moves between the alveolus and blood vessel because of an increased amount of blood flowing through due to a higher heart rate and cardiac output.

This amount is often the greatest in people who have high aerobic and cardiovascular fitness that helps in endurance activities such as long distance running (see *Breathing regulation*).

Pulmonary vascular system

The arteries and veins that carry blood flowing to and from the *lungs*. Blood with a low oxygen content flowing from the right ventricle of the *heart* is carried by the pulmonary arteries to the alveoli (microscopic sacs where gas exchange takes place) in the lungs.

The blood absorbs oxygen, changing its colour from blue to red, and flows back through the pulmonary veins to the left atrium and left ventricle of the heart where it is pumped into the *peripheral vascular system* to the cells of the body.

Pulmonary ventilation

See *Breathing*.

Pulse

The rhythmic increase and decrease in *blood pressure* in the arteries, which can be felt in areas close to the skin, such as the radial pulse at the front of the wrist just below the base of the thumb and carotid pulse in the neck next to the Adam's apple.

The increase in pressure occurs with each *heartbeat* that pumps blood from the ventricle of the *heart* into the arteries. The pulse is used to measure *heart rate*, which is the number of heartbeats per minute.

Pulsed short wave

See *Diathermy*.

Pyruvate

The chemical produced when pyruvic acid is added to water. Pyruvic acid is the end process of the breakdown of glucose in the *glycolytic system*, which produces adenosine triphosphate (ATP), the main source of energy for muscle contractions.

It is taken as a supplement with the aim of improving the impact of *aerobic training* and performance in endurance activities such as *long distance running*, and to assist with weight loss.

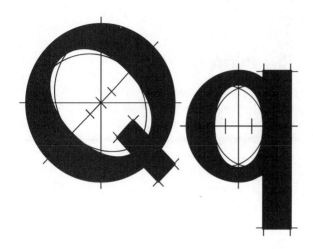

Quadriceps contusion

An injury caused by a direct blow into the front of the *thigh* from a part of the body of an opposing player or a piece of equipment. It is most common in contact sports such as *football* codes, *basketball* and *ice hockey*, and ball sports such as *lacrosse* and *cricket* where a ball often travels at high speed.

Diagnosis

The injury is a *muscle contusion* that causes a specific area of tenderness, swelling and pain that is aggravated by contracting or stretching the muscle. In severe cases the pain may interfere with sleep.

Blood from contusions located in the lower third of the quadriceps muscle may track down to the knee and irritate the *knee joint*. It is important to assess the severity to determine the treatment and return to sport.

A mild (grade 1) contusion usually does not stop activity, and it may not even be remembered. There may be soreness after cooling down or the next morning. Moderate (grade 2) contusion also usually doesn't stop activity; however, it is usually remembered. Tenderness is felt when pressed firmly

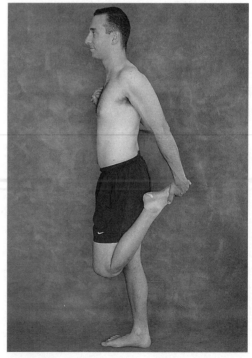

Flexibility exercise of the right quadriceps muscle following a contusion injury

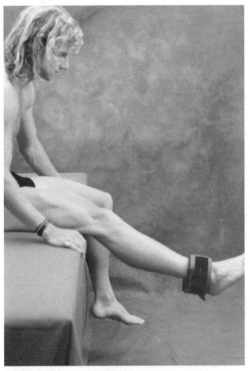

Concentric strengthening exercise of the right quadriceps muscle following a contusion injury

with the hand. Often it causes a limp and may stiffen up. Severe (grade 3) contusion is remembered and quickly causes loss of strength, difficulty with walking and the skin shows obvious signs of bleeding.

Treatment

Moderate and severe contusions are treated somewhat differently to mild contusions. The most important period for all grades is in the first 24 hours following the injury when *rest* with crutches is necessary until weight bearing is possible without causing excessive pain, combined with *ice, elevation* and *compression*.

Gentle *passive exercises* (which are the same as stretching, and should not aggravate the pain) and, later, *flexibility exercises* are recommended to prevent loss of range of movement of the muscle, which can be significant if not treated properly. Flexibility exercises should only begin on day three after the injury occurs for a moderate contusion and day four

for severe contusions. A mild contusion can begin on day one or two.

Not starting *massage or ultrasound therapy* in the first 48 hours and then only gently, is crucial for avoiding *myositis ossificans*, especially for moderate and severe contusions. Heat and alcohol should be avoided to prevent more bleeding.

Return to sport

The timing of return to sport is mainly guided by pain and the response of the muscle to treatment. General guidelines based on the severity are: mild, 3 days to 1 week; moderate, 2 to 4 weeks; severe, 4 to 8 weeks. Prevention of another contusion can be achieved by wearing *thigh padding*.

Quadriceps strain

An acute injury of the front *thigh* muscle that is caused by a sudden explosive force that usually occurs during sprinting, jumping or kicking. It is associated with insufficient *warm-up*, reduced flexibility, excessive muscle fatigue and muscle imbalance that creates an abnormality affecting *running biomechanics*.

Diagnosis

The painful area is easy to pinpoint, the muscle is tender to firm pressure and, if the strain is severe, swelling and bruising are present.

There are three degrees of muscle *strain*. Mild (grade 1) strain does not force a stop to activity, and is usually noticed after cooling down or the following day. Moderate (grade 2) strain causes reduced muscle strength and pain that prevents continued participation as soon as the injury occurs. Severe (grade 3) strains significantly reduce strength and immediately prevent continued participation, but may be less painful than moderate strains.

Occasionally it may be difficult to distinguish between a mild (grade 1) quadriceps contusion and mild (grade 1) strain. A contusion usually causes pain almost immediately, and bruising may be obvious soon afterwards. *Diagnostic ultrasound* examination may be helpful for differentiating between the two injuries.

Treatment and return to sport

The treatment of a quadriceps strain is the same as that for a *quadriceps contusion*, except it is important to include *strengthening exercises* and avoid sharp acceleration and deceleration movements in the early stages of injury. Return to sport for mild strains requires 3 to 5 days; moderate 2 to 3 weeks; severe up to 10 weeks.

Quadriplegia

Partial or complete loss of the ability to move the legs, trunk and arms and feel sensations, usually accompanied by bladder and bowel control impairment. The most common cause is damage to the *spinal cord* following a road accident. The impact on muscles is *atrophy* and hypotonia (reduced *muscle tone*).

The heart, diaphragm of the lungs and other organs continue to work because the nerves come directly from the brain, not via the spinal cord. Some of the muscles and sensations in the arms may not be affected, depending on the spinal cord level damage. Moving around can be achieved by using a wheelchair. Participants in exercise and sport are called *wheelchair athletes*.

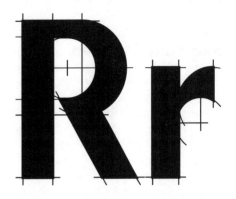

Radial tunnel syndrome

See *Posterior interosseus nerve entrapment.*

Radiofrequency neurotomy

A technique used for treating neck pain and some cases of low back pain. It is recommended when a zygapophysial joint of the *neck joints* or *low back joints* has been identified as the cause by a test called a *diagnostic nerve block.*

The technique involves inserting a needle close to the two small nerves that supply feelings of pain for the joint, heating the needle to 85°C (185°F) for 90 seconds, which damages the nerve and stops it from producing pain sensations.

The procedure should take from 45 minutes up to 3 hours, depending on the number of joints treated. The pain relief usually lasts for 9 to 12 months. The technique may need to be repeated if the nerve grows back and pain returns. An alternative method involves applying alcohol to damage the nerves.

Radiological investigation

A test that provides an image of bones, muscles, tendons, joints, ligaments, nerves and organs such as the brain and heart. The images are used to confirm the *diagnosis* already made according to the information gathered in the history and physical examination.

The most commonly used methods include *X-rays, diagnostic ultrasound, magnetic resonance imaging (MRI), CT scan,* arthrogram, *SPECT* and *bone scan.*

Each one uses a different type of invisible energy wave, such as high frequency sound waves in ultrasound, and has specific injuries and body parts that it is best suited for. For example, X-rays are good for finding simple broken bones but not for detecting a bone stress fracture. An MRI or CT scan is more suited for this task.

Radiologist

A doctor who has received medical training recognised as a specialisation to perform *radiological* investigations, such as X-rays, ultrasound, magnetic resonance imaging (MRI) and CT scan.

Radionuclide scan

A radiological investigation that produces an image of blood flow in a specific organ in the body. It involves being injected with a radioactive substance that is carried by the blood to the organ. A synthetic substance called technetium is used in a *bone scan*.

The radiation given off by the substance is called gamma rays, which are similar to X-rays. The dosage is considered to be minute and easily within safe limits. It is detected by a gamma camera, which contains a scintillation crystal and produces the image on a screen.

Radius distal epiphysis fracture

A break in the lower end of the radius above the thumb-side of the *wrist joint*, most commonly found in young female gymnasts.

It is usually due to an overuse injury called a *growth plate fracture*, which is caused by excessive repeated forces on the bone that cause pain and reduced range of movement of wrist extension (backwards movement).

An X-*ray* may be recommended to confirm the diagnosis. It is best treated with a plaster cast *immobilisation* for 3 to 4 weeks and reducing the forces on the wrist through changes to training. It can take 3 to 6 months to settle down.

Radius head fracture

A break in the upper end of the radius (outer forearm bone) just below the *elbow joint*. It is the most common fracture around the elbow, almost always resulting from a fall onto an outstretched hand.

Most radius head *fractures* are minimally displaced or undisplaced, making them very difficult to diagnose on an X-ray. The recommended treatment

is a splint, which is a form of *immobilisation* called protected mobilisation. Return to sport can be expected within 6 to 8 weeks.

If the fracture is displaced the required treatment is *open surgery* and *internal fixation* or excision. For comminuted fractures the treatment is surgical excision of the bone pieces.

Range of movement

The amount of movement that is available in a *joint* and associated ligaments, *muscle* or the neural sheath of *nerves*. It is also called a measure of *flexibility*, stretchability or range of motion. It can be performed with the assistance of an outside force, such as a therapist, which is called a *passive movement*, or as an *active movement* when performed without assistance.

Measurements

Measurements of range of movement are performed in a number of situations such as: during a *physical examination* when making a diagnosis of an injury or disease; as part of the continuing assessment during a *rehabilitation* program to check if progress is being made; during *strength training* to make sure that flexibility is not lost as a consequence of muscle strength imbalance; and in an assessment of a *biomechanical abnormality*.

Joint

For movements such as bending, straightening and turning it is calculated in terms of degrees, with the *anatomical position* or *neutral joint position* as the starting point. For example, 180 degrees of shoulder joint abduction occurs when you lift your hands and arms up and clap them above your head. If you are sitting in a chair right now, it is likely that your knee joints are bent at right angles or 90 degrees of knee joint flexion. These movements can be measured actively or passively.

For sliding (accessory) movements it is calculated in terms of distance (cm, mm or in) or as a percentage or grade of the normal amount that can be expected at that joint. They can only be measured passively.

Muscle

It is usually measured passively, though it can also be done actively, either as a *concentric* (shortening) or *eccentric* (stretching out) muscle contraction.

It is usually described as an angle that is measured in degrees, with the *anatomical position* or *neutral joint position* as the starting point. For example, the flexibility of the hamstring (back thigh muscle) can be measured by having a person lie down on their back on a bed. The leg of the hamstring being measured is lifted upwards at the hip joint keeping the knee straight until a stretching feeling is felt in the muscle. At this point the angle or range of movement at the hip joint can be measured.

An alternative method of measuring the hamstring is by standing and trying to touch your toes. For instance, reaching the floor with the fingers is a measure of the flexibility of the muscle.

Neural sheath

The range of movement of this structure is measured as part of a *neural tension* test. It is only measured as a passive movement.

Reading the play

See *Situation awareness*.

Rear foot valgus

A defect in the structure of the foot that causes the heel and rear section of the foot to point outwardly, leading to excessive *foot supination* during walking and running.

Rear foot varus

A defect in the structure of the foot that causes the heel and rear section of the foot to point inwardly, leading to excessive *foot pronation* at the subtalar joint during walking and running.

Reconstructive surgery

A surgical procedure that involves replacing diseased or injured tissue with healthy tissue. The most common example in exercise and sport is reconstructive surgery in the knee for *anterior cruciate ligament (ACL) tear*. It involves taking a section of a nearby muscle tendon, called a graft, and placing it in the same location as the anterior cruciate ligament.

Another common example of reconstructive surgery is bypass surgery for *coronary heart disease*, which involves removing a vein from the leg and using it to create a bypass around a blocked coronary artery, a blood vessel that supplies blood to the heart muscle.

Recreational

A term used to describe participation in exercise or sport at an informal level. Examples include walking with a friend, playing a social game of tennis and being a member of a netball team in an organised competition. Usually no money is received after winning an event. In fact participants often have to pay for the right to participate. It is the most popular form of physical activity.

Red blood cells

Cells that carry oxygen in the *blood* from the lungs to all the other cells of the body. Oxygen attaches to an iron-containing protein in red blood cells called *haemoglobin*, which gives blood its red colour. When red blood cells hand over oxygen to other cells they usually absorb back carbon dioxide, a metabolic waste product, which gives them a blue colouring.

Red blood cells (also called red blood corpuscles or erythrocytes) are disc-shaped and just small enough to squeeze through a capillary. There are billions of red blood cells in the average adult, and they make up more than 40 per cent of the volume of blood. The structure of the membrane of the cell varies from person to person, hence the different blood groups.

Red blood cells are formed from stem cells, which are found in the red *bone marrow* in the internal cavity of long bones. Stem cells are the immature prototypes for both red and white blood cells and platelets, which are stimulated to form blood cells by a hormone produced by the kidney called *erythropoietin (EPO)*.

The body will produce more erythropoietin and hence more red blood cells when it consistently senses that the level of oxygen being absorbed from the lungs into red blood cells is low, such as during *altitude training*.

Referred pain

Pain felt in one location that is caused by a damaged structure in another location some distance away. Examples include headache caused by the upper neck muscles, left arm pain caused by a heart attack, and pain in the hamstring muscle due to a low back joint injury.

While in most cases damaged structures cause *pain* to be felt locally, referred pain is not uncommon. The perception of pain at a point distant to the source of the pain is thought to be due to the brain misinterpreting the origin of a painful stimulus.

Structures like muscles, ligaments and joints in one part of the body can have their pain-sensing nerves (called nociceptors) connected to the same nerves in the spinal cord as nociceptors from other parts of the body. For example, signals from pain-sensitive structures in the spine of the neck may converge in the spinal cord with signals from the shoulder.

The brain is, therefore, unable to distinguish between the two signals. If the nerve from the shoulder to the spinal cord is dominant it can even take over the signal.

Types of referred pain

RADICULAR PAIN

Nerve root compression pain, which affects the large spinal nerves that branch off from the spinal cord. This is usually described as a sharp, knife-like, shooting pain in a relatively narrow band called a dermatome. It is a fairly predictable and can be used to identify the nerve root being compressed. Radicular

pain may be accompanied by pins and needles, numbness and muscle weakness.

SOMATIC PAIN

Pain caused by damage to a joint, spinal disc, ligament or muscle that may be felt locally as well as referred. For example, a *low back joint* spinal disc can cause low back pain and referred pain into the buttock and lower limb as far as the foot. If both are present, the pain tends to concentrate proximally near the spine.

Most cases of referred pain from the spine are somatic (about 95 per cent). It is felt in a wider area and more diffusely than radicular pain and is usually a static, dull ache, which is hard to localise. It is not accompanied by neurological abnormalities. It may even cause tenderness of a structure where the pain is felt.

Unfortunately, pain referred from somatic structures is not felt in a predictable area, as is radicular pain. Attempts to use areas of pain distribution, called sclerotomes, should be done with caution.

AUTONOMIC PAIN

Pain can be referred by the *autonomic nervous system*, the collection of neurons (nerve cells) that conducts the communications to and from the internal organs or viscera such as the intestines, heart and lungs and blood vessels throughout the body.

These nerves can be affected by *neural tension*. The sympathetic trunk, located just in front of the costovertebral (rib and spine) joints in the thoracic spine, is particularly susceptible to damage and may explain unusual symptoms such as nausea, temperature changes and changes in the amount of sweating that may accompany pain.

Diagnosis and treatment

Referred pain is a reminder that just because someone's pain does not fit into a recognised diagnosis, it does not mean that the pain does not exist.

While it is not possible to map out distinct patterns of referred pain, there are common sites that tend to emanate from particular regions.

A diagnosis of referred pain requires an accurate history, physical examination and possibly tests and investigations. A *history* may reveal pain that is a dull aching, poorly localised, deep-seated, moves from point to point, long-standing and fails to improve with local treatment.

In the *physical examination* the aim is to reproduce the referred pain by stressing the site of the source. This is achieved by local palpation if the source is muscle, by passive or active joint movement or with a neural tension test.

Inability to reproduce the referred pain does not necessarily exclude the diagnosis. Any significant abnormality of joints, muscle or neural sheath at a site that is a possible source of the referred pain should be noted. The best means of confirmation is to treat the abnormality and if an improvement is achieved, it is likely that the treated area was contributing significantly to the pain.

Reflex

An action that occurs automatically in reaction to a sensory stimulus. For example, a reflex reaction occurs when a muscle is suddenly overstretched. Sensory receptors in the muscle spindle send this information back to *neurons* in the spinal cord, which are programmed to immediately send instructions to stop the stretch in order to prevent the muscle from being damaged. A sudden blow against a tendon can cause a reflex muscle contraction.

Common sources of referred pain

Site of referred pain	Source of pain
Occipital headache	• Upper cervical spine
Shoulder	• Lower cervical, upper thoracic spine • Periscapular soft tissue
Lateral elbow	• Lower cervical (C5–6) • Upper thoracic
Chest wall	• Thoracic spine
Sacroiliac region, loin	• Thoracolumbar junction
Groin	• Sacroiliac joint, thoracolumbar junction, upper lumbar spine
Buttock, hamstring	• Lumbar spine, sacroiliac joint • Gluteal muscles
Lateral knee/thigh	• Lumbar spine

Other reflexes are more complex, such as shivering in response to the cold and the primitive reflexes of newly born babies. The latter are suppressed as the brain develops, though some can appear in certain situations in adults, such as the reaching reflex of the arms is a protective reflex in response to a sudden fall.

Reflex sympathetic dystrophy (RSD)

See *Complex regional pain syndrome (CRPS)*.

Reflexology

A method of diagnosis and treatment based on reflex points in the feet and the hands. These points represent the different parts and organs of the body. Tenderness at these points when firmly pressed with the thumbs or fingers is an indication of illness or disease.

Massage of these points triggers physiological changes in the body, including improvements in circulation and energy movement in the nervous system and lymphatic flow that promote health and reduce illness.

Rehabilitation

Treatments and activities that aim to restore the body back to its former condition after disease, injury or surgery. In general this includes a full return to performing daily living tasks at work and home, and during exercise and sport.

Different types of rehabilitation include *cardiac rehabilitation* following a heart attack, *stroke* rehabilitation and *sport rehabilitation* for an injury.

Commencement
Rehabilitation should start as early as possible, usually beginning after first aid and treatment is given to ensure that the injury or disease has settled down. For example, *RICE (rest, ice, compression and elevation)* followed by appropriate treatment, then sport

rehabilitation is recommended for an acute injury. For a *heart attack*, cardiac rehabilitation begins when the condition has been medically stabilised, which can take from 24 hours up to several weeks.

Method

Each person needs to be treated as an individual in rehabilitation. Some people are overzealous and may need to be held back when recovering from an injury. Others are hesitant and lack confidence and require considerable psychological support and encouragement (see *Psychology of rehabilitation*).

The rehabilitation program should be clearly understood and planned with realistic, approximate time frames. It is important to set short-term goals; for example, the removal of a brace or recommencement of walking for an injured joint; and long-term goals, such as a return to sport or recommencing work.

It is also important to understand the rationale behind the program. For example, if lack of flexibility contributed to an injury, an ongoing program should be included to gradually improve flexibility beyond the pre-injury level. If facilities such as a gymnasium, pool or exercise devices are available, the program may take advantage of them.

Rehydration

See *Hydration*.

Reiter's syndrome

A disease that causes *inflammation* of the joints leading to loss of flexibility, morning stiffness, pain, often at night, fever, skin rashes and conjunctivitis. It usually affects one or two joints, including the knee, ankle, low back and sacroiliac joint.

It is associated with a recent urinary tract infection or gastrointestinal infection that leads to an excessive response of the immune system. The diagnosis is based on the symptoms. Treatments include *non-steroidal anti-inflammatory drugs (NSAIDs)*, *flexibility exercises* and *strengthening exercises*.

Relative body fat

The percentage of a person's total body weight that is composed of fat. It is a measure of *body composition*. The opposite measure is fat-free mass.

The greater the relative body fat in an athlete, the worse the performance in sports where strength, speed, endurance and jumping are involved. For example, if two athletes are competing to see who can jump the highest, both athletes weigh 100 kg (220 lb), but athlete X has 15 per cent relative body fat (15 kg/331 lb) and athlete Y has 5 per cent (5 kg/211 lb), athlete Y has 10 kg (22 lb) more body tissue made up of predominantly muscle. In most cases athlete Y would win the competition.

Exceptions to this rule include *ultra long distance sports*, where additional fat provides extra stores of energy, and swimming, where fat increases buoyancy and makes it easier to move through the water. In general, women tend to have a higher relative body fat than men due to the affects of *oestrogen*.

The most commonly used and practical method of measuring relative body fat is the *skin fold test*. More sophisticated methods used in research include *densitometry*, *electrical impedance*, dual-energy X-ray absorptiometry and *magnetic resonance imaging (MRI)*.

Relative rest

See *Rest*.

Repetition maximum (RM)

The number of times a weight can be lifted before a muscle reaches the point of fatigue. It is a method of measuring the strength of a muscle or group of muscles, aerobic fitness and endurance. It is mostly used as a measurement to determine the recommended *overload* in a *strength training* program.

One repetition maximum (1-RM) equals the maximum weight that can be lifted once. 15-RM equals the maximum weight that can be lifted fifteen times. Heavier weights have a smaller number for the repetition maximum.

Repeatedly lifting a heavy weight 5-RM or lower leads to increased *strength*. Increased muscle size is best achieved with a moderate weight of 5 to 14-RM. Lifting a light weight 18-RM or higher results in a form of *aerobic training*.

Reproductive system

The organs and tissues responsible for reproduction in human beings.

Females

In a female the reproductive system includes two ovaries and fallopian tubes that connect to the uterus, cervix, vagina and female hormones. Each ovary contains thousands of eggs (ova, plural of ovum). Each month the reproductive organs prepare a woman's body for *pregnancy* in a process called the menstrual cycle, whose timing is determined by female hormones such as *oestrogen* and progesterone. If pregnancy does not happen, *menstruation* occurs. These cycles cease between the age of 45 and 55 in a process called *menopause*. Failure to fall pregnant can be due to a number of *fertility problems*.

Males

The reproductive system of a male includes the two testes, penis and male hormones. Sperm are pro-duced in the testes of males from the age of puberty due to the effects of the sex hormone *testosterone*. Sperm take about 72 days to grow to maturity before being passed out of the body, called an ejaculation, through a tube called the vas deferens, connecting the testes to the penis. About 200 to 400 million sperm mixed with fluid called semen are passed out of the penis in an ejaculation.

Only one sperm is allowed to penetrate an ovum during fertilisation, which is the start of pregnancy. Each sperm contains half of the genes of a male's normal cell. The ovum also contains half of the genes of a female's normal cell. When a sperm penetrates the ovum they are joined together to form a new combination of genes unique to the embryo (and eventually the baby that is born).

Resistance

The *load* or amount of weight that is placed on a muscle during a maximum strength test such as *repetition maximum (RM)* and in a *strength training* program that aims to increase strength.

Resistance training

See *Strength training*.

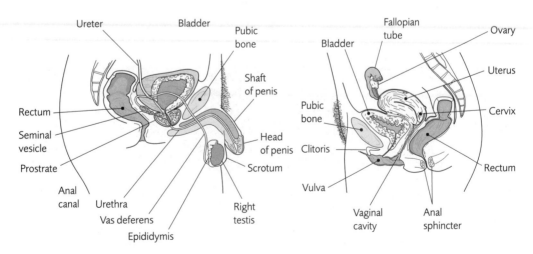

Reproductive system

Respiration

Breathing air in and out of the lungs, and moving oxygen and carbon dioxide between the lungs and the blood. It is also called external respiration to differentiate it from internal (or cellular) respiration, which is the movement of oxygen and carbon dioxide between the cells and the blood.

Respiratory system

The organs and tissues that are responsible for the exchange of oxygen and carbon dioxide between the outside air and the body. It is also called the external respiratory system to differentiate it from the internal respiratory system, which is the movement of oxygen and carbon dioxide between the cells and the blood. The respiratory system is intimately linked to the *cardiovascular system*, which includes the heart and blood vessels.

Respiration involves *breathing* in air that flows through the nose and mouth, down the upper respiratory tract and into the *lungs* that are made up of round tubes, which can be thought of as being like a large, leafy upside down oak tree that has a hollow trunk, branches, twigs and leaves. For example, the trunk of the tree is like the *trachea* (windpipe) and each leaf is the *alveolus*, which is a tiny air space where *pulmonary diffusion*, the movement of oxygen and carbon dioxide into and out of the blood, takes place. The lungs are suspended within the chest in a lubricated sac called the *pleura*. The main breathing muscles are the diaphragm and rib muscles.

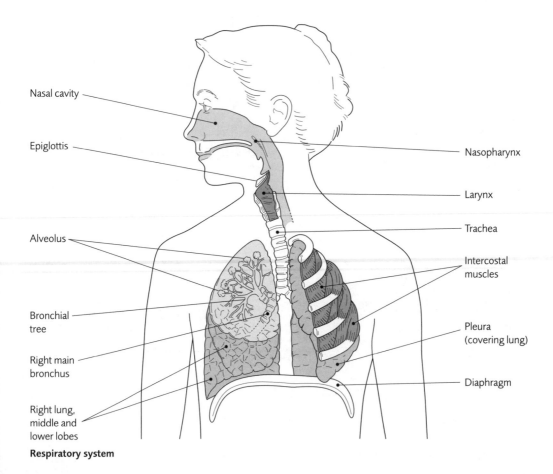

Nasal cavity

Epiglottis

Alveolus

Bronchial tree

Right main bronchus

Right lung, middle and lower lobes

Nasopharynx

Larynx

Trachea

Intercostal muscles

Pleura (covering lung)

Diaphragm

Respiratory system

Exercise and sport

The frequency and depth of breathing, which determine the volume of air breathed in and out, is called *breathing regulation*. Exercise and sport cause an increased demand for oxygen to be supplied to the muscles and the need to remove carbon dioxide produced by the working muscles. The breathing volume is increased according to these changes.

Rest

Inactivity or reduced activity. In exercise and sport it is used as a form of treatment for an injury, as one of the stages of a training program and as a tactic in a competition event.

Injury

As a treatment, rest means that activity using the injured part of the body should be ceased in order to avoid aggravating the injury, to allow it to heal properly and reduce feelings of pain. This applies equally to an acute injury that begins suddenly due to a single incident and an overuse injury, which develops over a period of weeks or months due to an accumulation of excessive forces.

An *acute injury* usually requires complete rest from aggravating activities such as using crutches to take weight off a broken bone or to stop playing tennis after a shoulder tendon tear. It should be done as one part of the combination of treatments called *RICE (rest, ice, compression and elevation)*.

An *overuse injury* may require complete rest or just a reduction in activity, such as running shorter distances or playing tennis less frequently for a mild tennis elbow injury.

'Relative rest' is a term used to describe maintaining fitness while allowing the injured part to heal. No matter what type of injury, a fitness program can always be designed. For example, with a leg injury that prohibits running, fitness may be maintained by performing activities such as cycling, swimming or aqua running. A tennis player with a leg injury that prevents running can maintain skills by standing on the court and practising strokes. Relative rest is an integral part of a *sport rehabilitation* program.

Training

Rest is used as part of training, such as *tapering* to replenish energy stores before a competition, like swimming heats and finals or a triathlon, as part of the *periodisation* of a fitness program to give easy days and easy weeks.

The aim is to allow the body to recover and recuperate, and thereby reduce the risk of developing an overuse injury or *overtraining syndrome*. In *interval training* it is used as a technique to achieve high levels of fitness.

Competition

During competition a rest may be required for a player who has yet to recover full match fitness after an injury, or as a tactic to save a player for a later part of the match when the opposition is more likely to be tired.

Resting metabolic rate (RMR)

A measure of the amount of energy the body needs to keep all the basic body functions working, such as breathing, body temperature and heartbeat. In most people it requires 60–75 per cent of energy used each day. Additional energy is required to do activities like exercise and sport.

RMR varies from person to person. It is lower in older aged people. *Stress* causes an increase. Men have a higher RMR than women because of a tendency to have more muscle. RMR is shown as *kilojoules* or Calories per day. The normal range is 5000–10 000 kJ or 1200–2400 Calories per day.

RMR can be measured accurately in a clinical laboratory. The subject is required to sleep for 8 hours after 12 hours of fasting. It is calculated according to the amount of oxygen breathed in, fat-free body mass, body surface area, age and other factors. Usually an estimate is made based on respiratory exchange ratio (RER), standard values multiplied by an estimate of the amount of oxygen breathed in for that person's height, weight and build.

Metabolic equivalent (MET) is a scale of measuring energy expenditure during physical activity such as aerobic training like running or swimming, where RMR = 1.0 MET = 3.5 mL oxygen per kilogram body weight per minute (3.5 ml/kg/min).

Retinal detachment

The back layer of the *eye* separates or lifts away, causing flashes of light or the appearance of a 'curtain' spreading across the field of vision. This may occur months or even years after the original injury. It is more likely to occur in people with *diabetes* and *hypertension*. The recommended treatment is immediate surgery to re-attach the retina.

Retrocalcaneal bursitis

An inflammation of the bursa that protects the *Achilles tendon* from friction due to rubbing against the back of the heel bone (calcaneus). It is an overuse injury caused by excessive and repeated physical forces on the bursa over a period of weeks or months, as can occur in running.

This injury causes the same pain as an *Achilles tendinosis*, except that the tenderness when the tendon is pressed firmly with the fingers is felt close to the heel bone. The recommended treatment is *rest* from aggravating activities, *flexibility exercises* and *strengthening exercises*, *non-steroidal anti-inflammatory drugs (NSAIDs)* and in some cases a *corticosteroid* injection into the bursa. Return to sport usually takes up to two to three weeks.

Return to sport

See *Sport rehabilitation*.

Rheumatoid arthritis

A disease that causes *inflammation* of joints leading to swelling, loss of flexibility, morning stiffness, pain, mild fever, and eventually, deformities. It usually affects more than one joint, in particular the wrist, fingers, hip, knee, feet and toes. In 15 per cent of

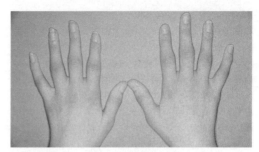

Rheumatoid arthritis of the fingers

cases only one joint is affected. It is characterised by attacks that come and go. Women are more likely to be affected than men.

The disease is caused by the *immune system* attacking the body's own tissues in the joints, which is called an autoimmune disorder.

The diagnosis is based on the symptoms, *X-rays* and blood tests that check for antibodies called rheumatoid factor. Treatments include *non-steroidal anti-inflammatory drugs (NSAIDs)*, anti-rheumatic medications, *flexibility exercises, strengthening exercises* and *hydrotherapy*. In severe cases surgery may be recommended (see *Hip joint replacement* and *Knee joint replacement*).

Rib contusion

Bruising to the ribs due to a sudden forceful incident, such as a collision with another player into the *chest*. A more severe blow causes a *rib fracture*. The diagnosis and treatment are the same. Return to sport is permitted when the pain settles down, usually between 1 to 3 weeks.

Rib fracture

A break to one of the bones that make up the cage-like structure of the *chest*. It is caused by a sudden forceful event, such as a collision with another player or piece of equipment.

The chest pain is aggravated by breathing in deeply and coughing. A physical examination reveals tenderness over one or more ribs when pressed firmly

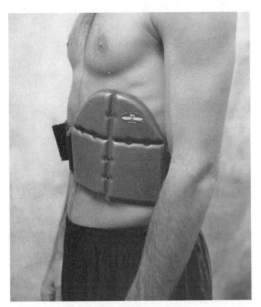

Protective padding after rib fracture

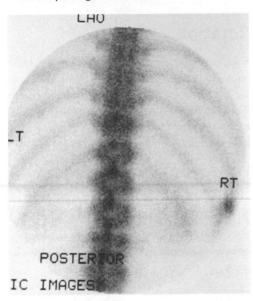

Bone scan of rib stress fracture

with the fingers. The most likely rib fractures are numbers 5 to 10.

Diagnosis, treatment and return to sport

A diagnosis can be confirmed with an *X-ray*, though it is not absolutely necessary because the recom-

mended treatment is based on the amount of pain. In mild cases the injury is usually not a fracture, but rather a *rib contusion* (bruising).

In severe injuries a *pneumothorax* (punctured lung) can be caused by a piece of broken bone. If several ribs are broken in at least two places the chest wall moves inwards instead of outwards during breathing in, which is called a *chest flail segment* (see *Medical emergency*).

It is also important to be checked for injury to one of the other nearby organs, including the liver, spleen and kidneys (see *Abdominal injuries*).

Treatment for a rib fracture includes *analgesics* and deep breathing exercises to prevent lung collapse. Return to sport is permitted when the pain settles down, usually between 3 to 6 weeks. Protective padding is often used in contact sports.

Rib stress fracture

A microfracture in one of the ribs that develops gradually due to an accumulation of repeated, excessive muscle traction on the bone during specific activities. A stress fracture of the first rib is most often seen in *baseball* pitchers, which tends to heal poorly. Stress fractures of the fourth and fifth ribs are most common in *rowing, canoeing* and kayaking.

Treatment for this *stress fracture* injury includes rest from the aggravating activity for at least 6 weeks, until there is no tenderness in the bone when pressed firmly with fingers. *Throwing biomechanics* and *scapular biomechanics* should be assessed and treated in both of the above injuries.

RICE (rest, ice, compression and elevation)

A combination of treatments for an *acute injury* that should be applied within 24 hours, but may be effective up to 72 hours after an injury has occurred. The main aims are to avoid aggravating an injury further, to allow it to heal properly, reduce feelings of pain and minimise bleeding, oedema and swelling.

The problem with bleeding is that the blood accumulates around damaged tissue and compresses adjoining tissues, which causes tissue anoxia and further damage. *Oedema* and *swelling* lead to increased fluid pressure on the damaged tissues, and may inhibit healing, cause pain and lead to muscle *spasm* and *atrophy*.

Rest aims to prevent further damage and aggravation of the injury. *Ice* reduces the flow of blood and oedema formation by causing vasoconstriction (narrowing) of the blood vessels. Both rest and ice also reduce pain. *Compression* usually involves using a bandage to place pressure on the injured area to reduce bleeding and oedema formation. *Elevation* involves raising the injured part high enough to encourage the blood and oedema to flow away.

At the same time as doing RICE, the following should be avoided because they increase bleeding and oedema formation: any form of heat (see *Heat therapy (superficial)*) such as a hot bath or heat rub or liniment; *massage* performed vigorously; and the consumption of *alcohol*, which acts as a vasodilator (widening the diameter of the blood vessels).

Role

The set of responsibilities, tasks and goals given to a player in a team. They can be formal and informal. The formal aspects are usually a combination of behaviours that are common to all the team, such as attending training on time, and behaviours specific to the individual. Informal aspects are those dynamics that develop on their own with minimal intervention.

They are usually *personality* and skills-driven, such as the player who takes on the role of inspiring fellow players with acts of courage.

Rolfing

A method of diagnosis and treatment that aims to restore the health of the fascia, a relatively inelastic connective tissue. According to Rolfing, *fascia* can be damaged not only by injury or bad posture, but also emotional trauma, which throws the body out of alignment.

Treatments include techniques for stretching and deep *massage* therapy, which can be quite painful. Hellerwork is based on similar principles and techniques.

Rollerblading

See *In-line skating*.

Roller-skating

Roller-skating was invented in 1735 to keep enthusiastic participants in ice-skating occupied during summer when ice was scarce. Ball bearings and shock absorbent wheels have made the activity easier to do. Fitness requirements and injuries are similar to *in-line skating*.

Rotation

A turning movement that moves the body around a vertical mechanical axis through the spine. For example, left rotation of the *neck joints* turns the face to look over the left shoulder. Left rotation of the *low back joints* turns to face the chest and abdomen towards the left.

Rotator cuff strain

An acute injury of one or more of the supraspinatus, subscapularis, infraspinatus and teres minor muscles of the *shoulder joint* that is caused by a sudden excessive force.

Causes
It is associated with not performing a sufficient warm-up, reduced flexibility, excessive muscle fatigue and muscle imbalance that creates an abnormality affecting *scapular biomechanics* or *throwing biomechanics*.

It is most likely in sports that involve sudden bursts of power during arm activities such as *tennis*, *squash* and *throwing sports*. Tendon tears most commonly occur in above 40 year olds due to degenerative changes such as *tendinosis*.

Diagnosis

There is usually a sudden 'twinge' in the shoulder area during an activity, such as a tennis serve, followed by pain and a noticeable inability to perform that activity.

There are three degrees of muscle *strain*. Mild (grade 1) causes pain, but no loss of strength. Moderate (grade 2) causes reduced muscle strength and pain that limits movement. Severe (grade 3) substantially reduces strength, though in some cases it may be less painful than a moderate strain.

Tendon strains are either a partial or complete tear. A partial tear often allows continued playing on the day, but at night the pain causes an inability to sleep on the shoulder. The diagnosis may be confirmed with *diagnostic ultrasound* or *magnetic resonance imaging (MRI)*.

Treatment and return to sport

Mild to moderate muscle strains respond quickly to *rest* from the aggravating activity and *ice*, followed by *flexibility exercises, strengthening exercises* and *massage*. Return to sport is often possible after 1 to 3 weeks, depending on the severity, though a severe tear may require up to several months.

A partial tendon tear requires ice and rest followed by strengthening and flexibility exercises. Return to sport may require up to 4 weeks. A complete rupture may need surgical repair followed by 12 weeks of rest and *shoulder rehabilitation*.

Rotator cuff tear

See *Rotator cuff strain*.

Rotator cuff tendinitis

An injury of the tendons of the rotator cuff muscles in the shoulder joint due to an inflammation that lasts for up to a week, but following continued aggravation develops into a *rotator cuff tendinosis*.

Tendinitis is much less common than was previously believed because by the time of the shoulder is checked by a health practitioner, it has usually already developed into a tendinosis.

Rotator cuff tendinosis

An overuse injury of one or more of the supraspinatus, subscapularis, infraspinatus and teres minor muscle tendons of the *shoulder joint* that is caused by a gradual accumulation of repeated excessive forces over a period of weeks or months. The supraspinatus is the most commonly affected tendon.

Causes

Excessive forces may be associated with an abnormality of *throwing biomechanics* or *scapular biomechanics*, sudden increases in aerobic training

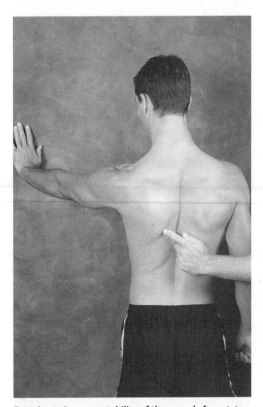

Exercise to improve stability of the scapula for rotator cuff tendinosis

intensity or volume *overload*, poor equipment selection and poor technique for a particular activity.

It is most common in sports involving overhead arm movements, such as *swimming*, *throwing sports* and racquet sports like *tennis*. Freestyle and butterfly swimmers are particularly vulnerable because they develop excessive strength of the internal rotator muscles of the shoulder.

Initially the injury causes inflammation of the tendon, called *tendinitis*. However, continued aggravation leads to the development of *tendinosis*, a degenerative condition that breaks down the cells in the tendon.

Diagnosis

The pain is usually felt some time after activity or first thing the following morning. In the earlier, less severe stages of the injury, pain is reduced by activity such as a warm-up, only to return after activity. However, a more severe injury causes stronger pain that continues throughout the activity.

A physical examination may find weakness of external rotator muscles, a loss of range of movement of internal rotation (turning arm inwards), *myofascial trigger points* and abduction movement (lifting arm out sideways) may reveal *shoulder impingement*. The diagnosis can be confirmed with ultrasound or *magnetic resonance imaging (MRI)*.

Treatment and return to sport

It is essential to reduce the amount of overhead movements, either completely or partially, depending on the severity. Correction of abnormalities in throwing or scapular biomechanics is often required for recovery and prevention of re-injury.

For example, for swimmers it can involve *strengthening exercises* for external rotator muscles of the shoulder to restore the balance with internal rotators or *motor re-education* to improve stability.

Other treatments include *ice*, electrotherapy such as *ultrasound therapy* and *interferential therapy*, *massage* and *dry needling* of myofascial trigger points. If all of the above are not successful a *corticosteroid* injection may be prescribed. Full return to sport can take 3 to 6 weeks in mild cases and 3 to 6 months when severe.

Routine

Activities that are planned in advance prior to a competition, tournament or performance of a specific skill. The aim is to prepare mentally and physically in order to consistently achieve the best performance.

Pre-competition routine is a timetable of activities for the 24 to 48 hours beforehand that provide an overall structure with the aim of achieving the optimum *arousal* zone by the start of competition. The routine can continue through the competition and for the few hours afterwards.

Specific skills that can benefit from performing a routine include kicking for a penalty goal in soccer and shooting for a foul shot in basketball.

Rowing

Rowing involves using two hands to grasp an oar for propulsion. Sculling involves grasping a single oar in each hand. The first organised rowing races were between Oxford and Cambridge universities in England in the 1820s, which later became known as the Henley Royal Regatta. Rowing events for men were first included in the 1900 Olympic Games. Dragon boat racing is a rowing competition between crews of 25 that is most popular in Asian countries.

Fitness and injuries

The main physical requirements are *strength training*, *aerobic training* and *interval training*.

The most common injuries are *low back pain (non-specific)*, *thoracic pain (non-specific)*, *rib stress fracture*, *de Quervain's tenosynovitis* (wrist), extensor tendinosis *(tennis elbow)*, *patellar tendinosis* (knee), *patellofemoral joint syndrome* (knee) and *iliotibial band friction syndrome* (knee).

Rowing machines

Fitness equipment for stationary rowing that can be an effective form of *aerobic training*.

The simplest models use hydraulic pistons for resistance to the oars. Flywheel types are more expensive and use a rotating belt around a wheel for resistance. There are no indications that a rowing machine achieves greater improvements in aerobic fitness than outdoors rowing, though it is certainly more convenient.

Rugby boots

See *Football boots*.

Rugby League

A sport that developed in the late 1800s in England as a simplified version of *Rugby Union*. The first governing body was founded in 1895, when 22 clubs from the north of England seceded from the Rugby Football Union over wages.

Rules
Rugby League is played between two teams of 13 players on a rectangular field with two goalposts and

Rugby league players

cross bar. The aim of each team is to score tries by carrying the ball into the end zone (3 points) and kicking goals after a try (2 points), a penalty kick (2 points) or a dropped goal (1 point). The attacking team is given five consecutive turns to move the ball forward. After the fifth turn the ball is handed over to the opposing team.

Fitness and injuries
The main training requirements are *strength training* and *aerobic training*. The most common injuries are *shoulder dislocation, shoulder instability, acromioclavicular (AC) joint sprain* (shoulder), *concussion*, lacerations (see *Face pain and injuries*), *rib fracture, medial collateral ligament (MCL) sprain* (knee) and *ankle sprain*. Players should wear *mouthguards* and correct *football boots*.

Rugby Union

Rugby Union originated in England in the 1830s as an adaptation of soccer. In 1871 the Rugby Football Union codified rules and the first match between England and Scotland was played. In 1895, 22 clubs broke away to play a new variation called *Rugby League*.

Rules and equipment
Rugby Union is played between two teams of 15 players. Players are allowed to use their hands to catch and throw an oval ball sideways or backwards but not forwards, run with it and kick it. The field is rectangular, with two goalposts and a cross bar at each end.

The aim is to score tries by running the ball into the end zone (5 points) and kick goals over the cross bar (2 points). Other features of the game include the scrum and line out. The attacking team is permitted unlimited turns to move the ball forward.

Fitness and injuries
The main physical requirements are *strength training* and *aerobic training*. The most common injuries are *shoulder dislocation, shoulder instability, acromioclavicular (AC) joint sprain* (shoulder), *concussion, Cauliflower ear* (face), *rib fracture, medial collateral ligament (MCL) sprain* (knee), *meniscus tear* (knee)

Rugby Union players forming a scrum

and *ankle sprain*. Players should wear *mouthguards* and correct *football boots*.

Rules modifications

Rules for a sport adapted from the adult version to suit the skills, abilities and needs of the participants. They are adapted for different groups including *children* and young *adolescents*, people with a *disability* and *older athletes*.

These modifications also help to reduce the risk of injury or illness. Adult men and women usually play sport according to the same rules. Exceptions include Grand Slam tennis where men play best of five sets and women only three sets, and the tee in women's golf is set closer to the pin.

Children

Most sports have a special set of rules for competition and training for younger age groups that are adapted from the adult version. The modification can involve reducing the amount of playing time, reducing the size and hardness of equipment, shortening the length of a season, de-emphasising the competitive

focus, simplifying the rules so that they are easier to understand and reducing the playing field or surface.

For example, there is a version of basketball called 'mini-basketball' for 5 to 12 year olds that uses a smaller ball, reduced court size and lowered backboard and basket.

The main aim is to allow children to learn the basic skills of the game, such as throwing the ball into the basket before moving on to more competitive levels, reduce the risk of injury and illness by decreasing the physical contact between players, lower the intensity of running and enhance positive experience and decrease humiliation.

Runner's high

Exhilaration, euphoria and positive physical sensations, such as reduced pain and extra energy, during exercise or sport. It was first noticed in long distance runners; however, it can occur during any high-intensity physical activity lasting more than 30 minutes.

It usually occurs suddenly and is unexpected. It is regarded as a form of natural intoxication that is most likely attributed to the body's release of a chemical substance called *endorphin*, which has heroin-like effects.

Runner's nipples

See *Nipples*.

Running

See *Middle distance running, Long distance running, Sprinting* and *Jogging*.

Running biomechanics

The movements and positions of the joints and muscles of the legs, pelvis and lower back during running. It involves a repeating cycle of activities divided into two phases: stance and swing.

Stance phase
The stance phase is divided into three stages: contact, midstance and propulsive. These stages differ according to the speed of running. The following is a description of slow running (which is similar to walking biomechanics).

Contact begins when the foot first strikes the ground, called the heel strike, and finishes when the

rest of the foot makes contact with the ground. Midstance is when the foot is flat on the ground. The propulsive phase begins with the heel lifting off the ground and finishes when the forefoot and toes push off the ground, called toe-off.

In *jogging, long distance running* and *middle distance running* there is a tendency for both the heel and forefoot to strike the ground together at the start of the contact stage.

In *sprinting* the forefoot may be the only contact with the ground throughout the stance phase. In addition, the feet strike the ground closer to an imaginary straight line running down the middle of the body and the toes turn to point in the same direction as the running direction. This is called a narrow *angle and base of gait*.

Swing phase
In the swing phase the foot is carried through the air towards the next heel strike. It is divided into three stages: follow through, forward swing and foot descent.

After push off at the end of the propulsive stage the other leg is still at the end of the swing phase before heel strike. As a result, both feet are off the ground for a time called the flight phase. This differs from walking biomechanics where both feet are in contact with the ground after push off for a time called the double support phase.

The faster the running speed, the longer the flight phase and the shorter the stance phase for each

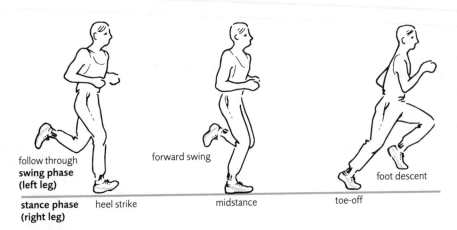

follow through
**swing phase
(left leg)**

forward swing

foot descent

**stance phase
(right leg)** heel strike   midstance   toe-off

Swing and stance phases of running biomechanics

stride. In sprint running the flight phase is longer than the stance phase.

Subtalar joint

At the moment of heel strike the subtalar joint (see *Foot and toes*) is in slight *supination* (a movement that contributes to *inversion*, turning the sole to face the midline).

The joint then begins *pronation* (a movement that contributes to *eversion*, turning the sole to face away from the midline), taking it past the *neutral joint position* and causing an eversion of the heel that helps absorb the shock of ground contact.

At the start of midstance the joint begins to supinate. This moves the heel back past the neutral position to inversion. During the propulsive stage the joint continues to supinate and becomes more inverted.

Forefoot and first ray

At heel strike and throughout the stance phase the forefoot (see *Foot and toes*) is locked in slight pronation, making a solid platform for pushing off during the propulsive stage. The first ray (first metatarsal-medial cuneiform joint at the base of the big toe) bends backwards (dorsi flexion) and internally rotates (inversion) during contact and remains in this position during the propulsive stage.

The movements at the *ankle* joint, *knee joint*, *hip joint* and *pelvis* are the same during walking, jogging and long, middle distance and sprint running, except that the faster the speed, the larger the range of movements.

Ankle

During contact the ankle joint plantar flexes (bends downwards). During midstance it is dorsi flexed (upwards bending). During the propulsive stage plantar flexion occurs once again.

Knee

During contact the knee flexes (bends) to 15 degrees and the tibia internally rotates. During midstance the knee extends (straightens) and the tibia externally rotates. During the propulsive stage the knee flexes again, but the tibia continues to externally rotate.

Hip

At heel strike the hip joint is slightly flexed (bent) and internally rotated. From contact through to the propulsive stage, the hip extends (straightens) to the neutral position and then backwards. External rotation begins in midstance and continues through propulsion.

Pelvis

At heel strike the pelvis is in the neutral position. From contact through to propulsive stages of the stance phase there is a *pelvis anterior tilt*. In the midstance stage there is an upward *pelvis lateral tilt* that is a result of a downward lateral tilt of the pelvis on the other side. This occurs because the other leg is going through the swing phase. There is also a forward *pelvis transverse rotation* of the side of the pelvis going through the swing phase.

Biomechanical abnormalities

A deviation from any of the above movements is called a biomechanical abnormality. It is associated with an increased risk of developing an *overuse injury*. The most common abnormalities that affect running include *foot pronation*, *foot supination*, pelvis anterior tilt and pelvis lateral tilt.

Running shoes

Footwear designed to cope with the physical demands of running and jogging. The two most important features are shock absorption and those that take into account abnormalities of running biomechanics.

Shock absorption

Each step creates an impact in your foot that equals a force of three to four times body weight and the average runner takes over 500 steps per kilometre (800 steps per mile). The most commonly used shock absorption materials are compartments filled with air or gel, carbon-fibres and reinforced rubber. They all provide great comfort for athletes; however, reinforced rubber is most effective for protecting against injuries.

Research has found that compartments filled with air or gel may even provide too much comfort, causing a perception that the foot is experiencing a

A running shoe with midsole dual-density

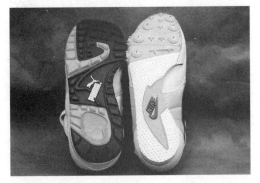

The latest shape of running shoes. The left shoe is straight. The right shoe is curved

reduced impact that does not match with reality, tricking the muscles not to work as hard as they should. Excessive comfort may also exacerbate a biomechanical abnormality in the foot such as *foot pronation* and *foot supination*.

Biomechanics

The recommendations take into account common abnormalities of *running biomechanics*. Runners with excessive foot pronation should wear dual-density

midsoles. These are more rigid in the medial (inner) half. A foot that supinates too much needs a single-density midsole.

In *shoe* making, the last, which is the shape of the shoe when viewed from below, is also an important physical feature for compensating for abnormal foot biomechanics. The recommendations are:

- Straight: The best shape to correct too much pronation. However, many athletes complain that a straight last feels uncomfortable, heavy and slow.
- Semi-curved: Feels less bulky and restrictive than the straight last; however, it is not as effective at compensating for too much pronation. On the other hand, a good midsole and strong heel counter can make up for it.
- Curved: This is the best shape to correct too much supination.

For people with normal foot biomechanics the recommended shoe is determined by their body weight: over 75 kg requires a semi-curved last with dual-density reinforced rubber and under 75 kg, a semi-curved last with single-density rubber.

Participation in sprinting needs to take into account the running spikes, which can decrease the stability and lead to an increase in the risk of *Achilles tendinosis*. This problem can be fixed by raising the midsole height of the shoe.

Rupture

A complete or severe *tear* of a ligament, disc, tendon or muscle.

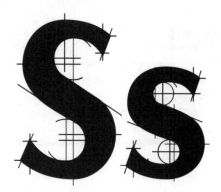

Sacroiliac joint pain

An overuse injury of the joint at the back of the large ring-shaped bone called the *pelvis*. It can cause pain in the low back and sacrum, and may refer pain into the buttock, groin or genitalia.

It usually begins as a small ache that gets worse over a period of weeks or months due to an accumulation of excessive forces. In most cases there is no specific diagnosis, which makes the injury similar to *low back pain (non-specific)*.

Diagnosis and treatment

The pain can make it difficult to walk up stairs and roll over in bed. A physical examination usually finds stiffness in the joint and reduced flexibility of the psoas major and rectus femoris muscles of the *hip joint*.

Treatment includes *mobilisation* of the joint, *massage* and *flexibility exercises*. If these treatments fail a *corticosteroid* injection into the joint may be recommended.

Sacrum

See *Pelvis* or *Buttock*.

Sarcomere

See *Muscle contraction*.

Saturated fats

A type of *fat* found in foods made from animals, such as red meat, chicken and dairy products and plants such as coconut. It is also found in large amounts in most confectionery, including cake, biscuits, chips, ice cream and chocolate.

When eaten in high amounts over a long period of life it is associated with an increased risk of cancers, such as bowel cancer, and raised levels of the bad cholesterol *low density lipoprotein (LDL)* and reduced levels of the good cholesterol, *high density lipoprotein (HDL).* LDL gets deposited in the walls of arteries and blocks the flow of blood, causing *coronary heart disease. Polyunsaturated fats* and *mono-unsaturated fats* decrease LDL and increase HDL levels.

Eating a *diet for good health* involves a low-fat intake that is evenly divided between the three types of fat. For many people this means: reducing the amount of saturated fat, such as kicking the fatty snack habit, trimming the skin off chicken, eating lean red meats and reduced-fat dairy products; and increasing the use of monounsaturated oils, such as almond or olive and polyunsaturated fats, which come in two types—omega 3, mainly in fish, and omega 6, from plants such as sunflower.

Scalp injury

See *Face and scalp skin injury.*

Scaphoid fracture

A break of a small bone in the wrist located at the base of the thumb (see *Hand and finger joints).* The usual cause is a fall onto an outstretched hand.

Diagnosis, treatment and return to sport

X-rays may not always detect a *fracture* in the early stage after an injury. *Magnetic resonance imaging (MRI)* or *bone scan* is recommended or, if these are unavailable, the wrist should be placed in a plaster cast anyway for 12 days and then X-rayed again.

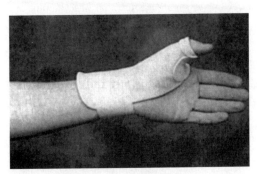

A protective brace for a scaphoid fracture

The treatment is *immobilisation* in a plaster cast for 8 weeks. After removal of the cast *flexibility exercises* and *strengthening exercises* are required. Soon afterwards return to sport may be permitted. Wearing a protective *brace* is recommended for up to 8 weeks.

Delayed or non-union

Scaphoid fractures face a risk of delayed or non-union. After removal of the cast the wrist should be X-rayed again and if the union is not complete, then a plaster cast for another 4 to 6 weeks is required. If that fails the recommended treatment is *open surgery* and *internal fixation* or *bone graft* if there is avascular necrosis (bone cell death).

Scapular biomechanics

The movements and positions of the scapula (shoulder blade) and muscles that attach to it during upper limb activities, such as throwing and swimming.

The scapula is intimately connected to the *shoulder joint,* which connects the shallow, saucer-shaped glenoid cavity of the scapula and the ball-like head of the humerus (upper arm bone).

The ligaments and rotator cuff muscles of the shoulder joint, including the supraspinatus, subscapularis, infraspinatus and teres minor muscles, are designed to improve the stability of the joint by holding the head of the humerus firmly into the glenoid cavity.

In addition the scapula muscles help keep the glenoid cavity in the best position to maintain maximum contact with the humerus head during movements of the shoulder. These muscles are called the scapular stabilisers. The coordination between all the different muscles that move the shoulder joint and the scapula is called scapulo-humeral rhythm.

Scapula movements are an important part of *throwing biomechanics, swimming biomechanics, tennis biomechanics, water polo* biomechanics and *volleyball* biomechanics.

Biomechanical abnormality

A deviation from normal movements and positions is called a *biomechanical abnormality.* It is associated

Muscles involved in scapular movements

Movement	Prime movers	Secondary movers
Retraction	• Rhomboid major/minor • Trapezius	
Protraction	• Serratus anterior	• Pectoralis minor
Upward rotation	• Trapezius (upper and lower) • Serratus anterior (upper and lower)	
Downward rotation	• Rhomboids (major/minor)	• Latissimus dorsi • Pectoralis minor
Elevation	• Trapezius • Levator scapulae • Rhomboids	
Depression	• Latissimus dorsi • Pectoralis minor	

with an increased risk of developing an overuse injury in the shoulder such as *shoulder instability*, *rotator cuff tendinosis*, *shoulder impingement* and *glenoid labrum injury*, as well as *neck posture syndrome*.

Scapular fracture

A break in the shoulder blade bone usually due to a crushing force, such as a fall on the *shoulder joint* or direct violence. The *fracture* usually heals well using a broad arm sling for *immobilisation*.

Scheuermann's disease

A disease of the *thoracic spine joints* that causes pain and later develops excessive bending forward posture (kyphosis).

It is the most common cause of pain in the middle section of the back in adolescents. It is one of a number of types of *osteochondrosis*, which cause a softening of bone that makes it vulnerable to being deformed. The cause is unknown.

The top and bottom sections of the main body of the vertebrae become deformed. The diagnosis is confirmed with an *X-ray*.

The recommended treatments aim to prevent progress of the kyphosis, including *mobilisation, massage, flexibility exercises* and *strengthening exercises* for the abdominal muscles. A *brace* may also be helpful. Surgery may be required if the kyphosis is greater than 50 degrees, or if signs of irritation of the *spinal cord* are present, such as pins and needles and numbness.

Screening

An assessment of current health status that aims to detect the existence of or risk of developing ill health, disease and injury.

Recommendations

A screening assessment should be performed for all *elite* athletes. It should be done at the earliest opportunity, preferably prior to joining a team or starting a training program. The initial screening is a full, wide-ranging history, physical examination and tests.

Subsequent screening focuses on the problems detected and the success of the prescribed treatment. Screening also should be conducted once a year, such as at the end of the season, so that surgery and rehabilitation can be planned.

Recreational athletes usually only require a *medical clearance* that gives them the go-ahead to start participating in exercise and sport.

General health

A *history* includes questions such as personal details, past medical history, family history, habits such as smoking and alcohol, allergies, medications and previous vaccinations, nutrition like vitamins and minerals, sport participation history, body weight variation and perceived body image.

Questions are also asked about signs and symptoms that can indicate a health problem, such as chest pain and dizziness for the heart and vomiting and diarrhoea for the gastrointestinal system. Women are asked gynaecological questions.

A *physical examination* includes common checks such as blood pressure measurement and an assessment of the ear, nose and throat, as well as checks relevant for problems detected in the history.

Musculoskeletal system

Screening of the *musculoskeletal system* aims to assess the status of any current injuries to muscles, joints, ligaments and bone, deficits resulting from previous injury and identifying unrecognised injury.

A physical examination also aims to find signs and symptoms that indicate an increased risk of an injury developing, such as stress fracture, chronic joint strain and muscle tendinosis.

Problems that may be found include excessive training *overload*, poor *shoe* selection, inappropriate running *surface* and *biomechanical abnormalities*. The latter is one of the strongest predictors for injury. Each sport has its own specific biomechanical problems. For example, chronic ankle sprains and pain on the lateral (outside) aspect accounts for nearly 50 per cent of all basketball overuse injuries.

Additional tests

These tests may be performed either routinely or as required based on the history and physical examination. They include *urinalysis, blood test, skinfold test, lung function tests* and *video analysis*.

Scrotum

The pouch that hangs beneath the base of the penis that contains the testicles (see *Reproductive system*). It may be injured due to a sudden blow during exercise and sport. Minor injuries cause pain and mild swelling.

The recommended treatments include *analgesics, ice*, bed rest and elevating the scrotum for comfort by placing a rolled towel between the legs. Major injuries may cause the testicle to rupture (tear) leading to severe *swelling*, which may require surgery.

Scrum pox

See *Herpes simplex virus infection*.

Scuba diving

An underwater activity that allows continuous breathing by using equipment that provides compressed air in tanks. First developed by Jacques Cousteau in 1943, this equipment enables a diver to stay under water for extended periods of time compared to *breath-hold diving*. The duration depends on the depth of the dive (deeper dives are shorter).

The pressure of water increases with the depth of a dive: at 10 m (33 ft) it is twice the air pressure at the surface; and at 20 m (66 ft) it is 3 times the surface pressure. The air that is breathed in from the tanks must be equal to the water pressure, which is provided by a regulator valve.

Care needs to be taken to avoid health risks of breathing compressed air, particularly the accumulation of excessive amounts of oxygen, nitrogen and carbon dioxide in the tissues of the body, which can cause *oxygen poisoning, decompression sickness, nitrogen narcosis* or spontaneous *pneumothorax. Eardrum rupture* is another injury associated with scuba diving.

Sculling

See *Rowing*.

Seizures

A sudden, uncontrolled burst of electrical activity of the *neurons* in the brain. A person who experiences more than two seizures is usually diagnosed with *epilepsy*. A seizure can also occur that is not due to epilepsy, such as severe *fever, hypoglycaemia* (excessively low blood glucose) in a person with diabetes, following a head injury that causes *concussion*, and as part of an episode of *syncope* (fainting).

Selective nerve root block (SNRB)

A test used to check whether a nerve root in the spine is the cause of pain. It is used most often for *nerve root compression* (an injury that causes knife-like pain located in the low back and/or leg in a well-defined area, and may be associated with pins and needles or numbness) when insufficient improvement has been achieved after 3 months of treatment.

The test involves inserting a needle through the skin into the space in the spinal canal adjacent to the nerve root (see *Low back joints*). An anaesthetic is injected into the area bathing the nerve root. The test is positive if there is relief of the pain.

Selenium

A mineral that has an essential role in the activities of many enzymes and combines with vitamin E to act as an anti-oxidant. Only tiny amounts are needed in the body, less than 100 (µg) (micrograms) a day. It is found in foods such as meat, fish and dairy products (see *Minerals*). There is no evidence that supplementation can improve performance in exercise and sport. It may even be dangerous when taken over the long term.

Self-confidence

Possessing a high level of expectation that you will succeed. In exercise and sport it is a state of mind that minimises the intrusion of *anxiety*-provoking thoughts, such as thinking about losing a game or not performing a skill in a desired manner, which can interfere with performance levels and lead to an increase in *stress* and over-*arousal*.

Self-confident people are more likely to fulfil their potential in exercise, fitness, skill and health goals. Even though it is not a guarantee of success, in sports where there is a small difference in physical competence between players, it can enable one player to succeed over another.

However, it should be remembered that *over-confidence* might occur when too much anxiety is blocked out. A small amount of anxiety is a helpful tool for preparing to perform successfully by focusing one's thoughts on specific problems that may need to be solved.

Self-talk

A stream of thoughts about one's performance that can be positive or negative.

Negative self-talk involves inappropriate thoughts such as 'I can't get this shot' or 'I never play well against this opponent'. Positive self-talk draws on past positive experiences such as 'I've been here before, I know I can do it' or 'Focus on the job at hand', which can reduce *anxiety* and achieve the optimum *arousal* zone.

The most common expressions of negative self-talk can be replaced with positive self-talk. Giving positive feedback at appropriate times during training and competition can reinforce positive self-talk. At the elite level sport psychologists may use a microphone transceiver to talk to an athlete wearing an earpiece.

Sensation

Information about your body and the world outside of it that enters your consciousness, such as pain, hunger, thirst, vision, hearing, strength and agility.

Sensory-motor integration

A stimulus that causes a reaction. For example, a firm tap on a muscle tendon causing a reflex muscle contraction, which involves an interaction within different sections of the nervous system.

Receptors belonging to the *sensory nervous system* in a section of the muscle called a muscle spindle send information about the stretch of the tendon caused by the tap to neurons in the spinal cord. These neurons are programmed to immediately pass it on to neurons belonging to the *motor nervous system*, which send instructions back to the muscles to stop the stretch by producing a muscle contraction.

The sensory-motor integration that occurs in the brain is much more complex. It potentially involves many more pieces of information. For example, the cerebellum is a part of the *brain* that coordinates movements by collecting information from every part of the body about their position, how hard the muscles are working and the body's overall posture, and sends instructions directly to muscles telling them to change actions and movements where necessary.

Sensory nervous system

The neurons (nerve cells) that collect information about the body and the outside world, which is sent to the brain and spinal cord.

Sensory *neurons* have special receptors that can detect specific types of information. For example, receptors that detect touch on the skin send this information to the sensory cortex of the brain.

There is also sensory information we are usually not conscious of, like blood pressure. This information is carried through the *autonomic nervous system.*

Other sensory receptors that are important in exercise and sport include: thermoreceptors for *temperature*, nociceptors for *pain*, chemoreceptors for the content of the *blood*, photoreceptors for vision and muscle *reflex* receptors that have endings that wrap around a single muscle fibre.

Sensory information also can be gathered by different types of receptors and combined to produce specific senses, such as *proprioception* for joint position and movement.

Sesamoiditis

An overuse injury of the two small bones located on the underneath surface of the head of the first metatarsal in the ball of the big toe (see *Foot and toes*).

It causes pain in the big toe that feels worse when putting weight through the ball of the foot, and feels less painful when walking on the outside border of the foot. It is due to an accumulation of excessive physical forces over a period of weeks or months during activities such as *long distance running*, *dancing* and *baseball* pitching.

Treatment includes *ice, non-steroidal anti-inflammatory drugs (NSAIDs)* and padding to reduce the pressure. If this fails a *corticosteroid* injection is recommended or, as a last resort, surgery to remove the bones.

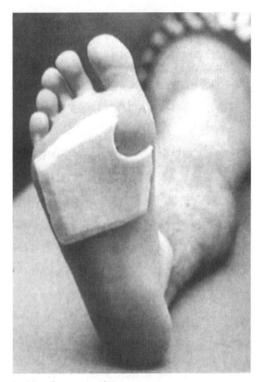

Padding for sesamoiditis

Set

A number of repetitions of a specific activity performed consecutively. For example, lifting a dumbbell 8 times is called a set of 8 repetitions. Three sets of eight = 24 repetitions. It is mostly used in *strength training* programmes. A set is also used for scoring in *tennis*.

Sever's disease

An inflammation of the heel bone (calcaneus) at the attachment of the *Achilles tendon*. It occurs most commonly in adolescents and is due to an accumulation of repeated, excessive traction imposed by the tendon on the bone over a long period of time, weeks or months.

The injury is associated with excessive amounts of running and the stage in life when the thigh and shinbones grow faster than the muscles and tendons, causing them to lose *flexibility*. It is considered to be a sub-group of a bone disease called *osteochondrosis*.

The diagnosis can be confirmed with an *X-ray*. An assessment to check for abnormalities of running biomechanics, such as excessive *foot pronation*, is recommended.

Treatment consists of *rest* from aggravating activities such as running, *ice*, gentle *flexibility exercises* for the calf muscles, *massage* and a heel raise (a wedge of rubber can be adhered to the inside sole of the shoe). Return to sport can take 6 to 12 months or, if severe, up to 2 years.

Sex

The traditional advice from coaches over the years has been not to have sex the night before a competition event. The reasoning was that abstinence increases aggression by channelling sexual energy onto the playing field or to save all one's energy for competition. However, there is no good scientific evidence to support these claims.

These days the standard recommendation is to leave it to athletes to decide for themselves to do what they feel is best, with the proviso not to spend the whole night before a game chasing after sex.

There is a theory based on research that shows having sex can raise *testosterone* levels during the next 24 hours. As a result, it is suggested sex the night before might give athletes involved in aggressive competitive sports an advantage.

Research has confirmed that short bursts of exercise can increase *testosterone* levels and therefore libido. But there is also clear evidence that *overtraining syndrome* and *overreaching* not only cause excessive fatigue and other symptoms, they also lower the sperm count and decrease libido.

Shiatsu

A traditional Japanese method of diagnosis and treatment based on pressure points and *massage* techniques using the thumbs and palms of the hand to apply deep pressure to clear blockages and restore the flow of energy.

Shin

Most of the lower leg between the knee and ankle. It contains the tibia (large, front shin bone) and fibula (smaller, outer-side shin bone), nerves and blood vessels, and a small synovial joint, the superior tibiofibular joint. The muscles, which produce movements of the *ankle* and *foot and toe joints*, are divided into three compartments by strong, inelastic fascia:

- Deep posterior compartment: flexor hallucis longus, flexor digitorum longus and tibialis posterior.
- Anterior compartment: tibialis anterior, extensor digitorum longus, extensor hallucis longus, peroneus tertius.
- Lateral compartment: peroneus longus, peroneus brevis.

The superior posterior compartment contains the gastrocnemius and soleus (calf muscles), which are in the *calf*, the back section of the lower leg.

Shin chronic compartment syndrome

Shin pain caused by excessive pressure on a group of muscles in the lower leg. It is an overuse injury, where pain gradually builds up over a period of weeks or months due to an accumulation of excessive physical loads placed on the muscles, in particular running.

Causes

The muscles in the *shin* are grouped into compartments surrounded by fascia, a thick, slightly elastic layer of fibrous connective tissue. The muscles expand in volume in the compartment during running due to contractions; however, this normally does not cause pain. But excessive physical forces can cause inflammation that ultimately leads to reduced elasticity of the fascia, and the muscle expansion during running causes increased pressure and pain.

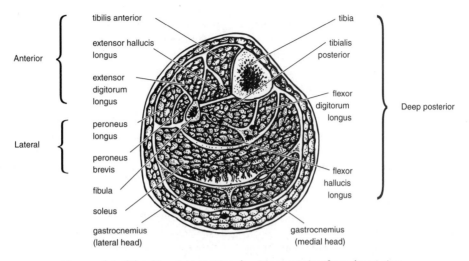

The muscles of the shin—cross-section showing a superior (from above) view

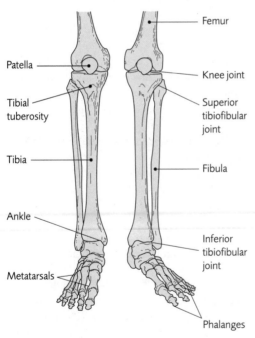

Bones of the shin

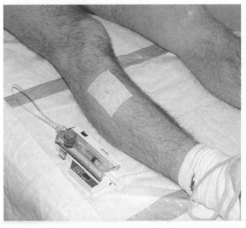

Pressure measurement for shin chronic compartment syndrome

Diagnosis

There are three types of shin chronic compartment syndromes. The two most common are deep posterior and anterior. The least common is the superficial posterior.

The deep posterior compartment, containing the flexor hallucis longus, flexor digitorum longus and tibialis posterior muscles, usually causes pain in the inner section of the shin towards the back or calf pain, often described as tightness or a bursting sensation.

The anterior compartment, containing the tibialis anterior, extensor digitorum longus, extensor hallu-

The excessive forces may be due to too much running, an abnormality of *running biomechanics* such as *foot pronation* and wearing inadequate *shoes*. Some people are simply born with a tight fascia.

cis longus and peroneus tertius muscles, causes pain felt on the outer side of the shin towards the front.

The superior posterior compartment, containing the gastrocnemius and soleus muscles, causes pain felt in the calf (see *Calf and Achilles tendon pain and injuries*).

In general, pain begins during running and ceases with rest. Occasionally it is associated with muscle weakness, numbness or pins and needles. The diagnosis is usually confirmed with compartment pressures measurements using a tube called a Stryker catheter during rest and activity.

Treatment and return to sport

The recommended treatment for both compartment syndromes is *rest* from running, *massage* and correction of any *biomechanical abnormality*, especially excessive foot pronation. Surgery is usually required to perform a fasciectomy (removal of a window in the fascia), fasciotomy (splitting the fascia) and stripping the periosteum from the tibia.

Shin guard

A tough, protective thermoplastic material that protects the *shin* bone and nearby muscles against direct blows, such as by a hockey ball or stick, or in *soccer* against kicks from opponents. A blow from a hockey ball struck with full force from 1 m (3 ft) away can shatter a guard. Blows can also strike the leg outside the guard from behind and just above the ankle.

Shin pain and injuries

Causes

Pain in the shin can be caused by an acute or overuse injury. An *acute injury* causes pain that begins suddenly due to a single incident such as a direct blow into a bone, which is common in contact sports.

An *overuse injury* causes pain that gets worse over a period of weeks or months due to an accumulation of excessive forces that cause microtrauma. In the early stages it causes only minor pain and stiffness. But later it becomes severe enough to seek medical care, either gradually or due to a sudden aggravating event. In rare cases tumour or blood vessel problem is the cause.

The tibia and fibula bones and the muscles and associated structures of the *shin* are the main sources of pain. Infrequently it is another structure such as the low back, which is called shin *referred pain*.

Diagnosis

Making the diagnosis involves combining information gathered from the *history, physical examination* and relevant tests.

For overuse injuries the relationship between pain and exercise is an important clue. Pain that improves after warming indicates *tibia periostitis*. Pain worsening with exercise and accompanied by tightness that disappears relatively quickly with rest suggests *shin chronic compartment syndrome*. Pain increasing during jumping, also present at rest or at night, indicates a *tibia stress fracture* or *fibula stress fracture*.

Acute injury due to a direct blow may be a bone fracture. A *tibia fracture* causes pain at the front or inner-side and in many cases prevents walking or running. A *fibula fracture* causes pain on the outer-side and in most cases walking is possible.

Radiological investigations can help diagnose shin pain, such as a *bone scan* for stress fracture. Other helpful tests include compartment pressure testing for shin compartment syndrome.

Shin splints

The popular term for a group of injuries that cause pain in the shin, particularly associated with running sports. The specific injuries that cause this type of shin pain include *tibia stress fracture, tibia periostitis* and *shin chronic compartment syndrome*.

Shoes

The most important wardrobe item in exercise and sports that involve walking, running, jumping and skiing because it reduces the chances of injuries in the foot, leg, knee, hip and low back.

Causes of shin pain

Common	Less common	Not to be missed
• Tibia stress fracture • Fibula stress fracture • Tibial periosteal contusion • Tibia fracture • Fibula fracture • Shin chronic compartment syndrome • Tibia periostitis	• Popliteal artery entrapment syndrome	• Osteoid osteoma • Osteosarcoma • Peripheral vascular disease • Acute compartment pressure syndrome

QUICK REFERENCE GUIDE

Shin

Acute injury: Pain caused by a sudden force

Tibia fracture .... Did you receive a sudden blow to the shin and now feel pain at the front or inner side?

Fibula fracture .... Did you receive a sudden blow to the shin causing pain on the outer side?

Tibia periosteal contusion .... Did you get a knock or kick onto your shin bone that has left a painful lump?

Overuse injury: Pain that has gradually worsened over a period of weeks or months

Tibia stress fracture .... Do you have shin pain that gets worse with exercise, possibly associated with pain at rest or at night?

Tibia periostitis .... Do you have shin pain that warms up with exercise, and gets worse after you cool down?

Shin chronic compartment syndrome .. Do you have shin or calf pain that gets worse with exercise, but ceases when you stop exercising?

Fibula stress fracture .... Do you have pain at the front of your shin that gets worse with exercise, but ceases when you stop exercising?

Selection

Each activity or sport places specific stresses and forces on the foot. The reaction of each person's foot to these stresses and forces is called the *biomechanics*, which may be normal or abnormal.

Aches and pains in the leg or back is a sign that you may need an assessment by a sport podiatrist or physiotherapist to identify a *biomechanical abnormality*.

You can also check for a biomechanical abnormality by assessing your shoes. All shoes normally show wear on the outside and heel area. However, excessive wear on the inner sole, for example, is an indication of too much *foot pronation*, causing excessive foot flattening and increased risk of tibial stress fracture. Too

much *foot supination* (outward turning movement) is indicated by excessive wear on the outer section.

Another method of checking your foot involves lying on your stomach and drawing a line along the Achilles tendon and continuing down to the calcaneus (heel bone). If the line on the calcaneus deviates in a sideways direction towards the outside when standing up, there is too much pronation. A line deviating in a sideways direction towards the inside indicates too much supination.

A final word on selecting the right shoe: make sure that the shoe is designed to take into account the stresses and forces of your sport and, if you have been feeling aches and pains in your lower limb or

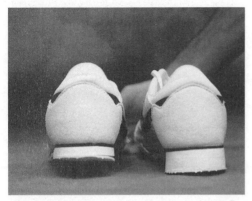

The upper rear part of the running shoe is called the heel counter

Sections of a sport shoe

back, it also may need to correct a biomechanical abnormality.

The most common used sport shoe designs are *running shoes, football boots, ski boots, tennis shoes, walking shoes, cricket shoes, golf shoes, basketball shoes, netball shoes* and *cross-training shoes.*

A shoe that can fix the biomechanical abnormality of excessive foot pronation, for example, is one with a straight last (the shape of the shoe when viewed from below), which reduces pronation in the rear foot.

General features of shoes

UPPER

The outer and most visible section of a shoe. The heel counter fits around the calcaneus bone and holds the heel in. It should be made of a firm, rigid plastic that provides stability.

The front section, called the toe box, does not have special physical features. Its main role is to protect the foot from the environment, such as the heat or cold, and skin abrasions. The mid-section con-

tains the lacing or velcro bands that hold the foot inside the shoe.

MIDSOLE

The upper layer of the flat, bottom section that makes direct contact with the foot inside the shoe. It contains most of the important physical features for running shoes, particularly shock absorption. Materials that may be used include compartments filled with air or gel, carbon fibres and reinforced rubber.

LAST

The shape of the shoe when viewed from below, which possesses important physical features for abnormal foot biomechanics such as too much pronation movement.

OUTSOLE

The outer covering of the sole of the shoe. It influences the shoe's grip on the surface, such as football boots with screw-in studs. It also determines durability, with a high carbon content lasting the longest.

Short bones

Bones that are shaped like a cube, trapezoid or scaphoid. The small bones of the *wrist joint*, called the carpal bones, are classical examples. They tend to have a thin layer of compact *bone* and thicker spongy bone compared to *long bones.*

Short wave therapy

See *Diathermy.*

Shortness of breath

Excessive difficulty with breathing and increased *breathing rate.* This is a normal response during high-intensity exercise in order to maintain oxygen supply and remove carbon dioxide from the blood.

However, an excessive difficulty may be a symptom of an underlying disease such as *asthma,* particularly if it is associated with wheezing or chest tightness. If chest pain is also present it may be an indication of disease such as a heart attack (see *Chest pain and injuries*).

Types of shortness of breath

Three different types of shortness of breath, acute, chronic or intermittent, provide an indication of the underlying cause.

Acute: begins suddenly for the first time

- *Heart attack*
- *Lung infection*
- *Asthma* attack
- Spontaneous *pneumothorax*
- Pulmonary embolism (see *Deep vein thrombosis (DVT)*)
- *Lung aspiration* of foreign body (can occur in athletes with dental prosthesis or those who chew gum)

Chronic: is present over a long period of time

- *Coronary heart disease*
- Anaemia (see *Iron deficiency*)
- *Diabetes*
- *Obesity*
- *Asthma*

Intermittent: occurs irregularly

- *Asthma*
- *Mitral stenosis*
- *Stress*
- *Anxiety*

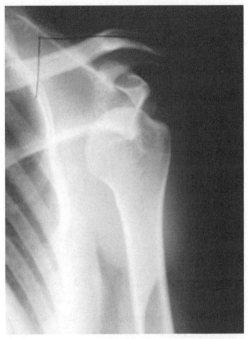

X-ray of an anterior (forward) shoulder dislocation

Shoulder dislocation

An acute injury that displaces the joint between the two bones of the *shoulder joint*. It is one of the most common acute injuries in exercise and sport.

Causes

In most cases the displacement forces the head of the humerus (arm bone) in an *anterior* (forwards) direction most commonly due to a fall onto an out-stretched arm forced above the head and turned outwards, or a direct blow to the back of the shoulder.

The displaced humeral head often causes a *glenoid labrum injury*, most often a Bankart lesion. A direct blow to the front of the shoulder can cause a posterior dislocation, although this is uncommon.

Diagnosis

The dislocation is often associated with a feeling of the shoulder popping out and a sudden, severe pain. There may be a history of *shoulder instability*. The physical examination usually finds a prominent humeral head and a hollow below the acromion (upper tip of the shoulder blade).

Anterior dislocations occasionally cause neuropraxia (see *Nerve injury*) of the axillary nerve, resulting in reduced skin sensation on the outer shoulder. An X-ray is recommended to detect any associated *fractures*. Posterior dislocation causes reduced range of external rotation (outwards turning).

Treatment and return to sport

The aim is to re-establish the normal connection of the shoulder joint as soon as possible, and then allow the ligaments, joint capsule and muscles to heal. This may occur spontaneously or can be performed by a medically trained person, sometimes under general anaesthetic.

Usually the joint is held in a sling for 3 weeks. Treatments also include *flexibility exercises, strengthening exercises*, particularly *isometric strengthening* for the internal rotator muscles.

Because of the high rate of recurrent dislocation in younger athletes, an *arthroscopy* should be considered particularly if a Bankart lesion of the glenoid labrum is suspected. These athletes often require open surgical reconstruction of the ligaments to reduce the risk of recurrent dislocation. Return to sport usually requires at least 2 to 3 months of *shoulder rehabilitation*, and up to 6 months before contact sports can be played again.

Shoulder impingement

Pain caused by pinching of the rotator cuff tendons within the sub-acromial space at the top of the *shoulder joint* that has become too narrow to allow them to pass without causing pain.

The top border of the sub-acromial space is made up of the coracoacromial ligament, the acromioclavicular (AC) joint and the underside of the acromion, a bony projection of the scapula (shoulder blade) that is commonly known as the tip of the shoulder. The bottom border is the upper part of the head of the humerus (the round head of the arm bone).

The space normally becomes slightly narrowed when the shoulder performs an abduction movement (lifted outwards and upwards). If impingement is present it will cause a painful arc of abduction movement, usually between 70 and 120 degrees.

There are a number of different potential causes. It may be a sign that there is an underlying injury such as *rotator cuff tendinosis* or *rotator cuff strain*; that one of the shoulder structures is abnormal; for example, a congenital abnormality of the acromion called os acromiale; or an abnormality of *scapular biomechanics*.

Shoulder instability

Reduced ability to maintain the normal connection between the two bones of the *shoulder joint*. It is usually due to damage to the ligaments, joint capsule, glenoid labrum or muscles. The instability may affect these structures in an anterior (forwards), posterior (backwards) or inferior (downwards) direction, or it can be multidirectional.

Anterior instability
Damage can occur because of a previous acute injury, such as a *shoulder dislocation*, or an overuse injury, most likely in sports involving repeated over-

head activities such as *baseball* pitching, javelin, swimming and *tennis*. It is also associated with an abnormality of *scapular biomechanics* and *throwing biomechanics*.

The most prominent symptom is shoulder pain. The history can also include episodes of *dead arm syndrome* and 'catching' associated with a *glenoid labrum injury*. In severe cases activities such as yawning or rolling over in bed may result in a subluxation or dislocation. Special tests such as the apprehension test can be used to confirm a diagnosis.

Treatment
Strengthening exercises are recommended. Surgery to repair the instability is often required if strengthening fails. In some cases surgery may be recommended as the first treatment. However, tendon transfers such as the Putti Platt procedure have poor results for people who want to return to sport. *Shoulder rehabilitation* is essential after surgery.

Posterior instability
Overuse is the most common cause of posterior instability. Most cases can be treated with strengthening exercises for the posterior stabilising muscles. If these measures fail, then surgery should be considered.

Multidirectional instability
Multidirectional instability involves a combination of anterior, posterior or inferior. It is usually an overuse injury, often associated with generalised ligament looseness throughout the body, which can be confirmed by examining the wrists, elbows and knees. Treatment may involve strengthening exercises and *motor re-education* of the shoulder stabilisers. If this fails surgery may be attempted.

Shoulder joint

A ball-and-socket *synovial joint* made up of the round head of the arm bone (humerus) and shallow saucer-shaped glenoid cavity. It is also called the glenohumeral joint. It relies on static and dynamic constraints to increase its stability and keep the two bones in contact.

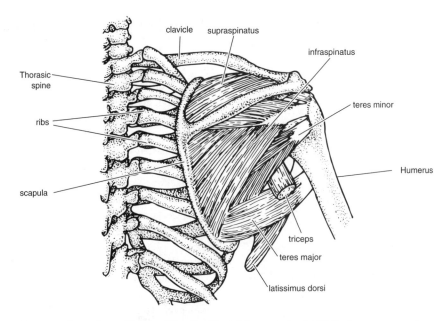

Anatomy of muscles and bones of the shoulder joint—posterior (behind) view

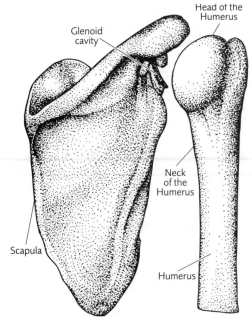

Bones of the shoulder joint

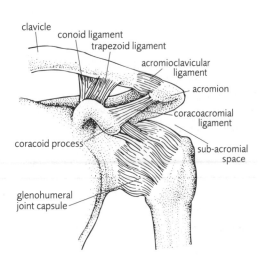

The ligaments of the shoulder joint (glenohumeral joint) and acromioclavicular (AC) joint

Stability

The static constraints are the joint capsule, glenohumeral ligaments and glenoid labrum, a ring of fibrous tissue attached to the rim of the glenoid cavity.

The dynamic constraints are predominantly provided by the supraspinatus and, to a lesser extent,

Muscles involved in shoulder (glenohumeral) joint movements

Movement	Prime movers	Secondary movers
Flexion	• Anterior deltoid • Pectoralis major (clavicular head) • Coracobrachialis	• Biceps
Extension	• Latissimus dorsi • Teres major • Posterior deltoid • Pectoralis major (sternocostal head)	
Abduction	• Deltoid (mid) • Supraspinatus	
Adduction	• Pectoralis major • Latissimus dorsi	
External rotation	• Infraspinatus • Teres minor	• Posterior deltoid
Internal rotation	• Subscapularis • Pectoralis major • Latissimus dorsi • Teres major	• Anterior deltoid

infraspinatus, teres minor and subscapularis muscles. They serve to control the position of the humeral head in the glenoid cavity.

The scapular stabiliser muscles, scapulothoracic, acromioclavicular (AC) and sternoclavicular joints also play an important role in shoulder movements. Normal shoulder function requires smooth integration and coordination between all these joints and muscles (see *Scapular biomechanics*).

Shoulder pain and injuries

Causes

Shoulder pain can be caused by acute or overuse injuries or disease. An *acute injury* causes pain that begins suddenly due to a single incident such as falling onto the shoulder, which is common in contact sports such as football codes, or a blow from equipment, such as an ice hockey stick.

An *overuse injury* causes pain that gets worse over a period of weeks or months due to an accumulation of excessive forces that cause microtrauma. In the early stages it causes only minor pain and stiffness. But later on, either gradually or following a sudden excessive force, it can become painful enough to seek medical care.

Diseases that may also cause shoulder pain include *osteoarthritis*, different types of inflammatory arthritis such as *ankylosing spondylitis* and *tumours*.

The *shoulder joint* and associated structures are the main sources of pain in the region. However, it is not unusual for *referred pain* to come from a distant structure, in particular the neck joints, thoracic spine joints or one of the internal organs of the chest and abdomen.

Diagnosis

Making a diagnosis involves combining information gathered from the *history*, including how the pain started, the *physical examination* and relevant tests.

For an acute injury the position of the shoulder at the time of impact is useful information. For exam-

Causes of shoulder pain

Most common	Less common	Not to be missed
Acute injury		
• Rotator cuff strain • Shoulder dislocation • Glenoid labrum injury • Clavicle fracture • Acromioclavicular (AC) joint sprain	• Rotator cuff tear • Scapular fracture • Biceps tendon (long head) rupture • Neck of humerus fracture	• Tumour • Referred pain from: heart attack; pleurisy; ulcer; spleen (left shoulder only); decompression sickness
Overuse injury		
• Shoulder instability • Rotator cuff tendinosis • Shoulder referred pain	• Biceps tendinosis • Osteolysis of the clavicle • Little Leaguer's shoulder • Coracoid process stress fracture	• Thoracic outlet syndrome

ple, a fall onto an outstretched arm forced above the head and turned outwards suggests anterior *shoulder dislocation*, which is also often associated with a *glenoid labrum injury*. A fall onto the point of the shoulder can cause a *clavicle fracture* (broken collarbone) or *acromioclavicular (AC) joint sprain*.

It is important to note the time of day that the pain is felt. Night pain is a common symptom of a complete tear of a rotator cuff (see *Rotator cuff strain*), though serious pathology such as a *tumour* also needs to be excluded. Unusual sensations such as sudden numbness and weakness are also significant, particularly for *shoulder instability* and *thoracic outlet syndrome*.

The diagnosis of an overuse injury predominantly relies on information about the activity that brings on the pain. For example, performing an excessive amount of throwing or freestyle and butterfly swimming are all associated with *rotator cuff tendinosis*.

A radiological investigation is often required to confirm the diagnosis, such as X-rays for a fracture and dislocation or *magnetic resonance imaging (MRI)* for shoulder instability and rotator cuff strain. *Arthroscopy* of the shoulder is often recommended to confirm a glenoid labrum injury. Other useful tests include blood tests for inflammatory arthritis such as *ankylosing spondylitis*.

QUICK REFERENCE GUIDE

Shoulder

Acute injury: Pain caused by a sudden force

Rotator cuff strain ....Did you feel a sudden pain in your shoulder while exercising or playing sport, which worsened when you cooled down and makes your arm feel a bit weak now?

Shoulder dislocation ....Did you displace your shoulder joint, causing it to remain out of its socket and had to be put back into place by someone else?

Clavicle fracture ....Did you fall onto or receive a blow to the point of your shoulder, which is causing pain and difficulty with arm movements now?

Acromioclavicular (AC) joint sprain Did you fall onto or receive a blow to the point of your shoulder, which is causing pain and difficulty with arm movements now?

Biceps tendon (long head) rupture Did you feel a sudden pain (and/or tearing sensation) at the front of your shoulder during exercise or sport, which has resulted in pain and weakness?

Overuse injury: Pain that has gradually worsened over a period of weeks or months

Rotator cuff tendinosis ....Do you have shoulder pain that started gradually, is aggravated by shoulder movements, is painful when starting activities and but then eases after warming up?

Shoulder instability ....Did your shoulder pop-out and pop back into place without any assistance?

Biceps tendinosis ....Do you have pain at the front of your shoulder that came on gradually and is aggravated by arm and shoulder movements (e.g. tennis or ten pin bowling)?

Shoulder referred pain.................Do you have pain around your shoulder, but also in your neck and possibly down your arm and into your hand?

Shoulder referred pain

Pain felt in the shoulder that is caused by a damaged structure in another location some distance away. The most commonly involved structures are the neck joints, thoracic spine joints, a nearby muscle or the neural sheath. The *referred pain* may be wholly or partly the source of the pain.

Diagnosis and treatment

The diagnosis is based on excluding a local cause of pain and positive signs that the cause is referred pain.

For example, a diagnosis of pain referred from the right side of the *neck joints* to the front of the right shoulder is considered likely if local diagnoses, such as rotator cuff tendinosis and anterior shoulder instability, are excluded and a physical examination finds reduced *range of movement* of neck lateral flexion (sideways bending) and tender and stiff sliding (accessory) movements of the right side neck joints.

This diagnosis is then tested with right side neck joint *mobilisation*, a treatment involving a practitioner pushing the joints with the hands. If the shoulder pain is reduced, the diagnosis is supported.

Muscles in the neck, upper thoracic spine and scapular regions may also refer pain into the shoulder pain, particularly *myofascial trigger points* in the trapezius, infraspinatus, levator scapulae and rhomboids, which can be treated with *massage* and *dry needling*. The neural sheath, which is the outer covering of nerves, is assessed and treated with the upper limb *neural tension* test.

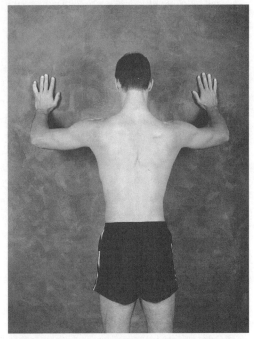

Wall push-up strengthening exercise for shoulder rehabilitation

Shoulder rehabilitation

Treatments and activities that aim to restore the damaged shoulder back to its former level or better in order to regain performance as quickly as possible and with the smallest risk of re-injury.

It is recommended for injuries including *glenoid labrum injury*, *shoulder dislocation*, *shoulder instability* and third-degree *rotator cuff strain* (complete tear), particularly those that have been treated with surgery.

A strengthening exercise using rubber tubing for shoulder rehabilitation

Throwing and catching basketball exercise for shoulder rehabilitation

A closed chain exercise for shoulder rehabilitation

Treatment and return to sport

It follows the four stages of *sport rehabilitation*:

1) The aim of the initial stage is to reach 90 degrees of passive or active assisted shoulder abduction (outwards) movement 3 weeks after surgical repair of glenoid labrum injury, shoulder dislocation and shoulder instability, and 90 degrees passive or active assisted abduction by 4 to 6 weeks for repairs of third-degree rotator cuff strain (complete tear).

Treatments include *ice, heat therapy (superficial), flexibility exercises, motor re-education, massage* and *mobilisation*.

Strengthening exercises should not be done for individual muscles in the initial stage, but rather for the group as an integrated unit using *closed chain exercises*, which involve performing movements when the arm is fixed, such as leaning the hand against the wall and moving the body.

2) The intermediate stage corresponds with resumption of normal activities of daily living, achieving normal *range of movement* and strength and the commencement of some sporting activity as part of *skills training* for rehabilitation.

3) The advanced stage begins with the commencement of functional activities related to the sport, *power* training and *endurance training for muscles* of the arms.

4) The final stage is return to sport, which involves full participation in training and competition. A full return is permitted if the clinical examination doesn't find abnormalities, particularly of *throwing biomechanics* and *scapular biomechanics*.

Shoulder subluxation

A partial dislocation of the *shoulder joint*. It causes less severe displacement and pain than a full dislocation. The diagnosis and treatment is the same as for a *shoulder dislocation*, except that the recovery and return to sport is quicker.

Sinus tarsi syndrome

An overuse injury of the small blood vessels, ligaments and fat pad in the small sinus tarsi canal that forms part of the subtalar joint of the *ankle*.

It develops gradually due to an accumulation of repeated, excessive physical forces over a period of weeks or months that is often associated with excessive *foot pronation* or forced ankle eversion (turning outwards movement), such as during high jump take-offs.

The pain is often felt in a vague area on the outer side of the ankle, is more severe in the morning, may diminish with exercise, but can be exacerbated by running on a curve in the direction of the affected ankle. Diagnosis is confirmed with an anaesthetic injection into the sinus tarsi.

The recommended treatment includes *rest* from aggravating activities, *ice*, *non-steroidal anti-inflammatory drugs (NSAIDs)* and *mobilisation* of the subtalar joint, followed by *strengthening exercises*, *flexibility exercises* and *proprioception training*. An injection of *corticosteroids* may be helpful.

Skateboarding

fracture (wrist), *supracondylar fracture* (elbow) and patellar *fracture* (knee). Wearing a *helmet*, wrist guards, elbow pads and knee pads, is recommended.

Situation awareness

The ability to take in many pieces of information and accurately assess the future actions in a game of sport.

For example, a soccer defensive player needs to anticipate where the opposing forward player may run to in order to receive the ball, and a baseball fielder should be aware if there are hitters on base and where to throw the ball if it is hit to him.

Situation awareness can make a player stand out, such as performing a high number of steals (cutting off a pass between opposing players) in basketball. It is also called 'reading the play'.

Skateboarding

There are two types of skateboarding, street and ramp. Street skating is a form of transport and uses objects to perform 'tricks' such as the 'handrail', riding down the handrail of an outdoor staircase. Ramp skating uses mini-ramps, semi-circles and large U-shapes.

Injuries
The most common injuries are *head injury*, *concussion*, *Colles fracture* (wrist), *radius distal epiphysis*

Skeletal muscle

Muscle that creates the movements performed in exercise and sport. There are more than 600 skeletal muscles in the body. The largest is the gluteus maximus in the buttock. The smallest muscles are in the face. *Kinesiology* and *biomechanics* are two areas of science that study how skeletal muscles and joints produce movements.

Anatomy
Each skeletal muscle has two parts: the belly, where *muscle contractions* are produced to create movement; and the *tendon*, aponeurosis or *fascia*, which connect the belly to a *bone* or connective tissue.

The shape and size of the belly and tendon, aponeurosis or fascia varies from muscle to muscle. Each design produces a different amount, direction and force of contraction and movement. Skeletal muscle is one of three types of *muscle* in the body.

Skeleton

The hard and rigid internal framework of the human body. It is made up of 206 *bones* that are connected together by *joints*. Most of these joints are flexible and allow movement. The skeleton provides a solid structure for *skeletal muscles* to attach to and produce the contractions that create movement. It also protects internal organs, such as the spine that encases the spinal cord.

The average male skeleton weighs more than a female. The female pelvis tends to be wider than a male, due to a wider birth canal for childbirth. The end of bone growth and full bone maturation occurs, on average, two to three years earlier in females compared to males. The skeleton is part of the *musculoskeletal system*.

Ski boots

Footwear designed to cope with the physical demands of skiing. *Downhill skiing* boots are usually stiff with a high ankle cut to protect the ankle, though it makes knee injuries more common in a slow twisting fall where release of the ski boot binding fails to occur and the fixed boot sustains a rotational force, which is exerted through the lower leg and into the knee. Care should be taken not to make the binding too tight.

The action of skiing requires *foot pronation* (inward turning movement) to edge the downhill ski into the slope. Skiers with excessive pronation of the foot, a common biomechanical abnormality, face an increased risk of knee injury, which can be reduced by wearing an *orthotic* placed in the boot to restore the foot into a neutral position.

Skier's thumb

See *First MCP joint sprain*.

Skills training

Regular participation in activities that aim to increase the efficiency and outcome of performance in a sport and minimise the risk of injury. For instance, skills training can be done to learn a sport for the first time, such as tennis, or to increase the chances of kicking a goal in football in an experienced player.

It involves performing a high number of repetitions of the same movements, preferably following the supervision of a coach to detect faults and provide advice. It can also include psychological work such as *visualisation* and theoretical instruction.

Sport rehabilitation

Skills training may be included in a *sport rehabilitation* program when recovering from an injury.

It is introduced to regain or improve skill levels. Activities are commenced during the intermediate stage of the program after adequate strength, flexibility and proprioception have been regained and continued until return to sport commences.

The program begins with the most basic level of skills; for example, a tennis player recovering from a knee injury hitting shots while seated in a wheelchair. The aim is to progress gradually through tasks of increasing difficulty.

Sport skills training for rehabilitation of a leg injury for a basketballer

Individual drill
- Defensive stance
  - Stationary
  - Side to side
  - Pivoting
- Dribbling
  - Forwards/backwards
  - Side to side
  - Zigzag
  - Cross-overs
- Shooting
  - Foul shots (no jump)
  - Dribble and shoot (no jump)
  - Dribble, jump shot, rebound alone
- Lay ups
  - Alone
- Rebounding
  - Post moves
  - High post
  - Low post

Team drills
- Set play
- One on one
- Half court play
- Full court scrimmage
- Match practice
- Match (off bench)
- Match (start)

Sport skills training for rehabilitation of an arm injury for a tennis player

Ground strokes

- Forehand, backhand, gradually increase time from 5–20 minutes

Serving

- Service action without ball, 10 repetitions
- Half pace serves, 10 repetitions
- Gradually increase 50 per cent to 100 per cent serves, 10 repetitions
- Gradually increase repetitions to 40 with break after each set of 20

Overhead shots

- Slow at first, 15 repetitions
- Gradually increase speed

Match practice

- Initially 15 minutes
- Gradually progress to one set, two sets, full match

Skin

Outermost covering of the body, which protects the organs and tissues inside the body from the outside environment. This includes waterproofing the body when immersed in water, fending off physical injury, providing a barrier to infectious organisms and buffering against the heat and cold.

The skin contains many neurons (nerve cells) that give us information about the outside environment, and the activities and movement that the body is involved in. It also contributes to the maintenance of a constant internal temperature.

A skin disease called psoriasis may be associated with *psoriatic arthritis*. Yellowing of the skin may be associated with *hepatitis*. Skin itching is one of the symptoms of *decompression sickness* in scuba divers. Other skin illnesses include *herpes simplex virus infection*, *athlete's foot* and *jock itch*.

Structure

The skin itself is an organ; in fact, the largest in the body. It is made up of a thin outer layer called the epidermis and a thicker inner layer called the dermis. Beneath them lies the subcutaneous layer.

The epidermis is made up of cells that sit on top of one another in layers. The bottom cells are the

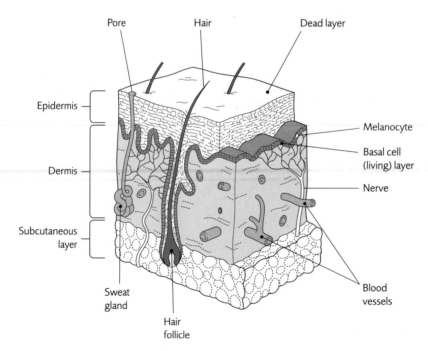

Skin structure and features

newest ones and as they grow they migrate outwards. By the time they get to the top these cells are dead and form a tough protective covering. This process takes about six weeks in the average adult.

The dermis is mostly made up of connective tissue fibres and contains specialised skin structures including hair follicles, sweat glands and sebaceous glands, that produce oil, and blood vessels and nerves.

Skin bumps

See *Cholinergic urticaria.*

Skin fold test

The most commonly used and practical method for assessing the amount of body fat in an athlete. It involves using a pincer device that grasps a fold of body tissue and provides a measurement of its thickness in millimetres. This thickness is a good estimation of the amount of fat in an athlete's *body composition* because it is stored in the subcutaneous tissue (the layers below the *skin* surface).

Method
There are seven standard sites in the test, and at least three sites should be measured to provide a result.

The sum of the measurements is used as a reference point for subsequent assessments, which can be done weekly in elite athletes during a training program or when recovering from an injury. A reasonably accurate calculation of body density and *relative body fat* also can be made, but it requires using a special equation.

- Triceps: A vertical fold is raised on the midline of the posterior surface of the right arm.
- Subscapular: A fold is raised just below and to the right of the inferior angle of the right scapula in the natural fold that runs obliquely downwards.
- Biceps: A fold is raised at the midline of the anterior surface of the right arm.
- Supraspinale: A natural fold is raised obliquely level to the undersurface of the tip of the anterior superior iliac spine.

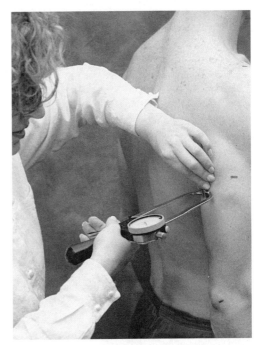

Triceps skin fold test

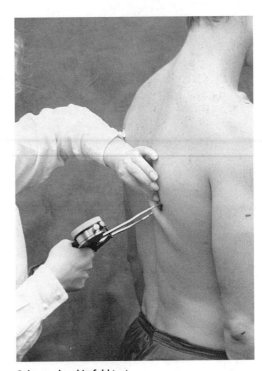

Subscapular skin fold test

381

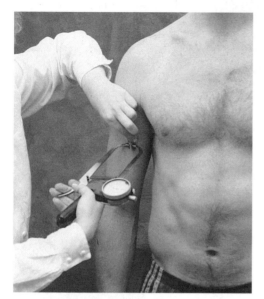

Biceps skin fold test

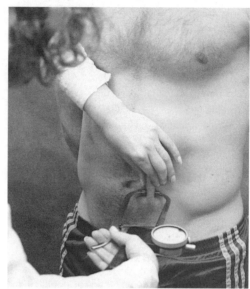

Abdomen skin fold test

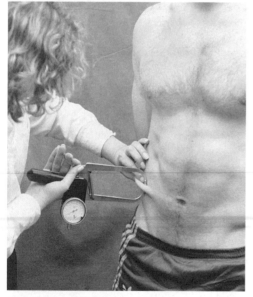

Supraspinale skin fold test

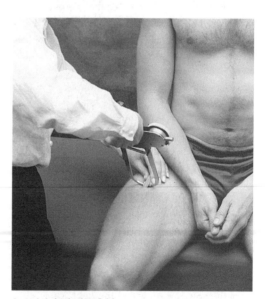

Anterior thigh skin fold test

- Abdomen: A vertical fold is raised adjacent to the left of the umbilicus so that all the subcutaneous fat is raised parallel to the fold.
- Anterior thigh: With the athlete sitting, a fold is grasped parallel to the long axis of the femur halfway between the crease at the top of the thigh and top of the kneecaps.
- Medial calf: With the athlete placing the foot on a chair so that the knee is flexed at right angles, a fold is grasped on the inner side of the calf where the muscle bulk is greatest.

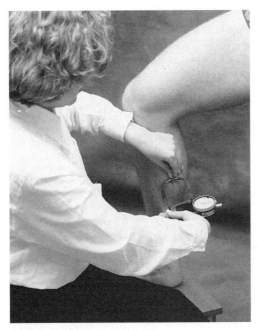

Medial calf skin fold test

Skin injury

Injury to the *skin* is common in exercise and sport, especially where collisions and contact with opponents, equipment and the ground frequently occur. Damage to underlying structures such as tendons, muscles, blood vessels and nerves can also occur at the same time. The main concern is when an injury causes bleeding, such as an abrasion, laceration or puncture wound.

Treatment

Applying direct pressure with a compression bandage and elevating the injured part to reduce blood flow to the injured area are the recommended treatments for a bleeding wound.

If the wound is open and clean, the wound edges should be brought together, either by the use of adhesive strips in a small wound or by suture of a larger wound.

A contaminated wound should not be closed. It is important to prevent infection by first removing all dirt and contamination. This can usually be achieved by simple washing with clean water. Occasionally, extensive washing and scrubbing is required, which should be done as soon as possible after the wound occurs.

Antiseptic solution should be applied and, if the wound is severely contaminated, *antibiotics* should be commenced to prevent infection. Tetanus injections may also be required. Natural health recommendations include using tea tree oil for at least 3 days, followed by calendula and hypericum ointments for speedy wound healing.

Wounds should be observed for signs of infection, such as redness, swelling, pain and increased

Skinfold measurements in elite athletes of various sports

Sport	Men (mm, sum of seven sites)	Women (mm, sum of seven sites)
Basketball (guard/forward)	67 (45–100)	77 (41–132)
Cycling	54 (26–85)	62 (34–90)
Gymnastics	42 (28–60)	38 (27–58)
Hockey (field)	59 (38–108)	88 (48–140)
Rowing, lightweight	45 (36–65)	73 (55–105)
Rowing, heavyweight	67 (46–111)	88 (61–119)
Skiing, alpine	51 (31–82)	59 (31–87)
Skiing, Nordic	46 (27–77)	74 (57–108)
Swimming	54 (34–108)	80 (45–155)
Track and field, sprint	56 (54–58)	60 (45–84)
Track and field, middle distance	39 (26–68)	59 (37–111)
Triathlon	40 (28–60)	56 (34–89)
Volleyball	57 (37–80)	91 (36–148)
Weight lifting	75 (34–190)	Not available
Water polo	70 (36–120)	96 (46–161)

tenderness, as well as increased temperature locally or *fever*, which affects the whole body.

Skull fracture

A break of one or more of the bones in the upper part of the *head*, including the occipital, parietal, frontal, sphenoid and temporal. It occurs due to a sudden forceful blow to the head such as striking the ground.

The main concern with this *fracture* is brain injury (see *Concussion*). If the injury does not cause an open wound it is left to heal itself. However, an open wound requires *antibiotics* to prevent infection (particularly meningitis), and surgery to drain blood and remove bone pieces where necessary.

Sleep and rest

An important part of the recovery process after high-intensity *aerobic training* and competition. Athletes may require up to 10 to 12 hours sleep at night. Afternoon napping is a useful method of catching up on sleep.

Lack of sleep over a long period of time may cause sleep deprivation, including persistent *fatigue* and possibly *overtraining* syndrome. Recovery can be achieved simply by devoting a weekend to long sleeps.

Slipped disc

See *Nerve root compression*.

Slow-twitch (ST) muscle fibre

A type of *muscle fibre* that produces contractions that are best suited for endurance events, such as a marathon run, and low intensity activities, such as walking. These *muscle contractions* are due to a high efficiency of adenosine triphosphate (ATP) production, the main source of energy in muscles.

Physiological features

Slow-twitch (ST) are slower than *fast-twitch (FT) muscle fibres* at generating a contraction: 110 microseconds compared to 50 microseconds. This is due to a slow-working enzyme for releasing energy from ATP, called slow ATPase.

FT fibres can also trigger off a quicker contraction because they have the ability to absorb calcium ions at a faster rate. In addition, the neuron from the *motor nervous system* that brings signals from the brain to switch on ST muscle fibres is slower and reaches a smaller number of fibres compared to FT. As a result, when ST fibres are switched on they generate less force and power. On the other hand, it is produced more consistently over a longer period of time.

Exercise and sport

Most muscles in the body contain an even mix of ST and FT fibres. The amount of force and power required for an activity determines the number of each that get switched on. If you are walking, the ST fibres are predominant. Breaking into a fast sprint switches on more of the FT fibres.

At the start of a long distance run your brain will switch on mainly ST fibres, though not all of them at once. As the run progresses more and more ST fibres get switched on. At one point the brain will run out of ST fibres and swap over to FT fibres.

This may explain why fatigue comes in stages during a marathon run and the great mental effort that is required to keep up the same pace towards the end of a race when the brain is trying to switch on muscle fibres less suited to endurance.

Athletes with a higher proportion of ST fibres in their muscles are more likely to achieve high levels of fitness during *aerobic training* and perform better in endurance activities such as *long distance running*.

Snapping hip

A snapping noise usually located in the outer side (lateral aspect) of the hip. It most commonly occurs in ballet dancers, gymnasts and hurdlers. Fibres of the tensor fascia lata or gluteus maximus muscles sliding over the greater trochanter produce the noise during abduction movement (leg is lifted outwards) of the *hip joint*.

It is usually not painful and clears with rest, correction of poor technique and abnormalities of *running biomechanics* if any are present, *massage* and *flexibility exercises* for hip muscles.

Snowboarder's ankle

See *Talus lateral process fracture*.

Snowboarding

Snowboarding is a hybrid of skateboarding and surfing. After an initial cult following in the 1960s it is the fastest growing snow sport in the world.

Equipment and fitness

Snowboards are like large skateboards. Riders stand on the board side-on, the front foot placed at a 45-degree angle pointing forward and takes most of the body weight. The back foot controls the steering. Both feet are fixed to the board in bindings that do not release during a fall.

The fitness requirements are *aerobic training* for long hours of activity, *flexibility training* and *strength training*, primarily for the legs.

Injuries

The most common injuries are *Colles fracture* (wrist), *scaphoid fracture* (wrist), *elbow medial collateral ligament sprain*, *radius head fracture* (elbow), *shoulder dislocation, acromioclavicular (AC) joint sprain* (shoulder), *medial collateral ligament (MCL) sprain* (knee), *ankle sprain* and *talus lateral process fracture* or 'snowboarder's ankle' (foot and toes).

Soccer

It is claimed that soccer originated from bizarre eleventh century tales of English citizens kicking the decapitated heads of Norman enemies through the streets during victory celebrations. In the modern era Cambridge University established the 'football association' in 1863. Soccer is called football in most parts of the world. There are more than 200 million participants in soccer worldwide.

Rules and equipment

Outdoors soccer is played on a large rectangular field. Two teams compete to score goals by kicking or heading the ball into the net. The ball must not be struck or caught with the hands.

Indoors soccer is played on a basketball-sized court, with a smaller goal and ball. Modified versions of soccer for children include reductions in the field and ball size.

Soccer player kicking for goal

Fitness and skills

Soccer skills include kicking and heading the ball and evasive running involving speed, endurance and quick changes of direction. The fitness requirements include *aerobic training* and *speed training*.

Injuries

The most common injuries include *concussion* (head), *osteitis pubis* (hip and groin), *adductor tendinosis* (hip and groin), *quadriceps contusion* (thigh), *hamstring strain* (thigh), *quadriceps strain* (thigh), *anterior cruciate ligament (ACL) tear* (knee), *medical collateral ligament (MCL) strain* (knee), *gastrocnemius strain* (calf), *soleus strain* (calf), *ankle sprain, Pott's fracture* (ankle) and *PIP joint dislocation* (finger) for goal-keepers.

Soccer boots

See *Football boots*.

Sodium

See *Minerals*.

Sodium bicarbonate

A chemical that is taken as a supplement to increase the concentration of bicarbonate in the *blood*.

The purpose is to reduce acidity leading to a delay in muscle fatigue and improved performance in *anaerobic training*. It is also used as an antacid to relieve *gastrointestinal reflux* (heartburn) by neutralising and reducing the amount of acid in the oesophagus and stomach.

It is recommended for exercise and sport involving maximal anaerobic activity lasting from 1 to 7 minutes. The recommended dose is 300 mg per kilogram (135 mg per lb) of body mass. However, gastrointestinal side effects such as nausea and vomiting can be severe in many athletes. People with heart disease or kidney disease should not take it.

Sodium cromoglycate

A medication that prevents an *asthma* attack by reducing the release of chemicals, which cause airways narrowing. However, it does not reduce symptoms once an attack has occurred. The usual dose is 20–40 mg immediately before exercise. Its greatest effect lasts for up to 2 hours. It has little or no side effects.

Soft tissue therapy

See *Massage*.

Softball

Softball originated in the United States as an indoor version of baseball in the late 1800s. It was first played outdoors in 1895.

Two teams take turns to bat and field. The 'hitter' stands at the 'home' base of four bases arranged in a diamond. The pitcher throws a ball with an underarm action. The fitness, skills and injuries in softball are similar to *baseball*.

Soleus strain

An injury of the deep *calf* muscle. It is usually associated with a build up of muscle tightness over the preceding days or weeks secondary to an abnormality of running biomechanics such as excessive *foot pronation*.

Diagnosis, treatment and return to sport

Often this muscle *strain* causes more pain during walking and jogging than sprinting. Tenderness is felt when the muscle is pressed firmly with the fingers on the outer side of the calf.

Treatment includes using a heel raise (a wedge of rubber adhered to the inside sole of the shoe), electrotherapy such as *ultrasound therapy* and *laser*

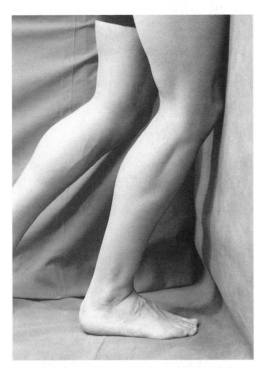

Flexibility exercise following soleus strain

therapy, flexibility exercises, strengthening exercises and *massage*.

Somatic nervous system

The collection of *neurons* (nerve cells) that conduct the conscious communications in the body that is in our voluntary control. In exercise and sport these communications occur to and from skeletal muscles and involve sensations including pain, touch, space, body and joint position and movement, heat, vision and hearing.

Spasm

An involuntary muscle contraction. It may occur after an injury to protect the damaged structures, by preventing movement. If pain and inflammation from the joint injury persist, muscle spasm also can continue and may lead to chemical and mechani-

cal stimulation of pain-sensing nerves in the muscle, which increases the risk of developing muscle *fibrosis*.

Special Olympics

Competition events across a wide range of sports only for people with an *intellectual disability*.

Specificity

Selecting activities to be included in a *training* program that maximise the chances of achieving specific goals, such as increased fitness and improved performance in a sport. For example, a sprint runner should do strength training and interval training to improve strength, power and anaerobic fitness.

Specificity is based on the fact that there are different types of *fitness* and skills that are unique for each sport. It is important to identify these components prior to developing a training program. Specificity is one of the four main principles of training.

SPECT

A test that combines a *bone scan* with tomography to produce images of body tissue. It is the acronym for 'single photon emission computed tomography'. The tomography is a method where images of slices of the body are put together to form a three-dimensional image. It may be recommended for injuries such as *pars interarticularis stress fracture* of the low back.

Speed training

Regular participation in activities that aim to increase speed of performance. It is achieved through *strength training*, training to increase power such as *plyometrics* and *Olympic-type weight lifting* and *skills training*, which is used to improve technique. For example, an increase in running speed can be achieved by doing strength training by lifting weights, plyometrics and learning how to move the arms and legs more efficiently during running.

Gains achieved through speed training may make the difference between winning and losing in a close competition. However, it should be noted that most of the speed that an athlete possesses is inherited.

Spinal cord

A long and narrow organ located inside the spine. Together with the brain the spinal cord makes up the *central nervous system (CNS)*.

It begins at the lower end of the *brain* and ends in the low back just above the tailbone. It mostly carries a two-way flow of communications between the brain and the rest of the body through millions of nerve fibres (also called axons), which are the long thin branches of *neurons* (nerve cells) whose cell bodies are located in the brain.

There are also neurons whose cell bodies are located in the spinal cord and conduct their own communications without consulting the brain, in particular *reflex* activity.

As the spinal cord passes down through the spinal canal, it sends off two large branches called the ventral and dorsal nerve roots at each vertebra level.

Within the spinal canal they rejoin together to form a larger *spinal nerve*, which exits the spinal canal through a hole called the intervertebral foramen. Each spinal nerve is named according to the vertebra level it exits from the spinal canal; for example, C5 is the fifth cervical spinal nerve.

Spinal fusion

A surgical procedure that involves fusing two vertebrae (spinal bones) together to prevent the disc and synovial joints from moving. It is most commonly performed for *low back joints*, when symptoms are excessively severe due to an injury such as *nerve root compression*, or after *conservative treatments*, such as physiotherapy and medication have failed. The procedure involves obliterating the disc and joint fea-

tures and inserting bone cells that grow to connect the bone ends together. It can take up to 3 to 4 months for a fusion to fully take hold and return to contact sports permitted, though simple activities may be commenced after 6 to 8 weeks.

Spinal injury

An acute injury to the spine due to a sudden excessive force. It can affect any part of the spine from the neck down to the low back. For example, a fall where the head strikes the ground can cause a neck (cervical) spinal injury, or an opponent's knee striking the back in a collision can cause a low back (lumbar) spinal injury. The primary concern is damage to the spinal cord, as well as the bones and joints of the spine, leading to long-term paralysis.

Treatment
A suspected spinal injury should be treated as a *medical emergency*, which includes ensuring that breathing and circulation are normal, and transporting the person off the field of play to a hospital as quickly as possible to minimise the chances of long term damage.

Spinal injury is suspected until proven otherwise by the following symptoms:
- Loss of consciousness for any amount of time.
- Conscious and complaining of numbness, pins and needles, weakness trying to perform a movement or inability to move at all or pain in the neck, middle back (thoracic) or low back.

Transporting a person with a suspected spinal injury from the field of play requires not moving the neck nor any other part of the spine because a damaged bone or joint may injure or further injure the spinal cord.

This is best achieved by keeping the injured person lying on the back on a firm, flat surface such as a spinal board, with the neck held in a *neutral joint position* (no rotation movement or sideways, forward or backwards bending). If the patient is unable to lie on their back; for example, due to vomiting, the person should be lying on the side while keeping the neck neutral.

One member of the transportation team needs to be responsible for keeping the neck still when moving the injured person from the field of play. Four other people should carry the spinal board.

If the injured person with a suspected spinal injury has no breathing problems, the helmet can remain in place during transport. However, if there are breathing problems requiring mouth-to-mouth resuscitation (see *Medical emergency*) the helmet may need to be removed by holding the neck in a neutral joint position from below while a second person removes it from above by pulling on the ear pads.

Spinal nerves

The 31 pairs of nerves that are part of the *peripheral nervous system*. As the spinal cord passes down through spinal canal it sends off two large branches called the ventral and dorsal nerve roots at each vertebra level. Within the spinal canal they rejoin together to form a larger spinal nerve, which exits the spinal canal through a hole called the intervertebral foramen (see *Low back joints*).

Each pair corresponds to a vertebra in the spinal column. For example, there are five lumbar (low back) vertebra bones, which means there are five pairs of spinal nerves. Each spinal nerve is named according to the vertebra level it exits from the spinal canal; for example, C5 is the fifth cervical spinal nerve. Just outside the spinal column each spinal nerve divides into two branches, ventral and dorsal ramus. Each spinal nerve carries a two-way flow of communications of the *neurons* that make up the *motor nervous system* and *sensory nervous system*.

Spirometer

See *Lung function tests*.

Spleen

An organ in the upper left side of the abdomen underneath the lower ribs that removes old red blood cells and helps to fight infections by producing some of the white blood cells used in the *immune system*.

It can be directly injured leading to rupture and bleeding in high-speed and contact sports such as *motor sports*, *horse riding sports* and football codes such as *American football*, *Australian Rules football* and *Rugby League*.

A spleen injury is a *medical emergency* that may require surgery for immediate removal. It can cause pain in the abdomen and, sometimes, refers pain into the shoulder. The spleen also can become enlarged during infections such as *glandular fever* and malaria.

Spondylolisthesis

A vertebra or part of a vertebra in one of the *low back joints* that has slipped forward. It is usually due to a defect in the bone that develops during childhood. Uncommonly it is associated with *pars interarticularis stress fracture*. The vast majority involve the L5 vertebra slipping on the sacrum (S1).

The diagnosis is usually made with an *X-ray*. The severity of the slippage is graded from mild (grade I) to severe (grade IV). Pain is usually located in the low back and sometimes spreads into the legs, aggravated

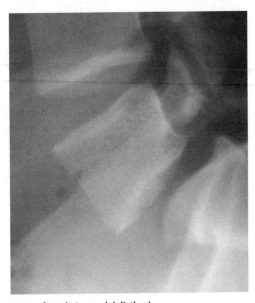

X-ray of grade I spondylolisthesis

by bending backwards. Many people with a grade I slippage do not even have pain.

The recommended treatment for grades I and II that are causing pain is *rest* from aggravating activities, *mobilisation*, *strengthening exercises* for the abdominal and extensor muscles and *flexibility exercises* for the hamstring.

Return to sport is permitted once bending backwards does not cause pain. People with grade III and IV injuries should not be permitted to play high speed or contact sports. In severe cases of low back pain a surgical procedure called a *spinal fusion* is recommended.

Spontaneous pneumothorax

See *Pneumothorax*.

Sport

Formal and highly organised activities that are governed by a set of rules and played competitively between individuals or teams, such as golf, tennis, basketball and football.

Participants play at three levels of competition: *recreational*, or informal; *non-elite*, or amateur; and *elite*, or professional. Many sports also can be performed as a form of *exercise* like cycling and swimming.

Sport rehabilitation

Treatments and activities that aim to restore an injured part of the body back to its former level to regain sport performance as quickly as possible and with the smallest risk of re-injury.

There are four stages in a sport rehabilitation program:

1) The initial stage begins immediately from the time that the injury occurs or, if it is a severe injury, when it is medically stable, and ends when almost full, pain-free *range of movement* is achieved.

2) The intermediate stage corresponds with resumption of normal activities of daily living and commencement of some sporting activity, primarily skill-related, and fitness maintenance that avoids stressing the injured area.

3) The advanced stage begins with the commencement of functional activities related to the sport.

4) The final stage is return to sport, which involves full participation in training and competition.

Throughout the program the *psychology of rehabilitation* should be taken into account, including dealing with fears, feelings of loss and excessive grief response.

Principles

Pain, range of movement and ability to perform exercises, sport-related activities and home-activities are the best guides to progress. If there is an adverse response, the intensity or volume of the program should be reduced.

In the early stages the type of activities should not directly stress the injury. Later in the program activities can be done to test if the injury has made a full recovery. When commencing activities that directly stress the injury, the time spent performing them must be increased very gradually.

An integral part of return to sport is sufficient recovery. For example, a runner may initially run every third day, then every second day, then two out of every three days, etc. Fitness can be maintained with swimming or cycling on non-running days.

Progress can be made from simple to complex movements. For example, a basketballer dribbling slowly in a straight line, then gradually increasing speed and introducing turns.

Return to sport

Judging the correct day to return to sport can tread a fine line between being keen to start, and making sure that all the physical and psychological rehabilitation goals have been reached.

Return to sport should only be permitted when the following criteria have been met:

• time constraints for normal healing have been observed

- pain-free full range of movement (a minor loss may be acceptable in certain sports)
- no persistent *swelling* (some minor swelling may be tolerated)
- adequate *strength* (at least 90 per cent compared to the uninjured limb) and endurance
- good *flexibility*
- joint stability (this may be controlled by a brace or tape and good muscle control)
- good *proprioception*
- adequate *aerobic fitness*
- skills regained
- no persistent *biomechanical abnormality*
- psychologically ready
- coach satisfied with training form.

For example, throwing can be started again after a shoulder or elbow injury beginning with 20–30 throws of 10 m (33 ft) each. If there is no abnormal pain by the next day, the number of throws and distance thrown can be increased every second or third day until eventually reaching 50–60 throws of 25 m (82 ft) each. Re-commencing participation in in-line skating should begin with only 30 minutes a day or every second day and increase in 5–10 minute increments every second or third day.

Sports bras

Bras designed to prevent excessive movement of the breasts during exercise and sport that cause pain and discomfort.

A good sports bra should give support of the *breasts* from above, below and the sides. The best ones are made of a material that is firm, mostly non-elastic, non-abrasive and have good absorptive quality. The straps should be of non-stretch material and, ideally, criss-crossed or Y-shaped at the back, with no seams or ridges in the *nipple* area, and no fasteners or hooks.

The sports bra should be individually fitted and be comfortable both at rest and with vigorous activity. There should also be provision for a plastic cup to be placed over the bra or the insertion of padding for contact sports such as martial arts and football.

Sports drinks

Drinks that have been prepared to meet the fluid and energy needs of people participating in exercise and sport.

Stages of sport rehabilitation

Stage	Functional level	Sport	Rehabilitation treatments
1. Initial	Poor	Substitute activities (e.g. swimming, cycling)	• RICE (rest, ice, compression, and elevation) • Electrotherapy • Flexibility exercises • Isometric strengthening • Stability program
2. Intermediate	Fair	Isolated skills training (e.g. basketball shooting)	• Electrotherapy (less) • Flexibility exercises • Strengthening exercises • Proprioception training • Stability program
3. Advanced	Good	Commence agility training and skills training	• Strengthening exercises • Flexibility exercises • Stability program • Functional exercises • Proprioception training
4. Return to sport	Good	Full	• Strengthening exercises • Power • Flexibility exercises

Sports drink

They contain varying amounts of *carbohydrates* and mineral salts diluted in water. The carbohydrates should be able to leave the stomach and be absorbed from the intestines into the body as quickly as possible.

Sports drinks may have advantages over plain *water*, such as for athletes participating in day-long, multiple events where carbohydrate replenishment is required and eating solid food is too difficult.

Selection

The research has yet to show conclusively which is the best drink. Fructose is emptied quickest from the stomach, but it is absorbed slowly from the intestines and large amounts may cause diarrhoea.

Glucose polymers, which are long chains of *glucose*, may leave the stomach quicker than glucose. Probably the most important fact is that too much

carbohydrate, greater than 10 per cent concentration, slows down emptying of the stomach.

According to the current state of knowledge, it is recommended to drink a carbohydrate solution of 4–8 per cent carbohydrate concentration, with a mixture of different carbohydrates.

The mineral salts include sodium, potassium, chloride and magnesium (see *Minerals*). They are added to replace those lost in sweat. However, the only one of concern is sodium, which can be lost in large amounts in ultra-long distance athletes.

In addition, the sodium may enhance fluid absorption in the small intestine and stimulate thirst, which helps by prompting more fluid intake. The ideal concentration of sodium in sports drinks is 10–25 mmol/L (millimoles per litre) = 23–58 mg/100 ml = 7–17 mg/oz. Other mineral salts are only lost in tiny amounts and can be easily replaced in a balanced diet.

Sports medicine

The provision of health services for the physical and psychological needs of people participating in exercise and sport.

It involves the prevention, diagnosis, treatment and rehabilitation of injuries, illness and disease, and the improvement of performance through training, nutrition and psychology.

It takes into account the specific needs of children, adolescents, females, older people and those with permanent disabilities, and a wide variety of situations such as high altitude, under water and in hot and cold environments.

Sports medicine team

It is difficult for any one practitioner to develop all the skills required in sports medicine. As a result, it is ideally suited to a team approach. Professionals from different disciplines provide specialised skills to provide optimal care for the athlete and improve each other's knowledge and skills.

The wide range of professions and skills include: *general practitioner* (family physician), *sports physician, orthopaedic surgeon, radiologist, physiotherapist* (physical therapist), *massage therapist, podiatrist, nutritionist, psychologist, sports trainer, osteopath, chiropractor, acupuncturist, exercise physiologist, biomechanist,* nurse, occupational *therapist, orthotist,* coach and *fitness trainer.*

Sports nutrition

The scientific study of the amount and type of food and fluids required by people participating in exercise and sport, which varies according to the level of participation.

People participating in high-intensity exercise and sport need to ensure optimum nutrition to reach maximum performance levels.

Specific goals include; maximising *energy supply*; achieving ideal body *weight*; ensuring an optimal intake of *vitamins* and *minerals*; *precompetition eating* and *pre-event meal*; aiding recovery from intense training and competition with *post-activity eating* and maintaining adequate *hydration.*

Different types of training require specific diets, such as *aerobic training diet, fat-loss diet* and *strength training diet.* The same applies for children and adolescents (see *Sports nutrition for younger athletes*) and female athletes (see *Women's sports nutrition*).

Participation in low- to moderate-intensity exercise and sport, such as a person walking briskly for 30 minutes on most days of the week, requires a balanced *diet for good health.* Specific nutritional needs also may be required if an illness or disease is present and in changing environmental conditions like hot weather.

Sports nutrition for younger athletes

The scientific study of the food requirements for children and adolescents participating in exercise and sport.

Nutrition at this age sets the foundations for adult life, both in terms of physical development and eating habits. It is also a time of nutritional risk. Adolescents tend to skip meals, snack frequently and rely

A peanut butter sandwich is a highly nutritious snack

heavily on fast foods. Girls, more often than boys, may become obsessed with achieving a slim figure. Participation in exercise and sport places extra demands on their food and fluid intake.

Energy

Children and *adolescents* involved in exercise and sport have high-energy requirements. During the growth spurt of puberty it may be difficult to satisfy energy needs. Fortunately they are great snackers at this age. Highly nutritious snacks can play an essential role in providing energy. Examples include:

- wholemeal dry biscuits topped with low-fat cheese and tomato, or peanut butter, honey and banana
- wholegrain toast topped with ricotta cheese and jam

- toasted English muffin with maple syrup
- fruit loaf
- pita bread with dips such as hummus, yoghurt and cucumber
- fresh fruit salad
- frozen yoghurt
- low-fat muesli bar
- low-fat ice cream with fruit
- smoothie drink made of low-fat dairy or soy products
- low-fat rice pudding
- rice salad
- baked potato with low-fat topping, such as cottage cheese
- pumpkin soup and toast
- baked beans on toast
- corn on the cob with wholegrain pepper
- boiled noodles with soya sauce.

Protein

The protein needs per kilogram of body weight are higher in children and adolescents due to growth and in those involved in exercise and sport they are greater still.

An intake of 2 g per kilogram (0.9 g per lb) of body weight is recommended. This amount should be 12 per cent of the total energy intake. Good sources of *protein* include lean meat, low-fat dairy products such as cheese and milk, chicken without skin, fish, legumes, rice, eggs, nuts and seeds.

Carbohydrates

Carbohydrates are the most important source of energy for athletes. In the young athlete it may be difficult to meet these needs without supplementing with refined carbohydrates such as sugar.

However, a delicate balance is required because too much can reduce the percentage of protein in the total energy intake. Good sources of *carbohydrates* include rice, pasta, breads and cereals, fruit, starchy vegetables and legumes.

Fat

Fat intake should be 25–30 per cent of the total energy intake, or 70–90 g a day for the young athlete. It should include an even balance between the three types of *fat*: monounsaturated (olive oil, avocado), polyunsaturated (margarine, fish) and saturated (red meat, dairy products).

Vitamins and minerals

An adequate *vitamin* and *mineral* intake is essential for the young athlete. This can be supplied by a healthy diet without the need to resort to supplementation. Eating a diet too high in refined sugars, such as soft drinks which are rich in energy but contain little to no vitamins and minerals, can cause a deficiency, such as vitamin B group deficiency.

Two minerals that are particularly important are *calcium* and *iron*. A lack of calcium can increase the risk of *osteoporosis* in later life, particularly in females. *Iron deficiency*, with or without anaemia, can have a negative impact on athletic performance. Females are at greater risk because of increased iron losses due to *menstruation*. In some cases supplementation may be necessary.

Sports physician

A doctor who has received an additional medical degree recognised as a specialisation to provide medical services for people participating in exercise and sport.

Services are provided for professional, elite and non-elite sportspeople, teams and clubs, as well as for the general population. The services include being the first contact for people who need a diagnosis and treatment, and deciding when to refer to another practitioner.

Sports psychology

The scientific study of the internal workings of the mind of people participating in exercise and sport. It looks at how emotions, thoughts, memory, intelligence, learning and motivation interact and influence performance, behaviour and physical health.

Many exercise and sports-related problems (including persistent illness or injury, *tiredness* and fatigue, failure to meet team goals, poor performance and failure to master a specific skill) can be due to psychological factors. For example, excessive *anxiety* can have a negative impact on ability to kick the winning goal at the end of a game.

Alternatively, regular participation in exercise and sport can reduce the need for antidepressant medication in people with *depression*.

Psychological techniques that are utilised to treat problems include controlling *arousal* levels, *visualisation*, *progressive muscle relaxation*, *centring*, devising a pre-competition and skills acquisition *routine* program, positive *self-talk*, *goal setting*, *behaviour modification*, *autogenic training*, *flotation tank*, *music* and *massage*.

Sports psychology for younger athletes

The scientific study of the workings of the mind of *children* and *adolescents* participating in exercise and sport. It looks at the special characteristics and needs of this age group in terms of their emotions, thoughts, memory, intelligence, learning and motivation, and how they affect outward manifestations such as performance, behaviour and physical health.

It is generally recommended that children should participate in exercise and sport to have fun, improve skills and experience social interactions with their peers. Some children, however, can experience negative outcomes such as *stress* and *anxiety*, particularly when problems such as the *ugly parent syndrome* are present. Coaches also can ignore the personal needs of children under their care by not giving enough positive feedback and too much negative feedback.

The recommendations for ensuring a long-lasting positive experience for children in sport include:

- Be reasonable in the demands placed on young athletes' time, energy and enthusiasm.
- Teach them that the rules of their sport are mutual agreements that no one should evade or break.
- Whenever possible young athletes should be grouped together in team sports to give everyone as much chance of success as possible.

- Avoid overplaying the talented children and give 'average' players equal time.
- Never ridicule or yell at a child for making a mistake.
- Winning is only part of the motivation for playing.
- Fun and enjoyment are more important.
- Be enthusiastic.
- Develop *sportsmanship* including respect for opponents as well as the judgment of umpires, referees, officials and opposing coaches.
- Avoid use of derogatory language based on gender, race or religion.
- Remain informed and up-to-date on the principles of children's growth and development in exercise and sport.

Sports rub

See *Analgesics (topical)*.

Sports trainer

A person who has completed training and is recognised as being qualified to prevent, assess and treat sport injuries and illness, including providing first aid and *taping*. Sports trainers usually work for sport clubs, teams and organisations.

Sportsmanship

Participating in a sport within the bounds of decency and morality. It involves playing without gaining an advantage other than that acquired through skills, good luck and factors out of one's own control such as the weather.

It also involves treating opposing players and officials with decency, such as lending equipment, showing care when a player is hurt and shaking hands with opponents at the end of a game. These acts are designed to counter and provide a balance to the tendency to label the opposition as the 'enemy'.

Opposition players shaking hands at the end of a game is part of sportsmanship

Spot reduction

The mistaken belief that strength training for a particular muscle is the most effective way to reduce weight off the same part of the body. For example, doing sit ups for the abdominal muscles does not necessarily make the stomach smaller or less flabby. It just makes the abdominal muscles stronger.

Sport science research has shown that any reduction in stomach fat that is achieved is coincidental. Moderate-intensity *aerobic training* such as brisk walking, is the best method of burning off fat. Of course, eating a *fat-loss diet* is also essential for losing weight. *Strength training* may be helpful too.

Even then, the reduction in fat occurs throughout the whole body. Some areas lose more than others, depending on your body's genetic programming. If you're lucky more will come off the abdomen. But there are no guarantees.

Sprain

A tear or excessive stretch of a *ligament* or *joint capsule* due to an external force that is too strong to withstand, which is called an acute injury. For example, the foot twisting too far can damage the ligaments of the ankle joint.

An *articular cartilage acute injury* or *bone bruise* may also occur at the same time. In a few cases a sprain can be an overuse injury, which is due to an accumulation of excessive forces over a period of

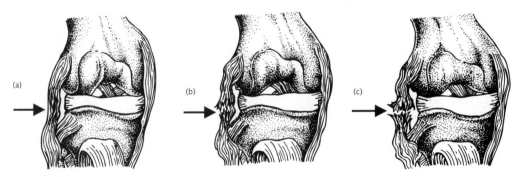

Sprains—(a) grade 1; (b) grade 2 (c) grade 3

weeks or months, such as an *elbow medial collateral ligament sprain*.

Diagnosis and treatment

A *history* and *physical examination* is usually sufficient to make a diagnosis.

MILD (GRADE 1)

Only a few of the fibres of the ligament or joint capsule are torn. A physical examination of the joint movements finds that the stability is normal.

The immediate treatment is first aid to minimise *swelling* and bleeding, including *RICE (rest, ice, compression and elevation)*, followed by gentle *active exercises*. Subsequent treatment aims to find a balance between allowing enough rest to permit the ligament to heal at the same time as encouraging movement so that stiffness and weakness are kept to a minimum. A *sport rehabilitation* program is usually recommended to help with return to sport.

MODERATE (GRADE 2)

A large number of fibres are torn. Also called a partial tear. It causes significant pain and swelling, perhaps bruising. The joint shows an abnormal amount of laxity and instability.

The first aid is the same as for a mild sprain; however, the subsequent treatment is given with greater care to ensure full healing and a longer time for rehabilitation and return to sport.

SEVERE (GRADE 3).

The ligament or joint capsule is completely torn across the width. Also called a rupture. In many cases less pain is experienced because nerves are completely torn as well. Swelling and bruising can be severe. The joint movements show an excessive amount of laxity and instability.

The first aid is the same as for a mild sprain, followed by conservative treatments such as a plaster cast, bracing or a bandage, or surgery may be recommended to reconnect the torn ends or replace the ligament.

Sprinting

A group of sports including the 100 m, 200 m, and 400 metres, 4 × 100 m and 4 × 400 m relays, and 400 m hurdles. The fitness requirements for shorter distances are anaerobic training such as *interval training*, *strength training* and *skills training* for activities such as the start and jumping for hurdlers. Maximum speed achieved by 100 m sprinters is 100 per cent. However, the 400 m sprinter can only achieve 90 per cent maximum speed due to muscle *lactate fatigue*, also requiring *aerobic training*.

Injuries

Detection of *running biomechanics* abnormalities can prevent injuries. The most common injuries include *tibia stress fracture* (shin), *fibula stress fracture* (shin), *shin chronic compartment syndrome*, *Achilles tendinosis* (calf), *navicular stress fracture* (foot and toes), *low back pain* (non-specific), *adductor muscle strain* (hip and groin), *quadriceps strain* (thigh) and *hamstring strain* (thigh).

Sprinting for children and adolescents

Recommended training guidelines for children and adolescents participating in *sprinting*, which minimise the risk of injuries.

Training sessions per week should not exceed three for children and adolescents up to 14 years. From 15 to 18, training can be held up to five times per week. The maximum amount of time per training session should not exceed 1½ hours, including a warm-up.

The general recommendations for *running shoes* also apply for children and adolescents. Children may wear spikes from the age of 10. Hard surfaces such as bitumen and concrete should be avoided, and grass and dirt used as much as possible.

Squash

Squash originated in the early 1800s between inmates of English prisons who were surrounded by four walls. Today there are 15 million players in over 120 countries.

It is a racquet sport between two players on an indoor four-walled court. The squash ball is

Squash player

golfball-sized and made of rubber. The ball is hit so it strikes the front wall. It involves a high level of *aerobic training*.

Injuries

The most common injuries include *rotator cuff tendinosis* (shoulder), *low back pain (non-specific)*, *gastrocnemius strain* (calf), *soleus strain* (calf), *anterior cruciate ligament (ACL) tear* (knee), *meniscus tear* (knee) and eye injuries, *orbit blow-out fracture* and *subconjunctival haemorrhage*. Wearing goggles is highly recommended.

Stabilisers

See *Instability*.

Stages of change

A model that aims to help people change their behaviour in relation to their health. Examples include helping a non-active person to become regularly active, and helping a cigarette smoker to give up smoking for life.

Developed in 1982 by two US psychologists, Dr James Prochaska and Dr Carlo DiClemente, the model states that rather than suddenly changing behaviour in a fit of inspiration, change goes through a series of five stages. The following is a description of each of the stages with regards to exercise and playing sport. They apply equally to eating a healthy diet and quitting smoking.

1) Not thinking about change (pre-contemplation)

People at this stage can't even see they have a problem. They are either in denial or lack awareness, and have no intention of changing their behaviour in the near future. They often feel unfairly pressured to change by family, friends or society in general. They can get defensive and angry and resist offers to help them change.

It does not help to tell a person at this stage that the local gym is offering half-price membership. The only potentially helpful actions are providing information about the dangers of not doing exercise and the benefits of being active.

2) Thinking about change (contemplation)

People at this stage are aware that their exercise habits are unhealthy and seriously considering making a change, but haven't made a commitment yet.

If you are at this stage you are definitely open to receiving information. That may be one of the reasons you are reading this book. You feel you need to work out the causes of your current unhealthy lifestyle and what the potential solutions offer you. But deep down inside your mind is still weighing up whether you are really going to change. You will not start making plans until the advantages outweigh the disadvantages.

3) Definite plans to change (preparation)

You have decided the advantages of changing now outweigh the disadvantages. You have made a commitment and intend to change your lack of exercise within the next month.

Your awareness of what is required is high, though final adjustments are still necessary. You may have even already started making a few minor modifications; for example, you may have done some exercise every now and then.

Your plans not only include what you will eat and what exercise to do, but how to make sure you don't back out on giving it a proper go.

Helpful actions include practical information about the different types of exercise available, particularly what is best for you in terms of timing, convenience, location, equipment, facilities and cost. It is also worthwhile to choose a day to start, called 'Being Active Day'.

A key question for qualifying for the next stage is finding out: How much is enough exercise? According to the definition of *exercise for health* it is at least 30 minutes of moderate-intensity exercise, which is the equivalent of brisk walking, on most if not all days of the week.

4) Starting to change (action)

You have actually started doing regular exercise at the correct amount and continued for up to 6 months. Undoubtedly, you and everyone else can see the improvement.

But it is not the end of your efforts if you are going to achieve a lifelong change. You are still vulnerable to temptations and pitfalls. There is a great risk that you will go back to your previous unhealthy lifestyle. You need to keep going and consolidate your change.

Helpful actions include having a rescue plan in case you drop out. If that happens it doesn't mean you have failed. You just need to be prepared to look at why it happened and how to rectify the situation.

5) Staying changed (maintenance)

You have been doing exercise for more than 6 months. However, you must continue to consolidate your gains and avoid temptations and pitfalls. This still requires diligence and effort.

Though at the same time it is getting easier as you build up your positive experiences and confidence. If you keep this up for 5 years you will most likely never fall out of the habit or stop doing exercise, except when you experience injuries or health-related problems.

Staleness

See *Overtraining syndrome*.

Standing biomechanics

The positions of the joints and muscles of the legs, pelvis and lower back when standing upright.

Efficient or correct biomechanics include the following: the right and left legs are symmetrical; the subtalar (talocalcaneal) joint is in a *neutral joint position*, where it is neither in pronation nor supination (see *Ankle*); the midtarsal (talonavicular and calcaneocuboid) joints of the foot are in maximal pronation (see *Foot and toes*); the forefoot is perpendicular to the midline of the heel; the *ankle* joint is neutral; the tibia (inner-side leg bone) is perpendicular to the ground; the *knee joint* is neutral or slightly extended; the *hip joint* is neutral; and a slight *pelvis anterior tilt* position. The *weight-bearing line* for each leg passes through the anterior superior iliac spine of the pelvis, the patella and the second metatarsal bone.

Stationary cycling

See *Exercise bike*.

Stepping (stair climbing) machines

Fitness equipment designed to simulate climbing stairs. Regular use can be an effective form of *aerobic training*.

The stepping machine has two pedals. The user stands with one foot on each pedal and presses down on one pedal followed by the same action with the other foot, repeated in cycles as if climbing up stairs. The resistance with each step can be adjusted.

The two main models are: (1) dependent action, with the left and right pedals linked so that when one depresses the other rises; and (2) independent action, where the pedals are connected to and rise and fall to the rhythm of a machine. There are no indications that a stepping machine achieves greater aerobic fitness than climbing real stairs, though it can be more convenient.

Stepping (stair climbing) machine

Sternoclavicular joint sprain

Pain in the upper front of the *chest*, where the clavicle (collarbone) is connected to the top of the breastbone, due to a sudden, forceful single incident, usually a fall on the shoulder. It commonly occurs together with an *acromioclavicular (AC) joint sprain*.

Diagnosis, treatment and return to sport

A diagnosis is required to determine the severity of the *sprain*. A mild sprain requires 1 to 2 weeks to recover. A moderate sprain 2 to 3 weeks. Severe sprains cause a subluxation or *dislocation*.

An anterior subluxation (partial displacement), which forces the clavicle forwards in the direction of the front of the chest, is more common and treated with *immobilisation* in a figure-of-eight bandage for 1 to 2 weeks.

Anterior dislocations are immobilised for 3 to 4 weeks in a clavicular strap. A posterior dislocation,

which forces the clavicle inwards, is potentially dangerous because of the close proximity of the subclavian veins and artery, the trachea (windpipe), oesophagus, heart and lungs. The recommended treatment is to reconnect the joint under general anaesthesia as soon as possible followed by immobilisation with a figure-of-eight strap for 4 weeks.

Steroids

See *Anabolic steroids*.

Stiffness

Reduced *flexibility* or stretchability of a joint, ligament, muscle or neural sheath. A measurement of stiffness is called *range of movement*.

Stimulants

Drugs that increase the activities of nerves. There are two groups: the central nervous system stimulants, such as *amphetamines* and *caffeine*, that reduce drowsiness and increase alertness; and the sympathomimetic drugs that influence the sympathetic nervous system, such as *ephedrine*.

Stinger

See *Neck burner*.

Stitch

A sharp pain in the left or right upper abdomen underneath the ribs that is usually felt during high-intensity exercise. It is most likely due to *spasm* of the diaphragm (the main breathing muscle), or trapping of gas in the upper portion of the large intestine. Avoiding high-*fat* and high-*protein* foods and eating mainly *carbohydrates* may help prevent a stitch.

Strain

An injury to a muscle or tendon when some or all of the fibres are torn due to a single event where the external forces are greater than the strength of the tissue to withstand them.

Muscle

The most common *muscle* strains are in the lower limbs, including the quadriceps (front thigh), hamstring, calf and hip adductors (groin muscles). The most common upper limb muscle strains include the supraspinatus and pectoralis major.

Factors that make a muscle strain more likely include insufficient *warm-up*, reduced *flexibility*, excessive fatigue, muscle imbalance, previous injury and *biomechanical abnormality*.

DIAGNOSIS AND TREATMENT

A *history* and *physical examination* are usually sufficient for making a diagnosis. However, *diagnostic ultrasound* or *magnetic resonance imaging (MRI)* can determine the severity of a muscle or tendon tear.

MILD (GRADE 1)

A small number of fibres are torn causing pain and no loss of strength. Return to sport usually occurs after 1 to 2 weeks.

Treatment aims to provide first aid through *RICE* (*rest, ice, compression and elevation*) to reduce pain, swelling and bleeding, followed after 2 to 3 days by treatments to encourage healing though protection of the torn muscle and electrotherapy such as *interferential therapy* and *ultrasound therapy*, massage, *flexibility exercises* and *strengthening exercises* as part of a *rehabilitation* program.

MODERATE (GRADE 2)

A significant number of fibres are torn that cause reduced muscle strength and pain that limits movement. It requires 2 to 3 weeks before a full return to sport can be made.

Treatment is the same as for a mild strain, however with greater care to ensure full healing and a longer time for rehabilitation and return to sport.

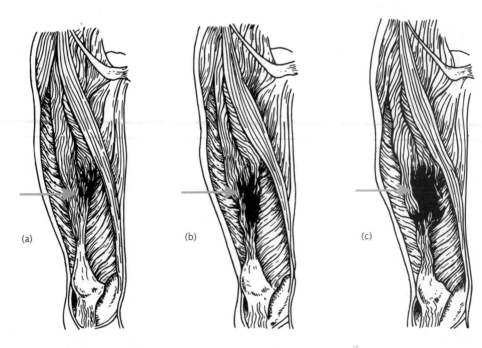

Strain—(a) grade 1; (b) grade 2; (c) grade 3

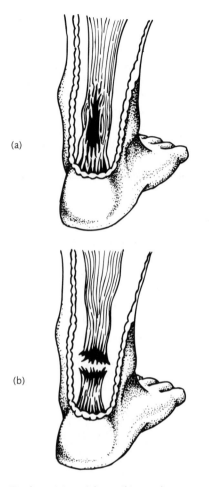

(a)

(b)

Tendon—(a) partial tear; (b) complete rupture

SEVERE (GRADE 3)

A complete *tear* across the width of the muscle near the junction of the tendon. Also called a rupture. It causes severely reduced strength, but often less pain than moderate tears if nerve fibres are also completely torn.

The treatment is the same as for a mild strain; however, the treatment and rehabilitation require up to 6 months before a full return to sport. Occasionally surgery to repair the tear is required.

Tendon

Tendon tears most commonly occur in people greater than 40 years involved in sports requiring sudden bursts of power, such as sprinting in tennis and squash. The tears are due to degenerative changes in the tendon. The most common sites are the *Achilles tendon* and supraspinatus in the *shoulder joint.*

DIAGNOSIS AND TREATMENT

The diagnosis and severity can be confirmed with *diagnostic ultrasound* or *magnetic resonance imaging (MRI)*, though a *history* and *physical examination* are usually sufficient. The severity is either a partial tear or complete rupture.

PARTIAL TEAR

Initial treatment for partial tendon tears begins with first aid including *RICE (rest, ice, compression* and *elevation)*.

Rest continues until pain and inflammation clears. *Strengthening exercises*, particularly *eccentric* contractions, should be commenced when: there is no local tenderness on palpation; a full pain-free stretch can be performed; no morning pain or stiffness; and no pain in response to resisted activity.

Return to sport should be a gradual process. For example, treatment for a partial Achilles tendon tear begins with light jogging, increasing the distance and speed over a period of 4 weeks. Wearing a heel raise inside the shoe helps to reduce the tension on the tendon.

COMPLETE RUPTURE

People frequently report hearing a 'snap' or feel as if they've been 'hit by a car', followed by immediate pain and severe weakness when this injury occurs.

A physical examination of the tendon finds a defect that is often easy to feel. Diagnosis can be confirmed with a clinical test; for example, a calf squeeze (Thomson's) test for an Achilles tendon rupture.

Complete tendon ruptures or tears may be managed without surgery in older aged patients, usually *immobilisation* for 4 to 8 weeks, initially in a non weight-bearing plaster cast followed by a walking cast. Younger athletes usually require surgery followed by similar immobilisation.

After removal of the plaster cast *sport rehabilitation* and return to sport should commence as described for a partial tear.

Strength

The maximum amount of force that can be produced by a muscle or group of muscles. It is important to check strength when performing *strengthening exercises* and for *strength training*.

Measuring strength

The most common method of measurement used for strength training of an uninjured muscle is the maximum weight that can be moved through a single full movement, called one *repetition maximum (RM)* = 1-RM.

A number of methods are used to measure the amount of strength in a muscle following an injury.

Manual muscle testing involves a practitioner comparing the injured muscle to the uninjured muscle (for instance, comparing the right calf to the left calf) or the normal strength expected. A system of grades that is commonly used is:

Grade 0: no muscle contraction.

Grade 1: muscle contraction but no movement of body part.

Grade 2: able to move body part with assistance of gravity.

Grade 3: able to move body part against gravity.

Grade 4: able to move body part with weight attached.

Grade 5: able to move body part with normal strength for that person.

Functional testing is using a specific activity that the muscle is primarily involved in producing, such as hopping on one leg for the calf muscle. Machine testing involves using devices such as the computerised KinCom (see *Isokinetic strengthening*).

Strength training

Regular participation in activities that aim to achieve an increase in muscle strength for general good health, to improve performance in a specific sport or for cosmetic reasons.

Method

The muscles that need to be strengthened should be selected, which follows the training principle of *specificity*. For instance, a general strengthening program for an older aged person includes strengthening exercises for muscles from the major regions of the body, in particular, the chest muscles, upper back muscles, shoulder muscles, buttocks, quadriceps and hamstring.

In addition, muscles should be strengthened on both sides of a joint in order to prevent an imbalance that can increase the risk of injury. Strengthening both the quadriceps (front thigh muscle) and hamstring (back thigh muscle) is a good example.

Frequency and load

The current *strength* of the muscles to be strengthened should be measured to provide a starting point. An increase in strength is only achieved when an *overload* is placed on a muscle that causes it to work until it feels fatigued.

A common training overload is 80 per cent of maximum strength, as measured by the maximum weight that can be moved in one full movement, which is called one *repetition maximum (RM)* = (1-RM). However, it may be recommended to have a lower overload with certain conditions such as *osteoporosis*.

A strength training program would involve lifting this weight for a set of 10 repetitions repeated three times for a total of 30 repetitions in each session. Generally, two to five sessions per week are recommended, though gains can be achieved by doing just one session. At least 1 day off each week is essential to prevent injuries.

A *fitness trainer, physiotherapist* or other health professional can give advice on the correct overload and number of repetitions. *Flexibility exercises* should be done at the same time to prevent reduced flexibility in the muscles that are being strengthened.

Strength gains

With each gain in strength over a period of weeks or months the number of repetitions and amount of weight can be gradually increased. This is called 'progressive overload'.

In the above example, the muscle will feel fatigued towards the end of each set of 10 repetitions. However, after a period of time, usually measured in weeks, the fatigue will decrease. When the repetitions can be completed without fatigue a new overload amount is required. This is achieved by increasing the volume of training; for example, from 10 to 15 repetitions per set.

After these repetitions can be completed without fatigue the maximum strength should be tested again. If it has increased the intensity can be increased by adding weight and the repetitions should be reduced back to 10 per set.

The strength gains that can be achieved with progressive overload range from 25–150 per cent over a year. Specific types of training include *isometric strengthening, isokinetic strengthening* and isotonic strengthening *(see Strengthening exercises).*

Olympic-type weight lifting and *plyometrics* are training to increase *power.* Special guidelines are available for *strength training for children and adolescents* and the *older athlete.*

Physiology of strength gains

Strength gains are due to two mechanisms. Nerve changes are the main reason during the first few months of training. They occur at the *motor unit* where a motor nerve switches on a group of muscle fibres. Not all of the motor units switch on their muscle fibres when lifting a weight in a muscle that has not been strengthened. The motor units also switch on in a haphazard manner. Strength training increases the overall number that switch on and the number that switch on at the same time.

Hypertrophy of muscles begins to contribute to increased strength after a few months of training. It is most pronounced in adult males due to the effect of the hormone, *testosterone. Women in sport* and *children* and *adolescents* tend to show smaller signs of increased muscle size, but continue to gain strength because of nerve changes.

Strength training diet

The recommended foods for an athlete participating in a strength training program, such as weight lifting. The diet is high in protein for muscle growth and tissue repair and high in carbohydrate and fat for energy.

Foods

An intake of 60–65 per cent of the energy supply from *carbohydrates* is recommended to ensure that glycogen stores are replenished and maintained, and 25–30 per cent *fat* or higher if carbohydrate intake is not sufficiently meeting energy needs.

Protein primarily helps the strength training athlete to achieve lean body mass gains of 0.5–1.0 kg (1.1–2.2 lb) per week, which increase muscle bulk. The recommended intake is 1.2–1.7 g per kilogram (0.5–0.8 g per lb) of body weight, which equals 120–136 g for an 80 kg (176 lb) athlete, which equals about 10–15 per cent of energy supply.

Supplementation with *amino acids,* in particular branched chain amino acids such as valine, leucine and isoleucine, is suggested as a means to delay fatigue and aid recovery by promoting muscle growth.

However, protein requirements can be achieved with diet alone, such as drinking fruit smoothies mixed with milk powder. In addition, excessive protein intake above the recommended levels may even be detrimental because additional protein is stored away by the body as fat and in extreme cases can lead to *heat illness, gout* and *calcium* deficiency.

Strength training for children and adolescents

The recommended training guidelines for children and adolescents participating in activities to improve strength are a precautionary measure to minimise the risk of injuries.

Strength training for children and adolescents can achieve a number of benefits, including increased strength, better motor skills and improved performance in sports where strength is important.

A strength training program should only be developed and implemented under the supervision of a professional trainer or coach. It should never replace other types of training.

Guidelines

Correct technique for lifting weights should be taught, the equipment must be the correct size, maximal intensities should not be reached until around the age of 16 and sudden bursts of strength should be avoided.

Correct technique can be taught by, at first, performing the movement without a weight. After weights are introduced, at any time that the technique falters, the weight should be reduced. In general the athlete should be aiming to do high repetitions at a low intensity below 80 per cent of a 1-RM (see *repetition maximum (RM)*), which is the maximum weight that can be lifted once.

The maximum number of training sessions per week, including strength training, should never exceed three for children up to the age of 14, with a maximum of 1½ hours per session. Exceptions may be permitted for elite athletes.

Risky activities that should be avoided include:
- Bouncing up from the bottom position of a squat which can cause knee damage and muscle injuries.
- Squatting with knees tilting or rotating inwards which can cause excessive pressure on the knees.
- Standing press (pulling down on a lever to lift a weight in the standing position) which can place excessive stress on the spine.
- Bench press (pulling down on a lever to lift a weight in the lying on the back position) which places excessive stress on the low back.

Strengthening exercises

An activity that aims to increase the strength of a muscle. It is usually performed as part of the treatment for an injury. Exercise to increase strength for general health reasons or cosmetic appearances is called *strength training*.

Method
Muscles to be strengthened should be assessed for their current *strength* in order to set goals for improvement and measure progress. This is usually done during a *physical examination*.

The types of exercises that can be selected include isotonic strengthening, which is the most common type of strengthening for a sport injury as well as a strength training program, *isometric strength-*

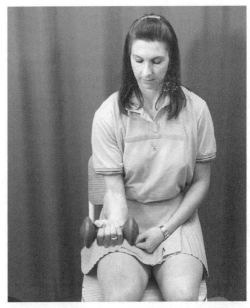

Using a dumbbell is an isotonic strengthening exercise

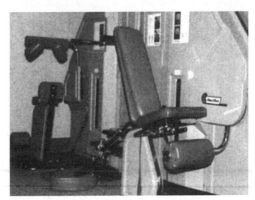

Nautilus machine for variable resistance isotonic strengthening exercise

ening (usually performed after surgery and injuries such as a *dislocation*) and *isokinetic strengthening*.

Isotonic strengthening
This involves moving a fixed weight or load with the aim of improving muscle strength. Examples include lifting a dumbbell and performing a sit up.

One advantage isotonic strengthening has over isometric and isokinetic strengthening is that the exercises tend to more closely resemble the natural movements required in sports, particularly when performed as a *closed chain exercise*. For example, squatting is a useful strengthening exercise of the quadriceps muscle for basketball, where a small squat is produced before jumping straight up from a standing position in basketball.

Usually the movement is repeated back and forth. This involves both *concentric* (muscle shortening) and *eccentric* (muscle lengthening) contractions. An eccentric contraction performed before a concentric contraction can achieve quicker strength gains because it causes an increase in the concentric force than otherwise would have been generated. *Plyometrics* is a form of strength training that involves sudden and explosive activities that take advantage of this effect.

Eccentric isotonic strengthening on its own is important in the treatment of *tendinosis* injuries such as Achilles tendinosis. However, eccentric exercising also has the potential to cause *delayed-onset muscle soreness (DOMS)* or muscle damage if used inappropriately. Consequently, eccentric programs should commence at very low levels, then progress gradually to higher intensity and volume (see *Overload*).

Isotonic strengthening can also be performed against variable resistance using exercise machines such as KinCom (see *Isokinetic strengthening*) and Nautilus and Eagle Universal. Although the specific amount of weight is constant, the resistance varies throughout the range of motion in an attempt to match the *muscle length* relationship. This results in the muscle working at, or near, maximal resistance throughout the range of motion.

Factors that help maximise strength gains during sport rehabilitation include: an adequate *warm-up* to increase body temperature and metabolic efficiency; a clear understanding of the exact instructions for performing the exercise; and a comprehensive *flexibility exercise* program to restore or maintain full range of movement.

Stress

A disturbance in a person's current physical or psychological state. Factors that cause stress may be positive or negative.

In physical terms, a positive stress is the forces generated through the leg during walking that stimulate growth and increase density of bone that is healing after a *fracture*. In contrast, a *stress fracture* of the tibia (shin bone) is a negative stress, where an excessive amount of ground forces are experienced due to, for instance, running an excessive number of kilometres wearing shoes that do not provide sufficient shock-absorption.

In psychological terms, stress also can be positive in certain circumstances. There are some people that perform well when faced with a dangerous or challenging situation. The body releases *adrenaline* and cortisol hormones, similar to the 'fight or flight' response, that have physical effects such as increased heart rate and also psychological ones such as focusing the mind on the task at hand and quicker reaction times.

However, many people have a negative response to psychological stress. In athletes it can cause high *anxiety* levels and a state of over-arousal. In the long term it can lead to anxiety disorders and *depression*. Physical manifestations include *gastrointestinal system* problems, *shortness of breath*, heart *palpitations*, fatigue, *tiredness*, muscle aches and pain, *amenorrhea* (absence of menstruation), a depressed *immune system* and being a trigger for *asthma*.

Treatment

Psychological techniques that can be recommended to reduce the negative impacts of stress include *visualisation*, *progressive muscle relaxation*, *centring*, devising a pre-competition and skills acquisition *routine* program, positive *self-talk*, *goal setting*, *behaviour modification*, *autogenic training*, *flotation tank*, *music* and *massage*.

Belief systems and other methods that may be used include *meditation*, *yoga*, and exercise and sport themselves. Natural health supplements that may be recommended include *ginseng*, *vitamins* and *minerals*. Regular participation in exercise and sport also can reduce stress (see *Exercise for health*).

Stress fracture

A microfracture in a bone that develops gradually due to an accumulation of repeated, excessive forces associated with an aggravating activity, such as running.

Stress fractures were first reported in military recruits in the 1800s. As with *overuse injuries* in general, they have become more common in people who exercise and play sport during the last two decades. The most commonly affected bones are the femur (thigh bone), tibia (large, front shin bone) and fibula (smaller, outer-side shin bone) and tarsal navicular and metatarsal bones of the foot.

Causes

Bone responds to excessive forces with a painless condition called 'bone strain', which is characterised by increased bone cell (osteoclast and osteoblast) activity and usually only detected coincidentally when a bone scan is used to look for another problem in the same area.

A bone strain can develop into a bone stress reaction, which has further increased bone cell activity, which may be tender when pressed firmly with the hand.

Women diagnosed with an *eating disorder* or *disordered eating*, *amenorrhea* (absence of menstrual periods), *osteoporosis* or *delayed menarche* have an increased risk of developing stress fractures (also see *Female athlete triad*).

Diagnosis

Stress fractures usually cause pain and tenderness over the fracture site. Often a recent change in training intensity (see *Overload*) or taking up a new activity is the cause. It is primarily diagnosed based on the history of the pain and a physical examination by a doctor.

A radiological investigation can be ordered to confirm the diagnosis. An *X-ray* may fail to show a stress fracture until after it has been present for some time, up to several months. A more sensitive examination is a *bone scan*, which finds a 'hot spot'.

It may be difficult to precisely localise the site, especially in the foot where numerous small bones are in close proximity. In these cases a *CT scan* or *magnetic*

Stress fractures according to site and the likely associated sports and activities

Bone	Sport or activity
Coracoid process of scapula (shoulder blade)	Trapshooting
Scapula (shoulder blade)	Running with hand-held weights
Humerus (upper arm)	Throwing, racquet sports
Olecranon (elbow)	Throwing/pitching
Ulna (elbow)	Racquet sports (especially tennis), gymnastics, volleyball, swimming, soft-ball, wheelchair sports
Rib, first	Throwing, pitching
Rib, second to tenth	Rowing, kayaking
Pars interarticularis (low back spine)	Gymnastics, ballet, cricket fast bowling, volleyball, springboard diving
Pubic ramus (front lower pelvis)	Distance running, ballet
Femur (thigh bone) neck	Distance running, jumping, ballet
Femur (thigh bone) shaft	Distance running
Patella (kneecap)	Running, hurdling
Tibia (shinbone) plateau	Running
Tibia (shinbone) shaft	Running, ballet
Fibula (lower leg)	Running, aerobics, race-walking, ballet
Medial malleolus (ankle)	Basketball, running
Calcaneus (heel)	Long-distance military marching
Talus (ankle)	Pole vaulting
Navicular (foot)	Sprinting, middle distance running, hurdling, long/triple jumping, football
Metatarsal (foot) general	Running, ballet, marching
Metatarsal (foot) base second	Ballet
Metatarsal (foot) fifth	Tennis, ballet
Sesamoid bones of the foot	Running, ballet, basketball, skating

resonance imaging (MRI) may be performed to show the exact site and extent of the fracture.

Treatment

Treatment generally requires relative *rest*, which means avoiding the activity that is causing the excessive forces, with the majority of stress fractures healing within six weeks.

However, it is not uncommon for some stress fractures to experience complications, most often delayed union or non-union of the fracture.

Healing is assessed by the absence of local tenderness and the ability to perform the aggravating activity without pain. In most cases it is not useful to monitor healing with an X-ray or bone scan.

The return to sport should be a gradual process in all cases.

Stress inoculation

A psychological method that involves being exposed to gradually increasing levels of *stress* associated with a specific stressful event. Increasing levels may begin with pictures or *visualisation* of the event, followed by activities associated with it and, lastly, the event itself. Also called desensitisation.

Stretching

See *Flexibility exercises.*

Stroke

Damage to part of the brain due to reduction of the blood supply or a leakage of blood through a blood vessel into the *brain*. The symptoms that occur vary according to the severity of the damage and its location. For example, a severe stroke causes sudden death. A mild stroke, also called a transient ischaemic attack (TIA), may cause no symptoms or temporary symptoms.

Causes

The main causes of a stroke are narrowing of the arteries called atherosclerosis, blockage of an artery due to a blood clot or a burst wall of an artery leading to bleeding within the brain or in the outer layers covering the brain, often called a haemorrhage or burst aneurysm.

The main risk factors include *hypertension* (high blood pressure), *diabetes, coronary heart disease* and unhealthy levels of *cholesterol*. It can also be caused by air emboli that block an artery due to *decompression sickness*.

Diagnosis and treatment

Any one or more of the following are a warning sign that a stroke is happening, including: sudden numbness or weakness of the face, arm or leg on one side of the body; feeling confused or difficulty speaking; sudden eyesight problems; dizziness; loss of balance; and sudden, severe headache.

If a stroke is suspected it should be treated as a *medical emergency*, requiring transport to a hospital as quickly as possible to prevent permanent damage to the brain. The emergency treatments aim to maintain normal breathing, circulation, feeding and fluids. Blood thinning drugs may be required if the cause is a blood clot or artery narrowing.

The symptoms of permanent damage include sensation loss or alterations, reduced ability to make the muscles work normally resulting in loss of movement or exaggerated movements, usually on one side of the body; loss of memory; loss of speech and the ability to understand speech; and behaviour and emotions that differ from the normal for that person.

Stroke *rehabilitation* is recommended to help regain losses caused by brain damage. It may include physiotherapy, occupational therapy and speech therapy.

Stroke volume

The amount of blood pumped out of the left ventricle of the *heart* with each heartbeat. In the average adult standing up and at rest it is between

60–80 mL (2–2.7 fl oz) of blood, in unfit people 50–60 mL (1.7–2 fl oz) and fit people 80–110 mL (2.7–3.7 fl oz). The amount of blood pumped out of the left ventricle of the heart per minute is called *cardiac output*.

Exercise and sport

During exercise and sport stroke volume can double, due to three mechanisms. The first is an increased amount of blood filling up the left ventricle, which stretches the muscles of the heart prior to a contraction, resulting in a stronger contraction. The increased filling is a response to a number of factors including an increased heart rate and widening of the diameter of the arteries and veins.

The second mechanism is the muscle fibres of the left ventricle produce a stronger contraction due to activation of the *sympathetic nervous system*.

The third mechanism is a widening of the arteries that reduces the peripheral resistance, which makes it easier for the left ventricle to pump out blood.

Subchondral bone

The bone that lies immediately beneath *articular cartilage*, a layer of tissue covering the ends of two bones that are connected together to form a *synovial joint*. Subchondral bone is typical of *bone* tissue, containing deposits of calcium and phosphate embedded among osteoblasts and osteocytes.

Articular cartilage is made up of cells called chondroblasts and chondrocytes. The deepest layer of articular cartilage contains a mix of articular cartilage and calcified bone cells. These transitional layers from articular cartilage to subchondral bone are collectively called osteochondrum. An acute injury of subchondral bone is called a *bone bruise*.

Subconjunctival haemorrhage

Bleeding beneath the outer layer of membrane (conjunctiva) that surrounds the *eye* and seals it off from the outside environment. It causes a bright red area in the white of the eye. It only needs treatment if it affects a large area or causes photophobia (sensitivity to light).

Subluxation

A partial dislocation of a joint. See *Dislocation*.

Substance abuse

Excessive drug use to achieve desired psychological and physical effects. Drugs are initially used as either a recreational habit or following a legitimate prescription, but afterwards a psychological and physical dependency develops.

The most commonly abused substance is *alcohol*. Other substances include *caffeine*, nicotine in tobacco, prescribed drugs such as tranquillisers, and illegal substances such as *cocaine*, heroin and marijuana (see *Cannabinoids*).

Treatments for substance abuse include counselling from a psychiatrist, psychologist, social worker or drugs counsellor, developing supportive personal relationships, participation in groups or organisations such as Alcoholics Anonymous, and the prescription of medications, such as methadone for heroin.

Subungual haematoma

Bleeding under the toenail, usually due to a sudden blow, though sometimes also caused by repeated pressure associated with an overuse injury. It causes pain in the toe and gives the toenail a black colouring.

Treatment involves using a heated needle or paper clip to puncture a hole through the nail to release the collection of blood.

Sudden death

An unexpected death that occurs during participation in exercise or sport. It is a rare event that is usually caused by underlying heart disease.

In people under the age of 35 years the most common cause is a structural congenital cardiovascular abnormality, such as *hypertrophic cardiomyopathy*.

In the over 35 years age group coronary artery disease leading to a *heart attack* is the leading cause. Other less common causes are *mitral valve prolapse, aortic stenosis, myocarditis* and side effects from drugs such as *erythropoietin (EPO)* and *anabolic steroids*.

Superficial

The anatomical direction pointing towards the outer surface of the body, or a body part located closer to the outer surface. For example, the superficial group of muscles in the front compartment of the forearm are the muscles located closest to the outer surface. Also called external for hollow structures like blood vessels. It is the opposite of *deep*.

Superior

The anatomical direction pointing upwards in the body towards the head. It is used to describe the surface of any part of the body that faces upwards or a body part located above another part. It is the opposite of *inferior*. Also called cranial.

Supination

A movement of a *synovial joint* that means rotation in a direction pointing away from the midline of the body. For example, turning the hands so that the palms face upwards involves supination of the elbow. The axis of the rotation movement is usually through the centre of the bone that is moving, similar to a pen that is being rotated between your thumb and fingers.

It is most commonly used to describe movement in the *elbow joint, ankle* and foot (see *Foot and toe joints*). Supination is also known as external rotation at the shoulder and hip joints. It is the opposite of *pronation*.

Supplementation

The regular ingestion of a nutrient, vitamin or mineral in addition to those eaten in foods with the aim of preventing disease and illness, such as osteoarthritis, coronary heart disease and cancers, or improving performance in exercise and sport (see *Ergogenic aids*).

Commonly used supplements include *creatine, Beta-hydroxy methylbutyrate (HMB), sodium bicarbonate, colostrum, fat-burning stacks, pyruvate, amino acids, antioxidants* and *vitamin and mineral supplementation*.

Supracondylar fracture

A break across the lower end of the humerus (arm bone) just above the *elbow joint*. It is more common in children around the age of puberty than in adults. It is often due to a fall on an outstretched arm, either from a height or a bicycle.

Treatment

The *fracture* should be treated as a medical emergency due to the risk of damage to blood vessels and nerves. It is managed by checking the radial and ulnar *pulses* in the wrist of the arm, and skin colour and temperature, and receiving treatment at a hospital as quickly as possible.

Treatment for unstable fractures is usually *open surgery* and *internal fixation* followed by *immobilisation* in a plaster cast for 4 to 6 weeks. Stable fractures are treated with a plaster cast.

The most common complication after healing of the bone is stiffness, particularly an inability to fully straighten (extension of) the elbow. This can be prevented with early *flexibility exercises, strengthening exercises* and *mobilisation*. Children need 8 to 12 weeks to make a full return to sport. Adults require 3 to 6 months.

Surface

Exercise and sport are played on different surfaces including roads, courts, fields, floors, tracks, sand and more. The type of surface can influence the selection of playing equipment and the risk of developing an *overuse injury*.

One mechanism of injury is the ground reaction force that is created when the feet impact on the ground. For a walker on a hard surface the force is equal to twice body weight, a runner three to four times body weight, and a jumper five to 12 times body weight. The greater the force and more often that it is generated, the greater the stresses on muscles, joints, ligaments and bone.

The hardness of a surface is also important when a part of the body, such as the head, strikes the surface after a fall.

Hard surfaces include concrete, artificial grass and rubber tennis courts. Slightly softer surfaces are wooden floors, dirt tracks and clay tennis courts. Grass is softer; however, it depends on the water content. Drier grounds are associated with a higher risk of injuries. Watering dry grass is recommended. On the other hand, excessively loose surfaces, such as mud, can increase the risk of injury.

Surgery

A procedure that involves cutting or breaking through the skin or entering the body through an orifice to treat injury and disease. Surgery has a major role to play in the treatment of an acute injury, such as a bone fracture or meniscus tear, in some cases of overuse injury and in many diseases such as osteoarthritis and coronary heart disease.

The decision to have surgery is not taken lightly. While in some cases it is clearly essential or the most effective choice of treatment, it can be more expensive and is sometimes associated with risks including infection of wounds, *deep vein thrombosis*, pulmonary embolism and side effects of general anaesthesia.

Surgery is performed by surgeons with a specific area of specialisation, such as orthopaedic surgery for exercise and sports injuries and osteoarthritis. Within this speciality there are sub-specialisations, such as surgeons who only perform *reconstructive surgery* of the knee or *joint replacement* surgery.

There are two types of surgery: *arthroscopy* and *open surgery*. Surgery is also called radical treatment. Non-surgical treatments such as drugs, manual therapy such as massage, exercises and mobilisations, nutrition and psychology are collectively called *conservative treatment*.

Suture

A *fibrous and cartilaginous joint* between two bones of the skull in adults that does not allow movement due to a strong ligament that securely fixes the bones together (like superglue) and which has a near-perfect fit between the ends of the bones, which have a jagged-shape. It is also used to describe stitching used to close wounds either after a *skin injury* or *surgery*.

Sweat

The liquid produced by sweat glands in the *skin*. It consists mostly of water and tiny amounts of sodium chloride.

It evaporates from the skin surface in a dry air environment, which causes a drop in temperature of the blood flowing past in the skin and, as a result, the core body *temperature*. It produces 80 per cent of the body's heat loss, which makes it the primary method for preventing *heat illness* during exercise and sport. Sodium loss also can be high in endurance athletes.

Sweating is controlled by the *autonomic nervous system*. It occurs in response to being active and emotional responses including fear and anxiety. There are nearly 3 million sweat glands in the skin.

Sweet spot

See *Tennis racquet*.

Swelling

An excessive accumulation of fluids or blood in body tissue that is visible to the eye. It is a sign that an injury has occurred or a disease is present.

In exercise and sports-related injuries the swelling can be due to *oedema* produced by inflammation or bleeding. Bleeding into a joint is called a *haemarthrosis*, and in muscles, a *muscle contusion*.

Not all oedema or bleeding is visible. For example, oedema of the joints of the spine can't be observed because the joints are too deep inside the body. In contrast oedema of the knee joint is usually visible.

Swelling caused by bleeding usually occurs quicker than oedema. This can be a helpful clue for diagnosis. For example, a ruptured anterior cruciate ligament tends to cause bleeding into the knee joint that causes swelling within 2 hours, whereas a meniscus tear takes 6 to 24 hours to develop swelling. Bleeding causes more intense and severe pain than oedema.

Diagnosis and treatment

Checking for the presence and extent of swelling is part of the inspection of the body conducted in the *physical examination*. The best method in the arms and legs is to compare the injured side to the uninjured side. The extent of swelling can be given a qualitative amount (mild, moderate or severe) or be measured, such as using a measuring tape for swelling of the knee.

One of the main aims of treatment for an injury is to reduce the swelling as soon as possible after it occurs and throughout the recovery period. Excessive swelling that lasts for too long can delay recovery and be associated with an increased risk of injury recurrence.

Treatments used to reduce swelling include *RICE* (*rest, ice, compression and elevation*), *active movement* exercises, *electrotherapy, massage, non-steroidal anti-inflammatory drugs* (NSAIDs), *corticosteroids, acupuncture* and natural health supplements including *bromelain, curcumin* and *flavonoids*.

Swimmer's ear

See *Ear infection*.

Swimming

Swimming was popular in ancient times, as evidenced in Roman Empire swimming pool ruins. Competition swimming began in Australia in the 1800s. Events were included in the first modern Olympics in 1896.

The four styles are freestyle, breaststroke, backstroke and butterfly. Races include 50 and 100 m sprints, middle distances of 200, 400, 800 and 1500 m, and long distance swimming, greater than 1500 m. *Ultra long distance sports* include distances such as the 28.5 mile/45 km Manhattan Island marathon swim in New York.

Skills and fitness

Recreational swimming is primarily aerobic training with benefits for health and disease (see *Exercise for health*). In competition swimming sprinters require *strength training* and *anaerobic training*, while longer distances require more *aerobic training*. *Flexibility training* and *skills training*, particularly starts, turns and finishes, are also essential.

Injuries

The most common injuries include *rotator cuff tendinosis* (shoulder), *shoulder instability, biceps tendinosis* (shoulder), flexor tendinosis (*Golfer's elbow*), *thoracic pain (non-specific)* (middle back), *patellofemoral joint syndrome* (knee) and *fat pad impingement* (knee).

World champion butterfly swimmer Petria Thomas of Australia

Swimming biomechanics

The movements and positions of the joints and muscles during swimming. The upper limbs provide 90 per cent and the lower limbs 10 per cent of the forward propulsion in all swimming strokes. The force of this forward propulsion must overcome the drag force of the water. Keeping the body as horizontal as possible minimises the drag force.

In freestyle, butterfly and backstroke there are two phases to the swimming stroke: the pull through and recovery. The pull through does not follow a straight line in freestyle but rather an S-shape. The propulsion begins one-third of the way into the phase when the elbow is bent (flexed) and above the hand. The recovery phase involves the opposite shoulder joint movements to the pull through.

Biomechanical abnormality

A deviation from any of the above movements or poor technique is called a *biomechanical abnormality*. It is associated with an increased risk of developing an injury in the shoulder region, particularly *rotator cuff strain* and *rotator cuff tendinosis*.

The risk of *shoulder impingement* injury is increased due to abnormalities of *scapular biomechanics* (shoulder-blade bone movements) and technique abnormalities, such as an excessively

Common technique errors that increase the risk of overuse injury according to swimming stroke

Swimming stroke	Common technique errors
Butterfly	• Entering the arms into the water too far outside the line of the shoulders or with the arms too close together
Backstroke	• Pull through with elbows extended which result in a straight pull through instead of an S-shaped pull through • Insufficient body roll
Freestyle	• A line of pull through that crosses far beyond the midline • Striving for too much length in the stroke • Insufficient body roll
Breast stroke	• Excessive elbow extension

straight arm during the recovery phase and insufficient body roll.

Swimming for children and adolescents

There are recommended training guidelines for children and adolescents participating in *swimming*, which are a precautionary measure to minimise the risk of injuries (see table, p. 414).

Sympathetic nervous system

The collection of *neurons* (nerve cells) that conduct communications with organs such as the heart and lungs. In general the communications are not in our voluntary control and involve sending instructions to the organs to increase their level of activity. For example, during exercise and sport it increases the heart rate and amount of blood pumped by the heart, widens the diameter of the lungs' airways to increase the amount of oxygen breathed in, dilates the blood vessels in muscles to allow more oxygen and nutrients to reach the muscle fibres and increases the amount of glucose released by the liver into the bloodstream.

The sympathetic neurons make up one half of the autonomic nervous system; the other half is the *parasympathetic nervous system*, which works in opposition to the sympathetic neurons.

The sympathetic system tends to cause a mass response during exercise and sport, but also in response to fear, hence the term 'flight or fight'. It also causes the release of *adrenaline*.

Symphysis

A *fibrous and cartilaginous joint* that only allows a small amount of movement and provides a large degree of stability. A fibrous and cartilaginous pad or disc acts like a tough glue to hold the two bones together in the joint, though it has some give in it when strong forces are experienced.

Recommended swimming training for children and adolescents

Age (years)	Frequency and duration	Development	Activities	Competition
3–4	• Whenever in bath, pool, beach, etc.	• Confidence in water • Ability to submerge and open eyes • An extension of play ground activities	• Blowing bubbles • Looking underwater • Jumping • Kicking on front or back with help from parent	• None
5–7	• Two 20-minute sessions a week in warm, waist-high water	• Basic water skills and stroke technique aiming to achieve 25 metre front and back crawl and symmetrical breast stroke	• Learn to dive, float, kick and dog paddle with the help of kickboards and other aids • Gradually build up to learning basic strokes	• None
8–9	• Two to three sessions per week, 45 minutes each session	• Learn more advanced skills and technique with the aim of swimming 25–50 m using basic strokes	• Introduce turns, bent arm backstroke and whip kick breast stroke, using training clock for rest and departure intervals, and working in group to promote cooperation	• Join swimming club for self–improvement and fun
10–12	• Three to five sessions per week, 60 to 90 minutes each session	• Introduction to competition and strengthen stroke technique	• Introduce butterfly and increase training distance to 500 m, possibly up to 2000 m for some individuals • Use relay changeovers to promote group rather than individual participation	• Highest level of competition possible at school, intra and inter–club and state
13–16	• Five to nine sessions per week, 90 to 120 minutes each session • Training fits in to a seasonal program of competition peaking for one or two competitions	• Maximise opportunities to develop all strokes over various distances	• Maintain a mixed bag of training with long distance workouts with all strokes • Introduce strength training with own body weight and light weights together with stretching	• Competition at high levels including regional, state, national and international

For example, the head of a baby pushing through the pelvic canal during childbirth causes a slight separation of the pubic symphysis that connects the front ends of the pelvis bone. The *disc* between the spinal bones is classified as a symphysis.

Synchronised swimming

A sport that involves one or more swimmers performing movements to music in a swimming pool. It first developed in the USA in the 1930s and became an Olympic sport in 1984. Competitions involve either solo, duet or teams of four or eight swimmers performing compulsory set movements and movements of their own choice. Competitors are scored according to execution and style, similar to gymnastics and diving.

Syncope

A group of symptoms including generalised weakness and loss of tone in the muscles, inability to stand upright and *loss of consciousness*. There also may be vomiting, nausea, paleness or ashen grey colour of the face, and very often the face and body are bathed in cold perspiration. Feeling faint and a lack of strength with a sensation of impending loss of consciousness is called pre-syncope.

Causes

Syncope may be due to reduced blood flow to the brain caused by blood loss, mechanical obstruction of the return of blood to the heart such as the *Valsalva manoeuvre* in weight lifting, pooling of blood in the lower limbs and emotional disturbances. It also may be caused by *hyperventilation*.

Other causes not due to an accident or acute injury, include an underlying disease or illness such as *coronary heart disease, aortic stenosis, mitral valve prolapse, hypertrophic cardiomyopathy, Marfan's syndrome, heart attack, stroke, heat illness, hypothermia, hypoglycaemia* (low blood sugars), *hyponatremia* (low blood sodium), *asthma* attack, *pneumothorax* (spontaneous) and *anaphylaxis* caused by an allergy or exercise.

Diagnosis and treatment

If syncope occurs immediately when ceasing an activity, such as at the end of an endurance event, it is most likely due to pooling of blood in the lower limbs. The treatment is to be put in a head-down position with the legs and pelvis elevated, usually leading to a quick recovery.

If syncope occurs during an activity one of the above diseases or illnesses should be suspected, which should be treated as a *medical emergency*.

Synergist

A muscle that assists the muscle that is the prime mover for a specific movement. For example, in the *elbow joint* the supinator muscle is the prime mover of supination (outward rotation). Biceps is the synergist.

A synergist can also help to fine-tune the direction of a movement. For instance, lifting the thigh upwards and slightly sideways involves the hip flexor muscles working as the prime movers and the abduc-tor muscles as synergists to determine the exact amount of sideways movement.

Synovial fluid

A clear, thick, viscous fluid that acts as a lubricant to reduce friction and make movements smooth and easy in a *joint, tendon sheath* or *bursa*. It is produced by synovium, which is a tissue that forms the inner lining of these structures. In a joint the synovial fluid also provides nutrients to the cells of the articular cartilage.

Synovial joint

A joint that allows smooth and easy movement between two bones, at the same time as providing stability and shock absorption.

Anatomy

The connection between two bones is made secure by a tough but flexible fibrous *joint capsule* that is shaped like a tube with each opening attached firmly around the circumference of the bones.

This creates an enclosed joint cavity that is filled with a lubricant called synovial fluid, which is

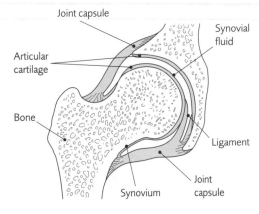

Anatomy of a typical synovial joint

produced by the inner lining of the joint capsule, called synovium. The two bones within the cavity are covered in smooth *articular cartilage* that reduces friction between them and also acts as a shock absorber. *Ligaments* provide the capsule with additional support.

Most joints in the body are synovial. Each joint allows movements such as bending the elbow and straightening the leg. Accessory movements, which are involuntary sliding movements, are necessary for normal joint function. The different shapes of the bones that make up synovial joints, such as the ball-and-socket, pivot, condylar, saddle, ellipsoidal and hinge joints, allow a specific number of movements.

For example, the condylar *knee joint* primarily allows bending (*flexion*) and straightening (*extension*).

System

A group of interconnected *organs* or body parts that perform a specific set of functions. For example, the *gastrointestinal system* is made up of the mouth, oesophagus, stomach, liver, gall bladder, pancreas, intestines, bowels and anus. They work together to bring food and fluids into the body, break down the food and absorb it and the fluids into the blood to be transported to the cells.

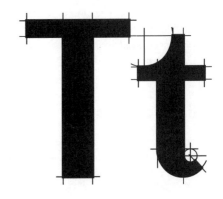

Table tennis

A sport originally called ping-pong after an English company trade name in the early 1900s. Table tennis was adopted as the name in 1921, the first world championships were in London in 1927 and it became an Olympic sport in 1988. A competition match is the best of three or five games. Each game is won by winning 21 points.

Fitness and injuries

The primary physical requirements are *strength training*, *skills training* and *flexibility training*. The most common injuries are *rotator cuff tendinosis* (shoulder), *shoulder instability*, *tennis elbow*, *thoracic pain (non-specific)* (middle back) and *adductor tendinosis* (hip and groin).

Tai Chi

Tai Chi was developed by ancient Chinese warriors to assist in fighting wars. It was later modified into gentler forms, the classical or chen style and the most gentle, yang style. Tai Chi involves performing a movement routine in a slow and coordinated

manner. Visual imagery assists in the learning process and creates a calm ambience. Exercises for relaxation, breathing and warming up are conducted before the movements.

Performing Tai Chi in a park

Injuries

The yang style is low-intensity *aerobic training* and has a low injury rate. The most common injuries for chen style are *medial collateral ligament (MCL) sprain* (knee), *patellofemoral joint syndrome* (knee) and *quadriceps strain* (thigh).

Talar dome injury

An injury of the articular cartilage and underlying bone of the upper section of the talus bone in the *ankle* joint. It is not uncommon for this injury to occur together with an *ankle sprain* or *ankle medial ligament sprain*, particularly if it involves a twist when landing on the foot from a jump.

It is more likely to be diagnosed quickly if it causes a large fracture, which can be detected on an X-ray. However, in many cases the injury is only diagnosed after there is persistent pain following an ankle sprain. The recommended radiological investigation to confirm a diagnosis is *bone scan* or *magnetic resonance imaging (MRI)*, followed by a *CT scan* to

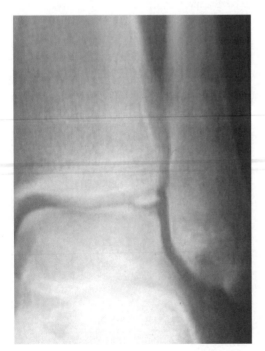

X-ray of a talar dome injury

identify the degree of severity (ranging from grade 1 to grade 5).

Grades 1 and 2 are treated with gentle *flexibility exercises, strengthening exercises*, stationary cycling and *rest* from aggravating activities such as running.

If this fails to bring improvement after 2 to 3 months an *arthroscopy* is recommended to remove any bone fragments and repair the articular cartilage (see *Articular cartilage acute injury*). An arthroscopy is recommended immediately for grades 3, 4 and 5, followed by the same treatment as provided for an ankle sprain.

Talus lateral process fracture

A break in a bone of the foot near the *ankle* joint. Often a result of a snowboarder's high jump landing on the nose of the snowboard causing a sudden excessive compression force. It is popularly known as 'snowboarder's ankle'.

It is commonly mistaken for a simple *ankle sprain*. An *X-ray* using a mortice view may confirm the diagnosis. The recommended treatment is usually *immobilisation* in a short plaster cast or, if the broken bone is displaced, *open surgery* and *internal fixation* with a metal wire.

Talus stress fracture

A microfracture in the squat bone that makes up the lower half of the *ankle* joint, causing pain on the outside of the ankle. It develops gradually due to an accumulation of repeated, excessive physical forces over a period of weeks or months associated with running such as *athletics* and *football* codes.

It may be more likely if there is excessive *foot pronation* or a poor technique, like 'planting' the pole too late during a *pole vault*. Diagnosis is confirmed with a *bone scan*. Treatment consists of *immobilisation* in a plaster cast for 6 weeks, followed by a gradual return to sport as part of a *sport rehabilitation* program.

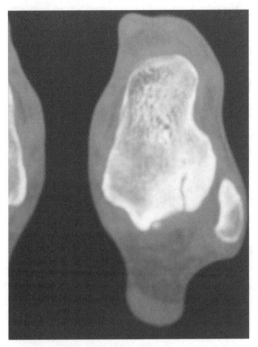

CT scan of a talus stress fracture

Taping

The application of adhesive tape to the skin to protect and support muscles and joints. It is used to prevent injuries, protect an injury that is healing and reduce pain.

Protection and support is achieved by increasing stability and providing joint and muscle position awareness. Stability is increased because the tape acts as a second or external ligament to a *joint* or body region.

It is applied to an area of skin that is relatively immobile, and is aligned in such a way as to restrict a particular movement or posture. For example, taping for an ankle sprain caused by excessive inversion (turning ankle inwards) aims to restrict this movement.

Increasing joint and muscle position and awareness, which is called *proprioception*, occurs because the adhesion of tape to the skin provides an additional sensory input. This can help improve the coordination of muscle activity and reinforce the attainment of postures or movements that minimise pain or the risk of injury.

Tapering

A period of rest and recuperation before participation in a competition event. The aim is to be in the best possible condition for achieving *peak performance* during competition, which may be a single event such as a triathlon or a group of events such as running in heats and finals. Tapering is done as part of the *periodisation* of a training program during the pre-competition stage.

Training for competition begins with a conditioning stage that lasts for a number of weeks or months, where the main goal is a gradual build up of fitness and skills. During this stage muscles and joints tend to experience minor damage.

Tapering gives the body a chance to heal this damage, replenish energy stores and provides a psychological break. It involves participating in activities at a lower intensity of training that is still sufficient to maintain fitness levels achieved during the conditioning phase. Tapering should be accompanied by *pre-competition eating*.

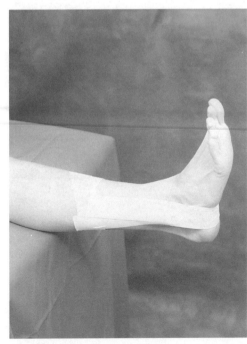

Taping for an ankle sprain—stirrups

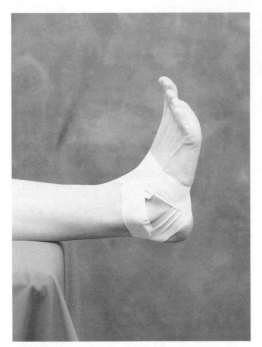

Taping for an ankle sprain—heel lock

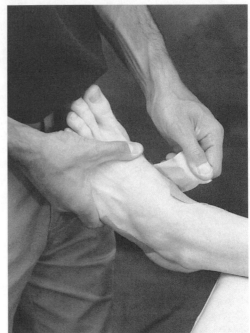

Taping for plantar fasciitis

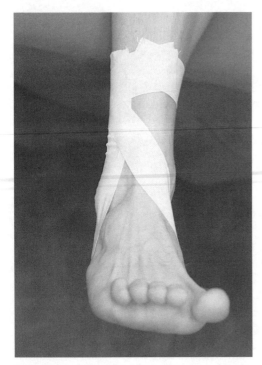

Taping for an ankle sprain—figure six

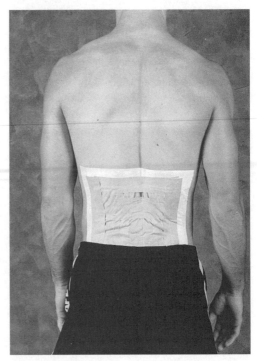

Taping for low back pain

Taping is also called strapping. A *brace* is a specially designed piece of equipment that has the same prevention aims as taping.

Neck pain

Taping is recommended for *neck posture syndrome*, which is pain associated with a round-shouldered and forward-chin posture. Tape applied to the neck and shoulder region pulls on the skin each time a round-shouldered and forward-chin posture occurs, which provides a sensory reminder to adopt the upright posture. An alternative to taping if skin aggravation occurs is an elasticised brace that pulls the shoulders back.

Ankle sprain

Even though one taped ankle looks the same as the next to the untrained eye, in fact there are a number of different techniques that can be selected for an ankle sprain. The selection depends on the movements that caused the sprain in the first place, and the severity of the damage and loss of stability.

Nine out of 10 *ankle sprains* are caused by extreme inversion (inward turning movement) of the ankle joint combined with varying amounts of plantar (downwards) or dorsi flexion (upwards) movements.

Up to four techniques applied in combination may be required for a severely sprained ankle, including a 'figure six', 'stirrups', 'half figure eight' and 'heel lock'. Taping should be continued throughout the healing period and after the injury has healed to prevent recurrent sprains.

Taping is preferred over wearing a brace because it can be tailored to a person's specific type of ankle sprain. However, a brace is better than nothing and may be required if taping causes adverse skin reactions.

Patellofemoral joint syndrome

The McConnell taping technique is recommended for people with knee pain caused by *patellofemoral joint syndrome*, which is caused by malignment of the patella (kneecap) that mostly occurs in sports involving walking and running.

The aim of taping is to relieve pain in the short term, while exercises are performed to improve vastus medialis muscle coordination and strength to achieve a long-term recovery.

Taping may be required continuously for up to several weeks, and then only during aggravating activities for up to 3 months if the muscle is severely weak or uncoordinated. However, the aim should be a maximum of 6 weeks wherever possible to avoid dependence and adverse skin reactions.

Plantar fasciitis

Taping is highly recommended for people with *plantar fasciitis*, an inflammation of the attachment of the plantar fascia at the calcaneus (heel bone). It aims to provide short-term relief, while the long-term treatment is a referral to a podiatrist for prescription arch supports, or *orthotics*. Taping can be continued until the orthotic is worn in.

Low back pain

Taping for low back pain aims to increase stability, prevent aggravating movements and provide joint and muscle position awareness for *motor re-education* to help maintain a lumbar lordosis (inward curve of the low back). It is most often used during the acute (early) stage of *low back pain (non-specific)*.

It is applied when standing up or lying face down. Strips of tape are placed according to the painful movements that need to be prevented. A maximum of 1 week is recommended for continuous taping. Alternatively, it can be applied for 2 to 3 weeks only during aggravating activities.

Adverse reactions

Problems that can be caused by taping include reduced blood circulation due to excessive tightness, which can be checked by feeling for a normal *pulse*, and skin irritation.

When the tape is applied the skin should be cleaned and shaved, an underlying layer of hypoallergenic elastic dressing can be used to protect the skin from the adhesive, the tape should avoid creating skin wrinkles or gaps that can lead to blisters and the edges of the tape should not cut the skin, especially at sensitive areas like the *Achilles tendon*.

After application the circulation should be checked. Removing the tape should be done gently to avoid damage, regardless of the condition of the skin. If the skin condition is good it may be better to leave the old tape on the skin and place a new layer over it.

Tarsal coalition

An inherited defect of the subtalar or midtarsal joints in the foot where the bones are fused together and may cause pain (see *Foot and toes*).

It is usually first noticed in adolescents beginning sports participation or a person aged 20 to 30 complaining of pain after vigorous activity, such as running, or an injury such as an *ankle sprain*. Treatment includes *mobilisation, flexibility exercises, strengthening exercises* and *orthotics* to correct any biomechanical abnormality. Surgery may be needed in a young person with severe symptoms or if these treatments fail to control the pain.

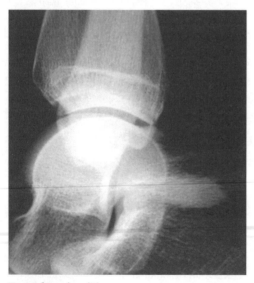

X-ray of tarsal coalition

Teamwork

The actions and thought processes of a group of people cooperating with each other to achieve shared objectives. It follows the saying that a champion team will always beat a team of champions.

A winning team requires teamwork

It involves having an understanding of group dynamics, setting up a process for communication and interaction between the individual members, *coach* and management staff, finding a balance between individual needs and those of the team, providing support for individuals, possessing a willingness to compromise, allocating responsibilities, defining team goals, and developing a team identity and cohesion.

Problems can arise within a team; for example, players feeling uncertain about their *role* or having a role they are uncomfortable with. Problems can be addressed through counselling, *goal setting* and *behaviour modification*. Although coach–player communications are essential, it should also be recognised that players may not find it easy to be totally frank with a coach and an alternative means of communications should be made available, such as via the team captain.

Tear

An injury that is a separation or narrow opening in a ligament, joint capsule, meniscus, disc, articular cartilage, nerve, tendon or muscle caused by trauma.

In most cases the tear is an *acute injury* due to a single event where external forces are stronger than the strength of the tissue to withstand them. Infrequently it can be due to an accumulation of smaller forces over a period of time, usually weeks or months, which leads to an *overuse injury*. The diagnosis and treatment is the same as for a *strain*.

Temperature

A measurement of the amount of heat, usually in degrees of Celsius, C, or Fahrenheit, F. The human body is normally kept constantly around 37°C (98.6°F), which is the optimum temperature for the cells engaged in *metabolism*. Maintaining this temperature is called thermoregulation. It involves achieving a balance between the mechanisms of heat gain and heat loss.

Heat gain and heat loss
Heat gain occurs through heat produced in the body, by muscle activity and metabolism, and from the outside environment. Heat loss occurs through conduction (direct contact with an object or the air), convection (the movement of air close to the body), radiation (heat energy in the form of infrared rays), evaporation (*sweat* on the external skin or clothing is converted from liquid to gas) and in faeces, urine and respiration.

Evaporation is usually the main method of heat loss during physical activity, contributing up to 80 per cent during endurance activities such as long distance running. However, conduction becomes more important when immersed in cold water, increasing by up to 23 times.

Thermoregulation
The hypothalamus of the *brain* acts like a thermostat to sense the temperature of blood flowing past it, which is called the core body temperature. It is most accurately measured with a rectal thermometer, though the mouth is a reasonable approximation.

The hypothalamus sends signals to the body in response to excessive changes in temperature. For example, when the temperature falls it tells the muscles to start shivering to create heat. When the temperature rises the hypothalamus switches on sweating. Temperature-sensing nerves in the skin also make a contribution.

In response to participation in exercise and sport it is normal for the body to heat up. However, temperatures above 41°C (105.8°F) start to cause damage to organs and cells.

Temperatures above 43°C (109.4°F) cause proteins, which make up the structure of most of the body, to fall apart (see *Heat illness*). Conversely, temperatures below 34°C (93.2°F) cause organs to shut down, leading to loss of consciousness. Below 28°C (82.4°F) the body appears to be dead (see *Hypothermia*). See also *Fever*.

Temporomandibular joint pain

Pain, clicking or locking of the one or both of the joints that open and close the mouth (see *Head*). The injury develops due to an accumulation of excessive physical forces on the joint over a period of months or even years. Treatment includes *mobilisation* and *flexibility exercises*.

Temporomandibular joint sprain

An acute injury to one or both of the joints that allow the mouth to open and close, causing pain and movement abnormalities. In severe cases a *dislocation* can occur.

The recommended treatment is *rest* by limiting mouth opening and closing movement for 7 to 10 days in severe cases and eating a soft diet and taking *analgesics* for pain relief. Return to *collision* sports such as football should be avoided for up to 2 weeks and boxing for at least 6 weeks.

Tendinitis

An overuse injury that causes inflammation of a *tendon*. The symptoms can include pain, tenderness, swelling, restricted movement and weakness. It is usually due to excessive forces associated with an aggravating activity.

Inflammation is the body's response to an injury. If the injury is continually aggravated the inflammation remains and develops into a chronic degenerative state, best described as tendinosis.

Tendinitis is a lot less common than was previously thought. Scientific research has studied tendons diagnosed with tendinitis and found only a few inflammatory cells, but many degenerated cells. It appears that most injuries that are diagnosed as a tendinitis, such as rotator cuff tendinitis of the shoulder and patellar tendinitis of the kneecap, are really a *tendinosis*.

Tendinitis is more likely to occur in association with paratendinitis, which belongs to a group of injuries called *paratenonitis*, and in association with inflammatory arthritis.

The recommended treatments include a combination of more than one of the following: *nonsteroidal anti-inflammatories (NSAIDs)*, *ice*, *rest*, *massage* of the tendon, electrotherapy such as *ultrasound therapy* and *high voltage galvanic stimulation*, *flexibility exercises* and *strengthening exercises*. If the above treatments are not successful, a *corticosteroid* injection may be recommended.

Tendinopathy

See *Tendon overuse injury*.

Tendinosis

An injury of a *tendon* characterised by an area of degeneration. It is an overuse injury caused by a gradual accumulation of repeated excessive forces associated with a biomechanical abnormality, sudden increases in training intensity or volume such as running a greater distance or at a faster speed, incorrect selection of *shoes* and equipment, and poor technique for a particular activity such as a swimming stroke.

Diagnosis

In the early, mild stages it may be painful at the start of the aggravating activity but then diminishes during the activity; for example, a runner who can 'run through' the pain, for it only to return after cooling down, frequently not until the next morning. At a later stage when the injury becomes worse the pain is felt throughout the activity and, when severe, also during other activities.

A physical examination finds tenderness and thickening of the tendon. Obvious *swelling* and crepitus (a grating sound when two rough surfaces rub against each other) may be present, although crepitus is usually a sign of associated tenosynovitis (see *Paratenonitis*).

The most common sites for tendinosis are *rotator cuff tendinosis* of the shoulder, extensor tendinosis of the elbow, more commonly known as *tennis elbow*, *patellar tendinosis* of the knee and *Achilles tendinosis* in the leg.

Treatment

Tendinosis often takes a long time to recover fully, particularly if symptoms have been present for some months.

The recommended treatments include relative *rest* (doing activities that maintain fitness but avoid aggravating the injury), electrotherapy, *massage* and *non-steroidal anti-inflammatory drugs (NSAIDs)*, though the effectiveness of the latter is not proven for tendinosis injuries.

Correction of *biomechanical abnormality* is essential for recovery and prevention of re-injury. *Strengthening exercises*, in particular *eccentric* contractions, which have a specific positive effect on tendon strength compared with concentric exercises, *taping* and *motor re-education* are also recommended.

If these treatments are not successful *corticosteroid* injection or surgery may be recommended.

Degree of severity of tendinosis and symptoms

Degree of severity	Symptoms
Mild	Pain after activity only—pain that disappears with activity
Moderate	Pain with sporting activity but not with activities of daily living
Severe	Pain during activities of daily living

Tendon surgery may involve stripping of the *tendon sheath*, release of adhesions, removal of degenerative tissue and repair if there is a partial tear (see *Tendolysis*).

Tendolysis

A surgical procedure that involves cleaning out fibrous scar tissue and adhesions in a *tendon* that are preventing free movement and causing pain. It is performed when conservative treatments, such as physiotherapy, exercises and massage, have failed to achieve an improvement for an overuse injury of a tendon called *tendinosis*.

Tendon

The section of a *muscle* that connects to a bone. It is a tough structure mostly made up of parallel bundles of *collagen* fibres that do not stretch when they transmit the force of contractions generated by a muscle. At the same time it is also flexible and can be bent around bones.

Tendons tend to be shaped like a cord or strap, though with various widths and lengths. For example, the *Achilles tendon* is short and wide, whereas the tendons at the back of your hand are long and narrow.

Tendons are a bright white colour due to having a small number of blood vessels. Aponeurosis and *fascia* are made up of the same cells as tendons, but come in different shapes. Some tendons are covered in a *synovial sheath* to protect them from excess friction against bones. Tendons also contain *neurons* from the sensory nervous system that give feedback about the position and movement of a muscle.

Tendon graft

A surgical procedure that involves taking a *tendon* from one part of the body and placing it in another part that has been damaged by injury. It is mostly done to repair injury of the flexor tendons in the hand. The most commonly used tendon in a graft is the palmaris longus, a tendon that comes from a small muscle in the forearm and attaches to the soft tissue underneath the skin in the palm of the hand.

Tendon overuse injury

An injury to a tendon that is caused by repeated excessive physical loads over a period of weeks or months until it causes enough pain to seek medical care. They are a very common *overuse injury*.

Because *tendons* have a relatively poor blood supply, they may not be able to cope with sudden, increased loads during training, such as running a greater distance. The injury begins with tissue deformation, followed by individual tendon fibre death and ultimately a large area of tendon failure.

The most common type of injury is a *tendinosis*, which is often mistakenly diagnosed as a *tendinitis*. There is also a group of tendon injuries called *paratenonitis*.

Tendon sheath

An outer protective covering for *tendons*. It reduces friction caused by rubbing against a tough fibrous band, called a retinaculum, that holds down tendons in the *wrist joint* and *ankle*. The inner lining of the sheath is similar to the synovium in a joint capsule. It produces *synovial fluid*, a thick, viscous liquid that acts as a lubricant.

Tendon transfer

A surgical procedure that involves changing the position of a *tendon* so that the muscle performs different movements or the same movement at a different joint. It is performed if another tendon has been damaged beyond repair.

For example, each finger has two tendons that both perform the movement of straightening out, called extension (see *Hand and finger joints*). If both get damaged in the same finger, the finger next to it can spare one of its two tendons without impact on its ability to straighten out.

Tendon transfer also may be performed when a nerve has become paralysed and the muscles that normally perform movements at a joint can no longer be switched on.

Tennis

Tennis originated with ancient Greek and Roman ball games that were refined during the Middle Ages in European royal courts and monasteries. Royal tennis is still played today. The modern game was developed during the 1800s. The word tennis probably derives from the French who called out 'tenez' to warn opponents before hitting the ball. Tennis is played by millions of people worldwide, making it the third most popular sport.

Rules and equipment

Tennis is a racquet sport played between one or two players (singles or doubles) standing on opposing sides of a net strung across a court. Play starts with a serve and is continued with ground strokes, including fore-hand, backhand, volley and smash. A match is completed when one side wins a fixed number of sets.

Rules and equipment are modified for children, including a smaller playing area, lighter racquets and shorter games.

Fitness, skills and injuries

Singles tennis is high-intensity *aerobic training*. Doubles tennis is moderate-intensity. *Skills training* for eye–hand coordination and technique is important. Correct *tennis shoes* and good equipment (see *Tennis racquet*) help prevent injuries.

The most common injuries are *tennis elbow, rotator cuff tendinosis* (shoulder), *rotator cuff strain* (shoulder), *glenoid labrum tear* (shoulder), *low back pain (non-specific), patellofemoral joint syndrome* (knee), *gastrocnemius strain* (calf), *soleus strain* (calf), *Achilles tendinosis* (calf) and *ankle sprain.*

Tennis biomechanics

The movements and positions of the joints and muscles during tennis.

In efficient tennis biomechanics the upper limbs contribute 50 per cent of the force generated in tennis, and the trunk and lower limbs the other 50 per cent.

Most of the upper limb force comes from the shoulder, with the elbow and wrist maintaining set positions, slightly flexed (bent) and the wrist slightly extended (bent so that the back of the hand is moved closer to the back of the forearm). Exceptions include forearm pronation (turning inwards) when hitting topspin forehand strokes.

Serving and strokes are divided into two phases, cocking and deceleration (follow through). For example, the serve involves abduction and external rotation of the *shoulder joint* during cocking, and combined adduction and extension and internal rotation during deceleration with the external rotation muscles (posterior deltoid, infraspinatus and teres minor) providing most of the slowing down force. The tennis racquet striking the ball dissipates some of the force of the arm and therefore the amount of the work these muscles need to do for deceleration.

Playing tennis

Poor backhand technique is an abnormality of tennis biomechanics that increases the risk of injury such as tennis elbow

The scapula provides a stable base for all of the shoulder muscles to create the movements of both phases. In many serving motions, the feet and body are actually off the ground when this rotation reaches its maximum peak. The entire stable base of the arm, in this situation, rests on the scapula rather than on the feet or the ground.

Therefore *scapular biomechanics*, in particular the stability of the scapula in relationship to the entire moving arm, play an important role.

Biomechanical abnormality

A deviation from any of the above movements, poor technique or equipment selection is a *biomechanical abnormality*, which is associated with an increased risk of developing an overuse injury in the shoulder and elbow regions.

Elbow injuries such as *tennis elbow* are the most common, probably due to abnormalities including the dominant activity of the wrist extensors, poor backhand technique and inadequate racquets. The

most common shoulder injuries are *shoulder instability*, *rotator cuff strain* and *rotator cuff tendinosis*.

Tennis elbow

An overuse injury of the tendon of the extensor carpi radialis brevis muscle near the *elbow joint* that gradually gets worse over a period of weeks or months, or suddenly starts after a single incident like attempting a hard backhand stroke.

Causes

It is most common in racquet sports like *tennis* and *badminton*, but can also be work-related like bricklaying or associated with leisure activities such as knitting. It affects all ages, though most commonly 40 to 50-year-olds.

The extensor carpi radialis brevis is a muscle that bends the hand backwards at the wrist (extension). If the muscle repeatedly experiences excessive loads controlling the wrist joint in a backwards position, for example, when gripping the tennis racquet, a degeneration of the tendon, called a *tendinosis*, may

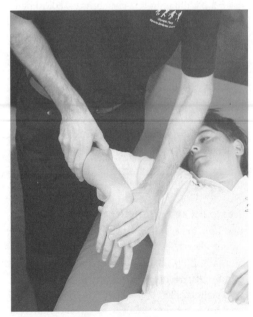

Treatment to increase the flexibility of the extensor carpi radialis brevis muscle for tennis elbow injury

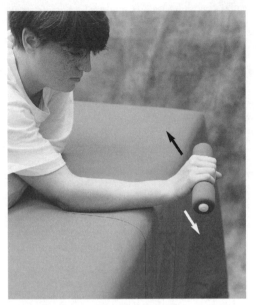

Strengthening exercise of the wrist extensor muscles for tennis elbow. Black arrow is the direction for a concentric exercise. White arrow is eccentric

occur leading to a gradual build up of pain or a sudden onset. *Inflammation* also may be present, though it is uncommon. The correct medical name for this injury is extensor tendinosis. The outdated name is lateral epicondylitis.

Diagnosis

Mild cases with a gradual onset usually feel pain during a warm-up, some time after the real activity begins or first thing the following morning. Severe cases cause pain that is easily stirred up by gentle activities such as turning the car ignition key, stiffness that is often felt in the morning and firm pressure on the tendon causing a sharp pain.

Treatment and return to sport

Rest from the sport is essential to reverse the degeneration. It may involve playing less frequently or a complete stop, lasting from a week up to a few months, depending on the severity.

Treatments to correct biomechanical abnormalities are essential for recovery and prevention of re-injury, including *flexibility exercises, strengthening exercises*, particularly *eccentric* contractions, wearing

an elbow brace and correction of factors such as poor stroke technique through *skills training*.

Other treatments include *ice* and *non-steroidal anti-inflammatory drugs (NSAIDs)*, electrotherapy such as *ultrasound, massage* and *dry needling* of myofascial trigger points. *Extra corporeal shock wave therapy* is a new treatment that uses high frequency sound waves that may have some success.

If all of the above treatments fail a *corticosteroid* injection may be prescribed. Surgery to remove degenerated tissue is a treatment of last resort.

A gradual return to sport is required over 3 to 6 weeks. For tennis this can involve practice sessions (with rest days in between) starting with performing tennis strokes without a ball, followed by gently hitting a ball from the service line for 10 minutes and lastly full strength shots against an opponent.

Tennis racquet

The equipment used to hit the ball in *tennis* should be best suited to the skills of the player and minimise the risk of an injury.

Injury prevention

The impact between a tennis ball and racquet produces a significant amount of force that is transferred into the hand and up the arm. Excessive force is associated with an increased risk of injuries such as *tennis elbow*. It may occur due to the type of racquet, the string tension and *tennis biomechanics*.

Modern wide-body racquets made of light and stiff materials generate more power in the stroke, however they provide much less shock absorption than the older style wooden racquets. The 'sweet spot' is the centre of the racquet face, also known as the centre of percussion, which makes a tennis shot feel good. Missing the 'sweet spot' due to a poor playing technique increases the forces transferred to the arm.

Excessive forces can be reduced by: increasing size of the racquet face; increasing the weight of the racquet, for example, by adding tape to the head and handle; increasing grip size; lowering string tension; gripping higher up on the handle during strokes; and improving tennis technique.

Tennis shoes

Footwear designed to cope with the physical demands of *tennis*, which involves sudden running acceleration combined with side-to-side movements.

The material of the upper section of the *shoe* should be made of solid leather (not synthetic) to hold the foot firmly on top of the midsole, which is the upper layer of the flat, bottom section that makes direct contact with the foot inside the shoe. The upper rear section (heel counter) should be firm to help protect the ankle from sprains.

The midsole should be made of reinforced rubber for good shock absorption, especially if most play is on hard surfaces, such as Rebound Ace.

Tenoperiosteum

A thin membrane of connective tissue that connects a muscle or its tendon to the outer layer of bone called the *periosteum*.

Tenosynovitis

See *Paratenonitis*.

Tenovaginitis

See *Paratenonitis*.

Testicle

See *Scrotum*.

Testosterone

A *hormone* that is responsible for the development of sexual characteristics around the time of *puberty* in males, in particular contributing to an increase in height and amount of muscle.

It also has been shown to have an effect on aggression, probably due to direct stimulation of brain receptors. Synthetic forms of testosterone and other similar hormones belong to a group of drugs called *anabolic steroids* that are banned by the International Olympic Committee (IOC) and most other sport organisations.

Therapeutic cloning

A treatment that involves growing replica cells for a person suffering from a disease or injury.

It is a new technology that is still under development. The potential benefits include replacing the brain cells in a person with Parkinson's Disease and replacing damaged tissue due to participation in exercise and sport, such as a ligament tear or bone fracture. A different type of cloning involves growing a replica of a whole organism, such as an animal like Dolly the sheep.

Method
The DNA is removed from a person's cells and implanted into an oöcyte (a female ovum or egg cell that is ready to be fertilised) that has had its own DNA removed to create a hybrid cell. A stimulus is given to this hybrid cell, such as an electric shock, to make it think it has been fertilised.

After five days of multiplying and growing the hybrid cells have become a large group of cells called a blastocyst. A number of cells are removed and grown in a dish (called a culture) to produce a population of embryonic stem cells that have the potential to be differentiated into any other type of mature cell in the body, such as bone, muscle, nerve or ligament. These differentiated cells are then transplanted into the recipient.

Thermal gear

Clothing worn by athletes to retain heat. It is made of neoprene, a wetsuit-like material, and designed to fit tightly on the body part. The aim of heat retention is to prevent *hypothermia*, increase blood flow and reduce chronic inflammation of a muscle tendon or joint; for example, *patellar tendinosis*.

Thermoregulation

See *Temperature*.

Thigh

The upper leg located between the hip and pelvis above and the knee below. The groin is the inner section of the upper leg (see *Hip joint*).

The thigh contains the femur, the longest bone in the body. The front (anterior) contains the quadriceps muscle, which has four parts: rectus femoris (upper and middle), vastus lateralis (outer or lateral side), vastus intermedius (middle) and vastus medialis (inner or medial side).

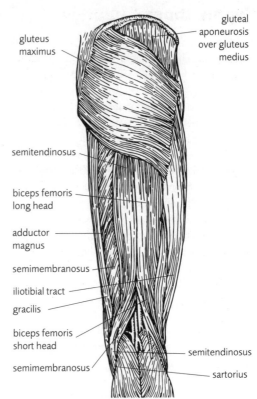

Muscles of the back (posterior) of the right thigh

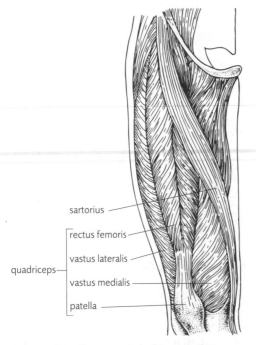

Muscles of the front (anterior) of the right thigh

The back (posterior) contains the hamstring muscle, also in four parts: semitendinosus (inner or medial side), semimembranosus (outer or lateral side) and biceps femoris long head and short head (middle).

The quadriceps and hamstring produce most of the *knee joint* movements, and also have a role in hip joint movements.

Thigh padding

A piece of equipment like a pair of short pants with thick padding in the section around the thigh. It is worn to protect against bruising called *muscle contusion* of the quadriceps (front thigh muscle), which is caused by a high-impact blow from other players.

Thigh pain and injuries

Causes

Pain in the thigh can be caused by acute or overuse injuries. An *acute injury* causes pain that begins suddenly due to a single incident such as a direct blow, which is common in contact sports.

An *overuse injury* causes pain that gets worse over a period of weeks or months due to an accumulation of excessive forces that cause microtrauma. In the early stages it causes only minor pain and stiffness. But later on, either gradually or following a sudden force, it becomes painful enough to seek medical care. In rare cases a tumour can cause pain.

The quadriceps, hamstring and femur (thigh bone) are the main sources of pain in the *thigh*. However, it is not unusual for the source of pain to come from another structure, particularly the low back and hip joint, which is called *thigh referred pain*.

Diagnosis

Making the diagnosis involves combining information gathered from the *history*, *physical examination* and relevant tests.

The pain's location is most important for an acute injury. For example, sudden back of the thigh pain when striving for extra speed during running can indicate a *hamstring strain*, or front of the thigh pain when kicking a ball may be a *quadriceps strain*.

A direct blow into the back of the thigh suggests a *hamstring contusion*. A direct blow to the front of the thigh indicates a *quadriceps contusion* (cork thigh or Charley horse), often the outer section or inner portion slightly above the kneecap. A number of injuries also refer pain into the back of the thigh from the low back or buttock, including *back-related hamstring injury, ischiogluteal bursitis, hamstring origin tendinitis, piriformis impingement, ischial tuberosity apophysitis* and *ischial tuberosity avulsion fracture*.

Radiological investigations can confirm a diagnosis; for example, diagnostic ultrasound for *myositis ossificans* or a bone scan if a *stress fracture* is suspected.

Thigh posterior cutaneous nerve entrapment

A nerve in the back of the thigh that is compressed by swelling or scarring in the piriformis muscle, and which causes *buttock* pain that may spread into the back of the thigh.

Causes of front of the thigh pain

Common	Less common	Not to be missed
• Quadriceps contusion (Cork thigh, Charley horse)	• Thigh referred pain	• Perthes' disease
	• Femur fracture	• Osteosarcoma (of the femur)
• Quadriceps strain	• Femur shaft stress fracture	
	• Anterior superior iliac spine apophysitis	
	• Anterior superior iliac spine avulsion fracture	
	• Myositis ossificans	

Causes of back of the thigh pain

Common	Less common	Not to be missed
• Hamstring strain	• Hamstring origin tendinitis	• Iliac artery endofibrosis
• Hamstring contusion	• Ischiogluteal bursitis	• Tumour
• Thigh referred pain	• Hamstring tendinitis	
	• Thigh posterior cutaneous nerve entrapment	
	• Ischial tuberosity apophysitis	
	• Ischial tuberosity avulsion fracture	
	• Piriformis impingement	
	• Myositis ossificans	

Thigh

Acute injury: Pain caused by a sudden force

Quadriceps contusion
(Cork thigh, Charley horse) ....Did you get a knock into the front of your thigh from an opponent or piece of equipment?

Myositis ossificans ....Did you have a quadriceps or hamstring contusion 1 or 2 months ago and now you are still feeling pain that is aggravated by running, worse at night and associated with increased tightness of the muscle?

Quadriceps strain ....Did you feel a sudden pain at the front of your thigh during sprinting, jumping or kicking?

Hamstring strain ....Did you feel a sudden pain and tearing sensation in the back of the thigh during running?

Hamstring contusion ....Did you receive a direct blow to the back of the thigh from an opponent or piece of equipment?

Overuse injury: Pain that has gradually got worse over a period of weeks or months

Back-related hamstring injury ....Has the pain started gradually over a period of weeks or months, is hard to pinpoint and has associated pain and stiffness in the low back?

The diagnosis can be confirmed with a *nerve conduction test*. The recommended treatment is surgery to release the muscle and free up the nerve, followed by a gradual return to sport over a period of 4 to 6 weeks. Treatments such as *massage* and *flexibility exercises* are generally unsuccessful.

Thigh referred pain

Thigh pain caused by a structure in a location some distance away. Usually it is the sacroiliac joint, *low back joints*, a nearby muscle or neural sheath. The *hip joint* also can cause pain in the front of the thigh.

Diagnosis and treatment

The diagnosis is based on excluding a local cause of pain and positive signs that the cause is *referred pain*. For example, a diagnosis of pain referred from the right side low back joints to the thigh is considered likely if *mobilisation* treatments reduce the pain.

Muscle *myofascial trigger points* should be treated with *massage* and *dry needling*. Prone knee bend

neural tension test for the front of the thigh and the slump neural tension test for the back are treated with mobilisation and *flexibility exercises*.

Thirst

A sensation that causes a desire to drink fluids. It is stimulated by nerves located in the hypothalamus in the lower part of the *brain* that detect high levels of sodium and glucose in the blood.

It is an unreliable guide of the need to replenish water levels in the body during exercise and sport because participation in physical activity causes a drop in circulating glucose, which counters the effect of increasing sodium levels due to fluid loss (see *Hydration*).

Thoracic outlet syndrome

Compression of nerves and blood vessels in the region between the neck, armpit and the chest. It can cause any one or more of the following: neck and shoulder pain, numbness or tingling of the entire arm or forearm and hand, muscle weakness and skin coolness.

It may be due to poor neck and shoulder posture, congenital abnormalities such as a cervical (extra) rib (see *Chest*) or tight neck muscles. Treatments may include posture improvement, muscle *flexibility exercises* and in severe cases surgery to remove a cervical rib.

Thoracic pain (non-specific)

Pain located in the middle section of the back that does not have an exact diagnosis. Fortunately in more than 90 per cent of cases it is unnecessary to identify the structure causing the pain because treatments can achieve improvement anyway. In a number of cases the pain is also felt in the sides or front of the chest, which is the same pain caused by a *heart attack* (see *Chest pain and injuries*).

The method of diagnosis and treatment for thoracic pain involves careful assessment and detection of abnormalities of the *thoracic spine joints* and associated muscles.

These abnormalities are treated using the techniques detailed below. One abnormality is treated at a time. Comparing the amount of pain and movement before and after the treatment provides an assessment of its effectiveness. If the treatment is not effective, a different technique should be attempted.

Joints
The most common abnormalities are pain and loss of *range of movement* in one or more of the joints. Treatments include *mobilisation, manipulation, traction* and *flexibility exercises* to increase range of movement.

Muscles
Abnormalities that are often found include *myofascial trigger points* in the paraspinal muscles and general areas of *fascia* thickening. Myofascial trigger points are treated with *massage* and *dry needling*, and fascia thickening with massage only.

Thoracic spine joint referred pain

Pain felt in the sides or front of the chest due to an overuse injury of the *thoracic spine joints*. It is the most common cause of chest pain in young people who play sport. The diagnosis and treatment is the same as for *thoracic pain (non-specific)*.

Thoracic spine joints

The joints of the middle spine that connect the neck to the low back and allow movements of the chest and abdomen.

It is made up of 12 bones in a column one on top of the other, called the thoracic vertebrae, and numbered from top to bottom T1 to T12. Each vertebra, beginning with T1, has three joints with the vertebra below; the central and forward-located (anterior) joint is the *disc*; and the two backward-located (posterior) *synovial joints*, one on each side, are called the zygapophysial joints (Z-joints).

The thoracic column curves outwards in the middle, a kyphosis. The thoracic vertebrae also connect to the ribs to enclose the *chest* at the costovertebral joints. The thoracic spine joints allow six types of movements of the chest.

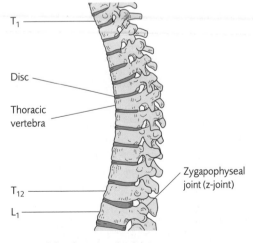

Bones of the thoracic spine joints

Thoracic spine joints range of movement and muscles

Movement	Range of movement	Muscles producing movement
Flexion (bringing the chest forward)	90 degrees	• Rectus abdominus
Lateral flexion (bringing chest sideways to the left and right)	30 degrees	• Iliocostalis thoracis • Longissimus thoracis
Extension (bending chest backwards)	30 degrees	• Longissimus thoracis • Spinalis thoracis • Iliocostalis thoracis
Rotation (turning chest to the left and right)	30 degrees	• Rotatores thoracis • Semispinalis thoracis

The spine protects the *spinal cord*, where at each thoracic vertebra level two large branches come off the spinal cord, the ventral and dorsal nerve roots, which form a larger *spinal nerve* exiting through a hole called the intervertebral foramen. Each spinal nerve is named according to the vertebra level it exits from; for example, T4 spinal nerve.

Thoracic spine pain and injuries

Causes

Pain in the middle of the back, called the thoracic region, may be caused by an *overuse injury*. The pain usually gets worse over a period of weeks or months due to an accumulation of excessive forces that cause microtrauma. In the early stages it causes only minor pain and stiffness. But later it becomes severe enough to seek medical care. Diseases that cause pain include *Scheuermann's disease, coronary heart disease* (see *Chest pain and injuries*) and *tumours*.

The *thoracic spine joints* and associated structures are the main sources of pain. However, there is little consistency to the type and location of the *pain* produced by each structure. Fortunately over 90 per cent of thoracic pain improves without an exact diagnosis.

When the painful structure can't be identified, it is described as *thoracic pain (non-specific)*. Radiological investigations such as *X-rays, CT scan* and *magnetic resonance imaging (MRI)* are rarely required in people with thoracic pain because the results usually can't identify the painful structure. Exceptions include diseases such as *Scheuermann's disease* and *tumours*.

Thorax

The anatomical region of the body more commonly called the *chest* or chest cavity.

Throat injury

An acute injury to the throat due to a sudden excessive force. An injury can be due to penetration of a sharp object, such as a water skier being thrown against a tree branch or, more commonly, being struck by a blunt object such as the elbow of another player or a piece of equipment such as a hockey stick.

The primary concerns are an injured larynx or trachea (windpipe) may block the airway and reduce *breathing* ability and major blood vessels passing through the throat may be damaged.

Treatment

A throat injury that is suspected of compromising breathing should be treated as a *medical emergency*, which includes a doctor or someone trained in first aid placing a tube to clear the airways followed by transporting the injured person to a hospital as quickly as possible.

A blocked airway should be suspected if the following symptoms are present:
- hoarseness, grating or creaking sounds when breathing
- drooling
- throat pain
- shortness of breath
- distress when breathing.

Throwing biomechanics

The movements and positions that occur in the joints and muscles of the body, particularly the shoulder and elbow, when throwing an object.

Throwing is divided into four phases: 1) wind up (preparation); 2) cocking; 3) acceleration; and 4) deceleration (follow through), which take just under 2 seconds to complete. The time sequence is 1.5 seconds (80 per cent of total) for the wind up and cocking phases, 40 milliseconds (2 per cent) for the acceleration phase and 0.3 seconds (18 per cent) for deceleration. It can move a ball at speeds of up to 150 km/h (93 miles/h). The following is a description of the efficient biomechanics for a right-handed baseball pitch.

Wind up

The body rotates so that the *hip joint* and shoulders are at 90 degrees to the target. The lower half of the body goes into a forward moving 'controlled fall'. In baseball pitching hip flexion of the lead leg raises the *centre of gravity*.

Cocking

Cocking positions the body to enable all body segments to contribute to ball propulsion. In the upper limb the *shoulder joint* is raised up (90–100 degrees abduction), lifted backwards (horizontal extension) and is externally rotated so that the ligaments are tight and store elastic energy.

The scapula (shoulder blade) is retracted (moved closer to the spine) and elevated. The internal rotation muscles of the shoulder are stretched. There is a counter-clockwise rotation and lateral flexion (sideways bending) of the trunk, which abruptly places the throwing arm behind the body. The leading leg is internally rotated and extended placing the foot forwards on the ground.

Acceleration

Acceleration is an explosion of strength due to the release of elastic energy and forceful contraction of the internal rotation muscles of the shoulder.

This explosion causes the two opposing bone surfaces to separate. To counter it the rotator cuff muscles also forcefully contract. Forward propulsion of

Wind up (preparation)—throwing biomechanics

Cocking—throwing biomechanics

Acceleration—throwing biomechanics

Deceleration (follow through)—throwing biomechanics

the arm is assisted by contraction of the anterior chest wall and spine. This phase concludes when the ball is released from the hand.

Deceleration
Shoulder external rotation muscles slow down the momentum of the acceleration phase. In addition, the spine and abdominal muscles cause the trunk to rotate forward to slow down the arm.

Biomechanical abnormality
A deviation from any of the above movements or a poor throwing technique can cause a *biomechanical abnormality*, which can increase the risk of developing an overuse injury. For example, repeated pitching for weeks or months can cause increased range of movement of external rotation of the shoulder joint, which may lead to anterior *shoulder instability* and *shoulder impingement* syndrome. Children may suffer *Little Leaguer's shoulder*.

Repeated throwing can also produce structural changes at the elbow, in particular *elbow medial collateral ligament sprain* and *ulnar nerve compression* in adults and *Little Leaguer's elbow* in children.

The most common throwing technique problems are 'opening up too soon', which increases stress to the anterior (front) shoulder and medial (inner) elbow structures and 'hanging', which is a characteristic sign of fatigue. Abnormalities of *scapular biomechanics* may also cause injuries.

Throwing sports

Sports including discus, hammer, shot put and javelin. The discus was in the ancient Greek Olympics. It involves throwing a round 22 cm (8.6 in) diameter disc, weighing 2 kg (14.4 lb) for men and 1 kg (2.2 lb) for women. Cannonball throwing, a popular military recreational pursuit through the centuries, was formalised in 1860 as the sport of shot put throwing a 7.26 kg (16 lb) ball for men and women 4 kg (8.8 lb).

Hammer throwing, where a heavy ball attached to a wire is spun around and thrown as far as possible, originated in Ireland in 2000 BC. Throwing an olive-wood stick as far as possible was in the ancient

Greek Olympics. Modern javelins are hollow metal tubes, weighing 800 g for men and 600 g for women.

Fitness and injuries
The main physical requirements are *strength training*, *flexibility training* and *skills training* for correct technique. The most common injuries are *rotator cuff tendinosis* (shoulder), *biceps tendinosis* (shoulder), *elbow medial collateral ligament sprain*, *ulnar nerve compression* (elbow), flexor tendinosis (*Golfer's elbow*) and *low back pain (non-specific)*.

Throwing sports for children and adolescents

Training guidelines for children and adolescents participating in *throwing sports*, such as shot put, discus, hammer and javelin, and for *baseball*, which minimise the risk of overuse injuries.

Training sessions per week should not exceed three for children and adolescents of all ages. The maximum time per training session should not exceed 1½ hours, including a warm-up.

Throws permitted for each session should not exceed 20 for children and adolescents up to the age of 14 and 40 from the age of 15. Because javelin is more demanding than the other throwing sports, the total number of throws should be two-thirds of the above recommendation.

Thumb

See *Hand and finger joints*.

Tibia fracture

A break in the large, front *shin* bone due to an excessive, sudden force, such as a fall.

Diagnosis, treatment and return to sport
The *fracture* is usually extremely painful, causes swelling and bony deformity and may be visible through damaged skin (called a compound fracture),

which requires immediate hospital treatment. Walking or running is impossible in cases of a displaced fracture. The diagnosis is confirmed with an X-*ray*.

Most fractures can be treated with *immobilisation* in an above-knee plaster cast for 6 to 8 weeks, followed by a hinged knee cast for another 10 to 12 weeks. Surgery may be required if the fracture is displaced.

After removal of the plaster a *sport rehabilitation* program is required, including *flexibility exercises* for the knee joint, *strengthening exercises* for the quadriceps and hamstring muscles, and aerobic training beginning with swimming. Return to sport is permitted when *range of movement* and muscle *strength* are normal. Return to contact sports usually requires 6 months.

A combined fracture of the tibia and fibula, often due to indirect violence such as landing from a jump on a twisted foot, is treated the same as above.

Tibia periosteal contusion

An acute injury of the *shin* that causes damage to the *periosteum*, the external thin outer layer of bones due to a sudden, blunt force. Though not a common injury, they are most likely to occur in contact sports such as *soccer*, *hockey (field)* and *basketball*.

It can be extremely painful at the time and cause momentary paralysis of muscles in the region, but usually settles down quickly. Persistent pain may occur because of bruising under the periosteum.

The recommended treatment is *ice* and *rest* from aggravating activities. The time required before return to sport is up to 2 weeks for severe contusions. A *shin guard* should be worn afterwards for protection.

Tibia periostitis

Inflammation of the large, front *shin* bone that causes pain that gradually builds up over a period of weeks or months due to repeated, excessive forces, particularly running.

It is often associated with a running biomechanical abnormality, particularly excessive *foot pronation*, which causes the tibialis posterior and soleus muscles

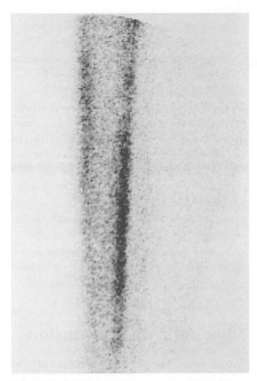

Bone scan of tibia periostitis

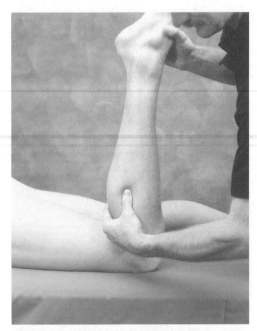

Massage of soleus muscle for tibia periostitis

that attach to the tibia to pull excessively on the bone's outer covering, the *periosteum*. This injury is popularly known as 'shin splints'. It is also called medial tibial stress syndrome, traction periostitis and inflammatory shin pain.

Diagnosis

Pain is felt along the inner (medial) border of the tibia that usually decreases after warming up during training or exercise; however, it gradually comes back after exercise and is worse the following morning. The bone is tender when pressed firmly with the fingers, usually at the junction of the lower third and upper two-thirds of the tibia. A diagnosis is confirmed with a *bone scan*.

Treatment and return to sport

The aim of the initial treatment is to reduce inflammation with *rest*, *non-steroidal anti-inflammatory drugs (NSAIDs)* and *ice*, followed by treatments including *flexibility exercises*, correct selection of *shoes*, *orthotics* for a biomechanical abnormality and *massage* of the thickened muscle fibres of the soleus and tibialis posterior adjacent to their bony attachment.

Return to sport should recommence on alternate days only when walking is pain-free and bone tenderness has cleared, which may take 1 to 2 weeks if the injury has been caught in the early stages. However, full recovery and return to running can take up to 6 months if it is detected late.

Tibia stress fracture

A microfracture in the large, front *shin* bone that causes pain that develops gradually due to an accumulation of repeated, excessive physical loads associated with running over a period of weeks or months. This injury is popularly known as 'shin splints'.

Causes

One of the major causes of the *stress fracture* is an abnormality of running biomechanics, particularly excessive *foot pronation* or a rigid, *pes cavus* foot that

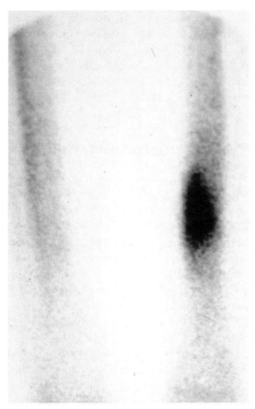

Bone scan of tibia stress fracture

results in reduced shock absorption, which increases the impact pressure on the bone. The risk is increased in female athletes with low oestrogen levels, such as in *female athlete triad*.

Diagnosis

Most stress fractures of the tibia are located along the inner-side (medial) border of the bone. The pain is easy to pinpoint, often sharp, either constant or increasing during exercise such as walking and getting worse with running or high-impact *aerobics*.

Pain may be felt during the night and can be worse the next morning compared to the night before. The bone also feels tender when pressed firmly with the fingers.

Most of the medial border fractures are transverse (horizontal) to the bone. Sometimes they may be along the length, called a longitudinal fracture, usually in the lower one-third of the tibia. Both types are treated the same. However, there are a small number of fractures located in the anterior (front) cortex, which are treated with greater caution and sensitivity.

Radiological investigation with either a *bone scan* or *magnetic resonance imaging (MRI)* can confirm the diagnosis and the exact location of the fracture. In addition, a fracture located in the inner-side (medial) third of the anterior cortex causes a vague, dull ache that in many cases does not get severe enough until it becomes a full fracture that shows up on an X-ray as a 'dreaded black line'.

Treatment

The recommended treatment for a medial border tibial stress fracture involves an initial period of *rest*, sometimes requiring non-weight-bearing on crutches. Alternative forms of exercise, such as swimming, cycling and water running, should be performed to maintain fitness. Pain may continue during this period due to soft tissue thickening below the fracture, which can be treated with *massage*.

Once there is no pain during walking and the tenderness of the bone when pressed firmly with the fingers completely disappears, slow jogging can be started again. This usually takes 4 to 8 weeks. It is also important to treat factors that have precipitated the stress fracture, such as low oestrogen levels and biomechanical abnormality.

Anterior cortex fractures are vulnerable to getting worse, in particular, delayed union, non-union or a complete fracture. The recommended treatment is *immobilisation* (protected mobilisation) using a long pneumatic air splint.

Return to sport is permitted when cortical bridging of the fracture is found on an X-ray. If this is not achieved after 4 to 6 months it is recommended to perform *open surgery* and *internal fixation* of an intramedullary rod or *bone graft*.

Tibial external torsion

A structural abnormality of the large, front *shin* bone (tibia) that causes excessive outwards rotation and results in abducted walking and running biomechanics and excessive *foot pronation*.

Tibial internal torsion

A structural abnormality of the large, front *shin* bone (tibia) that causes an in-toed walking pattern and lateral *instability* of the ankle joint.

Tibial plateau fracture

A break in the top end of the large, front shin bone (tibia) within the *knee joint*. It most commonly occurs in high-speed sports, such as *downhill skiing* and wave jumping during *windsurfing*, due to landing on both feet and compressing the knee joint bones against each other. Because the bone lies beneath the articular cartilage of the tibia within the knee joint, the risk of *osteoarthritis* is increased even after healing.

The *fracture* usually causes severe pain and inability to take weight on the leg. The diagnosis is confirmed with an X-ray, which also shows the size of the gap in the broken bone. Minor gaps are treated with *immobilisation* in a hinged knee *brace* for 6 weeks. Major gaps require *open surgery* and *internal fixation*, followed by a return to sport in 10 to 12 weeks.

Tibial varum

A structural inwards bowing of the large, front *shin* bone (tibia) that causes the foot to be inverted (turned outwards) when the heel strikes the ground during walking and running, which forces excessive *foot pronation* movement and can increase the risk of injury.

Tibialis anterior tendinosis

An overuse injury causing pain on the front of the *ankle* that gradually gets worse over a period of weeks or months due to repeated and excessive activity of the tendon. It is associated with reduced *range of movement* of the ankle joint, downhill running and excessive tightness of strapping or shoelaces over the tibialis anterior tendon at the front of the ankle.

Treatments include *rest* from the aggravating activity, *ice*, *mobilisation* of the ankle joint, *strengthening exercises*, particularly *eccentric* muscle contractions, *massage* and *flexibility exercises*. Non-steroidal anti-inflammatory drugs (NSAIDs) also may be recommended.

Tibialis posterior tendinosis

An overuse injury causing pain on the inside of the ankle that gradually gets worse over a period of weeks or months due to repeated and excessive stretching of the tendon. This injury is associated with activities involving *ankle* joint eversion (turning outwards movement) such as in speed ice skating and running on tight bends, particularly when a biomechanical abnormality called excessive *foot pronation* is present. The initial response is a tendinitis that gradually leads to *tendinosis*, which is a degeneration of the tendon.

Treatments include *rest* from the aggravating activity, *ice*, if required, *analgesics* for pain relief, *strengthening exercises*, particularly *eccentric* muscle contractions, *massage* and *flexibility exercises*. Non-steroidal anti-inflammatory drugs (NSAIDs) also may be recommended. A foot *orthotic* may be required to correct excessive foot pronation.

Tinea pedis

See *Athlete's foot*.

Tiredness

A feeling of fatigue that can be a normal or abnormal response to participation in exercise or sport. It can be a normal response to performing exercise and sport at the maximum limits of fitness. Fatigue is also the goal of training to increase fitness or strength, which involves doing an activity at an *overload* level.

Normal tiredness is usually easily reversed with a day or two of rest. Abnormal tiredness is defined as

Causes of abnormal tiredness in athletes

Common	Less common	Not to be missed
• *Overtraining syndrome*	• Chronic mild *dehydration*	• *Tumor*
• *Flu*	• *Exercise-induced asthma (EIA)*	• *Coronary heart disease*
• *Upper respiratory tract infection*	• Deficiency of *Magnesium, Zinc, Vitamin* B	• *Heart attack*
• *Glandular fever*	• Jet lag	• *Myocarditis*
• *Carbohydrate depletion*	• Anaemia (see *Iron deficiency*)	• *Diabetes*
• *Protein depletion*	• *Stress*	• *Hepatitis*
• Insufficient sleep	• *Anxiety*	• *HIV*
• *Chronic fatigue syndrome (CFS)*	• *Depression*	• *Eating disorders* (anorexia
• *Iron deficiency*	• *Ankylosing spondylitis*	and bulimia)
	• Medications such as *Beta-blockers, Antihistamines*	• *Pregnancy*
		• *Post-concussion syndrome*

tiredness that does not disappear after a 3-day break from activity and undisturbed, long sleeps. Persistent tiredness causes deterioration in training and competition performance.

Diagnosis

Making a diagnosis of the cause of abnormal tiredness involves combining information about the symptoms, including a training diary and nutrition diary, a physical examination and relevant tests.

A training diary can help with identifying the details of the tiredness, such as when it occurs, how long it lasts and the aggravating factors. For example, if it only occurs in hot weather the fatigue suggests chronic mild *dehydration*.

A training diary can identify whether there is excessive overload or sufficient recovery time. If not, the problem may be *overtraining syndrome*. The amount of sleep and bed rest should also be noted, indicating whether there is insufficient sleep.

A sore throat or discomfort with swallowing may indicate a *common cold* or *glandular fever*. A post-exercise cough, wheeze or chest tightness suggests *exercise-induced asthma*. Psychological factors that cause tiredness include *anxiety, stress* and *depression*.

A 7-day food and fluid intake diary can identify whether there is *carbohydrate depletion, protein depletion* or an *eating disorder* such as anorexia or bulimia. *Gastrointestinal bleeding* and heavy menstrual bleeding are indications of *iron deficiency*.

Coronary heart disease may be the cause if there are also symptoms such as *palpitations*, ankle swelling or chest pain. Absence of periods may be due to *pregnancy*. Jaundice, which is a yellowing of the skin and whites of the eyes, suggests *hepatitis*.

Tissue

A collection of *cells* that carry out a specific set of tasks. For example, muscle tissue contains cells called muscle fibres whose primary task is to perform contractions. There are many types of tissues such as *connective tissue, nerves*, blood vessels and *bones*.

Toes

See *Foot and toes*.

Tooth avulsion

A tooth that is forced out of its socket in the gum and jaw bone due to a sudden blow by another player of piece of equipment. Fortunately the tooth can be saved for replacement.

It should be retrieved and handled by the crown. If it is dirty it should be washed with sterile saline solution, milk or sucked clean under the tongue. If the injured person is conscious and alert, the tooth should then be reimplanted and taken for immediate treatment, preferably within 60 minutes.

If the injured person is not fully alert, the tooth can be stored in sterile saline solution or cold milk until medical help arrives. If the tooth is only loosened, it should be repositioned, followed by treatment from a dentist as soon as possible.

Tooth fracture

A break in the tooth due to a sudden forceful blow by another player or piece of equipment. Pain can be caused when the tooth is exposed to air, heat or cold, which is usually a sign of a crown fracture that exposes the outer layer over the nerve (dentine) and requires urgent treatment.

Any fragment of tooth that comes loose should be placed in milk to preserve it and improve the chances of a successful re-attachment. Enamel chip fractures are not painful, but do require treatment from a dentist.

Torticollis

See *Wry neck*.

Total hip replacement

See *Hip joint replacement*.

Total knee replacement

See *Knee joint replacement*.

Trachea

The large round tube that carries air between the lower part of the throat in the front of the neck and down into the *lungs* in the top of the chest (see *Respiratory system*). It is also called the windpipe. In the average adult it is 10–11 cm (4–4.3 in) long. At the end it divides into two tubes called the left and right bronchus. The trachea is made up of 20 rings of firm cartilage that prevent it bending too much and causing a blockage (like a drinking straw). At the same time it is flexible and moves with movements of the neck.

Track and field

See *Athletics*.

Traction

A treatment that involves pulling on a joint in a direction that widens the space between the joint surfaces. It has traditionally been recommended to reduce pain caused by *nerve root compression* by reducing the pressure in a herniated disc, widening the intervertebral foramen and stretching the spinal muscles. It may be performed manually by a practitioner or a traction bed and harness.

Training

Regular participation in an activity with the aim of increasing *fitness* and skill levels. For example, walking briskly for 30 minutes on most days of the week increases aerobic fitness. Baseball hitting practice improves motor and eye–hand coordination skills.

Increased fitness and skills can achieve positive effects, ranging from improved performance in a sport through to general health benefits. For instance, lifting weights to increase the strength of the muscles in the arms, trunk and legs can improve the distance of golf shots. Increased aerobic fitness reduces the risk of illness and disease such as a *heart attack*.

The main principles of training are *periodisation*, *overload*, *specificity* and *individuality*.

Doing a *warm-up* before training is an essential measure to reduce the risk of injuries associated with training. A *warm-down* should be done afterwards, particularly if it has involved high-intensity activities. Other helpful treatments and techniques include post-exercise *massage*, getting enough sleep and *rest* and eating a healthy diet.

The different types of training include *aerobic training*, *anaerobic training*, *strength training*, *speed training*, *agility training*, *flexibility training*, *cross training* and *skills training*.

Trampolining

The trampoline was developed in 1936 by George Nissen from Cedar Rapids in Iowa, inspired by circus trapeze artists bouncing on safety nets. The first official American championships were held in 1954. Trampolining was included in the 2000 Olympics.

Fitness, skills and injuries

Competitions are based on the difficulty and successful completion of manoeuvres. The most difficult is a triple somersault and one-and-a-half twist. The physical requirements are similar to gymnastics and diving, including *flexibility training*, *strength training* and *skills training*.

The most common injuries are *head injury*, *concussion*, *Colles fracture* (wrist), *radius distal epiphysis fracture* (wrist), *supracondylar fracture* (elbow) and *shoulder dislocation*.

Transcutaneous electrical nerve stimulation (TENS)

A treatment for pain and muscle spasm provided by a portable electrical device that produces a direct electric current via conducting pads placed on the skin. The treatment causes a comfortable pins and needles sensation.

There are two types of stimulation, high frequency (conventional) or low frequency (acupuncture-like). High frequency electric currents selectively activate large diameter, non-noxious sensory nerve fibres and inhibit the transmission of *pain* signals from the spinal cord and perception of pain sensation.

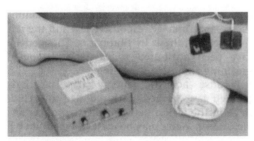

Transcutaneous electrical nerve stimulation (TENS) treatment for the knee

Low frequency currents cause *muscle contractions*. It may be used for *myofascial trigger points* or *acupuncture* points. The pain relief may be achieved through *endorphins* release, and lasts longer compared to high frequency currents.

Transient hypertrophy

Muscles that feel and look larger immediately after a *strength training* session. It is due to swelling in the muscle fibres caused by an accumulation of clear fluid from the blood called *oedema*. It only lasts for a maximum of a few hours until the oedema is reabsorbed back into the blood. It may be associated with *muscle soreness*.

Transplant recipients

People who have undergone an organ transplant operation. The main types are kidney, liver, heart, bone marrow and heart/lung. They are evenly divided between men and women, and across all age groups.

Exercise and sport

Transplant recipients participate in all forms of exercise and sport, except long distance events such as running more than 10 km (6 miles). This restriction is due to an increased risk of *heat illness* and dehydration caused by a side effect of the drugs, cyclosporin and corticosteroids, that are taken to prevent rejection of the transplanted organ by the immune system.

In addition, it is advisable to avoid exercise and sport if the outside air temperature is greater than 28°C (82.4F°), ensure adequate *hydration* before and during activity by drinking copious fluids, have wet towels available to relieve heat illness and to stop participation if the *heart rate* rises above 100.

Cyclosporin can also cause high blood pressure. Corticosteroids increase appetite and cause weight gain. When taken together they also act to increase the risk of *diabetes*. Regular participation in exercise and sport can help to reduce or prevent all of these side effects.

Corticosteroids place athletes at a slightly increased risk of muscle strain, joint articular cartilage wear and infection. Wounds and cuts should be properly cared for. One of the psychological side effects of corticosteroids is excessive optimism, which may cause athletes to be overzealous in their participation and more prone to injury. Care also should be taken to avoid exposure to the sun because transplant recipients have an increased risk of skin cancer.

A new organ can make the recipient physically more capable than the average person of their age, as would be expected in a 60-year-old heart recipient with a 30-year-old heart. However, most transplant recipients are physically unwell prior to their operation and many can find it difficult to adjust to their new status. Exercise and sport may be a highly effective means of demonstrating to oneself and others a new ability to lead a healthier and more active life.

Despite a persistent perception that transplant operations are excessively complicated, costly and indicate poor long-term health, recipients actually live longer and have a much improved quality of life. Kidney transplants have a 95 per cent success rate as measured by organ taking and survival.

Transtheoretical model

See *Stages of change*.

Travel health

The prevention, diagnosis and treatment of travel-related injuries, illness and disease. It is important for people who play sport and participate in physical activities overseas.

Preparation for travel includes being well-versed about the travel destination in terms of climate, altitude, level of pollution, accommodation, food, water, illness and disease and the existing health services.

Method

Recommended measures include *heat acclimatisation, altitude sickness* prevention, booking accommodation with air-conditioning in hot climates and adequate bed sizes, particularly for tall athletes like basketballers who require extra-long beds, arrangements for adequate diet such as high carbohydrate meals, ensuring a clean drinking water supply, treatments for *traveller's diarrhoea*, vaccination requirements and *jet lag* prevention and treatments.

Traveller's diarrhoea

An increased amount, frequency or fluidity of faeces movement out of the bowels associated with travel to foreign countries. It is caused by eating food and water in foreign countries that contain bacteria that are different to the normal bacteria found in the gastrointestinal system.

Diarrhoea usually occurs in the first week after arrival and commonly lasts between 24 and 48 hours. It is often associated with mild *fever*, abdominal pain and a general feeling of illness, with the latter possibly lasting for a few days.

The risks of developing traveller's diarrhoea can be reduced by drinking bottled water, eating freeze-

Vaccination recommendations for travel health

Basic (essential)	Recommended	Regional (depends on travel destination)
• Tetanus	• Hepatitis A (frequent international travel)	• Malaria
• Diphtheria		• Typhoid fever
• Measles	• Hepatitis B (contact sports especially)	• Japanese encephalitis
• Mumps		• Cholera
• Rubella	• Influenza (annual vaccination)	
• Poliomyelitis	• Rabies	• Meningococcus
		• Yellow fever

dried cultures and yoghurt, and avoiding raw foods that may have been washed in local water.

Treatment of traveller's diarrhoea includes appropriate fluid and electrolyte replacement, and anti-diarrhoeal medications such as loperamide and *antibiotics* if symptoms are severe.

Treadmill

Fitness equipment designed for stationary walking and running. Regular use can be an effective form of *aerobic training*. The design and cost of models varies considerably. In general they include a device for moving the surface under the feet and altering the effort required to walk or run.

The simplest models are non-motorised. Walking or running provides the power, so that the leading foot of each step pushes the tread surface back over a smooth underneath surface or a series of rollers. The treadmill speeds up and slows down according to the effort. More expensive models are motorised and can be set at different speeds. Both non-motorised and motorised models can be adjusted to simulate uphill slopes.

The most common design faults of treadmills are being too narrow, too short and not sturdy enough, all of which increase the risk of falling off.

There are no indications that a treadmill achieves greater aerobic fitness than outdoors walking or running. However, it can be more convenient by permitting walking at home and in all weather conditions.

A treadmill is often used in medical tests such as an *exercise ECG test* for assessing coronary heart disease and *aerobic fitness* tests.

Treatment

A measure or activity that is designed to prevent, cure or relieve the signs and symptoms of an injury, illness or disease. For example, ice can reduce the swelling after an ankle sprain. A painkilling medication can relieve a headache. Coronary bypass surgery can make a diseased heart beat more effectively.

The effectiveness of each type of treatment should be evaluated by comparing the symptoms and signs before and after treatment.

Injury

The two main types of injuries that occur due to participation in exercise and sport include an *acute injury* that causes pain that begins suddenly due to a single incident and *overuse injury*, which causes pain that gets worse over a period of weeks or months due to an accumulation of excessive forces. Treatments provided for both types have the following aims:

- Minimise the initial damage.
- Reduce the associated pain and inflammation.
- Promote healing of the damaged tissue.
- Maintain or restore the *range of movement, flexibility, strength, proprioception* and *fitness* during the healing phase.
- A *sport rehabilitation* program focusing on the most relevant activities to enable a return to the exercise or sport.
- Assess and correct any factors that increase the risk of the injury recurring or another related injury occurring.

There are many effective treatments for injuries. However, no single treatment is wholly effective for every injury. There is also considerable variation in individual responses to particular treatments.

The ideal treatment program often combines different treatments in an attempt to maximise effectiveness. Treatments commonly recommended for exercise and sports-related injuries include:

- *rest, ice, compression* and *elevation* (also see RICE *(rest, ice, compression and elevation)*)
- *drugs* and *ergogenic aids*
- *immobilisation*
- *electrotherapy*
- *heat therapy (superficial)*
- *mobilisation*
- *manipulation*
- *traction*
- *strengthening exercises*
- *flexibility exercises*
- *massage*
- *motor re-education*
- *biofeedback*

- *proprioception training*
- *muscle energy techniques*
- *neural tension stretching*
- *acupuncture*
- *dry needling*
- *open surgery*
- *arthroscopy*
- *sport rehabilitation.*

Triangular fibrocartilage complex sprain

An acute injury that causes pain located on the medial (little finger-side) of the *wrist joint*. The triangular fibrocartilage complex lies between the ulna (inner forearm bone) and the carpal bones. It is the major provider of stability for the distal radio-ulnar joint. It is made up of fibrocartilage, ligaments and the extensor carpi ulnaris tendon sheath.

The injury is usually caused by a sudden and excessive adduction movement (bending the little finger-side of the hand towards the body), often during *gymnastics*, *diving* and racquet sports such as *tennis*.

Diagnosis, treatment and return to sport

The injury causes pain that is aggravated by resisting wrist dorsiflexion movement (forcefully pressing the back of the hand against a wall), a clicking sensation with wrist movements and reduced grip strength.

Mild *sprain* (grade 1) causes pain and minor swelling. Moderate sprain (grade 2) causes significant pain and swelling and perhaps bruising. A severe sprain (grade 3) can cause severe swelling and bruising, though sometimes less pain if nerve fibres are torn. *Magnetic resonance imaging (MRI)* can confirm the diagnosis.

The recommended treatment is *RICE (rest, ice, compression and elevation)* followed by wearing a protective *brace*, *flexibility exercises* and *strengthening exercises*. Return to sport can take 1 week for a mild sprain, up to 6 weeks for a moderate sprain and 12 weeks for a severe case. An injury that does not heal properly or is re-injured can lead to *distal radioulnar joint instability*.

Triathlon

A sport invented by the San Diego Track Club in California in the early 1970s that involves swimming, cycling and long distance running. The first official event was held in Hawaii in 1978. It is also known as ironman and ironwoman.

The distance for each event varies. In the 2000 Olympics it was a 1500 m ocean swim, 40 km road cycling race and 10 000 m run. The Ironman Triathlon in Hawaii is a 3.8 km (2.4 mile) swim, 179 km (112 mile) cycle and a marathon (42.2 km/26.2 miles). The training required and most common injuries are similar to the specific sports, *swimming*, *cycling* and *long distance running*, though the overall fitness demands are much greater.

Triglycerides

A type of fat used for fat storage in the body. It is made up of three fatty acid molecules and a glycerol, and is located in the fat cells in adipose tissue. When required for energy in the body such as for muscle contractions, it is broken down into its constituent parts and the free fatty acids are carried in the blood to the muscles where they undergo *fat metabolism*.

Triglycerides are found inside plaques, which are damaged sections of arteries affected by *atherosclerosis*, which cause narrowing or a blockage of these arteries, such as in *coronary heart disease*. The recommended level of triglycerides in the blood is less than 4mmol/L (356 mg/dL) if you have a low risk of coronary heart disease and less than 2 mmol/L (178 mg/dL) if your risk is high.

Trochanteric bursitis

An overuse injury that causes inflammation of the bursa that protects the gluteus medius muscle tendon from excessive friction due to rubbing against the greater trochanter bone of the upper femur (thigh bone). It is usually due to excessive and repeated forces on the bursa over a period of weeks or months. It is most commonly seen in *long distance running*.

The pain is usually on the outer side (lateral aspect) of the *hip joint*, though it may also spread down the outside of the thigh. It can be aggravated by activities such as climbing stairs and getting out of a car. It is often associated with an abnormality of running biomechanics, in particular, *pelvis lateral tilt*.

The recommended treatment is *ice* and *rest* from aggravating activities, *non-steroidal anti-inflammatory drugs (NSAIDs)*, *flexibility exercises* for the gluteus medius and correction of biomechanical abnormalities. A *corticosteroid* injection may be required if these treatments fail.

Trying too hard

The main characteristic of an athlete described as suffering from the 'overmotivated-underachiever syndrome'. Other features include possessing moderate to high intelligence, highly analytical thought processes, being obsessed with achieving inappropriate and unrealistic goals, training excessively, a high rate of chronic injuries and illness, *tiredness* and *overtraining syndrome*.

Turf toe

See *First metatarso-phalangeal (MTP) joint sprain*.

Tumour

A collection of cancer cells. A tumour occasionally can cause pain that appears to be an exercise or sports-related injury. For example, testicle cancer can present as a groin injury, such as *osteitis pubis*.

Pain caused by a tumour tends to be more constant and does not vary intensity in association with activity, is felt more at night and can be severe enough to cause a person to wake up. Tumours also cause *fever*, loss of appetite, weight loss and a general feeling of illness (malaise). Specific types of cancer that affect bones and joints include *osteosarcoma* (malignant) and *osteoid osteoma* (benign).

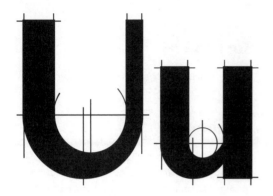

Ugly parent syndrome

Negative parental behaviour that has a detrimental impact on younger athletes. The problem is usually excessive expectations and pressure on the child to perform successfully.

Competition is a good thing during childhood and adolescence; however, having fun and enjoying sport is more important. If it all gets too much a child may drop out, exhibit unusual behaviour or experience a physical ailment such as headaches, stomach aches and muscle pains. In addition, there may be sleep disturbances, emotional volatility, *tiredness* and *depression*.

The guidelines for parents supporting a young athlete's participation in exercise and sport in a positive manner include:
- Don't force participation if a child is unwilling.
- Focus on the efforts and performance rather than the end outcome (winning or losing).
- Set realistic participation goals.
- Teach children that an honest effort is as important as a victory, so that the result of a game is accepted without undue disappointment.
- Encourage participation according to the rules.
- Never ridicule a child for making a mistake.
- Remember that a child is involved in a sport for his or her own enjoyment, not the parent's.
- Children learn by example from adults.
- Adults should show good sportsmanship such as applauding good opposition play. If there is a disagreement with an official it should be taken up through the appropriate channels rather than making public criticism.
- All verbal and physical abuse should be removed from the playing field, particularly derogatory language based on sex, race or gender.
- Respect should be shown to the coach.

Ulcer

A wound that causes a loss of tissue in the lining of an organ, such as the *gastrointestinal system* or *skin*. Gastrointestinal or peptic ulcers include gastric ulcers of the stomach and duodenal ulcers of the upper small intestine.

Ulcers cause pain when exposed nerves become irritated. A duodenal ulcer can refer pain into the left *shoulder joint*. Severe ulcers can cause *gastrointestinal bleeding*.

The most common cause of gastrointestinal ulcers is bacteria called Helicobacter pylori (H.pylori), which infects the lining, making it vulnerable to the corrosive effects of acid. Other causes include excessive *non-steroidal anti-inflammatory drugs (NSAIDs)* and *aspirin*. Antibiotics are the best treatment for H.pylori. Antacids only relieve the symptoms without treating the cause.

Ulnar nerve compression

A nerve compressed by swelling in surrounding muscle and fibrous tissue that causes pain on the inner (medial) side and back of the elbow, and pins and needles or numbness along the inner (medial) side of the forearm, fifth finger and half of the fourth finger.

The compression is located in the ulnar groove near the *elbow joint*, popularly known as the funny bone. The main causes include excessive throwing and a biomechanical abnormality of *throwing biomechanics*.

The recommended treatment is *massage* to the nerve and, if required, *neural tension* stretching. If this fails, surgical transposition of the nerve may be required. The ulnar nerve may also be compressed in the wrist, called *handlebar palsy*.

Ultra long distance sports

Sports that involve continuous activity for long periods, such open ocean swimming in the Manhattan Island marathon swim (45 km/28.5 miles) and running more than a marathon (42.2 km/26.2 miles).

The physical requirement for these sports is predominantly *aerobic training* based on *periodisation*. Women have an advantage over men in this sport because of extra stores of body fat (see *Women in sport*). The most common injuries are similar to *long distance running*, *swimming* and *cycling*.

Ultrasound diagnosis

See *Diagnostic ultrasound*.

Ultrasound therapy

A treatment of high frequency sound waves that penetrate the skin and are absorbed in the tissues to a depth of 2–5 cm (1–2 in).

The absorption of pulsed ultrasound waves causes non-thermal effects, which are the most appropriate treatment for an *acute injury*. These effects include: increased intracellular calcium, skin and cell membrane permeability, mast cell degranulation, chemotactic factor and histamine release, macrophage responsiveness and protein synthesis by fibroblasts, all of which are due to the creation of microscopic air bubbles and micro-streaming within the cells.

The thermal effects, which are achieved by using a continuous and uninterrupted dosage, include acceleration of metabolic rate, reduction or control of pain and muscle spasm, alteration of nerve conduction velocity, increased circulation and increased muscle, tendon and ligament flexibility. It is more commonly recommended for an *overuse injury*.

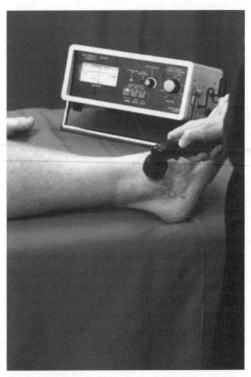

Ultrasound therapy for the lateral (outer side) ankle

Treatment

A gel is used to provide constant contact between the machine head and the skin. The recommended dosage for injuries is the lowest intensity needed to achieve the desired effect and the highest frequency that will transmit the sound waves through the tissues to the injured tissue.

Upper respiratory tract

The nose, mouth and throat. They form the beginning of the *respiratory system* and *gastrointestinal system*, and sound production such as words, cheers and boos.

The passages of the nose and mouth join up at the top of the throat, also called the pharynx. The bottom end of the pharynx divides into two passages. The back passage takes food and liquids down into the stomach through the oesophagus. The front passage takes air into the lungs through the trachea. The *common cold* is an infection of the upper respiratory tract.

Urethra

A tube that carries urine from the bladder to the penis in males (see *Reproductive system*) and to an opening just above the vaginal entrance in females (see *Urinary system*). The male urethra is much longer than the female's. The flow of urine is controlled by the *bladder*. *Urinary tract infection* is more likely to affect the urethra of men rather than women, who are more likely to have the infection in the bladder.

Injury

The urethra can be injured due to a sudden blow during sport, such as a fall astride in cycling causing pain just behind the pubic bone above the genitals and sometimes blood in the urine (haematuria).

If a urethral injury is suspected, the injured person should try not to urinate until a medical check up can be conducted. A severe injury that causes rupture (tearing) of the urethra requires immediate surgery. *Pelvis fracture* may also occur.

Urinalysis

An analysis of the contents of urine, which is the fluid excreted from the *kidneys*. The contents can help confirm a diagnosis, monitor a disease or detect *drugs banned in sport*. For example, a *pregnancy* test involves measuring the amount of HCG hormone. A urinary tract infection can be diagnosed based on bacteria in the urine. *Anabolic steroids* are detected in the urine.

Urinary system

The organs responsible for clearing the blood of waste products produced by the cells and excess water, salt and acids. It is made up of two *kidneys* that are like filtering machines and their drainage organs, the ureters, *bladder* and *urethra* (also see *Reproductive system*).

Illnesses associated with the urinary system include *urinary tract infection* and *incontinence*. A doctor should check blood in the urine, called

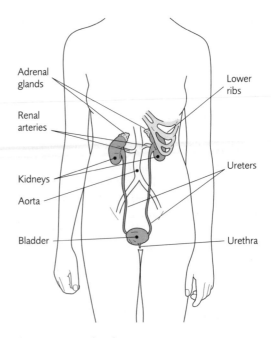

Adrenal glands

Lower ribs

Renal arteries

Kidneys

Aorta

Bladder

Ureters

Urethra

Urinary system (female)

haematuria, as soon as possible. Injuries to the urinary system can occur to the kidney, bladder and urethra.

Urinary tract infection

An infection of the kidney, urethra or bladder, usually caused by bacteria. The main symptom of a urethra infection, which is more common in men, is a burning sensation when urinating.

A bladder infection, which is more common in women, may cause a frequent need to urinate, *incontinence*, pain in the groin or lower abdomen and blood in the urine, which is called *haematuria*. The bacteria usually enter the urinary system from the rectum area. *Wheelchair athletes* are also at risk of bladder infections.

A diagnosis is confirmed with a urine test, which can also identify the type of bacteria. The recommended treatment is *antibiotics*, drinking lots of fluids to maintain *hydration* and clean personal hygiene in the genital region.

Urine test

See *Urinalysis*.

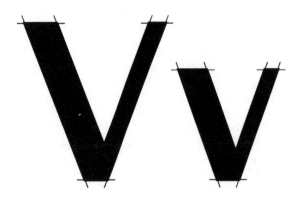

Vacuum cupping

A massage technique that uses a device that creates a negative pressure over the skin that is transmitted to the muscles and other tissues below. It involves applying oil to the skin, placing the cup portion of the device against the skin and pulling on a lever of a pump to create the vacuum, which draws upward and stretches the muscle.

It is used for injuries such as for the anterior compartment of *shin chronic compartment syndrome*, thickening of the medial aponeurosis of the soleus (calf muscle) or muscle tightness in the *iliotibial band friction syndrome*.

Valsalva manoeuvre

A *weight lifting* technique that aims to increase stability of the chest during a lift. It involves closing the epiglottis, the flap of tissue that blocks air from passing from the throat (pharynx) into the voice box (larynx), and forcefully contracting the diaphragm, abdominal and rib muscles in order to increase the pressure in the lungs pushing outwards in the chest (see *Respiratory system*).

Because it can cause the collapse of large veins in the chest bringing blood back to the heart and reduce the amount of blood that gets pumped around the body it should not be done without supervision.

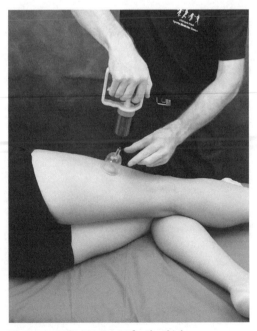

Vacuum cupping treatment for the thigh

Varicose veins

Large, twisted and blue veins that are visible through the skin, usually in the legs. They are caused by defective one-way valves that allow deoxygenated (blue) blood to pool in the veins instead of flowing towards the heart. They are also found in the anus (called haemorrhoids).

Varicose veins of the legs are treated by wearing elastic stockings, regular walking, avoiding standing up without moving, and putting the feet and legs up when sitting. In severe cases sclerotherapy is required, a procedure that empties the veins of blood and then injects them with a solution to seal them.

Vegan

A person who does not eat meat, fish or animal products such as eggs and dairy products (see *Vegetarian*).

Vegetables

See *Fruit and vegetables*.

Vegetarian

A person who does not eat meat and fish. Other variations include: vegans, who don't eat meat, fish nor their products such as milk and eggs; ovovegetarians, who eat eggs but no dairy; and lactovegetarians, who eat dairy but no eggs.

It is possible to be a vegetarian and participate fully in exercise and sport, though it does require strict attention to the nutritional intake, particularly ensuring a sufficient *energy supply*, *amino acids*, *iron*, *calcium* and *vitamins* (particularly vitamins A, B_{12}, riboflavin and D).

There are plenty of food sources that may not be rich in these nutrients, but can be eaten in sufficient amounts to provide an adequate intake, such as nuts, grains and dark green leafy vegetables for calcium.

The benefits of a vegetarian diet include a high *fibre* intake, which is associated with a reduced risk of colon cancer and intestinal conditions, and low *fat* intake for weight loss and *coronary heart disease* and *diabetes* prevention.

Vein

A strong, yet pliable tube carrying blood flowing from the cells of the body to the heart of the *cardiovascular system*. In most veins the blood is blue-coloured because the cells have removed the oxygen. It also has a high content of wastes such as carbon dioxide. The exception is the veins of the *pulmonary vascular system*, which carry oxygen-rich, red-coloured blood from the lungs back to the heart.

Structure

Each vein is made up of three layers of tubing. The inner tube is smooth, the middle layer is made of muscle and elastin fibres and the outer layer is a tough fibrous tissue. It is similar to an *artery*, but thinner and less muscular and elastic. Within each vein at various points are one-way valves to ensure that the flow of blood upwards from the legs to the heart is not overcome by gravity.

Major veins pass through the middle of the leg muscles so that when they are active and contract (such as during walking), they squeeze the veins and force the blood upwards. Two common diseases of veins are *deep vein thrombosis* and *varicose veins*.

Ventilation rate

See *Breathing rate*.

Video analysis

The use of video to assess the *biomechanics* of a specific activity. It can help with the investigation of the proficiency of a specific sport technique, such as throwing a baseball, and making a diagnosis of an injury by looking for abnormal movements and postures.

For example, the biomechanics of running is an analysis of the movements and positions of the foot, ankle, knee, hip, pelvis and lower back. With so many moving parts a video can be used to observe all the detail and identify a *biomechanical abnormality*.

An analysis can have implications for both effectiveness, for instance running speed, and the chances of developing an injury, particularly an *overuse injury*.

Visualisation

A psychological technique that involves imagining a physical activity in the mind in order to reproduce it during competition. It uses memories and thoughts to recreate the visual images and other senses such as touch, sound and smell that represent the activity. It is best performed 'looking out' from within, rather than being a spectator from the outside.

For example, a competition downhill skier waiting at the top of a slope prior to clearance to begin the run, may have the eyes closed and move the head from side to side at the same time as picturing him or herself shifting body weight, changing direction smoothly, feeling the wind against their face and finally racing over the finish line.

Visualisation is used for factors that athletes have complete control over, as well as those that are out of their hands. This includes controlling excessive levels of *arousal*, enhancing skills acquisition and maintenance, implementing *stress inoculation* and preparing an athlete for anticipated scenarios during a competition event.

Some people can visualise with ease, whereas others need to practice. It must be performed exactly as required. For example, if the skill is a pole vault technique, then it must be imagined in its entirety and at competition speed.

It should be performed before training sessions, beginning three to four times a week for 10 minutes a day (two 5-minute sessions) progressing to six or seven times a week during the last two weeks prior to a competition or tournament. Visualisation should not be performed just before falling asleep because it acts as a stimulant. It is also called imagery and mental rehearsal.

Visually impaired athletes

People with visual difficulties who participate in exercise and sport. The impairments range from correctable conditions through to blindness. The most common causes of blindness among athletes include retinitis pygmatosa and congenital abnormalities such as infection during pregnancy.

The classifications of visual impairment for exercise and sport are:
- B1: No light perception at all in either eye or some light perception, but an inability to recognise the shape of a hand at any distance or in any direction.
- B2: Can recognise the shape of a hand and the ability to perceive clearly is up to a visual acuity of 2/60 (a person can see at 2 m/6.6 ft what is normally seen at 60 m/55 yd). The visual field is less than 5 degrees, which is like looking through a keyhole compared to looking through a doorway.
- B3: Can recognise the shape of a hand and the ability to perceive clearly is a visual acuity of 2/60 to 6/60. The visual field varies between more than 5 degrees and less than 20 degrees.

Exercise and sport

Visually impaired athletes participate in a wide range of sports such as wrestling, judo, track and field, cricket, swimming and equestrian. Goalball is a game developed for this disability grouping.

Track and field is easiest for athletes in the B3 class. B1 athletes must have a guide runner to keep to the designated lane. The problem for fast B1 runners is finding fast enough guides who don't want to compete as athletes in their own right.

B1 class swimmers require less assistance. They receive a tap on the head from an official standing outside the pool to tell them to turn at the end of a lap.

Goal ball is a game for athletes in the B1 class. B3 athletes can participate but must wear goggles to block out vision. It is played on an indoor court with small soccer nets and a weighted ball with a bell inside. Three players per team, wearing protective padding, roll the ball into the nets to score goals and throw themselves on the ground in front of the ball to prevent goals. Audiences are not allowed to cheer or applaud until the end of play so as to allow participants to clearly hear the ball.

Injuries

Injuries are similar to those experienced in the general population. The exceptions are injuries associated with reduced *proprioception* during running and walking activities, which causes exaggerated movements of the legs and feet. The knees are lifted higher and the feet strike the ground with a sudden 'slap' rather than the slow, controlled movement, which generates excessive forces resulting in an increased risk of leg and foot *stress fractures* and pain.

Treatment for these injuries requires special verbal instructions and tactile feedback to correct the exaggerated movements. For example, instructing the running or walking athlete 'not to lift the knees too high with each stride'.

Vitamin and mineral deficiency

A lack of *vitamins* and *minerals* that can cause illness or disease. In many cases the cause is the body's needs exceeding the intake, such as in pregnant and breastfeeding women, people who have recently had a severe illness or surgery, women taking the oral contraceptive, strict vegetarians who eat no dairy foods or eggs and when taking certain drugs such as antibiotics, aspirin and hydralazine.

An unhealthy lifestyle also increases the risk, such as that of heavy alcohol drinkers, cigarette smokers and severe weight-loss dieters eating less than 3000 kJ (720 Cal) a day, who most commonly experience a mild lack of B1 (thiamine), which causes fatigue, irritability, depression and a loss of appetite.

Vitamin and mineral supplementation

Taking vitamins and minerals in addition to those found in foods eaten in the diet. It is only recommended for people suffering from a *vitamin and mineral deficiency* and in people participating in exercise

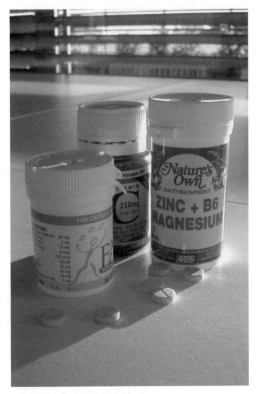

Vitamin and mineral supplements

and sport training at high *overload* levels, but only as a short-term measure for up to 2 weeks.

It has been suggested that supplementation can prevent disease and illness such as osteoarthritis, eye disease, coronary heart disease and certain cancers, including the colon and stomach, and improve performance in exercise and sport. However, there is not enough scientific evidence to support these claims. As a result, it is recommended that maintaining a diet rich in all vitamins and minerals should be sufficient.

There is also a concern about potential side effects of supplementation, especially when taken at mega-dosages such as at 1000 times the normal diet. For example, excessive vitamin A can cause the skin to turn yellow within two months due to liver disease.

In addition, just focusing on the vitamins and minerals in supplements ignores other lesser known *antioxidants*, such as carotenoids, polyphenols and *flavonoids*, which help make up the red, orange and yellow colouring, in fruit and vegetables, that may also be beneficial.

Exercise and sport

VITAMIN C

Strenuous exercise can cause an increased need for this vitamin. However, studies indicate that an adequate intake of foods rich in vitamin C is sufficient.

VITAMINS A, D, E AND K

Very few studies have been done on vitamins A, D and K. There are indications that vitamin E does have an antioxidant effect by helping to maintain red blood cells during exercise and assist in muscle recovery following strenuous exercise.

VITAMIN B COMPLEX

This group of eight vitamins combine to ensure proper digestion, muscle contraction and energy release. In most cases it appears that the dietary requirements of an athlete can be met through increasing foods rich in vitamin B complex.

Vitamins

A group of compounds that is essential for health. They release energy and contribute to the proper functioning of substances such as enzymes and the genetic material in cells. Except for niacin and vitamin D, they can't be produced by the body and must be obtained from the diet. There are 13 known vitamins, eight in the vitamin-B complex, and the other five are vitamins A, C, D, E and K.

Much of our knowledge about vitamins comes from observing what happens to a person who doesn't eat enough of them, which was not uncommon up until the early part of the last century in industrialised countries. For example, brittle bone disease is due to a lack of vitamin D, and scurvy is caused by an inadequate intake of vitamin C.

Vitamin and mineral supplementation is regarded as a means of living longer and healthier lives and, in exercise and sport, maximising performance. However, some of the more popular claims are not backed by scientific study. For example, taking vitamin C to prevent the flu and colds has been investigated by many studies, which have consistently found that it

has no effect. Though once you do have a cold it can give partial relief from symptoms. Other unproved benefits include prevention of grey hair with pantothenic acid and vitamin B$_6$ for pre-menstrual tension.

Volleyball

Volleyball was invented in 1895 by William G Morgan, the physical director of the Young Men's Christian Association (YMCA) in Holyoke, Massachusetts, for people who found basketball too vigorous. It first became an Olympic sport in 1964. Beach volleyball was first played in California in 1930 and included in the 1996 Olympics.

Indoor volleyball is a game played between two teams of six players. Beach volleyball is played between two players on a sand court. The players use their hands to hit a ball over a high net without it touching the ground. A team is allowed only three touches of the ball before it must be returned over the net.

Defence in volleyball

Vitamins: Food sources, major functions and possible importance in exercise and sport

Vitamin	Food sources	Major functions	Possible importance in exercise and sport
Water soluble			
Vitamin C (ascorbic acid)	Green leafy vegetables, parsley, capsicum, citrus fruits, currants, berry fruits, tropical fruits, tomatoes	• Maintenance of connective tissue, cartilage, tendons and bone • Facilitates absorption of iron • Role in wound healing and muscle repair • Protects against free radicals	• Antioxidant • Increased iron absorption • Formation of adrenaline (epinephrine) • Promotion of aerobic energy production
Vitamin B₁ (thiamine)	Meat (especially pork), yeast, wholegrains, nuts, all vegetables	• Energy production through carbohydrate metabolism • Nerve and heart function	• Energy production from carbohydrate • Haemoglobin formation
Vitamin B₂ (riboflavin)	Milk and milk products, yeast, organ meats, eggs, wholegrains, green leafy vegetables	• Energy production through fat, protein metabolism • Necessary for growth and development	• Energy release from carbohydrate and fat
Niacin/nicotinic acid	Meat, liver, fish, eggs, yeast, some green leafy vegetables, peanuts, wholegrain products	• A vital component of co-enzymes concerned with energy processes	• Energy release from carbohydrate and fat
Vitamin B₆ (pyridoxine)	Mainly high protein products, wholegrains, yeast, cereals, vegetables, peanuts, bananas	• Role in protein metabolism • Role in glucose metabolism	• Energy production from carbohydrate • Formation of haemoglobin and oxidative enzymes
Vitamin B₁₂ (cyanoco-balamin)	Liver, meat, dairy products, oysters, sardines (not generally found in plant foods)	• Formation of genetic materials • Development of red blood cells	• Red blood cell production
Folic acid	Liver, meat, fish, green leafy vegetables, orange juice	• Formation of genetic materials • Maintenance of normal red cell production • Co-enzyme in amino acid production	• Red blood cell production
Pantothenic acid	Meat, poultry, fish, grain, cereals, legumes, yeast and egg yoke	• Central role in carbohydrate metabolism, fats and proteins • Role in nerve cell growth and function	• Carbohydrate and fat synthesis
Biotin	Meat, egg yoke, fish, nuts, vegetables (also formed in intestines by bacteria)	• Synthesis of carbohydrates, fats and proteins • Role in nerve cell growth and function	• Carbohydrate and fat synthesis
Fat soluble			
Vitamin A (retinol)	Liver, dairy foods, green leafy vegetables and fruits	• Essential for normal growth and development • Essential to prevent night blindness • Maintenance of surface cells such as skin and lining of the gut	• Antioxidant • Prevention of red cell damage
Vitamin D (calciferol)	Eggs, butter, liver, fish oil, fortified margarine (also manufactured in the body by the action of sunlight on the skin)	• Growth and mineralisation of bones • Aids in absorption of calcium and phosphorus from the diet	• Calcium transport in muscles
Vitamin E (alphatoco-pherol)	Wheat germ, vegetable oils/margarine, nuts, seeds, whole grain products, green leafy vegetables	• Red blood cell production • An antioxidant, may protect cell membranes	• Antioxidant • Prevention of red blood cell damage • Promotion of aerobic energy production
Vitamin K	Liver, meat, green leafy vegetables, soya beans, cauliflower, cabbage	• Important in the blood clotting mechanism • Facilitates action of some bone and kidney proteins	• Nil known

Fitness and injuries

The physical requirements include *aerobic training, speed training, strength training* and *flexibility training*. Treating abnormalities of *throwing biomechanics* can prevent injuries. The most common injuries include *rotator cuff tendinosis* (shoulder), *shoulder impingement, shoulder instability, hand and finger pain and injuries* such as fractures and dislocations, *anterior cruciate ligament (ACL) tear* (knee), *patellar tendinosis* (knee) and *ankle sprain*.

Volume of training

See *Overload*.

Vomiting

The involuntary, uncontrollable expulsion of the contents of the stomach out of the mouth due to stimulation of the vomiting centre in the brain.

It can be stimulated by many factors such as a gastrointestinal infection or excessive eating or drinking, *stress* or *anxiety*, and circulating substances in the blood such as the side effects of drugs. Vomiting also can occur due to participation in exercise and sport, particularly soon after a meal. Prevention of vomiting involves the same measures used for preventing *gastrointestinal reflux*.

VO$_2$

The volume of oxygen breathed in during an activity. Oxygen is used in *aerobic metabolism* in the cells of the human body, such as the breakdown of glucose that occurs in *carbohydrate oxidation*.

VO$_2$ max

A method of measuring aerobic fitness. It is based on the maximal or greatest volume of oxygen that can be breathed in and consumed by a person during an activity.

It is usually measured by having a person run on a treadmill at increasing speeds and using specialised machinery to monitor the gases breathed in and out. An unfit person will reach a certain speed and not be able to breathe in more oxygen. The speed will be faster for a fit person. It is accurate for assessing a wide range of fitness levels, from elite marathon runners through to people recovering from a *heart attack*.

Aerobic fitness is mostly determined by the efficiency of oxygen usage in muscles. Men have a higher VO$_2$ max than women because they tend to have a greater amount of muscle and a superior capacity to carry oxygen in the blood to muscles. VO$_2$ max is also called maximal oxygen uptake and aerobic capacity.

Measurement

Calculations are based on the amount of oxygen breathed in per kilogram of a person's weight, per minute (millilitres/kilogram/minute). An unfit person can have a VO$_2$ max of less than 20 mL/kg/min. The average fit and active young male has 48 ml/kg/min. Young females have 40 mL/kg/min. Super fit athletes like cyclist, Lance Armstrong, have a VO$_2$ max above 80 mL/kg/min.

Aerobic training

VO$_2$ max can be used to make recommendations for *aerobic training*, by determining the required intensity of an activity during training in order to increase aerobic fitness.

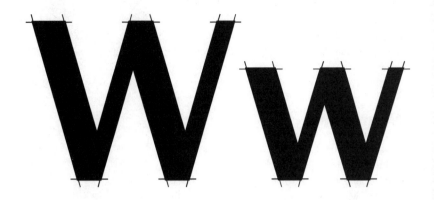

Waist–hip ratio

A method of assessing the amount of fat in the abdomen. It involves measuring the circumference of the waist at the navel and dividing it by the circumference around the hips. For women, a ratio of more than 0.8 is overweight and an increased risk of disease and ill health. For men it is more than 0.9. (see *Overweight*)

Waist size

A method of assessing the amount of fat in the abdomen. It involves measuring the size of the waist. It is also considered an accurate measure of risk of coronary heart disease and stroke in men. Overweight is defined as a measure greater than 100 cm (40 in). (see *Overweight*)

Walking

A recreational physical activity for health and fitness (see *Exercise for health*) and an athletic sport, also called race walking, where the striding foot has to touch the ground before the rear foot looses contact (see *Walking biomechanics*). It was first included in the 1908 Olympics. Race distances are usually 10, 20 or 50 km. The fitness requirements and injuries that are experienced are similar to *long distance running*. The best walking shoe is the same as the recommended *running shoe*.

Walking biomechanics

The movements and positions of the joints and muscles of the legs, pelvis and lower back during walking. The stance phase when the foot is in contact with the ground makes up 60 per cent of the step and the swing phase, which moves the foot through the air, is equal to 40 per cent.

The biomechanics is similar to slow *running biomechanics*. The main difference is at the start and end of the swing phase both feet are in ground contact, which is called the double support phase.

A deviation from normal movements is a *biomechanical abnormality*. It is associated with an increased risk of developing an *overuse injury*. The most common abnormalities are *foot pronation* and *foot supination*.

Walking shoes

Footwear designed to cope with the physical demands of walking. The best recommendation is to select a *running shoe* because the physical demands are similar.

Warm-down

Activities performed after participation in high-intensity training or competition. The aim is to reduce *muscle soreness* and *delayed-onset muscle stiffness* *(DOMS)*, which are aches and pains not caused by an injury that develop up to 48 hours after the training or competition has been completed.

The activities maintain blood flow to the muscles to help clear away the accumulation of swelling and products of metabolism such as *lactate*, which are part of the normal response to high-intensity *aerobic training* performed to overload and during heavy competition.

A warm-down also may be important in sports such as squash where there is a risk of a strain on the heart due to insufficient blood supply as a result of blood pooling in the tissues.

Method

A warm-down should be performed for 5 to 15 minutes. The activities are similar to a *warm-up*, including low to moderate-intensity exercise such as walking, slow jogging and basic skills of the sport. *Flexibility exercises* (also called stretching) only need to be performed by athletes who have a tendency to stiffness or are recovering from an injury that has caused reduced *range of movement*.

Other treatments and techniques that are recommended include *post-activity massage, whirlpools and spas, sleep and rest, post-activity psychology* and *post-activity eating*.

Warm-up

Preparing the mind and body for activity to prevent injury and illness and achieve the best performance.

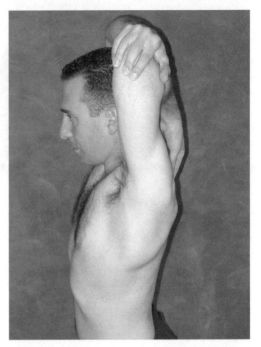

Flexibility exercise for the triceps muscle of the upper arm

A warm-up should last for at least 5 minutes for exercise such as brisk walking or jogging, 10 minutes for sports such as tennis and golf, and 20 minutes for games such as netball and football, beginning with general activities followed by sport-specific and individualised exercises.

General

General activities are performed for a minimum of 10 minutes, including walking and slow jogging progressing to running and callisthenics including arm, neck, trunk and leg movements.

Flexibility exercises (also called stretching), which aim to prevent muscle tears, are considered to be an essential component of a general warm-up. The reasoning is that a muscle tear occurs when it is stretched too far during sport. Animal studies have found that increasing the temperature of muscle tissue increases the length that it can be stretched. Therefore, it is believed that stretching exercises increases bloodflow to the muscles and, hence, the temperature.

However, in recent years it has been observed that muscle tears also occur when the muscle is in the middle of its stretchable length (see *Range of movement*) and contracting at the time of the tear, for example, during running or taking off for a sprint. The mechanism of the injury in these cases may be an uncoordinated contraction of the muscle, which causes the muscle to rip itself.

Specific

Flexibility exercises are a general prevention measure, but also specifically after a previous injury has caused a *biomechanical abnormality* and as part of a self-treatment program to treat reduced *flexibility*.

Signs that flexibility may be reduced include: 1) exercise or sport associated with exceptional aches or pains; and 2) feeling tightness associated with *running biomechanics* abnormality. Joint hyperflexibility should not be stretched.

Activities that replicate the sport's *motor skills* and psychological skills are also recommended. Replication prior to a game or event must avoid fatigue.

Sports that require explosive bursts of strength such as a 100 m sprint, will replicate at a level significantly less than 100 per cent, perhaps only 75–90 per cent. In contrast, soccer and Australian Rules football, which demands endurance as well as explosive strength, requires warming up closer to 100 per cent levels.

AUSTRALIAN RULES FOOTBALL

Where possible this should be performed out on the field. Running styles should be varied including: alternating movements such as 'high-knees' and 'butt-kicks'; backwards, forwards and sideways running; and running and jumping to mark the ball. Ballistic exercises include high kicks, tuck jumps and body contact such as partner or tackle-bag shoulder bumps.

Ball handling should be included with running, such as picking up the ball from the ground, bouncing and handballing. Each player should practise their specific skills on the field, such as kicking for goal or punching the ball in defence.

SOCCER

Where possible the warm-up should be performed out on the field. It should include kicking and heading the ball, and specific skills used most often by that player such as sliding for defenders, twists and dives by forwards and jumps and leaps by goalkeep-ers. The overall time for the warm-up should be up to 20 minutes.

TENNIS

Elite tennis players have a highly developed warm-up routine including hit-outs on a practice court before a game and going through the entire repertoire of shots and serves for up to 10 minutes on the court.

Recreational players should copy the main aspects of this routine, including sprinting forwards, backwards and sideways over a distance of 10 m/yds and stationary exercises including swinging the racquet to simulate the serve, forehand and backhand strokes. This should be followed by practice hitting and serving on the court for at least 10 minutes.

CRICKET

The specific activities depend on whether the team is batting or fielding, with the latter including the slips fieldsman practising slips catching, outfielders performing long sprints, bending and throwing and midfielders moving quickly forwards, backwards, upwards and sideways to catch or stop fast moving balls.

Water

A simple molecule of two hydrogen atoms and one oxygen atom (H_2O). It is essential for life. Around 60 per cent of the body weight of humans is made up of water. It provides the ideal environment for the billions of cells in the body to perform their chemical activities.

Water levels in the body have to be maintained to ensure optimal performance in exercise and sport, prevent *heat illness* and maintain *hydration*.

It is also suggested that drinking 2–3 L (70–100 fl oz) a day is beneficial for good health, though scientific studies show that the amount required depends on how active you are, the outside environment and any history of a medical condition, such as kidney stones. For example, for a person with a fairly inactive life, one litre (35 fl oz) a day may be sufficient.

Water purity

There is much discussion about the safety of tap water and the benefits of filters and bottled water. Water authorities claim that tap water is safe due to their own filtration and/or the addition of chlorine, which kills off water-borne bacteria.

People who don't accept these reassurances may choose to use water filters, though they need to be replaced regularly to avoid a build up of bacteria, and filtered water must be drunk or refrigerated immediately to prevent a build up of bacteria inside them.

Bottled water is a safe option; however, it is costly. A cheaper alternative is to bottle tap water, keeping a small gap of air at the top, and placing it overnight in the fridge to allow the chlorine to evaporate out, but still remaining bacteria-free due to the refrigeration. Even though some people swear by the medicinal benefits of mineral water, it has no proven nutritional value.

Water polo

Water polo was invented in Great Britain in the 1870s. The first international water-polo match was in London in 1890 between England and Scotland. It was first included in the 1900 Olympics.

The game is played in a swimming pool with a minimum depth of 1.8 m (2 yds), between two teams of seven players. The aim is to throw the ball into the opposing team's net. Injuries can be prevented by treating abnormalities of *swimming biomechanics* and *throwing biomechanics*. The most common injuries are *rotator cuff tendinosis* (shoulder), *shoulder impingement* and *shoulder instability*.

Weight

The heaviness of an object. It is a useful measurement in health, such as the height–weight charts for babies that indicate whether growth is occurring within the normal range.

In adults the *height–weight chart* according to gender is often used to determine if a person is overweight. However, a more accurate method for deciding if a person is at risk of developing coronary heart disease is *waist–hip ratio* and *waist size*, which are methods for assessing the amount of fat around the abdomen.

Weight-bearing

Any activity or position of the body where contact is made by the feet or hands with the ground. Standing, walking, running and hand standing are common examples.

It is called weight-bearing because it involves feeling the force of *gravity* that is pulling our weight towards the centre of the earth and, as a result, against the surface of the ground.

Weight-bearing can be reduced partially or completely (called non weight-bearing) by taking weight off the feet, for example, by sitting, lying down, using crutches or a walking stick, or by immersing oneself in a body of water where gravity is partly neutralised by buoyancy. This is often an important part of the early the treatment of injuries in the leg and foot.

Weight-bearing line

An imaginary line that represents where the centre of the weight of a body falls to the ground. For example, when standing on both feet there are two weight-bearing lines, one for each foot. The weight-bearing line is parallel to the line of gravity that represents an imaginary line between the body's *centre of gravity* and the ground.

Weight lifting

In Greek mythology Atlas was a weight lifter. The sport originated in ancient times, and in the modern era was performed in the circus and theatre. It was included in the 1896 Olympics. It is also an activity recommended for good health (see *Exercise for health* and *strength training*).

There are two types of sport weight lifting: 'snatch' and the 'clean and jerk'. The barbell is lifted from the floor to arm's length overhead in a single movement in 'snatch'. In 'clean and jerk' the barbell is lifted first to the shoulders and then overhead to arm's length. In both types the lift must be held overhead for 2 seconds or the referee's signal. The winner lifts the heaviest weight first.

Weight-lifting competition

The most important physical requirement is strength and power through *strength training*. The most common injuries are *low back pain (non-specific)*, *rotator cuff tendinosis* (shoulder) and *patellar tendinosis* (knee).

Weight loss

See *Overweight*.

Weight station

Fitness equipment for *strength training*, such as lifting weights. Equipment designs include different metal frames and systems. The simplest are weight stacks, free weights that can be lifted or moved by pulling a bar. The most expensive are hydraulic and pneumatic-machines.

Weight stations enable the user to adopt a variety of positions, such as standing, sitting and lying so that strengthening can be directed at specific muscles.

The most common design fault is lying on a padded bench to perform hamstring (thigh muscle) strengthening, which increases the risk of *low back*

pain (non-specific). A bench that folds up into a V-shape or placing a pillow under the low back can reduce the risk.

Wheelchair athletes

People who use a wheelchair to move around during exercise and sport. Some of the more common reasons for using a wheelchair include traumatic *paraplegia* and *quadriplegia*, spina bifida, poliomyelitis, *cerebral palsy*, non-ambulant *les autres* athletes and amputation (see *Amputee athletes*). To be eligible to compete in this category an athlete must have at least a 10 per cent loss of function of their lower limbs.

In the initial stages of rehabilitation people in wheelchairs exhibit a great enthusiasm for sport and exercise. However, a significant proportion drop out at a later stage, never to participate again. It is likely

Paralympic gold medal winner Louise Sauvage from Australia

the current levels of participation in exercise and sport among people who use a wheelchair mirror that of the general population, which means a high degree of inactivity.

The majority of wheelchair athletes are male, and there is a wide range of ages similar to the general population. The largest group is 15 to 24 year olds with traumatic spinal cord injuries.

Exercise and sport

The most common activities include athletics, basketball, quad-rugby, shooting, swimming, tennis, weight lifting, snow skiing, racquetball, water skiing, lawn bowls and parachuting.

The benefits of exercise and sport are the same as for the general population. In addition, adequate fitness levels help with confidence and self-esteem and are necessary to be able to independently complete transfers in daily life, such as lifting oneself from the wheelchair to the toilet.

Injuries

The risk of injury may be increased because, in addition to participating in exercise and sport, people in wheelchairs already use their arms and hands extensively to complete transfers and move around in their daily life.

The most common injury in the shoulder is *rotator cuff tendinosis*. Treatment is the same as for the general population, except that rest is next to impossible due to the need to use the upper limbs during transfers in daily life. The most common elbow injuries are *tennis elbow* and *golfer's elbow*. *Blisters* may develop due to overuse of the hands.

Problems with body temperature regulation including *hypothermia* and *heat illness* are more likely the higher the level of spinal cord injury. Good prevention measures include dressing for extra warmth in cold weather and ensuring adequate *hydration* before, during and after exercise and avoiding the hottest part of the day.

Pressure sores of the skin and *urinary tract infections* due to fluid retention are a risk for all people in wheelchairs. Athletes also face an increased risk of *osteoporosis* and, as a result, bone fracture following a fall from the wheelchair, which is more likely

to occur to participants in basketball and quad-rugby. Wheelchair athletes require fewer kilojoules in their diet compared to the general population.

Hyperreflexia, which is a physiological reaction to a full bladder, full bowel or an abscess in the gluteal region, may also occur. It causes raised heart rate resulting in *hypertension* (high blood pressure), which can lead to *stroke* if severe. It affects people with a spinal cord injury above T6. Excessively motivated athletes have been known to intentionally cause this condition, by not emptying the bladder, to enhance their performance during competition.

Wheeze

See *Asthma*.

Whey protein

An *amino acid* supplement that is a by-product of cheese and casein production taken with the aim of increasing muscle mass during strength training (see *Strength training diet*).

Whiplash

Damage to the discs, muscles, ligaments and the neural sheath of the *neck joints* caused by a sudden, rebound, back and forth movement that is common in car accidents and sports due to a collision with an opponent or the ground. Pain caused at the time of the injury usually gets worse over the first 48 hours.

Treatment includes *immobilisation* with a soft neck collar for 3 to 7 days and *analgesics*, followed by gentle *flexibility exercises*, *mobilisation* and *massage*.

Whirlpools and spas

A hot bath with jets of water creating movement and bubbles. It is used to prevent *muscle soreness* and *delayed-onset muscle stiffness* (DOMS) after high-intensity training and competition. The effect is to increase blood flow to the muscles to help clear away accumulation of swelling and by-products of metabolism such as lactate.

White blood cells

Cells that have an essential role in *inflammation*, the body's response to an injury, and the *immune system* in the fight against infections.

There are millions of white blood cells in the *blood*, though they make up less than 5 per cent of its volume. The general name for white blood cells is leukocytes or white blood corpuscles. There are three types: granulocytes, monocytes and lymphocytes.

Granulocytes come in three types: neutrophils (also called phagocytes), basophils and eosinphils. Neutrophils attack and destroy invading foreign bodies by gobbling them up. Pus is mostly made up of neutrophils. Monocytes behave like neutrophils. Lymphocytes come in two main types, B-lymphocytes and T-lymphocytes. They produce antibodies that can remember an infection caused by a foreign body, like the measles virus, so that if another invasion occurs at a later time a quicker and stronger immune response can be mounted to fight it.

Wind chill

Increased heat loss due to the movement of air past the body, due to the effects of convection (see *Temperature*). The faster the wind speed, the greater the heat loss. For example, if the temperature is –1°C (30.2°F) in still air, wind speeds of 16, 32 and 48 km/hr (10, 20, 30 miles/h) reduce the temperature to –9°C (16.0°F), –16°C (4.0°F) and –19°C (–2.0°F).

Wind speed can be estimated easily. If you feel the wind in your face the speed is at least 16 km/per hour (10 miles/h). Small tree branches moving and snow and dust being raised is approximately 32 km/per hour (20 miles/h). Large tree branches moving is 48 km/h (30 miles/h). Note that cyclists can generate these wind chill factors on a still day.

Windsurfing

The first patented windsurfing equipment was invented in 1968 in California and by 1988 it had become an Olympic sport. It involves standing on a surfboard and, when the wind catches the sail, staying upright by holding onto a horizontal pole attached to the mast at chest height, and half-sitting in a harness.

Fitness, skills and injuries

Windsurfing involves *aerobic training, strength training* and *skills training* to learn starts and sailing. Basic windsurfing is moving in a straight line. Advanced is moving in a zigzag, called tacking. Pumping includes jumps over and up the front of waves. The most common injuries are *low back pain (non-specific), ankle sprain, medial collateral ligament (MCL) sprain* (knee), *carpal tunnel syndrome* (wrist) and *neck pain (non-specific).*

Women in sport

Women have been performing heavy physical activities since civilisation began. However, recognition for their athletic skills has been a long slow battle that has only made significant advances in recent times.

At the ancient Olympics women were given their own version called the Games of Hera that received scant attention. At the first modern Olympics in 1896 women were not allowed to participate at all. From 1900 events were gradually introduced, though female track and field didn't make an appearance until 1928 and the women's marathon was not run until 1984. Slow progress has also affected other sports.

A recent survey of daily newspapers found that the reporting on all women's sport combined was less than that given to horse and dog racing. Another problem is that the media coverage that does exist devalues women's participation by emphasising sex appeal (or lack of it) or superficial features such as clothing.

Greater recognition of female athletes can provide an important role model for girls and women in general society. One benefit may be encouraging more females to become physically active, which may reduce health problems later in life, such as *osteoporosis* and *coronary heart disease*.

Parents can have an influence on their daughters by encouraging all their children, not just sons, to be involved in sport. An additional benefit is that female teenagers who participate in physical activity tend to have a higher self-esteem.

Performance comparisons: women and men

Even though the performance differences between women and men tend to draw the most attention, there are far more similarities.

Prior to puberty there is little to no difference between girls and boys. The changes begin due to the impact of the sex hormones of puberty that cause the average male to attain a larger size and, in particular, a greater proportion of muscle, which gives them an advantage in strength and speed as they become *adolescents* and adults.

Even then, many female athletes are able to beat male competitors. In *ultra long distance sports*, such as open ocean swimming, women have an advantage over men due to larger stores of body fat and, as a result, hold the world records. Other comparisons in performance include:

- Men are substantially ahead in sports such as weight lifting, shot put and 100 m sprint where explosive strength and muscle *power* is dominant.
- Men are moderately ahead in soccer, hockey (field) and long distance running such as the marathon where strength and speed still dominate, but the gap is narrowing.
- Women and men are more or less the same in equestrian (many competitions are not separated), shooting, archery and bowls because the skills dominate rather than strength or speed.

Bones

Females begin the initial growth spurt in puberty before men, but by the end of adolescence men are, on average, 10 per cent taller than women. This contributes to the average male being 11 kg (24 lb) heavier than the average female.

Women have shorter limbs than men, especially the upper arm, and as a result less power due to a shorter lever action. They also tend to have a wider carrying angle at the elbow. Men usually have wider shoulders and narrow hips.

Women have a wider pelvis in relation to their shoulders. Combined with a shorter height, this gives women a lower *centre of gravity* and possibly, greater stability and better *balance* compared to men. The wider pelvis also causes a greater inward slant of the femur (thigh bones) that connects the hip to the knee joint, which may increase the risk of knee problems such as *patellofemoral joint syndrome*.

Body composition

The average female has a greater tendency to store body fat due to the effect of the sex hormone *oestrogen*, and the average male tends to have more muscle due to *testosterone*. In women the fat tends to store around the buttocks, hips and thighs. In men it tends to be in the abdomen and upper parts of the body.

Strength

For many years the differences in *strength* between women and men were thought to be due to testosterone. It is now realised that they are in large part due to women not participating in strengthening activities, and the gap between the sexes is much smaller than previously believed.

Strength gains in women are due to improved efficiency in the recruitment of *motor units* in the first 6 to 8 weeks of strength training in women and men. Then men start getting stronger due to increased muscle mass. On the other hand women continue to gain strength by improving their motor unit efficiency, which is why women don't bulk up like men.

It appears unlikely that women will ever become, on average, as strong as men. But some sport science researchers say we may be surprised at how narrow the gap becomes.

Physiology

Cardiovascular responses, such as *stroke volume* and *cardiac output*, are similar between men and women. Women have a lower stroke volume due to a smaller left ventricle and lower blood volume (the result of women's smaller body size), but compensate with a higher *heart rate* in response to activity.

Women have fewer red blood cells than men, which causes a lower oxygen-carrying capacity (see *Haematocrit*). Respiratory responses are similarly influenced by size differences compensated by increased *breathing rates*.

Women have a VO_2 *max* that is, on average, 25–30 per cent less than men's. This is mainly due to greater relative body fat and to a lesser extent, less red blood cells and reduced mechanical efficiency because of a wider pelvis. Women are capable of making the same improvements in VO_2 max during *aerobic training* that are achieved by men.

Women's sports nutrition

The scientific study of the food and fluid requirements for women participating in exercise and sport. Women have a higher degree of *iron deficiency* compared to men because of lower iron stores and loss of iron through menstrual blood loss, which may be compounded by inadequate iron intake in female athletes on severe weight loss diets.

Calcium intake may need to be increased in athletes who have lost their menstrual periods, called *amenorrhea*, which is associated with reduced levels of oestrogen that can increase the risk of the bone thinning and weakening disease called *osteoporosis*. The recommended treatment includes oestrogen replacement therapy and a calcium intake of 1200 to 1500 mg per day.

Other menstrual irregularities that may occur due to a severe weight loss diet include oligomenorrhea (see *Amenorrhea*) and luteal phase defects.

Wrestling

Works of art from 3000 BC depict wrestling in Babylonia and Egypt, and the sport was included in the ancient Greek Olympics. In modern times two types have developed: Greco-Roman and freestyle. Both involve forcing an opponent to touch the ground with some part of the body other than the feet or forcing the opponent into a certain position, usually lying on the back.

The main physical requirements are *strength training* and *agility training*.

Wrist dislocation

See *Carpal joint dislocation*.

Wrist ganglion

An injury that involves the formation of a cyst in one of the tendon sheaths near the *wrist joint*. It can be located in any tendon and deep enough not to be visible to the eye. The cyst can vary from a pea-size to, less frequently, golf ball-size.

A *ganglion* is often painless and does not require treatment and may go away spontaneously. A painful ganglion is treated with an *aspiration* needle, sometimes also with a *corticosteroid* injection. If this fails surgery is recommended.

Wrist joint

The joint that connects the forearm to the hand. It is made up of small joints between the two forearm bones (radius and ulnar) called the inferior radio-ulnar joint, and eight small bones called the carpal bones, arranged in two rows of four; the first row starting from the thumb-side includes the scaphoid, lunate, triquetrum and pisiform; the second row is the trapezium, trapezoid, capitate and hamate.

The wrist moves as a single unit, except the inferior radio-ulnar joint, which is involved in forearm turning movements (supination and pronation) that also occur at the *elbow joint*.

Many of the muscles that move the wrist joint and finger joints originate in the forearm and elbow and form tendons that pass through the wrist. Blood vessels, such as the radial artery, are used for checking the *pulse*, and nerves including the radial, median and ulnar, also pass through.

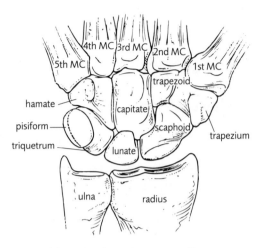

Bones of the wrist joint (MC = metacarpal)

Muscles involved in wrist movements

Movement	Primary movers	Secondary movers
Flexion	• Flexor carpi radialis • Flexor carpi ulnaris • Palmaris longus	• Flexor digitorum superficialis • Flexor digitorum profundus • Flexor pollicis longus • Abductor pollicis longus
Extension	• Extensor carpi radialis brevis • Extensor carpi radialis longus • Extensor carpi radialis ulnaris	• Extensor digitorum • Extensor indicis • Extensor pollicis longus
Abduction	• Flexor carpi radialis and Extensor carpi radialis combined	• Abductor pollicis longus
Adduction	• Flexor carpi ulnaris and Extensor carpi ulnaris combined	
Internal rotation and External rotation	• Combination of above muscles	

Wrist joint sprain

An acute injury that causes torn ligaments or joint capsule of the *wrist joint*. It usually occurs due to a fall onto an outstretched hand or a sudden force on the hand such as trying to stop a running opponent in a contact sport.

Diagnosis, treatment and return to sport

A sprain can occur in three degrees of severity. Mild *sprain* (grade 1) tears only a few of the fibres of the ligament or joint capsule, but enough to cause pain and minor *swelling*. Moderate sprain (grade 2) tears a large number of fibres, causing significant pain and swelling and perhaps a bruise.

A severe sprain (grade 3) completely tears or ruptures a ligament, leading to severe swelling and bruising and excessive laxity and instability during wrist movements. X-rays are usually recommended to exclude a bone fracture.

The immediate treatment includes *RICE (rest, ice, compression and elevation)* to reduce the swelling and bruising, followed by gentle *flexibility exercises* soon after. Subsequent treatment aims to find a balance between allowing enough rest to permit healing, while encouraging movement so that stiffness and weakness do not develop. Return to sport usually takes about 1 week for mild sprains, up to 6 weeks for moderate sprains and up to 12 weeks for severe cases.

Wrist pain and injuries

Causes

Wrist pain can be caused by an acute or overuse injury, or disease. An *acute injury* causes pain that begins suddenly due to a single incident, usually falling onto an outstretched hand.

An *overuse injury* causes pain that gets worse over a period of weeks or months due an accumulation of excessive forces that cause microtrauma. In the early stages it causes only minor pain and stiffness. But later on, either gradually or following a sudden force, it becomes painful enough to seek medical care. Diseases affecting the wrist include *rheumatoid arthritis* and *gout*.

The *wrist joint* and associated structures are the usual sources of pain. However, it is not unusual to have *referred pain*, which comes from another structure, in particular the neck joints.

QUICK REFERENCE GUIDE

Wrist

Acute injury: Pain caused by a sudden force

Colles fracture ....Did you fall onto your outstretched arm and now feel pain at the back of the wrist?

Scaphoid fracture ....Did you fall onto your outstretched arm and now feel pain at the base of the thumb?

Triangular fibrocartilage
complex sprain ....Did you fall onto your outstretched arm and now feel pain that is aggravated by resisted movement, such as pushing the back of your hand against a wall?

Radius distal epiphysis fracture ....Are you a child or adolescent with pain in the back of the wrist that is aggravated by resisted movement, such as pushing the back of your hand against a wall, and is associated with gymnastics or other activities that cause impact on the hand?

Overuse injury: Pain that has gradually worsened over a period of weeks or months

de Quervain's tenosynovitis ....Do you have pain and/or swelling in the tendons on the back of your wrist or forearm that is aggravated by wrist movements?

Wrist ganglion ....Do you have a swollen lump on the back of your wrist or hand, which may or may not be painful?

Carpal tunnel syndrome................Do you have wrist pain that is worse at night and/or numbness and tingling (pins and needles) in the fingers?

Handlebar palsy ....Do you have wrist pain and/or numbness and tingling (pins and needles) in the little finger and inner side of the fourth finger?

Kienbock's disease ....Are you a child or adolescent with pain on the palm-side or back of the wrist caused by gymnastic or other activities that cause impact on the hand?

Diagnosis

Making the diagnosis involves combining information gathered from the *history*, *physical examination* and relevant tests.

How the injury occurred is important for diagnosing an acute injury. For example, a fall onto an outstretched hand may result in a *scaphoid fracture* or *triangular fibrocartilage complex sprain*. The pain's

Overuse wrist injuries according to Pain location

Posterior (Back)	Anterior (Front)	Medial (Little finger side)	Lateral (Thumb side)
• Wrist ganglion • Kienbock's disease • Carpal joint dislocation • Posterior interosseous nerve entrapment • Osteoarthritis • Radius distal epiphysis fracture	• Kienbock's disease • Carpal tunnel syndrome • Capitate osteochondrosis	• Triangular fibrocartilage complex sprain • Distal radioulnar joint instability • Carpal joint dislocation • Handlebar palsy	• Scaphoid fracture (delayed or non-union) • de Quervain's tenosynovitis

Causes of wrist pain and injuries

Most common	Less common	Not to be missed
Overuse injury		
• Wrist ganglion	• Capitate osteochondrosis	
• de Quervain's tenosynovitis	• Kienbock's disease	
• Inferior radioulnar joint instability		
• Wrist referred pain	• Handlebar palsy	
• Carpal tunnel syndrome		
Acute injury		
• Colles fracture	• Hook of hamate fracture	• Carpal joint dislocation
• Scaphoid fracture	• Triangular fibrocartilage complex sprain	• Radius distal epiphysis fracture
• Wrist joint sprain		
Disease		
		• Gout
		• Rheumatoid arthritis

location is also important. For example, pain felt on the back of the wrist following a fall may indicate a *Colles fracture.*

Pain location (see table above) and associated activities also help to diagnose an overuse injury. For example, pain felt after repeated wrist movements followed by stiffness suggests *de Quervain's tenosynovitis.* Pain aggravated by bearing weight on the hands during gymnastics indicates *Kienbock's disease* or *distal radioulnar joint instability.* Pain felt worse at night, with or without pins and needles or numbness, is a sign of *carpal tunnel syndrome.*

Radiological investigation is often required; for example, *X-rays* and *magnetic resonance imaging (MRI)* for a Colles fracture. It should be kept in mind that some injuries take time to emerge on X-ray, such as scaphoid fracture. Other useful tests include blood test for rheumatoid arthritis and joint fluid for gout.

Wry neck

Sharp neck pain and difficulty moving the head, usually caused by a sudden, quick movement or it may appear after a long sleep. The two types of wry neck are Z-joint and disc (see *neck joints*).

Z-joint

This injury is usually caused by a sudden movement and is more likely in younger-aged people. The sharp pain fixes the neck in a bent forward (flexion), turned (rotation) and bent to one side (lateral flexion) position due to muscle spasm. Treatment includes *ice, transcutaneous electrical nerve stimulation (TENS), interferential therapy, mobilisation* (if muscle spasm is present) or *manipulation* (if there is no spasm).

Disc

This injury usually appears after waking up in the morning due to a long sleep with the neck in an awkward position. It tends to occur in older-aged people. The pain is often strongest in the lower neck and upper thoracic spine. Treatment can involve *immobilisation* with a neck collar, *non-steroidal anti-inflammatory drugs (NSAIDs), massage* and *mobilisation.*

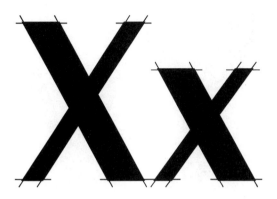

X-rays

An invisible electromagnetic form of energy with a short wavelength that passes through solid objects like the human body. German physicist Wilhelm Roentgen discovered them in 1895.

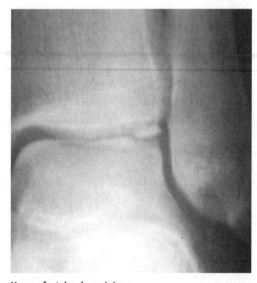

X-ray of a talar dome injury

It is used to produce images on a film to confirm a *diagnosis*. These images are also called plain X-rays or radiography.

An X-ray involves a machine sending out a low dosage of X-rays through the body part where the injury is located and onto a film on the other side. Certain parts of the body, particularly bones, absorb some of the X-rays, whereas those that pass through form images on the film.

Despite the availability of newer and more sophisticated radiological methods, X-rays continue to give a great deal of information regarding bony abnormalities, such as *fractures*, *dislocations*, calcification, joint conditions like *osteoarthritis* and diseases like cancer *tumours*. They are also easily available, relatively cheap and simple to perform.

Usually more than two views, perpendicular to each other, are required for a diagnosis. The two conventional views are the anteroposterior (front to back) and lateral (from the side). Special views may give further information, such as the oblique view to detect pars interarticularis defects of the low back.

X-rays also can be used as a treatment for specific medical conditions, which is called radiotherapy.

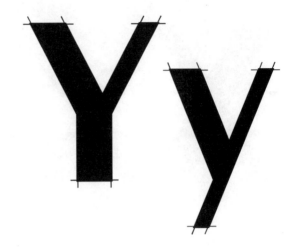

Yoga

Yoga is an activity and spiritual belief system that originated in India. It is translated from Hindu as 'union of the mind, body and spirit'. The most popular form is Hatha yoga. Other forms are Satyananda, Iyengar, Ashtanga and Power yoga.

All the forms have two common activities: breathing control (Pranayama) and physical postures (Asanas). Breathing involves four stages: inspiration, expiration and a brief pause after each. Breathing control may be practised once a day for 15 to 20 minutes, or twice a day for 10 minutes.

Physical postures include variations of standing on all fours, headstands, lying on the back, stomach-lying, squatting and sitting, such as the classical 'lotus position'.

Satyananda is the gentlest form of yoga, with breathing control given great importance. Iyengar is more active, with participants expected to push their physical limits. Ashtanga is similar to Iyengar, but involves continuous movement between physical postures. Power yoga is similar to Ashtanga.

Health benefits

Yoga reduces the risk of *hypertension* (high blood pressure), *stress, headaches,* migraines, *osteoarthritis* and medication-use in *asthma*. It involves *aerobic training, flexibility training* and *strength training*.

Injuries

The most common injuries are *low back pain (non-specific), meniscus tear* (knee) and *thoracic pain (non-specific). Hypertension* (high blood pressure) may be aggravated by headstands.

Yoga posture—Utthita Parsvakonasana

Younger athlete

Athletes who are children and adolescents. Infancy begins at birth and ends after 1 year. *Children:* 1- to 10-year-old females, and 1 to 12 in males. *Adolescents:* 10- to 19-year-old females, and 12 to 22 males. In their latter years many adolescents participate as equals against adults.

Zinc

A mineral that is essential for enzymes involved in the formation of proteins, such as genetic material, wound healing, the immune system and normal growth and development of the sex organs. It is found in tiny amounts in the body called trace elements.

The recommended daily intake is 12 mg in women and 15 mg in men. Zinc deficiency can cause reduced levels of performance in exercise and sport, as well as loss of appetite, hair loss, skin problems and increased frequency of the *common cold*.

It is recommended to keep a diet rich in zinc such as lean meat, poultry, wholemeal grains and seafood (see *Minerals*). There is no evidence that supplementation improves performance in athletes with normal zinc levels. In fact, it may even cause symptoms such as nausea, vomiting, headaches and tiredness. It also can be dangerous if taken over the long term, including an increased risk of *coronary heart disease* and *iron deficiency* due to side effects of reduced iron absorption.

Further reading

Bannister, L.H. et al. (eds) 1995, *Gray's Anatomy*, 38th edn, Churchill Livingstone, New York

Brukner, P. & Khan, K. 2002, *Clinical Sports Medicine*, 2nd edn, McGraw-Hill, Sydney

Mackenzie, F. 1999, *Penguin Guide to Family Health*, Penguin, Melbourne

Smith, T. et al. (eds) 1994, *Reader's Digest Encyclopaedia of Family Health* Reader's Digest, Sydney

Stanton, R. 1999, *Rosemary Stanton's Fat & Fibre Counter*, Wilkinson's Books, Australia

Wilmore, J.H. & Costill, D.L. 1999, *Physiology of Sport and Exercise*, 2nd edn, Human Kinetics, Champaign, Illinois

Weinberg, R.S. & Gould, G. 1999, *Foundations of Sport and Exercise Psychology*, 2nd edn, Human Kinetics, Champaign, Illinois

Credits

Unless otherwise specified below, all photographs and illustrations in *The Encyclopedia of Exercise, Sport and Health* are from Peter Brukner and Karim Khan, *Clinicial Sports Medicine*, McGraw-Hill, Sydney, 2002.

Photos on pp. 10, 18, 27, 54, 81, 100, 113, 130, 152, 197, 284 (left), 292, 396 (left), 398, 412, 417, 422 (top), 456, 463 (top and bottom) and 472 are © Australian Sports Commission, reproduced by permission.

Photo on p. 17 courtesy Gridiron Australia Ltd; p. 38 courtesy Victorian Amateur Football Association Baseball; p. 41 courtesy Victoria Baseball Association; p. 42 courtesy Basketball Victoria; p. 95 (bottom) courtesy Victorian Women's Cricket Association; p. 206 courtesy Ice Hockey Australia; p. 355 courtesy Rugby League Victoria; p. 356 courtesy Victorian Rugby Union; p. 385 by Carlos Furtado/ courtesy of Soccer NSW; and p. 426 courtesy Tennis Victoria.

Illustrations on pp. 36, 51, 70 (top), 74, 79, 93, 122 (bottom left), 133, 165, 181, 183 (bottom), 185, 194 (bottom), 240 (bottom), 268, 270, 278 (top), 283, 291, 297, 299 (bottom), 312 (left), 347, 348, 367 (bottom left), 380, 415, 433 and 450 are by Lorenzo Lucia.

Photos on pp. 60, 70 (bottom), 95 (top), 119, 137, 144, 200, 205, 216, 258, 262, 392, 393 and 455 are by Tabitha King.

Index

(continues)